Inclusive Leisure Services

Third Edition

Inclusive Leisure Services

Third Edition

John Dattilo, Ph.D.
Penn State University

Venture Publishing, Inc.

For Amy, David, and Steven

"We have so much for which to be thankful."

Table of Contents

List of Figures and Tables

Acknowledgments

My appreciation is extended to the many people who have experienced some form of oppression whom I have come to know in my personal and professional life. Their comments helped to enrich this book and have greatly influenced my ideas. This book has evolved over the past three decades while I have taught and conducted research. Students enrolled in courses I have taught on inclusive leisure services have influenced the content of the book. Their feedback concerning the material I present in class helped shape the content of this third edition of the book.

I wish to thank several colleagues and friends who worked with me to expand the focus of the third edition of this book beyond disability to include considerations for a variety of individuals who have experienced oppression. A new chapter on civil rights legislation was primarily developed by Ben Hickerson to improve our understanding of the legislation, which creates a solid foundation to better understand the Americans with Disabilities Act and guidelines associated with universal design. To further broaden the scope of the book, I invited Elisabeth Weybright to help develop a chapter that addresses unique considerations for leisure service delivery to older adults. In addition, Junhyoung Kim lent insight into providing leisure services to individuals who are immigrants or members of ethnic or racial minorities and have experienced some form of oppression as a result of their ethnic background or race. David Scott made an important contribution to another chapter that has been added by addressing economic challenges many people around the world encounter that limit their opportunities to experience leisure.

I have not forgotten the people who helped me in developing the first and second editions of the book who continue to deserve my recognition: George Alderson, Brenda Arnold, Michele Barbin, Leslie Black, Amanda Darley, Mary Ann Devine, Bonnie Godbey, Lynda Greer, Diane Groff, Douglas Kleiber, John McGovern, William Murphy, Roger Nielsen, Susan St. Peter, Kathleen Sheldon, Ralph Smith, Marlee Stewart, Mary Ulrich, Brent Wolfe, Robin Yaffe, George Lauer, Richard Yocum, and the entire Venture staff.

There have been a variety of readings that have influenced my thinking that are reflected in the new edition of this book. Although there are many articles and books that I have read that helped me to evolve my thinking, there are a few books that had a major impact on me, and, if you are interested in pursuing further reading on the topic, that I would recommend: Leonard Pitts, Jr.'s *Forward from this Moment*; Randy Pausch's *The Last Lecture*; Shannon Sullivan and Nancy Tuana's *Race and Epistemologies of Ignorance*; Jackie Leach Scully's *Disability Bioethics*; Juan Williams' *Thurgood Marshall: American Revolutionary*; Dorothy Herrmann's *Helen Keller: A Life*; Joseph Shapiro's *No Pity*; John Hockenberry's *Moving Violations*; the Dalai Lama's *Ethics for the New Millennium*; and Mitch Albom's *Tuesdays' with Morrie*.

It is my desire that this text will assist readers in understanding the importance of inclusive leisure services. I am hopeful that this knowledge is applied to develop leisure services that welcome all people so that they experience enjoyment and leisure.

J. D.

Chapter 1
Be Ethical

If we are to achieve a culture rich in contrasting values,
we must recognize the whole gamut of human potentialities.
And so we are a less arbitrary social fabric,
one in which each diverse human gift will find a fitting place.
-Margaret Mead

Orientation Activity: Ethical Assumptions

Directions Alone: Read the eight statements presented below and describe why you think these assumptions are listed at the beginning of this book

Directions with Others: Divide into small groups and discuss your interpretation of the statements with other members. After a specified time, share your responses with the entire group.

1. All people deserve our respect and to be treated with dignity.
2. Everyone has the right to self-determination.
3. With great power comes great responsibility.
4. Inclusion is good.
5. Diversity enriches our world.
6. No one can be reduced to one characteristic.
7. We ought to consider perspectives that differ from our own.
8. Critical and constructive thinking contribute to a more just society.

Debriefing: Addressing fundamental ethical assumptions is one way to begin to approach our learning on a given topic. The assumptions require interpretation that will be specially provided in the chapter and more broadly addressed throughout this book. Consider the following questions when reflecting on the activity:

- Which of these assumptions do you think are the most important? Identify reasons why you selected these particular assumptions.
- Which of these assumptions have you spent limited time thinking about?
- Select one of the assumptions. What is the relationship between that assumption and providing inclusive leisure services?

Introduction

Listening to Students: Responding to their Wishes

Students and practitioners have requested to hear more from me in this third edition of the book. As a researcher, I have been taught and give credence to the position that as an individual related to seeking truth, my singular perspective is limited and insufficient to speak authoritatively. I have learned that when making statements, it is important to substantiate my contentions by, ideally, identifying research that supports the contentions, or, at the very least, identifying supportive positions espoused by topical authorities.

Students and practitioners argue that I have been either providing services to people who have experienced barriers to their leisure, have been consuming and contributing to research, or teaching others about concerns related to diversity and oppression for over 35 years. They tell me that I should, by now, be able to synthesize my experiences and the research to say something worthwhile. They share that by including what they view as unnecessary and numerous citations in the book to support my contentions, I tend to distract them from the lessons they are trying to learn from me.

I appreciate these individuals' perspectives; after all, they are the audience for whom the book is written. Their consistent comments highlight my struggle to be a humble researcher and to be an effective educator. In this third edition of the book I have tried to reach a compromise in letting my voice come through more clearly while not losing sight of the research that is often responsible for my positions and, most importantly, the voices of the people who are the focus of this text.

Broadening the Conversation: Widening the Lens

In this edition of the book, I have attempted to more broadly address the topic of inclusion. I invited a few knowledgeable individuals to work with me on some new chapters. These colleagues have taught me much and have expanded my knowledge and perspective. The new chapters contain additional information that is based on knowledge and experience that extends beyond my limited perspective that I think is important to include here.

This third edition of the book represents an evolution with the intent of broadening the scope of this book. Clearly, there are many other groups of individuals who have been oppressed on grounds other than ability, age, ethnicity, race, and socioeconomics. However, I hope you learn that there are general principles applicable to all individuals who experience barriers inhibiting their leisure participation.

Broadening the Conversation: An Example

At age 12, English poet William Ernest Henley (1849–1903) contracted tuberculosis with associated complications that ultimately resulted in amputation of his leg when he was 25. While recovering in the hospital, Henley wrote "Invictus," a Victorian poem published untitled in his 1888 *Book of Verses*. The title "Invictus" (Latin for *unconquered*) was added by Arthur Quiller-Couch when it was included in *The Oxford Book of English Verse* (1900).

> *Out of the night that covers me,*
> *Black as the pit from pole to pole*
> *I thank whatever gods may be,*
> *For my unconquerable soul.*
> *In the fell clutch of circumstance,*
> *I have not winced nor cried aloud.*
> *Under the bludgeonings of chance,*
> *My head is bloody, but unbowed.*
> *Beyond this place of wrath and tears,*
> *Looms but the Horror of the shade*
> *And yet the menace of the years,*
> *Finds and shall find me unafraid.*
> *It matters not how strait the gate,*
> *How charged with punishments the scroll*
> *I am the master of my fate:*
> *I am the captain of my soul.*

Nelson Mandela, 1993 Nobel Peace Prize winner, who was elected President of South Africa in 1994, found this poem to be inspirational during his imprisonment from 1962 to 1990. Later, Mandela shared the verse with Francois Pienaar, Captain of the South Africa Rugby Team, to inspire a connection and facilitate reconciliation between Black and White South Africans through efforts of the National Rugby Team. The team went on to win the 1995 Rugby World Cup held in South Africa. A 2009 Warner Brothers film, which borrowed its name from Hensley's poem, depicted Mandela's story of connecting with the successful rugby team to unite a divided country.

As I explored the background of this poem and the connection between William Hensley's experience of acquiring a disability and Nelson Mandela's efforts as a human rights activist committed to promoting national reconciliation and global peace, I could not help but think about this edition of the book and my experiences with inclusion. My initial professional experiences associated with inclusion, and the focus of the first two editions of this book, were specifically concerned with disability.

As my thinking and the book evolved, I have come to realize that there is much to learn about the broader idea of diversity and inclusion from the specific domain of disability. As a result, many of the examples contained in the book relate directly to disability but can be applied to any person who has been oppressed.

This book is about connecting more broadly to the issues of oppression and promoting civil rights. I found the poem "Invictus" to be inspirational; I also hope the story behind it provides you with a better understanding of the evolution of my thinking and the rationale for the revisions to this third edition.

The Purpose of the Book

With this book I encourage leisure service professionals to develop and implement programs that are inclusive of all people, regardless of their individual characteristics. Throughout the book, information is provided to create opportunities for all people to engage in leisure pursuits together.

Hopefully, this book will help us to become more relaxed in our interactions with people who possess different characteristics. There is value in coming into contact with diverse people and getting to know them. Karen Mihalyi stated (Bogdan & Taylor, 1992, p. 6):

It's difficult at first when you are not familiar with a group you have a stereotype about. [For example,] if you are not used to relating to people with disabilities, you are not sure how to. You don't want to make a mistake, do something that might offend them. So you hold back. Now I dive right in and hope that people know I am trying my hardest. I am really losing my self-consciousness around people with disabilities. At first I think I listened mostly. I listened to people and read some—mainly by people who had disabilities. But my ease mostly came by getting close with people, hearing their stories and loving them.

This book is designed to educate future and current leisure service professionals about attitude development and actions that promote positive attitudes toward people who have experienced discrimination and segregation. Development of positive attitudes toward all people is important since negative attitudes are an extremely difficult barrier to overcome; if attitudes are not properly addressed, they can result in stigmatization, discrimination, segregation, and isolation.

This book is intended to provide current and future professionals with suggestions on ways to facilitate meaningful leisure participation by all participants, while respecting everyone's rights. To achieve this end, this book contains five distinct sections.

The first section is designed to create an awareness of important concepts such as ethics, inclusion, attitudes, and barriers to leisure involvement. Details are provided about the nature of attitudes, ways to enhance our attitudes, and strategies to improve other's attitudes.

The second section addresses specific considerations for embracing diversity, such as the impact of human rights guidelines and civil rights legislation, how to be compliant with the letter of the law and, more importantly, ways to embrace the spirit of the law. Also, this section includes techniques on how to celebrate culture by considering ethnicity, race, and the impact of immigration. There is information on ways to promote healthy aging and approaches to support leisure participation of older adults. The section concludes with suggestions how to provide leisure services for people who are experiencing economic challenges.

In response to the conclusion that training is needed for leisure service providers on ways to include people who have been oppressed in community recreation programs, the third section of the book presents readers with specific strategies to facilitate participation. The strategies include facilitating self-determination, providing leisure education, promoting social interactions and friendships, applying principles of universal design, and being an advocate.

The fourth section of the book identifies specific issues especially relevant to providing leisure services for people with disabilities, such as ways to demonstrate respect through use of sensitive terminology and how to support the families of those people. Methods for making adaptations to materials, activities, instruction, and the environment are also presented in this section.

This fifth and final section introduces readers to people with different physical, cognitive, and sensory disabilities, their characteristics, and methods for including them in community leisure services. The specific descriptions and pictures of the people were chosen to provide a diverse introduction to people with disabilities who are living within their communities. However, after examining the broad definition of disability as defined by the Americans with Disabilities Act (ADA), it became clear that an overview of each disabling condition presented within the confines of this text would be an unmanageable task. Therefore, a sampling of disabilities was chosen, including physical limitations, cognitive limitations, and sensory limitations. The final chapter addresses the topic of assistive technology and the impact that technology can have on enhancing leisure involvement for people with limitations.

The chapters are organized in a similar manner and contain segments designed to enhance learning. Each chapter begins with an *orientation activity* to familiarize the reader with the content presented in the chapter and to provide an opportunity to interact with others about the topic. The orientation activities provide an experiential preview of what is to come in the chapter and set the educational climate.

These orientation activities are immediately followed by *debriefings* to maximize learning associated with the activities. The debriefings consist of a brief discussion about the orientation activity and a few questions requiring the reader to reflect on the activity. I encourage you to attempt to answer these questions that are designed to assist you in processing the orientation activity.

Next, each chapter contains an *introduction* designed to briefly acquaint the reader with the topics to be covered in the chapter. The *content* of each chapter follows the introduction and comprises the majority of the chapter. A variety of questions and possible responses are posed throughout each chapter.

Concluding sections, or final thoughts, offer readers additional examples and a chance to reflect on the information presented in each chapter. The chapters finish with several *discussion questions* to encourage the reader to review the material, identify important aspects of the content, and engage in problem solving.

In this chapter the following questions are addressed:

- What are the underlying ethical assumptions of this book?
- What is the value of reading this book?
- What is the problem?
- How can we make a difference?

What are underlying ethical assumptions of this book?

I think it is useful to discuss some underlying ethical assumptions that I have in regards to the information presented in this book. I believe that it is fair to present these ideas so that you understand the rationale for including the material I have selected to present.

Later in the book specific civil rights laws that directly impact leisure service delivery are presented. These laws are accompanied by suggestions on how to comply with the legislative acts. In this first chapter, however, I address ethical considerations. I believe a quotation from Thomas Friedman (2008, p. 192), author of the book *Hot, Flat, and Crowded*, provides insight into why I begin with a discussion about ethics:

> *Ethics are not laws. They are not imposed by the state. Rather, they are norms, values, beliefs, habits and attitudes that are embraced voluntarily—that we as society impose on ourselves. Laws regulate behavior from the outside in. Ethics regulate behavior from the inside out. Ethics are something you carry with you wherever you go to guide whatever you do.*

The way in which I have arrived at these ethical assumptions is based on a variety of conditions. My experiences and reflections as a person within our society and as a leisure service practitioner contributed to these assumptions. In addition, my reading and reflection on relevant literature and other informative media shaped these beliefs. My discoveries as a clinician and researcher impacted my perceptions. Finally, my observations of what appear to be operative assumptions within the professions associated with the topics addressed in this book also contributed to development of these ethical assumptions.

The following sample of underlying assumptions is addressed in this section:

- All people deserve our respect and to be treated with dignity.
- Everyone has the right to self-determination.
- With great power comes great responsibility.
- Inclusion is good.
- Diversity enriches our world.
- No one can be reduced to one characteristic.
- We ought to consider perspectives that differ from our own.
- Critical and constructive thinking contribute to a more just society.

Assumption #1: All people deserve our respect and to be treated with dignity.

The thread that connects the many individuals and groups addressed in this book is the fact that each person has and/or does experience oppression in some manner. Oppression involves the domination and repression of one group by another group that is privileged to be in power.

Oppression of any group works to deteriorate a society. Although initially it may appear that oppressors benefit by dominating another group of people or other individuals, the actions are not justified when considering the humanity of the oppressed.

An important antidote to oppression is to consider our common humanity and to demonstrate respect for each individual. Respect involves being considerate of another's rights by treating the person with dignity. Dignity is the condition of being valued by others that results in a proper sense of pride and self-respect.

When we regret what we say and do or how we speak or act toward another person, our behaviors often stem from a lack of respect for another human being. Conversely, when our actions reflect respect for people, we are likely to feel good about our interactions and engage in positive discourse.

According to the co-founders of the *Dignity Project*, as reported on its website, the Global Dignity Initiative is an autonomous non-profit, non-criticism, and non-partisan project, identified as "inspiration-based," with the goal of commending and encouraging best-practice and dignity-centered leadership. The mission of the Dignity Project is to implement globally the universal right of every human being to lead a dignified life, by using a new language and a mindset to approach issues of poverty, peace, and progress. The Global Dignity Initiative offers the following principles:

- Every human being has a right to lead a dignified life.
- A dignified life means an opportunity to fulfill one's potential, which is based on having a humane level of health care, education, income, and security.
- Dignity means having the freedom to make decisions on one's life and to be met with respect for this right.
- Dignity should be the basic guiding principle for all actions.
- Our dignity is interdependent with the dignity of others.

And how do we know how to demonstrate respect? We take our lead from the people whom we serve and allow them to teach us how to treat them with dignity and respect. As a result, the oppressed become teachers of the oppressor.

Assumption #2: Everyone has the right to self-determination.

Since many people can benefit from leisure services, we are in a position to assist many people; however, to avoid being paternalistic, which results in neglecting individual choice and personal responsibility, it is helpful to consider that everyone has the right to self-determination.

Over decades of research, Edward Deci, Richard Ryan, and colleagues have concluded that the three fundamental psychological needs that are the basis for motivation and characterize self-determination are autonomy, competence, and relatedness (Figure 1.1). Ryan and colleagues (2011, p. 38) provided the following description of these three needs:

> *__Autonomy__ describes actions that are self-endorsed and volitional rather than controlled or compelled, and autonomy support includes methods that foster or encourage voice, initiative, and choice and that minimize the use of controls, contingencies, or authority as motivators. A second psychological need is the need for __competence.__ This concerns the psychological need to experience confidence in one's capacity to affect outcomes. The third is the need for __relatedness.__ This involves the need to feel connected with and significant to others.*

Although three components of self-determination have been identified, the salience of each of these components varies across individuals and cultures. *Salience* involves the degree to which something is relevant or important to the individual.

For example, people who possess a more collectivist perspective (including many people with heritage in Asia) may find the need for relatedness to be more salient than the need for autonomy.

Given the interaction of autonomy, competence, and relatedness, many people's sense of self-determination is affected by a variety of socially influenced factors including gender, race, ethnicity, and class. Scully (2008, p. 161) observed that:

> *... what actually makes autonomy possible is not detachments, but the social relationships that provide the conditions for experiencing and maintaining self-determination.*

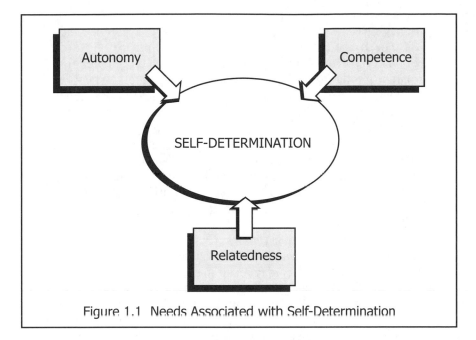

Figure 1.1 Needs Associated with Self-Determination

Assumption #3: With great power comes great responsibility.

I realize as the author of this book I am immediately placed in the role of an authority and, as such, I am a privileged individual who is in a position of power even though I present ideas from a limited perspective. People are *privileged* when they enjoy resources and advantages that provide them with opportunities other people do not possess. Since some people are privileged, then others must be oppressed; these are the individuals who are the subject of this book.

I am humbled by being in this position of privilege and feel an important responsibility. I am especially uncomfortable as I speak on behalf of or about individuals who possess characteristics that I might not possess. These individuals may have directly experienced forms of oppression that I have not.

My intention in writing this book is to share ideas that might assist people personally to improve their relationships and professionally to provide effective leisure services by becoming more responsive to diversity and practicing inclusion. I am, however, limited in my perspective by each of the characteristics associated with my privilege in society. Some of those characteristics include being a middle-aged adult (age), male (gender), Caucasian (race), having considerable financial and intellectual resources (class), being raised Christian (religion), being heterosexual (sexual orientation), living in the United States (residence), and having at least average physical and cognitive abilities (disability). Within the culture I was raised and currently live, each of these characteristics is associated with privilege.

In her chapter titled "The Problem of Speaking for Others," Linda Alcoff (1995) warned that speaking about and speaking for others is problematic because both of these actions require us to represent others; as a result she suggested that when doing so we must constantly work to empower people who have been oppressed with our descriptions. Similarly, Gayatri Spivak (1999) concluded that as a result of the challenges of representation, complete understanding of other people is impossible; consequently, efforts to represent others must be based on working responsibly within the context of such impossibility. More recently, Amy Histerberger (2007, p. 74) wrote that since authors, teachers, and researchers hold a position of power and authority, speaking about others "requires a commitment to an ethical involvement in the representation of 'others'" and, therefore, we must be self-critical as we strive to empower those who have been oppressed.

I feel it is important that I guard against presenting material in a paternalistic manner. *Paternalism* involves an approach to relationships in which the desire to help, advise, and even protect may result in neglecting individual choice and personal responsibility. Although the intention to care for others is responsible, disregarding people's ability to take control of their lives is often disrespectful. Russ Shafer-Landau (2010, p. 33) in describing the fundamentals of ethics, identified the problem of paternalism as it relates to self-determination:

> *It's a good thing to be able to exercise autonomous choice, and this explains what is objectionable about paternalism—someone's limiting your liberty against your will, but for your own good.*

As a teacher, author, and researcher, I must work to avoid being paternalistic. Similarly, leisure service professionals must also guard against approaching interactions, relationships, and service delivery in a paternalistic manner.

The mere fact that people are hired as leisure service providers places them immediately in a position of power. Power involves the capacity to control and influence other people and their actions. Often participants view leisure service providers as role models and consciously or unconsciously imitate and incorporate providers' behaviors into their behavioral repertoires.

In their book on ethical decision making associated with recreation and leisure, McLean and Yoder (2005, p. 197) concluded by encouraging students and professionals in the leisure service field to make a difference:

> *Whether you realize it or not, you are incredibly privileged. You have a chance to make a difference in the world. If you are reading this book, you're probably either already in leisure and recreation or you are considering or preparing for a career in this field. But with this privilege comes an awesome responsibility: We can make decisions based on only our own wants and needs, we can continue as before without thinking about our actions, or we can be a part of creating a better world by actively deciding to do so. As society slowly but surely recognizes the importance of leisure and recreation,*

*even more authority will be granted to us and even more will be
expected of us. In that respect, times have never been better or
worse for our field. Much promise and many challenges await
leisure services personnel in every imaginable setting. You will
need to carefully weigh the consequences of your decisions and
actions, consider the obligations and rights of all people, and
strive to live a virtuous life both professionally and privately.*

Considering the words of McLean and Yoder and the mantra of Spider-Man as shared with him by his uncle Ben, *with great power comes great responsibility*, it may be helpful to reflect on the idea that each time we interact with the people we serve we influence them in some way. Hopefully, this will lead us to recognize and eliminate any unconscious sense of superiority and remind us to be humble and respectful of the people whom we serve.

Assumption #4: Inclusion is good.

Inclusion involves people living together in the same community so that they share experiences and develop an appreciation for one another. The practice of inclusion promotes valuing of differences in each other by recognizing that each person has an important contribution to make to our society. *Diversity* is associated with variety; within the context of this book the term 'diversity' is used to address the variety associated with humans relative to ethnicity, socioeconomics, gender, ability, sexual orientation, race, and age.

Inclusion implies that everyone deserves to be given a chance to be a part of a community from the beginning of their lives. Including all people in a pluralistic society can be challenging but ought to be embraced. A *pluralistic society* is a diverse public comprised of groups of different ethnic, religious, political, or other dissimilar backgrounds.

Pluralism is a condition of society in which numerous distinct ethnic, religious, or cultural groups coexist. Pluralism assumes that race, gender, ethnicity, sexual orientation, class, disability and other such variables shape our experiences in relation to how we think about ourselves, and how we view and are viewed by others.

Assumption #5: Diversity enriches our world.

We value diversity when we are not only aware of differences, but we are also accepting and respecting of differences. Embracing people so that they feel included is a responsibility of all professionals who provide services to others.

Intolerance of difference and ambiguity leads to prejudice and bigotry. *Intolerance* involves an unwillingness or refusal to accept people who are different in some way from the person or the group in power. Intolerance occurs when actions are motivated by biases and hatred of individuals or groups based on characteristics including age, ancestry, color, disability, national origin, political belief, race, religious creed, sex, sexual orientation, gender identity, or veteran status. Acts of intolerance damage our society and result in unreasonable harm to the dignity, safety, and well-being of those who encounter this malicious form of discrimination.

Openness and comfort with difference and ambiguity promotes tolerance. *Tolerance* is the deliberate act of an individual or organization to refrain from disapproval, censure, or violence against the beliefs of another, despite a disagreement with those beliefs. This definition narrowly identifies tolerance as the absence of negative behaviors. When considering this narrow definition, Cooke (2004, p. 25) provides the following insight:

> *tolerating other individuals or groups implies a feeling of superiority over them. This is in direct conflict with the current philosophical foundation of diversity discussions, which recognizes that no one culture is intrinsically superior to another.*

A perhaps more useful approach involves the idea of embracement. *Embracement* is the ability and commitment to recognize, respect, engage, and negotiate differences while accepting the belief that human beings are diverse in many ways including their appearance, speech, behavior, and values. It also includes a belief that everyone ought to have the right to live in peace. This broader approach is sometimes inferred when using the word *tolerance,* although is more in keeping with the notion of *acceptance,* which implies inclusion.

The notion of embracing all individuals into leisure service is a result of humility and self-acceptance originating from a sense that we have nothing to prove and that an opposing perspective is not a threat. According to Simpson (2003; p. 31):

> *when a person is truly humble, the thought of condemning, rejecting, or ostracizing other people, their actions, or their ideas is not the natural way of reacting and if it were not for the we-versus-them mentality, there would be no need to guard against intolerance.*

True inclusion goes beyond tolerance toward embracing and recognizing the value of diversity and difference. When we embrace diversity we include individuals and groups as people who are part of the whole and appreciate what they bring to our group or, more generally, society (Figure 1.2).

Assumption #6: No one can be reduced to one characteristic.

For each person's sense of identity there is the intersection of many characteristics including age, gender, race, ethnicity, class, religion, sexual orientation, and ability. A unique combination of characteristics gives each of us our individuality. Our individuality distinguishes us from all other people.

Some people mistakenly think that a particular characteristic such as being short of stature, Jewish, or gay becomes *the* defining feature of the individual and that a person focuses on that characteristic continuously. Humans are

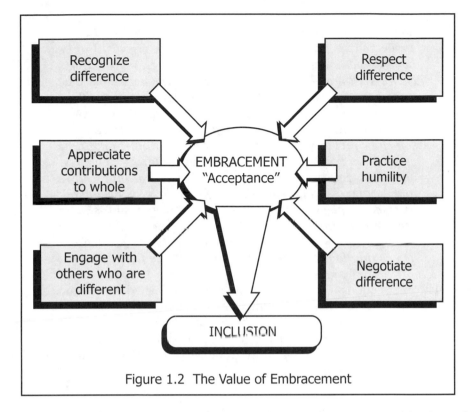

Figure 1.2 The Value of Embracement

complex and our sense of identity comes from a numerous combination of characteristics, including our leisure interests and patterns. The relevance of different characteristics shifts depending on the situation. Scully (2008, p.141) speaks to this issue:

> *Any theory of common political cause around identity must take into account that groups are made up of people with multiple, simultaneous, and sometime noncontinuous commitments and allegiances . . . no subject's identity may be explained wholly in terms of one category.*

When attempting to interact with other people it is helpful to consider that individual characteristics such as being blind, Hispanic, Mormon, female, or impoverished, are important and relevant in many situations and are not to be ignored; however, they are only one part of the complex individual whom you encounter. Leonard Pitts (2009, p. 154–155) addresses this issue specific to being African American:

> *I am a linear descendent of Mississippi slaves. My ancestry—and I suppose this is true of all ancestries—is a fundamental part of who I am, a wellspring of challenge and pride, my spiritual and emotional home. I am black. That's not, however, all that I am. I'm also a man. I am a native of*

Southern California. I am a husband and a father. I am a comic-book geek. I am a Christian. I am in my 40s. I am a hope-to-die Lakers fan. I am, in other words, many things, each relevant to different circumstances and occasions. The same is true of everyone. Of course, not one of the many things I am puts people on edge quite like blackness. Which is why some well-meaning people think it would be best if we could somehow factor race—alone, of the things I am—out of the picture . . . maybe if you're white, just ignoring blackness altogether comes to seem like a good idea. But that's naïve and faintly insulting. How do you foster equality by making an essential piece of who I am vanish? Decent people should seek balance instead—to make race neither smaller than it is nor larger. Because race is neither a defining facet, nor a demeaning facet, of individual identity. It's a facet, period.

The intersections of multiple identities and associated oppressions can all work together and have led to a multitude of social movements and organizations. The notion of intersectionality includes the belief that although every person possesses a variety of characteristics it is helpful to consider that each of these characteristics hold the potential to contribute to the way we are perceived by others and the opportunities we receive (Figure 1.3).

Assumption #7: We ought to consider perspectives that differ from our own.

Providing leisure services can be challenging, given that people living in diverse situations within our community consider different elements of an experience to be important to a meaningful existence. As a result, developing comprehensive leisure services requires careful attention to cultural factors and contexts.

It is helpful to develop an understanding that various perspectives exist and are important to consider when attempting to meet the needs of a diverse clientele. A perspective is an evaluation or assessment of a circumstance or situation from one person's point of view.

Although many examples presented in this book are associated with research, legislation, and service delivery based on situations primarily associated with the United States (U.S.), my intention is try to communicate perspectives and principles that are more global in nature. Globalization involves the consideration of what is happening throughout the world and attempting to consider perspectives that may be different than those of a particular culture.

When I consider some of the many perspectives that are held by individuals across the world, I recognize my perspective of issues is limited. The more I realize how narrow my perspective is and, subsequently, my need to broaden my perspective, I feel humility. As I encounter opportunities to become more humble, I believe I grow as an individual.

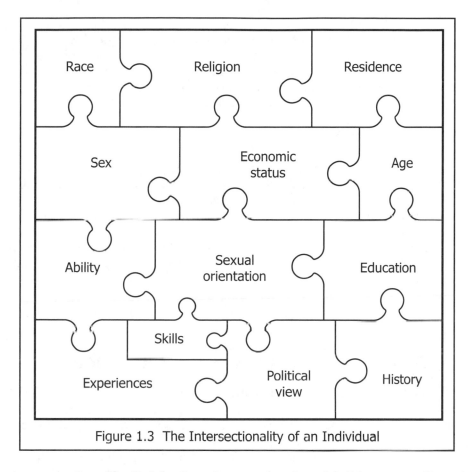

Figure 1.3 The Intersectionality of an Individual

Assumption #8: Critical and constructive thinking contribute to a more just society.

I challenge readers to not accept anything I present at face value; rather, I encourage you to think critically about the issues I raise and decide for yourself what you believe about these issues. Critical thinking involves clarifying the meaning and significance of what is being presented and to determine if there is sufficient explanation to accept the information as being true. In this way, people are encouraged to think for themselves and to analyze others' behaviors and material closely before accepting the information. I encourage readers to analyze the information presented in this book and then form their own opinions.

I think it is important as we learn new information for us to apply critical thinking. The practice of critical thinking can and does challenge unreasoning prejudice and discrimination of all kinds and encourages us to be fair and reasonable.

I also believe we then have the responsibility as we critically examine something to actively engage in the process of constructive thinking. Constructive thinking involves building on initial ideas that help to improve or advance ideas. This position is supported by Colby and her colleagues (2002, p. 14) who stated that:

> *Colleges and universities should encourage and facilitate*
> *the development of students' capacities to examine complex*
> *situations in which competing values are at stake, to employ*
> *both substantive knowledge and moral reasoning to evaluate*
> *the problems and values involved, to develop their own*
> *judgments about these issues and in respectful dialogue with*
> *others, and then to act on their judgments.*

So, while it is helpful to critique information, it is also important to offer alternatives, offer ways to successfully be inclusive. My intent in writing this book is to provide some information in a constructive manner so that readers will increase their knowledge and skills associated with providing inclusive leisure services.

The book is designed to either start you thinking about creating inclusive leisure services or help you to expand your current thinking on the topic; however, it is my hope that as you gain experience, you choose to use critical and constructive thinking to move beyond the suggestions contained in this book by discovering and creating innovative ways to foster inclusion (Figure 1.4).

What is the value of reading this book?

With each day that passes, communities are becoming more diverse. While many of us view this increasing diversity as a sign of the health and vigor of culture, the broad range of linguistic, cultural, ethnic, and ability differences challenges today's professional.

As a result, leisure service professionals provide programs to individuals with a variety of interests and characteristics and are expected to work with and have an understanding of individuals from many cultural, racial, and ethnic backgrounds. Miller and Schleien (2006, p. 10) speak to the status of inclusive recreation and the need for leisure service professionals to promote inclusion:

> *Signs exist signaling that we are on the verge of the "tipping*
> *point" when the provision of inclusive services becomes*
> *state-of-the-art across North America. It is likely that inclusive*
> *recreation will transform from a legally mandated service*
> *that agencies address primarily because it's the law (and*
> *politically correct), to an embraced and genuine philosophy*
> *that welcomes and accommodates people of all abilities. . . .*
> *We have that power to make a difference. It is important to*
> *keep in mind that if we don't continue on this path of progress,*
> *we are at risk of losing gains.*

To facilitate inclusion it is helpful to develop an awareness of and appreciation for diversity and an interest in involving all citizens in our programs. A variety of people suggest that experiences designed to educate others about inclusion should include information about diversity, specific conditions, and

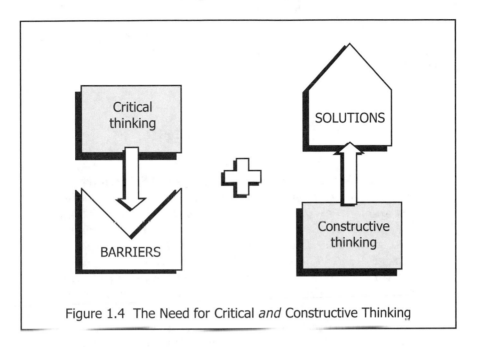

Figure 1.4 The Need for Critical *and* Constructive Thinking

relevant legislation, as well as encouragement of appropriate attitudes and skills needed to promote inclusion. Some professionals are calling for the hiring of personnel with these characteristics and the continued training of these professionals.

Leisure service professionals have identified a need to train staff on issues related to diversity and disability awareness, sensitivity toward all people, and methods for modifying programs so that they can be inclusive. Research findings support observations that leisure service personnel are perceived as not being equipped to conduct inclusive programs, both in terms of staff-to-participant ratios and knowledge regarding activity adaptations and programming techniques.

For example, after surveying over 300 professionals, Herbert (2000) concluded that staff should acquire greater knowledge of inclusive practices. Also, Anderson and Heyne (2000) conducted a series of focus groups with leisure services providers and participants and concluded that, relative to inclusive leisure, service providers lacked awareness, acceptance, and information, and they needed assistance with promoting social inclusion, physical access, communication, and networking between agencies and consumers.

Leisure service providers are in an excellent position to enhance the lives of people who have been oppressed in some manner. Services we design can improve participants' sense of competence and self-determination. The ability to make choices and take control of their lives can permit all individuals to match their skills to the challenges presented in community recreation opportunities.

Once we recognize our ability to enhance the quality of life for all people, we can develop strategies to promote inclusive leisure services. We can build on people's talents and opportunities and know that all people bring important contributions to community life.

What is the problem?

Ignorance is of increasing concern. The public discourse of anti-intellectualism poses ignorance as a positive alternative and antidote to elitism, and in polls of the U.S. population, one of the most elite populations of the world, reveal alarming ignorance about world geography and history as well as current events. The problem is not explainable by lack of access to resources for knowledge and information, nor is it a problem that decreases with the advantage of class. It is, or appears to be, a willful ignorance.

As noted in the quote above from Linda Alcoff (2007, p. 39), a major challenge for the world is ignorance. This challenge often stems from the inability or unwillingness of people to engage in meaningful dialogue with other people who are different from them in some way (Figure 1.5).

This lack of interaction results in people not developing an understanding of the common humanity that exists between them; rather, this ignorance can be exacerbated when people discriminate and segregate individuals. *Exacerbation* occurs when an already negative situation becomes worse. Again, Leonard Pitts (2009, p. 152) provides a helpful description of this problem specific to the U.S:

[O]ur level of intercultural dialogue in this country is abysmal. . . . a significant portion of the insult and hurt feelings that pass between races, genders, sexual orientations, [and] religions, probably grows not out of intent, but ignorance. . . The problem is that we live cookie-cutter lives, go through our days hemmed in by comfort zones, cloistered by our perspectives, surrounded by people who look and sound like us. We don't know the exotic-looking people who live just across the street, just down the block, just around the corner. All we know is that they are, in some highly visible way, Not Like Us.

Ignorance exists within people of privilege, who are oblivious to the life experiences and living conditions of those who have been oppressed. People who are privileged tend not to consider factors for which they are advantaged such as with class, ability, gender, race, or ethnicity; as a result, they often do not readily detect acts of discrimination and oppression. Norine Dresser (1996, p. 8) made the following reflection:

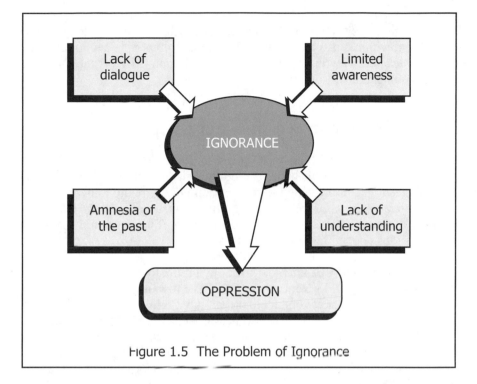

Figure 1.5 The Problem of Ignorance

I wrote Multicultural Manners because I wanted to ease the conflicts and misunderstandings that happen to all of us every day. My experience as a teacher has convinced me that we really want to understand and accept each other; most of our failures stem from ignorance rather from bad intentions.

Often members of privileged groups fail to learn about people less fortunate, and at times refuse to recognize their shared humanity with these individuals. Unfortunately, many people of privilege perceive the goals of those who are oppressed to be in opposition to theirs. In describing this distinction associated with race in the U.S., Mills (2007, p. 35) stated:

Inevitably, then, this will affect white social cognition—the concepts favored (e.g., today's "color blindness"), the refusal to perceive systematic discrimination, the convenient amnesia about the past and its legacy in the present, and the hostility to black testimony on continuing white privilege and the need to eliminate it to achieve racial justice.

Across the world and throughout history, people have been and are oppressed because of the ignorance of others. Oppression has occurred because people possess a particular characteristic related to age, gender, race, ethnicity, class, sexual orientation, or religion, which is not embraced or accepted by people in power.

By reading this section of the chapter, you will have concluded that there is a problem within our society, and that it stems from people's ignorance. This ignorance leads to viewing other people as having an inferior status resulting in oppression and discrimination.

How can we make a difference?

Hopefully, as you read this book you will become concerned about the importance of including all people in community leisure services. Although many suggestions are presented in this text on how to relate to people, *I have found one idea that helps me most to guide my interactions with all people,* including those who have experienced some form of oppression. I ask myself these questions depending on the situation:

- When I encounter a man older than me, I think to myself, if that were my father, how would I want others to behave toward him?
- When I encounter a woman older than me, I think to myself, if that were my mother, how would I want others to behave toward her?
- When I encounter a child, I think to myself, if that were one of my sons, David or Steven, how would I want others to behave toward that child?
- When I encounter a woman about my age, I think to myself, if that were my wife, Amy, how would I want others to behave toward her?
- When I encounter a man my age, I think to myself, if that were me, how would I want others to behave toward me?

I use my answers to these questions to help determine my actions toward all individuals. When I do this, I am then more likely to act toward people with kindness, dignity, and respect.

Since I have spent some of my life interacting with, befriending, and providing services to people with some very challenging conditions, I have been asked: "How do you know if a person will respond to you, that the person even knows you are there, or if your efforts to include that person work?" My response to this question is always the same. I tell people that sometimes I am not sure whether a person is aware I am there; however, *I always assume that the person is aware of me and that the person benefits from my contact.*

I would much prefer to assume that a person is benefiting by my actions and be wrong, than to assume that they could not, and not give them the chance. As I explain this concept I often share the quotation by Baer (1981) when he responded to the question "Why should we proceed as if all people are capable of learning under instruction?"

> *If I proceed in this way, sometimes—perhaps often—I will be right, and that will be good. What will be good is not that I will have been right (much as I enjoy that), but rather that some children who we otherwise might have thought could not learn will learn at least something useful to them. (p. 93)*

As you read this text, you may notice that the chapter titles and the various headings used throughout the book begin with action verbs. I intentionally included these words to encourage readers to take action and implement what has been learned.

When we gain knowledge about inclusion, we have a responsibility to advocate for the empowerment of people who have been oppressed in some manner. We also have the responsibility to promote their inclusion into the community, and, more specifically, to promote their inclusion in leisure opportunities within communities. To help emphasize this point, Fulghum (1989, p. 107) stated:

> *I do not want to talk about what you understand about this world. I want to know what you will do about it. I do not want to know what you hope. I want to know what you will work for. I do not want your sympathy for the needs of humanity. I want your muscle. As the wagon driver said when they came to a long, hard hill, "Them that's going on with us, get out and push. Them that ain't, get out of the way."*

Final Thoughts

Although there is tremendous potential for leisure to enhance the lives of all individuals, this potential is not being fully realized in the lives of many people who experience oppression. One solution is to educate leisure service professionals on ways to promote inclusion.

The broad issue of human rights is concerned with reconfiguring how people who have been oppressed are viewed first, and foremost, as human beings. These individuals who have legal and moral rights and responsibilities that are the same as people who have been privileged. Hopefully, by getting to know some people through this book, we can avoid creating stereotypes, and we will see the value in providing inclusive leisure services.

I began this chapter presenting some values associated with offering inclusive leisure services. Colby and colleagues (2003, p. 13) identify values that college graduates should strive to develop such as those presented in this book.

> *These values include mutual respect and tolerance, concern for the rights and the welfare of individuals and the community, recognition that each individual is part of a larger social fabric, critical self-reflectiveness, and a commitment to civil and rational discourse and procedural impartiality.*

I realize there may be some information presented in this book with which you disagree or that even may contribute to feelings of discomfort; however, often discomfort leads to change. The saying "necessity is the mother of invention" has relevance here. If we are uncomfortable, we then are motivated to change. When we desire change, we have many options of what to change including changing our perspective about particular ideas.

Discussion Questions

1. What is the association of William Ernest Henley's poem "Invictus" to this book?
2. What is the relevance of the concept of oppression to this book and how is it related to respect?
3. What are the three primary components that make up self-determination?
4. What is the relationship between the concepts of intolerance, tolerance, and embracement?
5. What is our responsibility associated with being in positions of privilege and power so that we avoid being paternalistic?
6. How might a global perspective influence our sense of humility?
7. What is the relevance of critical and constructive thinking to developing inclusive leisure services?
8. What is the relationship between ignorance and discrimination?
9. Why is poverty a consideration when providing leisure services?
10. What can leisure service providers do to help include all people into the services they provide?

Chapter 2
Celebrate Inclusion

Inclusion is recognizing that we are one
even though we are not the same.
-Shafik Abu-Tahir

Orientation Activity: Consider Inclusion

Directions Alone: Read the lyrics presented below and the statement quoted above. Write a paragraph describing what you think the authors meant when they wrote these words.

It's been a long time coming; Up the mountain kept runnin'
Souls of freedom kept hummin'; Channeling Harriet Tubman
Kennedy, Lincoln, and King; We gotta invest in that dream
It feels like we're swimming upstream;
It feels like we're stuck in-between A rock and a hard place,
We've been through the heartaches; And lived through the darkest days
If you and I made it this far, Well then hey, we can make it all the way
And they said no we can't, And we said yes we can
Remember it's you and me together . . .
-will.i.am – Lyrics from "It's a New Day"

Directions with Others: Divide into small groups and discuss your interpretation of the statements with other members. After a specified time, share your responses with the entire group.

Debriefing: Inclusion does not mean we are all the same or we all agree; rather, inclusion means that we celebrate our diversity and differences with respect and gratitude.

Inclusion does not mean that people are oblivious to individual differences. This sentiment is similar to the notion of "color blindness" that infers that all people are the same and we do not notice differences.

Inclusion develops a community in which all people are knowledgeable about and supportive of other people. That goal is not achieved by some false image of homogeneity in the name of inclusion. Consider the following questions when reflecting on the activity:

- How do you define inclusion?
- How does the statement by Shafik Abu-Tahir relate to inclusion?
- What did you learn by doing this activity?

Introduction

The lyrics presented at the beginning of this chapter provide a place to begin to discuss the idea of inclusion. Inclusion is a way of looking at the world and helping people come together. As people come together, they get to know one another, begin to understand one another, and develop an appreciation for one another.

The use of metaphors can be a way for us to learn about inclusion. For example, Eileen Szychowsky (Wheat, 2000, p. 78), a woman participating in a rafting trip, made the following observation:

> *In this perfect setting, the beauty, power, and fragility of the Grand Canyon reflect who we are as a society. Each rock layer within the canyon is a thing of unique beauty. However, it is the contrast of colors, shapes, and textures [that] only in unity become the Grand Canyon. Likewise, when individuals within our society, regardless of color, nationality, sexual orientation, ability, or disability work in unity, we too, become things of beauty and wonder.*

This metaphor may be helpful to consider when we attempt to develop leisure services that are inclusive. To address the topic of inclusion, several questions are discussed in this lesson:

- What is leisure?
- What is diversity?
- Why are some people excluded?
- What is inclusion?
- What is integration?
- What is a community?
- What do people want from their communities?
- Whose responsibility is it to create inclusive communities?

What is leisure?

Although the terms "recreation," "free time," and "leisure," may often be used interchangeably, there appears to be some consensus about how these terms are defined. Typically, *recreation* is defined as an activity developed by a society and designed primarily for fun, enjoyment, and satisfaction such as swimming, table games, and dance.

The notion of recreation, therefore, relates directly to the activity and is independent of the participant's feelings and experiences. People who participate in recreation activities may experience enjoyment and satisfaction, or they may encounter failure, rejection, and feelings of helplessness.

> For example, soccer is identified across the world as a recreation activity, an activity people engage in to have fun and experience enjoyment. However, if I am ill, feel incompetent in dribbling the ball, or I feel forced to play soccer because of peer pressure, I am engaging in a recreation activity but I may not be happy or having a good time.

Similarly, *free time* often describes time that is not obligated—time when daily tasks, such as responsibilities associated with family, work, or home maintenance, are not being attended to. When people are not busy performing specific required tasks, they possess free time. Although many people experience enjoyment and satisfaction during their free time, this free time may trigger feelings of boredom, anxiety, and despair in others.

> For instance, people who are chemically dependent and have abused substances such as alcohol may view free time as a difficult time since that is when they typically make decisions that lead to further substance abuse. Therefore, some treatment approaches, such as Alcoholics Anonymous, work to "fill up" people's free time with meetings.

Leisure is a complex concept that is multi-dimensional (see Figure 2.1, p. 26). Through participation in *leisure*, people:

- perceive freedom to engage in the experience
- feel positive emotions such as enjoyment
- find their experience to be meaningful
- are intrinsically motivated to engage in the experience
- find their experience to contribute to their sense of identity
- become self-determined

Leisure, then, is an experience, a process, and a subjective state of mind. As a state of mind, leisure transcends time, environments, and situations. Leisure allows us to express our *freedom*, and that it is an inalienable human right. For that reason, we must make every effort to help all people become involved in active leisure participation. The challenge lies in finding ways to remove barriers to participation while providing opportunities to develop the skills, awareness, and understanding needed to freely choose participation in various leisure experiences. The goal in providing leisure services, then, is to help individuals develop the skills and opportunities needed to feel free to participate in such chosen experiences.

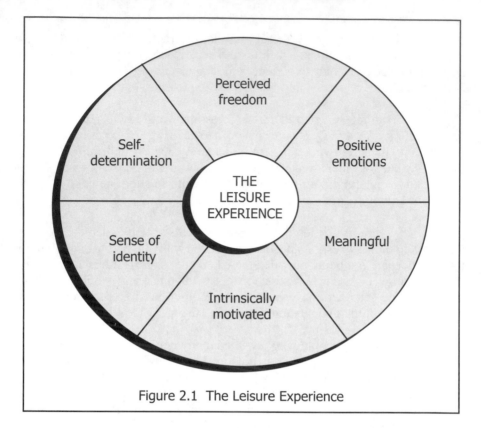

Figure 2.1 The Leisure Experience

To engage in leisure is to express talents, demonstrate capabilities, achieve one's potential, and experience a variety of *positive emotions* associated with participating in enjoyable and *meaningful activities*. Typically, these positive emotions include such feelings as enjoyment, happiness, excitement, relaxation, and joy that lead us to be intrinsically motivated to participate.

Intrinsic motivation refers to the motivation one has for doing the activity because of the expected pleasure of participation in the activity itself, not because of expected results or external rewards. Russell (1996, p. 48) provided the following illustrations to help us to better understand the notion of the leisure experience:

> *Leisure gives us a sense of living for its own sake. Cross-country skiers often exclaim about the sensations of peacefulness and physical exertion while gliding along. Artisans may explain their interest in working with clay on the potter's wheel because of the elastic, smooth substance responding to their hands. Dancing could be described as moving to a rhythm. Hikers often stress the experience of being a part of the beauty of the natural environment. These are all intrinsic rewards.*

Another dimension involves the types of activities or particular contexts in which we engage; many activities and contexts that are identified in a particular culture as "recreation" often are conducive for encouraging positive emotions. Leisure is associated with time in which we feel we have the knowledge and skills to participate and that we are free from responsibilities and obligations. After interviewing people of over 10 different ethnic backgrounds, Livengood and Stodolska (2004, p. 202) concluded that:

> *[a]ctivity was not perceived as the most salient feature of their leisure lives. In fact, our study showed that the activity itself was secondary to the freedom to do the activity of choice in an unrestricted manner.*

Leisure also affects our *sense of identity.* Leisure involvement should positively influence our perceptions of ourselves. In discussing positive ways to view ourselves and others, Fulghum (1989) illustrated the role leisure can play in defining our identities:

> *Making a living and having a life are not the same thing. Making a living and making a life that's worthwhile are not the same thing. Living the good life and living a good life are not the same thing. A job title doesn't even come close to answering the question "What do you do?" But suppose that instead of answering that question with what we do to get money, we replied with what we do that gives us great pleasure or makes us feel useful to the human enterprise? (p. 65)*

The perceptions, attitudes, and feelings of the individual during a certain time and within a particular context or activity influence the leisure experience. Since our perceptions are culturally influenced, roles and meanings associated with gender, race, ethnicity, class, and ability affect whether we experience leisure and the way we experience leisure. In addition, leisure involvement can satisfy a variety of needs associated with self-determination including expressions of autonomy, connectedness, and competence.

As stated previously, *self-determination* involves being autonomous with the perceived freedom of having options and making choices, having a sense of competence with the belief and confidence of being successful, and developing a sense of connection with others that promotes a sense of affiliation and affection. Leisure provides a context and opportunity to express self-determination and is also a means to contribute to perceptions of being self-determined.

The practical value of knowing what contributes to experiencing leisure leads us to concentrate on facilitating the leisure experience. In turn, learning how to facilitate leisure makes it possible for us to reduce or eliminate constraints and barriers to leisure participation. A particular kind of leisure expression that involves spontaneity, purposelessness, creation of an imaginary world, pleasure, and self-expression—activity that can range from fairly aimless and disorganized activity to very complex—can be identified as *play.*

In summary, free time exists when people are not consumed by require-ments associated with work or requirements of daily living. Recreation is typically associated with activity designed to be fun but might not result in people experiencing positive emotions. Finally, leisure and play depend on and emphasize the perspective of the individual and are associated with intrinsic motivation and self-determination. In addition, leisure and play transcends time, environments, and situations.

What is diversity?

We are living in a diverse world. *Diversity* is the existence of difference or variety resulting in recognition that two or more things have unlike characteristics or elements. These characteristics or elements include a multitude of variables such as race, ethnicity, national origin, gender, age, ability, and sexual orientation, as well as veteran status, prior life experiences, socio-economic background, communication styles, physical characteristics, learning styles, educational background, geographic location, work experience, and any other characteristics that make individuals distinct. Katie Coffroad (2005, p. 20) warned that:

> *When asked to characterize diversity, most agencies typically focus on race, ethnicity, national origin, gender, abilities, religion, sexual orientation, and veteran status. Diversity is, however, much more. It is also about prior experiences, socioeconomic backgrounds, communication styles, physical characteristics, learning styles and all other unique characteristics that make individuals distinct.*

While the word *diversity* often implies differences between cultural groups, the word also refers to differences that exist *within* cultural groups. It is helpful if we work to avoid making generalizations about a particular group of individuals that share one common characteristic but likely possess many other attributes that are different.

Nancy Miller and Catherine Sammons (1999, p. 1–2) wrote about diversity and difference and encouraged us to understand and then change our reactions:

> *Everybody's different. Some of us have differences that no one notices, while others are different in various apparent ways. We all look different from each other, sometimes by chance, sometimes by choice. Our behavior patterns have incredible variety, even within our own families. We all have unique physical strengths and limitations as well as different learning capabilities, creative talents, and social skills. Everybody reacts to difference . . . some attract us, some surprise or frighten us, and some aren't important to us at all. Our reactions to differences are sometimes complex and confusing. We often want to be open-minded and feel*

comfortable about other people's differences but find that some unfamiliar difference make us feel tense and judgmental . . . we cannot avoid reacting to differences. What we do after our first reaction, however, is based on our learning and choices.

Why are some people excluded?

The same excuses being used to exclude people with disabilities were used to segregate people of color. However, as presented in detail later in the book, the U.S. landmark decision of *Brown v. Board of Education* (1954) stipulated that state laws establishing separate public schools for students who were Black and White, which resulted in the denial of children who were Black to receive equal educational opportunities, was unconstitutional. The decision sent a clear message to U.S. citizens, as well as other countries, that *separate is not equal*.

Any situation stipulating that some people are segregated because they are different is a civil-rights issue. It is discriminatory when any group of people must earn the right to be included in their communities.

Historians agree that segregation of people has been practiced for centuries across the globe, and there are entrenched attitudes, laws, policies, and structures that work against achieving inclusion. However, it is helpful to consider that the alternative to segregation is not *dumping* individuals into groups and ignoring their individual differences; rather, inclusion involves developing ways to build communities that acknowledge and celebrate individual differences. Consider the words of Martin Luther King, Jr. (Carson, 1998, pp. 8, 12):

> *For a long, long time I could not go swimming until there was a Negro YMCA. A Negro child in Atlanta could not go to any public park. In many of the stores downtown I couldn't go to a lunch counter to buy a hamburger or a cup of coffee. I could not attend any of the theaters . . . I could never adjust to the separate waiting rooms, separate eating places, separate rest rooms, partly because the separate was always unequal and partly because the very idea of separation did something to my sense of dignity and self-respect.*

People are often excluded because they possess a characteristic that is somehow different from the mainstream of society or from those in power. This difference can come in the form of race, ethnicity, religion, sex, age, sexual orientation, ability and any other characteristic in which people can differ. Therefore, leisure service providers should address the challenge of including all people, regardless of characteristics, in meaningful leisure services.

What is inclusion?

To be *included* is to be considered a part of the whole, a part of a group. *Inclusion* then involves the presence of someone or something in a group. When using the word *inclusion* in the context of people who have been oppressed in some manner, there is an assumption as identified in the previous chapter that inclusion is good. It is an ethical responsibility that society welcomes all people so that they feel included in society.

To achieve inclusion, many people stress the importance of creating a sense of belonging. For example, Charlie Bullock, Mike Mahon, and Charlie Killingsworth (2010, p. 78–79) stated that:

> *Inclusion gives people equal opportunity to grow and develop to their fullest potential. The fundamental principle of inclusion is the valuing of diversity within the human community. When inclusion is fully embraced, we abandon the idea that children or adults have to become "normal" in order to contribute to the world. We begin to look beyond typical ways of becoming valued members of a community, and in so doing begin to realize the achievable goal of providing all people with an authentic sense of belonging.*

The following are characteristics of inclusion that can be embraced by leisure service providers:

- recognize we are one, yet we are different
- create chances for others to experience freedom to participate
- value each person and value diversity
- support participation

Recognize We Are One, Yet Different

An inclusive philosophy means the greater the diversity in a given community, the more it is capable of creating new visions. Sayeed (1999, p. 14) stated:

> *Inclusion—the word itself conjures a picture of belonging, of being part of woven threads of colorful fabric which are the communities we live in.*

Similar to the metaphor of the Grand Canyon, the image of colorful fabric helps to capture the spirit of inclusion.

A man that devoted much of this life promoting the inclusion of all people was Dr. Martin Luther King, Jr. He asked people to put aside the clashes among groups and to endorse a more inclusionary view of their society. By developing leisure services that are inclusive, we promote ideals expressed by Dr. King and other wise leaders such as Mahatma Gandhi, Helen Keller, the Dalai Lama, Nelson Mandela, Mother Teresa, and many other perceptive individuals.

Create Chances for Others to Experience Freedom to Participate

A valuable aspect of inclusion involves the creation of opportunities for all people. Inclusion does not mean, however, that people must participate in groups characterized by being diverse. What inclusion does mean is that all people should feel welcome and supported to participate in community programs of their choosing. Inclusion involves people being in the community from the beginning so that they are raised in an environment that accepts them and celebrates their diversity.

It is not a problem if some people choose to participate in groups that are homogeneous. Homogeneous groups mean that people within those groups have certain identified similarities.

> For example, people may participate in a woman's bowling league, an evening social sponsored by Alcoholics Anonymous, a fraternity formal, a luncheon for the Sons and Daughters of Italy, a recreation majors' club tailgate, or a wheelchair basketball tournament.

The important point to remember is that people attend these groups because they freely choose to participate rather than because they feel they have few or no other options. Therefore, these individuals perceive that they have choices.

> As a specific illustration, research about people associated with one particular ethnic group supports the conclusion that some people participate in recreation activities sponsored by ethnic organizations designed to attract a homogenous groups. They participate in these activities in an attempt to preserve their ethnic culture in a pluralistic society.

However, a problem arises if people are relegated to participating in activities only experienced by a homogeneous group. This practice is discriminatory since these people perceive they do not have options.

Value Each Person and Value Diversity

An understanding of cultural diversity issues is crucial for leisure service delivery. As identified in the first chapter, if professionals are to provide leisure services equitably and continue moving forward toward a pluralistic society, awareness of cultural diversity can be helpful. This awareness can help us to avoid focusing only on privileged members and excluding those who are marginalized. Leisure service professionals will increasingly be required to develop programs to enhance the quality of life and leisure in pluralistic societies.

> For instance, although ethnic-oriented recreation activities allow immigrants and their descendants to come together

and preserve their culture, an obstruction to their freedom would exist if these individuals only felt welcome in activities sponsored by their ethnic organizations. Inclusion, then, intends to empower people to participate in recreation activities of their choosing rather than constrain them by limiting their opportunities.

Within inclusive communities, each person's talents are recognized, encouraged, and supported to the fullest extent possible. Inclusive communities view each person as an important and worthwhile member with responsibilities and a role to play in supporting others; all individuals have a mutually valued presence.

Diversity is valuable, not just to be tolerated, accepted, or even accommodated, but to be *valued and celebrated*. Inclusive contexts focus on:

- recognizing capacities of people
- realizing there is an array of contributions to be made
- believing that all people are inherently worthy
- doing one's best and helping others do the same

By assisting all people to feel they are valued members of a community, we can develop more effective leisure services. In addressing the role of leisure service providers in creating inclusion Dan Hibbler and Kim Shinew (2002, p. 32) stated that:

> *Too often, simply acknowledging diversity translates into focusing on differences, whereas celebrating diversity involves promoting mutual respect for a multitude of factors that differentiate one person from another. Practitioners must be exposed to, and embrace, the concept that differences enhance an agency.*

Support Participation

Fundamental to inclusion is the belief that everyone can benefit and participate in community leisure programs. *Participation* involves people actively taking part in an event or activity. Based on the belief that everyone belongs and everyone is welcome, an inclusive community views a problem as a sign that help is needed, not that a person must go elsewhere to solve the problem.

Therefore, rather than providing *special services*, programs that are only for people with unique characteristics, such as people with disabilities or those of a particular ethnic background, professionals work within the context of ongoing inclusive activities to support participation and interdependence. When we provide *supportive services* we take the "can do" approach that involves believing that with the appropriate supports, people can enjoy meaningful leisure experience with others in their communities.

Once we accept the premise that people possess similarities as well as differences from one another, we can work to eliminate the belief that some people must earn their way into a program by being like everyone else. When this belief is eliminated we then can focus on finding adequate support for individuals so that they can participate to the greatest extent possible.

> Support can come in the form of offering assistance to someone experiencing a challenge that exceeds their current skill level, being willing to make a change to a scheduled event, allowing someone to take additional time to complete a task, or modifying the rules to an activity.

Typically, family members who have experienced the success of inclusion during school hours want their children to continue participating in inclusive leisure services after school. Kyle Glozier (2000, p. 14), an insightful and mature eighth-grade boy who happens to have cerebral palsy, made the following comments about inclusion:

> *Including kids with disabilities from the very beginning will begin to change society as a whole. Together we can teach society to not push people with disabilities out of the way, forgetting that we deserve our rights as citizens of the United States. . . . When I ask my brother, Nigel, "How do you feel having me as your brother?" he answers, "Good. I like you. You're nice." And when I asked my brother Jason, the same question, he says, "You're okay, but you're really scary when you're mad" . . . If all people are exposed to people with disabilities at an early age, the disability makes no difference at all. They see just another person. They see past the disability. This is how we need to see society change.*

Inclusion is about ensuring choices, having support, having connections, and being valued. People can make many choices because they have friends, family, and community to support them.

The need for *connections* becomes obvious when you consider that every reference ever given for an internship, job, credit application, or housing application has been a person with whom we have connected. People have connections and support from others because they are valued. Though people may lack certain talents that are valued by our society, those who know them have found qualities in them they like. For example:

> Diane values Larry because she can tell him anything and knows that Larry will not share the information with others. Maria appreciates Erica because she will not quit working at something until it is done. Others value Marty because he is an optimist. None of these traits are dependent on a deep intellect or great physical prowess.

What is integration?

Integration has been important to all civil rights movements to create a context for people who had previously been segregated to be synthesized into society. *Integration* involves the movement of disenfranchised members of a society into the mainstream of community life, allowing them to gain full access to opportunities, rights, and services available to those who have been privileged. Someone in a society is *disenfranchised* when that person has been deprived of a right that privileged members of the society receive.

Integration has been desired globally for people who have been persecuted as a result of their religious practices, ethnic and racial heritage, age, sex, sexual orientation, and ability. However, some people are abandoning the term *integration* when discussing best practices for people who have been disenfranchised, since it implies that the goal is to return someone who has been excluded back into the mainstream of community life.

Inclusion, unlike integration, does not depend on being segregated in the first place; rather, all individuals have the right to be included in opportunities and responsibilities available in their communities. The phrase *a part from the start* is central to the notion of inclusion. This distinction is important because it moves the concept of inclusion of people into community-based programs from preferred best practices to an ethical mandate (Figure 2.2).

The question for those delivering leisure services is no longer, "How do we integrate some people who were previously excluded?" but rather, "How do we develop a sense of community and mutual support that fosters success among all members of our community?" If we can develop a feeling of community and support within all of our leisure participants, we will likely succeed and the goal of inclusion will be achieved.

What is a community?

When addressing the idea of community, it is helpful to consider that a *community* is often identified as a context that contains a sense of place, people, and a feeling of belonging. A *sense of place* is developed from where people live, work, recreate, and generally spend time. The *people* who comprise a community are individuals with whom we interact and develop relationships. A feeling of *membership or belonging* is based on a sense of connection with the group of people in a particular context.

In a community, there are varied tasks to be performed. Members of the community engage in interesting and satisfying roles that also benefit the group as a whole. By fulfilling roles, people meet their responsibilities as members of a community. In his book, *The Last Lecture*, Randy Pausch (2008, p. 175) had this to say about rights, responsibilities, and communities:

> *We've placed a lot of emphasis in this country on the idea of people's rights. That's how it should be, but it makes no sense to talk about rights without talking about responsibilities.*

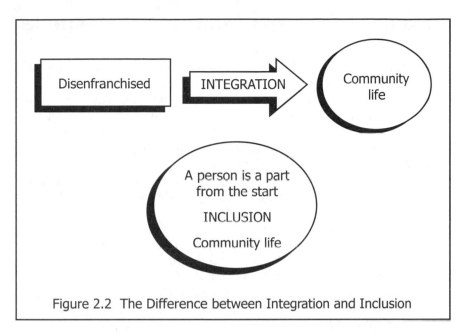

Figure 2.2 The Difference between Integration and Inclusion

Rights have to come from somewhere, and they come from the community. In return, all of us have a responsibility to the community.

Community members are given *respect* and they enrich the community with their variety. A community flourishes when its members continually develop and apply their talents in mutually enriching ways. Scully (2008, p. 148–149) describes community in this way:

> *"Community" implies a distinctive pattern associated with a "group" or "collective." We speak of communities rather than groups at times when we want to convey the idea that the bonds between members are something more than a contract between rational decision makers. . . . The language of community carries a greater consciousness of mutual responsibility, with all the benefits and burdens that entails.*

Although a sense of place is often considered an important aspect of developing a feeling of community, some people feel that it is the connections that we make within that place that are most critical. Taking this a step further, clearly our sense of community is shaped by where we are and who we know; however, *the essence of community comes from how we feel.* If we feel membership and belonging, we will then perceive that we are a member of a community.

What do people want from their communities?

Rosa Parks, a respected African American woman among many members of her community who will be discussed in more depth later in the book, refused to give up her bus seat to a man who was Caucasian on the afternoon of December 1, 1955. As a result of her decision, she was arrested and incarcerated. Ms. Parks' actions were the stimulus for the bus boycott in Montgomery, Alabama, and a year later when the boycott ended, segregation on buses was ruled unconstitutional.

Why did Ms. Parks make such a decision that would result in her incarceration? What did she want from her community? Rosa Parks (1992, p. 116) wrote of the fateful day:

> *People always say that I didn't give up my seat because I was tired, but that isn't true. I was not tired physically, or no more tired than I usually was at the end of a working day. I was not old, although some people have an image of me as being old then. I was forty-two. No, the only tired I was, was tired of giving in.*

So what did Rosa Parks want from her community? For that matter, what do all people who differ relative to age, gender, ability, socioeconomic status, race, religion, ethnic background, sexual orientation, education level, political affiliation, and language want? Frankly stated by Marsha Forest and Jack Pearpoint (1995, p. 1), individuals say:

> *"I want to be included!" This simple statement is being spoken, signed, key-boarded, whispered, and shouted by people of all ages, shapes, sizes, colors, and cultures. Many are making the request for themselves while others are asking for their friends or aging relatives. It is a simple request and the answer is equally easy: Welcome!*

When people want to be included in their communities, what do they mean? Based on a study exploring experiences of adults who had been oppressed residing in their communities, Walker (1999) concluded that when these adults had positive community experiences, they described their community as providing:

- a sense of safety
- a feeling of being known, a sense of identity
- familiarity with people and places
- a feeling of being liked or accepted
- a sense of accommodation

Parks are valuable aspects of any community and safety is an important concern for people accessing leisure services and facilities and developing a sense of community.

In a story describing the rebirth of Atlanta's Selena Butler Park, May (2011) suggested that professionals responsible for park operations leave lights on at night, work to increase police patrols, support neighborhood monitoring programs and promote safe and affordable public transportation.

It is helpful for us to work for inclusion of all people so that everyone is socially connected as we exchange and share responsibilities. Inclusion means that people become full, active, learning members of the community. Angi Sullivan and Mary Beth O'Brien (2001, p. 72) stated that:

In a perfect world, inclusion would just happen, but in reality, an inclusive community must be fostered through conscious efforts.

Many groups of oppressed people have been influenced by the social and political awareness created by global human rights movements. These people can identify with struggles of other disenfranchised people to achieve inclusion and meaningful equality of opportunity.

Disenfranchised groups are comprised of individuals who collectively have been deprived of their legal and moral rights or privileges, rights and privileges that are enjoyed by other members of that society. Inclusive leisure opportunities are a basic civil right for all human beings because people, regardless of ability or any other defining characteristic, deserve the opportunity to experience meaningful leisure. In describing their model of building a life of meaning, Cynny Carruthers and Colleen Hood (2007, p. 278) reported that:

All people desire a life of meaning wherein they can experience pleasure, participate equally in relationships with others, and make a contribution to their community and world. Building strengths and resources, empowering clients, and cultivating capacity contribute greatly to building a life of meaning.

Whose responsibility is it to create inclusive communities?

Although people who have been disenfranchised have greater possibilities to be welcomed into their communities than past generations, many people continue to experience constraints to leisure participation or be forced into segregated services. The responsibility for advocating and facilitating inclusion must shift from families to leisure service providers. Segregated recreation programs may have served a purpose in the past, but now many families and professionals believe all individuals should have the option of participating in activities with their peers.

Researchers have interviewed people with disabilities and their families and find that most participants report that specialized, segregated programs were available for people with disabilities in their communities; however, they express a desire for more inclusive leisure services. For example, Anderson and Heyne (2000, p. 25) reported that one parent stated:

> *We try to keep our daughter out of segregated programs as much as possible. There's a Saturday afternoon thing for people who are disabled, but we haven't taken her to those. We would prefer to have her go to the Y and be a part of the rest of the gang.*

We are encouraged to develop inclusive services that reflect the values and norms of a host of diverse groups. As discussed in the previous chapter, agencies that are truly inclusive not only tolerate difference but also embrace and celebrate differences.

Leisure service providers are in an excellent position to facilitate and enhance experiences of others. It is important to have as our goal to provide leisure services that reach all members of the community, treat everyone fairly, and help eliminate discrimination. A sense of community can be developed in various contexts in which leisure services are provided.

As a case study, Dawson and Liddicoat (2009) examined participants and families of a summer camp that was based on the promotion of self-determination via choice, empowerment of campers, and social engagement of staff with campers. The most prominent theme that emerged from their research was that the camp environment created an opportunity for participants to be a part of a supportive community.

Clearly, the community belongs to everyone, and everyone, regardless of knowledge and skills, belongs to the community. Inclusive leisure services can be a major avenue for promoting this sense of community.

Final Thoughts

Mother Teresa, Nelson Mandela, the Dalai Lama, Mahatma Gandhi, Martin Luther King, Jr., Helen Keller, and many other people who have dedicated their lives to promoting human and civil rights have shared a vision of inclusion. For leisure service professionals, this vision is a daily journey that may be assisted by the following:

- welcome all people to every aspect of our services
- provide all people with meaningful choices
- be knowledgeable about and supportive of others
- encourage interactions among people
- celebrate diversity and difference with respect and gratitude
- recognize and encourage each individual's talents
- view inclusion as a legal and ethical mandate

As we move forward with inclusion, we can take comfort knowing that inclusion enriches the lives of people who differ in age, gender, ability, socioeconomics, race, religion, ethnic background, sexual orientation, education level, political affiliation, and language.

The importance of inclusion was noted by Sakari Moberg (2003), who conducted a cross-cultural study of 1,636 education professionals, and found that most respondents felt that inclusion enhances social justice.

Social justice involves those actions that promote equality and solidarity to create a fair and just society that values human rights and recognizes the dignity of all people. Perhaps a fitting way to end this chapter is to share a sentiment from the Dalai Lama (1999, p. 164):

In order for us to overcome our tendency to ignore others' needs and rights, we must continually remind ourselves of what is obvious: that basically we are all the same. I come from Tibet; most of the readers of this book will not be Tibetan. If I were to meet each reader individually and look them over, I would see that the majority do indeed have characteristics superficially different from mine. If I were then to concentrate on these differences, I could certainly amplify them and make them into something important. But the result would be that we grew more distant rather than closer. If, on the other hand, I were to look on each as one of my own kind—as a human being like myself with one nose, two eyes, and so forth, ignoring differences of shape and color—then automatically that sense of distance would decrease. I would see that we have the same human flesh and that, moreover, just as I want to be happy and to avoid suffering, so do they. On the basis of recognition, I would quite naturally feel well disposed toward them. And concern for their well-being would arise almost by itself.

Discussion Questions

1. What is meant by the words "recreation," "free time," and "leisure?"
2. What is intrinsic motivation?
3. What is a disability according to the U.S. Americans with Disabilities Act?
4. What are examples of disabling conditions?
5. What are some characteristics associated with disabling conditions that can influence an individual's ability to experience leisure?
6. What is a community and what do people want from their communities?
7. Why are some people with disabilities not included in their communities?
8. What does inclusion mean?
9. What are some things we can do to value diversity?
10. How does the notion of "freedom of choice" relate to providing inclusive leisure services?
11. How are the Grand Canyon and a colorful fabric all metaphors for inclusion?
12. Why is the word "inclusion" used more than the word "integration" to describe the focus of leisure services for people with disabilities?
13. Whose responsibility is it to create inclusive communities?
14. What can we do to create inclusive leisure services?

Chapter 3
Understand Attitude Development

Injustice anywhere is a threat to justice everywhere.
-Martin Luther King, Jr.

Orientation Activity: Examine Differences and Similarities

Directions Alone: Record the following headings at the top of the page: name, difference, and similarity. Think of several people you know and list their names in the first column. Try to identify something about you and that person that is different. Once you have determined a difference, identify something that you and the person share or have in common.

Directions with Others: Move about the room and talk with each person. Identify something about the two of you that is different and record this characteristic. Once you have determined one difference, identify something the two of you have in common. Continue moving about the room finding new people to interview.

Debriefing: The individual qualities of people make them interesting. Why we like some people or why we respect other people is not necessarily due to our similarities, but frequently because they possess unique characteristics.

However, it is helpful to begin relationships with the belief that we share common characteristics. When we develop a bond with people we can accept their differences. If we encounter people who happen to be different from us and we work to identify and focus on similarities with those individuals, it is more likely that we will include that person and accept the differences. Respond to the following questions related to the orientation activity:

- What was most difficult aspect of the orientation activity?
- How did you feel when you talked about similarities with another person as compared with differences?
- How do you feel when you meet people and these people primarily focus on how you are different from them?
- How do you feel when you meet people and these people primarily focus on how you are similar to them?

Introduction

People who have been oppressed in some manner, such as immigrants or people with disabilities, not only experience the challenge of trying to master the dominant language or the actual physical, cognitive, or emotional tasks associated with their particular disability, but they also experience the often larger barrier of negative attitudes of society.

> For example, people who are immigrants and are learning the native language or anyone who is traveling in a foreign country who does not know the language will have challenges communicating with others. However, their communication can be severely impaired if people they encounter have negative attitudes about them. Conversely, their communication can be enhanced if people they meet have a positive attitude about them and are willing to be creative and work toward mutual understanding.

Negative attitudes toward people represent a major obstacle to successful adjustment. Throughout the world, various groups, including older adults, ethnic and racial minorities, and individuals living in poverty, are either not fully accepted or are discriminated against and devalued by those sharing the mainstream cultural perspective.

Unfortunately, negative attitudes of members of a community toward these disenfranchised people may halt the progress of inclusion efforts or deprive them of assistance necessary to ensure success. It is not the actual characteristic of the person as much as society's perception of that characteristic that poses the greatest barrier to leisure pursuits. As an illustration of a negative attitude and associated deplorable actions, the following is an excerpt from a newspaper article (Police say coach, 2005):

> *A T-ball coach allegedly paid one of his players $25 to hurt an 8-year-old mentally disabled teammate so he wouldn't have to put the boy in the game, police said Friday. Witnesses told police that [the coach] didn't want the boy to play in the game because of his disability. Police said the boy was hit in the head and in the groin with a baseball just before the game and did not play. He [the coach] was arrested on charges*

including criminal solicitation to commit aggravated assault and corruption of a minor.

Since a goal of this book is to encourage acceptance of diversity, examples that promote positive attitudes of acceptance are provided to counteract the type of appalling actions described above. Our attitudes play a critical role in supporting equal access to leisure services. Attitudes can create positive forces for change or can create major barriers.

The principles presented here apply to any person who is perceived as being different from those who are in power and privileged within our society. Therefore, it is valuable to remove barriers to leisure and stimulate development of approaches that facilitate meaningful leisure participation for all people. This chapter is designed to answer the following questions:

- Whose attitude matters?
- How are attitudes formed and expressed?
- What happens when we focus on differences?
- How can labels influence expectations?

Whose attitude matters?

The attitudes held by everyone influence people's inclusion in a community, so they are all important. However, specific to this discussion, the attitudes of leisure service professionals greatly influence community inclusion. A willingness to accept individuals into leisure programs is critical if inclusion is to work.

Unfortunately, attitudes of some professionals are not very supportive of inclusion. After interviewing professionals working for 13 different leisure service agencies, Germ and Schleien (1997, p. 32–33) reported that respondents identified negative staff attitudes as the number one barrier to inclusive community recreation:

> *One administrator suggested, "My staff have a resistance to learning about people with disabilities. They fear the inclusion experience." Supervisors also agreed with them, "My instructors are afraid. They have high expectations for themselves and they don't want to feel like failures." Administrators, supervisors, and program instructors acknowledged "fear" to be the primary attitudinal barrier for staff. Fear of shouldering responsibility for people with disabilities, failing to provide an enjoyable program for all participants, and addressing internal feelings and misgivings about disabilities were prominent stumbling blocks.*

Devine and Kotowski (1998) provided the following description that may be useful when considering the influence leisure service professionals might have on a person's life:

> *Mrs. K., a woman with gray hair who is somewhat stooped over and carrying an oxygen bottle, approaches the community swimming pool. She stops to rest on the bench outside the pool entrance. After resting, Mrs. K. enters and approaches the reception desk. She sits down again and raises her voice to get your attention. Mrs. K. asks if someone can come out from behind the desk and get her money as there is a long line of patrons waiting to pay and she can't stand for long periods of time. She also asks for assistance with opening the locker room door because it is too heavy for her to open. Mrs. K. has emphysema and goes to the pool several times a week to swim, one of the few activities in which she can still participate. Your attitude toward this woman and others like her contributes to their interest and willingness to continue participation in activities. In other words, your attitude matters when it comes to welcoming and including people with disabilities in recreation programs.*

How are attitudes formed and expressed?

To consider the impact of attitudes on our interactions with others, it may be helpful to examine how attitudes relate to our beliefs, our intentions, and our behaviors. Fishbein and Ajzen (1975) provide a frequently cited description of the relationship among:

- antecedents
- beliefs
- attitudes
- intentions
- behaviors

Antecedents are conditions that exist before beliefs, attitudes, and intentions are formed, and they exist prior to the occurrence of behaviors. Antecedent conditions set the stage for beliefs to develop.

A variety of circumstances can influence development of people's beliefs, such as their communities, past experiences, families, friends, and individual characteristics. These various conditions are considered antecedents to the development of beliefs.

> For example, Johari, a summer camp counselor, finds herself raising her voice with campers who are identified as being at-risk. She considers the antecedents that exist prior to her raising her voice and notices a pattern that when the youth begin to talk to each other and laugh while she is providing directions, she begins to raise her voice. By focusing on the antecedents, Johari now understands the situation better and can make a plan to positively change her behavior.

People's *beliefs* involve what they perceive to be true. These beliefs are composed of an individual's perception of information that has been available. Beliefs that are acquired may or may not be correct.

Convictions people have based on their beliefs influence development of their attitudes. Beliefs often refer to generally accepted tenets of society. In our society beliefs about many people who have been oppressed are often associated with thoughts that somehow these individuals are less able than other people.

> For instance, one particular belief that is presented in this book is that everyone wins when leisure services are inclusive.

A learned predisposition to respond to a given object, person, or idea in a consistent manner is identified as an *attitude*. This consistent manner can be either negative or positive. Once people develop an attitude about a group of people, when they encounter a person affiliated with this group they will tend to respond to this person in a similar way. Therefore, attitudes result in positive or negative feelings about some person, object, or issue.

> As a case in point, Tanner, a leisure service supervisor, mistakenly has the attitude that, a person who is Hispanic is lethargic and not motivated to work. As a result of this negative attitude, Tanner does not hire Edwardo, a qualified applicant who would be ideal for the advertised position.

Intentions indicate how much effort a person plans to exert to perform a behavior. People anticipate behaving a particular way based on the information they have acquired throughout their lives and the attitudes they have formed. However, what people *intend* to do is not always what they *actually* do.

> For example, based on the material presented in this book, Chun Hua, a recent graduate from a university, intends to promote inclusion and to develop inclusive leisure services in her first professional employment situation.

Attitudes impact behaviors. A *behavior* is any observable and measurable act, response, or movement by an individual that can be detected with at least one of the five senses. When clearly described, behaviors generally mean the same thing to different people.

As an illustration, while acting as a guide for a tour, you walk across a busy intersection and watch Irving, an older gentleman who is on the tour, slip and fall to the ground. As you move toward him to provide assistance, you observe the behavior of Tiva, an adolescent girl, as she speaks to the man and hold his arm to help him up.

As seen in Figure 3.1, antecedents, beliefs, attitudes, intentions, and behaviors are interrelated in a dynamic process of attitude development and expression. Each component of the process influences, and is influenced by, another. Therefore, when one component of the process is altered, the other components change accordingly.

Ulrich and Bauer (2003, p. 23) provided these insights about what is our responsibility associated with this dynamic process of attitude growth and demonstration:

> *After years in Nazi concentration camps, psychotherapist Viktor Frankel wrote in "Man's Search for Meaning" (1984) that each of us must find our own larger sense of what is happening to us, a "guiding truth" for our attitudes, beliefs, and actions, and then we must be willing to take responsibility for the choices we make.*

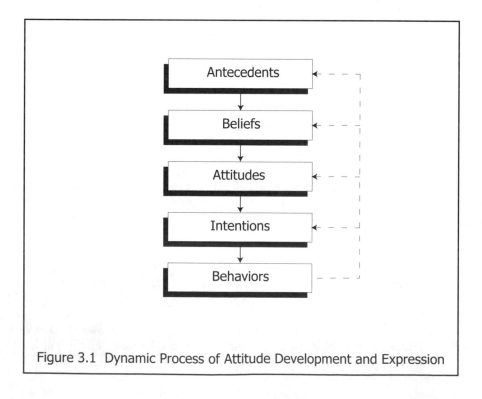

Figure 3.1 Dynamic Process of Attitude Development and Expression

What happens when we focus on differences?

People who possess differences associated with characteristics such as race, age, religion, ability, and sexual orientation can experience *stress* when interacting with one another. Tension between two different people might occur because neither person knows what the other expects. Nalini Krishnankutty (2007, p. A6) wrote:

> *as President Clinton once told interviewer Tim Russert on NBC's "Meet the Press," "The biggest problem confronting the world today is the illusion that our differences matter more that our common humanity." There is no doubt that we need to nurture this common humanity to live peacefully in the future.*

The perception of a person as being *different* results in personal stress, which can cause a strain in interactions as well as fear, anxiety, avoidance, and segregation. For example, Wanda, who has a physical disability, illustrated this point when she said:

> *People don't talk to me because of the way I am . . . they just kind of look at me and not really know what to say because they feel uncomfortable maybe, but I don't feel uncomfortable.*

When we respond to people's characteristics rather than their conduct, we may treat a given characteristic as a reason to exclude someone we think is different. We may feel no need for further justification because we attribute the consequences to the differences we see. We may neglect the other characteristics that we may share.

Some problems we experience interacting with other people are based on the way we see these people. Often, if we see similarities we share with other people, there is a good chance that the interactions we have with them will be positive. However, if we focus solely on the differences that exist between us, interactions can be strained. When talking with his friend and student, Mitch Albom, Morrie Schwartz stated (Albom, 1997, p. 156):

> *The problem, Mitch, is that we don't believe we are as much alike as we are. Whites and Blacks, Catholics and Protestants, men and women. If we saw each other as more alike, we might be very eager to join in one big family in the world, and to care about that family the way we care about our own.*

The stress many people who are privileged experience when interacting with people who have been oppressed can be traced to perceptions of these individuals as being different. To clarify what occurs when a person is viewed as different, the following terms are described:

- stigma
- stereotype
- discrimination
- segregation

Stigma

Irving Goffman (1963), a noted sociologist, developed a theory of *stigma*, which he defined as an undesired *differentness* that separates the person from others in society—not merely a difference, but a characteristic that deeply discredits a person's moral character. A person with a stigma is perceived as not quite human.

> For instance, Jason, who is gay, may be negatively valued by Cassandra. Cassandra defines Jason by the single attribute of being gay and devalues him.

Personal and social identity of a person comes into question because of a disability. The marginal social position of people who have devalued observable characteristics spreads through everyday life. Living with stigmatized characteristics can transform ordinary social concerns, such as shopping for clothing and meeting strangers, into socially demanding tasks.

Stigma involves a person not being valued because that person possesses an attribute that deviates from the norm. An attribute perceived as negative interferes with people's perceptions of positive attributes and creates a perception of undesired difference from what was anticipated. Once people become aware of their stigmatized label, their self-perceptions are negatively affected.

Stereotype

A major problem encountered by people who have been oppressed is being stereotyped. A *stereotype* is a standardized mental picture of members of a group that represents an oversimplified opinion, attitude, or judgment.

> For example, some people believe that individuals receiving psychiatric services are a threat to society. This response is based on a stereotype frequently presented in the media. In truth, very few people experiencing mental health problems pose a threat to anyone.

Stereotypes of people can result in evaluating them as a category, rather than as individuals. In an effort to explain why stereotypes exist, Allport (1954, pp. 20–21) reported the following:

> *We like to solve problems easily. We can do this best if we can fit them rapidly into a satisfactory category and use this category as a means of prejudicing the solution. So long as we can get away with coarse overgeneralizations, we tend to do so.*

Although it may be convenient to apply a stereotype to a group of people, it is fundamentally inaccurate. Schuman and Olufs (1995, p. 300) stated:

> *We know that any group stereotype, in any particular case, is wrong. That includes good and bad stereotypes. Every person in every group is not identical. But what has never been at issue is the question of individual identity: Each of us is unique. No matter what color we are, what sex we are, what religion we are.*

One practice associated with stereotyping that has come under close scrutiny is racial profiling. *Racial profiling* occurs when race is used by law enforcement or private security officials, to any degree, as a basis for criminal suspicion in non-suspect-specific investigations. Discrimination based on race, ethnicity, religion, nationality, or on any other particular identity undermines the basic human rights and freedoms to which every person is entitled.

One of the problems with racial profiling is that it associates a particular characteristic, race, with specific negative behaviors associated with criminal activity, such as terrorism or illegal immigration. This practice promotes stereotyping of individuals who possess a particular characteristic that is not necessarily directly related to behavior. It would be beneficial is we heeded the advice of Krishnankutty (2007, p. A6):

> *For although we all smile in the same language, we stereotype in the same way too, forming opinions about entire groups without realizing that these groups are just like us: nothing more and nothing less than a collection of individuals.*

It important that we respond to each other relative to our behaviors as opposed to a characteristic in which we do not have control. Leonard Pitts (2009, p. 146–147) tells this story to address this issue:

> *I'm standing on a subway platform waiting for the train. A group of teenage boys is standing nearby and I'm watching them with a wary eye. You know the type. Loud and profane city kids dressed like street thugs. Hats to the back, shirts hanging open, pants sagging low so you can see their drawers. When the train pulls in, I wait to see which car they board. Then I board another. You will have a hard time convincing me I did not do the right thing. Don't take that as an argument in favor of stereotyping. It's illogical to make sweeping judgments about a person based on some accident of birth or circumstance. None of us choose the color of our skin, the nation of our origin, the orientation of our sexuality, the ability or disability or our limbs, the religion of our forbearers. How stupid, then, is the person who attempts to draw conclusions about us by observing these things over*

which we had no control. . . . I often hear such kids insist that dress is neutral and how dare you stereotype them based on what they wear. Fine. It's the argument you would expect them to make. But it is an abrogation of responsibility for adults to encourage them in that delusion. Better to explain to them that what you show to the world, how you allow yourself to be perceived, will have profound implications for the way people treat you. This is a fact of life that has little to do with stereotyping, racial or otherwise. I mean, I perceived a threat by those boys on the subway platform and acted accordingly. Anyone who thinks that constitutes racial stereotyping needs to understand something. They were white.

Discrimination

> *. . . if you only have love for your own race*
> *Then you only leave space to discriminate*
> *And to discriminate only generates hate*
> *And when you hate then you're bound to get irate*
> *Madness is what you demonstrate*
> *And that's exactly how anger works and operates*
> *Man, you got to have love just to set it straight*
> *Take control of your mind and meditate*
> *Let your soul gravitate to the love y'all*

These lyrics, from the song "Where is the Love?" performed by The Black Eyed Peas, capture the problematic relationship between discrimination and anger. *Discrimination* involves a person making a distinction categorically rather than individually about another person, then acting differently toward that person. The act of discrimination results in people who are in positions of power distancing themselves from, avoiding, and excluding people in low-status social categories.

> For example, Toby, an adolescent who is deaf, is interested in registering for some instructional leisure classes. Lydia, the recreation director, may automatically think that Toby does not like to dance. The inaccurate distinction was based on the category of deafness rather than on Toby's individual interests and abilities. Following that inaccurate distinction, Lydia may not offer programs that involve dance to Toby.

Discrimination includes failing to make reasonable modifications in policies, practices, or procedures when such modifications are necessary to afford goods, services, facilities, privileges, advantages, or accommodations to individuals with disabilities unless the entity can demonstrate that making such modifications would fundamentally alter their nature. The following is an example of a situation that depicts discrimination in a recreation context.

Gloria, an energetic and sensitive adolescent who is blind, went to an amusement park with her friends. Although her friends were required to pay admission, she was given free admission to the park. When stopping for lunch, a waitress asked her friends what Gloria wanted to eat. Ride attendants asked her friends if they thought she was capable of holding on properly during the ride. Gloria was refused admittance to the merry-go-round because the attendants were concerned that she might injure herself. The attitudes that Gloria experienced occurred, in part, because people focused on her disability rather than her ability. Gloria's enjoyment and fun was reduced by the discriminatory attitudes and behaviors of the park personnel.

People who experience discrimination in most cultures include those who have limited financial resources and those who are currently be homeless. The various challenges of people who encounter financial barriers are described in detail in a subsequent chapter in the book. In reference to discrimination encountered by people with limited financial resources, Monika Stodolska (2010b, p. 108) stated:

Affluent participants may look down on those who cannot afford quality equipment or who are perceived to be "out of place" in some leisure venues or locations. A younger person from an underprivileged background who is admitted on scholarship to a prestigious school may be looked down upon by his or her peers who are socialized to different leisure activities and leisure spending patterns. Children and adolescents who cannot afford brand-name apparel are often too embarrassed to participate in many activities for the fear of ridicule from their more affluent counterparts.

Shapiro (1993, p. 25) clearly described the problems people with disabilities experience as a result of the many forms of discrimination in the following statement:

Often the discrimination is crude bigotry, such as that of a private New Jersey zoo owner who refused to admit children with retardation to the monkey house, claiming they scared his chimpanzees. It may be intolerance that caused a New Jersey restaurant owner to ask a woman with cerebral palsy to leave because her different appearance was disturbing other diners. Resentment may have led an airline employee in New York to throw a 66-year-old double amputee on a baggage dolly—"like a sack of potatoes"—his daughter complained, rather than help him into a wheelchair and aid him in boarding a jetliner. Others may feel that disabled

> *people are somewhat less than human and therefore fair game*
> *for victimization, as when a gang of New Jersey high school*
> *athletes raped a mildly retarded classmate with a baseball*
> *bat in 1989.*

The consequences of discrimination, including limited access to resources, restricted movement, and fewer opportunities, are often experienced by people without social or financial power. Discrimination can lead to exclusion of people from community life.

> Thun (2007) reported that between 1993 and 2003, 35 countries enacted antidiscrimination laws to promote human rights and equality. Unfortunately, the study observed that discrimination against many different individuals still occurs throughout the globe in areas such as recreation.

In the introduction to the book *Diversity and the Recreation Profession*, Maria Allison (2000, p. 7) made these comments about understanding discrimination:

> *Discussions of diversity are difficult. Often, it is uncomfortable*
> *to talk about issues of race and ethnicity, gender, sexual*
> *orientation, social class, age, and physical ability. Many*
> *individuals suggest that they are "colorblind" or that these*
> *factors do not influence behavior toward others, but the reality*
> *is that sometimes, even unconsciously, race and ethnicity,*
> *gender, sexual orientation, social class, age, and physical*
> *ability do influence how we treat others.*

In his book, *Thurgood Marshall: American Revolutionary*, Juan Williams described an incident that occurred when Marshall was a college student that influenced his thoughts about discrimination. He was hired by a man he befriended at a club—where he was employed as a waiter—to work a private party at the man's expensive home. Marshall had the following interaction with the man's wife (Williams, 1998, p. 45).

> *The woman showed him a room full of toys abandoned by her*
> *grown children. Thurgood mentioned that he knew people in*
> *Old West Baltimore who worked with handicapped children*
> *and that they would love to have the toys. The woman got*
> *excited and immediately offered to donate the toys to the*
> *children. A moment later, however, she asked Thurgood if the*
> *kids were black. "Yes, Ma'am," he told her. Her face suddenly*
> *red and drawn tight, she responded, "I'm not going to give*
> *them anything."*

If people experience discrimination at some point in their lives within a particular context such as recreation, they may anticipate that they will be discriminated against in the future. Anticipation of discrimination may influence an individual's leisure decisions, including the selection of activities and the choice of where and with whom to participate. These observations are supported by identified by Livengood and Stodolska (2004, p. 186–187):

> *[n]umerous research studies reported minorities to experience discrimination in leisure settings such as parks, campgrounds, recreation areas, pools, beaches, golf courses, and forests. . . . Discrimination has been shown to affect quality of recreation experience, to prevent people from frequenting leisure places of their choosing, and to force people to isolate themselves during their leisure engagements.*

Discrimination can result in people's confinement to groups only composed of individuals possessing similar characteristics. When people elect to participate in segregated programs even when their motivation is to avoid discrimination, members of society may view these groups as alien and undesirable. In conclusion, Kyle Glozier (2000, p. 14), who has been attending inclusive schools since kindergarten, made the following comments about discrimination:

> *Discrimination is when people don't allow people of other races, religions, sexual orientations, or abilities to go to all the places they want.*

Segregation

Segregation occurs when an individual or group is isolated in a restricted area because of discrimination. People who are stigmatized, stereotyped, or identified as deviant may experience segregation.

Segregation results in individuals receiving treatment that is different from other people. Segregation is based on the belief that people who have been given similar labels have the same needs and that they can best be served together in a congregated environment that leads to further stigmatization and isolation.

Monika Stodolska (2010b, p. 97) provided a description of segregation among ethnic and racial minorities in the United States:

> *Many ethnic and racial minority groups still face large degrees of segregation in their residential, employment, and leisure patterns. In fact, many urban areas are more ethnically and racially segregated now than they were 10 or 20 years ago. Many members of ethnic and racial minorities are significantly ethnically enclosed during the leisure time. Research has shown that the primary leisure companions of many members of ethnic and racial minorities are people from their own ethnic groups.*

Segregation has been practiced for centuries, and there are entrenched attitudes, laws, policies, and structures that work against achieving inclusion. The previously accepted way of dealing with differences among people was segregation, a method which communicates the message that we do not want to accept everyone or that some people are not worth the effort to make the accommodations necessary to include them.

Some brief history about segregation in the United States may be helpful. Kunen (1996, p. 40) stated:

> *In its ruling on Plessy v. Ferguson, announced May 18, 1896, the Supreme Court declared laws mandating that "equal but separate" treatment of the races "do not necessarily imply the inferiority of either race" and cited the widely accepted propriety of separate schools for white and colored children. In dissent, Justice John Harlan remarked, "The thin disguise of 'equal' accommodations . . . will not mislead anyone, nor atone for the wrong this day done." But the thin disguise endured for a half-century, until a series of school-segregation cases culminating in Brown v. Board of Education of Topeka. "Separate educational facilities are inherently unequal" and violate the Constitution's equal protection guarantee, a unanimous Supreme Court ruled on May 17, 1954. A year later, the court ruled that school districts must admit Black students on a nondiscriminatory basis "with deliberate speed" and instructed the federal courts to retain jurisdiction "during this period of transition."*

Segregation separates people from their own culture and denies them the right to participate in the complex and ever-changing society. Segregation increases physical and social distance, which results in constructing the world as *us* and *them*. In his autobiography (Carson, 1998), Dr. Martin Luther King, Jr. wrote about segregation:

> *The underlying philosophy of democracy is diametrically opposed to the underlying philosophy of segregation, and all the dialectics of the logicians cannot make them lie down together. Segregation is an evil; segregation is a cancer in the body politic, which must be removed before our democratic health can be realized. There was a time that we attempted to live with segregation. There were those who felt that we could live by a doctrine of separate but equal and so back in 1896, the Supreme Court of this nation through the Plessy v. Ferguson decision established a doctrine of separate but equal as the law of the land. But we all know what happened as a result of the doctrine; there was always a strict enforcement of the separate without the slightest intention to abide by the equal. (p. 90)*

As the U.S. civil rights movement has shown us, we are aware that different services resulting from segregation are clearly not equal. For example, when people with disabilities are segregated from their peers who do not have disabilities, they may not learn a full range of behaviors. Instead they may only model those behaviors exhibited by people with whom they have the most contact, other people with similar disabilities.

Segregation is related to the practices of exclusion. *Exclusion* involves the barring of a person from contact with others, often from the mainstream of society, resulting in the person being disadvantaged and often not regarded as human. Exclusion can hinder the quantity and quality of interpersonal relationships as well as affect a person's development. It involves ignoring someone's physical and social presence.

Seclusion, on the other hand, involves individuals being removed from social contact while still maintaining a sense of value. At times we may seek a secluded place that is quiet and removed from activity so we can focus on our thoughts.

When people of a similar characteristic congregate, it is difficult, if not impossible, for each person to be treated as an individual because of the tendency of people to generalize and stereotype them. Wolf Wolfensberger and colleagues spoke to the issue of congregation when they described the occurrence of *deviancy transference*. They reported that deviancy transference occurs when people with physical disabilities are grouped together with people with mental disabilities. It is likely that in such groupings, all the individuals will be suspected of having both mental and physical limitations.

Bengt Nirje and Wolf Wolfensberger led what was described as the *normalization reform movement*. The movement started in Sweden and Denmark, before spreading to the United States and Canada during the 1970s. The normalization movement focuses human services on making available to all people with disabilities patterns of life and conditions of everyday living that are as close as possible to the typical circumstances and ways of life enjoyed by most people within a society.

Societal behaviors motivated by negative attitudes have resulted in the isolation of various groups of people from the social mainstream and the denial of benefits and opportunities available to people of privilege. In spite of advances toward inclusion, segregated recreation programs continue to exist, especially for people with disabilities.

In addition to these segregated programs, people are excluded from community recreation programs in subtle ways. Subtle actions that encourage segregation include avoiding social contacts with people because interactions may be uncomfortable or inconvenient and forbidding or preventing one's children from playing with children that happen to be different in some way.

In summary, perceptions of *differentness* can stem from people being stigmatized. Once people are stigmatized, negative stereotypes can develop. If negative stereotypes exist, then actions such as segregation and discrimination follow (see Figure 3.2, p. 56).

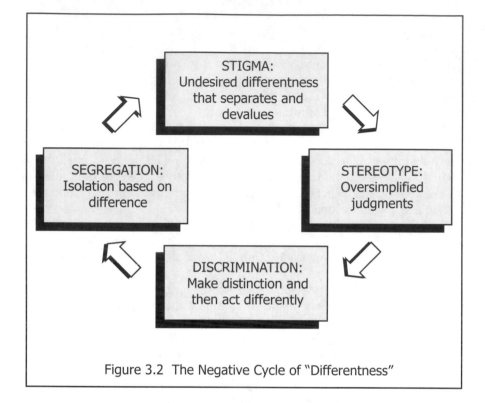

Figure 3.2 The Negative Cycle of "Differentness"

How can labels influence expectations?

If some people develop negative attitudes toward a group of other people, they begin to develop expectations that can be destructive. Three possible reactions can occur that results in people who are viewed negatively being stifled:

- self-fulfilling prophecy
- over-exaggeration assumption
- spread phenomenon

Self-Fulfilling Prophecy

The *self-fulfilling prophecy* can be described as how a person's expectation for another person's behavior can become an accurate prediction of the person's behaviors simply because it exists.

> For example, Robert, a young adult, is labeled homeless. As a result, some people's expectations for Robert to be a successful participant in a program can be extremely limited. Some labels imply deficiencies that produce expectations that interfere with his development and pursuit of happiness.

The self-fulfilling prophecy requires interaction of two people. Initially, a person becomes aware of an expectation of another person (Figure 3.3). This first individual comprehends this expectation and retains the information. Next, this person must communicate the expectancy to the other person.

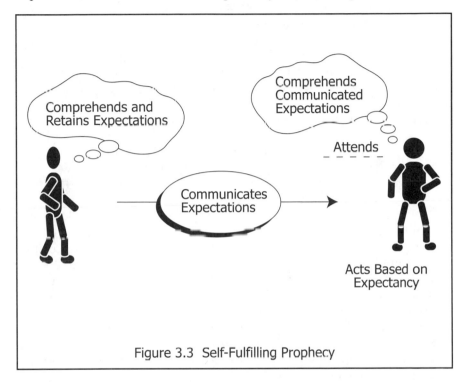

Figure 3.3 Self-Fulfilling Prophecy

Once this communication has occurred, the other person then must attend to this communication, comprehend, and act upon the expectancy. Negative labels may generate negative expectations. A description of a recent video by Leonard Pitts (2009, p. 194) illustrates the chilling power of the self-fulfilling prophecy.

> *"Can you show me the doll that looks bad?" The two baby dolls are identical except that one has pale skin, the other is dark. The little black girl, maybe 5 years old, has been holding up the pale doll, but in response to the questions, she puts it down and picks up the other. "Why does that doll look bad?" the interviewer asks. Because it is black," the little girl says. "And why do you think that's the nice doll?" asks the interviewer, referring to the light-skinned doll. "Because she's white." "And can you give me the doll that looks like you?" The dark-skinned girl reaches for the light-skinned doll, jiggling it as if she really wants to pick it up. In the end, with palpable reluctance, she pushes the black doll forward. You might be forgiven for thinking you have happened upon one of the "Doll Tests" conducted by Dr. Kenneth Clark beginning*

late in the 1930s, tests that helped persuade the Supreme Court to strike down segregation in its Brown v. Board of Education decision. But this is a new doll test, conducted by Kiri Davis, a 17-year-old student from New York, for A Girl Like Me, her short film about black girls and standards of beauty. Be warned: If you have a heart, the new doll test will break it.

An individual bearing a deviancy-related label is expected to behave in a consistent way that is negative. The mere identification of a person who needs assistance from professionals can instill the belief that the person is not quite human. Although these examples demonstrate how the self-fulfilling prophecy can have negative impacts, positive results are also possible.

> For instance, when Rosenthal and Jacobson (1968) led teachers to believe that randomly selected students would improve substantially during the next school year, the students did achieve more than their classmates.

Unfortunately, when the self-fulfilling prophecy is applied to people with who have been oppressed, the results typically involve lowered expectations, reduced participation, and decreased performance. The hope is that this book helps contribute to a self-fulfilling prophecy that raises expectations and performance levels of all people who have not been members of the privileged.

Sometimes we accept as truth what others communicate to us about ourselves. The tendency of individuals to accept negative stereotyping about themselves is often referred to as *internalized oppression*. **Internalized oppression** occurs when an individual comes to accept these stereotypical beliefs as truths and acts upon them (Brown, 1992).

> For instance, a negative belief held by some professionals is that people with disabilities are not capable of participating in community recreation programs. As a consequence, people with disabilities might be relegated to segregated programs and they may not even try to enroll in other programs, or they may feel excessively thankful to be given a chance to participate. People who feel grateful might be uncomfortable in asking for reasonable accommodations to enable them to participate.

Over-exaggeration Assumption

If we overestimate or over-exaggerate the extent to which certain characteristics such as being Asian, a woman, an older adult, or using a wheelchair, influence mental status, individuals can experience difficulty developing relationships. Some privileged people assume that certain people who have been oppressed think about the particular characteristic that has resulted in their oppression all the time. When these people encounter a person who is a member of an oppressed group, such as those who are a member of a racial minority, they wrongly assume that that characteristic should be the focus of the discussion rather than more relevant topics.

> For example, when riding on a gondola during a ski trip, Jerry encounters Sheila, a woman about his same age. With a bright smile, Sheila says, "Hi, the powder sure is terrific today!" Jerry responds, "Yeah, but it must be really hard for you to ski since you have only one leg."

Some people may avoid interaction with people who are different from them in some observable way either to prevent potentially embarrassing situations or to avoid having to respond to what they expect are extremes of happiness or despair. This tendency for others to reduce interaction can make it difficult to develop relationships and to access necessary supports within communities. If people become aware that having a particular characteristic does not have as great an impact as might be expected, they might find it less threatening to interact with these people.

Spread Phenomenon

An ***attribute*** is a quality, property, or characteristic associated with someone or something. The tendency to associate an additional negative attribute with a person who has another negative attribute is known as the ***spread phenomenon***.

> For example, people may:
> - speak loudly to an individual who is blind
> - believe that a person with an intellectual disability lacks physical skills
> - assume that a person with a speech impairment is not mentally alert.

Ruth, who uses a communication aid to help her to interact with others, made the following statement about the spread phenomenon (Crossley, 1999, p. 9):

> ***People in the community tend to equate one's speaking abilities with one's intelligence. The misconceptions on the part of those around a non-speaking person can be both painful and dangerous to that person, as it usually means he or she will be treated in a sub-human manner.***

The spread phenomenon further *handicaps* a person with a disability. Although people with disabilities may be limited in only one aspect of their life, many people believe that these people are handicapped in all situations.

> For example, Anthony, who uses a wheelchair, is seated in a restaurant with his wife, Sylvia, and a waitress asks Sylvia

if she would like to order for him. The waitress may assume that because Anthony is in a wheelchair he is helpless, unable to talk, or could not order dinner for himself. If the waitress feels uncomfortable with Anthony and his chair, she may limit communication with him by talking with Sylvia who does not have an observable disability. In this situation, the waitress's reaction most likely created discomfort for Anthony and Sylvia and reduced their enjoyment of the intended leisure experience.

The generalization of a particular characteristic to all aspects of a person's life that is a result of the spread phenomenon is extremely detrimental. During an interview, Lori, a woman who has had a spinal cord injury and uses a wheelchair, illustrated the occurrence of the spread phenomenon:

One thing that really does perturb me is . . . a lot of times people will act like something is wrong with your mind because you're in a chair. They'll come up and they'll ask somebody else, "What happened to her?" like I can't talk for myself. They'll talk to whoever I'm with instead of talking to me . . . I don't like that; I don't appreciate that at all.

The following example illustrates the effect of the spread phenomenon.

Subot approached Mareeka, a woman who he knew was deaf. Subot handed Mareeka a note that said: "Can you read?" Maria wrote back: "No!" Maria's sarcastic reply to the note clearly indicates her ability to read. It appears that Subot assumed that her sensory impairment affected Mareeka's other abilities. Subot may have assumed that because Mareeka is deaf she also could not read.

Final Thoughts

Development of attitudes is intertwined with antecedents, beliefs, intentions, and behaviors in a dynamic process. Unfortunately, negative attitudes may arise when people make contact with others who possess different characteristics.

If a specific characteristic such as a person having a particular religion or a person who is older results in the individual being perceived as deviant, viewed in a stereotypical way, excluded from participation, discriminated against, or segregated from others, the result can be the devaluation of individuals. *Devaluation* involves the reduction of the perceived importance or worth of someone or something. Unfortunately, devaluation can result in abuse, neglect, and people having limited exposure to the things that make life pleasurable.

Benefits people gain in segregated settings can be equaled and exceeded in inclusive surroundings. Involvement with people who are within the mainstream of society has allowed individuals to upgrade their skills, expand their choices of community activities, and increase their active participation.

> For example, the music video, Standing Outside the Fire (Yates & Brooks, 1993) depicts a teenage boy who participates in an inclusive classroom, can drive the family car, and rejects Special Olympics in favor of joining his school track team. At one point in the video the coach sees the youth with Down syndrome looking at the sign-up sheet for a track meet and nudges the boy toward a separate sign-up sheet for Special Olympics. The boy sneers at the Special Olympic poster and defiantly signs his name on the track meet list.

Although behaviors that reflect negative attitudes can limit opportunities for many people who have been oppressed, negative attitudes and subsequent behaviors can be changed. Leisure service professionals can play an important role in improving everyone's attitudes about others.

Discussion Questions

1. How do antecedents and beliefs influence the development of attitudes?
2. What is an attitude?
3. How do cognitive, affective, and behavioral predispositions relate to the expression of attitudes?
4. How do people's intentions relate to their attitudes?
5. How are attitudes manifested in a way that other people are influenced by these attitudes?
6. What is the relationship between stress and the development of negative attitudes toward other people?
7. What is meant by the words "stigma," "discrimination," "stereotype," and "segregation?"
8. What is the relationship between segregation and exclusion?
9. How does the self-fulfilling prophecy occur and what is its impact on people who have been oppressed?
10. What is meant by the "spread phenomenon" and how does it influence people's feelings about people who have been oppressed?

Chapter 4
Enhance Your Attitude

Things do not change, we do.
-Henry David Thoreau

Orientation Activity: Identify Significant Experiences

Directions Alone: Select a member of an oppressed group of which you are not a member. For example, if you are Caucasian you might select a person who is African, if you do not possess a disability you may select a person with an intellectual disability, or if you are Christian you may select someone who is a Buddhist. Record a brief answer for each of the following questions. Also record any questions you have as you are completing the exercise.

Directions with Others: Divide into small groups and discuss the specific questions assigned. After a specified time, discuss your responses with the entire group.

1. What was your first experience with a person who has been oppressed?
2. How do you feel about the experience?
3. How do the people who raised you view people who have been oppressed?
4. What events do you think had an impact on their attitudes?
5. In what ways have the attitudes of the people who raised you affected your attitudes?
6. How were their attitudes communicated to you?
7. How do you think your peers view people who have been oppressed?
8. What events do you think had an impact on their attitudes?
9. In what ways have their attitudes affected yours?
10. How were your peers' attitudes communicated to you?
11. What indirect exposure to people who have been oppressed have you experienced (e.g., books, films, jokes, television)?
12. Has this exposure been generally positive or negative?
13. How would you describe your reactions to the exposure?
14. What direct contact to people who have been oppressed have you experienced?
15. Has this contact been generally positive or negative?
16. How would you describe your reactions to the direct contact?
17. How would you summarize your current feelings or attitudes toward people who have been oppressed in general?

Debriefing: Many attitudes we have today are a result of our earlier experiences with people who possess different characteristics than our own. At times, we may have directly encountered these people. The way our parents, siblings, or friends interacted with other people may have strongly influenced the way we now think.

We are also exposed to people who are different from us in indirect ways. The manner in which books, magazines, movies, and television programs present people who have been oppressed such as women, members of racial minorities, and older adults influences our perceptions of those people. Consider the following questions when reflecting on the orientation activity:

- What are advantages of improving your attitude toward people who have been oppressed in some way?
- What barriers do you envision as you consider improving your attitudes toward these individuals?
- Do you anticipate your attitude toward people who have been oppressed improving?

Introduction

In response to the observation that attitudes of recreation professionals significantly impact the leisure opportunities of all people, strategies that reduce or eliminate prejudice toward individuals who have been oppressed have been identified. Development of these strategies has been further encouraged by civil rights legislation mandating the inclusion of all people.

The outcome of legislation mandating inclusion and equal opportunity will, unfortunately, be unpredictable until people develop positive attitudes toward individuals for whom the legislation is designed to protect. As a result, examination of ways to positively influence attitudes of professionals toward individuals who have been oppressed might be useful. The following questions are addressed in this chapter:

- How can we cultivate a sense of professional competence?
- What are considerations when doing a simulation in a wheelchair?
- What can help to process simulations?
- What are responses to doing a simulation?
- What else can we do?

How can we cultivate a sense of professional competence?

Professionals' perceived ability to work with people who are different from them relative to their religious beliefs, the color of their skin, gender, sexual orientation, ability, class, and other characteristics, is identified as a sense of *professional competence*. This sense of competence is directly related to people's attitudes.

Leisure service professionals who perceive themselves as more competent tend to be more positive in their attitudes toward all people being included into their programs. Attitudes toward people who are different from the leisure service professional in some manner can be improved as a result of exposure to a course on inclusive leisure services.

People responsible for professional preparation can play an important role in enhancing positive attitudes and perceived competence in providing leisure services for all people. Academic preparation and experience influence attitudes and perceived competence directly and indirectly.

> For example, previous exposure to courses about people with disabilities has been linked to development of favorable attitudes toward these individuals (Rees, Spreen, & Harnadek, 1991). More favorable attitudes and greater perceived competence are likely to lead to beneficial learning experiences.

Attitudes toward people who have been oppressed can be improved in many ways. People can be provided with information via presentations, discussions, readings, and videos. In addition, we can encourage people to examine their attitudes and consider ways to enhance those attitudes. We also can make vicarious experiences available to people. *Vicarious experiences* are those situations that require people to take the place of another person such as when participating in a simulation. Another way to make a positive impact on people's attitudes is to create opportunities for direct contact with people who have been oppressed such as through field work or guest speakers. The use of multiple methods provides positive changes in attitudes toward others.

> As an illustration, Rizzo and Vispoel (1992) reported that a planned, systematic intervention using all these procedures had a positive effect on attitudes toward providing services for people with disabilities. In addition, examination of one's own attitudes has also been used as an agent of attitude change.

It appears that a particularly important variable in professionals' offering of effective inclusive leisure services is their sense of competence. If professionals feel competent, that is, if they feel that they have the knowledge and skills needed to offer such services, they will be more likely to do so.

> For example, after surveying 111 recreation professionals, Conatser and Block (2001) concluded that the best predictor of attitudes toward inclusion was the professionals' competence in working with individuals in an inclusive context. Conversely, Engelbrecht, Swart, and Eloff (2001) found that a lack of self-competence and insufficient training is a major stressor for human service providers in inclusive settings. After surveying

133 college students, Kowalski and Rizzo (1996) found that the more competent students felt, the more favorable their attitudes were toward inclusion, and the belief that professional preparation programs play a vital role in enhancing both positive attitudes and perceived competence. Similarly, Soodak, Podell, and Lehman (1998) interviewed 188 professionals trained to provide services to the general public and found that the higher their sense of competence, the more likely they were to support inclusion.

This chapter presents information on methods that can influence attitudes and cultivate a sense of professional competence. Among those methods are the following (Figure 4.1):

- attending presentations and discussions
- developing awareness of personal attitudes
- making direct contact
- participating in simulations

The first strategy focuses on indirect exposure through presentation and discussion of information and methods that help facilitate inclusive participation in programs. The second technique is the development of awareness of what attitudes people possess and possible ways their attitudes were formed. This technique of self-awareness is designed to help people become more responsive to information that may improve their attitudes. The third strategy, direct contact with people, can facilitate development of an understanding and appreciation of people's lives and thus improve attitudes. Finally, the fourth strategy, simulation, promotes a vicarious experience of other people's conditions that may enhance development of positive attitudes.

Attend Presentations and Discussions

Professionals' attitudes or behavioral intentions toward inclusion can be modified by having them attend presentations and engage in discussions related to inclusion.

As a case in point, Stainback, Stainback, Strathe, and Dedrick (1983) had professionals read and discuss materials on inclusion. They reported that the presentation of reading materials and subsequent small group discussions modified attitudes and behavioral intentions of professionals toward inclusion. Similarly, Austin, Powell, and Martin (1981) examined use of class presentations to modify leisure studies students' attitudes and found that presentations positively influenced their attitudes.

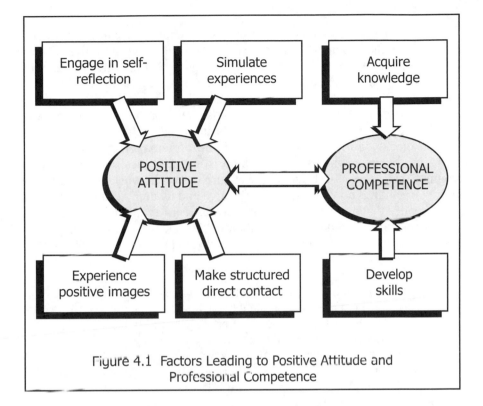

Figure 4.1 Factors Leading to Positive Attitude and Professional Competence

These findings support the value of presenting information to leisure service students and professionals on methods to facilitate successful inclusion of all people.

There are many ways to attend presentations and discussions associated with inclusion. If you are a student reading this book associated with a face-to-face course, then you already are attending multiple presentations associated with the course. If you are enrolled in an online course, the presentations may be presented over the web.

On many college campuses, there are talks that are given by nationally and internationally known people. These talks are often not associated with a formal course and address relevant issues promoting civil rights and including people in human services.

There are other opportunities that are available to both students and professionals, including state, regional, national, and even international conferences. These are just a few of the possible ways to attend presentations and discussions that increase your ability to provide inclusive leisure services.

Develop Awareness of Personal Attitudes

An important aspect of developing positive attitudes about inclusion and people who have been oppressed involves examination of one's attitudes and values. Once we become aware of our values, we are more prepared to assume responsibility for making our own decisions.

We all carry with us beliefs and biases. Although we can have much in common with the people for whom we provide services, we are often different in many ways relative to ability, racial background, cultural affiliation, ethnic heritage, religion, or sexual orientation. Examining our values might help us avoid making value judgments about others and minimize the extent to which we impose our view of the world in a professional relationship. Self-reflection is a way professionals can become actively involved in their development, as they consciously work to shape what kind of professional they will become.

As we begin to understand our beliefs and attitudes, we will come to recognize that we all have biases and that our view of the world is not universal, nor are our cultural norms absolute. Cartledge and Kourea (2008, p. 353), who recommended that human service professionals learn about their own and other cultures and come to understand how their beliefs and biases can influence their interactions with others who are culturally different from them, provided the following examples:

> Some youth who have been socialized to look away rather than make eye contact when directed by an adult are not necessarily being disrespectful. Similarly, people who associate with a cultural group where "overlapping speech" is typical and accepted, may be unaware that this practice in unacceptable in some contexts. Understanding these motives and helping these participants be socially successful is one of the responsibilities of service providers.

People tend to think at least partially in categories; therefore, it is helpful if we become seriously self-critical about the inferences we make about other people. If we acknowledge that various groups of people have been stigmatized and underserved, those thoughts may begin to sensitize us to address leisure interests and needs of all members of the community.

If we want to help facilitate social inclusion, it can be useful for us to start by examining our attitudes. Leisure service providers are encouraged to conduct self-evaluations to help ensure that they are providing inclusive and fully accessible programs.

As we examine how we feel about different issues, we become more aware of how we think about these issues and more able to improve our actions. With self-awareness comes an ability to take more responsibility for our actions. Barry (1997, pp. 143, 156) spoke to this interaction between awareness and responsibility:

> *Certainly there is no more necessary rule for responsible living than to know what we feel, think, and believe; to be aware of factors that contribute to our emotions, thoughts, and beliefs; to know who and what have influenced our attitudes, values, and habits—why we choose one thing instead of another, or follow, perhaps the more rather than the less traveled path. . . . The opinions and customs we have absorbed*

in growing up, the ones we hold and practice, may be rational or irrational, fair or biased, liberating or diminishing. So can our conscience. Being responsible, therefore, is heeding but not hypnotically following the "inner voice" of conscience. It is challenging that voice, critically conversing with it, and always pressing it into discourse with other consciences.

To develop competence in serving diverse groups, it is helpful for us to begin by gaining an awareness of attitudes, beliefs, and knowledge about our culture as well as an understanding of other cultures. Many individuals have warned us that it is easier to acknowledge that diversity exists than to do something about it. Enough is being learned about various aspects of diversity that leisure service providers can apply some of the findings to their programs immediately.

To enhance peoples' attitudes toward individuals who have been oppressed in some manner, we can use awareness activities; however, it is helpful if we process these awareness activities. *Processing* is the umbrella term for a set of facilitation techniques designed to assist people in describing, reflecting on, analyzing, and communicating about experiences. Processing helps people to transfer or generalize what they have learned in an activity-based experience to other life contexts such as their home, community, work, or school.

The act of processing involves not only attending to the immediacies of the experience but also relating important aspects of the experience to future issues. Processing can be used to help participants:

- increase awareness of issues prior to an experience
- promote change while an experience occurs
- reflect on, analyze, or understand an experience after it ends
- promote assimilation of the experience

While processing often involves some form of dialogue or discussion in group settings, it can occur through activities such as journal writing, one-on-one conversations, writing activities, drawing, or drama. Processing moves participants' attention from general awareness to: acknowledging responsibility, making choices, and applying these choices to other areas of life. By processing the experience with participants, we can help them learn how their experiences might be relevant to their lives. Processing helps people make sense of their experiences.

Make Direct Contact

Evans (1976) observed that a strain in social interactions, including uneasiness, inhibition, and uncertainty experienced by people who are privileged when interacting with people who are oppressed. This strained interaction appears to contribute to development and maintenance of negative attitudes. One useful response to these negative attitudes, then, is to reduce such strain by structuring positive experiences. These structured experiences present positive images of people who have been oppressed.

A *structured experience* associated with inclusion is one that promotes mutually respectful interaction between people and is often the key to promoting inclusive services.

> For example, in preparation for a structured interaction at the beginning of a cooking class, Yahimba, the instructor, obtains pairs of cooking utensils such as whisks, wooden spoons, and peelers. When participants arrive, they are given a name tag and one utensil. At the beginning of the class, Yahimba asks participants to locate the other person who has the same utensil, learn the person's name, and share one story about a positive cooking experience.

A considerable amount of research has been conducted that demonstrates the value for individuals who are privileged when they make direct contact with people who have been oppressed.

> Rowe and Stutts (1987) observed improved attitudes when college students participated in inclusive internships. Minke, Baer, Deemer, and Griffin (1996) surveyed over 300 teachers and found that those in inclusive settings reported more positive views of inclusion and higher ratings of competence than those not exposed to inclusion. Folsom-Meek, Hearing, Groteluschen, and Krampf (1999) surveyed almost 3,000 college students and found that those who had worked with diverse people displayed more positive attitudes than those without such experience. Krajewski and Flaherty (2000) interviewed 144 high school students and found students who reported more frequent contacts with diverse groups held more favorable attitudes toward inclusion. Shinew, Glover, and Parry (2004) interviewed 195 urban community gardeners; most gardeners found the direct contact with others helped them feel connected to their community, a sense of belonging, and that gardening brought diverse people together successfully. Devine and O'Brien (2007) interviewed inclusive camp participants and found when campers got to know each other on a personal level, they learned new things, viewed each other as similar rather than different, and focused on how each person contributed to the group.

Taken together, research supports the general conclusion that the quality of contact between people strongly influences development of positive attitudes toward people who possess different characteristics. Structuring the inclusive environment to promote positive contact is critical for positive inclusive leisure experiences. For instance, Charlsena Stone (2003, p. 171) explored leisure professionals' cultural competencies and concluded that:

It is important to have direct interactions with people from diverse cultural backgrounds in order to learn more about their value systems and cultural norms, how they live in society, why they hold certain beliefs, and the relationship of those beliefs to recreation and leisure.

Based on what is identified as contact theory, one way to promote positive encounters is by structuring activities that require close personal interactions to occur and develop. According to Mary Ann Devine (2004),

Contact theory has been applied to inclusive leisure contexts and may be a framework from which to implement services to counter ambivalence . . .

Contact theory was developed by Gordon Allport (1954), who identified that under appropriate conditions, interpersonal contact is one of the most effective ways to reduce prejudice between majority and minority group members. Allport proposed that properly managed contact between groups and individuals should reduce stereotyping, prejudice, and discrimination, and ultimately lead to better interactions. He provided suggestions to manage group interactions that included:

- present both groups to be of *equal status*
- engage both groups in activities and share a *common goal*
- structure the activity so that members of both groups are *interdependent* to achieve this common goal
- support contact and interaction between groups and members by an *authority* that both groups acknowledge

The manner in which contact is structured can make the difference between an encounter being positive or negative. The direction of attitude change depends on the conditions under which contact has occurred; favorable conditions produce positive attitude shifts, while unfavorable conditions produce negative attitude shifts. Structured experiences with people who differ regarding some basic characteristics facilitate positive attitude shifts.

> For example, Beck and Dennis (1996) assessed attitudes of 186 fifth graders, some involved in an inclusive situation and others not. Results from previous research and this study indicate that structured, interactive programs designed to increase positive attitudes are more useful in effecting positive attitudes than programs where children are simply placed in physical proximity to one another and given limited instruction regarding interaction and communication.

To increase the likelihood of long-term behavior change, experiences that include opportunities for direct exposure to individuals who present positive images of people who have been oppressed can be helpful. The direct exposure could involve interacting with people who are guest lecturers, working on a specified task with a person, or conducting inclusive programs.

Problems can result from people developing images of others with whom they have not yet had direct contact.

> In his memoir titled Moving Violations, John Hockenberry (1995) suggested that if you get close to people, stereotypical images begin to break up, but they do not go away easily. When people experience repeated direct contact with other people who may be different from them, their differences become so familiar that these differences become part of people's personal comfort zone.

Inclusion is not possible if people only read and talk about people who are different from themselves. The more we do things with people who are different from us, the more likely we can develop an appreciation and, hopefully, acceptance and understanding of other people. John Callahan, a successful cartoonist who created the cartoon series *Pelswick*, the first television show to feature an animated character in a wheelchair, made the following observation about making contact with people (Hauser, 2001, p. 19):

> *If you hang around someone who's disabled, within just a few days, hours—or, in my case, minutes—you'll realize that he or she is just another person on the street.*

There is also support for the belief that vicarious contact that may occur by watching videos and television can have a positive impact on people's attitudes. Yoo and Buzinde (2012) concluded that:

> *[d]espite the fact that racial/ethnic stereotypes are developed and learned culturally, they can nonetheless be altered through individual direct contact with a member of the depicted group or via indirect experience, such as viewing of a televised program.*

Participate in Simulations

To alter attitudes toward people who find themselves in different situations than you, distorted ideas supported by deeply felt emotions must be confronted. An initial step in this educational process is to focus on the individual at an emotional level. One strategy that affects people at an emotional level is participation in simulations.

> As an example, after a five-hour program that included a disability simulation, children's attitudes toward other children

with disabilities were more positive than their attitudes prior to the educational program (Jones et al., 1981).

Through simulations, participants can develop some sensitivity to experiences that other people encounter on a regular basis.

Over the years, many students have returned to my office after working as a leisure service professional. When they talk about the course on inclusion, they typically remember the simulation in which they participated, and they report to me how it continues to influence the way they deliver services and their sensitivity to the needs of individuals.

Sayne (1996, p. 24) provided an interesting description of a special event sponsored by a parks and recreation department that provided the chance for members of the community to participate in an entire day of simulations:

> *What would drive perfectly healthy, nondisabled boys and girls to partake in recreational activities such as wheelchair basketball, blindfold baseball and chin-ramp bowling? Why would Ed, who doesn't even wear glasses, be writing his name in Braille? And why would Lindsey, whose teacher would be the first to tell you, has no problems talking, be practicing sign language? "It's simple," explains nine-year-old Lindsey, as she eagerly walks with her friends to the next station. "This is a way to learn about people who have different abilities; it's hard to know what people go though unless you try it yourself." . . . Ten-year-old Marianne says it is definitely working. "I have a younger brother who has been diagnosed with CP (Cerebral Palsy)," said Marianne. "This helps me to understand a little better some of the things he's going through at home."*

Simulations can be effective in changing attitudes; however, it is useful if the simulation requires participants to observe reactions of other people. Movement through a largely unfamiliar group of people as a single role-player may further enhance realism, allowing the person to experience the possible frustrations of the condition, but, perhaps more importantly, to experience other people's reactions.

Many individuals have participated in simulations while enrolled in introductory courses related to diversity and disability. The rationale for the assignments is often to encourage participants to become more sensitive to the requirements placed on individuals and to develop an awareness of the barriers, both physical and attitudinal, that confront some people.

Simulations are learning experiences, as opposed to recreation activities. The primary intent of a simulation is to develop sensitivity rather than simply provide participants with a "fun" experience. However, it is hoped that participants experience enjoyable and amusing moments during the simulation.

What are considerations when doing a simulation in a wheelchair?

One specific example of a simulation requires participants to pretend they have paralysis of the legs and use a wheelchair to move. The duration of the simulation can vary according to the learning situation, but a simulation brief in duration may not have the desired effect.

When giving directions for a simulation, it is helpful to provide extensive information and guidelines regarding the preparation, implementation, and evaluation of the simulation. These directions help to increase the chance that participants will approach the task in a mature and understanding fashion.

> Eichmiller (1990) interviewed several college students who participated in a simulation that required them to use a wheelchair for half a day. One student, Chrissy, said she had not thought about it before, but in the future her attitude would not be patronizing. "People think they (people with disabilities) are in need of constant assistance. Now I realize that they're not. To have people constantly offering help makes you feel childlike," she said. The class prepared students for what they might encounter, including people staring. "Definitely, yes," people stared, Chrissy said. "People were more friendly than usual then they would stare at my legs," she added. Although she does not think that anyone without a disability could fully understand, Deborah reported that after the simulation, she could relate much more to those with disabilities.

There are several considerations associated with participating in a simulation using a wheelchair. It is helpful to prepare for the situation, actually participate in the simulation, and take time to evaluate the experience.

Preparation

Participants are encouraged to place themselves in challenging situations but to use sound judgment. It is recommended that participants carefully *preplan all experiences* before charging ahead. Providing sufficient time to arrive at planned destinations on time is a necessity.

Often, participants will experience that even the "best-laid plans" will lead them into the unexpected. Therefore, when possible, participants are encouraged to have a friend accompany them. The participant's friend should assist only when absolutely necessary.

In some cases, it may be advisable for participants to *describe the assignment in advance* to people with whom they have close relationships. This advance notification is done to avoid family members and close friend being taken off guard by the participant resulting in possible duress by these concerned individuals.

Typically, it is suggested that if a transportation system is in place specifically for people with disabilities, participants in the simulation should not use this transportation service. Participants are also discouraged from conducting their simulation with another person using a wheelchair. In any simulation, participants should *discuss personal concerns or reservations* about the experience with the person supervising the simulation.

Implementation

Throughout the experience, participants should attempt to *remain in the wheelchair as much as possible*. If, for any reason, participants must get out of the wheelchair, such as if the person is alone and stuck in the mud, the person should attempt to do this discreetly while others are not watching. This may mean that participants might need to wait a few moments before breaking character.

If it is unavoidable to break character in front of other people, such as in a situation when the participant is in danger, then the person should attempt to briefly explain the situation truthfully to those present. However, it is hoped that participants do not break character during the time they are using the wheelchair.

When encountering acquaintances, participants are encouraged to explain to them that the experience is an assignment and provide them with the rationale for the simulation. The most appropriate responses to questions about participants' condition while they are conducting the simulation are those that are direct and honest.

When conducting the simulation, it is valuable to spend some time engaged in leisure pursuits, especially those that require movement. Many students have described their experiencing playing Frisbee, basketball, and catch, and they report that these experiences were valuable. In addition, it is helpful to travel outside to experience physical challenges associated with architecture and the ecology. An important consideration for the simulation is to be in a social situation so that observations of people's reactions can be noted.

Evaluation

After completing the simulation, participants will not know what it is like to actually have the particular disability, due to many physical and psychological factors that exist in actual disabling conditions. However, participants will increase their awareness of having a physical disability and associated attitudinal and physical barriers.

Although using a wheelchair can be extremely challenging, many people who use wheelchairs view them as liberating. For example, Paul Kuzuo (2002), p. 20) made the following observation:

> *Many able-bodied people think of a wheelchair as "confining" and restricting." However, to anyone who is unable to walk, or has a difficult time walking, a wheelchair is actually "liberating" and a means to mobility and independence. It's*

like what glasses (or contact lenses) are to the person who has difficulty seeing or reading something.

In certain situations, participants of a wheelchair simulation may experience more problems than an individual who regularly uses a wheelchair due to lack of skill and problems with the wheelchair. In other situations, participants may experience less difficulty as they realize that they can literally walk away from the experience.

In response to employees of a hospital participating in a simulation requiring them to use a wheelchair, Scott Balko had a few suggestions for participants that illustrate the limitations of such an educational experience. He recommended that people conduct their simulation for one year. During this year, participants should get a skin ulcer that does not heal so that plastic surgery is required, experience some urinary tract problems, encounter calcium deposits, have some muscle atrophy, experience respiratory problems such as pneumonia, and encounter cardiovascular problems. In conclusion, Balko warned people participating in an educational simulation that it is no game.

Balko's sentiments are a reminder that although participation in educational simulations of disabling conditions can heighten awareness, once participants have completed the simulation, they will not know what it is like to be disabled for a considerable length of time. Figure 4.2 summarizes the suggestions for simulation participation.

What can help to process simulations?

To enhance the effectiveness of the simulation, participants are often encouraged to record their impressions of the experience. The organization of such a report might include the following:

- consider ethical issues
- evaluate social reactions
- recognize environmental barriers
- describe personal reactions
- identify professional implications
- plan actions for advocacy

Consider Ethical Issues

There are a variety of ethical considerations that arise when participating in a simulation. Perceptions of people who have the actual conditions that are being simulated are important to consider; these are people who must deal with the

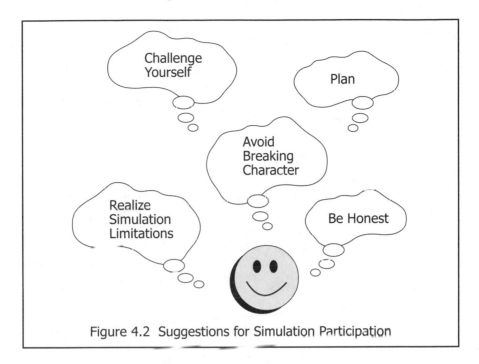

Figure 4.2 Suggestions for Simulation Participation

circumstance on a long-term basis. It is helpful to reflect on how these individuals feel about the learning experience, given that once the simulation is completed, participants immediately stop experiencing the barriers associated with the condition. Taking into account the limitations of a simulation are important in understanding the experience.

Another inherent aspect of a simulation that is conducted in public is related to the act of deception. It is helpful for participants to describe any ethical issues experienced in having misled people during the simulation and how these issues were handled. Identifying any other ethical issues that this experience has raised can also be valuable.

Evaluate Social Reactions

Social reactions that participants experienced appear to be critical in influencing development of positive attitudes toward people with disabilities. Identification of the verbal and nonverbal responses of people who were encountered can be very revealing.

Participants are encouraged to describe specific communication behaviors and avoid making assumptions about people's intentions. Identifying specific examples of different people's reactions can help participants become aware of how they would now treat people with disabilities.

Recognize Environmental Barriers

Another consideration is the environmental barriers that participants experienced. A description of various *architectural barriers,* those barriers that were created by humans, such as steps, heavy doors, and holes in the pavement, can be identified.

Observation about *ecological barriers,* those barriers that are found in the natural world, such as steep hills and marshy areas, can help provide insight into the experience. Participants' encounters with these barriers and their responses to them can be informative.

Describe Personal Reactions

When attempting to process the simulation that has influenced participants' emotions, a section of the report devoted to personal reactions can be helpful. Participants may attempt to explain their feelings before, during, and after the simulation. This comparison can develop insights that were not initially apparent to the participants. Trying to find the answers to such questions as: "What was your response to your abilities and disabilities?" and "How did you feel about other's reactions?" can help participants develop insights into the lives of people with disabilities.

Identify Professional Implications

It is helpful for participants to describe a possible career that they plan to pursue. Participants are then encouraged to provide specific examples of how this simulation experience will improve their ability to successfully meet the demands of their intended career responsibilities. Identification of specific actions that could be taken as a professional to provide accessible programs helps individuals develop action plans for inclusive leisure services. Figure 4.3 summarizes the suggestions for developing a reflective paper associated with a simulation.

Plan Actions for Advocacy

Engaging in a simulation can be the impetus for subsequent efforts that advocate for people who have been oppressed. One action that can be taken is to generate plans that can immediately be undertaken to advocate for an improvement in the quality of life for various individuals who have experienced oppression. These efforts can occur in many contexts including school, work, and in the community. It is helpful to identify who might be involved in these efforts and what mechanisms might need to be established to complete these actions. In addition, the simulation can act as a stimulus for a long-term commitment to eliminating discrimination and oppression of various groups who are currently disenfranchised.

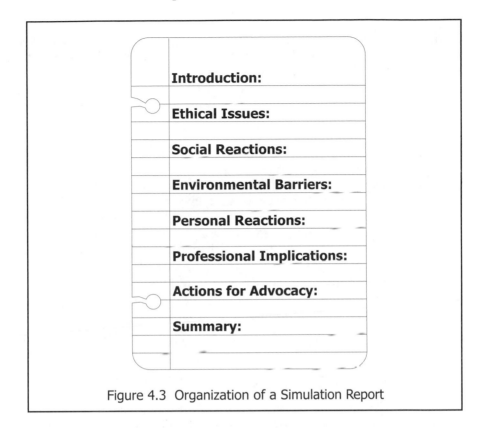

Figure 4.3 Organization of a Simulation Report

What are responses to doing a simulation?

After examining student papers associated with completing wheelchair assignments across many courses on inclusive leisure services, Williams and Dattilo (2005) reported that reactions of students to the wheelchair simulations have been remarkably consistent over the years with the most typical outcomes being:

- heightened awareness of challenges experienced by people who use wheelchairs
- an enhanced appreciation for their own abilities
- newfound empathy for people with disabilities

Yaccino, a former student in recreation and leisure studies, reported on her experience of participating in a simulation that required her to use a wheelchair for half a day. She stated that she always felt slightly uneasy when she was around people with disabilities:

> *It was always very scary to me. I was always very intimidated. It's made me much more comfortable being around people with disabilities. It's opened my eyes to how people with disabilities are treated in our society. And how to treat people with disabilities in a way that is appropriate.*

Yaccino said using the wheelchair showed her just how many barriers exist for people using wheelchairs. She explained that she still does not know what it is like to have a disability because she was able to stand up and put the chair away.

After completing a simulation we do *not* know what it is like to actually have the particular disability. In response to this, several students expressed their opinions and feelings.

> Linda reported that: "You can only understand to a point. I could build my upper body strength, but I couldn't get used to the staring." Nancy explained that "I sat in with a student who uses a motorized wheelchair. He thinks everybody should spend time in a wheelchair. He told me, 'You'll definitely learn from this.'" Dave admitted that: "Normally girls will look at me, but when you're in the chair, it's like you're being looked right over. They don't see you, they see the chair." Bob reported that "I think I will, in the future, approach a person with a disability differently. I won't just look at their disabilities, but at their abilities." Nancy exclaimed that, "It was definitely an eye-opening experience!" Dave added, "You don't forget an experience like that." "Even now (two weeks after the simulation), I'll go somewhere and take note if places are accessible," Deborah said. "Will this stick with me? Definitely!"

Young (1990) reported that being temporarily disabled was an "eye-opening experience" for him. His strongest realization was how inaccessible the world is for people with disabilities. He observed that although many buildings have access ramps, some were angled too steeply or were in such a state of disrepair that efforts at access were hazardous. What was most surprising and disconcerting to him was the number of public facilities that had no access ramps.

At times, he felt a sense of outrage at his helplessness and dependency upon the graciousness of others that he withdrew from the public. Young expressed the feeling that seeing himself as a burden to others was quite sobering. Throughout his experience, he reported that many of his friends were generous with their time and energy. Yet, Young reflected that the many years most people spend learning to be self-sufficient are difficult to ignore, and the desire for self-sufficiency can lead one to eliminate events and activities where self-sufficiency is not possible.

Young's comments teach us that although it is helpful to provide assistance when required, it is even more effective to help people with disabilities access community recreation programs and create a supportive and accessible environment that allows people to participate as actively as possible without the need for assistance.

A person who responded to Young's letter has a friend, Brian, who will use a wheelchair for the remainder of his life. The anonymous writer stated that if people would increase their awareness of people with disabilities, all would benefit. Although awareness has improved in the last few years, communities have a long way to go to provide a workable public transportation system, restrooms that have doors that open easily, curb cuts on both ends of sidewalks, seating that does not relegate some people to out-of-the-way areas, and usable ramps. Finally, the writer suggested that it is not an issue of "them and us"; rather, we are all in this together. Those people who today consider that they are not disabled may acquire a disability at any time.

> Thompson and Vierno (1991) reported that Don Smitley likes to refer to people who do not use wheelchairs as "shoe-bound." He relates using his wheelchair to others using shoes and said, "You would only think about shoes if they are uncomfortable, and I view the wheelchair the same way."

The world-renowned violinist, Itzhak Perlman (1987) suggested that if people would like to become sensitive to the indignities and frustrations experienced by people with disabilities, they should spend a day or two in a wheelchair. Perlman (p. 26) provided the following guidelines for people engaging in a wheelchair simulation:

> *Tell yourself that you cannot get up, then try to get into a car. Try to go shopping or use the toilet in a restaurant. See what it feels like to be all dressed up and have to ride to your appointment in a freight elevator with the garbage. I can tell you how that makes me feel—furious. . . . What we need is an attitude that we're all human beings, and as such, we all care about each other.*

It is helpful to consider that there can be negative effects associated with doing a disability simulation. Some researchers have identified some of these undesirable consequences.

> For instance, French (1996) found that some participants engaged in a wheelchair simulation reported that they felt embarrassed and unattractive while completing the simulation assignment. Given the positive effects reported in the literature about participating in disability simulations as well as the negative effects, researchers have conducted a meta-analysis of disability simulation research. Flower, Burns, and Bottsford-Miller (2007) closely examined 10 studies examining effects of disability simulations. They reported that the current research does not support any suggested harmful effects of disability simulations.

What else can we do?

If we are interested in developing authentic and respectful professional relationships with people who differ from us, then a step toward greater inclusion has been taken. When detecting the other person's difference, it may be helpful to consider that it is natural to notice differences, and it is fine to have a negative impression of a difference—at first.

> For example, our negative impression may be related to the fact that a person who is missing an arm is new to us, or that we were not expecting to see a person with an amputation in the current context, or that the disability is disturbing to us.

In any event, after detecting a difference, it is helpful to pause before acting on this first impression. Miller and Sammons (1999) suggest ways to improve how we interact with a person who happens to be different from us:

- decide what to do
- take action by looking
- take action by talking
- take action by doing
- debrief the encounter

Decide What to Do

After detecting the other person's difference, the next step is to think about the difference so we can decide what to do next. Although this process can take only a few seconds, it helps us to gain control of our actions and take actions that reflect our goals and values, rather than taking action based on our sometimes uncomfortable or negative first impression of differences.

Take Action by Looking

If we can see, the first action we typically take when encountering a person is to look at that person. Once we see someone who looks or acts different from us, we stare, turn away, or acknowledge them. *Staring* involves a long, direct examination that implies an evaluation or judgment that often causes the person being stared at to feel uncomfortable. *Turning away* means that the person who rotates away attempts to ignore the individual whom she or he initially saw.

The other choice we have after seeing people who act or look different from us is to acknowledge them in a nonjudgmental way; looking at a person's face is what we do in most situations, and smiling is typically a safe behavior. Consider that the difference you detect about a person is only one attribute they possess among many others. Thinking in this way may help us to positively regard a person rather than staring or turning away.

Take Action by Talking

After we see people, the next action that we typically engage in is talking to them. Sometimes we might have difficulty speaking to a person we perceive to be different because we may think that there is only one correct thing to say to the person, and, of course, there is not. Miller and Sammons (1999, pp. 92–93) offer some important examples:

> In situations that call for quick and easy accommodation, such as holding a door for a person who uses a walker or explaining the type and location of foods at a buffet for a person who is blind, there's no need to talk about the difference. You might think that it would be rude to ignore the person's disability—but you wouldn't ask questions about his other characteristics, such as personality, hair color, or shoe size when these features aren't relevant to the situation. When the disability is relevant to the situation, however, you have a lot of choices about what to say. Your options include acknowledging the difference, asking for information, and asking whether assistance is needed while waiting for a response before helping.

Take Action by Doing

Much of this book is designed to assist you in determining what might be the most appropriate action when encountering people who have been oppressed. Generally, if people are in need of assistance, it is helpful if we help the person only after our offer of assistance has been accepted, that we accommodate differences whenever possible, and that we work to include all people into our programs. The remaining chapters in the book are designed to help identify actions that reflect respect and sensitivity to all people.

Debrief the Encounter

To debrief a situation, reflect on the interaction and then think about the next possible encounter with that person or to a similar situation. When debriefing it is helpful to consider what happened, how we felt about what happened, and what could happen next time.

Final Thoughts

Education of leisure service professionals about the capabilities of individuals who are different from them in some way may improve their attitudes. To maximize the usefulness of such educational attempts, the following strategies can be employed:

- experience positive, indirect exposure through readings, discussions, and videos
- complete self-awareness exercises, and associated briefings
- participate in simulations
- encounter positive, direct contact with individuals in a variety of contexts

The strategies presented in this chapter intend to help people who are privileged in some manner reduce their discomfort around people who have been oppressed. A reduction in discomfort will increase the likelihood of positive attitudes being developed.

As we develop more positive attitudes toward others, leisure opportunities for individuals who have been oppressed will increase. When opportunities to experience leisure increase, the quality of life for all individuals often is enhanced.

By using strategies presented in this chapter, we can begin to gain a sense of professional competence. It might be helpful to consider the observations that our belief in our ability is the most important factor in our professional effectiveness and thereby the success of people we serve.

Discussion Questions

1. How can you cultivate a sense of professional competence?
2. What is the value of attending presentations and engaging in discussions about people who have been oppressed?
3. How can you become aware of your attitudes toward people with disabilities?
4. What is the value of participating in simulations of disabling conditions?
5. What are some guidelines to follow when conducting or participating in a simulation requiring the use of a wheelchair?
6. How can you encourage people to learn from a simulation?
7. What have been some responses of people who have participated in a simulation of a disabling condition?
8. What is the value of participating in situations that provide you with an opportunity to become familiar with a person with a disability?
9. What are some techniques you could use to improve other people's attitudes about people with disabilities?
10. What is the value of reducing some people's discomfort around other people who happen to have disabilities?

Chapter 5
Improve Others'
Attitudes

It is the greatest of all mistakes to do nothing
because you can only do a little. Do what you can.
-Sydney Smith

Orientation Activity: Examine
Societal Attitudes

Directions Alone: Record your feelings about the person making each statement. What might you say if the person directed the statement to you?

Directions with Others: Find a person and discuss the implications of one statement on recreation participation. Make notes as you talk for later discussion. Once you finish discussing your responses, find another person and discuss another statement.

1. She could not belong to the ceramics class; she's got the mind of a 6-year-old, even if she is 48 years old.
2. We want the underprivileged kids at the recreation center—that's why we have special classes for them.
3. She really should be with the other girls on the cheerleading team rather than playing football.
4. He can play in the volleyball league; however, if his cerebral palsy becomes a problem, then he must leave.
5. If she insists on wearing that veil, then she will not be able to participate in our program.
6. I do not want to give our campground space to that group of Chicanos; I bet they will be loud and offend other campers.
7. That woman is just too old to participate in our tennis program; she'd be better off playing in a bridge league.
8. Our movie theater offers discounts to handicapped people with proper identification.
9. I do not mind if she is a lesbian, but if she openly talks about it, we will need to move her to a different program.
10. It is expensive to make our resource room accessible to the disabled; it is better if they order resources from home.

11. That boy needed to get a scholarship to participate in this program; you'd think his parents could give him the money.
12. Sure she wants to learn sports, but our clinics are not set up for retarded people.

Debriefing: People often fear what they do not know, what is different, and what makes them feel vulnerable. Negative attitudes based on fears create barriers to full participation in society for a variety of individuals.

Conversely, positive attitudes create opportunities for people that enable them to pursue active participation in their communities. Development of positive attitudes can begin with exposure to individuals that allow people to develop an understanding of and an appreciation for those that differ from them. Consider the following questions when reflecting on the activity you have recently completed:

- What are the problems associated with the statements?
- What attitudes might be represented by these statements?
- How can you change these statements to reflect positive attitudes?

Introduction

Ignorance resulting from a lack of exposure can facilitate the development of negative attitudes. A direct result of ignorance is fear, as illustrated in the following quotation by Bart, who has an observable physical disability:

> *People do not know how to act towards you. They're afraid they'll say something wrong, they're afraid that they'll do something different that will make you upset; they don't know how to act with you.*

Fear can be a privileged person's strongest feeling when encountering someone who has been oppressed.

> For example, according to Murphy (1990), a researcher who has paraplegia, people with disabilities serve as constant, visible reminders to people without disabilities that they are vulnerable; people with disabilities represent a possibility that is feared.

If those who are privileged have previous exposure to oppressed people, they can develop positive attitudes toward these individuals. The following studies illustrate this point:

> Stewart (1988) reported that students who participated in an inclusive university weight-training course improved their attitude toward diversity significantly more than participants in a university weight-training course that was not inclusive. As

another example, Kisabeth and Richardson (1985) documented significant positive changes in attitudes of students as a result of a person with a disability being included in a university racquetball class.

The challenge to leisure service professionals is to determine ways to provide exposure to diversity, to foster development of positive attitudes toward all participants. The two primary questions addressed in this chapter are:

- How can we adopt inclusive beliefs that help improve attitudes?
- What actions can we take to improve others' attitudes?

How can we adopt inclusive beliefs that help improve attitudes?

This section provides some ways to think about and treat people with disabilities. The ways of thinking presented in Figure 5.1 set the stage for beneficial contact and development of positive attitudes. They include the following imperatives:

- focus on similarities
- view all people as part of humanity
- adopt a person-centered approach

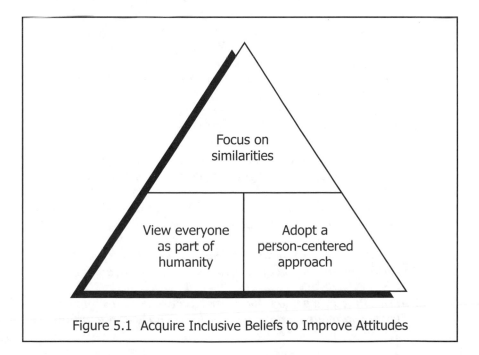

Figure 5.1 Acquire Inclusive Beliefs to Improve Attitudes

Focus on Similarities

In the case of groups that are already disadvantaged, ignoring similarities adds to their challenges. If we focus only on other peoples' differences, we will develop a dissimilar impression of those differences than if we perceived them within a system that includes similarities as well. The words of the Dalai Lama (Dalai Lama & Cutler, 1998, p. 2) are relevant as he described the art of happiness:

> *Wherever I meet people, I always have the feeling that I am encountering another human being, just like myself. I find it is much easier to communicate with others on that level. If we emphasize specific characteristics, like I am Tibetan or I am Buddhist, then there are differences. But those things are secondary. If we can leave the differences aside, I think we can easily communicate, exchange ideas, and share experiences.*

Positive relationships are often established between people who believe they share common characteristics. Many factors encourage the feeling that two people belong together in some way. When a common bond between individuals is developed by focusing on similarities, people's ability to accept differences is enhanced.

Differences between people can be viewed negatively by requiring conformity, or differences can be seen as exciting opportunities to learn new ways of looking at the world. Diversity is what allows people to grow and learn. Shapiro (1993, p. 4) emphasized this point when he stated that people with disabilities:

> *[n]o longer see their physical or mental limitations as a source of shame or as something to overcome in order to inspire others. Today they proclaim that it is okay, even good, to be disabled. Cook's childhood polio forced him to wear heavy corrective shoes, and he walked with difficulty. But taking pride in his disability was for Cook a celebration of the differences among people and gave him a respectful understanding that all share the same basic desires to be full participants in society.*

The orientation activity presented at the beginning of this chapter was provided to encourage readers to begin considering the implications of focusing on similarities with people and identifying differences between people. Statements by Alonzo who we interviewed following his rehabilitation from a spinal cord injury, emphasizes this point:

> *I forget that I'm in a wheelchair sometimes; I totally forget that I'm different than anybody else, and it just doesn't bother me.*
>
> *I'm still the same person that I used to be . . . I just sit down instead of stand up all the time . . . can still have as much fun*

as I ever wanted to and ever did . . . I'm still able to do things
that I used to do and want to do.

View All People as Part of Humanity

Similar to some of the ethical assumptions presented in Chapter 1, Bogdan and Taylor (1992) reported that when people are accepting of individuals, they often describe them as possessing characteristics of **humanness**. Consequently, the differentiating characteristic, such as having a different religion, color of skin, sexual orientation, or ability, is viewed as secondary to the person's humanness. The authors offer four primary dimensions of acknowledging someone's humanness (Figure 5.2):

- attribute *thinking* to the other person
- see *individuality* in the other person
- view the other person as *reciprocating*
- define *social place* for the other person

Belief in these dimensions enables people who have been privileged to define people who have been oppressed as people like them.

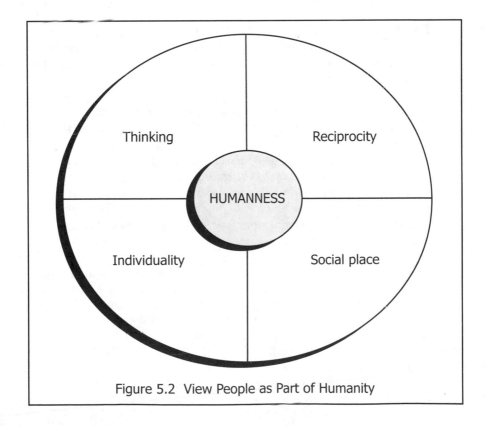

Figure 5.2 View People as Part of Humanity

Attribute Thinking to the Other Person. The dimension of assuming that each person, regardless of their cognitive status, can think means that each individual has the capacity of free will and can make meaningful choices. People have preferences about what they enjoy in their free time. It is important that we provide all people opportunity to express these preferences and participate in enjoyable and fun activities so that they experience the positive emotions associated with leisure participation.

See Individuality in the Other Person. The belief that *each person is a unique individual* suggests that everyone can contribute to the community. Each individual brings something distinctive to a recreation program and can make a unique contribution to the situation. As we are exposed to one another we learn new ideas and gain different perspectives on life.

View the Other Person as Reciprocating. *Reciprocity* implies that there is a give and take between people and that each person has the ability to make a contribution in some way. When reciprocity occurs, feelings and actions are mutually beneficial. Reciprocity is the key characteristic of a friendship or successful close relationship.

All people have the capacity to give something in an interaction as well as to receive something. In addition, many people who are oppressed in some way express the desire to help other people as a result of being helped themselves.

Define Social Place for the Other Person. The dimension of *defining a social place* is based on the notion that since people are social beings, each person has the right to be a part of society that includes social networks, organizations, and institutions. Bogdan and Taylor (1992, p. 289) stated that:

> *Within these social groups, individuals are given a particular social place. The concept of role is often used to describe a person's social place, but social place is not merely a matter of playing a social role. It is also a matter of being defined as being an integral part of the group or social unit. There is a personal dimension to roles. Roles are particularized for each social unit and personalized by each occupant. Through fulfilling particular social roles, social factors are defined as being part of humanity.*

If we consider that each individual possesses the dimensions of humanness—that is, if we attribute thinking to the other, see individuality in the other, view the other as reciprocating, and define social place for the other, we then will tend to treat each person we serve with dignity and respect. In doing so, we increase the chance that each interaction we have will create a positive experience for all people involved.

Adopt a Person-Centered Approach

A helpful approach for facilitating access of all people to community leisure services is to adopt a person-centered approach to the delivery of services. The *person-centered approach* is a way to provide services that are designed to focus on each individual's abilities and interests and to encourage every person to feel important, have hope, and dream about developing relationships and a sense of community. According to Bui and Turnbull (2003, p. 23), the defining features of person-centered services include:

- a circle of support directed by the participant
- involvement of family and friends
- personal relationships as the primary form of support
- focus on capacities and assets of the participant
- emphasis on community settings, services, and supports
- tolerance of setbacks, uncertainty, and disagreements
- shared actions through creative problem-solving

This approach is based on the belief that every person is unique and has the potential for growth and development. It is helpful to focus on what participants can do, rather than what they are currently unable to do, and then attend to whatever barriers prevent the inclusion of people into leisure services.

A person-centered approach is based on the assumption that in an ever-changing world, one constant factor is our *shared humanity*. Roberts, Becker, and Seay (1997) reviewed several person-centered models and identified the following common elements: support for inclusion is invited, connections between people are made, expectations are envisioned, problems are solved, and progress is celebrated. The authors described this approach by stating:

> *Our shared humanity should be what compels us to treat each other as unique human beings with unknown potential for growth and learning. A strong person-centered philosophy helps us respond to each other, first in terms of our human needs, and second in terms of our more individual requirements.* (p. 75)

What actions can we take to improve others' attitudes?

The next section describes some specific strategies to help people develop more positive attitudes about those who have been oppressed.

In response to the following warning by Kenneth Stern (2002, p. 1–2), author and the American Jewish Committee's expert on anti-Semitism and bigotry, these strategies go beyond traditional forms of education to provide experiences designed to enhance people's attitudes.

Many would like to believe that education is a sufficient antidote to bigotry, but the facts demonstrate otherwise. There have always been too many very well-educated bigots. Just ask the Southern blacks who were victimized, not only by the lynchings of the Ku Klux Klan in the 1950s and 1960s, but also by the powerful local white "citizen councils" that spoke about "state rights" and whose members included well-educated community leaders.

Bigotry involves the stubborn intolerance of a person, belief, or opinion that differs from one's own. A **bigot** is a person who is devoted to his or her own opinions and prejudices, particularly opinions that reflect intolerance or animosity toward people who have different beliefs, or people who differ from them in regards to race, ethnicity, nationality, sexual orientation, disability, or religion. A bigot is hostile to such people on account of his opinions.

Leisure service providers can become actively involved in facilitating acceptance of all people, regardless of their personal characteristics or opinions, by members of our community. Some strategies that can help us achieve this goal include:

- structure interactions
- encourage extensive personal contact
- promote joint participation
- facilitate equal status
- foster cooperative interdependence
- develop effective communication
- create naturally proportioned groups
- model positive interactions
- encourage age-appropriate behaviors

Structure Interactions

Programs structured to promote positive interactions among participants tend to stimulate positive attitudes. Structured experiences consistently result in positive attitude changes, while unstructured contact does not. Leisure service providers can create a supportive inclusive environment and can take steps to ensure that the potential for appropriate contact between people is realized.

One way to encourage the presentation of structured interactions is to *promote positive interactions* between participants as one of the goals of each program. Plans can be developed to stimulate positive interactions and to devise methods for responding to negative interactions.

Inclusion is clearly beneficial to all people involved; however, it does require effort on the part of the leisure service professional. Simply placing people in the same environment does not ensure positive interactions among them. Planning ways to structure and promote meaningful interactions between participants can help professionals to increase the likelihood that the benefits of inclusion will be realized.

For example, at the start of a soccer program, Demetrius, the instructor, conducts ice-breaker activities designed to introduce participants to soccer and each other. One such activity involves participants being introduced to each other. Next, they stand in a circle and one player kicks a soccer ball to another person in the circle while simultaneously calling out the name of the person. Participants are then required on their next turn to kick the ball to a different person and continue in this way until every participant kicks the ball to each person in the circle.

Encourage Extensive Personal Contact

The goal of providing extensive contact between people is to increase communication and understanding.

For instance, Hoenk and Mobily (1987) reported that children who had extensive contact with diverse children in an inclusive play environment demonstrated more positive attitudes toward interacting with diverse peers than those with little contact. In addition, Rowe and Stutts (1987) demonstrated that an inclusive practicum experience that provided contact with diverse participants improved attitudes of undergraduate students.

When we use volunteers to assist people in an inclusive leisure program, we may wish to consider the implications of the volunteers' roles. One-time interactions that are brief in duration with people who have been oppressed, such as special events, may not create an environment that fosters positive attitudes by volunteers toward participants who have experienced oppression. If volunteers are placed in situations where they have ample opportunities to interact with individuals who have different characteristics from them, then they are in a better position to develop positive attitudes toward these individuals than if they were placed in situations where they encountered limited interaction with participants.

As an example, Elizabeth chooses to volunteer for a bowling league for older adults. The bowling league lasts for several months in the winter, and during that time Elizabeth meets and interacts with Bertha, an 83-year-old woman who is beginning to experience symptoms of Alzheimer's disease. During those months Elizabeth learns that she and Bertha grew up in the same neighborhood and have many things in common, including a love for bowling. This extensive contact has created an opportunity for Elizabeth and Bertha to become friends.

Promote Joint Participation

Agencies that offer inclusive leisure services have more of a chance to achieve the goal of frequent contact between people than those departments that do not actively promote inclusion. Participation in inclusive recreation activities can provide opportunities for people residing in the community to experience positive interactions that dispel existing stereotypes.

> For example, Jack is a toddler who enjoys a swimming class that he participates in with his father at the YMCA. He notices in amazement that one of the other children, Clarisse, who happens to have multiple disabilities, is yipping loudly. Jack looks to his father after observing and listening to Clarisse making these distinctive noises. Jack's father just smiles and says: "Sometimes people express their enjoyment differently than you do." Jack then smiles and nods to Clarisse.

Since participation in recreation activities offers us many opportunities for close personal contact, involvement in inclusive leisure services can provide an effective way to change societal attitudes. By facilitating inclusive leisure opportunities for all community members, we can contribute to the acceptance of all people. Mary Ann Devine and Brett Lashua (2002, p. 74) studied the way social acceptance is constructed in inclusive leisure contexts and provided this quotation of 12-year-old Elvis:

> *I use checkers, chess, and computer games to show my stuff. I mean this is how I can get them to see what I can do. I don't say that to them, I just say "Do you want to play this game?" And then I beat the pants off them [laughs].*

To conclude this section, a quote by James Rimmer (2007) seems appropriate as he commented on the importance of encouraging participation in physically active recreation and sports for children and youth:

> *There is that break point in youth sports where winning becomes the primary reason for playing . . . those who lose, and lose often, quit. And those who win, and win often, keep playing. Think of the irony of that; the winners keep playing and the losers are relegated to the sidelines. Shouldn't it be the opposite way? Those who lose need more time to play and practice rather than less time! Junior high seems to be that critical juncture where . . . those with the most talent move on, while others with less body weight, height, and coordination drop out. With rising obesity rates among youth . . . and the diminished opportunity to participate in youth sports, we're heading down a path of disaster.*

Facilitate Equal Status

Positive attitudes result from contact between individuals on an equal status basis. *Equal status* refers to participants assuming roles that result in similar degrees of respect from other participants. Inclusive recreation activities that bring people together on an equal basis have the potential for positively influencing the public's perceptions of people who have been oppressed.

To promote equal status of participants, we must clearly communicate the contributions that each individual makes to a given activity. We can direct participants' attention to insights they gain by being exposed to diversity among participants.

All participants can be encouraged to view their involvement with others as a means to facilitate leisure participation for the entire group, rather than simply helping those "less fortunate" people. We can take steps to avoid the experience reported by Wilhite (p. 21) and colleagues:

> *Molly talked about her embarrassment when one of her teachers asked in front of the class, "Who wants to be Molly's helper?" Molly explained, "I knew a few people in there, but not well. So nobody raised their hand which embarrassed everyone." Clearly, Molly was not being given equal status with her peers. A better approach might be if a buddy system was initiated for all participants and buddies were encouraged to help each other.*

Foster Cooperative Interdependence

We are dependent on one another across many aspects of our lives. We rely on friends, family, and community members such as merchants and law enforcement personnel to support us in different ways. In turn, we provide support to our families, friends and communities. We are all interdependent.

The use of cooperative activities can help to promote positive interactions and attitudes. In addition, when *common goals* rank higher than individual goals, improved relationships and positive attitudes occur. Positive attitudes result from contact between individuals that are friendly, cooperative, and aimed at a common goal. Jones (2004, p. 64) reported that:

> *[c]ommunity recreation agencies should enlarge their offerings to include structured activities that foster cooperation in order to provide inclusive recreation programs.*

For the goal of *cooperative interdependence* to occur, each person is equally dependent on the other for achieving desired goals. We can provide many different recreation activities, such as team building, trust development, and adventure recreation that require cooperation and contributions by all participants.

The focus of the recreation activities can be on the process of *collaboration*, working together to meet a challenge rather than obtaining a product or winning. Examples of cooperative activities include:

- gardening when everyone is assigned a particular task
- making a paper-mâché project when everyone adds a layer
- bowling when the highest possible team score is desired
- making a quilt when working with a group
- cooking when everyone completes a step in the preparation

Develop Effective Communication

Clear communication between people can reduce interaction strain. Since some people want to express attitudes that are acceptable to and respectful of people who differ from them in various ways, it becomes clear that they can benefit from learning about how their behaviors can offend other people.

> For instance, Cook and Makas (1979) reported that people differ in their perceptions of what constitutes positive attitudes toward people with disabilities. To people with disabilities, positive attitudes mean either removing the special category of disability entirely, or promoting attitudes that defend their civil and social rights. However, for people without disabilities, positive attitudes reflect a desire to be nice, helpful, and ultimately place people with disabilities in a dependent situation. Therefore, people without disabilities may actually be perceived by people with disabilities as expressing negative attitudes in spite of good intentions.

It is helpful if people are educated about civil rights issues. In situations in which a person makes a statement or behaves in a way that is demeaning or insulting, those who are affected are justified in correcting the error. However, if the correction is accompanied by negative emotions that are reflected in a person's angry voice tone or demeanor, the content of the correction is likely to be lost.

Negative reactions to a person's failed attempts at positive interaction may discourage the person's good intentions and create further misunderstanding and discomfort. Communication, particularly the sharing of one another's expectations, can be valuable in reducing barriers that contribute to discomfort.

Create Naturally Proportioned Groups

The company a person keeps influences perceptions of this person. Inclusion is almost impossible if individuals are grouped together solely on the basis of a particular, often stigmatized, characteristic. When people with the same characteristics are placed together in an activity this conveys to others the idea that such people *belong together*.

It is difficult to see the person and not the category when the individual is surrounded by others who share similar salient characteristics. If people who are devalued are placed in an environment in numbers that are too large for the social systems around them to relate to and assimilate, then these individuals will probably experience rejection, hostility, and efforts at segregation.

However, if a person is seen associating with people who we view positively, then we tend to view that person in a positive manner. In response to this occurrence, Wolfensberger (2000, p. 114) advocated the idea of natural proportions by stating that people:

> *[a]re apt to acquire—or retain—positive images and role expectancies by being associated with people who are perceived as competent, vigorous, moral, distinguished, etc., and who occupy positive roles. However, in order for such positive image transfer to take place, it is generally important that only a small number of devalued persons be associated with, or juxtaposed to [placed close together, side by side], a much larger number of valued ones, because it is the majority—and even predominant—identity of any social grouping that is apt to define its individual members in the eyes of observers.*

The formation of ***natural proportions*** involves developing groups of people that resemble demographics of the society. Most leisure service professionals who have been interviewed consider natural proportions helpful in increasing the chance of inclusion.

> For example, there are approximately 80 people going on a rafting trip with eight rafts. Of those people, eight of them have some type of disability. Groups that are formed that have approximately one person with a disability for every raft meet the condition of natural proportions for people with disabilities.

Model Positive Interactions

One way to promote positive attitudes toward all people is to model behaviors intended to make the person feel welcome. Children model behaviors of adults who are in leadership positions.

We can act as change agents by modeling positive behaviors and social acceptance toward including all people. This reduces resistance to inclusion by community members and improves their attitudes.

Devine and colleagues (1998, p. 72) provided the following example of effective modeling, specific to sports but relevant to all leisure services:

> In front of others, treat all teammates the same as everyone else. It's not, "Team, meet Johnny, our special teammate."

Instead, it should be, "Team, meet Johnny. He bats left-handed and plays outfield."

Encourage Age-Appropriate Behaviors

One specific suggestion to help people develop more positive attitudes about people who have been oppressed is directly related to people with intellectual disabilities. Some individuals with intellectual disabilities participate in leisure activities that are typically engaged in by those who are younger than them. If we encourage these individuals to participate in activities and with materials that are typically associated with children, such as toys, negative stereotypes about them are perpetuated.

However, if individuals with intellectual disabilities use materials and participate in activities appropriate for their age, they may be viewed more positively. *Age-appropriate activities* reflect the interests and attitudes that are commensurate with a particular age group.

Leisure service providers are encouraged to select recreation activities based on activities performed by peers in a wide variety of inclusive community environments. Age-appropriate activities might reduce the stigmatizing perceptions about adults with intellectual disabilities.

Participating in age-appropriate activities may lead others to view adults with disabilities as capable of taking on more complicated and advanced tasks than would otherwise be expected.

One example of promoting age-appropriate leisure participation is associated with an adolescent boy, Jason. As a child he loved to listen to any toy that emitted sounds and flashed lights. When he got older, his parents bought him a portable video game. This game was extremely reactive with sounds and lights that flashed. Jason very much enjoyed playing the video game. Now that he is older, Jason enjoys playing video games with his friends in video arcades, movie theater lobbies, and bowling alleys.

The strategies presented in Figure 5.3 intend to promote beneficial contact and positive attitudes.

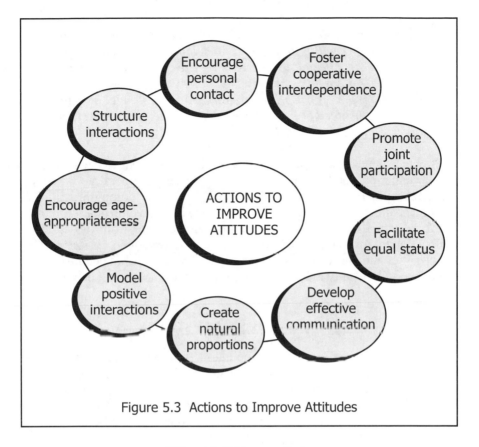

Figure 5.3 Actions to Improve Attitudes

Final Thoughts

Although behaviors that reflect negative attitudes can limit opportunities for people who have been oppressed, these negative attitudes and subsequent behaviors can be changed.

> As an illustration, after conducting in-depth interviews with over 50 youth ranging in ages from 6–18, Bunch and Valeo (2004) found that those youth who attended an inclusive school developed more diverse friendships, demonstrated lower degrees of abusive behavior, and advocated for diverse peers more than those youth attending schools that contained segregated services.

Leisure service providers can play an important role in changing participants' attitudes so they reflect acceptance and understanding of diversity. We can teach people about the importance of equal access and equal opportunity; principles that were articulated by U.S. President Barack Obama (2010):

Equal access. Equal opportunity. The freedom to make our lives what we will. These aren't principles that belong to any group or any one political party. They are common principles. They are American principles. No matter who we are—young, old, black, white, Latino, Asian, Native American, gay, straight, disabled or not—these are the principles we cherish as citizens of the United States of America.

Structuring interactions, encouraging extensive personal contact, promoting joint participation, facilitating equal status, fostering cooperative interdependence, focusing on similarities, developing effective communication, and modeling positive interactions are ways that may help develop positive attitudes toward individuals who possess different characteristics from those who are privileged. Perhaps, with increased contact with people who possess different characteristics and the awareness of a highly visible presence of people who have been oppressed, negative feelings toward these individuals can be eliminated.

Discussion Questions

1. What is the value of structuring interactions when people who possess different characteristics are participating in recreation programs?
2. What is an example of how to structure a situation to promote positive interactions between diverse participants?
3. How can you encourage extensive personal contact between diverse participants?
4. What are some methods that promote joint participation between diverse participants?
5. What is the value of facilitating equal status among participants in a recreation program?
6. How might you encourage participants in your recreation programs to be of equal status?
7. How might you foster cooperative interdependence with people participating in your recreation program?
8. What are some ways you can encourage people you encounter to focus on people's similarities rather than their differences?
9. What are some strategies to increase effective communication that would help improve attitudes of people you encounter?
10. What are some specific techniques you could use to improve people's attitudes toward people who have been oppressed?

Chapter 6
Be Aware of
Psychological Barriers to Leisure

*I have learned that success is to be measured not so much
by the position that one has reached in life,
as by the obstacles which one has overcome by trying to succeed.*
-Booker T. Washington

Orientation Activity: Whose problem is it?

Directions Alone: Read the following scenario and write a brief paragraph describing its relevance to understanding people with disabilities.

Directions with Others: Divide into small groups and have each person describe his or her interpretation. When everyone has presented his or her ideas, determine how many different interpretations there were. Discuss your response with the entire group.

> I thought my wife was losing her hearing, so one day I decided to test it. I quietly walked in the front door and stood 30 feet behind her. "Suzanne," I said, "can you hear me?" There was no response so I moved 20 feet behind her. "Suzanne," I repeated, "can you hear me?" Still there was no reply. I advanced to 10 feet and asked, "Now can you hear me?" "Yes, dear," Suzanne answered, "for the *third* time, yes!"

Debriefing: Many of us have observed that a number of people confront problems when they try to experience leisure. Some rarely initiate contact with others, some do not follow rules and misbehave, some withdraw from participation, and others indicate a lack of interest in available leisure services.

If we view these problems as originating from the person as a result of their disability or other characteristics, little can be done to facilitate inclusive leisure services. If problems experienced by people are viewed from the perspective that professionals, family members, and community members contribute to these problems, then leisure service professionals can assist these individuals in many ways.

> For example, some people who speak slowly may rarely attempt to communicate because others control communication exchanges by not allowing sufficient time for them to make a statement or answer a question. Other people may withdraw from

participation as a result of repeated failures within a program. Without intervention these people may begin to feel helpless.

This chapter highlights some of the barriers encountered by people who have been oppressed and the role leisure service professionals may play in overcoming them. As you consider the orientation activity, ask yourself the following questions:

- What are some problems people with disabilities encounter when participating in community recreation programs?
- How might recreation professionals contribute to these problems?
- What can be done to overcome these problems?

Introduction

When asked to describe the leading barrier they experience, people who have been oppressed consistently report that negative attitudes are the most devastating. These negative attitudes, described in previous chapters, do not occur in isolation.

To illustrate the impact of negative attitudes upon a particular group who have been oppressed, those people with intellectual disabilities, a "Multinational Study of Attitudes Toward Individuals with Intellectual Disabilities" (2003) was conducted across 10 countries, with at least one country from each continent, involving over 8,000 respondents. The overall conclusion of the study was that the general population lacks an appreciation for the range of capabilities of people with intellectual disabilities, and respondents have low expectations of how much these individuals can achieve. The study demonstrated that although some progress has been made in changing the public's perceptions about people with intellectual disabilities, much work remains.

The barriers associated with negative attitudes that are described in this chapter include: reactance, learned helplessness, controlling environments, unresponsive and negative environments, direct competition, and boredom and anxiety. In addition, the following questions are addressed:

- Why do some people want unavailable things?
- Why do some people give up their freedom?
- What happens when people experience controlling environments?
- What happens when people experience unresponsive and negative environments?
- What happens when we emphasize direct competition?
- How does arousal influence participation?

Why do some people want unavailable things?

The experience of freedom involves a set of behaviors that requires physical and psychological skills. To experience *freedom,* individuals must have the knowledge and understanding that they are able to make a choice. Behaviors that are free include only those acts that are realistically possible for the individual.

In his 1966 book titled *A Theory of Psychological Reactance*, psychologist Jack Brehm reported that given a set of free behaviors, ***reactance*** will occur when any of these behaviors is eliminated or threatened. The relationship between freedom and reactance is illustrated in Figure 6.1.

Reactance increases the desirability of the eliminated or threatened behavior—the behavior becomes more attractive to the individual.

> For instance, if a child is to select one recreation activity from several attractive alternatives (e.g., hiking, dancing, or reading), elimination of one activity (e.g., hiking) will result in that activity becoming even more desirable (Figure 6.2, p. 104).

A person who experiences reactance will be motivated to remove the threat to the free behavior or regain the lost free behavior. When reactance occurs, the person tends to engage in the threatened free behavior, engage in behaviors that imply continued engagement in free behaviors, and encourage other people of similar abilities and status to engage in threatened or eliminated behaviors.

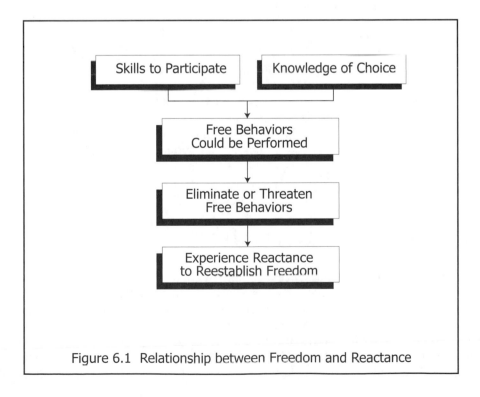

Figure 6.1 Relationship between Freedom and Reactance

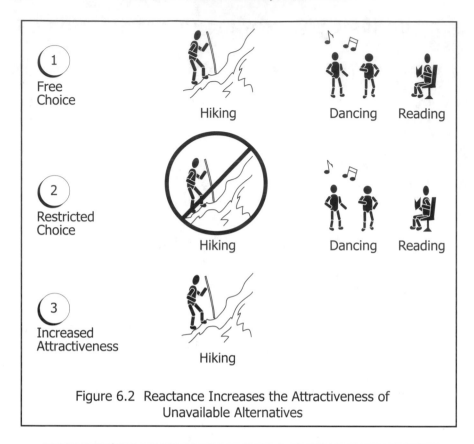

Figure 6.2 Reactance Increases the Attractiveness of Unavailable Alternatives

As an illustration, David, Tawanda, Steven, and Pheodora are playing a basketball game. The youth are told by Jerome, a leisure service professional, to stop yelling obscenities. Steven continues to yell obscenities, Tawanda increases her use of obscenities, Pheodora reduces her use of obscenities but increases her physical aggression, and David encourages the other players to use obscenities. All four youth have responded in slightly different ways, but all illustrate the principle of reactance.

Why do some people give up their freedom?

When people expect to influence a certain outcome, but find their control and freedom jeopardized, initially they exert more effort to establish control such as through reactance. However, the perception of *helplessness* occurs if people become convinced that further attempts will not produce a desired outcome.

After conducting a series of experiments that began with animals and then moved to humans to better understand the state of depression, psychologist Martin Seligman (1975) proposed the theory of learned helplessness. Seligman described *helplessness* as a psychological state that frequently results when events are uncontrollable—that is, those events that are independent of a person's voluntary actions. Reinforcement or punishment can modify voluntary actions. Certain consequences of voluntary behavior will increase or decrease the chance of the behavior occurring.

As individuals are exposed to uncontrollable events, they begin to learn that responding is futile. They feel that it just does not matter what they do because they will fail and therefore they learn to be helpless.

Learned helplessness undermines a person's motivation to respond, reduces the ability to learn that responding works, and results in emotional disturbance such as depression or anxiety. The occurrence of learned helplessness is presented in Figure 6.3.

People find it difficult to assess their ability to control a situation when they first encounter events that are troublesome for them to control. Often, people initially assume that the cause of difficulty is unstable and specific to the situation. Therefore, they increase their attempts to exert control. They often feel that their failure may be related to factors that could change the next time they try, such as the difficulty of the activity, the people associated with the activity, their luck, or the amount of effort and concentration they expend. However, if they are still unable to gain control after repeated attempts to do so, they may begin to assume the outcome is uncontrollable and will experience helplessness.

A person will eventually give up the desire for freedom when reestablishment of freedom proves impossible. The length of time required for people to stop believing that they have freedom to engage in the eliminated or threatened

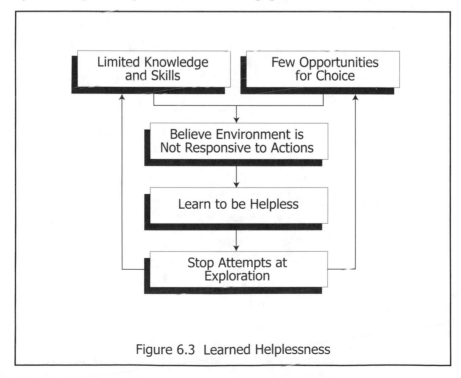

Figure 6.3 Learned Helplessness

free behavior depends in part on the certainty of elimination. The more apparent the inability to experience the free behavior becomes, the more quickly the person will give up that freedom.

Once people perceive the absence of a relationship between their actions and the desired consequence, they attribute their helplessness to a cause. Two types of learned helplessness—personal and universal—are presented in Figure 6.4.

When people expect outcomes to be dependent on others' actions and not their own, ***personal helplessness*** is experienced. This personal helplessness results from failures that erode self-determination.

> As an example of personal helplessness, Laura may be on her first ski trip with a group of peers. She may see other people receiving instruction in snow skiing and think that it is fine for those people to learn to ski. However, Laura believes that she could never learn to do it.

Some people may expect outcomes not to be dependent on their own actions or other people's actions. This is identified as ***universal helplessness***, and it produces feelings of hopelessness.

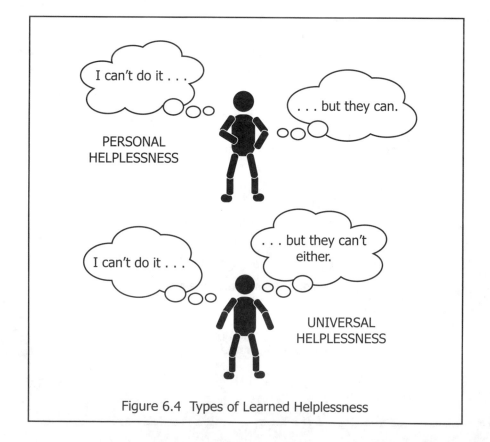

Figure 6.4 Types of Learned Helplessness

As an illustration of universal helplessness: Matthew may decide not to attend a program on volunteerism. He chooses not to attend the program because he thinks that nobody really wants anyone else's help. Also, Matthew believes that even if other people try to help, it would not do any good.

In each situation, the outcome expectancies are not absolute; rather, they are on a continuum ranging from total dependence on one's responses to very limited control of a situation. People do not necessarily adopt the perception of helplessness or mastery in every situation. Our challenge is to try to move participants in our programs away from perceptions of helplessness toward a more mastery-oriented orientation. Learned helplessness may be revealed in these aspects of behavior:

* *cognition*—the way they think
* *emotion*—the way they feel
* *motivation*—their interest in an activity

These consequences of helplessness are important considerations as we try to promote meaningful leisure participation for people.

Cognition

People who learn to be helpless will experience difficulty understanding that their responses produce outcomes. Consequently, they will have problems learning to take control of their lives.

For example, Talie, who is attending a dance class, may feel that no matter how hard he tries he will never learn to dance. As a result of this belief, he finds it difficult to concentrate and learn what is presented.

Emotion

People who expect outcomes to be independent of their responses will tend to become depressed. As individuals attribute their negative outcomes to internal, stable, and global factors and attribute their positive outcomes to external, unstable, and specific behaviors, their self-esteem decreases.

For instance, each time Ozza experiences failure in outdoor adventure recreation activities, she attributes her failures to her ability—which is internal, stable, and global—and she attributes her successes to luck—which is external, unstable, and specific. Therefore, Ozza's self-esteem may be lowered and she may become unhappy.

Motivation

People who expect their responding to be futile will reduce their initiation of voluntary actions. Some people have less knowledge and fewer skills than their same-age peers. Consequently, they are given fewer opportunities to make choices and demonstrate self-initiated leisure participation. Repeated futile experiences result in the perception that one is helpless. With the perception of helplessness comes an elimination of attempts to explore the environment. As exploration decreases, opportunities to experience enjoyment also decline.

> As a case in point, Cleo feels that no matter how hard she tries to learn the martial art of judo, she will never learn it. Because of Cleo's beliefs, she will not be motivated to attend judo class.

People respond to failure in different ways on different occasions. The manner in which people react to failure depends on their perspective. Their responses may be categorized as a mastery orientation or a helplessness orientation (Figure 6.5).

Mastery Orientation

For some people, failure can result in increased effort, intensified concentration, increased persistence, heightened sophistication of problem-solving strategies, and enhanced performance. When people respond in this way, they are identified as having a *mastery orientation*.

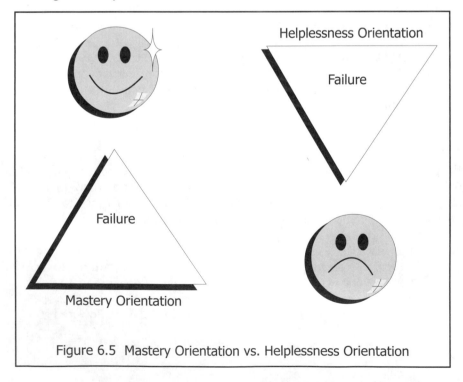

Figure 6.5 Mastery Orientation vs. Helplessness Orientation

If they assume a mastery orientation, they perceive their mistakes are rectifiable. In addition, they view their failure as a result of a lack of effort and therefore look forward to the future. People with a mastery orientation emphasize the positive aspects of their failures and/or engage in active problem solving.

Helplessness Orientation

Others may respond to failure with curtailed effort, reduced concentration, decreased persistence, a deterioration of problem-solving strategies, and a disruption in performance. These responses are indications that a person has learned to be helpless.

If people come to expect that they cannot control outcomes, they might perceive that their mistakes are inevitable and view their failure as a result of a lack of ability. Individuals who have a *helplessness orientation* tend to dwell on the present and focus on negative aspects of a situation. Therefore, they stop attempts at solving the problem associated with failure.

What happens when people experience controlling environments?

A controlling environment does not respond to people's initiatives; however, it does demand behaviors from individuals. When an environment directs and controls people, they often become motivated by external rewards; they experience external motivation.

> For example, Mahteka, a baseball coach, may emphasize to her players the need to win the championship trophy. The enjoyment associated with participation in a baseball league may be reduced for many of her players as a result of their coach's focus on external rewards.

The presence of certain rewards and deadlines that pressure people toward specific outcomes tends to undermine intrinsic motivation, promote compliance or defiance, and inhibit enjoyment. Deci and Ryan (1985, p. 57) noted:

> *Research has substantiated that extrinsic rewards and controls can affect people's experience of self-determination. In such cases, the events will induce a shift in the perceived locus of causality from internal to external, a decrement in intrinsic motivation for the target behavior, less persistence at the activity in the absence of external contingencies, and less interest in and enjoyment of the activity.*

Many researchers have demonstrated the effects of a controlling environment. Typically in these studies children are engaging in some activity, such as drawing, and then experimenters offer to pay the children for the products they produce. Productivity increases while rewards are offered; the children draw more. However, when rewards are withdrawn, children demonstrate what is called, ***overjustification effect***, when these children show less interest in the activity than they did before rewards were offered and they show less interest than children who were not offered rewards. Such studies show that intrinsic motivation can be undermined by extrinsic rewards.

The relationship between motivation and overjustification is illustrated in Figure 6.6. Certain extrinsic rewards such as money, prizes, and food, tend to decrease intrinsic motivation.

> As a classic example, Deci (1971) had two groups of children work on a set of puzzles. Half of them were given a dollar for each puzzle they solved, and the others received no reward. All children were observed in a subsequent free-choice period, and the researchers found that the children who received the rewards spent significantly less free-choice time with puzzles than did those who were not rewarded. In a similar study, Orlick and Mosher (1978) first provided children with a free-choice period. Next, the children played in either a reward condition where they received a task-contingent trophy or a no-reward condition. Four days later, they returned for free-choice period. The children who had participated to obtain the trophy displayed a decrease in free-choice time spent on the task, as compared to those who did not receive any rewards. These results suggest that extrinsic incentives can undermine intrinsic motivation for interesting recreation activities. Ryan, Williams, Patrick, and Deci (2009) warned that practitioners can decrease participation in physically active leisure pursuits by being pressuring or controlling.

What happens when people experience unresponsive and negative environments?

Some individuals experience ***unresponsive environments***, those situations that do not react to their initiatives. As a result of these unresponsive environments, outcomes are perceived to be unrelated to their behaviors. In this type of an environment, the relationship between an action and associated consequences is not clear and cannot be mastered by the individual.

Environments that contain ***negative feedback*** that is not contingent on a person's behaviors also tend to reduce motivation. When we provide general, nonspecific praise or criticism to participants as they attempt to learn a new leisure skill, we will inhibit rather than stimulate learning. Participants will have

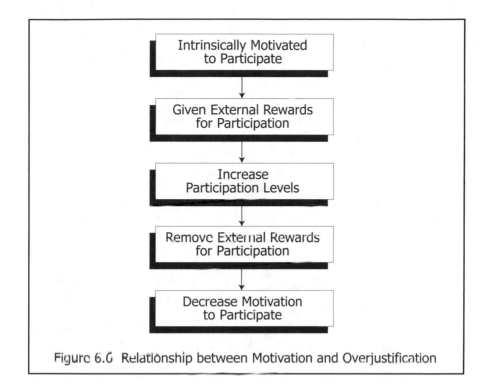

Figure 6.6 Relationship between Motivation and Overjustification

difficulty determining effects of their actions when we fail to provide them with informational feedback.

> As an illustration, when Paulo, the instructor in a painting program, only tells participants that they need to work harder even after they have made considerable progress, they may become frustrated. At the same time, if participants complete their projects and Paulo never seems to have time to provide useful feedback, they may lose their desire for the activity.

What happens when we emphasize direct competition?

Competition can make many recreation activities fun and exciting. In activities such as swimming laps or shooting baskets, people can engage in *indirect competition* when they compete against themselves, striving to surpass some internal standard they have set. This indirect competition provides purpose and direction and is the basis for satisfaction when the standards are met.

Direct competition, which involves pitting oneself against another, can also be fun, exciting, and challenging, and can encourage intrinsic motivation. Doing well in a competitive situation provides clear competence feedback and could enhance a person's intrinsic motivation. However, focusing on winning rather than on doing well at an activity is problematic. The focus on winning can impair performance and lead to aggression.

> As an illustration, Deci, Betley, Kahle, Abrams, and Porac (1981) had two groups of children work on puzzles, with each student working in the presence of another person. Children in one group were instructed to solve each puzzle faster than the other child, while children in the other group were told to solve the puzzles as quickly as they could. When given a chance for free choice afterwards, the direct, face-to-face competition led to a decrease in intrinsic motivation. In a similar example, Vallerand, Gauvin, and Halliwell (1986) reported that competition undermined the intrinsic motivation of children. The children worked with a motor task, and those who directly competed at it spent less subsequent free-choice time working with the activity than those who had not experienced such competition.

Many people tend to experience competition as controlling and feel like they have to win. When they do win, although they feel satisfied, participants are less intrinsically motivated for the activity itself. They will be motivated to continue competing and will still want to win; however, the activity itself will no longer be inherently rewarding

> For example, Weinberg and Ragan (1979) demonstrated that participants who won a competition were more eager to compete again than those who had not, but less eager to engage in the activity in the absence of the competition.

Another problem associated with direct competition is that sometimes parents and guardians of children who are involved in recreation activities that are designed for direct competition, typically youth sports, focus heavily on performance. As a result of this focus, a message might be sent to a participant that what is most important is their performance as opposed to who they are. Fred Engh (2007, p. 55), founder of the National Alliance for Youth Sports, concluded that:

> *What is so detrimental to the kids is that they get the impression that their parents care more about their accomplishments than about them as unique individuals. It makes them anxious rather than setting them at ease. So, parents often forget that what their six-year-old needs from them is warmth, caring and support to help develop good character and friendships. Instead, young children are expected to perform in everything—including sports—at professional, not kid, levels.*

How does arousal influence participation?

Recreation activities can offer people opportunities to control their lives, increase their personal development, experiment with roles, and take part in self-appraisal. However, recreation activities are not necessarily positive, nor do they necessarily produce positive results.

Boredom and anxiety may occur because of an incompatible match between skill level and challenge. As seen in Figure 6.7, too little challenge coupled with a high skill level is likely to produce boredom. ***Boredom*** is the condition that exists when a person perceives a situation to be uninteresting and unchallenging.

Conversely, too much challenge and too little skill may produce anxiety. The state of ***anxiety*** exists when a person is involved in a situation that challenges the individual beyond the current skill level and results in being worried about something negative happening or being impatient because of a desire to have something else happen.

Activities that involve people performing at their maximum level or that require them to "stretch" and expand their skills to some degree are likely to be motivating. People tend to gravitate to recreation activities that provide them with challenges that require some effort and concentration while permitting some degree of success.

As a classic illustration of how arousal influences participation, people are given the choice to play ring toss. They are first

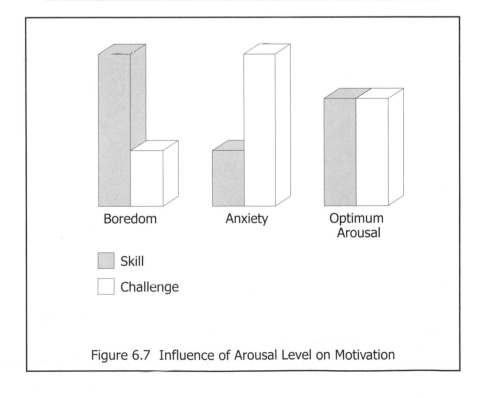

Figure 6.7 Influence of Arousal Level on Motivation

instructed to throw several rings to a post placed near their feet where they consistently achieve ringers, one a few feet away where they have about a 50% success rate, and one several yards away where they rarely, if ever, make a ringer. After being given the chance to throw at each post, participants are asked to throw rings toward the post of their choosing. Which position do you think participants select most often? Is the most selected post the one at their feet, the one in the middle or the one far away? Interestingly, although some participants selected the post close to them and others selected the one far away, most participants chose the post in the middle because it required them to concentrate and afforded them the opportunity for success. They generally reported that throwing rings at the post at their feet was boring and throwing at the post far away was frustrating.

Although from time to time all of us become bored in various situations, when people consistently experience boredom during their free time they can encounter a variety of related problems.

For example, after a review of the literature, Lee, Mittelstaedt, and Askins (1999), concluded that boredom in general (and boredom in free time in particular) can lead to problems such as drug abuse, delinquency, vandalism, hostility, stress, and depression.

Alternatively, if challenges are too high, an individual becomes frustrated, then worried, and eventually anxious. Anxiety brings on negative expectations about personal success in an activity. These negative expectations occur when people believe their skills are insufficient to be successful in a situation. When people experience repeated failure while engaged in various activities, their fears may increase and result in anxiety.

Final Thoughts

There are several explanations of human behavior that provide insight into the problems people experience relative to their leisure participation. An understanding of barriers helps to clarify difficulties experienced by some individuals in becoming self-determined. Sensitivity to barriers such as reactance, learned helplessness, overjustification, boredom, and anxiety should help professionals design leisure services that alleviate these barriers rather than contribute to their development.

Barriers to leisure may occur in many different ways. The hope is that leisure service providers will respond in a positive manner to people who have encountered a variety of challenging barriers to their leisure participation. And that these individuals rather than feeling helpless, bored, and anxious in addition to other negative experiences, will be empowered to take control of their free time. This control should lead to people's perceptions of being self-determined and encourage them to experience the enjoyment and satisfaction associated with meaningful and rewarding leisure participation, such as the experience of Charles St. Germain as described by Phil Taylor (2010, p. 80):

> *Sometimes the world moves too fast for 12-year-old Charles St. Germain. A friendly game of soccer with other boys can seem like chaos, leaving him agitated and shaken. At other times it's Charles who moves too fast for the world, or at least his brain does, giving in to impulses so easily that he has been known to walk away in mid-conversation if something catches his attention. Such are the symptoms of autism, which can leave a person feeling out of step, unable to adjust to the rhythms of the world around him. But when he has a golf club in his hands, Charles, whose condition was diagnosed when he was five, seems to find the perfect beat. He discovered the game two years ago. "And since that day," says his father, "he has been a different boy." . . . Without a lesson, Charles displayed a swing that was smooth and sweet as syrup, and he was soon lofting the kind of impressive drives that have made him a rising star among young golfers in the province [Montreal], routinely shooting in the high 70s and low 80s.*

Discussion Questions

1. What is the leading barrier to participation as reported by people with disabilities?
2. How can reactance influence leisure behavior?
3. What causes people to perceive helplessness?
4. What is learned helplessness?
5. What are two types of learned helplessness?
6. What are the three consequences of helplessness?
7. What are the two different reactions people experience to the interaction of failure and helplessness?
8. How does the overjustification effect undermine intrinsic motivation?
9. What are two types of competition and how do these influence motivation?
10. What is the relationship between skill, challenge, boredom, and anxiety?

Chapter 7
Uphold Human and Civil Rights

Benjamin Hickerson and John Dattilo

There comes a time that people get tired . . . Tired of being humiliated,
tired of being kicked about by the brutal feet of oppression.
-Martin Luther King, Jr.

Orientation Activity:

Directions Alone: Review the material presented in Chapter 3. On a blank piece of paper take a couple minutes to write a paragraph that describes the relationship between stigmas, stereotypes, discrimination, and segregation. Next, take a couple more minutes to compose a paragraph describing the connection between these concepts and human and civil rights.

Directions with Others: After composing the two paragraphs described in the "directions alone," move about the room. Introduce yourself to another person and learn their name. Next, share a key point from your introductory paragraph and have the person share a key point from their introductory paragraph. Follow this same process with the second paragraph and then locate another person. Repeat the procedure with a few other people.

Debriefing: Behaviors motivated by negative attitudes result in isolation of people from the social mainstream and deny them the benefits and opportunities available to people of privilege. In spite of advances toward inclusion, segregated recreation programs continue to exist, especially for people with disabilities. In addition to these segregated programs, people are excluded from community recreation programs in subtle ways.

Subtle actions that encourage segregation include avoiding social contact with people because interactions may be uncomfortable or inconvenient. Perceptions of *differentness* can stem from people being stigmatized. Once people are stigmatized, negative stereotypes can develop. If negative stereotypes exist then actions such as segregation and discrimination follow.

Human rights are freedoms that are perceived to exist as a condition of being human. Consider them as natural liberties that are inalienable and inherently created at birth. Civil rights are equal protections of citizens of a country from their government. There are many connections between the development of attitudes and human as well as civil rights. Here are a few questions to help you debrief this learning activity.

- Why do you think there are global declarations of human rights?
- Why do you think civil rights legislation exists?
- What is the relationship between attitude development and human and civil rights?

Introduction

Since this book is intended to educate future and current leisure service professionals about attitude development and actions that promote positive attitudes toward people who have experienced discrimination and segregation, a chapter devoted to addressing human and civil rights seemed to us to be important. Global human rights declarations and more national and local civil rights legislation are designed to promote inclusion of all people into their communities and, more broadly, into society.

In the first section of this book, information is presented about inclusion and the various attitudinal, sociological, and psychological barriers. These barriers may prevent people from experiencing inclusion in their communities, and more specifically, into recreation programs and leisure opportunities. In this chapter we address the issues of human rights declarations and civil rights legislation that have been pursued to provide formalized ways to encourage the development of inclusion.

These declarations and legislative acts are helpful to understand so that all agencies and personnel providing leisure services can be sure to meet these important guidelines and laws. However, in our estimation, it is most important is that leisure service professionals understand and embrace the spirit of human rights declarations and civil rights legislation.

Although there has been progress with the advancement of human rights, much work is still needed. Pegg and Compton (2004, p. 6) wrote:

> *There remains a significant percentage of the world's population who are denied access to basic services, opportunities, and full inclusion into the fabric of society. Many regions across the globe, including developed countries, continue to isolate many citizens and as a result are unable to fully participate in the mainstream activities of society. There is no greater challenge to the global community than to optimize opportunity for all people. Integral in creating opportunity is the need to assure access and inclusion of all persons to education, health care, employment, recreation, and leisure services.*

The following questions are addressed in this chapter:

- What is meant by human and civil rights?
- What are significant historical events that have influenced human and civil rights?
- What are guidelines for promoting human and civil rights?
- How can we promote human and civil rights?

What is meant by human and civil rights?

Human rights are basic freedoms that all people should be entitled to regardless of nationality, sex, national or ethnic origin, race, religion, language, or other status. These rights consist of those that are social and political, such as the right to life, liberty, and freedom of expression. Often people freely express themselves through the way in which they choose to participate in leisure.

Rights that are cultural and economic including the right to participate in culture, the right to food, and the right to work and receive an education are all considered to be human rights. Leisure is an expression of self that is culturally embedded.

In the U.S. Declaration of Independence, Thomas Jefferson simply categorized human rights as "life, liberty, and the pursuit of happiness." While many people may perceive human rights as inalienable privileges, previous and current generations across the globe have struggled to ensure that formalized governments recognize a broad interpretation of these rights.

The terms *human rights* and *civil rights* are often used interchangeably. While on a basic level this mixture of terms is accurate, *civil rights* are better defined as protections allowed to a citizen of a country from their government; such as the right to receive fair and equal treatment under the law or to vote. Much like human rights, most civil rights include safety, the ability to move or relocate freely, freedom of thought and expression, choice of religion, and protection from discriminatory practices.

What are significant historical events that have influenced human and U.S. civil rights?

Throughout history there has been conflict surrounding human and civil rights. There have been some factions of the human race working for the rights of all people while other factions have fought to promote the rights of specific groups at the expense of others. The actions of groups that have fought for the rights of specific groups over others have resulted in the oppression of people who were not included in the privileged group or groups.

One person who devoted much of his life working to achieve human rights was Mohandas Gandhi. In describing the leadership qualities of Gandhi, Howard Gardner (1995, p. 277) wrote:

He stressed that human beings belonged to the same species; that their frequent, often-violent struggles were fundamentally illegitimate, and that human beings needed to resolve their conflicts peacefully. It was not the right for any human group to subjugate another; members of the species must learn to face one another as equals, unafraid. Slavery or subjugation was not just wrong in principle; it was deeply wrong in practice—it had to be opposed.

Subjugation involves the act of a person or group forcing another person or group into submission—thus, bringing individuals, a group, or even a nation under the control of another.

On a global level, the progression of civil rights has not been straightforward. Civil rights vary from nation to nation based on a complex equation including the stability of the government, political powers, level of industrialization, and support from foreign nations.

Unlike the philosophy of Gandhi, advancements in human and civil rights are often precipitated by major conflicts, typically wars and protests. These wars involve the clashing of groups of people, with some who are working for human and civil rights and others who are fighting for the advancement of some and the oppression of others.

The following points in history will be used to provide an overview of historical events that have influenced human and civil rights, especially in the United States:

* The Early Years
* The Revolutionary War and the U.S. Constitution
* The Civil War and the Emancipation Proclamation
* World War I and Women's Suffrage
* World War II and the United Nations
* The Cold War and the Civil Rights Movement

The Early Years

The concept and discussion of human rights have existed for centuries. Early philosophers, such as Aristotle, pondered over societies where people should have rights to influence public policy and be in possession of property. Greater developments took place during the 18th century during the Enlightenment, a cultural and scientific movement that developed many of the foundations of modern society.

Enlightenment philosophers placed an emphasis on the importance of equal rights for all individuals regardless of race, religion, gender, or color (Edmundson, 2004). These public thoughts, as well as legislative documents such as the U.S. Constitution (1787), seemed to indicate that human rights were becoming a universal concept.

The Revolutionary War and the U.S. Constitution

The American Revolution was a political upheaval staged by 13 colonies in North America with the purpose of separating from governance by the British Empire. The colonies rejected the notion that the Parliament of Great Britain could govern them without allowing political representation and joined together to form the United States of America.

These political issues coupled with a restriction of the independent social and economic development of the U.S. led to the rebellion known as the American Revolutionary War, fought between 1775 and 1783. During this period, the U.S. declared their independence from British rule (1776) and began to frame the new order of the country. Following successful separation from British rule, the U.S. drafted the Constitution (1787), a document establishing the framework for the government as well as the natural rights of citizens.

The most commonly known U.S. civil rights are those discussed in the U.S. Bill of Rights (1791). This document amended, or added, 10 specific statements to the U.S. Constitution (1787) with the purpose of protecting citizens from a tyrannical federal or state government. However, when the amendments were made, these rights were not extended to many Americans. Different rights and laws were applied to people of color (i.e., racial and ethnic background), women, and people with disabilities. See page 131 for more details about the Bill of Rights.

Prior to the legislation discussed later in this chapter, membership in an oppressed or disenfranchised group could result in a restriction of voting rights, employment opportunities, education, and independent living. Numerous individuals and groups were discriminated against for many years following the Bill of Rights and therefore membership in one of these oppressed groups is typically considered when the term "civil rights" is mentioned.

The Civil War and the Emancipation Proclamation

The war of the largest scale, and with the most casualties occurring on U.S. soil, was one of the first steps toward broader U.S. civil rights. A primary reason for the U.S. Civil War, fought between 1861 and 1865, was that many southern states did not agree with a growing movement intended to abolish or limit the ownership of slaves in the country.

African Americans, the predominant racial and ethnic minority group of the time, were being used for cheap labor, but were not allowed the freedoms or rights of citizens. Legal precedent set by the U.S. Supreme Court in the case of Dred Scott v. Sandford (1857) had determined that slaves were "*so far inferior that they had no rights which the white man was bound to respect.*"

Following the election of Abraham Lincoln as the 16th President of the United States, the following seven states seceded to create the Confederate States of America: South Carolina, Mississippi, Florida, Alabama, Georgia, Louisiana, and Texas. They were soon joined by Virginia, Arkansas, North Carolina, and Tennessee. These 11 states clashed with the remaining 25 states, known as the Union, in a series of bloody battles culminating in surrender by the Confederacy in April of 1865.

During the war, President Lincoln signed an executive order known as the *Emancipation Proclamation*. The Emancipation Proclamation was an executive order that became effective on January 1, 1863, that declared freedom for all slaves residing in all states rebelling against the Union. Once the Civil War ended, amendments 13, 14, and 15 were added to the U.S. Constitution to promote civil rights. See pages 131–132 for more detail about these amendments.

World War I and Women's Suffrage

Although the 15th Amendment to the U.S. Constitution enabled people of color to vote, no amendment or law had granted women's voting rights. Many years of advocacy were necessary to convince the United States that voting rights should be extended to all citizens regardless of their race, color, gender, choice of religion, or mental capacity. Suffrage is the word that describes the right to vote in public elections.

New Jersey was one of the first states to grant suffrage to women, but in 1807 these rights were rescinded. At the state and national levels, women were not allowed the right to vote for many years to come.

Margaret Fuller, an American journalist, was one of the most well-known advocates of women's rights. Unfortunately, upon her death in 1850, women were no closer to voting. Susan B. Anthony, a proclaimed admirer of Fuller, continued to advocate for women's suffrage by giving speeches across the United States. In 1869, she co-founded the National Woman Suffrage Association with the intent of assembling women to voice their opinions about their rights. As with her predecessor, Fuller, Anthony died in 1900, without voting rights having been granted to women.

Additional women's advocacy, including deriding the 15th Amendment allowing people of color to vote, had limited impact over the next 15 years. However, one seminal event in the global context provided the final push. In 1914, World War I began. This war, as interpreted by the Allied powers, was a war about democracy and freedom. Women questioned a war over democratic rights when people within those Allied countries were still discriminated against, and in response to their calls the 19th Amendment to the Constitution was written and passed in 1920, which gave suffrage to U.S. women.

World War II and the United Nations

One the most well-known and opposed violations of human rights happened as recently as the 1940s. During World War II, Adolf Hitler and the Nazi regime of Germany stripped the rights of many individuals based upon their characteristics and religious beliefs, creating a worldwide conflict driven partially by a protection of human rights. While it is widely discussed that Hitler's diabolical plan was to exterminate people of Jewish faith, his first target was to eliminate people with disabilities because of their dilution of the "pure" German ethnicity.

Following the Second World War, a new organization known as the United Nations (UN) was formed in 1945 to establish world peace and create uniform international government policies. Central to the formation of the organization was a discussion of the globalization of human rights.

The Cold War, UDHR and the Civil Rights Movement

The U.S. Civil Rights movement corresponded with what has been identified as the "Cold War," which lasted from 1947 to 1991. The Cold War began after World War II and is characterized by political anxiety and military tension between countries supporting communism, including what was known as the Soviet Union (often identified as the Eastern Bloc), and countries supporting democracy, including the United States and its allies. These countries did not engage in any official military clashes, but rather they expressed major philosophical differences in a variety of political and ideological encounters.

In 1948, delegate members from 56 nations debated over common human rights and drafted a document known as the Universal Declaration of Human Rights (UDHR) that laid a framework to be followed by each member country. The UDHR was adopted unanimously (with abstentions) by the UN General Assembly on December 10, 1948. More details on this declaration are presented on pages 128 and 130–131 While the document is not a binding treaty, it is generally regarded as a success for expanding human-rights awareness and compliance at the global level. According to the 14th Dalai Lama (Morgan, 2001, p. 132):

> *We need to think in global terms because the effects of one nation's action are felt far beyond its borders. The acceptance of universally binding standards of Human Rights as laid down in the Universal Declaration of Human Rights and in the International Covenants of Human Rights is essential in today's shrinking world. Respect for fundamental human rights should not remain an ideal to be achieved but a requisite foundation for every human society.*

During this time of foreign challenges associated with the Cold War, the U.S. was experiencing the culmination of some domestic changes that were focused on civil rights. The Civil Rights Movement in the United States can be described using the following categories:

- The Mistake: Separate is Equal
- The Correction: Separate is Not Equal
- Prominent Civil Rights Activists
- The Civil Rights Act

The Mistake: Separate is Equal

The 14th Amendment to the Constitution created "equal protection" for the rights of people of color, but this term was loosely interpreted for many years to follow. Starting in 1876, many states enacted laws commonly known as Jim

Crow laws. Jim Crow laws were laws that were enacted with the intention of segregating people of color from Whites. These laws that restricted access to public facilities, schools, and transportation were based on the premise that people of color were provided *"separate but equal"* accommodations. The constitutionality of this *"separate but equal"* doctrine was upheld in the U.S. Supreme Court Decision of Plessy v. Ferguson (1896).

In this case, Homer Plessy, a man born free from slavery and racially seven-eighths White, boarded a railroad car in Louisiana reserved for "Whites only." When Plessy refused to leave the car and retreat to the car marked for people of color, he was arrested and imprisoned. His legal argument of injustice was appealed to the U.S. Supreme Court because of the constitutional context, but the *"separate but equal"* doctrine was upheld.

Arguably, the greatest inequality of the *"separate but equal"* doctrine was the inadequate education provided for people of color. During this period, children educated in the public school system were separated by race. While Whites and Blacks were supposed to be offered equal facilities, teaching personnel, and learning materials; this rarely occurred, so that students who were Black received lower quality services.

In addition, there were a number of logistical concerns, such as requiring Blacks to travel far distances to school when there were "White" schools in the neighborhood nearby. The educational opportunities for Blacks were far inferior, and many civil rights advocates called for a much-needed change in these disparities.

In response to the mistake of *"separate but equal,"* the National Association for the Advancement of Colored People (NAACP) was established in 1909, with a mission to ensure the political, educational, social, and economic equality of rights of all persons, and to eliminate race-based discrimination. A slightly more lengthy statement of objectives is found on the first page of the NAACP Constitution, but in short, the principal objectives of the Association (NAACP, 2012) include:

- To ensure political, educational, social, and economic equality of all citizens.
- To achieve equality of rights and eliminate race prejudice among U.S. citizens.
- To remove all barriers of racial discrimination through democratic processes.
- To seek enactment and enforcement of federal, state, and local laws securing civil rights.
- To inform the public of the adverse effects of racial discrimination and to seek its elimination.
- To educate persons about their constitutional rights and to take all lawful action to secure these objectives.

The Correction: Separate is Not Equal

Brown v. Board of Education of Topeka (1954) is frequently identified as the case that ended racial segregation in schools; however, many cases had been previously filed with the same intent, following the ruling in *Plessy v. Ferguson (1896)*. A famous quotation from the Brown case, "Separate educational facilities are inherently unequal," is often quoted as "Separate is not equal"; a retort to the statement from *Plessy v. Ferguson*.

In the Brown case, 13 parents from the city of Topeka, Kansas, filed a class-action lawsuit against the Topeka Board of Education in the U.S. District Court for the District of Kansas. These parents obtained the support of the Topeka chapter of the National Association for the Advancement of Colored People (NAACP).

The 13 parents attempted to enroll their children in the neighborhood school closest to their homes. When the students were not allowed to enroll because these were designated as schools for "Whites only," the parents banded together to file the lawsuit.

Oliver Brown, the named plaintiff in the lawsuit, was chosen as the namesake for the case because he was a male, and the other litigants were females. The judges of the district court cited the precedent from *Plessy v. Ferguson (1896)* and ruled favorably for the Board of Education. However, the judges did indicate that segregation may have some negative effects for children of color, and the case found new life through an appeal to the U.S. Supreme Court. The Brown case (1954), as it is most commonly known, is actually a combination of five different desegregation cases, *Briggs v. Elliott, Davis v. County School Board of Prince Edward County, Gebhart v. Belton, Bolling v. Sharpe*, and *Brown v. Board of Education of Topeka*, that were collectively presented to the U.S. Supreme Court.

The justices of the Supreme Court unanimously determined to strike down the precedent of *Plessy v. Ferguson (1896)* and declared the segregation of public schools unconstitutional. Their interpretation expanded the suspicions of the district court, and held that although equal facilities and opportunities may be available for people of color, the general nature of segregation had psychological and social repercussions. The segregated schools may have provided Blacks with adequate education, but it still created an image of their inferiority in the American society.

Brown vs. Board of Education of Topeka (1954) was an important case for expanding civil rights for people of color, but the case only applied to education. During the 1950s, people of color still encountered segregation on public transportation and in public places, including restaurants and restrooms. Many people of color were tiring of this oppression and began to put pressure on the U.S. government to end segregation and provide greater protection for the rights of all people.

Prominent Civil Rights Activists

Thurgood Marshall was the lawyer who represented Brown et al. in *Brown v. Board of Education*. He earned this right through his history of arguing equality cases and from his role as the Chief Counsel of the NAACP. Marshall served as counsel in over 30 Supreme Court cases, and eventually became the first African-American Supreme Court Justice in 1967. In his book, *Thurgood Marshall: American Revolutionary*, Juan Williams (1998, p. 35) provided this description of Marshall:

> *Once, the principal sent him to the basement with a copy of the U.S. Constitution and told him he had to memorize it before he could leave. "Before I left that school," Marshall said later, "I knew the whole thing by heart." Thurgood's study of the constitution gave him an interesting perspective on the conflict between American ideals and the reality of how the law was twisted when it came to Black people. Sitting in a second-floor classroom and next to the window, he had a bird's-eye view of the Northwest Baltimore police station. He could see prisoners, mostly Black, being brought in by the all-white police. Often he could even hear as black suspects were questioned about crimes and sometimes hit with a club or brass knuckles to loosen up a confession.*

Martin Luther King, Jr. was one of the most well-known figures in the Civil Rights Movement. King, Jr. was a trained clergyman-turned-civil-rights-activist. He marched against White supremacist groups, staged sit-ins, and delivered speeches to large audiences all to admonish discrimination and segregation.

King's goal was to conduct all of these advocacy actions following the nonviolent social action methods of Gandhi. For his efforts, he was the youngest person ever to win a Nobel Peace Prize. Probably his most famous writing is the "I Have a Dream" speech. Here is a sample from this historic speech:

> *I have a dream that one day this nation will rise up and live out the true meaning of its creed: "We hold these truths to be self-evident, that all men are created equal". . . From every mountainside, let freedom ring. And when this happens, when we allow freedom to ring, when we let it ring from every village and every hamlet, from every state and every city, we will be able to speed up that day when all of God's children, Black men and White men, Jews and Gentiles, Protestants and Catholics, will be able to join hands and sing in the words of the old Negro spiritual: Free at last! Free at last! Thank God Almighty, we are free at last!*

King also organized a 385-day boycott of the Montgomery, Alabama bus system. The boycott was stimulated by the arrest of Rosa Parks, a Black civil rights advocate, for refusing to move to the "Blacks only" section of a public bus. Ms. Parks provided the following conclusion in her autobiography, *Rosa Parks: My Story* (1992, p. 187–188):

> *I have spent over half my life teaching love and brotherhood, and I feel that it is better to continue to try and teach or live equality and love than it would be to have hatred or prejudice. Everyone living together in peace and harmony and love . . . that's the goal that we seek, and I think the more people there are who reach that state of mind, the better we will all be.*

Ms. Parks, who was highlighted earlier in this book when we focused on the meaning of community and inclusion, demonstrated how the actions of one person help change policy within a country and help challenge acts of oppression and discrimination. For her actions and bravery, she was honored with a Congressional Gold Medal in 1999.

Altogether, this small sample of leaders and events illuminate the displeasure with segregation and the status of people of color during this time period.

The Civil Rights Act

Given the global advances in human rights as represented by the development of the Universal Declaration of Human Rights, as well as the advance in civil rights in the United States with the Bill of Rights, the Emancipation Proclamation, and *Brown v. Board of Education*, some people might have questioned the need for the U.S. Civil Rights Act. The memories of David Halberstam (2004, p. 4–5), a preeminent social historian, about life in the U.S. in the 1950s help to put this piece of legislation into perspective:

> *Looking back, the America of 1954 was so different from that of today that it is sometimes hard for me to believe it existed in my lifetime. In all too many parts of the South, Blacks could not register to vote, could not serve on juries and thus were deprived of the most basic justice. Black children went to neglected poverty-stricken elementary and high schools—whose schedules were often arranged so that they would not interfere with cotton picking—and could not go to the best state universities. The indignities inflicted on Blacks everyday were both small and large. They could not swim in local pools, eat at local restaurants, stay at local hotels; they could not go to local movie theatres through the main entrance and had to sit separated from the White audience in a ghetto area upstairs.*

As a response to such injustice and calls for equality, the U.S. government drafted the Civil Rights Act of 1964. This piece of legislation was intended to literally interpret and enforce two amendments of the Constitution already in existence, the 14th Amendment (which guarantees equal protection) and the

15th Amendment (which protects voting rights for people of color). See pages 132–133 for more detail about the Civil Rights Act.

> *Dudziak (2002) suggested that one of the major proponents for this legislation, John F. Kennedy, helped draft the proposal because of pressure from Communist nations during the Cold War.*

For one of the first times in U.S. history, a disenfranchised group brought attention to their struggles and advocated for their freedom without the context of a war or other political circumstances, or so it seemed. Similar to the passage of women's suffrage during World War I, the United States could not preach the gospel of democracy while many of the citizens in the country were still experiencing discrimination. A timeline of significant historical events that have influenced human and U.S. Civil rights is presented in Figure 7.1.

What are guidelines for promoting human and U.S. civil rights?

There are many documents that are helpful to consider when leisure service providers are working to promote human and civil rights. Some examples of such documents include:

- Universal Declaration of Human Rights
- The U.S. Bill of Rights
- Amendments to the U.S. Constitution
- The U.S. Civil Rights Act of 1964
- Title IX of the U.S. Education Amendments of 1972

Universal Declaration of Human Rights

The Universal Declaration of Human Rights (UDHR) of 1948 has 30 Articles, but Articles 1 and 2 of the document summarize the overall intent (The United Nations, 1943):

- **Article 1**. *All human beings are born free and equal in dignity and rights. They are endowed with reason and conscience and should act towards one another in a spirit of brotherhood.*
- **Article 2**. *Everyone is entitled to all the rights and freedoms set forth in this Declaration, without distinction of any kind, such as race, color, sex, language, religion, political or other opinion, national or social origin, property, birth or other status. . .*

In the first chapter of this book, the initial assumption presented, that all people deserve our respect and to be treated with dignity, is similar to the

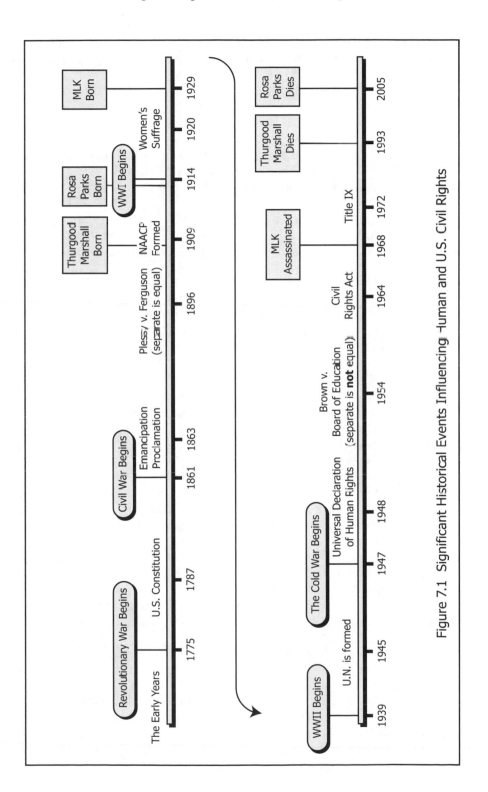

Figure 7.1 Significant Historical Events Influencing Human and U.S. Civil Rights

sentiments expressed in the first article of the UDHR. The word brotherhood appears to be used in this context to denote a feeling of fellowship and sympathy for other people, as opposed to focusing on males.

Many of the articles in the UDHR discuss civil and political rights that protect citizens from government power. Specifically, the following two articles directly address the issue of liberty and its antithesis, slavery.

- **Article 3**. *Everyone has the right to life, liberty, and security of person.*
- **Article 4**. *No one shall be held in slavery or servitude; slavery and the slave trade shall be prohibited in all their forms.*

The issue of discrimination that is described in detail in earlier chapters is addressed in Article 7. Article 10 directly associates the right to a fair public trial with the denouncement and repudiation of discrimination.

- **Article 7**. *All are equal before the law and are entitled without any discrimination to equal protection of the law. All are entitled to equal protection against any discrimination in violation of this Declaration and against any incitement to such discrimination.*
- **Article 10**. *Everyone is entitled in full equality to a fair and public hearing by an independent and impartial tribunal, in the determination of his rights and obligations and of any criminal charge against him.*

People throughout history have been persecuted because their religious beliefs differ from those who are privileged. Article 18 directly addresses the freedom of religion.

- **Article 18**. *Everyone has the right to freedom of thought, conscience and religion; this right includes freedom to change his religion or belief, and freedom, either alone or in community with others and in public or private, to manifest his religion or belief in teaching, practice, worship and observance.*

While the protection of civil and political rights are central to the UDHR, additional freedoms are addressed that have been described as economic, social, and cultural rights. Two of those articles address important rights associated with work and education and their role in the advancement of society.

- **Article 23**. *(1) Everyone has the right to work, to free choice of employment, to just and favorable conditions of work and to protection against unemployment.*
- **Article 26**. *(1) Everyone has the right to education. Education shall be free, at least in the elementary and fundamental stages. Elementary education shall be compulsory. Technical and professional education shall be made generally available and higher education shall be equally accessible to all on the basis of merit.*

Two articles are especially relevant to leisure service delivery. Leisure is specifically identified in Article 24, and cultural life is addressed in Article 27.

- **Article 24**. *Everyone has the right to rest and leisure, including reasonable limitation of working hours and periodic holidays with pay.*
- **Article 27**. *(1)* Everyone has the right freely to participate in the cultural life of the community, to enjoy the arts and to share in scientific advancement and its benefits.

The UDHR was written more than 60 years ago and is still a reference document for member nations of the UN. Each nation has had a variable growth process in adopting national legislation for civil, political and socioeconomic policies.

The U.S. Bill of Rights

The following are examples of civil rights detailed in the U.S. Bill of Rights of 1791 that contained ten Amendments to the **U.S. Constitution**. The issues of freedom of religion and free speech are identified in the very first amendment.

- **The 1st Amendment** disallows the government from establishing a uniform religion. It also empowers people to speak freely without consequences, publish free speech in the press, and gather peaceably in public.

The 4th and 5th Amendments focus on limiting control of government from infringing on citizens' privacy and right to due process of law.

- **The 4th Amendment** protects citizens from unreasonable searches and seizures conducted by agents of the government. Most commonly, this amendment is known for protecting "a right to privacy," or the ability to live and conduct business freely without unreasonable scrutiny from the government.
- **The 5th Amendment** establishes the practice of due process of law. Under this amendment, all individuals who have violated the law of the land are privy to consistent standards of legal procedure and interpretation.

Additional Amendments to the U.S. Constitution

Following the Civil War, three amendments were signed into law that further guaranteed the civil rights of people of color. However, the discussion from this chapter illuminated how these rights were not completely recognized until the Civil Rights Act of 1964.

- **The 13th Amendment (1865)** abolished slavery, or forced labor, in all member states of the U.S. This amendment extended freedom to many

Africans living in the U.S. who were forced into slavery through unpaid labor agreements.

- **The 14th Amendment (1868)**, commonly known as equal protection of the law, disallows federal and state governments from abridging or limiting rights and immunities, including due process, of citizens of color.
- **The 15th Amendment (1870)** disallows the government from using race, color, or previous status (e.g., slave) as a qualifier for the right to vote.

Since women have been a historically oppressed group in the United States and many other countries in the world, the 19th Amendment was enacted in the early 1900s and granted women suffrage. As stated previously, suffrage involves the right to vote in public elections.

- **The 19th Amendment (1920)** prohibits the federal government from discriminating against any citizen's voting rights based upon their sex.

The 15th and 19th Amendments to the Constitution granted voting rights for people of color and women, but this did not mean members of those groups were always able to vote. To circumvent voting rights, many states required voters to pass literacy tests or pay poll taxes to exercise their right to vote. Since members of minority groups had unequal access to education at this time, many of them were unable to pass the literacy tests. These unfair practices and standards were legal until the passage of the National Voting Rights Act of 1965.

The U.S. Civil Rights Act of 1964

In 1964, President Lyndon B. Johnson signed the most prominent piece of civil rights legislation into law. President John F. Kennedy had prefaced this historical law in a 1963 speech, but was assassinated before its passage through Congress.

The law was highly debated, as could be expected, by many of the politicians representing former Confederate states. A number of Senators opposing the bill participated in a 50+ day filibuster, or discussion of irrelevant topics to delay the passage of legislation, during which they attempted to develop an alternative solution. However, the bill eventually passed through the legislative branch and became standing law in the United States.

This act contains 11 major titles, each establishing the enforcement of equal rights for all protected classes (The National Archives, n.d.). A protected class is a person belonging to a group that has unique characteristics and cannot be discriminated against based upon these characteristics. The protected classes included in the Civil Rights Act of 1964 were:

- Race
- Color
- Religion
- National origin
- Sex

The first seven titles of the act had the greatest implications for eradicating discrimination in public places, schools, and places of employment.

- **Title I**. Required voter registration to be applied equally
- **Title II**. Disallowed segregation in public accommodations including hotels, restaurants, and theatres
- **Title III**. Prohibited state and municipal governments from denying protected classes' use of public facilities.
- **Title IV**. Authorized the U.S. Attorney General to file suits to continue desegregation of public schools
- **Title V**. Empowered the Civil Rights Commission
- **Title VI**. Prevented discrimination by government agencies receiving federal funding
- **Title VII**. Prohibited employers from discriminating against applicants, employees, and former employees belonging to a protected class

Following the Civil Rights Act of 1964, many Americans enjoyed greater freedoms than their ancestors. Lawsuits and special agencies, including the Equal Employment Opportunity Commission and Office of Civil Rights, were necessary to ensure these freedoms, but nonetheless they began to expand in the years to come.

Title IX of the U.S. Education Amendments of 1972

Following the Civil Rights Act of 1964, additional pieces of legislation were necessary to empower protected classes. Title IX of the Education Amendments of 1972 is a civil rights law that arguably has the most direct impact on leisure service providers.

This law, later renamed the *Patsy T. Mink Equal Opportunity in Education Act*, specifies that no public education system can deny benefits to students on the basis of sex. At the time of the law, female students were vastly underrepresented in colleges and universities. Most specifically, few of them were educated in sciences, technology, engineering, and mathematics.

The intent of Title IX was to increase female enrollments and stop discrimination against their educational pursuits. At face value, the law was associated with education, but the legal interpretation of the terms of the law had greater meaning:

> *No person in the United States shall, on the basis of sex, be excluded from participation in, be denied the benefits of, or be subjected to discrimination under any education program or activity receiving Federal financial assistance.*

The term "activity" implied that all facets of the schooling experience, including sport and recreation, were protected by Title IX. This meant that any opportunities and funding for sports must be split between men and women. Compliance with Title IX is determined by a three-prong test. Schools and universities can demonstrate that they are providing equal opportunities by:

- Substantial proportionality: A test that measures proportions of males and females at the school in question and determines if opportunities and funding are equal within a 5% threshold. For example, if a school is 55% male, no more than 60% of the sporting opportunities and funding can be dedicated to males.
- History and continuing practice of expansion: The school must demonstrate that it has taken steps each year to equalize opportunities for males and females. This test has lost relevancy over time because Title IX has been in existence for over 35 years.
- Accommodation of interests and abilities: The school must demonstrate that although opportunities are not equal for males and females, this standard is desired by the population.

Title IX is one civil rights law where the effects are easily identified. Since the law has come into effect, the number of college female varsity athletes has increased five-fold, high school female athletes have increased ten-fold, and professional women's sports are now widely recognized. See Figure 7.2 for a summary of guidelines that promote human and U.S. Civil rights.

How can we promote human and civil rights?

There are many ways that leisure service professionals can promote human and civil rights. A few examples include:

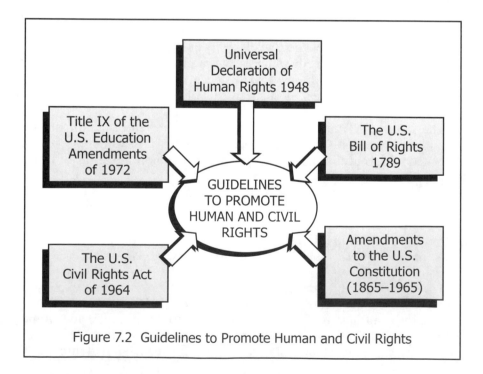

Figure 7.2 Guidelines to Promote Human and Civil Rights

- Be Aware of the History of Human and Civil Rights
- Comply with Civil Rights Legislation
- Analyze and Advertise Programs
- Monitor Employment Practices

Be Aware of the History of Human and Civil Rights

The creation of human rights declarations and civil rights laws move a society toward equality, but declarations and laws cannot create social change. People must adopt an inclusive philosophy for such declarations and laws to take effect both socially and politically. For example, in the U.S. slaves were freed during the Civil War in 1863, but over 100 years later, some politicians still voted against expanding the rights of people of color through the Civil Rights Act of 1964.

The historical context of the laws discussed in this chapter can help us analyze our practice and determine if we are providing services for a diverse population. We must realize that prejudices still exist in today's society, and inclusive services provide the possibility to overcome oppression.

Comply with Civil Rights Legislation

Although compliance with civil rights laws is a legal necessity, not all businesses follow the recommended guidelines. Compliance with civil rights laws:

- Protects our businesses from negative attention
- Helps us analyze the diversity of our programs
- Provides a map for a diverse staff

For a violation of civil rights law to be recognized, an individual or representative such as the *Office of Civil Rights* must file a complaint against an agency.

Public awareness of non-compliance with civil rights laws can be damaging to the image of an organization, especially if they intend to practice the concepts of inclusion. To avoid issues with non-compliance, we must be aware of current civil-rights legislation and frequently review the proportionality of our programs and employees.

Analyze and Advertise Programs

We can analyze our leisure services to determine if we are providing a breadth of activities. Some cultures prefer activities that differ from traditional recreation offerings. Providing a variety of programs may attract more participants from a broader array of backgrounds and allow the introduction of new activities to others.

Some people may not participate in traditional activities because of a historical bias indicating that their race or gender is not allowed to participate. Using advertising depicting a variety of participants may help attract atypical users. If a program can attract a diverse group, the concept of natural proportions should be used to help reduce the incidence of stigmas. The success of Title IX provides great evidence that if we give people opportunities, they will demonstrate and cultivate their interests.

Monitor Employment Practices

Leisure service providers must also analyze their employment practices. Title VII of the Civil Rights Act of 1964 requires that public and private businesses do not discriminate against hiring people belonging to protected classes. The hiring of a diverse staff can maximize the experiences of a diverse body of participants.

It is critical that we consider the idea that natural proportions exist for those who partake in the activities, and the people who guide and direct the activities. Providing a diverse staff is another opportunity for alleviating stigmas and increasing the comfort level of participants. See Figure 7.3 for a summary of ways to promote human and civil rights.

Final Thoughts

There are many people who have worked to promote human and civil rights throughout history. A particularly articulate person who was a leader in the U.S. Civil Rights movement who is quoted earlier in this chapter and in this book was the Reverend Martin Luther King, Jr.

In 1963, a few months before he delivered the famous "I Have a Dream" speech in Washington, D.C., to over 2,000 attendees and millions of television viewers, King was jailed for his nonviolent protests. While in jail, he wrote a 20-page letter that has come to be known as simply the "Letter from Birmingham City Jail." It seems fitting that we began this chapter with a quotation from Dr.

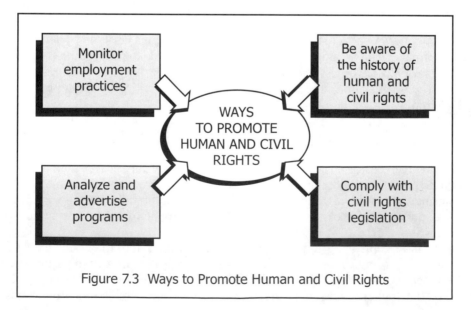

Figure 7.3 Ways to Promote Human and Civil Rights

King, and now we end the chapter with a section of that letter that seems to capture the frustration of people of color who lived in a country founded on principles of life, liberty, and the pursuit of happiness.

We have waited for more than 340 years for our constitutional and God-given rights. The nations of Asia and Africa are moving with jet like speed toward the goal of political independence and we still creep at horse and buggy pace toward the gaining of a cup of coffee at a lunch counter. I guess it is easy for those who have never felt the stinging darts of segregation to say "wait." But when you have seen vicious mobs lynch your mothers and fathers at will and drown your sisters and brothers at whim; when you have seen hate-filled policemen curse, kick, brutalize and even kill black brothers and sisters with impunity . . .when you suddenly find your tongue twisted and your speech stammering as you seek to explain to your six-year-old daughter why she can't go to the public amusement park that has just been advertised on television, and see tears welling up in her little eyes when she is told that Funtown is closed to colored children . . . then you will understand why we find it difficult to wait.

Discussion Questions

1. What is the distinction between human and civil rights?
2. What is the Universal Declaration of Human Rights (UDHR)?
3. How is the U.S. Bill of Rights of 1791 related to the U.S. Constitution of 1787?
4. What is the relevance of the Emancipation Proclamation to the U.S. civil rights movement?
5. What is the relationship between Jim Crow laws and the 14th Amendment of the U.S. Constitution?
6. What is the relationship of the court case *Plessy v. Ferguson* in 1896 to the court case *Brown v. Board of Education of Topeka* in 1954?
7. What was the purpose of the U.S. Civil Rights Act of 1964?
8. What are the implications of Articles 24 and 27 of the UDHR to leisure service delivery?
9. What are the implications of Title IX for leisure service delivery?
10. Why is it important for leisure service agencies to follow Title VII of the Civil Rights Act of 1964?

Chapter 8
Respond to the Americans with Disabilities Act

Ignorance of the law excuses no man.
-John Selden

Orientation Activity: Describe the ADA

Directions Alone: Write a brief paragraph describing the Americans with Disabilities Act (ADA). Write as if you are explaining the ADA to someone who is not aware of this legislation.

Directions with Others: Move about the room and share your description with someone. Have that person tell you what he or she learned from your description, recording any key points. Listen to that person's description. Tell the person what you learned from the description, making notes on important ideas you learned. Repeat this exercise with other people until you are given a signal to stop. Come together as a group and discuss what you have learned.

Debriefing: As a civil-rights legislative act for people with disabilities, the ADA guarantees the rights of full inclusion into the mainstream of American life. While there have been some improvements toward inclusion during the last decade, segregation and discrimination of individuals with disabilities continues to be a pervasive social problem. Reflecting on the orientation activity, consider the following questions:

- What are some implications of the ADA?
- Why is it necessary to have the ADA?
- Who is influenced by the ADA?

Introduction

The Americans with Disabilities Act (ADA) (Public Law 101-336) is a civil-rights law intended to eliminate discrimination against people with disabilities. It guarantees equal opportunities, full community participation, enhanced independent living, heightened self-sufficiency, and access to every critical area of American life. The ADA was signed into law in 1990 and then amended in 2010 to promote inclusion, independence, and equality of opportunity to contribute to society. This chapter, along with other chapters in this book, is designed to bring the spirit of the ADA to the field of recreation and leisure.

In 2010 the Kessler Foundation and the National Organization on Disability worked with Harris Interactive to survey Americans with disabilities that assessed their quality of life. Based on the survey data, researchers concluded that:

> *While there has been modest improvement among a few indicators, the general trend of the measures is that 20 years after the passage of the Americans with Disabilities Act (ADA), there has yet to be significant progress in many areas. For instance, although there has been substantial improvement reported in education attainment and political participation since 1986, large gaps still exist between people with and without disabilities with regard to: employment, household income, access to transportation, health care, socializing, going to restaurants, and satisfaction with life. In some instances, the spread has actually gotten worse since the inception of the survey in 1986. Since this survey was last conducted in 2004, America has undergone a significant economic downturn. Some areas measured in the survey, such as employment, poverty, and frequency of going to restaurants, were negatively impacted by the state of the economy. However, the consistency of the size of the gaps this year suggests that people with disabilities were affected as much, or more, by the recession.*

According to the ADA, public facilities including leisure agencies, restaurants, hotels, theaters, retail stores, museums, libraries, and parks cannot discriminate on the basis of disability. Private clubs and religious organizations are exempt. To respond to the ADA, we must make reasonable changes in policies, practices, and procedures so that discrimination and segregation do not occur.

It is hoped that the ADA will encourage and empower people with disabilities to explore preferences and pursue choices, including leisure choices. Lana Shaw (Spirit of ADA, 2000, p. 6) stated:

> *[The ADA] has definitely had a big impact on my life. With the passage of this act, I gained a sense of self-respect and equality that I had not felt in a long time. Doors have been opened and I have opportunities that so many others take for granted. No longer do people look at someone with a disability and shake their head in pity because now we are given a chance to be productive and influential citizens.*

Although the ADA has resulted in greater awareness of disabilities and barriers that prevent many people from participating fully in American society, evidence for real improvements in their lives, such as greater social inclusion, has been slow to materialize. According to Kaye (1998, p. 1):

While there are indications that many barriers in the built environment have been removed, improving accessibility of public buildings and some transportation systems, many problem areas remain. And low levels of participation in social, cultural, and commercial activities do not seem to have increased measurably since the ADA became law. People with disabilities continue to live in relative social isolation.

The following several questions are addressed in this chapter:

- Who is covered by the ADA?
- What are the major ADA titles?
- Who must comply with the ADA?
- How can we plan for inclusion?
- How can we make inclusion happen?
- What is considered an undue burden?

Who is covered by the ADA?

As described in previous chapters, the ADA applies to people with any type of *disability* that is a physical or mental impairment that substantially limits one or more major life activities. Although the ADA does not specifically say whether the law covers "correctable" disabilities, in 1999, the Supreme Court ruled on *Murphy v. UPS* and decided these types of disabilities, such as diabetes, are not covered.

Although the ADA covers mental impairments, many people are confused on how to make accommodations for these individuals. As a result, the *Equal Opportunity Commission in 1997* issued guidelines to help agencies determine how to make accommodations for people with mental illness. A goal of the ADA is to remove the stigma of talking about mental illness and coping with it. Unlike sometimes costly alterations, such as installing ramps or lowering drinking fountains, accommodating people with mental illnesses often requires little more than an attitude adjustment.

What are the major ADA titles?

The ADA contains five major titles, illustrated in Table 8.1 (see p. 142). *Title I* prohibits employers from discriminating against "otherwise qualified individuals with a disability" in any employment action. *Title II, Subtitle A* prohibits state and local government agencies from discriminating against people with disabilities in the provision of services and opportunities. *Title II, Subtitle B* prohibits providers of public transportation from discriminating against people with disabilities. *Title III* prohibits private entities that offer public accommodations, goods, facilities, and services such as restaurants, theaters, hotels, zoos, and museums from discriminating against people with disabilities.

Table 8.1 Major Titles of the Americans with Disabilities Act

Title I	Employment Practice
Title II, Subtitle A	Government Services
Title II, Subtitle B	Public Transportation
Title III	Public Accommodations by Public Agencies
Title IV	Communication Systems
Title V	Miscellaneous

The Department of Justice amended regulations implementing *Title II and Title III*, thereby adopting the 2010 ADA Standards of Accessible Design. Specifically, guidance is provided for:

- sale of tickets for *accessible seating*, seating available to people using wheelchairs
- use of *service animals*, a dog individually trained to do work or perform tasks that benefit a person with a disability
- distinction between wheelchairs and *other power-driven mobility devices*, a range of devices not designed for individuals with mobility impairments, such as a Segway, but which are often used by people with disabilities as their mobility device of choice
- details on *video-remote interpreting*, an interpreting service that uses video conference technology over dedicated lines or wireless technology offering high-speed, wide-bandwidth video connection that delivers high-quality video images
- reservations for places of lodging
- time shares, condominium hotels, and other places of lodging

Title IV requires the availability of communication systems for individuals with hearing impairments. *Title V* covers a variety of miscellaneous issues, including regulation and enforcement. Specific agencies enforce the different titles (Table 8.2).

Who must comply with the ADA?

The ADA addresses many issues that facilitate realization of the rights of each person. To ensure compliance with the ADA, leisure service providers consider the major groups targeted by the ADA, including:

Table 8.2 Who Enforces the ADA?

ADA Regulations	Enforcing Agency
Employment	Equal Opportunity Employment Commission (EEOC)
Buildings, facilities, rail passenger cars, and vehicles; Recreation facilities and outdoor developed areas	Architectural and Transportation Barriers Compliance Board (Access Board)
Transit	Department of Transportation
Telecommunications	Federal Communications Commission
Public accommodations; State and local public services	Department of Justice

- employers
- transit systems
- private agencies
- government agencies
- telecommunications

Employers

Employers may not discriminate against an individual with a disability in hiring, promotion, or other employment activity if the person is otherwise qualified for the job. Employers can ask about one's ability to perform a job, but they may not inquire if someone has a disability or subject a person to tests that tend to screen out people with disabilities.

Employers must provide reasonable accommodations to individuals with disabilities. This includes job restructuring and modification of equipment. Employers do not need to provide accommodations that impose an "undue burden" on business operations.

Undue burden implies that making a particular accommodation would result in a significant economic, administrative, or programmatic challenge that would prevent the agency from continuing their operation or offering their services and result in substantial difficulty in continuing to operate. Employers of fewer than 15 people are exempt from Title I, unless the employer is a state or local government.

Transit Systems

Public transit buses must be accessible to individuals with disabilities. Transit authorities must provide comparable transportation services to people with disabilities who cannot use fixed-route bus services, unless an undue burden would result.

Private Agencies

Private entities that offer goods, services, and facilities to the public may not discriminate against people with disabilities. Auxiliary aids and services must be provided to individuals with disabilities, unless an undue burden would result.

Physical barriers in existing facilities must be removed if removal is readily achievable, inexpensive, and easy to do. If not, alternative methods of providing the services must be offered, if they are readily achievable. All new construction and alteration of facilities must be accessible.

Government Agencies

State and local governments may not discriminate against qualified individuals with disabilities. All government facilities, services, and the information they communicate must be accessible.

Telecommunications

Companies offering telephone service to the general public must offer telephone relay services to individuals who use text telephones, teletypewriters (TTYs), or similar devices.

Although the ADA requirements vary according to the type of agency such as state funded or private and size of the agency, many procedures outlined by the ADA would be beneficial for any leisure agency to follow.

How can we plan for inclusion?

Planning is a critical aspect of the delivery of leisure services. During the planning phase, compliance with the ADA is considered. To encourage this consideration, the following suggestions are provided:

- determine essential eligibility
- complete a transition plan
- ensure coordination
- conduct a self-analysis
- provide notice of compliance
- adopt a way to handle complaints
- consider employment concerns
- develop inclusive services

Determine Essential Eligibility

The ADA requires that people who meet essential eligibility requirements, or could meet them with reasonable accommodations, be given the opportunity to participate in leisure programs regardless of age, sex, mental or physical ability, race, or religious beliefs. An individual meets essential eligibility requirements for participation in most leisure programs if the following conditions are present (see Figure 8.1): capacity, fee, rules of conduct, safety, relative skill, age, and residence.

Capacity. The person must register for the leisure program before other registrants have filled the program to capacity. The capacity of a program is based on factors such as the size of the facility, the number of staff available, and the amount of resources available.

For example, if a program has a capacity of 50, and Sylvia is the 51st individual desiring registration, she may be denied the opportunity to register. This may occur whether or not the individual has a disability. However, in this particular situation, Sylvia's name can be added to a waitlist with her contact information and if anyone drops out of the program she may be contacted.

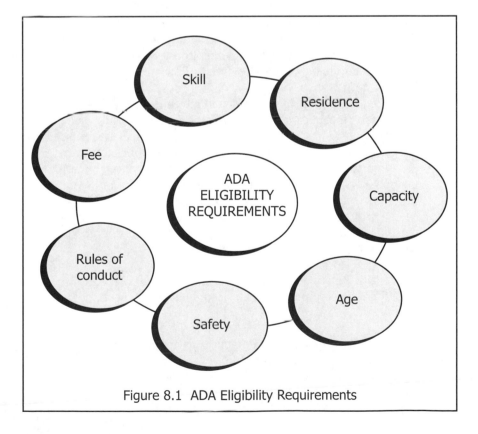

Figure 8.1 ADA Eligibility Requirements

Fee. The person must pay the appropriate registration fee for the leisure program. However, individuals may not be charged a higher fee to offset the costs of accommodations.

> For instance, if a fee of $40 is required for a one-hour golf lesson, and Antonio is registered for the lesson, he must pay the fee or have the fee paid by another, such as his parent, sibling, guardian, or sponsor.

Rules of Conduct. The person must agree to abide by any reasonable rules of conduct for participation in that leisure program. If an individual violates reasonable rules of conduct, the agency may suspend or modify that individual's involvement after reasonable accommodation has been made.

> As an illustration, in a swimming lesson, participants must not dive from the deck into the shallow end of the pool. In a sports program, players must not hit other participants. In a public outing to a theater, members of the audience must not speak so loudly during a performance as to disturb the listening of others in the audience. These examples are applicable to everyone, whether or not a disability is present.

Safety. Safety concerns may be a factor when a direct threat of imminent physical harm exists. This threat must be real, and not perceived. Employees must be cautioned against allowing their perceptions of an individual's disability to result in an inaccurate belief that the threat of harm is imminent.

> For example, if Althea, who has had a traumatic brain injury, previously harmed another participant and could not be reasonably accommodated, employees may elect to refuse her admission to a general swimming program. However, the opportunity to swim must still be offered through such methods as individual lessons. In addition, based on this one experience, some employees may assume that all people who have a traumatic brain injury pose a direct threat of imminent physical harm. This belief is based on a misconception and results in discriminatory treatment.

Relative Skill. Relative skill may be a factor in a few programs, such as highly competitive sports programs. This is applicable whether or not the person has a disability.

> For example, Ira could not register to participate in an annual musical performance for the public without basic competencies. Therefore, staff could refuse to allow Ira to perform in a concert, but they should consider providing other music options, such as joining a choir or enrolling in music lessons.

Age. The age of participants may also be a factor in an analysis of essential eligibility.

> For example, it is inappropriate for Terrance, a 15-year-old, to be registered in a program for children ages 3 to 5. Regardless of whether he has a cognitive impairment, it will likely be inappropriate to place Terrance with younger children.

Residence. If agencies exclude nonresidents from certain programs for legitimate reasons such as limited capacity, then nonresidents with disabilities may be excluded. However, whenever possible, services should be available to residents as well as nonresidents. No person living outside the geographic boundaries may be excluded solely because of disability.

> For example, where fees charged for nonresidents are higher than those for residents, that standard may be applied to people with disabilities.

Complete a Transition Plan

If an agency is not completely accessible, a transition plan for the removal of barriers and other structural modifications is developed. The transition plan identifies alterations required to achieve accessibility, the cost of the alterations, and a timeframe for when the alterations will be completed.

Ensure Coordination

It is important that at least one employee is designated to coordinate agency efforts to comply with the ADA and promote inclusion. This employee must have authority to make decisions regarding compliance, ensure cooperation of staff, and investigate alleged complaints against the agency. The name, office address, and office telephone number of this employee is made available to the public.

It is also helpful if at least one member of a leisure-services delivery agency has received specific training associated with including people with disabilities; however, many agencies do not have such a person. Miller, Schleien, and Bowens (2010, p.47) recommend that we:

> *[i]nvest more heavily in the hiring, preparing, and support of highly qualified inclusion facilitators. . . . Perhaps the inclusion facilitator's greatest challenge will be in addressing the "we/they" designations among program staff in order for these staff members to prepare environments and facilitate programs where participants also shed their "we/they" distinctions, resulting in real social inclusion.*

If departments do not have an inclusion facilitator, steps can be taken to prepare the agency to include people with disabilities into existing services. The support of people with disabilities and local agencies can be enlisted to teach staff about the ADA and how to include people with disabilities into existing services.

Conduct a Self-Analysis

To determine deficits in delivery systems and barriers to participation that result in discrimination against people with disabilities, we can initiate a self-analysis. Professionals must examine all leisure programs to determine how to accommodate a person with a disability who meets essential eligibility requirements for participation. Any architectural, transportation, communication, or service barriers should be identified.

Leisure service providers solicit input from interested people with disabilities or advocacy organizations. Ongoing self-analysis is available for public review, contains a list of the interested persons consulted, and provides descriptions of areas examined, problems identified, and modifications made.

Provide Notice of Compliance

The intent of the agency to comply with the ADA and how this intent will be achieved should be provided. Some agencies may report that compliance to the ADA will occur by making reasonable accommodations such as:

- changing rules, policies, and procedures
- removing architectural, transportation, and communication barriers
- providing auxiliary aids and services
- presenting notice of compliance in all agency materials

> For example, business cards and letterhead include the agency text telephone, otherwise known as the teletypewriter (TTY), number. The TTY enables people who have severe hearing impairments to use the telephone. Information on TTYs and other technology is presented in chapter on people, inclusion, and technology.

Adopt a Way to Handle Complaints

It is recommended that agencies develop a procedure for responding to complaints of noncompliance against the agency. The procedure should be similar to procedures established for employee grievances. It must allow for prompt attention to allegations of noncompliance.

Consider Employment Concerns

Agencies must consider alternate ways to address employee needs. For example, supplemental unpaid leave may be a viable option for qualified people with disabilities who, because of their disability, may require additional time away from work. Individuals associated with a person with a disability, such as a family member, may require additional unpaid leave.

Develop Inclusive Services

In many cases, the ADA has acted as a catalyst for promoting the inclusion of people with disabilities in community life. If compliance with the inclusion mandates stipulated in the law does not occur, a process is established to enforce adherence to the law.

A ruling by the U.S. Supreme Court in the case of Olmstead v. L. C. provided clarification of the ADA interpretation of unacceptable placement of individuals into segregated programs without a choice of participating in those that are more inclusive. The Olmstead case involved two Georgia women who lived in state-run institutions and had intellectual and mental health disabilities. Professionals determined that they could be appropriately served in a community setting, and the plaintiffs asserted that continued institutionalization was in violation of their right under the ADA to live in the most integrated setting appropriate. The court concluded that:

> *Unjustified Isolation . . . is properly regarded as discrimination based on disability . . . institutional placement of persons who can handle and benefit from community settings perpetuates unwarranted assumptions that persons so isolated are incapable or unworthy of participating in community life. (Perez, 2000, pp. 1, 11)*

See Figure 8.2 (p. 150) for the key points associated with planning for inclusion.

How can we make inclusion happen?

To actually make inclusion happen, the following suggestions are provided:

- purchase inclusive equipment
- advertise to everyone
- facilitate access
- make reasonable accommodations
- remove barriers
- provide resources

Purchase Inclusive Equipment

There are many things to consider when making purchases. This section examines ADA requirements related to purchasing:

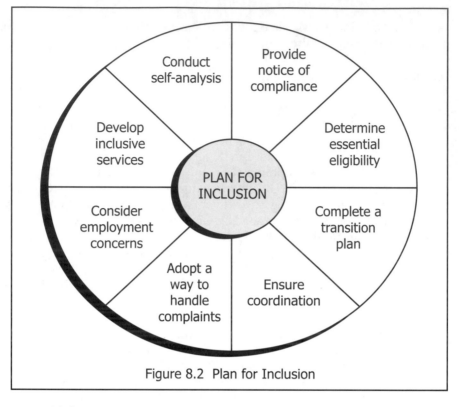

Figure 8.2 Plan for Inclusion

- vehicles
- furniture and equipment
- capital purchases

Vehicles. Under the ADA, agencies must ensure that requests for bids to buy or lease vehicles for transporting participants specify that the vehicles are readily accessible to and usable by people with disabilities. This requirement should be followed regardless of whether any individual with a disability is known to require use of such a vehicle. All donated or leased vehicles used for the transportation of participants need to be readily accessible to, and usable by, individuals with disabilities.

Furniture and Equipment. When leisure professionals purchase furniture and recreation equipment, a portion of the product must be accessible. The Architectural and Transportation Barriers Compliance Board issued the Americans with Disabilities Act Guidelines (ADAG) for building and facilities designated as play areas. These guidelines provide detailed information concerning the purchasing of equipment and construction of play areas. These regulations are described in the chapter on universal design.

Capital Purchases. Include consideration of access and use by people with disabilities for capital purchases. A *capital purchase* refers to equipment such as a computer, swing set, or boat, that becomes a major acquisition. Typically, capital purchases require a procurement request, unlike less expensive items sometimes purchased with petty cash. An agency should demonstrate that people with disabilities could access capital purchases or that a plan is in place for making the purchase accessible to all. Capital improvement plans must include removal of architectural and communication barriers.

Advertise to Everyone

A critical aspect of promoting inclusion and responding to the ADA is ensuring that people with disabilities are aware of our programs. Therefore, the following suggestions are provided when considering advertising leisure services:

- include a compliance statement
- provide alternative formats
- make advertisements accessible

Include a Compliance Statement. Agencies include a statement in all brochures and publications about compliance plans for the ADA.

> For example, the brochure should include a statement that the agency *does not* discriminate on the basis of an individual's disability, and the agency *does* make reasonable accommodations such as changing rules, removing barriers, providing auxiliary aids and services to enable a person with a physical or mental disability to participate.

It is also helpful to include a statement inviting people to communicate their needs. For example, a brochure may include the following statement:

> *To assist staff in planning programs, please call in advance of programs if you or a family member requires an accommodation.*

Provide Alternative Formats. It is important to develop brochures in alternative formats such as large print, Braille, and audio recordings for use by individuals without sight or by those with cognitive impairments. The creation of a brochure via an audio recording as part of the program and brochure planning process is easy and may have other uses.

> For example, when presenting a description of services to a group of children, a brief spoken "sound bite" can be more effective than a written one. Information on using technology to develop alternative formats is presented in the later chapter on people, inclusion, and technology.

Make Advertisements Accessible.

> *In recent years, more and more companies are showing people with disabilities in their print and TV ads, and the image of*

> *a person in a wheelchair has become a kind of shorthand: It suggests a corporate policy of inclusion in regard to both employees and customers . . . But for this message to actually be credible, the model in the ad must have a genuine disability and use the product she's selling.*

These above comments by Bruno (1997, pp. 58–59) identifies the importance of truth in advertising. Leisure service providers must ensure that brochure display areas are accessible to and usable by individuals with disabilities. Features of such displays include a shelf positioned at the correct height for an individual using a wheelchair, or making staff available to distribute brochures that may be out of reach of an individual in a wheelchair. A Braille message regarding the type of brochures available and how these may be obtained is made available.

> After surveying over 300 directors and staff affiliated with therapeutic adventure programs in the United States, Herbert (2000) reported that while directors followed hiring and promoting policies consistent with the ADA, promotional materials describing programs were not available in alternate formats such as large print, Braille, or audiotape.

Facilitate Access

Leisure service professionals must provide opportunities for people with disabilities to register for programs. People with disabilities can be a wonderful source of support, and soliciting their input can provide valuable information. The contributions people with disabilities can make toward helping to develop inclusive services can be very useful because of their perspective of the situation. This section considers the following methods of facilitation:

- modify registration
- make meetings accessible
- obtain input

Modify Registration. Professionals must be prepared to change registration procedures to accommodate an individual with a disability who, because of that disability, cannot register in the manner required by procedures. Alternative registration procedures may include, but are not limited to, mail-in registration, telephone registration, or personal registration by appointment.

As a precaution, personnel may request that a person provide proof of disability such as documentation from a physician or educational clinic in exchange for the opportunity to register in an alternative manner. However, personnel shall permit the individual accommodation in the registration process, pending submission of proof. If satisfactory proof is not provided within a reasonable time, or if proof is insufficient, the registration may be canceled.

According to the ADA, agency brochures must have a statement acknowledging the departmental policy of adherence to the ADA and must invite people with disabilities to register for any program they choose. Devine, McGovern, and Hermann (1998, p. 72) provided the following suggestions associated with a sport program registration and planning:

> *Each registration form must ask if potential participants need an accommodation to enjoy or participate in a program. When a registrant does require a special accommodation, you, your staff, or team volunteers must contact this individual before the session begins. Discuss the types of activities, the level of social interaction, and prerequisite skills, and ask if the registrant will require assistance to play the sport. Allow yourself plenty of time to secure staff, plan program changes, develop behavior plans, purchase or make adaptive equipment, and make other changes to allow successful inclusion.*

Make Meetings Accessible. It is necessary to ensure that any public committee or advisory group meetings are conducted in an accessible fashion. Notices for such meetings could include the following:

> *If you plan to attend the meeting and will require an accommodation because of a disability, contact our office at least one working day in advance of the scheduled meeting.*

Service providers must be ready on short notice to seek an interpreter or provide other accommodations necessary for participation by an individual with a mobility, sight, or hearing impairment, even if the notice requirement is not met. We should plan all meetings to be held in rooms without architectural barriers.

Obtain Input. It is critical to ensure that nominees for advisory boards, citizen panels, or other groups involved in guiding the agency include people with disabilities. Invitations to participate should be posted in large print or Braille or available in alternative formats. With the passing of the ADA in July of 1990 and its reauthorization in 2010, people with disabilities are more visible in society as a result of requirements associated with nondiscrimination. Because these individuals have now been recognized as an important market sector, especially to the travel and tourism industry, Peniston (1996, p. 29) concluded that:

> *Since the passage of ADA, the lodging industry has greatly improved services to people with disabilities, but this industry can continue to make strides by including the opinions of travelers with disabilities as important data to determining the future trends of hotel customer satisfaction.*

Make Reasonable Accommodations

A variety of agency procedures can be changed to help include people with disabilities into leisure services. The following areas are addressed in this section:

- modify services
- reassign programs
- adapt equipment

Modify Services. We must modify rules, policies, or practices that result in the exclusion of or discrimination against an individual with a disability, so that a person might meet essential eligibility requirements to participate in the program.

> For instance, a rule prohibiting the use of personal flotation devices in swimming pools may exclude Cybil, who has a physical impairment and requires additional support. The rule could be modified to permit certain types of flotation devices to accommodate Cybil. In another example, a policy requiring a driver's license instead of an identification card to fish would be discriminatory to individuals who are old enough to have a driver's license but do not currently have one due to impairments. As a final example, an agency that forbids all animals from entering particular areas of their facility such as dressing rooms and swimming pool areas is discriminatory. This rule must be revised to accommodate animals that provide mobility assistance to people with various visual and motor impairments.

Reassign Programs. The ADA requires that programs be reassigned from an inaccessible site to a site free of architectural barriers. We can consider bringing the leisure program to the participant at his or her home. In certain instances, home visits may be a less costly accommodation than transportation to and from a site where a transportation barrier exists. Home visits can be made when a person with a disability cannot attend a program and the inability to attend is clearly a result of the disability and not a choice made by the registrant.

Adapt Equipment. When equipment is integral to the leisure program, such as camping equipment or sports equipment, adaptive devices may be used to help a person with a disability. Such devices may alter the degree of strength or dexterity required to manipulate the equipment, such as a bowling ramp, or assist an individual in holding equipment, such as a brace or Velcro straps. Specific strategies for making reasonable adaptations to materials, activities, environments, participants, and instructional strategies are provided in a later chapter.

Reasonable accommodations can come in the form of adjustments to an agency policy, or specific supports, or services provided to an individual that enables that person to participate in leisure opportunities within their communities. The ADA includes reference to a number of specific accommodations to enable people to participate.

Based on a survey of over 200 recreation agencies throughout the United States, Devine (1999) reported that the most common accommodations provided for participants with disabilities included pool lifts, relocation of classes to accessible facilities, adapted sport and recreation equipment, sign language interpreters, formal inclusion plans, participant assessments, and Braille, large print, or audio recorded information.

Reasonable accommodations will vary, depending on the type of activity such as sports, crafts, social, or educational activities, the location of the program, whether it is an individual or group activity, whether it is competitive, recreational, or instructional, participant ages, and other factors. Generally, accommodations are not expensive and can occur by removing barriers, changing procedures, and providing assistance.

An example of how the ADA helped a person to receive a reasonable accommodation occurred in golf. Casey Martin was a professional golfer who has a congenital degenerative circulatory disorder manifested in a malformation of his right leg that causes him severe pain and atrophy in his lower leg. He is unable to walk for extended periods of time and is at risk of fracture or hemorrhaging when he does. When the PGA denied Martin's request to use a golf cart in a tournament, Martin sued under Title III of the ADA. He won because the court concluded "the provision of the golf cart to Martin was a reasonable accommodation to his disability, and that use of the cart did not fundamentally alter the nature of the PGA and Nike Tour tournaments" (Kozlowski, 2000). The PGA appealed, but on May 29, 2001, the Supreme Court confirmed that Martin has a legal right to use a golf cart during tournament play. Spousta (2005) quoted Martin as saying, "I'm not out here for a cause. I'm like everybody else. I just love the game and wanted an opportunity to play and make a living at it." Also quoted in the article is Kel Devlin, director of sports marketing for Nike Golf, "I anticipate we will have a long relationship with Casey. He's been a great ambassador for the game and for us."

Remove Barriers

A variety of barriers can impede inclusion. In addition to the major barrier of negative attitudes, we can systematically address removal of the following barriers:

- architectural barriers
- transportation barriers
- communication barriers

Remove Architectural Barriers. Architectural barriers that prevent people with physical impairments from entering a facility must be removed. Such barriers result in unlawful discrimination. If we provide services on several floors of a building, accommodations must be made to allow people with mobility impairments to access services on the upper floors. An immediate solution facilitating access would be to install an elevator. Although this is an excellent solution, other alternatives are possible, such as moving services to an accessible portion of the building.

Many leisure services provider own and operate historical facilities. Removing architectural barriers from a historical structure could compromise the integrity of the building. To avoid damaging the historical significance of a facility and still accommodate people with disabilities curators can develop a model to scale of upper floors and display this model on ground level. Also, a video presentation of the upper floors can be developed. Photographic and other displays of the upper floors can help to accommodate people unable to access the top floor. An audio recording or narrator to describe the upper floors is an additional option.

Remove Transportation Barriers. Not being able to participate in a program because of a transportation barrier may result in the exclusion of a person with a disability. When a program is made available to the public, and a person cannot get to the program because of a disability, these barriers must be removed when transportation is provided as a part of a program.

Remove Communication Barriers. If a person with a disability cannot understand communication media used because of a hearing, sight, or cognitive impairment, the communication poses a barrier to participation.

> As a case in point, to register for a leisure program, Leon must complete a registration form. This requires the ability to see and understand the words on the registration form. For Leon, who has a cognitive impairment, the written form is a communication barrier that can be removed by providing an employee to read the form to him. This accommodation could also help a person with a visual impairment.

Other actions that could be taken for people with visual impairments include providing audio recording that explain registration procedures or registration forms with Braille instructions.

> As another example, when providing food services, servers can prepare themselves for customers with visual and cognitive impairments by being ready to read the menu to customers and developing alternative menus, such as Braille or larger type.

Provide Resources

Providing assistance is one of the most important ways to promote inclusion and respond to the ADA. If we provide some very simple help to a person, it can make the difference between them being actively involved in leisure or being isolated and bored.

Although the ADA is designed to promote the independence of people with disabilities, everyone is dependent on others each day. By providing assistance we promote interdependence. The following ways to provide assistance are presented in this section:

- make aids available
- supply personnel
- conduct in-service training

Make Aids Available. We must provide auxiliary aids and devices that will enhance participation and communication. If a person with a hearing or sight impairment has registered for a leisure program, assistance must be provided to enable this person to have an equal opportunity to enjoy the program.

> For example, in a youth sport skills program, oral instructions and demonstrations will be used to teach participants. For Tzabar, who has a hearing impairment, the oral instructions will be difficult to interpret, even if he has some lip-reading ability. An appropriate accommodation may be providing an interpreter for Tzabar during the leisure program. Another accommodation may be teaching an employee elementary sign language, with an emphasis on terms used in the sport, and the eventual assignment of that employee to the sport skills program in which the individual with a hearing impairment has registered. However, care must be taken to ensure that the interpreting skill of the employee is adequate to the task.

Supply Personnel. Provide additional staff as needed. Sometimes a little help from another person can be the difference between someone becoming involved in a fun and meaningful activity or remaining at home alone.

> For example, a staff member can help Leonard, who has a cognitive impairment, with completing a registration form for a square dancing program. As another example, a volunteer at an amusement park, Sasha, is available to assist children with disabilities to ride roller coaster rides or to help children without disabilities whose parents may encounter difficulty due to restricted mobility.

Conduct In-Service Training. Conduct in-service training for agency personnel and volunteers. Training may include information such as programming strategies, adaptive techniques, principles of the ADA, use of sensitive language, or awareness of attitudinal barriers.

For example, training is provided for personnel and volunteers of a nature center on ways to present information that assist people with disabilities who are attending an interpretive tour.

See Figure 8.3 for the key points associated with how we can make inclusion happen.

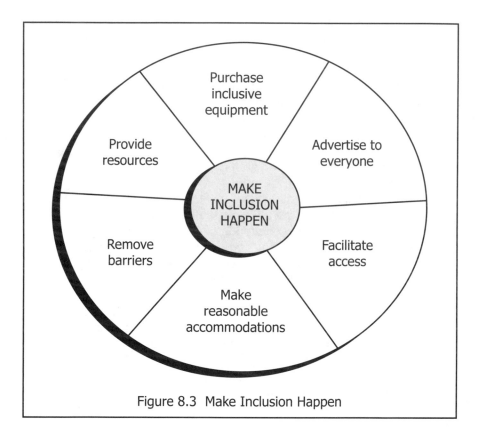

Figure 8.3 Make Inclusion Happen

What is considered an undue burden?

At times, making accommodations that include people with disabilities can result in an undue burden to various agencies. The ADA recognizes this possibility and provides directions for such instances. Undue burdens can occur in the following areas:

- economic
- administrative
- programmatic

Economic Burden

The Justice Department has not upheld the denial of an accommodation solely because of an economic burden. Because agencies vary greatly in size and cost of accommodations, they must determine the cost of the accommodation in comparison to the operating budget, availability of tax funds, number of employees affected, potential number of beneficiaries, nature and location of the program, and other factors.

> To address the topic of economic impact of the ADA, Shaw (1994) reported on statistics collected by the Job Accommodations Network, a federally funded consulting service that provides free information to employers and people with disabilities. Shaw stated that 15% of recommended accommodations needed to respond to the ADA cost nothing, 52% cost less than $500, and only 22% would cost more than $1,000.

Administrative Burden

An administrative burden is typically associated with an agency not having the necessary personnel to accommodate people. If there is a severe shortage of qualified personnel needed for a specific accommodation, an undue administrative burden may result.

> For example, if there were no certified interpreters in the area, the agency would be permitted to employ a noncertified interpreter who lived in the area.

Programmatic Burden

The third consideration includes an accommodation that results in a fundamental alteration of the nature of the program. This accommodation opposes the concept of "most integrated setting," but if the individual cannot leave his or her home because of a disability, home visits may be appropriate.

> For example, a home visit for Nelani, a woman who has a severe health impairment, could result in a fundamental alteration. If the program for which Nelani registered were a team sport, it would not be reasonable to bring the entire team and the opposing team to an individual's home. However, with a crafts program, instructional music program, or art program, a home visit can be an effective accommodation.

Final Thoughts

The ADA intends to improve the quality of life for people with disabilities by involving them in all aspects of life, including leisure services provided in their communities. Leisure service professionals deal with quality of life issues on a daily basis and have the opportunity to make compliance with the ADA a visible and positive statement for the entire leisure industry and for people with disabilities.

Although we have made progress with the ADA, there is still much work to be done. For example, after conducting an extensive survey, the Kessler Foundation and the National Organization on Disability (2010) concluded that:

> *There have been some improvements measured over the years that may be in part attributable to the implementation of the ADA of 1990. However, there is clearly much work to be done in order to narrow the very substantial gaps that still exist. Hopefully policymakers, employers, and the disability community will work together to translate these findings into actions and policies that will improve the lives of the millions of Americans with disabilities in the future.*

Leisure service providers who embrace the spirit of the ADA are in a good position to develop inclusive leisure services. The hope is that we move beyond simply accommodating people to openly including them in our programs. John Hockenberry's (1994, p. 33) comments emphasize these sentiments:

> *Our struggle for inclusion in this society is a test of whether American society truly wants diversity and freedom for all. . . . It is in this world that we celebrate our victories with legal symbols like the Americans with Disabilities Act. . . . Real inclusion is not measured in laws and lawsuits, but instead by what the community builds together in order to bring everyone together. Inclusion is a subway everyone can use, a building everyone can enter. There is no single definition of inclusion, but you'll know it when you see it.*

Discussion Questions

1. What is the purpose of the ADA?
2. Which leisure service agencies must comply with the ADA?
3. What are the different titles associated with the ADA and what major topics do each of them cover?
4. What should be considered in order to make purchases that are consistent with the intent of the ADA?

5. How can advertisements of leisure services respond to the ADA?
6. How can registration for leisure services be facilitated for people with disabilities?
7. What are essential eligibility requirements for the provision of leisure services?
8. What are some examples of reasonable accommodations for people with disabilities in leisure programs?
9. What is meant by the existence of undue burden?
10. How can we meet the spirit of the ADA?

Chapter 9
Embrace People with Disabilities

*When I recreate, I don't recreate with a bunch of
people with disabilities, I recreate with friends.*
-John Chambers

Orientation Activity: 54 Million Strong

Directions Alone: Read the following excerpt from Karen Wing (2006, p. 12)
and record the first five reactions that come to your mind after reading it.

> *Over 54 million strong, people with disabilities are considered
> America's largest minority group. They're also more than
> twice as likely to live in poverty as other Americans and only
> half as likely to be employed, according to David Stapleton,
> director of Cornell University Institute for Policy Research.
> And that's the good news. The situation was much worse
> before the 1960s, when the Disabilities Rights Movement
> began to dismantle structural and attitudinal barriers in
> society. The landmark Americans with Disabilities Act of
> 1990, which mandated curb cuts, wheelchair ramps, kneeling
> buses, and widened doors, has helped make the physical
> environment more habitable, but it has had little impact on
> the ways in which social institutions and attitudes affect the
> lives and choices of those with disabilities.*

Directions with Others: Divide into small groups and discuss your reactions to
the quotation with other members. After a specified time, share your responses
with the entire group.

Debriefing: There have been many advances for people with disabilities that
have occurred in various countries across the globe. For example, it has been
over 20 years since the Americans with Disabilities Act (ADA) was signed into
law in the United States. Similar legislative acts have occurred in other countries.
These pieces of civil-rights legislation have helped advance opportunities for
people with disabilities in many different arenas of life, including leisure.

Although progress has been made, much work is needed to move people who
have disabilities from being members of an oppressed group to the mainstream
of various societies. Reflecting on the orientation activity, consider the following
questions:

- What was most interesting to you about your reactions to the quotation?
- What is the connection between disability and poverty?
- What is your reaction to the conclusion about the limited impact of the ADA?

Introduction

As with any group of individuals who have been oppressed in some manner, typically people with disabilities want to have control of their leisure and connect with others while they participate in meaningful activities. All of us want to enjoy our life and have some level of choice on what to do, when we do it, where to do it, and with whom to do it.

People associated with various civil rights movements believe that all people desire similar things and should be treated with respect. For example, people with disabilities are not helpless *cripples*, nor are they courageous or heroic *super-achievers*. Most people are just regular people trying to lead meaningful lives, not to inspire, nor to be pitied. Mireya Navarro (2007) emphasized this point in her thought-provoking article titled "Clearly, Frankly, Unabashedly Disabled," published in the *New York Times:*

> **When Josh Blue won NBC's "Last Comic Standing" last season, he did so with riffs like this: "My right arm does a lot of crazy stuff. Like the other day, I thought someone had stolen my wallet." It's funny only if you know that Mr. Blue has cerebral palsy. The public image of people with disabilities has often hinged on the heroic or the tragic. But, Mr. Blue, 28, represents the broader portrait of disability now infusing television and film. The new, sometimes confrontational stance reflects the higher expectations among many members of the disabled population that they be treated as people who happen to have a disability, rather than as people defined by disability. "What we're seeing is less 'overcoming' and more 'just being,'" said Lawrence Carter-Long, the director of advocacy for the Disabilities Network of New York City, which last year started a film series, "disTHIS: Disability Through a Whole New Lens," celebrating unconventional portrayals of the disabled. The heart wrenching movie of the week and fundraising telethons striving for cures have given way to amputees rock climbing on reality shows. . . . "It used to be that if you were disabled and on television, they'd play soft piano music behind you," said Robert David Hall, a double amputee who plays a coroner on "CSI." The thing I love about "CSI" is that I'm just Dr. Robbins.**

The disability rights movement focused on acceptance of people with disabilities as people first and foremost and the persistent universal negative attitudes about people with disabilities. As such, the following questions are addressed in this chapter:

- What is the problem?
- What is a disability?
- How do attitudes create barriers for people with disabilities?
- How can we be responsive to the needs of people with disabilities?
- How can we emphasize the person first?
- How can we encourage autonomy?
- How can we involve participants?
- How can we meet the spirit of the ADA?

What is the problem?

Consistently across various cultures the characteristic of disability has and does result in extreme acts of discrimination. Julie Smart (2009, p. 177–118) speaks to this issue:

> *In spite of the long history and the universality of disability, almost without exception, people with disabilities have been discriminated against, with that discrimination ranging from minor embarrassment and inconvenience to relegation to a life of limited experience and reduced social opportunity and civil rights. . . . No other racial, cultural, ethnic, linguistic, religious, political, national, sexual orientation, or gender group has experienced this degree of pervasive and generalized prejudice and discrimination, which included killing babies with disabilities, forced sterilization, institutionalization, and mass murder.*

Disability is the one minority that anyone can join at any time—as a result of a sudden automobile accident, a fall down a flight of stairs, cancer, or disease. Most people were not born with their disabling condition; rather, they acquired the disability at some point in their life.

The incidence of disability is increasing globally as a result of a variety of conditions including the aging of the world's population, the spread of HIV, and the rise of tobacco-related disability. Historically, societies have tended to *isolate* and *segregate* individuals with disabilities. Despite some improvements, discrimination against individuals with disabilities continues to be a serious and pervasive social problem.

In the book *FDR's Splendid Deception*, chronicling Franklin Delano Roosevelt's disability and the intense efforts to conceal it from the public, Gallaher (1994) described the injustices people with disabilities have experienced throughout the years including: Spartans hurling them off a cliff to their death; Martin Luther believing they were fathered by the devil and that killing them was not a sin; people who were Jewish banishing them from communities, forcing them to beg along the road; American Indians burying alive newborn infants with disabilities; 18th-century societies confining them to asylums to be cared for and segregated; 20th-century Americans keeping them at home, out of sight, by families who felt embarrassment and shame about their presence, or institutionalizing them.

Discrimination against individuals with disabilities persists today in critical areas, such as recreation. Individuals with disabilities continually encounter various forms of discrimination. Examples include outright intentional exclusion, the discriminatory effects of architectural, transportation, and communication barriers, overprotective rules and policies, failure to make modifications to existing facilities and practices, exclusionary qualification standards and criteria, segregation, and relegation to lesser services, programs, activities, benefits, jobs, or opportunities.

Numerous studies have documented that people with disabilities, as a group, occupy an inferior status across the globe and are severely disadvantaged socially, vocationally, economically, and educationally. The continuing existence of discrimination and prejudice denies people with disabilities the opportunity to compete on an equal basis and to pursue those opportunities for which our free society is justifiably famous. Such discrimination costs billions of dollars in unnecessary expenses resulting from dependency and a lack of productivity. See Figure 9.1 for a summary of leisure barriers for some people with disabilities.

After surveying 997 adults with disabilities and 953 adults without disabilities, The National Office of Disability/Harris Survey of Americans with Disabilities (2000) reported that although there have been improvements in the lives of people with disabilities, they lag behind their peers without disabilities in employment and income. People who have disabilities are almost three times as likely to live in poverty. Since having discretionary income often enables people to enjoy themselves and take advantage of recreation activities such as eating at restaurants, going to movies, and attending sporting events, it is not surprising that people with disabilities report far fewer experiences associated with accessing entertainment, socializing, and going shopping. The survey revealed that when comparing people of similar ages and incomes, significant gaps still exist between people with and without disabilities, implying that factors such as lack of accessibility, negative public attitudes, and discomfort may be inhibiting people with disabilities from participating in these recreation activities.

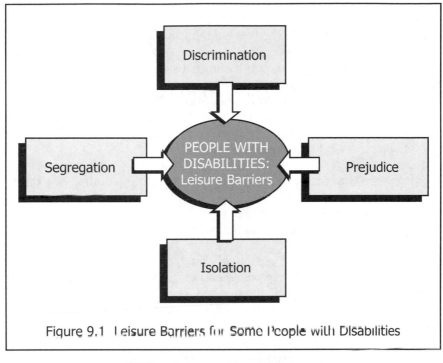

Figure 9.1 Leisure Barriers for Some People with Disabilities

What is a disability?

To understand issues surrounding people with disabilities and actions to promote inclusion, it is useful to clarify the identification of people with disabilities. According to the Americans with Disabilities Act (ADA, 1990), *a person with a disability* is anyone who has a physical or mental impairment that substantially limits one or more major life activity. Major life activities include seeing, hearing, speaking, walking, dressing, feeding oneself, working, learning, recreating, and other daily physical or mental activities. This broad definition incorporates many people, including individuals with:

- sensory impairments such as visual and hearing impairments
- communication disorders such as speech impairments
- cognitive disabilities such as mental retardation or brain injury
- physical disabilities such as cerebral palsy or multiple sclerosis
- chronic health disorders such as cardiac or pulmonary disease
- impaired mental health such as depression or schizophrenia
- chemical dependence
- HIV infection

Some people currently free of disease or impairment and not limited in major life activities may also be covered by the ADA. This includes *people who have a record of a disability*, such as a history of alcoholism or chemical dependence, mental or emotional illness, heart disease, or cancer. Other examples include *people who have been misclassified* as having a disability (e.g., intellectual disability or mental illness) when they did not.

In addition, the ADA covers *people who are regarded as having a disability*. An example of a person regarded as having a disability is an individual who has a significant facial deformity that does not limit major life activities. While the person is not physically or mentally restricted in performing activities, public reaction to the person's appearance may result in discrimination. Another example is *a person rumored to be, but who is not, infected with HIV*. In summary, a person with a disability is anyone who:

- has a physical or mental impairment substantially limiting one or more major life activities
- has a record of such impairment
- is regarded as having such impairment

The U.S. Supreme Court continually interprets the definition of disability stipulated in the ADA. Deciding who qualifies as an individual with disabilities is a challenging task that will require considerable effort in the future. For example, Fawley (1999, p. 12) reported that on June 22, 1999, the U.S. Supreme Court ruled that the ADA:

> *does not cover people who can use eyeglasses, medication or other treatments to correct their disabilities. Because people with diabetes can control their disease with insulin, they are not covered in the new version of the law. According to Joseph LaMountain, national director for the American Diabetes Association, "The bottom line is that a person with diabetes will first have to show that, even with treatment, he or she is substantially limited in a major life activity. Once that is shown, the person will then have to turn around and prove that with reasonable accommodation, he or she can do the job in question."*

There are many characteristics associated with disabling conditions that influence the ability of individuals to enjoy meaningful leisure. For example, people who have conditions that are *episodic* that result in sporadic performance (e.g., multiple sclerosis) have different concerns than people whose condition is *continuous* (e.g., cerebral palsy). The *age of onset that the disability* occurs will influence a person's approach to leisure; such as a person who is congenitally blind (blind at birth) as compared to someone who is adventitiously blinded (acquired the blindness) as an adult.

The *length of time the person has the disability* can also be an important consideration, such as the difference between someone who has recently recovered from a spinal cord injury as compared to someone who sustained the injury many years ago. The *prognosis of the condition that causes the disability* can affect people's leisure such as the difference between someone who has a static condition such as a hearing loss caused by medication taken as a child, compared to a hearing loss that is progressively deteriorating. The *severity of the condition* also influences a person's participation: a person with mental retardation who requires intermittent supports, for instance, may be able to participate to a greater degree than someone who needs pervasive supports.

The idea of ***heterogeneity***, the diverse nature of a particular category, group or condition, applies to groups who have been oppressed, including people with disabilities. Jackie Scully (2008, p. 21) speaks to the issue of heterogeneity:

> *The concept of disability also has to cover impairments with different origins: an arm can be missing because someone was born without it, lost it in an accident, or had it amputated to prevent the spread of cancer. It must also include impairments, like spinal cord lesion, that are present at all times; those that are intermittent, such as multiple sclerosis, and others that get progressively worse, like osteoarthritis. And it has to account for the fact that there are people with the same bodily variation who disagree on whether they are disabled at all.*

When considering these many factors that influence an individual's leisure participation, it becomes apparent that each person will have unique leisure needs and require different types of accommodations. Shapiro (1993, p. 5) identified the diversity associated with people who have disabilities with the following description:

> *There are hundreds of different disabilities. Some are congenital; most come later in life. Some are progressive, like muscular dystrophy, cystic fibrosis, and some forms of vision and hearing loss. Others, like seizure conditions, are episodic. Multiple sclerosis is episodic and progressive. Some conditions are static, like the loss of a limb. Still others, like cancer and occasionally paralysis, can even go away. Some disabilities are "hidden," like epilepsy or diabetes. Disability law also applies to people with perceived disabilities such as obesity or stuttering, which are not disabling but create prejudice and discrimination. Each disability comes in differing degrees of severity. Hearing aids can amplify sounds for most deaf and hard-of-hearing people but do nothing for others. Some people with autism spend their lives in institutions; others graduate from Ivy League schools or reach the top of their professions.*

There are indeed a variety of disabling conditions; however, a person with a particular disability may be very different from another individual with the same disabling condition.

For example, the National Office of Disability/Harris Survey of Americans with Disabilities (2000) reported that it is misleading to think of people with disabilities as a homogeneous group because disabilities vary in type and severity.

More recently, the Kessler Foundation and the National Organization on Disability (2010) concluded that:

> *[t]here is no single indicator of the quality of lives of people with disabilities. They face a range of challenges and have varied experiences and aspirations. This diversity is characterized not only by a broad spectrum of disability characteristics, specifically type and severity, but also by a range of personal characteristics and circumstances. Understanding this heterogeneity will be crucial toward properly equipping people with disabilities with the tools, skills, and opportunities they need to succeed.*

There are a numerous characteristics that influence the prevalence of disability. One characteristic is *age*; as people become older adults, the incidence of disability increases. Another important predictor of disability is *poverty*; those in poverty experience a higher rate of disability than those who have access to health care, especially prenatal care. *Education* is also correlated with disability, with people who are less educated having a higher incidence of disabling conditions.

Although the information presented in this section identifies how disability is defined by the ADA, it is helpful for us to focus on environmental and attitudinal barriers experienced by individuals that we can minimize as opposed to focusing on limitations within a person. Therefore, a person with a disability can be viewed as someone who needs an accommodation to function rather than someone who is impaired. This sentiment was reported by the Institute of Disability (2011, p. 7):

> *It is increasingly clear that disability is a complex social experience that, independent of the physical aspects of one's underlying condition or impairment, can contribute to poorer health outcomes. The root of this phenomenon, however, may well be based on the common observation that "It's not my disability that's my problem; it's how other people treat me because of my disability." Much like the experiences of more recognized disparity groups such as racial and ethnic minorities, this observation links disability to discrimination and the byproducts of discrimination: a lack of economic resources, power, and social standing.*

See Figure 9.2 for a summary of disability characteristics that influence people's leisure.

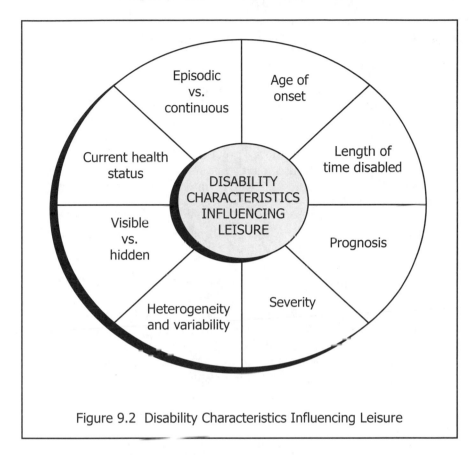

Figure 9.2 Disability Characteristics Influencing Leisure

How do attitudes create barriers for people with disabilities?

Many individuals possess negative attitudes toward people who have been disenfranchised. One group who has been consistently oppressed across various cultures is people with disabilities. As stated in the U.S. Americans with Disabilities Act of 1990:

> *Individuals with disabilities are a discrete and insular minority who have been faced with restrictions and limitations, subjected to a history of purposeful unequal treatment, and relegated to a position of political powerlessness in our society, based on characteristics that are beyond the control of such individuals and resulting from stereotypic assumptions not truly indicative of the individual ability of such individuals to participate in, and contribute to, society.*

People without disabilities can experience *stress* when interacting with people with disabilities. This discomfort can be created from ignorance or the perception that people with disabilities do not look or act the way most other people might.

> For example, Makas (1988) noted that people without disabilities reported greater emotional distress, exhibited higher physiological arousal, showed less motor activity, displayed less variability in their verbal behavior, expressed opinions less representative of previously reported beliefs, and terminated interactions sooner when interacting with a person who appeared disabled than when interacting with a person without disabilities.

This stress by people who do not have disabilities can create major barriers to inclusion for people with disabilities.

> As an illustration, Pivik, McComas, and LaFlamme (2002) interviewed youth with disabilities and their parents and determined that in addition to barriers created by physical environments and their physical limitations, the most devastating barriers are associated with negative attitudes that included intentional and unintentional attitude barriers. Intention attitude barriers consisted of youth actually isolating and bullying their peers with disabilities while the unintentional attitude barriers consisted of a lack of knowledge, understanding, or awareness.

As was presented earlier in this book, the major barriers to community involvement and leisure participation experienced by many people who are oppressed, including people with disabilities, are associated with stigmatization, stereotyping, discrimination, and segregation. These negative occurrences stem from negative attitudes that are often engrained into societal thinking.

To illustrate how engrained negative attitudes are in some societies, David Connor and Lynne Behoian (2006, p. 52) provided the following list of expressions. Later, they describe their reason for identifying these statements:

> *Can I ask a dumb question? What a limp response? Are you blind? You're so lame. That was short-sighted. He's crazy. They're insane. Your blind spot is ... Schizo! Another case of the blind leading the blind. Are you deaf? That's so retarded.*
>
> *Each of these statements contains a reference that reinforces the connection between disability and negativity, inferiority, undesirability, incompletion, and abnormality. The pervasiveness of such tolerated verbal expressions indicates the large, stereotypic perspective of our culture: Disability can never be a good thing. Within contemporary society, disability—unlike race, gender, sexual orientation, or age—is still somewhat of a free-for-all; a repository of bad*

associations and images; and a concept that people routinely look down on, devalue, and ridicule. With the overwhelming negative connotations of disability, how can people ever see disability as a natural part of human diversity, merely another bodily attribute, and one that we can frame in positive terms? In brief, how can we view disability as simply another way of being? (p. 52)

How can we be responsive to the needs of people with disabilities?

Weinum and Mitchell (1997) presented a model to encourage leisure service professionals to support and include every participant in programs and services, regardless of ability by:

- getting ready
- being willing
- being able

To *get ready*, it is helpful to prepare yourself and staff to accept inclusion as a process that begins with a customer service attitude. The authors suggest asking participants or family members for more information to increase the chance of success. It is useful to recruit staff members who are willing to learn or may already have the skills needed to work with a diverse consumer group. Knowing whom to contact for training on management strategies, crisis prevention, and disability awareness is important.

To *be willing* is an important next step. This step involves knowing the why and how of inclusion and know that everyone benefits from inclusion. As described later in the book, this step includes implementation of inclusive strategies.

To *be able*, involves a willingness to go the extra mile to include any individual. This is achieved when success stories are identified, as reported by participants and family members. It is helpful to identify the growth in numbers of people with disabilities who attend programs.

An example of one way to celebrate successes relative to inclusion was reported by Miller (2009, p. 40), when describing the practices of the Groton, Connecticut, Parks and Recreation Department, recipient of the 2005 National Institute of Recreation Inclusion's Excellence in Inclusion Award:

> Each season, the department publishes a program guide, Discover, which describes the activities and programs available to the general community. A cover story about the successful inclusion of an individual with a disability is published in at least one edition. Sharing success stories has been an effective

way for the entire community to see and hear about the department's efforts in making inclusion a reality.

Many people believe that to be responsive to the needs of people with disabilities, those who provide and fund services must make changes in the way they think about and serve these individuals. To achieve this change, Michael Kennedy and Lori Lewin (2010) suggested that the service system must shift from:

- seeing people as having limitations that prevent them from participating *to* seeing them as valuable citizens who contribute to their communities
- seeing people as service recipients *to* seeing them as individuals with rights and entitlements
- providing agency-controlled services *to* supporting person-directed services
- controlling people *to* empowering them

Another consideration when working to respond to the needs of people with disabilities is for us to consider that the focus of people with disabilities is often not on their disability. Relevant to the pursuit of leisure experience, as with any person, people with disabilities are interested in experiencing enjoyment, fun, and pleasure.

Harriet McBryde Johnson (2006, p. 254) lawyer, author, and a person who has a *congenital disability*, a condition existing at birth, stated that:

> *When nondisabled people start learning about disability, what seems most startling, most difficult to accept, is the possibility of pleasure. . . . We need to confront the life-killing stereotype that says we're all about suffering. We need to bear witness to our pleasures. I'm talking in part about the pleasure we share with nondisabled people [where there is] no impairment: disability makes no difference. But I'm also talking about those pleasures that are peculiarly our own, that are so bound up with our disabilities that we wouldn't experience them, or wouldn't experience them in the same way, without our disabilities.*

How can we emphasize the person first?

Realizing that participants are people first can create an important starting point for including all people in the services we provide. To encourage us to focus on the person first, leisure service professionals can:

- individualize accommodations
- focus on abilities
- match challenge and skills

Individualize Accommodations

A key to providing inclusive leisure services is to consider the individual needs of each participant. Each participant has different life experiences, different support systems, different health considerations, and different resources. Because many people possess differing levels of skills, and experience a variety of consequences as a result of different conditions, it is important for us to individualize any accommodation that we make.

Focus on Abilities

It is helpful to focus on participants' *abilities* rather than on their *disabilities*. Too often, assessments conducted identify what participants cannot do. Next, accommodations are designed to address this limitation.

A typically more useful procedure is to initially focus on the skills and abilities of participants and then work with the person and their support system to build upon these skills. Some professionals refer to this approach as a strengths-based practice. Hood and Carruthers (2007, p. 299) explained:

> *Strengths-based practice, at the most fundamental level, is based on the premise that all people have strengths and capacities that they can use [to] optimize their lives. It is, therefore, the responsibility of the helper to focus attention on the clients' strengths so that they may be further developed and used by clients to improve their lives.*

When people's abilities become the focus of attention, we are more likely to allow participants to be as independent as possible. As we focus on abilities, we tend to avoid stifling these people by making unnecessary adaptations that fail to capitalize on their skills; rather, we celebrate what can be achieved and move on from that point.

For example, when attending her first soccer practice, Regina is met by her coach who introduces himself to her. The coach then asks Regina, "What are some skills or talents you have that might help you play soccer?" Regina smiles and says, "When I am at the beach, I have fun building castles in the sand but I am even better at kicking them apart!" The coach responds, "That is a great place for us to begin Regina!"

Match Challenge and Skills

Leisure services contain experiences that possess a certain degree of challenge. Prior to providing leisure services, we can systematically assess the skills and interests of the people for whom the program is designed. Then, when conducting programs, we will be in a position to better achieve the delicate balance between the challenge of specific activities and participant skills.

If an imbalance exists between the degree of challenge of a program and participants' skills, barriers to leisure participation may be created. As discussed in previous chapters, if a specific activity is too easy for participants, boredom often results. However, if an activity is too difficult, frustration can occur.

One way to reduce leisure barriers is through adaptations and accommodations. Adaptations and accommodations can permit modifications of the challenge associated with participation to meet the abilities of the participants. Once adaptations are made, these changes must continually be adjusted to meet the changing skills of the participants.

How can we encourage autonomy?

Since a critical aspect of the leisure experience involves freedom to make choices, it is important that people perceive that they are autonomous. The following suggestions are provided to facilitate this sense of control and choice:

- facilitate independence and interdependence
- determine necessity of any accommodation
- view accommodations as transitional

Facilitate Independence and Interdependence

Any form of accommodation or adaptation should decrease the necessity of participants to rely on others for assistance. Accommodations and adaptations are made to provide participants with increased opportunities to actively participate in leisure as independently as possible.

Independence is important for many people with disabilities and so is interdependence. There are many people who you will read about in subsequent chapters who are role models—people who are highly independent but also who are extremely connected with other people in their community and thereby are interdependent. Rick Reilly (2003) wrote the following about Ben Cowen, an extremely determined youth who happens to have cerebral palsy:

> *The condition does not affect his intellect and he is a straight-A student. But his gait is cumbersome and he has the balance of a Times Square drunk. Yet there he is, competing for the Hanna High cross-county team in Anderson, S.C., dragging that uncoordinated, wobbly body over rocks and fallen branches. And people ask, why? "Because I feel like I've been put here to set an example," says Ben, 16. "Anybody can find something they can do and do it well. I like to show people that you can either stop trying or you can pick yourself up and keep going. It's more fun to keep going." . . . This is a kid who builds wheelchair ramps for Easter Seals, spends nights at assisted living homes, volunteers for Habitat for*

Humanity, plans to run a marathon and be a doctor. Boy, the youth of today, huh?

Determine Necessity of Any Accommodation

Because many people experience barriers to leisure participation, sometimes we may be quick to change a recreation program. Changes may be readily made to a given program because leisure services professionals may be skilled at making modifications.

However, sometimes these changes are made with the knowledge of general characteristics of a group rather than with explicit information about the specific participants. Although this may be practical in some situations, it may also create a problem. Some aspects of recreation programs may be changed when they need not be. Therefore, we must take note of any accommodation we make and examine each adaptation to determine its necessity.

View Accommodations as Transitional

Accommodations can permit active participation for people with a wide range of knowledge and skills. The very nature of leisure services implies that individuals will learn and change. As people learn and change, their skills and knowledge fluctuate.

If an accommodation was made at one time, it may no longer be appropriate because the individual has now acquired the knowledge and skills to participate without any accommodation. At that point, the accommodation may stifle the person and impair rather than encourage leisure participation.

Conversely, some people participating in recreation programs may possess degenerative or progressive conditions that require continual modifications. A previous slight accommodation to a particular activity may later be insufficient to provide the person with the opportunity to participate. We must be willing to adopt the view that any adaptation that is made may need to be altered in the future.

How can we involve participants?

It is important for leisure service professionals to involve people with disabilities in all aspects of program development. These individuals can provide a valuable perspective that helps to improve the delivery of inclusive leisure services. The following suggestions stimulate ways to include these individuals in the adaptation process:

- talk with participants
- determine feasibility of accommodation
- ensure safety of accommodation

Talk with Participants

In almost every aspect of planning, it is helpful to consult with participants regarding their opinions and desires. A critical task in helping people become motivated to participate is to encourage them to offer input into the chosen program. Active involvement in shaping leisure services can provide individuals with a sense of investment that may increase their motivation to initiate and maintain participation.

Discussions with participants may provide valuable information about ways to accommodate those who possess diverse knowledge and skills. These contributions by participants can instill in them feelings of control and commitment. When participants do not currently possess the skills to effectively communicate their feelings and ideas, then observations can be used to obtain input from these individuals.

Determine Feasibility of Accommodation

Including participants in the process of making accommodations that promote their active involvement in leisure services can provide a way to determine the feasibility and usability of any planned accommodation. If participants feel that the accommodation reduces the quality of the program in some way or limits their sense of enjoyment then their motivation may be reduced.

Asking participants their opinions and encouraging them to make suggestions can enhance our ability to make feasible accommodations. Discussions with people prior to and throughout the provision of services can help encourage active leisure participation.

Ensure Safety of Accommodation

The most critical element for us to remember when making changes and accommodations to any leisure service is safety. Commercially available equipment, materials, and games typically have been tested and retested to determine their safety for potential participants. Any time an adaptation is made to a piece of equipment or material, the previous research conducted by the manufacturers is compromised and associated safety claims change. As a result, we must examine and evaluate any service, material, or piece of equipment we adapt, and consider the implications to the safety of participants.

One strategy to help evaluate the safety of an adaptation is to actively seek participants' input regarding ways to ensure and increase the safety associated with a given aspect of a program. A summary of ways to involve participants in the inclusion process is presented in Figure 9.3.

How can we meet the spirit of the ADA?

The ADA helps set the stage for inclusion. However, even if agencies are in compliance with the ADA, people with disabilities still might not be included

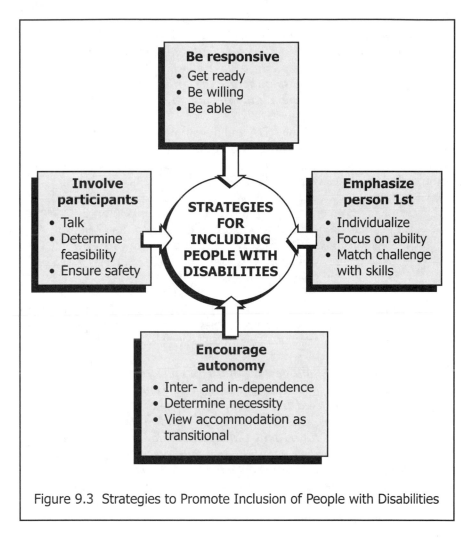

Figure 9.3 Strategies to Promote Inclusion of People with Disabilities

in various programs. Baylor (1996, p. 14) explained how the ADA mandates accommodation rather than inclusion:

> *ADA was designed to "accommodate" rather than to include. That is, it makes an assumption that if we accommodate people with disabilities, inclusion will automatically result. Unfortunately, it does not. I can be accommodated by a ramp, but I will be included if someone invites me in their door. . . . Changing architectural design is one thing; changing peoples' hearts is another.*

We must go beyond responding to the letter of the law and respond to the spirit of the law. It is critical that we be willing to take whatever actions necessary to help people become included in community leisure programs. Jill Smolowe (1995, p. 54) spoke to this point:

> *While the specific aim of the landmark legislation was to provide America's 49 million physically and mentally disabled people with access to public areas and workplaces, the larger spirit of the law was to puncture the stifling isolation of the disabled and draw them into the mainstream of civic life.*

Embracing the spirit of the ADA and developing inclusive leisure services allows us to contribute to the entire community. It is important that we respond to federal legislation such as the ADA, and it is also important to respond to the people with disabilities who are demanding leisure services.

> After interviewing 55 people with disabilities, Bedini (2000) found that having a disability could compromise leisure. She encouraged leisure services providers to ensure that their language, signage, titles, advertisements, and staff are appropriate and respectful of all participants.

Sometimes it is the little things that people do that can help encourage others to feel comfortable with being in a situation. For example, Smolowe (1995, p. 54) wrote:

> *It is often the small gesture that can make an inhospitable world seem welcoming. After a sunglasses vendor in Palatine, Illinois, advertised her sign-language skills, people with hearing impairments flocked to her stand to discuss frame shapes and lens tints. At the Chicago Botanic Garden, shelves and pulley systems enable wheelchair users to inspect a special exhibit. In the rest rooms there, a cheap innovation safeguards the disabled from the nasty scalding their legs routinely endure in public places: the hot-water pipes beneath the sinks are wrapped in insulation.*

When thinking about the ADA, it is helpful to focus on personal identity, where difference is not merely tolerated and accepted, but it is positively valued and celebrated. It is not simply a matter of providing laws that result in inclusion, but rather that the legislation creates a sense of moral obligation to ensure its enforcement. In discussing how people avoid personal responsibility, Barry (1997, pp. 72, 75) talked about the relationship between laws and morality:

> *Laws are intended to institutionalize the highest moral ideals of a people. Were we always true to those ideals, we'd need no laws—we'd be self-regulating. That we have legal limits in almost every area of our lives is public proof of the countless individual failures to honor some ideal or other, which law piled upon law can do little to alter. If we were more caring and considerate, more respectful and fair-minded, more understanding and empathetic, we'd have fewer laws because we'd need laws less.*

The intention of this book is encourage readers to create inclusive leisure that responds to the spirit of all human rights guidelines and civil rights legislation, including the ADA. There is extensive research highlighting the many benefits of inclusion for everyone. Commenting on this research, Ryndak and colleagues (2010, p. 38) reported that:

> *A comprehensive list of the research in support of those benefits would be lengthy and reveal increases in appropriate social behaviors, increased interactions with others, more positive affect, increased friendships, and improved communication skills.*

Ryndak and colleagues described how two brothers with similar significant disabilities and a 10-year age difference functioned as young adults after the older brother received segregated services, while the younger brother received services in inclusive settings. Following a review of the brothers' records subsequent to conducting interviews and field observations, the authors concluded that the brother who received services in an inclusive environment experienced more positive long-term outcomes.

Although progress has occurred in support of the inclusion of people with disabilities, more is needed. John McGovern (1996) offered the following examples of ADA compliance associated with leisure services:

- A woman with multiple sclerosis should be able to get in and out of a newly constructed swimming pool using a lift at the pool.
- A young boy who has autism spectrum disorder should have the same opportunity as his brothers and sisters to enjoy a summer camp by being assigned an extra staff member to him.
- An adolescent girl who is deaf should be able to understand the strategy discussed by her hockey coach thanks to a sign language interpreter provided by the league.
- A boy using a wheelchair should be able to get across a playground surface and enjoy the new and exciting playground equipment.

Final Thoughts

It is valuable for us to focus on principles that facilitate people's inclusion into community leisure services. Inherent at any level of leisure service delivery is the need to communicate to potential consumers the availability of services. Although inclusion is an ethical responsibility and a legislative requirement, it also presents an opportunity to address a worthy market sector. So, as attempts at marketing are made, it may be helpful to consider that, although people who have been oppressed in various ways may be a minority, they are many in number.

For example, people with disabilities have emerged as a consumer group with money to spend on leisure pursuits. Shapiro (1993, p. 36) described an incident that identified people with disabilities as a market to be targeted:

> *The Minneapolis-based Target department store chain put its first model with mental retardation, a young girl with Down syndrome, in a Sunday newspaper advertising insert in 1990. "That ad hit doorsteps at six a.m. Sunday and a half hour later my phone was ringing," recalls George Hite, the company's vice president for marketing. "It was the mother of a girl with Down syndrome thanking me for having a kid with Down syndrome in our ad. It's so important to my daughter's self-image," she said. That ad, one small picture among dozens in the circular, generated over two thousand letters of thanks to stunned Target executives.*

Not only are people with disabilities an important consumer group for leisure services and products, they also can be helpful in promotion and marketing efforts.

> As an illustration, April Holmes helped Michael Jordon launch the Air Jordon 2009. The carbon fiber prosthetic running technology used by Holmes and other athletes was the inspiration for the shoe design. Advertisements and press releases featured Holmes' exploits as a gold medal winner in the 100-meter race in the 2008 Paralympic Games.

Even though as a group, people with disabilities present an important market sector, there are numerous examples in every culture of people with disabilities being oppressed, stigmatized, discriminated against, removed from society, and segregated. In the book *Helen Keller: A Life*, Dorothy Herrmann (1998, p. 11) wrote specifically about people who were blind and deaf-blind:

> *For centuries, the blind, as well as the deaf-blind, were regarded as monsters, to be killed as quickly as possible. In ancient Greece, blind children were taken to mountaintops and left to starve to death or be eaten by wild animals. In Rome, a parent of a sightless child could buy a small basket in the marketplace in which to put their visually impaired offspring before throwing him or her into the Tiber. Other early societies sanctioned selling of blind children into slavery or prostitution, and in the Orient, blind women were routinely forced to become prostitutes. Even in Europe, blind children were often thrown in the streets by their parent to beg for a living.*

In spite of extreme injustices against people with disabilities, still there are success stories of people who have endured. One such triumphant individual was Helen Keller. Although she could not hear or see, Helen Keller made important contributions to society and positively influenced many individuals. Interestingly, Helen accepted her blindness and deafness as natural conditions, even though she lived in a society that regarded her life as a courageous battle against overwhelming disabilities. An often quoted statement by Ms. Keller is *Life is either a daring adventure or nothing.*

Annie Sullivan, Helen's teacher and life companion, wrote a speech that was delivered by Alexander Graham Bell at an 1894 convention when Helen was 14. As the inventor of the telephone, Bell considered his career to be the teaching of people who were deaf. In fact, the telephone was partly conceived with the hope that it might act as a hearing aid. The following is an excerpt of the speech Annie wrote in which she described Helen's personality and accomplishments (Herrmann, 1998, p. 97):

> *It is Helen's loving and sympathetic heart rather than her bright intellect which endears her to everybody with whom she comes in contact. She impresses me every day as being the happiest child in the world, and so it is a special privilege to be with her. The spirit of love and joyousness seems never to leave her. May it ever be so. It is beautiful to think of a nature so gentle, pure, and loving as hers; it is pleasant also to think she will ever see only the best side of every human being . . . So we see, pathetic as Helen's life always seems to those who enjoy the blessings of sight and hearing, that it is yet full of brightness and cheer and courage and hope.*

Discussion Questions

1. How is disability defined by the Americans with Disabilities Act (ADA)?
2. What is the connection between disability and poverty?
3. What are some examples of how negative attitudes influence leisure participation for people with disabilities?
4. What can leisure service providers do to meet the needs of people with disabilities?
5. What are ways we can focus on the person first when providing inclusive leisure services?
6. What are some strategies that would enable leisure service providers to encourage participant autonomy?
7. What are procedures we can develop that stimulate participant involvement in the development of inclusive leisure services?
8. What are some actions we can take to embrace the spirit of the ADA?
9. In what way are people with disabilities an important leisure service consumer group?
10. Why might Helen Keller be a role model for us?

Chapter 10
Promote Culture:
Ethnicity, Race, and Immigration

John Dattilo and Junhyoung Kim

There is a yellow one that won't accept the black one
that won't accept the red one that won't accept the white one.
Different strokes for different folks.
-Sly and the Family Stone

Orientation Activity

Directions Alone: Read the statement presented below and write a paragraph describing what you think the person meant when he wrote it.

> *It seems to me if I abhor intolerance, discrimination and hatred when they affect people who look like me, I must also abhor them when they affect people who do not. For that matter, I must abhor them even when they benefit me. Otherwise, what I claim as moral authority is really just self-interest in disguise.*

> -Leonard Pitts, Jr.

Directions with Others: Divide into small groups and discuss your interpretation of the statement with other members. After a specified time, share your responses with the entire group.

Debriefing: As leisure services providers, we work with participants who differ from us and each other relative to their ethnicity and race. Challenges arise when attempting to provide leisure services since people of different races and ethnicities often possess different interests and priorities. In addition, these challenges can be compounded if people have recently immigrated to the host country.

It is clear that although differences exist, that people of all races and ethnicities have strong similarities associated with their basic human needs. As Pitts describes above, if we are committed to providing inclusive leisure services, it is imperative that we consistently work to empower all people, especially those who have been disempowered and work to promote leisure for everyone. As we work to eliminate discrimination and promote inclusive leisure services it is important that we encourage inclusion for all people regardless of their characteristics.

One way we can be involved in the promotion of human rights is to offer people of diverse backgrounds the opportunity to experience leisure together and to actively welcome them into our programs. We are in a position to offer recreation activities that can promote positive interactions between them. Leisure services that promote interactions among diverse participants can be beneficial to everyone involved.

Introduction

The world is becoming more ethnically and culturally diverse.

> For example, the United States (U.S.) Census Bureau predicts by the year 2050 more than 50% of all residents living within the U.S. will be members of an ethnic minority (U.S. Bureau of the Census, 2008).

With an influx of new residents from different cultures to many countries across the globe, there are numerous challenges for these countries and their immigrants. This chapter is designed to address some of the challenges specifically related to promoting positive and meaningful leisure experiences. As mentioned in previous chapters, people are oppressed for many reasons including possessing cultural characteristics that are different from those who are privileged and in positions of power. Leslie Aguilar (2000, p. 201) speaks to the issue in the U.S.:

> *The flagrant racism of yesterday has decreased; today, customers are no longer barred from an establishment based on ethnicity or skin color. However, do not confuse physical access with outstanding consumer service. Many customers are treated with suspicion or encounter prejudice or stereotypes against them. For example, all too often African American consumers are ignored, as they cannot afford to pay for services, or are watched suspiciously, as if they might steal something. In many parts of the country, Native Americans and Latino consumers have similar experiences.*

Some of the material included in this chapter is adapted from an article titled: *Use of leisure education and recreation activities associated with Asian cultures to promote older Asian immigrants' well-being* by Kim and Dattilo (2011) and a chapter from the book *Leisure Education Program Planning: A Systematic Approach* (Dattilo, 2008) titled: *Multicultural Consideration for Leisure Education*. The following questions are addressed in the chapter:

- What are relevant terms when addressing ethnic and racial differences?
- What are challenges for immigrants and people of various ethnic and racial backgrounds?
- What happens when diverse people experience leisure together?
- What are outcomes of experiencing leisure among diverse participants?
- What are benefits of leisure services that promote contact with diverse participants?
- How can leisure services be designed to promote positive interactions?

What are relevant terms when addressing ethnic and racial differences?

When discussing cultural perspectives including ideas associated with race and ethnicity is can be helpful to begin with a discussion about relevant terms and their meanings. Therefore, the next section of the chapter will provide information about the following terms:

- Culture
- Acculturation and Assimilation
- Race, Ethnicity, and Minority

Culture

Culture is a pattern of beliefs, values, and behaviors that is socially transmitted from generation to generation through the spoken and written word, the use of certain objects, customs, and traditions. Culture influences communication patterns, methods of conveying messages, and the comprehension of information and exists not in the artifacts or festivals, but in how people think and feel. In addition, culture affects how we define ourselves and our perceptions of what constitutes leisure and how we partake in it.

Cultural factors, including racial and socioeconomic differences, can contribute to on-going alienation when certain behaviors are misread and unfairly judged.

> This conclusion is supported by Malaney and Shively (1995) who found that students of color in schools with a majority of Caucasians reported that it was more difficult to meet people with similar backgrounds and interests and that these students generally encountered social isolation.

Participants who experience rejection or exclusion because of their culture may choose not to attend programs. The individual's absence may be interpreted by leisure service professionals as disinterest.

Culture is what people need to know to be members of a community and to regulate interactions with other members of the same community as well as people from backgrounds different from their own. Every person has cultural identity; most people have multiple cultural memberships and have multiple identities.

Most individuals readily identify race (or races, for those who are multi-racial), nationality, ethnicity, and religion as cultural groups. Other examples include age, gender, sexual orientation, social class, education, language and communication style, level of ability, and in the region of the country, part of a city, or rural area in which one resides. Culture involves ways of living that evolve from the process of thinking, perceiving, believing, and evaluating within a group.

It is important for leisure service professionals to attend to cultural contexts for the benefits of leisure to be realized across cultural boundaries. This action will assist in sorting through the need to maintain or promote cultural heritage, traditions, and history while continuing to develop, change, and advance.

Acculturation and Assimilation

The degree to which a person is identifies as "different" often depends on the extent to which the individual is acculturated. *Acculturation* is the process by which people acquire cultural characteristics of the host culture. Cultural characteristics might include clothing choices, eating habits, entertainment choices, and language usage, including local slang.

Acculturation occurs at varying rates for different immigrant groups and for specific individuals. Factors influencing acculturation include such conditions as the:

- degree of acceptance by host culture
- amount of social support by ethnic community
- motivation of individual to be integrated into host culture
- length of time individual has resided in host culture

Some families may maintain their traditional dress, language, and values indefinitely, while others may adopt new customs immediately. When meeting an individual from a racial or ethnic group other than one's own, it can be helpful to consider that the person may have come to the country very recently or may be second or third generation.

The acculturation process involves many forms of adjustment that include physical, psychological, financial, spiritual, social, language and family. This process can be stressful for immigrants who have recently immigrated because they often have less knowledge about the healthcare system, a different set of accepted cultural social settings and resources, and a lower proficiency of the primary language of the host country.

Much research has linked the level of acculturation with immigrants' psychological stress, life satisfaction, well-being, and family conflicts. In particular, the cultural adjustment process is difficult for older immigrants who must adapt to a new social environment while attempting to decide whether to maintain their cultural values and beliefs or accommodate new social norms and values. Specifically, Berry (1980) proposed that immigrants experience a process of change in six areas of psychological functioning:

- language
- cognitive styles
- personality
- identity
- attitudes
- acculturative stress

> *Berry (2003) argued that as immigrants acculturate, a number of intergroup behaviors are modified and assimilated in positive ways and various psychosocial and behavioral changes occur for host or dominant members who have continuous contact with members of different ethnic and immigrant groups. These changes can vary as a function of characteristics such as age, social status, education level, and generational status. Mio, Barker-Hackett, and Tumambing (2008) suggest that a mutual change process between the hosts and immigrants may generate negative consequences such as misunderstandings, intergroup anxiety, and avoidance of contact associated with cultural, racial, and ethnic differences. As a result of the acculturation process and ethnic and cultural differences, groups of immigrants may face numerous challenges when they have contact with people who are in a host society.*

The word *assimilation* is a synonym for acculturation and is the process that occurs when a minority group gradually adopts the customs and attitudes of the host culture. People's view of assimilation varies across groups and across time. Pitts (2009, p. 129) explains about assimilation in the U.S.:

> *A tricky thing, assimilation. The Holy Grail of immigrants ever since Eastern Europeans started rushing to these shores late in the last century. You gave up your "funny-sounding" name, you hid your religion, you lost your accent, and you thereby "became American" – which almost always meant some close approximation of the, white, Anglo-Saxon, Protestant ideal. But many have come to a different understanding of what it means to be American. They've come to feel that it doesn't require them to give up identity and heritage, doesn't demand that they become Smiths and Joneses. Rather, it*

requires them only to believe in American Ideals: equality, democracy, justice, freedom. Including the freedom to be who and what you are.

The terms, acculturation and assimilation, have been addressed predominantly from the perspective of immigrant groups but they also apply to marginalized groups within the host population. In addition, acculturation is typically identified as a unidirectional process; however, acculturation may be viewed as a multidirectional process that entails both groups adapting, tolerating, and embracing each other.

Race, Ethnicity, and Minority

Although **race** is a term sometimes used to describe a group of people having genetically transmitted physical characteristics, it can be argued that race is socially constructed. Characteristics associated with race might include skin, eye, and hair color, facial features, height, and body type. According to Terry Long (2005, p. 3):

> *Understanding that race is a man-made classification that has more potential for harm than good is much more useful than being able to define race as a group of people who share certain genetic characteristics. The former represents understanding while the latter closely resembles a parrot mimicking simple words.*

As the number of individuals who are multiracial increases, there will be a greater chance that we will be providing services to people who have more than one racial background.

> As an illustration, being multiracial in the U.S. is complicated by a *hierarchy of color* based on two assumptions: that Caucasian is considered superior to other races and that privileges and power accorded to Caucasians are desired by those of other races. The hierarchy of color further dictates a social status system based on ethnic features and skin tone. Traditionally, an individual is considered to belong to the racial group of the darker skinned parent. A child who has a parent who is Caucasian and a parent who is Asian is usually identified as Asian, whereas a child with a parent who is Asian and a parent who is African American would be considered African American. Unfortunately, in many cases, these biracial classifications have been written into laws in the U.S.

Individuals with a multiracial background may have unique problems with their sense of identity. For example, they may not racially identify with the way they look, and may not automatically be accepted by the racial group with which they do identify. People with a multiracial background may actively reject the culture of one parent, or may choose to identify with a different racial group than do their siblings. They may change their racial identity over the course of their lifetime.

The terms *race* and *ethnicity* are sometimes used interchangeably even though historically their meanings have been different. Although race has been traditionally viewed as being primarily genetically transmitted, more recently, race is viewed similarly to ethnicity which is socially constructed. Ethnicity impacts leisure participation including activity choices, frequency of participation, participation location, types of activities, and the manner in which an individual participates.

The word **ethnicity** refers to an individual's membership in a group sharing a common ancestral heritage including the biological, cultural, social, and psychological domains of life. To self-identify, then, is to be willing to be perceived and treated as a member of the group such as Polish American, Gypsy, or gang member. Again, whenever possible, it is useful to ask individuals how they self-identify.

People of different groups are sometimes referred to as minorities. However, Texeira (2005, p. A10) asked the following question:

> *What do you call a minority that is becoming the majority? News that Texas is the fourth state in which non-Hispanic whites make up less than 50 percent of residents has renewed discussion about whether the term "minority" has outlived its usefulness; critics include both liberals and conservatives.*

Minority literally means smaller or fewer in number.

> For instance, in the U.S. the Navajo Nation is a minority group because there are fewer of them than of the larger society. The categories of people most often referred to as minorities are those of certain races such as Polynesian, religious such as Quaker, economic situations such as people without homes, political affiliations such as Libertarian, sexual orientations such as lesbian, and disability diagnosis such as having cerebral palsy.

The term *minority* is problematic because a person can be a member of a minority group in one culture but can be a member of the majority in another culture. In addition, the proportion of people associated with different cultures can change over time.

> As an example, White (1997) reported that if current demographic trends persist, midway through the 21st century whites will no longer comprise the majority of the U.S. population. The term *minority* is currently less-preferred than

terms or phrases that are more precise. The phrase people of color has been revived for use in formal contexts to refer to members or groups of non-European origin such as people who are of Asian descent, who are from the Pacific Islands, or who are Native Americans. Many people prefer the phrase *people of color* as a substitute for *minorities* because these groups are not in fact the minority in many parts of the U.S.

What are challenges for immigrants and people of various ethnic and racial backgrounds?

As much as Americans pride themselves on the notion that their national identity is premised on a set of ideals rather than a single race, ethnicity, or religion, we all know that for most of our history, white supremacy was the law of the land.

The statement above by Gregory Rodriguez (2010, p. 52) highlights one particular challenge associated with being a member of a racial or ethnic group who has been oppressed within the U.S. In spite of benefits of leisure involvement, immigrants and people who are not members of the dominant race or who do not comprise a portion of the most common ethnic background of a particular country may experience constraints to leisure. A brief explanation of the following barriers is presented in the next section:

- discrimination
- limited language skills
- lack of social support
- unaware of leisure resources
- minimal financial resources

Discrimination

As discussed in earlier chapters of this book, one of the most devastating constraints to leisure participation experienced by people who have been oppressed in some manner is *discrimination*.

For example, when studying the leisure behavior of American Muslims in the post-September 11 America, Livengood and Stodolska (2004, p. 183) conducted in-depth interviews with 25 individuals with varied ethnic backgrounds and found that:

> *... discrimination has affected leisure of Muslim immigrants directly through experiences in leisure-related settings and while engaged in leisure activities, by restricting the range of available leisure options and co-participants, by affecting their willingness to participate in leisure activities and by restricting their freedom of movement, travel, timing and location of activities.*

Discrimination is fueled by ignorance. Often, the less people understand and are aware of others, the more likely it is that they will develop stereotypes and engage in discriminatory practices. In describing how American Muslims experience life in the U.S. since 9/11, Halimah Abdullah (2011, p. D7) stated:

> *Despite a decade in which Muslim Americans have tried to show patriotism and educate non-Muslim friends and neighbors, polls show that many people with the United States remain wary of Islam or don't know much about it.*

Limited Language Skills

In addition, *language barriers* can hinder leisure participation and result in many people, often immigrants, feeling isolated from their community. Some immigrants struggle to communicate with others because they are not proficient speakers of the dominant language. Subsequently, these individuals experience barriers to communication and social interactions.

> For example, Mio and colleagues (2008) discovered that many older Asian immigrants report that they depend on their children to communicate with others and without help from their children they encounter numerous problems. Many immigrants to the U.S. live in households in which some family members cannot speak English creating challenges associated with their interpersonal communications that result in a sense of isolation (Sohng, Sohng, & Yeom, 2002).

Lack of Social Support

Although differences in cultural beliefs and language barriers may contribute to constrained leisure experienced by immigrants, the lack of social support and limited social networks may also create challenges for them. Researchers have found that lack of social support leads to psychological problems including anxiety, depression, and loneliness.

> For instance, Mio and colleagues (2008) examined immigrants' psychological concerns including anxiety, stress, loneliness, and isolation and found that respo ndents reported that a lack

of perceived social support led to them experiencing stress and loneliness; although community resources are available for immigrants, they may not use such resources because they fear rejection. Also, Hong and Ham (2001) interviewed immigrants and found that many reported feeling isolated from their relatives and friends who remained in their countries of origin.

Unaware of Leisure Resources

In general, immigrants often lack valuable information about leisure resources in the community and experience changes in their cultural values and beliefs, social circumstances, and social networks. Research demonstrates that this lack of information and experience of different social settings generates various constraints and participation patterns associated with cultural differences.

As an illustration, Im and Choe (2001) examined immigrants' attitudes toward free time physical activities and concluded that they could not actively participate in these activities because of barriers, such as busy daily schedules, a lack of reliable child care from their extended families, a lack of English skills and limited social networks. In another example, Tsai and Coleman (1999) found that international graduate students experienced a number of barriers to leisure, including a lack of community resources, time, financial support, and social relationships.

Minimal Financial Resources

Another barrier to leisure participation experienced often by immigrants and members of ethnic and racial groups who are not members of the dominant culture include *limited financial resources*. Monika Stodoska (2010, p. 101) provided this detail on the topic and other associated barriers to leisure:

> *... because of the disadvantaged position of many minority members, they often work long hours at physically demanding jobs and are constrained by lack of time and physical stamina necessary for active recreation. The necessity to take care of younger siblings in large families, lack of culturally appropriate child-care services, some religious restrictions on mixed-gender interactions, and preference for wearing clothing that restrict recreation participation of some religious minorities may constrain leisure participation.*

Immigrants and people who are not members of the dominant race or who are not members of the most common ethnic background of a particular country experience a variety of constraints to their leisure. As described above, these constraints can include language barriers that create communication challenges and restricted social interactions, limited awareness of leisure resources, and all the problems that are associated with poverty such as limited free time and poor health.

Considering the possible constraints identified in this section, it is helpful to note that if someone is a member of a minority group or is an immigrant they may not experience these barriers. Many of these variables create substantial social challenges; however, a major constraint that we can immediately address is negative attitudes and discrimination of services providers and the agencies they represent. See Figure 10.1 for a summary of leisure barriers experienced by some immigrants.

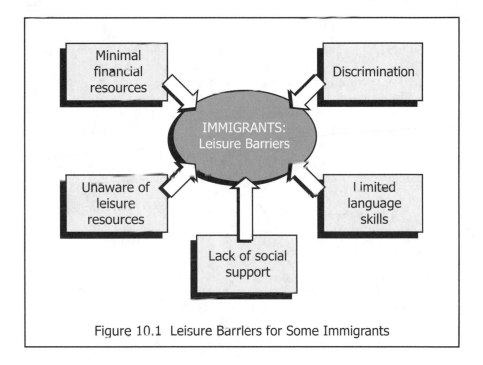

Figure 10.1 Leisure Barrlers for Some Immigrants

What happens when diverse people experience leisure together?

With the increasing globalization, interactions between members of culturally and racially different groups is a part of everyday life for many people. Some people report making contact with diverse people generates suspicion, fear, resentment, disturbance, and, at times, open conflict. Others propose that contact between individuals from different cultures has positive effects such as the creation of mutual understanding and development of positive attitudes.

Dixon and Rosenbaum (2004) observed that social networks that facilitate interactions with diverse people reduce anti-black and anti-Hispanic stereotypes. McLaren (2003) noted that friendships and acquaintances among people having different racial or ethnic backgrounds decrease prejudice. Emerson, Kimbro, and Yancey (2002) concluded that prior racial contact in schools and neighborhoods lead to more diverse extended social ties that helped to establish racially-diverse friendships.

There is support for the belief that when friendships and acquaintances occur through joint interactions, these relationships are associated with favorable attitudes. However, other researchers demonstrate that contacts between people from different cultures may yield negative feelings such as anxiety and prejudice, and create a context for conflicts.

For example, Stephan and Stephan (1985) reported that when two cultural groups are in contact without understanding and acknowledging different cultural backgrounds, anxiety and uncertainty develop and form negative stereotypes and prejudice. Such anxiety may inhibit positive social interactions and relationships between people of different cultural groups.

Some people positively react to different cultural values and beliefs and therefore, reduce their negative stereotypes while others do not.

For instance, when people immigrate to a new society, they bring their religions, customs, and languages. Cultural differences can arouse fears of cultural invasion, loss of national identity, and relative decline of the dominant culture and group. Cultural values of immigrants are not always consistent with the host culture and, therefore, can cause intercultural conflict and tension.

Interactions during leisure participation can reduce negative feelings when diverse group members have the opportunity to interact positively with one another. Unfortunately, in some countries including the U.S. often individuals with different cultural heritages do not interact.

As an example, in the U.S. Caucasians and Latinos continue to live in segregated communities (Martin, 2006). Most U.S. Caucasians live in predominantly Caucasian neighborhoods with a small percentage of people of color (Logan, 2006). In spite of the U.S. being identified as a multicultural society, some U.S. citizens have limited interactions with diverse people. According to Graham and Cohen (1997), people have a tendency to interact mainly with those similar to themselves, especially with regard to age, race, and gender. The quality of interactions is important because if the quality is low then people tend to avoid future interactions with diverse groups.

What are outcomes of experiencing leisure among diverse participants?

Regardless of ethnicity, culture, race, and other characteristics, individuals are intrinsically motivated to engage in meaningful activities because they have a desire to experience optimal positive well-being through leisure contexts. Although participants have different levels of socio-economic status and education, they often have similar goals when they participate in leisure services such as happiness, social interaction and a sense of connectedness, satisfaction, and a sense of competence and autonomy.

Even given these overarching similarities in motivations, there are some leisure participation motives that may be more important for different ethnic and racial groups.

> For example, McDonald and McAvoy (1997) concluded that Native Americans often visit outdoor recreation sites to maintain spiritual connections with nature. Also, Shaull and Gramann (1998) reported that many Hispanic Americans participate in leisure to help instill a sense of family cohesion.

Participation in leisure contexts that promote interactions between diverse participants can instill within participants a sense of belonging and create personal connections because the focus is on meaningful and enjoyable participation. This type of participation may alleviate negative consequences associated with cultural and racial differences and facilitate positive outcomes through meaningful participation. Leisure services can be designed so that close relationships between diverse participants are fostered.

Participation in leisure services that foster opportunities for positive interaction among diverse participants encourage people to establish friendships and reduce negative feelings toward group members who may not share certain characteristics. Services that promote positive interactions between diverse participants can lead to dynamic interactions and adaptations via the ability to:

- learn about others
- improve attitudes and behaviors
- generate friendships
- change perspective of the world

Learn About Others

When contact between diverse participants occurs in leisure contexts participants my initially learn about each other and different cultures. As participants get to know people who possess different characteristics they may reduce negative views of others and improve their attitudes.

> For example, Stephan and Stephan (1984) reported that Caucasians ("Anglos") had more favorable and positive attitudes toward those identified as "Chicanos" when they had engaged in previous interactions.

Leisure participation can enable diverse participants to learn from one another and develop positive attitudes toward specific groups.

> For example, Hugo and Melanie participate in a yoga class and experience an enjoyable way to relax and become more flexible. In addition to skill development, because the instructor communicates various aspects of the Hindu culture, participants are likely to learn about different cultural values and philosophical approaches.

Improve Attitudes and Behaviors

Leisure services that create a chance to interact with diverse people can help participants improve their attitudes and behaviors. Positive attitude changes can reduce prejudice and promote new respectful behavior.

> For instance, Jackman and Crane (1986) examined the relationship between Caucasians' racial attitudes to establishing personal connections with African-Americans and found that having repeated personal contacts between people of different backgrounds positively impacted their racial attitudes and, subsequently, their behaviors.

Based on these collective findings, it is likely that people who participate in leisure that facilitates contact with diverse participants will positively modify their behaviors.

> For instance, Janelle, who is African-American, participates in a Martial Arts class that exposes her to Eastern cultural values and beliefs. By doing so Janelle considers the perspective of people from Asia during interactions and increases the chance that she develops a positive attitude toward members of this group and treats those individuals with respect.

Develop Friendships

It can be valuable to offer leisure services that encourage participants to experience close social interactions that promote self-disclosure among diverse participants. Leisure participants can share information, skills, techniques, and related past experiences. These acts of sharing can lead to positive social interactions that become the foundation for more intimate relationships.

> As an example, Tai chi is offered by a leisure service agency. Kai is a Chinese immigrant who knows the movements of Tai chi and understands the philosophy of the technique. He volunteers by assisting participants with their form during class. This positive contact has led to enhancing other participants' understanding of the perspective of Chinese immigrants and has created a context for Kai to make new friends.

Change Perspective of the World

Leisure contexts that promote contact with diverse people can provide participants with insights about various cultures. As participants develop these insights they begin to reshape their worldviews that lead to more openness among diverse people.

> For example, Western cultures often emphasize individualism and independence and Eastern cultures often focus on collectivism and interdependence. Using a case report, Peregoy and Dieser (1997) demonstrated that although avoiding direct eye contact is identified as a symptom of low self-esteem in Western cultures such behavior is a way of demonstrating respect in many Eastern cultures.

Leisure services that promote positive interactions enable diverse participants to experience different cultural values and beliefs and facilitate a broad sense of social views.

> For instance, in individualistic cultures people often focus on their personal achievements and autonomy in terms of their choices, goals, and decisions. Alternatively, people raised in collectivist cultures often focus on positive social relationship. Also, people who have more individualistic values and beliefs tend to focus on personal achievement, whereas those who are more oriented toward collectivistic cultures tend to focus on social interactions and social harmony.

When people from a particular culture participate in leisure services that originate in a different culture, they may come to understand interests and desires of people from different cultures. This understanding can influence a person's overall perspective about the world. See Figure 10.2 (p. 200) for a summary of strategies of ways leisure services promote positive interactions and the associated benefits of these inclusive services.

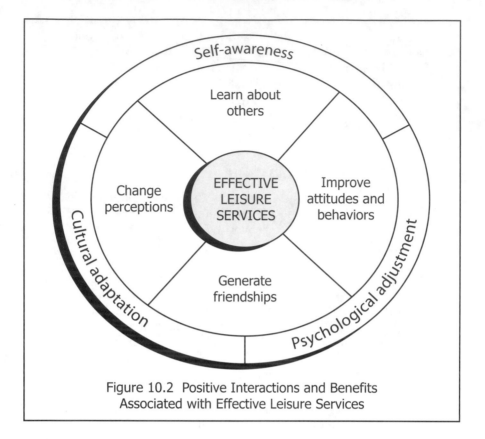

Figure 10.2 Positive Interactions and Benefits
Associated with Effective Leisure Services

What are benefits of leisure services that promote contact with diverse participants?

There are various benefits from engaging in leisure services that involve making contact with people of different cultures. The following three benefits are identified:

- self-awareness
- psychological adjustment
- cultural adaptation

Self-Awareness

Participants involved in activities that provide diverse interactions can potentially create a new, more complex identity. Individuals who experience cultural differences can develop the ability to cope with challenging situations and become open to new experiences that could lead to self-awareness.

Adler (1975, p. 22) argued that during encounters with people from different cultures, individuals often become aware of their values and cultural perspectives and suggested:

> *. . . paradoxically, the more one is capable of experiencing new and different dimensions of human diversity, the more one learns of oneself."*

Psychological Adjustment

Leisure contexts can create opportunities for participants to encounter people who having different perspectives. Participants can share with others the positive experiences of enjoyment, satisfaction, and self-determination.

As people make connections with diverse participants they may experience positive personal and psychological outcomes such as reduction of prejudice and anxicty and development of positive attitudes and behaviors.

> For example, Afanasi, who is a recent immigrant, experienced trauma and felt vulnerable as he struggled with cultural differences, family loss, prejudice and discrimination, language challenges, and limited social connections. Based on these challenges, he encountered difficulties adjusting to a new culture and became clinically depressed. After Afanasi began participating in a community soccer league he began to expand his social networks and increase his psychological support.

Cultural Adaptation

Leisure experiences can promote cultural adaptation. When immigrants interact with other people who have different racial or cultural backgrounds, they may encounter challenges and obstacles to engaging in healthy social interactions. These challenges can occur because of different customs, language and associated communication skills, and social norms. Nevertheless, participating in meaningful leisure pursuits may enable participants to negotiate these cultural differences and challenges.

If diverse participants share leisure experiences, they may discover previously unnoticed similarities in one another. People who experienced prior interactions with diverse people through shared leisure participation may maintain or develop social relationships with others who have different cultural values and beliefs in other contexts such as school or work. These positive encounters can lead to cultural adaptation.

How can leisure services be designed to promote positive interactions?

Given the diversity of people accessing leisure services, it is helpful to determine how to provide leisure contexts that promote positive interactions. In addition, it is valuable to encourage any person who avoids contact with specific groups to interact with members of these groups. The overall goal is to maintain social harmony diverse participants in spite of different cultural identities.

To encourage positive social interactions among diverse participants, leisure service providers may consider several strategies. The following techniques are a sample of approaches that may be used to facilitate positive interactions between diverse participants within leisure contexts:

- increase cultural awareness
- provide culturally diverse leisure experiences
- create leisure spaces that promote interactions
- offer cultural special events
- implement leisure education programs

Increase Cultural Awareness

Often leisure service managers have few ethnically diverse employees and these administrators have had limited prior experience serving multicultural groups. Based on this limited representation and exposure, it may be challenging to fully understand the complex nature of social interactions between diverse individuals and groups. Thus, it may be helpful to educate leisure service employees on ways to include people with various cultural backgrounds into the services they provide.

> For example, since a leisure service provider, Jason, had limited experiences serving Middle Eastern immigrants, he was having difficulty acknowledging their motives for participation. Jason was provided with information from his supervisor about traditions that are important to the leisure of many individuals from the Middle East, such as their religious beliefs, gender issues, and veiling and dressing habits. Subsequently, Jason now encourages positive interactions among participants and creates a variety of enjoyable leisure contexts.

Provide Culturally Diverse Leisure Experiences

Another way to promote positive interactions between people who differ in regards to ethnicity or race is to develop leisure services specifically designed to expose participants to diverse cultural situations.

> For instance, Jennifer, a leisure service manager understands that various recreation activities that can be used to teach participants from a Western society about beliefs and philosophies associated with Eastern cultures. As a result, Jennifer offers the following activities at the recreation center: dances such as Middle Eastern folk dancing and belly dancing, martial arts including Taekwondo and Karate, and fitness activities such as yoga and Pilates.

Participants involved in these activities may improve their cultural sensitivity and benefit from their participation. These experiences can be used as catalysts for purposeful and meaningful contacts and cultural adaptation.

Create Leisure Spaces that Promote Interaction

A variety of leisure spaces can be created to stimulate direct contact individuals of diverse backgrounds. Many playgrounds are designed to promote interaction between all children.

Another example of a specific type of leisure environment that is conducive for social interaction is community gardens. Shinew, Glover, and Parry (2004, p. 338) conducted research demonstrating positive effects of community gardens in urban settings and found that most participants felt that the activity brought together people of different races; the authors stated that:

> *Leisure settings can be ideal environments for interracial interaction to occur due to qualities of free choice and self-determination, which are important because they give individuals the opportunity to freely choose their companions without restrictions that often exist in work and other formal settings. Thus, interracial interactions that occur is leisure settings have the potential to be more genuine and sincere as compared to more obligatory interactions that take place in formal settings.*

Offer Cultural Special Events

Particular community events can promote cultural awareness and appreciation. These events can be developed to create positive experiences for participants and those providing the demonstrations, materials, and instruction.

Skill demonstrations, art festivals, and art exhibitions may all be venues for creating opportunities for people to learn about other cultures and interact with people who have different cultural backgrounds.

For instance, students and masters from martial arts studios may provide a demonstration in exchange for advertising their services. Such a performance setting may promote positive interactions between diverse audiences and performers. Also, international dance festivals can be offered that include various ethnic dances such as tango, Middle Eastern folk dances, and Hip-Hop. Dance teams can provide demonstrations, compete or have dance contests following instruction. Audiences and participants can share experiences and learn about different types of dance. Also, photography exhibits can be organized that document traditional leisure pursuits of other countries. Associated educational sessions can provide details about these activities. Pictures and illustrations can increase audience and participant awareness of different forms of leisure.

Cultural events can be helpful in creating positive interactions across diverse people. Leisure services that promote such interactions can result in participants who develop mutual understandings, adapt to a new culture, reduce their prejudice and anxiety, and generate friendships regardless of culture, race, and ethnicity. See Figure 10.3 for a summary of strategies that can be used to promote social interactions with diverse participants.

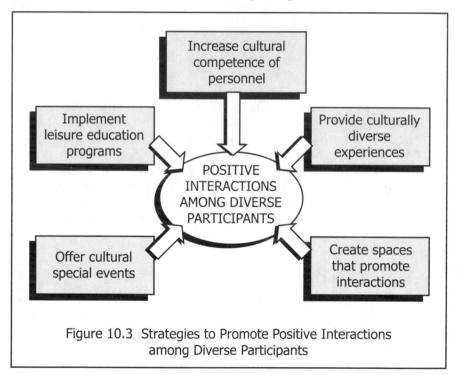

Figure 10.3 Strategies to Promote Positive Interactions among Diverse Participants

Implement Leisure Education Programs

In some situations there are a variety of leisure opportunities available to people of various ethnic and racial backgrounds. Unfortunately, many people encounter various challenges including language barriers, limited social networks, and limited knowledge of leisure resources.

These individuals can benefit from learning to redefine leisure in a broader perspective rather than simply a list of activities. As described in detail in Chapter 14, to help people cultivate social skills, gain knowledge of leisure resources, and encourage leisure involvement, we can educate these individuals about the importance of leisure and how they can use a variety of leisure services and resources. People can gain an appreciation for the benefits associated with leisure participation by attending leisure education classes.

Leisure education can be a process to help people of various ethnic and racial backgrounds to become aware of their abilities, talents, and interests.

> Leisure education programs may be designed to teach people to access leisure resources such as senior and fitness centers as well as hobby and social clubs in their communities. These venues can help people gain leisure and social skills that are valuable for developing connections within their communities.

Despite the availability of various leisure resources, some people may not fully utilize them because they may be unfamiliar with leisure resources. Leisure education programs can be designed to foster leisure participation through effective decision-making. Also, leisure education can help people establish new social networks that are regarded as the foundation of inclusion.

As described in Chapter 14, programs that include leisure awareness and appreciation, knowledge of leisure resources, development of leisure participation skills including activity skills, decision-making skills, and social skills, may be beneficial for many individuals including immigrants and people who are members of different ethnic and racial groups. Skills and knowledge acquired from such programs can assist individuals in pursuing optimal leisure involvement.

Final Thoughts

There are many leisure services that provide a context for developing meaningful personal contacts between people who are ethnically and racially diverse. We live in a diverse world where people are likely to regularly experience cultural and racial differences among people they encounter.

Recreation activities that promote positive interactions among diverse participants can encourage participants to develop an understanding of people who have different characteristics such as those related to ethnicity or racial heritage. These experiences have the potential to facilitate positive social interactions through cultural awareness, culturally diverse leisure experiences, leisure spaces that promote interactions, and cultural events.

Leisure services may contribute to reduced feelings of anxiety, prejudice, and negative stereotypes and foster cultural understanding, cultural adaptation, and improved cultural attitudes and behaviors. Contact created by shared leisure participation can facilitate development of meaningful relationships, discovery of personal similarities, and, in turn, produce positive feeling toward diversity and people who possess different characteristics. Such activities may alleviate negative effects caused by cultural differences and facilitate positive outcomes between people who differ relative to ethnicity, race and country or origin.

Finally, it can be helpful for us to be sensitive to the fact that people who are immigrants may experience challenges associated with their adaptation to a new culture and leisure constraints such as language barriers, cultural roles, limited social networks, and family dependence. By acknowledging these challenges, we can offer services that increase participants' awareness about the importance of leisure as well as encourages a sense of personal control and competence. Immigrants and others participating in leisure education can enhance their sense of personal leisure control and leisure competence as well as their psychological well-being.

We began the chapter with a quote from Leonard Pitts, Jr. (2009, p. 202) and now we will close the chapter with the response he gives to people who question why he writes articles about people who have been oppressed:

> *The most concise answer I can give is cribbed from what a white kid said some 40 or so years ago, as white college students were risking their lives to travel south and register black people to vote. Somebody asked why. He said he acted from an understanding that his freedom was bound up with the freedom of every other man.*

Discussion Questions

1. Why is it helpful to consider culture when providing leisure services?
2. How are the experiences of acculturation and assimilation similar and different?
3. What are some challenges to experiencing leisure that are some immigrants and members of other disenfranchised groups encounter?
4. Why is it useful to consider the impact of ethnic and racial differences on leisure participation?
5. What happens when diverse people experience leisure together?
6. What are some ways recreation activities can promote positive interactions?
7. What are aspects of personal growth that can occur through contact between diverse participants?
8. What strategies can leisure services providers use to promote positive interactions between diverse participants?
9. How can participation in leisure services promote cultural adaptation?
10. How might leisure education assist people of various ethnic and racial backgrounds?

Chapter 11
Sustain Healthy Aging and Older Adults

Elizabeth H. Weybright and John Dattilo

*It is not the years in your life but
the life in your years that count in the long run.*
-Adlai Stevenson

Orientation Activity

Directions Alone: Read the following portion of a conversation between Morrie Schwartz and writer Mitch Albom (1997, p. 117–119) from the book *Tuesdays with Morrie*. Next, prepare yourself to write for a few minutes—use a computer, pen and paper, or whatever works for you. When you are ready, check the time and give yourself four minutes to write a reaction to the conversation.

"All this emphasis on youth—I don't buy it," he said. ". . . the young are not wise. They have very little understanding about life. Who wants to live every day when you don't know what's going on? When people are manipulating you, telling you to buy this perfume and you'll be beautiful, or this pair of jeans and you'll be sexy—and you believe them! It's such nonsense."

Weren't you ever afraid to grow old, I asked?

"Mitch, I embrace aging."

Embrace It?

"It's very simple. As you grow, you learn more. If you stayed at twenty-two, you'd always be as ignorant as you were at twenty-two. Aging is not just decay, you know. It's growth. It's more than the negative that you're going to die, it is also the positive that you understand you're going to die, and that you live a better life because of it.

Yes, I said but if aging were so valuable, why do people always say "Oh, if I were young again." You never hear people say, "I wish I were sixty-five."

He smiled. "You know what that reflects? Unsatisfied lives. Unfulfilled lives. Lives that haven't found meaning. Because if you've found meaning in your life, you don't want to go back. You want to go forward. You want to see more, do more. You can't wait until sixty-five. Listen, you should know something. All younger people should know something. If you're always battling against getting older, you're always going to be unhappy because it will happen anyhow."

Directions with Others: Read the above portion of a conversation between Morrie Schwartz and Mitch Albom. Move into a small group of three to four people and discuss your reaction to the exchange. Ensure that each person has time to share their responses. Once finished, you may be asked to share your comments with the entire group.

Debriefing: From the moment we are born, we age; however, for most people, during the first 20 or so years, our bodies are growing and our minds are expanding. As we move into our 30s and 40s we stop physically growing, and we begin to detect some minor challenges associated with our aging.

> For example, when we engage in fitness activities, we might find that it takes us longer to get into shape and we quickly get out of shape when we stop exercising.

As we enter our 50s and 60s, we begin to experience physiological and biological declines to our bodies that are associated with the aging process.

> For example, we may need to increase the power of our eye glasses so we can read road signs when we are driving or we realize we may benefit from wearing eye glasses to read.

The changes continue to occur as we age. Although we experience physiological declines as we age, there are also benefits of aging, as aptly described by Mr. Schwartz. Each day we encounter learning opportunities—we have the chance to become wiser with each day that passes. It is amazing what we can learn from people who have many years of experience living. We also have chances each day to become better human beings. We can learn how to treat one another in a more caring and respectful manner.

Clearly, aging is one of those occurrences that can be viewed as a glass half empty or one that is half full. Morrie seems to view the process of aging and being an older adult as the glass being half full. The following are some questions to help you reflect on Morrie's comments.

- What do you think was Morrie's main point?
- How do you feel about Morrie's view of aging?
- How do you feel about how Morrie characterizes young adults?
- How do you feel about the concerns raised by Mitch?
- If you had a chance to speak with Morrie, what would you say to him?

Introduction

This chapter contains descriptions of common characteristics of aging and ways leisure service providers can promote healthy aging. Everyone who lives to be an older adult will experience the effects of aging. Aging is the inevitable and individual process of changeover tim including decreases in physiological, cognitive, and social skills such as reaction time, or increases in awareness and knowledge such as understanding of world events.

For the purposes of this chapter, the term older adults refers to the segment of the population that is 65 years of age and older, although some agencies (such as the Administration on Aging) define older adults as 60 years of age and older. The phrase 'older adults' is preferred by many older adults over words such as the 'elderly' or the 'aged.'

The group of people who are considered to be older adults is expanding across the world, and there are indications that this expansion will continue at an even faster rate in the future.

> According to the U.S. Census Bureau (2009), older adults in the United States account for an estimated 13% of the population (over 38 million). They are projected to comprise more than 16% (over 54 million) by 2020 and exceed 20% (over 80 million) by 2040. Not only will there be over twice as many older adults in the next 30 years, but they are living longer than ever. This same pattern can be found globally. There were 606 million older adults in the world in 2000, and this number is expected to triple in the next 50 years (United Nations, 2002).

In response to the rapid growth of this portion of our populations, the United States Older Americans Act (OAA) was signed into law in 1965, and established the Administration on Aging, which is currently housed in the Department of Health and Human Services within the federal government. This act was the first federal-level initiative to fund community services for older adults, including nutrition, supportive services, disease prevention and health promotion, caregiver support programs, and elder rights (Administration on Aging, 2009). The OAA (2006, Section 101, Objective 9) impacts leisure service professionals because it specifically states that individuals 60 and older are entitled to:

> *[e]qual opportunity to the full and free enjoyment of . . .*
> *participating in and contributing to meaningful activity within*
> *the widest range of civic, cultural, educational and training*
> *and recreational opportunities.*

This act identifies the importance of the provision of leisure services to older adults in local organizations such as senior community centers and area agencies on aging. Leisure is valuable not only because they are mentioned within the OAA, but also because leisure satisfies many needs and roles for older adults.

To address the topic of inclusion and aging, several questions are discussed in this lesson:

- What is ageism?
- What are changes that result from aging?
- What prevents older adults from experiencing leisure?
- What do older adults want?
- What are considerations for inclusion of older adults?

What is ageism?

Ageism is making an evaluation or judgment about an individual based solely on their age. These attitudes and stereotypes can be positive such as the belief that older adults are wise or they can be negative such as older adults are senile.

Perceptions that result from ageism can cause people to treat an individual differently because of their age and cause that person to experience discrimination. Older adults experience discrimination when younger individuals are given preferential treatment over older adults because those who are younger are assumed to be better and faster than older adults. Meneses and Monroe (2007, p. 25) expressed these sentiments about ageism:

> *As a result of ageism, older adults become a group of*
> *individuals that are being objectified and marginalized*
> *because they are no longer a member of the dominant group.*
> *Ageism also generates and reinforces fears and denigration*
> *of the aging process, and stereotypical assumptions regarding*
> *competence and the need for protection and legitimates the*
> *use of chronological age to mark out classes of people who*
> *systematically are denied resources and opportunities.*

As described in chapter 4, there are several possible ways to reduce negative attitudes and behaviors toward all people, including older adults. It is helpful for us to be aware of our beliefs and attitudes. Use the questions below to determine how you think about older adults.

- What do you think when you see an older adult?
- Do you offer to help them simply because they are older?
- Do you stay away because you are fearful of them?
- What stereotypes do you hold about older adults?
- What experiences shaped how you feel about older adults?

What are changes that result from aging?

As we age, natural changes in the body begin to take place, including physical and cognitive changes. Before we discuss these changes, consider the questions below and your experiences with older adults.

- What age-related changes have you noticed in adults whom you know?
- How do they deal with or compensate for these changes?

We will briefly review some changes associated the aging process and the impact they might have on engaging in leisure activities. McGuire, Boyd, and Tedrick (1996, p. 38–39) warned that assumptions should not be made about those getting older:

> *The gradual nature of the aging process allows most individuals ample opportunity to cope and adapt to the changes their bodies undergo. [Aging] is not synonymous with illness and disability. Most older adults are able to lead full, unencumbered lives well into old age. Many individuals are able to adapt and compensate for losses.*

Changes that occur through the natural aging process occur in several domains including:

- physiological
- cognitive
- social

Physiological Changes

Senescence is the term for physiological changes that occur to the body due to the aging process that include not only wrinkling of our skin or graying of our hair, but also many biological systems within the body. Changes occur to the cardiovascular system such as the weakening of the heart and to the respiratory system including a reduction in lung capacity. Freysinger (2000, p. 140–141) stated that:

> *While biological growth and development (or improvement) are associated with infancy, childhood, adolescence, and*

even young adulthood, as we move into middle age (typically defined as 40 or 45 to 65 years of age) the beginning of biological decline or decrements is expected. We tend to believe that such decline only accelerates in later adulthood. Certainly, research indicates that on average there is decreasing physical strength, flexibility, and endurance as we move into our forties and beyond. Our senses—vision and hearing in particular—also start to become less acute in midlife. There are hormonal changes: decreased production of estrogen in women and testosterone in men. Most dominant in our images of middle and later life are probably the overt physical changes that typically occur: thinning and/or graying hair, "laugh lines," "age spots," wrinkles, stooped posture, increased body fat, and decreased muscle definition. When such overt signs of aging are present, others often respond differently to us.

Although the physiological or biological changes listed below are common, it is helpful to consider that each individual is different and may experience different rates of decline over time.

- reduced muscle and bone mass
- decreased muscle elasticity
- stiffening of joints
- less efficient respiratory system
- less proficient cardiovascular system
- lost sensory abilities

Cognitive Changes

Cognition refers to brain functions such as learning, memory, and problem solving. Many older adults experience some impairment in cognitive functioning due to natural aging.

> For example, how well an older adult is able to attend to multiple processes is a main predictor of driving safety (McDowd & Shaw, 2000).

Often, cognitive changes are not as noticeable as physical changes, unless the individual has a disease or illness such as dementia. *Attention, reaction time*, and *memory* are three cognitive abilities that commonly change over time.

> Older adults are often stereotyped as "bad drivers," but in actuality they may have a more difficult time dealing with the multiple tasks that require their attention, such as safety hazards and surrounding traffic.

Older adults sometimes move slower due to physical limitations but also tend to process information slower than younger individuals. The time it takes an individual to react to a situation can lead to safety issues.

> Using the previous example, an older adult with a cognitive limitation may not react quickly enough to step on the brake pedal and may cause an accident with another vehicle.

Not all types of memory are impacted by the aging process. Memories that were created earlier in life and that are used regularly, such as the street where you were raised or a spouse's favorite meal, stay the same in the normal aging process. Other types of memory, including working memory, do decline slightly with age. Working memory includes both the storing and processing information.

> For example, if you were stopped by another driver asking for specific directions, you would have to take note of where the driver currently was and where the driver wanted to go. This involves remembering what the driver was asking as you mapped the route in your head. This task, using working memory, becomes more challenging with age.

As stated previously, it is useful to consider that the aging process is different for each individual. These declines do not happen to everyone and when they do, they occur in varying degrees.

Social Changes

As individuals age, so do their close friends and spouses. Issues such as aging, poor health, financial limitations, and death will limit the number of activity partners an older adult has to share various experiences. One way to help us understand the social changes that occur when people age is to consider the socio-emotional selectivity theory.

The *socio-emotional selectivity theory* postulates that as individuals age they will begin to reduce the number of people with whom they regularly interact.

> For example, an older adult may choose to focus on a small number of meaningful relationships with friends rather than having a large social network of coworkers and peers.

This theory is useful when considering the social activities and preferences of older adults. As the social network decreases, an older adult may choose to engage in recreation activities with only a specific group of friends and relatives.

What prevents older adults from experiencing leisure?

Before considering how to include older adults in leisure services, it is important to know why they avoid recreation and leisure experiences. In addition to the physiological, cognitive, and social changes associated with the aging process, additional barriers exist that can prevent older adults from experiencing leisure. Some of the more common constraints include:

- limited financial resources
- transportation challenges
- limited free time
- fears and safety concerns
- health impairments and disability

Limited Financial Resources

Many older adults are retired and, therefore, have a fixed income based on their savings and retirement accounts. Some may not be able to afford the cost of attending certain recreation programs. These individuals who may be on a fixed income often have skills that can be utilized by an agency.

> For example, Yoon is an older adult who immigrated from Korea over a decade ago. She is an amazing musician and is an excellent teacher. She and the local community center have worked out an arrangement that involves her providing music lessons to some children in exchange for a waiver of the annual membership fee.

Transportation Challenges

In addition to and related to financial concerns, transportation concerns can also prevent some older adults from engaging in enjoyable and meaningful leisure experiences.

> For example, Douglas would like to attend a pottery class that is held in the evening; however, he is uncomfortable driving a car when it is dark since it is more difficult for him to see oncoming traffic.

In addition to considering how a person will be transported to a program, the proximity of parking spaces to the facility is also important. Some people may be dissuaded from attending the program because the parking facilities are a considerable distance from the location of the program. The lengthy distance could raise concerns associated with physical limitations or safety issues resulting in an individual choosing not to attend the program.

Limited Free Time

Since many older adults are retired from their place of employment, they are perceived as having a great deal of free time. However, they often report a lack of free time. This lack of free time may be related to their financial situation. If people have less discretionary dollars, they will need to engage in home cleaning, maintenance and repairs themselves rather than hiring other people to complete these activities.

In addition, many older adults are often the main caregiver to their parents, spouse or significant other, friends, or even their aging children who may be experiencing an illness. These responsibilities in conjunction with their own age-related changes create substantial time constraints on their lives and limit their free time, not to mention the additional stress that occurs when a loved one is ill.

Fears and Safety Concerns

While participation in recreation activities can benefit older adults in many ways, some older adults may reduce participation because they are afraid they may become injured. When people feel discomfort while doing an activity, such as joint pain while walking, they may reduce how much they walk or stop walking altogether. Unfortunately, decreasing physical activity in this instance may only make joints stiffer.

Fear of falling is prominent among older adults and is a major health problem for community-dwelling, older adults. Such a fear can reduce physical independence, limit daily activities, and result in functional decline. People with a fear of falling often decrease physical activity, leading to reduced strength and balance. This may place them at a higher risk for falls and activity avoidance. Since a consequence of fear of falling is activity avoidance, which negatively impacts physical abilities, it may be helpful to encourage and support older adults in being physically active.

> In a study of 70 community-dwelling older adults, Hansma, Emmelot-Vonk, and Verhaar. (2010) identified that the second most common recommendation to reduce falls was to participate in an exercise program; unfortunately, only half the adults followed this recommendation.

The environment also impacts older adults' safety concerns. Inclement weather such as rain, ice, and snow is an additional safety concern to leisure participation due to fear of injury or illness.

Health Impairments and Disability

Health is often cited as the biggest barrier to physical activity in older adults. Health-related barriers can cause physical limitations, pain, fear of pain, and fear of falling. Voelkl and Aybar-Damili (2008, p. 187) reported the following:

> *The majority of the older-adult population report that at least one disability affects their activities of daily life. Limitations in activities because of health conditions are more likely to occur in advanced years. Twenty-eight percent of the population between age 65 and 74 and 50% of the population age 75 and older experience limitations in activities because of chronic health conditions.*

One of the more common physically disabling conditions often associated with aging is osteoarthritis. *Osteoarthritis* is defined as a slow, progressive, degenerative joint disease, coined the *aging disease*, that affects both men and women and is more prominent in adults age 50 and older. For more detail on osteoarthritis refer to Chapter 21 on physical disabilities.

One of the main illnesses associated with declines in cognition is dementia. *Dementia* is a unique diagnosis because instead of being an illness, it refers to a collection of symptoms including:

- memory loss
- language difficulties
- disorientation
- impaired judgment
- personality changes

These symptoms may be difficult to notice at first, but gradually worsen. The cognitive limitations are so severe that they cause impairment in social or occupational functioning. Alzheimer's disease is the most common type of dementia and is a progressive and fatal disease with no cure. Lifestyle strategies associated with healthy aging such as exercise, social activity, mental activity, and a balanced diet may offer some protection from or reserve against the disease. See Figure 11.1 for a summary of leisure barriers experienced by some older adults.

What do older adults want?

As individuals age, not only do their social networks change, but social roles change as well. They often move from identifying with an occupation, in which they have invested a lifetime of work, to being retired. After retirement, older adults continue to engage in enjoyable recreation activities that they participated in as young or middle-aged adults.

> A collaborative committee formed from several institutes within the National Institutes of Health has started the Cognitive and Emotional Health Project, which aims to identify the "demographic, social, and biological determinants of cognitive and emotional health in the older adult" (Hendrie et al., 2006, p. 14). Five independent factors were identified and appear to be

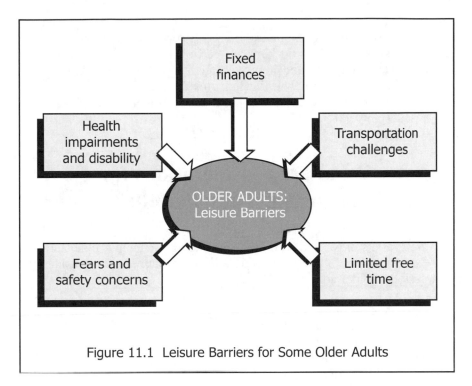

Figure 11.1 Leisure Barriers for Some Older Adults

consistent predictors of maintaining functioning. Three of these factors are: increased levels of physical activity or exercise, increased levels of cognitive stimulation, and increased social engagement.

Recreational activities can address these three factors by encouraging physical activity, providing intellectual stimulation, and facilitating social engagement. All people, including older adults, seek to experience leisure that fulfills specific needs or desires. Below is a list of these desires older adults may seek to satisfy through leisure:

- provide a socially useful service
- be a part of a community
- engage in meaningful leisure
- enjoy social activities with friends and family
- be recognized as an individual
- experience achievement and self-expression
- care for and protect their health

To address these needs, some individuals become more involved in their community following retirement by volunteering. Not only does this provide the individual with a sense of achievement, but it can also provide a socially engaging leisure pursuit. Older adults who participate in satisfying recreation activities report a higher quality of life.

For instance, Lloyd and Auld (2002) reported that there is a positive relationship between participating in leisure and physical activities and improved quality of life. This means that an older adult who participates in meaningful leisure activities tends to enjoy life more than someone who lacks satisfying activities.

What are considerations for inclusion of older adults?

There are a variety of ways to promote healthy aging and include older adults into leisure services. The following considerations are examples of considerations for inclusion of older adults:

- promote continuity
- provide novelty and challenge
- encourage physical activity
- stimulate mental engagement
- utilize technology
- encourage selection, optimization, and compensation
- communicate effectively
- provide intergenerational programs

Promote Continuity

Over the years, we develop leisure pursuits that bring meaning to our lives. Because participation in these activities meets many of our needs and increases our satisfaction and enjoyment, we want to continue to pursue these positive experiences.

Although older adults have the desire to continue to participate in activities that are familiar and meaningful to them, they may encounter challenges to their continued participation. As previously identified in this chapter, these challenges may result from barriers they experience as a result of ageism or physiological declines associated with aging.

As a result, it is helpful to be aware of the previous leisure participation patterns of individuals and to work with people to identify what may be preventing them from participating in their desired pursuits. To compensate for these constraints to leisure, many older adults can work with leisure professionals to make adaptations to leisure pursuits. Sometimes minor adaptations can be made to activity, equipment, and material that facilitate a person's continued leisure participation.

For example, Sophia has enjoyed playing cards at the local community center for many years. Lately she has been having difficulty holding the cards because of deterioration in her fine motor grasping skills. By simply using a block of wood with a slit cut in it where she places her cards allows Sophie the opportunity to continue to engage in an enjoyable activity that keeps were connected with her friends.

Provide Novelty and Challenge

Although, as previously described, many of us receive comfort from continuing our participation in activities we have previously enjoyed, we also desire novel experiences that come with trying new activities. New experiences can often bring excitement into our lives.

For example, since his 75th birthday, former President George H. W. Bush has been skydiving not once, but four times. He did a tandem skydive in 2009 to celebrate his 85th birthday. He shared his feelings about the experience with reporters, saying, "just because you're an old guy, you don't have to sit around. . . . Get out and do something. Get out and enjoy life." (Associated Press, 2009)

Sometimes leisure service providers are in a position to facilitate interactions between people and agencies that provide unique opportunities for people to experience novelty. These connections are often described as natural supports.

Natural supports are those people, equipment, or materials that typically are available in one's community that help a person engage in meaningful activities. It is valuable to set up systems to use natural supports because these supports that are embedded in the community are readily present and, therefore, encourage participation adherence. *Adherence* involves continued participation or involvement in a recreation activity or program over time.

Bullock, Mahon, and Killingsworth (2010, p. 73) provide a useful illustration of the use of natural supports that provide an opportunity for two men to experience a novelty:

John and the facilitator were exploring John's options for retirement. John lives in a rural setting and indicated that he "just wanted to go fishing." The two were having some difficulty figuring out how John could fish regularly because John could not drive and the river was two miles out of town. One evening, the facilitator was talking to a friend who told him that his dad (Larry) had retired recently and had taken up fishing with a vengeance, something he had always wanted to do. The light came on for the facilitator. Today, John and Larry go fishing three to four times a week, enjoy each other's company, and are catching lots of fish. This is natural support at its best!

Just because a person is older does not mean that he or she has a major physical or mental limitation. Enjoyable activities often have an element of challenge to them; it is important to match the difficulty of the activity to a person's skill level.

> For example, Cassandra, who resides at a retirement community, made the following comment: I like my stretch and tone class but the instructor is afraid he is going to work us too hard. I want to break a sweat but the instructor thinks we're too old to exercise like that.

Encourage Physical Activity

Research has demonstrated that physical inactivity can lead to declines in physical functioning and disability. Both low and moderate intensity activity protect against cognitive impairments.

> Results of the Canadian Study of Health and Aging indicate that individuals with cognitive impairments who participate in low-impact activities are almost 50% less likely than those who are physically inactive to develop further cognitive impairments (Laurin, Verreault, Lindsay, MacPherson, and Rockwood, 2001).

Adults with osteoarthritis may experience joint stiffness, and with disease progression their pain may also increase as a result of total joint failures. Apart from these symptoms, these adults often encounter challenges with mobility, range of motion and pain management.

> The Center for Disease Control (CDC) (2010) recommends older adults engage in 150 minutes of moderate intensity aerobic activity every week such as walking, swimming, and biking and muscle strengthening activities two or more days a week that work all major muscle groups; however, many older adults do not meet these recommended guidelines and remain physically inactive.

Low-impact physical activity such as walking and swimming has emerged to be an effective treatment for osteoarthritis in preventing and reducing pain and disability.

> Farhney, Kelley, Dattilo, and Rusch (2010) evaluated a goal-setting program on physical-activity engagement of older adults with osteoarthritis residing in the community. Results demonstrated an increase in physical activity levels after the program.

Recreation activity completed in the water, such as water aerobics or swimming, provides a context where individuals can typically participate with enhanced freedom of movement, greater independence, lower body temperature, less muscle stress, less energy expenditure, and less guarded actions associated with fear of falling. Activity in the water provides experiences of fun and challenge for many older adults. Water allows individuals to experience movement that can be performed on land with difficulty, if at all. Many people gain a sense of achievement as they learn to understand and control the different forces acting on their bodies in the water.

As older adults experience declines in physical functioning, they tend to stop engaging in physical activity. This creates a downward spiral, since reduced physical activity contributes to further reductions in physical functioning and development of health impairments. For this reason, it is important to match a desired recreation activity to the functional ability of the individual.

> For example, individuals who experience discomfort or painful physical symptoms such as shortness of breath or painful joints while engaging in physical activity should be informed about the physical characteristics of those activities and the benefits of participation. Shortness of breath could be interpreted as a symptom of a disease instead of a side effect of participation.

Stimulate Mental Engagement

Recent attention to lifelong learning over the last decade suggests that older adults are choosing to be learners and participate in learning experience during their free time as leisure pursuits. Adult education and lifelong learning often occurs in contexts that are conducive to leisure, since they are less formal than those typically experienced by children and youth.

Typically, lifelong-learning programs have identifiable learning outcomes but include no formalized assessment or certification completion and occur outside of traditional educational institutions and settings.

> Examples of these types of learning experiences include craft or home-maintenance retail-store classes, park and recreation courses, and art and cultural-organization programs.

Instructors in informal learning settings orient themselves toward the specific interests and needs of the learners. These programs are characterized by informality, interactivity and hands-on learning.

> Informal learning contexts can include topic-oriented leisure programs such as guided bird walks or night hikes, and home-craft classes such as furniture finishing.

In addition, it may be helpful to provide older adults with the opportunity to participate in recreation programs that are fun and stimulate their thinking.

Some programs focus solely on cognitive training including ACTIVE, which addresses memory, reasoning, and speed of processing. This program has been associated with improved memory abilities in older adults (Gamberini et al., 2008).

Activities that encourage problem solving such as crossword puzzles, board games, and card games can also promote improved cognition.

Schooler and Mulatu (2001) examined intellectual difficulty of recreation activities and found that more complex recreation activities were positively associated with a higher level of cognitive functioning.

Leisure professionals can provide services that increase enjoyment and stimulation for older adults and prevent cognitive decline. According to Stewart Brown (2009, p. 71):

Many studies have demonstrated that people who continue to play games, who continue to explore and learn throughout their life, are not only much less prone to dementia and other neurological problems, but are also less likely to get heart disease and other afflictions that seem like they have nothing to do with the brain. For instance, various studies have shown that only a small part of the risk of getting Alzheimer's disease is determined by genes. The majority of risk of Alzheimer's is attributed to lifestyle and environmental influences. One prospective study done at Albert Einstein and Syracuse Universities showed that people who had the most cognitive activity (doing puzzles, reading, engaging in mentally challenging work), the chances of getting Alzheimer's disease were 63 percent lower than that of the general population.

Studies have found links between some recreation activities, such as traveling, dancing, bowling, knitting, gardening, puzzles, and games, and delayed onset of Alzheimer's disease. Researchers have also discovered links between environmental enrichment and this disease. Given that play and leisure engagement are forms of environmental enrichment, these experiences can be instrumental in prevention of cognitive impairments such as dementia. Leisure and play's unique features, such as spontaneity, complete absorption, and fun, should help to stimulate the thinking processes of older adults.

Utilize Technology

There are a variety of technologies that can be used to deal with health-related changes that occur with aging. These technologies can help prevent health impairments, augment the environment so that it is more responsive to older adults, and provide a way to substitute for activities that individuals may be experiencing difficulty completing.

For example, Charness and Boot (2009, p. 256) offered insights about technologies that can be used to improve perceptual and cognitive functioning of older adults:

> *In recent years, numerous computer games and software packages have been developed and marketed to older adults seeking to attenuate or reverse age-related declines in perceptual and cognitive abilities. . . . Although far fewer older adults are gamers compared to younger counterparts, older adults are among the most active gamers, with many reporting playing almost every day (possibly because many are retired and have more free time).*

Interactive video games can offer a new, different, and stimulating activity for older adults. Game systems such as the Nintendo Wii or X-Box 360 Kinect provide older adults an activity using both physical activity and cognitive skills that can be used in a social or even intergenerational setting.

> For example, Weybright, Dattilo, and Rusch (2010) examined effects of Nintendo Wii bowling on attention and positive affect of older adults with a cognitive impairment. Results demonstrated that individuals were more attentive to the bowling game and enjoyed the activity more than comparable passive activities.

Encourage Selection, Optimization, and Compensation

Baltes and Baltes (1990) proposed that if these three strategies of selection, optimization, and compensation (SOC) are initiated, then successful aging will occur.

Although SOC is a general process of adaptation that can be applied to any stage of development, individuals vary in the degree to which they use each strategy. A more detailed examination of these three concepts follows.

Selection involves goal-setting. When older adults experience a decrease in skills and abilities, they must reconstruct their goal system, focus on important goals, or search for new goals.

> For example, when Rashall's arthritis becomes too severe to play tennis, he committed to another activity, walking.

Optimization refers to focusing on goal-relevant means such as time, effort, new skills, practice, and modeling, to accomplish goals and thus attain desired outcomes.

As an illustration, Mildred, a senior swimmer, competes in two events, the 100-meter freestyle and 200-meter backstroke, and is hoping to win her best event, freestyle, in an upcoming competition. Months before the competition, she realizes that her two events are held consecutively, with her best event second. She knows that competing in the backstroke may tire her and decrease her chances to win freestyle. Mildred decides to spend more time training for her best event (effort), gain more efficiency in the water by practicing her freestyle drills (practice) and, do what she has seen others do, use this first event as a warm-up instead of racing at full speed (modeling after others). Mildred is optimizing by spending more time and effort on her existing skills, by practicing and modeling others to achieve her desired outcome.

Compensation involves using alternative means to maintain a level of functioning when goal-relevant means are no longer attainable, by using adaptive equipment, acquiring new skills, obtaining resources, adapting time and effort spent, modeling compensation strategies, or receiving help.

For example, Efenia, who has a severe vision loss, may use a magnifying glass, an adaptive piece of equipment, to see small print when reading for pleasure or she may learn to use a talking computer, a new skill, to allow her to communicate with her children. Also, she may go shopping for books in the early morning, adapting her schedule, because the store is not as busy. Or, Efenia may go to a small local bookstore compared to a large discount center so it is easier to find what she needs, managing the effort spent, so that she has a greater chance of finding help if needed.

Communicate Effectively

When communicating with older adults, it is helpful to practice good public speaking skills. Speaking clearly, being articulate, facing the individual while making eye contact, and giving them plenty of time to respond are all important leadership skills that become even more essential when interacting with older adults. It is also useful to provide individuals plenty of time to respond to questions and to avoid jumping in and answering for the individual. For example, Rosco, a participant in a leisure-education fitness program, stated:

One of my biggest pet peeves is when people talk down to me. They assume I have a disability when, in reality, I can think just fine!

Given the safety concerns that many older adults have regarding getting to and participating in recreation activities, it is important to communicate effectively ways to increase safety for participants in recreation activities.

When considering safety, it is helpful to ensure that walking areas are properly lit. Also, it is important to maintain pathways so that they are clear and easy to access. Handrails and ramps are important to have in locations that are frequently accessed. These features can help someone with a physical limitation feel more comfortable and more easily participate in an enjoyable activity.

Provide Intergenerational Programs

One way to reduce negative attitudes about older adults is to provide intergenerational programs. Intergenerational programming is the offering of services that intentionally include both young and old individuals within recreation programs. Intergenerational programming can be facilitated by providing activities that both young and old enjoy.

> One example of such a program is children's story and reading programs. In these programs, older adults can be assigned to children to read stories to them and also help them to with their reading. Some programs include large couches that create a comfortable environment that often results in children learning against the adults or sitting on their laps.

Everyone wins when people of all ages participate together and experience leisure. Having personal experiences that include learning from or socializing with older adults can help people who are younger develop positive attitudes and associated respectful behaviors. Also, the relationships that develop between people of all ages help to validate the worth of the participants.

> For example, a study by Levy, Slade, Kunkel, and Kasl (2002) found that positive self-perceptions of aging can increase the life span of an older adult by almost eight years.

In addition to helping to reduce ageism and providing a meaningful context for older adults to engage in stimulating activities, intergenerational programs can be an effective way to address the reduction that occurs to older adults' social networks. Intergenerational programs can create a contact where older adults not only meet children, youth, and younger adults, but they also can meet and interact with older adults who are engaged in similar roles. See Figure 11.2 (p. 226) for a summary of strategies that can be used to include some older adults in leisure services.

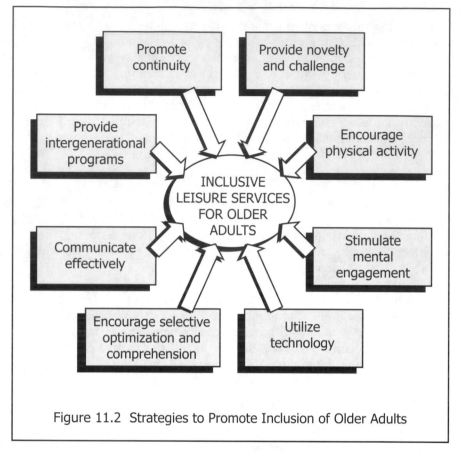

Figure 11.2 Strategies to Promote Inclusion of Older Adults

Final Thoughts

There are many people who are role models for healthy aging. Jimmy Carter, who served as the 39th President of the United States from 1977 to 1981, and his wife, Rosalynn, embody the spirit of healthy aging.

> For over 30 years after leaving office, Jimmy and Rosalynn Carter have actively promoted human rights throughout the world. The couple founded the Carter Center in 1982, a nonprofit organization that is dedicated to advancing human rights. These human-rights activities have allowed them to travel all over the world, see amazing sights, and enjoy meeting diverse people. The couple can also be found working on projects associated with Habitat for Humanity. In 2002, President Carter received the Nobel Peace Prize for his work to find peaceful solutions to international conflicts, to advance democracy and human rights, and to promote economic and social development through the Carter Center.

One way for leisure service providers to support healthy aging is to create inclusive leisure programs that address some of the unique considerations associated with aging and being an older adult. Older adults have had a lifetime to develop their leisure interests and habits and they have had a lifetime to develop important insights into life.

As an illustration, Sarah L. Delany (Sadie), who was 103 years old, and A. Elizabeth Delany (Bessie), her 101-year-old sister, were daughters of a man born into slavery. They agreed to work with Amy Hill Hearth to record their story, so that they could share their knowledge and experience with the next generation in their book titled *Having Our Say*. In their book, Bessie had this to say (1993, p. 186):

> *All I ever wanted in my life was to be treated as an individual.*
> *I have succeeded, to some extent. At least I'm sure that in the*
> *Lord's eyes, I am an individual. I am not a "colored person,*
> *or a "Negro" person, in God's eyes. I am just me! The Lord*
> *won't hold it against me that I'm colored because he made*
> *me that way! He thinks I am beautiful! And so do I, even with*
> *all my wrinkles! I am beautiful!*

Leisure service providers are in a position to promote health aging and respond to the desires of older adults and facilitate meaningful leisure experiences. The leisure experience is not necessarily just about the activity; instead, it is usually more about the meaning people connect with the activity and with whom they share their experience.

Discussion Questions

1. Why is it helpful for leisure service providers to learn about aging and older adults?
2. How does "ageism" influence the leisure involvement of older adults?
3. What are examples of physiological changes that are associated with aging?
4. In what way do older adults experience social changes?
5. What are some examples of common health impairments that occur as we age?
6. How might leisure service providers promote continuity in the lives of older adults?
7. Why is it helpful to provide the use of natural supports to promote leisure participation of older adults?
8. What are specific ways to encourage physical activity and stimulate mental engagement in older adults?
9. What are implications of selection, optimization, and compensation on leisure for older adults?
10. What are some characteristics of intergenerational programs?

Chapter 12
Address Income and Economic Challenges

David Scott and John Dattilo

Poverty is like punishment for a crime you didn't commit.
-Eli Khamarov

Orientation Activity: Whose problem is it?

John Scalzi writes a blog called *Whatever*. On September 3, 2005, he posted an entry called *Being Poor*. Scalzi offered over 60 examples of what it means to be poor. Below is a subset of what he wrote.

Directions Alone: Read the following statements. You may wish to go to Scalzi's (2005) website for a complete list. Write down your reactions to the statements.

Directions with Others: Read the following statements. You may wish to go to Scalzi's (2005) website for a complete list. Divide into small groups and discuss your interpretation of the statements with other members. Make sure everybody in your group has an opportunity to share his or her reactions. After a specified time, share your responses with the entire class.

- Being poor is hoping the toothache goes away.
- Being poor is coming back to the car with your children in the back seat, clutching that box of Raisin Bran you just bought and trying to think of a way to make the kids understand that the box has to last.
- Being poor is hoping your kids don't have a growth spurt.
- Being poor is Goodwill underwear.
- Being poor is feeling the glued soles tear off your supermarket shoes when you run around the playground.
- Being poor is relying on people who don't give a damn about you.
- Being poor is needing that 35-cent raise.
- Being poor is six dollars short on the utility bill and no way to close the gap.
- Being poor is crying when you drop the mac and cheese on the floor.
- Being poor is a six-hour wait in an emergency room with a sick child asleep on your lap.

Debriefing: Scalzi's blog received a great deal of attention and was even published in the *Chicago Tribune*. His statements provide a stark glimpse of what it means to be poor.

Many Americans, of course, struggle now and then to make ends meet. Many college students who are putting themselves through school understand clearly what it means to live on a fixed income. Few of us, however, can truly relate to what it means to be abjectly poor.

Too often we blame people for their own misery. Understanding what it means to be poor should provide us compassion and skills to aid people who are economically challenged. Consider the following questions as you reflect on this exercise:

- Can you describe an instance when you felt hungry because you could not afford to buy food?
- How would you go about paying bills when you knew you did not have enough money to make ends meet?
- How would it feel to be cut off from other people because they had more money than you?
- What would you tell your children if you could not afford to enroll them in little league, ballet, day camp, or swimming lessons?
- What are your feelings about people who are obviously poor?

Introduction

One group of people who tend to be significantly disadvantaged when it comes to leisure opportunities are those of lower socioeconomic status and those who are homeless. Regardless of their gender, racial and ethnic background, age, or ability status, these are people who have the least material resources to devote to recreation participation.

Given the above comments by Monika Stodolska (2010, p. 106), people who have low income, identified as living in poverty, or who are homeless encounter major challenges in experiencing leisure. In this chapter, we examine what it means to live with a low income and how a low income is related to our leisure involvement. In theory, leisure amenities are available to all us irrespective of our socio-economic status.

> For example, in the United States, publicly funded park and recreation amenities were actually created in the early 20th century so they would be accessible to people concentrated in low-income communities.

Today, around the world, leisure service providers struggle to meet the leisure needs of those who are economically challenged. This situation is exacerbated by the fact that inequality among Americans is on the rise. In this chapter, the following questions are addressed:

- What is social stratification?
- What is a low income?
- How is income related to life chances?
- What prevents people from experiencing leisure?
- How do we lessen constraints to leisure?

What is social stratification?

In virtually all societies, people have varying access to material and scarce resources. Sociologists use the term *social stratification* to refer to a hierarchical ranking of people based on wealth and power.

Although all societies are stratified, they differ strikingly in their degree of inequality. Small agrarian and foraging societies are relatively equal, while larger industrial and post-industrial societies are characterized by large disparities in wealth and power.

Many sociologists believe that powerful groups seek to perpetuate inequality over time. According to Charles Tilly (1999), they do this in two ways. The first of these is through *exploitation*, which occurs when powerful people take possession of resources and goods produced by others and prevent them from fully benefiting from their labor. The second mechanism is what Tilly described as *opportunity hoarding*. As the term suggests, this is the process of powerful groups taking control of scarce resources and limiting less powerful groups from accessing these resources through fees, rents, and prohibitions. Together, these mechanisms consolidate wealth, limit upward mobility, and perpetuate inequality.

Stratification, of course, exists across the globe, and there has always been inequality in regard to income and wealth. In many countries in recent years, however, income disparities have risen, with wealth becoming increasingly concentrated among the richest citizens.

> For instance, since 1980, incomes among U.S. wealthy have risen, but among the middle class and poorer they have remained constant or shrunk. According to Massey (2007), the richest 1% of U.S. citizens control approximately 40% of the national's total wealth. To put this in perspective, the top 300,000 U.S. citizens, collectively, earn as much income as the bottom 150 million (Johnson, 2007).

What is a low income?

The focus of this chapter is to increase understanding about those who lack wealth or, more simply, those who have limited income. What does it mean to have a low income? Perhaps the simplest definition of *low income* is the state of being poor or lacking material comforts. This definition comes close to the definition of poverty.

In 1964, the Social Security Administration provided an "official" definition of poverty, which was the smallest amount of money it cost to feed a family. In 2009, the poverty line for Americans living in the continental United States was $20,400 for a family of four (U.S. Department of Health & Human Services, 2009). According to this definition, there were 43.6 million people in the United States living in poverty in 2009. Put differently, 14.3% of U.S. citizens were defined as living in poverty, the highest poverty rate since 1994 (DeNavas-Walt, Proctor, & Smith, 2010).

Some groups are more likely to live in poverty than others.

For instance, according to the U.S. Census Bureau (2009), higher rates of poverty are reported among: people of color (Asian/Pacific Islands, Blacks, and Hispanics), those under the age of 18, and female-led households. In 2009, an astonishing 41.6% of U.S. female-led households lived in poverty, compared to 2.5% of households that included a married couple.

There is a human tendency to "blame victims" for their circumstances. In other words, people often believe that those with low incomes live the way they do because they do not work hard enough or they are somehow morally deficient. The reality is that many people living in poverty work long hours to barely make ends meet.

For example, U.S. citizens who hold minimum-wage jobs and support a family of four would have to work over 58 hours a week, 52 weeks a year, to live above the poverty-line threshold.

How is income related to life chances?

Level of income influences life chances—that is, opportunities people have to improve the quality of their life. In general, level of income is highly related to being able to access a variety of social services and amenities.

As an illustration, compared to others, low-income U.S. citizens are far more likely to be restricted in their choice of residence and neighborhood schools for their children, as well as in their access to food and health coverage (Scott & Munson, 1994). They are also far more likely than others to be victims of crime and family violence, experience drug addiction, mental illness, infant mortality, and come from a household where two parents are not present (Wilson, 1987). U.S. citizens with low incomes are also disproportionately homeless or close to being homeless (Trussell & Mair, 2010) and more likely to live in communities with high levels of environmental toxins (Evans & Kantrowitz, 2002).

What effect does a low income have on leisure behavior?

Several studies, such as those completed by Lee, Scott, and Floyd (2001) as well as Scott and Munson (1994), have documented that people who have low incomes are far less likely than others to:

- spend money on leisure
- travel
- participate in artistic activities
- participate in outdoor recreation activities
- exercise
- visit zoos
- visit local, state, and national parks
- use municipal public park and recreation amenities

As noted by Chubb and Chubb (1981, p. 94), a low income limits a person's access to a wide range of leisure resources:

> *The poor do not have the recreation rooms, landscaped backyards, automobiles, recreation vehicles, seasonal homes, and other amenities that enhance the recreation environment.*

Following World War II, a two-tier system of publicly funded park and recreation provision evolved in the U.S. On the one hand, there are suburbs and wealthy communities that enjoy strong financial support for parks and recreation. Residents in these communities have easy access to an array of quality park and recreation amenities. On the other hand, there are inner cities and poor communities that lack basic funding for municipal services. Residents in these areas have limited access to parks and recreation amenities.

Although people with low incomes may be dependent on publicly funded park and recreation facilities and programs for their leisure, the reality is they are less likely than their affluent counterparts to make use of these programs and facilities during their leisure time.

What prevents people from experiencing leisure?

If we are to better serve those who have low income, it is important to understand factors that constrain their leisure involvement. Obviously it costs money to do things, and people with low incomes have limited discretionary income. There are many ways, however, in which people with low income are constrained in their leisure beyond a lack of discretionary income.

> In fact, research has shown that people with low income report a wider range of constraints to leisure involvement than those who are more affluent (Scott & Munson, 1994).

Multiple constraints work concurrently to limit leisure participation among people with low income. Before proceeding, it is important to understand a little about how researchers have approached the study of leisure constraints. First, *leisure constraints* include those factors that limit people from:

- participating in recreation activities
- using of leisure services
- enjoying current activities
- developing leisure preferences

Early studies on leisure constraints tended to focus on factors that prevented people from participating in *desired* activities. Most of these factors were also thought to be physical and outside the control of the individual. From this perspective, people with low incomes were thought to be constrained in their leisure because they lacked discretionary income, recreation equipment, and accessible facilities

Although true, as we shall see, people with low incomes encounter several other problems in their pursuit of leisure. As discussed in previous chapters, characteristics that are correlated with low income include: problems with physical and mental health, disability, as well as being a member of an oppressed racial of ethic group. Stodolska (2010, p. 101, 107–108) stated that:

> *Poverty is also correlated with health problems and disabilities . . . psychological states of depression and low self-esteem, which can decrease the desire to participate in active, out-of-home leisure activities that require higher organizational involvement and social interactions . . . many members of ethnic and racial minorities are constrained by the lack of financial resources to participate in leisure activities.*

A crucial change in the way we think about leisure constraints occurred when researchers began to understand that constraints could also be internal and include such things as personality and individual dispositions.

Crawford and Godbey (1987) argued that constraints influence other facets of people's leisure beyond just participation. They recognized that constraints impact both leisure participation *and* leisure preferences. They proposed the following three types of constraints that help us better understand why people with low incomes are thwarted in their pursuit of leisure:

- intrapersonal
- interpersonal
- structural

Intrapersonal Constraints

Intrapersonal constraints are psychological states that prevent people from developing leisure preferences.

> Researchers have documented intrapersonal constraints among women with stereotypic feminine personalities (Henderson, Stalnaker, & Taylor, 1988), adolescents with low self-esteem (Raymore, Godbey, & Crawford, 1994), and people with disabilities who experience learned helplessness, as described in previous chapters.

These individuals are far more likely than others to report they lack interest, skills, confidence, and knowledge to participate in a range of leisure activities. Having a low income can prevent a person from developing leisure preferences in the following four ways:

- lack of formative experiences
- lack of information
- stigma
- poor health

Lack of formative experiences. Early childhood experiences in leisure tend to carry over into adulthood. This means the type of leisure activities we grow up doing are ones we tend to pursue as adults.

Likewise, our leisure as youngsters is very much related to our family's socioeconomic status. People who are relatively well-off are in much better positions than others to pass on to their children skills, knowledge, and appreciation of outdoor activities, sports, music, literature, and the arts. They do this by enrolling them in classes, lessons, and club memberships; providing them necessary equipment and transportation; and supporting them via attendance and encouragement. They also vacation regularly with their children, thereby providing them rich formative experiences in the great outdoors and exotic destinations. People who are well-off can take for granted that their children will be able to participate in a range of recreation activities that can be pursued in later life.

In contrast, many people who are poor lack financial resources to spend on leisure activities and travel. Growing up poor means they are unlikely to acquire the same skills, knowledge, and appreciation of recreation activities and leisure destinations. As a result, their leisure preferences tend to be limited to pursuits that are relatively inexpensive and ones that require little in the way of skill development. Importantly, as adults their knowledge of recreation activities and amenities tend to be more constricted than individuals who grew up in more affluent households. The following quotation reported by Erickson et al. (2009, pp. 537–538) shows how growing up poor limited one African American's knowledge of Rocky Mountain National Park:

> *We had the freedom [to] . . . go where we wanted to go, [but] we still didn't have the capital or the resources to be able to enjoy recreation. We spent so much time working trying to scratch out a living; we didn't have time for that type of recreation and relaxation. . . . For a very long time, those programs were dominated by people who had the money to do it. And typically, African Americans typically didn't.*

Lack of information. Leisure practitioners recognize that many people do not use amenities under their jurisdiction because they lack information about agency offerings.

> A nationwide study by Geoffrey Godbey and colleagues (1992) revealed lack of information was the second most frequently cited barrier, behind lack of time, given by U.S. citizens as a reason for not participating in locally sponsored leisure activities.

Lack of information can be particularly difficult for people who are poor. Because many people with low incomes are unable to afford to use community leisure services, they are unlikely to be included on agency mailing lists.

> As an example, Harnick (2010) reported that some leisure service agencies send advertisements about agency offerings only to current and past customers.

People who have low incomes are also less likely than others to have access to the Internet and other electronic media that provide information about community events and programs. Many people with low incomes are simply "out of the loop" when it comes to knowing about park and recreation opportunities in the communities in which they live.

Stigma. Many people with low incomes are stigmatized and are dependent on social welfare services for assistance. This is particularly true for people who are homeless or close to being homeless. Assistance comes in the form of food and clothing banks, shelter, counseling, and medical care. According to Trussell and Mair (2010, p. 516), receiving assistance comes at a steep price:

Many individuals receiving social assistance face high levels of depression and shame. They also experience the de-habilitating effects of isolation and loneliness.... The stigma associated with accessing social supports comes from the support structures themselves, but also from the broader society and the feeling of being looked down upon by others.

Receiving social assistance often requires people with low incomes to prove they are poor and eligible for public assistance, and provide caregivers information about their lives they would rather keep private. Baker Collins (2005) stated that people who receive regular assistance feel as though they live under a giant microscope and under constant surveillance.

Blatant intrusion into the lives of low-income people, according to Baker Collins, contributes to an erosion of dignity, self-esteem, freedom, and agency. All of these feelings are linked to diminished interest in accessing community leisure services.

Poor health. One of the costs of having a low income is inadequate access to health coverage.

> As an illustration, health coverage in the United States is viewed as a privilege and one that is apportioned unevenly by race, ethnicity, and social class (Massey, 2007). Many U.S. citizens who have low incomes do not have primary caregivers and must rely on emergency rooms for medical care.

Likewise, many people with a low income who work do not have the luxury of taking time off for being sick. Being absent from a low-paying job often means loss of wages or, worse, being fired. Many of these same jobs are physically demanding and leave workers tired and in constant pain. Journalist Barbara Ehrenreich (2001, p. 33) found out this the hard way because she wanted to see what it meant to be poor, so she took on low-paying jobs and found herself:

[t]ossing back drugstore-brand ibuprofens as if they were Vitamin C, four before each shift, because an old... repetitive injury in my upper back has come back to full-spasm strength, thanks to the tray carrying.

It is no wonder, then, that people who have low incomes are far more likely than others to report that illness and poor health prevent them from participating in leisure service programs.

> For instance, Scott and Munson (1994) studied how level of income was related to people' use of public parks in northeast Ohio. Level of income was the best predictor overall of why people said they did not use parks more often. In fact, 33% of people with low incomes said that poor health was a very

important constraint to their use of parks. Less than 3% of respondents in the highest income group reported poor health as a constraint. These results held true even when controlling for other factors, including age and gender.

Interpersonal Constraints

Interpersonal constraints are barriers that arise out of social interaction with friends, family, and strangers. Interpersonal constraints may shape both leisure preferences and leisure participation. Researchers have shown that interpersonal constraints may take the form of negative attitudes, harassment, scheduling problems, and lack of partners.

For example, fear of violence or harassment prevents many women and people of color from visiting public parks and recreation facilities (Bialeschki, 2005; Erickson et al., 2009).

The following three interpersonal constraints make leisure problematic for people with low income:

- worrying about safety
- feeling unwelcome
- experiencing isolation

Worrying about Safety. Many people who are privileged worry little about being assaulted or harassed while pursuing recreation activities. Many people who are poor, however, live in low-income neighborhoods where crime and physical assault are familiar experiences. In fact, fear of crime is among the most frequently reported reasons why many people with low income do not make greater use of community leisure facilities near where they live.

The park-use study reported earlier (Scott & Munson, 1994) revealed that over half of all low-income residents in northeast Ohio said that fear of crime was *very important* in limiting their use of parks in the area. In contrast, only 16% of people with high incomes felt that fear of crime limited their use of public parks. In the same study, 86% of low-income residents reported they might use parks more often if they were made safer.

Regrettably, safety concerns and fear of harassment are common barriers to leisure among people who have low incomes.

Feeling unwelcome. A related barrier to leisure among people with low incomes is feeling unwelcome when they use community services. Leisure service professionals may provide them inferior treatment and monitor their movements and actions lest they engage in criminal behavior. Affluent participants frequently treat people who are poor as outcasts and unworthy of civility.

> For instance, public parks and recreation facilities in the United States are sometimes touted as being places where people of all classes, races, and ethnicities can mix equally and without fear of ostracism. Theory and reality are very different. There are many examples of upper- and middle-class U.S. citizens who have sought to distance themselves from those who are poorer than they (Rosenzweig & Blackmar, 1992).

Some affluent people have gone so far as to create community associations that put restrictions on who is eligible to use local park and recreation amenities. Unhappily, many people with low incomes are often made to feel loathsome and inadequate by recreation workers and other visitors.

Experiencing isolation. A low income constrains leisure by undermining opportunities to interact with friends and family who are more affluent. Strapped for cash, people with low incomes are often unable to interact with friends and relatives who have the discretionary money to go out to bars, clubs, restaurants, or coffee shops.

They are also not able to join more affluent friends and family members who are able to go on vacation, attend a concert, go skiing, go to the movies, go to a ball game, visit a zoo, or go bowling. They may even avoid visiting a friend or family member in the latter's home because they may not have the discretionary income to extend a reciprocal invitation.

Relationships take time to nurture. But relationships are also frequently pursued in leisure contexts that require some exchange of money. For people who lack funds to meet in such places, opportunities to visit with friends and family members can be limited. Invitations from more affluent friends and family members may actually cease because they know their poorer relations do not have the money to go out. Sadly, having a low income can lead to a feeling isolated and being alone.

Structural Constraints

Structural constraints are factors that intervene between leisure preferences and participation; they are barriers that prevent people from doing what they would like to do. Structural constraints are how many professionals typically think about barriers and include those factors that are outside the control of the individual, including family life stage, family resources, and available opportunities and transportation. There are at least three structural constraints that make leisure participation problematic for people who have low incomes:

- fees and costs
- lack of accessible facilities
- lack of transportation

Fees and costs. Much has been written about the impact of fees and charges on limiting access to recreation and park programs among people with low incomes.

The general consensus is that fees and charges negatively impact the ability of people who have lower incomes to access leisure services (Burns & Graefe, 2006).

Even a modest fee to a swimming pool or recreation center may be enough to deter low-income earners from accessing these facilities.

Entrance fees, however, are the tip of the iceberg. In some leisure programs, participants are required to purchase equipment and uniforms. In youth programs, there are also informal norms about treating children to snacks after a game. Many children from middle-class and affluent families are now involved in club (select) teams that require extensive out-of-town travel. All these costs can be prohibitive for families who have limited means.

Lack of accessible facilities. Many people with low income reside in communities that are themselves impoverished. In some urban areas, the problem is exacerbated by the fact that wealth and potential tax revenues have migrated to affluent suburbs.

> As an illustration, Massey (2007) determined that over the last 30 years, poorer cities and communities throughout North America have struggled mightily to provide residents basic services. Furthermore, because of land acquisition decisions made in the past, these same communities are ones that have been historically deprived of parks and recreation amenities (Boone, Buckley, Grove, & Sister, 2009).

Today, people who have low incomes are far more likely than others to live in communities where there are only low quality park and recreation amenities of limited accessibility.

> To drive this point home, let's return to the study described earlier in the chapter from northeast Ohio (Scott & Munson, 1994). Of those who said they were infrequent visitors of public parks, a small fraction reported that parks were too far away. However, 33% of those respondents in the lowest income category (less than $15,000) said that accessibility was *very important* in limiting their use of public parks. In contrast, less than 6% of people in the highest income group ($50,000 or more) reported accessibility was a very important barrier to their use of public parks in northeast Ohio. These results have been replicated more recently by Mowen, Payne, and Scott (2005) and Shores, Floyd, and Scott (2007) and suggest that accessibility is a major constraint to leisure among low-income Americans.

Lack of transportation. To make matters worse, numerous people with low incomes lack reliable transportation. Many of these individuals do not own their own automobiles. The kind of vehicles that such individuals *do* possess are prone to frequent breakdowns.

People with low incomes are far more likely than others to be dependent on public transportation, which can be an inefficient means for accessing leisure resources. On the one hand, many recreation and park facilities—county parks, state parks, and national parks—are not on public transit routes. Those that are linked via public transit frequently require multiple transfers and stops. Outings to parks and other leisure settings that require public transit can be very time-consuming affairs indeed.

> Let's again return to the northeast Ohio study previously mentioned (Scott & Munson, 1994). Over one-third of low-income respondents who were infrequent users of public parks said they had no way to get to parks. Twenty-eight percent reported they lacked public transportation to parks. In contrast, less than 2% of high-income earners said they had no way to get to parks and less than 1% said they were unable to visit parks because they lacked access to public transportation. Significantly, individuals with low income were three times more likely than those with high income to say they would probably visit public parks more often in northeast Ohio if public transportation was available. In sum, lower-income Americans are transportation-disadvantaged—a condition that is not that much different than one experienced by people who have physical disabilities.

Relationships among Constraints

It is important to note that intrapersonal, interpersonal, and structural constraints are interrelated (see Figure 12.1, p. 242). Crawford, Jackson, and Godbey (1991) theorized that the three categories of constraints are related in a hierarchical fashion. This means that constraints are encountered, first, at the intrapersonal level. Intrapersonal constraints are the most powerful constraints, since they limit preferences and suppress motivations.

If preferences are formed, then people with low incomes need to surmount interpersonal constraints. Participation may be curtailed if the individual is unable to locate suitable partners or encounters unwelcome employees and/or recreation participants.

Finally, if both intrapersonal and interpersonal constraints are successfully negotiated, people with low incomes encounter structural constraints. If sufficiently strong, these constraints may result in low-income people not using community leisure services at their own desired level of intensity.

Elsewhere, Jackson, Crawford, and Godbey (1993) argued that intrapersonal, interpersonal, and structural constraints interact with one another in ways that further limit people's ability to access park and recreation amenities. How does this work with people with low incomes? As noted above, many people with lower incomes experience harassment (an interpersonal constraint) from

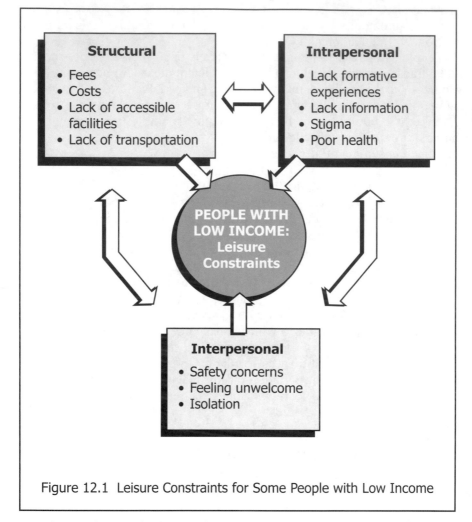

Figure 12.1 Leisure Constraints for Some People with Low Income

recreation workers and other participants. These experiences may be powerful enough to result in people developing negative attitudes, an *intrapersonal constraint*, about the activity and recreation locale. Transportation and accessibility problems, *structural constraints*, may prevent people from acquiring skills and knowledge, *intrapersonal constraints*, about what kinds of opportunities are available at recreation areas.

It is also helpful to recognize that constraints work in tandem. This means that multiple constraints *operate simultaneously* to make leisure problematic for people with low incomes.

> State and national park managers, for example, must recognize that fees and charges are only one set of barriers that limit those with low incomes from accessing the great out-of-doors (Shores et al., 2007).

People with low incomes lack adequate transportation, skills, and knowledge. They are also apprehensive about how they will be treated on site. These and other factors work simultaneously to limit leisure among those who have low incomes.

How do we lessen constraints to leisure?

Facilitating leisure among people with low incomes requires recognition of their barriers to participation. As noted, constraints may block participation in desired activities but they may also inhibit people with low incomes from developing leisure preferences.

Leisure constraints, however, are not insurmountable. Like anyone else, a person with a low income can negotiate constraints and participate in desired leisure activities. Leisure service agencies are in a position to facilitate leisure participation among people with low incomes. They need to include multiple strategies as they seek to lessen the constraints that inhibit leisure among people with low incomes. In this last section, six major strategies are described that facilitate leisure for people with lower income:

- engage in advocacy
- provide instruction
- improve safety
- welcome leaders
- make programs affordable
- enhance access

Engage in Advocacy

Leisure service agencies face formidable challenges serving people who have low incomes. The biggest challenge they face as they diversify program offerings is political.

> For example, a large proportion of U.S. citizens firmly believe that publicly funded leisure programs and facilities are already available to all, and practitioners' efforts to provide programs and services to people with low incomes are pointless and financially irresponsible (Scott, in press).

Indeed, many people who are affluent believe that if some people do not want to use park and recreation services, it is simply a matter of their own free will. At the same time, many people who are privileged are averse to sharing parks and other leisure spaces with people who are poor.

Public park and recreation agencies will need strong and influential allies as they advocate for improved leisure service delivery. If they are unable to rally support for diversifying programs, many people with low incomes will continue to encounter numerous obstacles to leisure.

Provide Instruction

As noted above, many people with low incomes lack formative experiences in many recreation activities. This means that leisure service agencies will need to create programs that include basic instruction in different activities.

> For instance, the Texas Parks and Wildlife Department (TPWD) seeks to do this by providing grants to municipalities and nonprofit groups who, in turn, create programs for low-income youth and family that introduce them to different outdoor recreation activities. Many of these programs include overnight camping trips to state parks where people learn how to set up a tent, cook over a camp fire, and learn about the natural history of the area. These programs help participants develop outdoor recreation skills and develop an appreciation for parks and outdoor activities. TPWD's grant program was created with the understanding that people with low incomes do not participate in outdoor recreation, in part, because they lack necessary skills and interest.

Improve Safety

People with low incomes are unlikely to use community park and recreation resources if they feel threatened on site or while traveling to the site. Scott and Munson (1994, p. 93) stated that, at minimum, leisure service personnel:

> *[m]ust be committed to bolstering existing law-enforcement programs, including highly visible car and bicycling patrols, facility surveillance, and strategic placement of telephones for receiving and responding to distress calls.*

In some low-income communities, park and recreation professionals have worked hard to eradicate gangs and others who make parks and facilities unsafe. They have done this through innovative programs that make parks and other facilities vibrant. The point is that parks and community facilities that are busy and full of people are perceived as less dangerous than ones that are empty and lifeless.

Welcome Leaders

Leisure service personnel must strive to be more welcoming to people with low incomes. Too often, visitors who have low incomes are made to feel undesirable and unworthy of quality service. Although most public park and recreation agencies provide employees diversity training, these efforts are often more symbolic than they are substantive.

If agencies are to better serve residents with low incomes, principles of inclusion must permeate the organization from top to bottom. This means that *all employees*—from locker-room attendants, custodial workers, and facility attendants, to recreation leaders and instructors, counselors, park rangers, and managers—must be committed to inclusion and helping all visitors feel welcome.

Consistent with ideas expressed elsewhere in this book, a guiding principle of inclusion is that visitors with low incomes are people first and deserve the same respect and treatment as other visitors.

> Trussell and Mair (2010) concluded that people with low incomes have the same needs as anybody else when it comes to feeling accepted and connecting to the broader community.

Make Programs Affordable

In these fiscally challenging times, leisure service agencies are typically opposed to reducing fees and charges to make programs and services affordable to people with low incomes. Even municipal recreation services are being called on to generate revenues via fees and charges in order to make programs sustainable. Although these trends have been criticized since they undermine social equity (More, 2002), the reality is that fees and charges are likely to be a permanent fixture of how public park and recreation agencies do business.

Nevertheless, there are at least two ways that agencies can make programs more affordable for people with low incomes. One strategy is to set aside set times during the week when facilities and programs are available at no charge. Cleveland Metroparks Zoo, which is located in northeast Ohio, does this on Mondays. Another strategy is to allow customers to volunteer in exchange for a fee waiver. The latter method not only makes programs and facilities affordable, but it also benefits the agency by providing valuable person power in areas in which the agency is understaffed.

Enhance Access

Leisure service agencies will need to be resourceful as they create strategies to make park and recreation services more accessible to people with low incomes. There are numerous ways they can do this.

Partnerships with transportation agencies may need to be fostered to ensure bus or van services are available to areas where there is a concentration of people living with low incomes. In other cases, where such efforts are not feasible, bringing park and recreation programs to the people may be the next best alternative.

These strategies are particularly important for people with lower incomes who live in areas that are relatively devoid of park and recreation amenities. Leisure service professionals must also strive to provide residents who have low incomes with reliable information about community services. Word-of-mouth continues to be the primary way people keep informed about leisure services. Agencies would do well to develop personal relationships with underserved constituents to ensure they have useful information about the range of program services available to them. See Figure 12.2 for a summary of strategies for providing inclusive leisure services for people with low income.

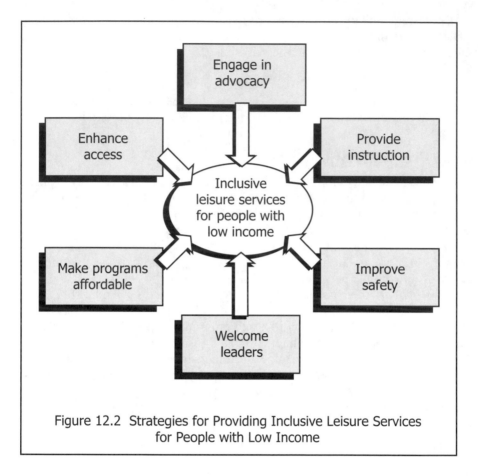

Figure 12.2 Strategies for Providing Inclusive Leisure Services for People with Low Income

Final Thoughts

I will never tire of repeating this: what the poor need the most is not pity but love. They need to feel respect for their human dignity, which is neither less nor different from the dignity of any other human being.

These words by Mother Teresa (Gonzalez-Balado, 1996, p. 35) reinforce many of the ideas and strategies presented in this chapter.

Most people who are affluent can take for granted that the communities in which they live will have a wide-range of interesting, safe, and accessible leisure services. They can also expect to receive friendly and reliable treatment from recreation personnel. They also have reason to believe that they can affect change in program delivery by serving on park and recreation boards or simply making their viewpoints known to personnel or city officials.

None of these things are taken for granted by people who have low incomes. They remain largely invisible. If we are to take seriously the idea that leisure services are open to all people, irrespective of their socioeconomic status, then leisure service professionals and their allies will need to work hard at changing how agencies currently operate, to avoid excluding people with low incomes and to create a more inclusive environment.

A person whose work and advocacy for people living in poverty is legendary was Mother Teresa, who was awarded the Nobel Peace Prize in 1979. She founded the order of Missionaries of Charity and devoted her life to working with and for people with low incomes. It seems fitting to end the chapter with a story that illustrates the character of some people who live in poverty. In the book titled *Mother Teresa. In My Own Words*, which was released before her death in 1997, José Luis Gonzalez-Balado included this story as told by Mother Teresa (1996, p. 16):

> *One night, a man came to our house to tell me that a Hindu family, a family of eight children, had not eaten anything for days. They had nothing to eat. I took enough rice for a meal and went to their house. I could see the hungry faces, the children with their bulging eyes. The sight could have not been more dramatic! The mother took the rice from my hands, divided it in half and went out. When she came back a little later, I asked her: "Where did you go? What did you do?" She answered, "They also are hungry." "They" were the people next door, a Muslim family with the same number of children to feed and who did not have any food either. That mother was aware of the situation. She had the courage and the love to share her meager portion of rice with others. In spite of her circumstances, I think she felt very happy to share with her neighbors the little I had taken her.*

Discussion Questions

1. What is social stratification and how is it perpetuated?
2. What does it mean to have a low income?
3. How is a low income related to life chances?
4. How do intrapersonal, interpersonal, and structural constraints differ from one another?
5. How do intrapersonal constraints inhibit leisure preferences and motivations among people with low incomes?
6. How do interpersonal constraints prevent people with low incomes from developing relationships and accessing leisure amenities?

7. What are the major structural constraints that prevent poorer Americans from accessing public park and recreation programs and facilities?
8. What are some strategies for reducing leisure constraints encountered by people with low incomes?
9. Why are advocates needed for poorer Americans?
10. Why is it important to alleviate intrapersonal, interpersonal, and structural constraints in tandem?

Chapter 13
Encourage Self-Determination

*Few human concerns are more universally
central than that of self-determination.*
-Edward Deci

Orientation Activity: The Choice Is Theirs

Directions Alone: Choose any recreation program that you might offer as a leisure services professional. While thinking of this recreation activity, record answers for each of the following questions. Be sure to include specific examples.

Directions with Others: One person will be assigned as recorder and will write the responses on a chalkboard or easel that all participants can see. Address each question and report the different methods identified. Attempt to produce as comprehensive a list as possible.

- How might we encourage participants to choose activities within a given recreation program?
- How might we determine what a participant has chosen if he or she does not speak?
- How might we encourage participants to make choices once we begin conducting a recreation activity?
- If participants do not have the skills to respond to a survey or interview questions concerning their enjoyment associated with a program, how might we determine if they are enjoying an activity?

Debriefing: Self-determination is a highly valued personal characteristic in many societies. If we identify self-determination and choice as important elements of leisure and enjoyment, then it appears logical to encourage participants to make as many choices as possible and to take responsibility for their participation.

Providing opportunities for participants to cultivate self-determination can be challenging and often requires systematic planning. The goal of enhancing self-determination has merit, since it appears that people's perceptions of freedom and their ability to determine their own participation patterns is more important than the specific recreation activity which they choose. The previous questions encourage leisure service professionals to provide opportunities for choices whenever possible within programs.

The fact that some participants may have fewer skills, respond in different ways, or exhibit behaviors not demonstrated by most participants does not preclude them from valuing their freedom and from experiencing enjoyment. Leisure service professionals are in an excellent position to facilitate self-determination for all individuals. Their support will help individuals experience leisure as much as possible. Consider the following questions related to the orientation activity:

- What is the value of encouraging participants to make choices and increase their sense of self-determination?
- What is the primary responsibility of leisure service providers to their constituents?
- Why is it important to provide opportunities for participants to become empowered?

Introduction

On December 25, 1971, Dr. Jesse Jackson encouraged the crowd he addressed to join him in his famous proclamation: "I am somebody." With this phrase, people announced that they view themselves as valued people who have much to share and contribute; they have a sense of self-determination. People learn that they are somebody by experiencing positive interactions with others that nurture and support their sense of inherent value as a human being and their sense of self-determination.

Self-determination is necessary for the optimal experience of enjoyment. Self-determination makes effort and the investment of attention worthwhile for a person. These factors bring about enjoyable involvement. This experience serves to develop competence, thereby reinforcing self-determination.

> After surveying over 500 human service professionals, Mason, Field, and Sawilowsky (2004) found that these professionals indicated that they would benefit from additional training on how to promote self-determination. After conducting an ethical analysis of the literature, Smith, Polloway, Smith, and Patton (2007) concluded that professionals need to assess and teach self-determination because it makes a significant difference in people's lives.

It is helpful to consider the impact of the way in which leisure services are delivered. These services are primarily designed to set the stage for people to enjoy themselves. At times, we become so concerned with keeping people busy that we lose sight of the more important goal of facilitating enjoyment. The following questions are addressed in this chapter:

- What is self-determination?
- How is intrinsic motivation related to self-determination?
- How is enjoyment related to self-determination?
- How can the environment stimulate self-determination?
- How can self-determination in leisure be facilitated?

What is self-determination?

As described in the first chapter of this book, Edward Deci and Richard Ryan and colleagues developed the self-determination theory that has been the foundation for development of many educational and leisure interventions. According to these researchers, ***self-determination*** results in having control over our lives in areas we value, making decisions without interference from others, and having the freedom to live as we choose.

Self-determined people exert control over what happens to them, when and where it occurs, and with whom it takes place. People's sense of self-determination is closely tied to their leisure. The following excerpt (Taylor, 2010, p. 84) describes a person who is clearly self-determined.

> *Anthony Robles can do it. Do what? Whatever you might think someone with only one leg can't do. Ride a bike? He learned it when he was five, with no more tumbles that you probably had. Run the mile? Technically, Robles "crutches" the distance, but he has done it in as little as eight minutes. If there's something Robles can't do because he doesn't have a right leg, he hasn't come across it yet. As for what he does best, he puts on his Arizona State wrestling singlet and twists another opponent into a human slipknot. Last season Robles was an all-American in the 125-pound class as a sophomore and finished fourth at the NCAA championships. Most people would call that amazing. Robles calls it an appetizer. For Robles, wrestling has been a way of showing that he's too strong, in every sense, to be held back just because one leg of his pants hangs empty. "You define yourself by what you can do, not what you can't," he says.*

Generally, people who perceive themselves as capable and self-determined can effectively deal with the challenges of day-to-day life and may avoid undesirable outcomes such as depression, distress, substance abuse, and physical illness. Self-determination involves the flexibility and ability to choose options and to adjust to situations when there is only one available option. By considering another person's choices, preferences, and aspirations, we can promote a sense of self-determination and communicate a sense of respect.

Wehmeyer (1998) proposed four essential characteristics of self-determination required for the individual to act autonomously. People who are self-determined:

- act on their own preferences without external pressure
- regulate their own behaviors by considering skills and the task, then formulating, implementing, and evaluating a plan
- initiate and respond in an empowered manner, believing in their ability to influence outcomes
- realize the impact of their actions that provide an accurate understanding of their strengths and limitations

As stated in the first chapter, self-determination is composed of the need for autonomy, competence, and relatedness. *Autonomy* involves the perception of having the opportunity and capacity to independently make choices and decisions based on needs, preferences, and interests. The ability or skill to successfully perform a task or do something that is determined to be proficient by comparing the behavior to a standard of performance is identified as having a sense of *competence*.

Although autonomy and competence are extremely important aspects of self-determination, few of us would choose to meet all our daily living demands independently, without assistance and support from others. The need for *relatedness* involves the desire to have the feeling of connecting with other people or experiencing a sense of belonging with a group. This sense of relatedness emphasizes the importance of interdependence. *Interdependence* includes the reliance on mutual assistance, cooperation, support, or interaction among people.

Given this need for interdependence, being self-determined includes being interdependent with family, friends, and others with whom we interact. Leisure service providers are encouraged to acknowledge this interdependence and focus on supporting participants to become self-determined within the context of interdependence.

Research supports the value of fostering self-determination skills daily by offering opportunities for participants to set simple goals, solve manageable problems, make choices and decisions as well as evaluate the outcomes of these decisions. However, Zhang, Landmark, Grenwelge, and Montoya (2010, p. 176) warned that because the concept of self-determination is rooted in the normalization movement originating in Europe, the values in most efforts to promote self-determination are connected to Anglo-European cultures and societies and stated that:

> *In recognition of this European origination and the fact that the U.S. society has become increasingly multiethnic and multilingual, researchers have begun to examine self-determination and its related practices within cultural contexts, especially non-Western and collective cultures. However, after conducting a cross-cultural analysis Chirkov (2009) concluded that research from diverse settings around the world supports the idea that self-determination universally has a beneficial role of promoting autonomous motivation. This finding supports research by Ryan and Deci (2006) identifying that autonomy is a significant issue across ages and cultures and is critical to wellness.*

It is important as we attempt to promote self-determined leisure participation that we consider the cultural perspective of each participant. By doing so, we can work to communicate respect for their perspective and focus on what is viewed by each individual as promoting their self-determination.

How is intrinsic motivation related to self-determination?

Intrinsic motivation involves the desire to engage in experiences that are interesting and satisfying for the purpose of feeling positive emotions associated with participation, rather than because of related consequences. This internal form of motivation energizes behavior and increases autonomy.

When people are intrinsically motivated, their performance of the behavior does not require external rewards or control. The experiences of interest, enjoyment, and excitement, for example, provide reinforcement for such behaviors. These are the experiences most often associated with leisure and recreation.

People who are intrinsically motivated will seek challenges commensurate with their competencies—they will avoid situations that are too easy or too difficult. The balancing act between competencies and challenges associated with intrinsic motivation is depicted in Figure 13.1. Individuals who are intrinsically motivated are more likely to learn, adapt, and grow in competencies that characterize development.

In comparison to intrinsic motivation, extrinsic motivation involves being interested in engaging in an activity because participation results in obtaining some separate consequence such as a reward.

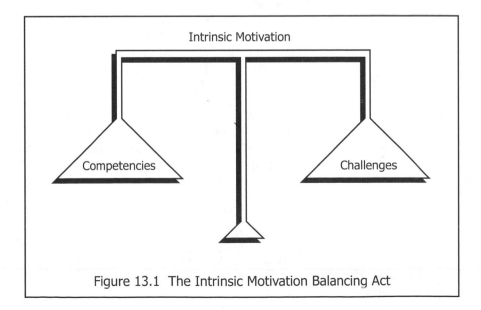

Figure 13.1 The Intrinsic Motivation Balancing Act

Deci, Koestner, and Ryan (1999) conducted a meta-analysis of over 100 studies and concluded that extrinsic rewards decrease intrinsic motivation across a range of activities and rewards. In interpreting these findings, Deci and Ryan (2008, p. 15) explained that:

> *In other words, when people were given extrinsic rewards such as money or awards for doing an intrinsically interesting activity, their intrinsic motivation for the activity tended to be undermined. That is, rewards led them to lose interest in the activity. There were, however, limiting conditions to this finding. For example, rewards that are noncontingent or are not specifically dependent on doing an activity or achieving some standard tend not to undermine intrinsic motivation of the target behavior.*

How is enjoyment related to self-determination?

Enjoyment is the feeling derived from investing one's attention in intrinsically motivating action patterns. The activity is often so compelling that one becomes deeply absorbed in it and loses consciousness of self and awareness of time.

Leisure service providers can bring about the experience of enjoyment. Whatever additional benefits enjoyment may bring, it is in and of itself a major reason for the provision of leisure services. Enjoyment is considered by many as the optimal experience that people pursue.

Csikszentmihalyi (1997) and colleagues have studied optimal experience for decades and they offer a helpful perspective. By examining experiences of dancers, rock climbers, writers, basketball players, artists, surgeons, and others who love their play and work, these investigations have isolated characteristics of enjoyment, or what they refer to as optimal experience. *Optimal experience* is the most desirable or favorable active involvement in an occurrence, situation, or event.

The word used to describe this subjective quality of the optimal experience is *flow*. The sense of movement that *flow* implies is created by the merging of action and awareness around the challenges provided by an activity and the feedback that defines a person's capability to meet those challenges. While many activities can create an optimal experience, the activity must become more challenging to keep up with participants' expanding skills so that flow is maintained.

As an example, most video games are based on this premise, with multiple levels that participants must pass through as they increase their competence associated with the game.

The experience of enjoyment is distinguishable from pleasure. ***Pleasure*** is the result of satisfying basic biological drives such as hunger, thirst, sex, and stimulation. Unlike pleasure, enjoyment is consistent with:

- concentration
- effort
- a sense of control
- competence

Enjoyment is often used colloquially as the equivalent of "fun," but it is being used here to reflect a considerable degree of psychological involvement as well. The research of Csikszentmihalyi and others show that concentration, effort, and a sense of control and competence are all critical aspects of the experience of enjoyment. Thus, if the goal is to facilitate enjoyment, leisure professionals should seek to understand these factors. See Figure 13.2 for a depiction of the conditions of enjoyment.

While there are other agendas for leisure professionals, establishing environments conducive to flow and teaching people to generate optimal experiences are especially important. Creating conditions that help concentration, effort, and a sense of control and competence, while promoting freedom of choice and the expression of preference, is the engineering of enjoyment. To do that, leisure service providers must understand self-determination and the factors that interfere with it (see Figure 13.3, p. 256).

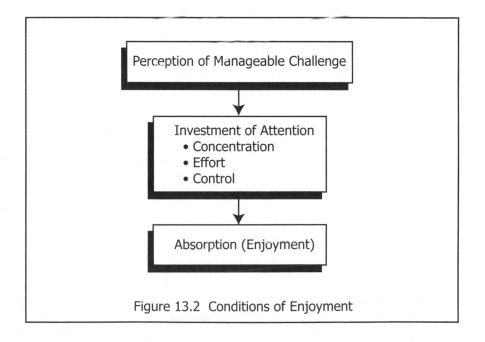

Figure 13.2 Conditions of Enjoyment

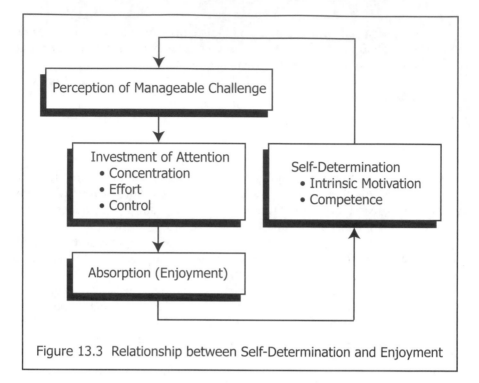

Figure 13.3 Relationship between Self-Determination and Enjoyment

How can the environment stimulate self-determination?

Self-determination occurs when people take control of their freedom. The environment can encourage self-determination by being responsive and informational, or it can discourage self-determination through controlling and unpredictable responses to behaviors.

A responsive and informational environment reacts to a person's initiatives, provides information about the person's competence, and encourages further action. It fosters intrinsic motivation and internal causality, resulting in self-determined behavior.

Events involving choice and positive feedback provide information to the person, thereby enhancing self-determination. By creating environments that are option-rich, responsive, and informative, we can increase the likelihood of participants becoming self-determined.

How can self-determination in leisure be facilitated?

Because self-determination involves a lifelong interplay between the individual and the environment, a supportive, responsive context is important when encouraging people to become self-determined. Optimum environments offer individuals the opportunity to express and further develop self-determination. To promote self-determination, it is important that we shift from services directed by professionals to services directed by participants.

Research supports the connection between self-determination and participation in recreation activities.

> For example, McGuire and McDonnell (2008) examined the relationship between recreation and self-determination for adolescents and young adults. They found that strong indication that an increased amount of time spent actively engaged in recreation predicted higher levels of self-determination. The researchers concluded that recreation may be a useful strategy for enhancing self-determination.

The challenge for service providers is to structure services so as to encourage self-determined leisure participation. Many strategies can facilitate self-determination. An environment that facilitates self-determination can be established by encouraging participants to:

- provide opportunities for choice
- promote communication
- respond to preferences
- foster active participation
- encourage empowerment
- increase competence
- advocate goal setting

Provide Opportunities for Choice

One characteristic common to most discussions of self-determination is choice; however, some families and professionals act in a paternalistic manner and make choices for people rather than allow participants to decide for themselves. Opportunities to express interests and preferences have been prevented by people who incorrectly assume that certain participants, such as older adults, people who do not speak the dominant community language, or those who have a disability, are incapable of making informed choices. When people are given choices they:

- engage in activities more
- increase their interest
- become more enthusiastic
- increase participation
- reduce challenging behaviors

We can encourage participants to make choices within activities if we present multiple and diverse options, such as what materials to use, with whom to participate, and when to stop an activity. Opportunities to make choices can also be facilitated during the course of an activity by simply following the person's lead and interests. To encourage self-determination, we can support initiation of activities by:

- providing participants with opportunities to express preferences
- allowing them to make choices regarding their leisure participation
- permitting them to experience outcomes based on their choices

Freedom of choice is vital to the pursuit of enjoyable, satisfying, and meaningful experience. Personal autonomy for people is an essential aspect of independent functioning and self-reliance. When people are encouraged to choose activities, they:

- are more enthusiastic about learning skills needed to participate
- more readily apply those skills to other settings
- are more likely to continue to participate in those activities

The ultimate goal of any leisure program is to facilitate self-initiated, independent use of free time with chronologically age-appropriate recreation activities. When we provide opportunities for individuals to make self-determined and responsible choices that reflect their needs to grow, explore, and realize their potential, their ability to experience leisure is enhanced.

> For example, Amy's favorite recreation activity is doing artwork. When she attends her art class she is encouraged to select the paper she will use; she chooses between different colors, sizes, and textures. In addition, she decides to use watercolors today rather than chalk or markers. After she has her materials, Amy is invited to position her easel where she prefers and begins her chosen project while carefully selecting her color scheme.

It is important to maintain a delicate balance between providing opportunities for choice and encouraging development of culturally normative, age-appropriate leisure behaviors. Sometimes people choose to exhibit behaviors that society has identified as being offensive or detrimental. It is helpful to redirect these people to participate in socially acceptable activities of their choosing that do not bring psychological or physical discomfort to themselves or other people.

Leisure instruction related to helping individuals determine the appropriateness of behaviors is often useful. All of us must learn that we are rarely completely free to do anything we wish. To experience leisure on an ongoing basis, we must learn to assert our rights as well as respect other people we encounter. The appropriateness of behaviors may vary according to the following:

- *location* such as the bedroom versus a public swimming pool
- *frequency* such as asking once versus asking several times

- *timing* such as laughing joke versus when someone is crying
- *relationship of people* present such as brother versus teacher

Encouraging participants to make choices and take charge of their lives is an important aspect of leisure service delivery. The earlier that opportunities for choices are presented to people, the more likely they will acquire behaviors associated with self-determination. An important action in trying to support all participants to become more self-determined is to invite them to try new experiences, while at the same time continuously offering opportunities for them to make choices.

Promote Communication

Effective communication facilitates involvement with others. However, for a variety of reasons, some people may take considerable time to formulate what they want to say. At times, professionals responding to these individuals do not provide them with adequate time to respond. This unwillingness to wait for people to take their turn results in the professional taking control of the conversation and often the entire situation.

Since the ability to choose to initiate involvement is critical to the leisure experience, it is helpful if people are encouraged to initiate interactions and share conversations. Construction of a supportive environment that is responsive to the communicative attempts is important. A supportive environment can be created when we approach the person, attend to the person, and wait at least 10 seconds for that person to initiate interaction. This will encourage leisure involvement and, more importantly, demonstrate respect for that person.

Since a perception of freedom to choose to participate in meaningful, enjoyable, and satisfying experiences is fundamental to the leisure experience, independent leisure participation is stifled when there is a reliance on a directive approach to service delivery. A *directive approach* to leisure services involves professionals maintaining control and limiting choice for participants.

When providing leisure services, it may be helpful to take a nondirective approach. A *nondirective approach* to service delivery involves participants being encouraged to provide input freely, resulting in practitioners strongly considering the individual's preferences and choices. Nondirective instructional strategies can help us avoid instilling a sense of dependency within our participants.

Since much daily communication is not verbally prompted, encouraging people to initiate communication is an important goal. As people engage in reciprocal exchanges stimulated by their ability to initiate interaction, their ability to communicate preferences, make meaningful choices, and experience leisure is enhanced. When communication is *reciprocal* the interaction is mutual, this is, the conversation is shared relatively equally between two people when the comments and thoughts of both parties are expressed, listened to, and respected.

Simply providing people who have limited communication skills with an alternative form of communication is not sufficient. It is valuable to provide specific attention to responding to their conversational attempts. It is important for us to be as responsive as possible to the communicative attempts made by people with limited communication skills.

If people do not initiate communication, these individuals can still be supported. Their actions can be supported by:

- providing them with objects they have requested
- returning greetings to them
- extending and expanding their comments

When people do not initiate interactions, professionals are encouraged to ask open-ended questions beginning with *what* and *how* as opposed to those questions that force people into a *yes/no* response.

Respond to Preferences

The most common way to determine someone's preferences is to ask the individual. However, some individuals may not currently have the verbal skills to communicate, or they may feel pressured to identify certain preferences that correspond with expectations of privileged individuals. Consequently, it can be helpful to observe individuals when they are presented with choices to determine if there is pattern in their selections.

Preference refers to a desire for an option following a comparison of that option against a continuum of other options. *Choice* refers to the act of selecting one option, ideally a preferred one, from among others that are simultaneously available. The distinction between choice and preference is subtle but important.

> For example, on the one hand, arbitrarily providing an option that is preferred by someone removes the opportunity for that person the pleasure of making the choice, such as taking Tonia to her favorite playground without having asked her to choose between going to different playgrounds. Conversely, helping someone to choose among options that are not preferred only substitutes for the kind of choice-making most people value, such as offering Tonia the opportunity to choose between tap, ballet, and jazz dance classes even though Tonia does not enjoy dance and would prefer to be playing sports such as soccer, basketball, or field hockey.

When attempting to provide leisure opportunities, it is valuable if we determine the person's preferences and create supporting opportunities for the person to choose among preferred options. Each day presents many opportunities for participants to express preferences and make choices about their leisure. These choices include not only what to do, but also where, when, and with whom to perform the activity. To respond to the needs of diverse participants, we can assess their preferences and develop strategies for determining the most preferred activities.

Foster Active Participation

Individuals who have been oppressed in some manner are often excluded from recreation activities, at times due to their assumed inability to perform independently. However, a person who is deemed unable to engage in an activity independently should not be denied the opportunity for partial participation.

Partial participation involves use of adaptations and assistance to facilitate leisure participation regardless of skill level. This approach affirms the right of people to participate in environments and activities without regard to degree of assistance required.

Through partial participation, individuals may experience the exhilaration and satisfaction associated with the challenge inherent in a particular recreation activity. The following is an example of partial participation:

> Miguel uses a walker, and his colleagues at work decided to enter a softball league sponsored by the community recreation and parks department. At the beginning of the season, a few rules were adjusted to facilitate his participation in league play. Instead of the ball being pitched to him, he hit the ball off a tee and after he made contact a teammate, Nicole, ran the bases. When his teammate scored a run, the team congratulated both Miguel and Nicole.

The principle of partial participation ensures that even those people who might never be able to acquire a large-enough complement of skills to completely participate in recreation activities could still learn enough to participate to some degree. There are some challenges that may arise when professionals have attempted to promote partial participation.

First, some professionals have narrowly defined participation as simply presence. When passive participation is the dominant form of participation, the practice becomes problematic. It is helpful to encourage active participation by all participants regardless of skill level.

Second, sometimes professionals fail to consider the person's preferences, long-term learning needs, family priorities, reactions of peers, and other socially validated, community-referenced guidelines. It is important to gain this information from the participants and their families.

Third, we may interpret "doing things independently" as doing them alone, which can result in too narrow a prescription for performance. The supportive presence of another person offers the opportunity to enhance an individual's participation. This supportive person can perform those parts of the activity that are determined by the individual encountering difficulty to be burdensome, overly time-consuming, stressful, or exhausting.

Encourage Empowerment

Empowerment may be defined as the transfer of power and control over the values, decisions, choices, and directions of services from external entities, such as service providers, to consumers of services. This results in increased motivation to participate and succeed and greater dignity for participants.

Service providers do not always allow people and their families the right to make their own major life decisions and, therefore, fail to empower various participants.

> For instance, people who experience communication barriers—such as immigrants who do not effectively know the dominant language of a particular culture or individuals with cognitive, physical, communicative, or sensory impairments—may encounter challenges in expressing preferences and being accurately understood by another person.

For many people who have been oppressed, the opportunities for learning and practicing decision making and self-direction are limited. The reasons that these individuals experience such powerlessness and lack of self-direction have less to do with their lack of abilities than with attitudes and practices of service providers, funding agencies, and social institutions.

Every person, regardless of his or her characteristics, has the right and ability to be empowered by communicating with others, expressing everyday preferences, and exercising at least some control over life. Each individual is to be given the choice, training, technology, respect, and encouragement to do so. It is valuable if leisure service providers create empowering environments in which people and their family members are given information to make choices as well as opportunities to exercise their choices.

Learning to make good choices requires experience with the process of ***decision making***, which involves choosing among viable alternatives and dealing with the consequences of decisions. When independent choice making is not feasible or safe, choice making can be adapted or supported, and individuals may partially participate in decision-making processes. The development of autonomy, the importance of choice-making, opportunities for self-initiation, and environmental manipulation all facilitate learning, enjoyment, and empowerment.

Making timely and correct decisions leads to a sense of personal effective-ness and interest that subsequently promotes investment of attention and enjoyment. People who do not possess the decision-making skills needed for activity involvement are more likely to acquire these skills if they participate in recreation activities and are given considerable autonomy in doing so.

Participants can be encouraged to evaluate their decisions, determine effects of their decisions, and decide whether they would act in a similar fashion in a similar circumstance. Encouraging people to locate facilities, learn about participation requirements, and obtain answers to questions can stimulate deci-sions about leisure involvement and empower them. Leisure service providers who want to empower all participants to become self-determined would do well to give participants as many opportunities as possible to practice making manageable decisions.

Increase Competence

Perceived competence refers to people's evaluation of their own ability to achieve tasks compared to others of the same age and gender. Perceived competence is an important feature of leisure because it results in feelings of personal control.

Psychological comfort is perceived when people compare their performance to standards adopted internally and feel satisfied with their performance. This comfort is important because it allows for the possibility that people may use a criterion other than social comparison to judge their competence.

People who have more free-time activities to choose from are in a better situation to experience leisure than those who do not. When making plans, leisure service professionals ought to prioritize activities that allow participants to perceive themselves as competent throughout their lives.

A *leisure repertoire* includes those activities an individual does for enjoyment and fun. Expanding a person's leisure repertoire would increase feelings of competence. It is helpful to consider the following phrase when examining the relationship between the opportunity for practice and engagement and a person's leisure repertoire:

> *The activities people do often for their leisure they will do well, and what people do well in their leisure they will do often.*

West and Parent (1992, p. 75) provided a note of caution when helping people to expand their leisure repertoires:

> *More activity does not necessarily mean a better quality of life. Some individuals may actually choose to engage in a few repetitive but highly enjoyable activities per week. The issue is ensuring that meaningful opportunities for choice are actually provided.*

Advocate Goal Setting

Self-determination includes attitudes and abilities that lead individuals to define goals and to take the initiative to achieve those goals. Activities with clear goals are more likely to lead to participant enjoyment. In many activities the goals are implicit, and therefore goal setting is not important.

> For example, when completing a painting, the main concern is to develop the skills which, when used, result in recognizing an aesthetically pleasing finished product.

One role of service providers is to encourage participants to set goals when they are not apparent and work toward achieving them—usually problem-solving in the process—within an environment which fosters interdependence. According to Deci (1995, p. 152):

*[g]oals need to be individualized—they need to be suited
specifically to the person who will work toward them—and
they need to be set so as to represent an optimal challenge.*

See Figure 13.4 for a summary of strategies that can help to facilitate
self-determination.

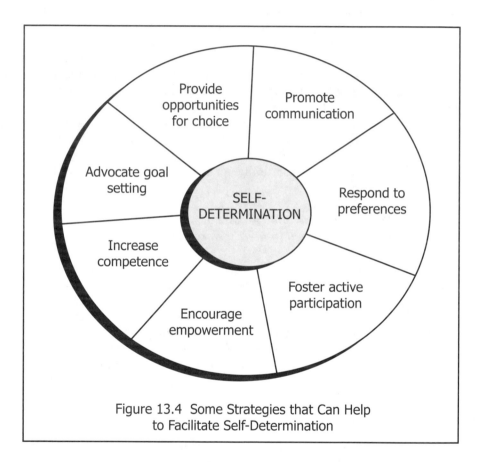

Figure 13.4 Some Strategies that Can Help
to Facilitate Self-Determination

Final Thoughts

In summary, self-determination is necessary for the optimal experience of
enjoyment. It makes effort and the investment of attention worthwhile for a
person. As seen in Figure 13.4, this experience of enjoyment serves in turn to
develop competence, thereby reinforcing self-determination.

All people need to have opportunities to take charge of their own lives. Their
experiences can be organized by principles that promote self-determination.

> Wehmeyer and Bolding (1999) surmised that if people are supported to make choices, participate in decisions, set goals, and experience control in their lives, they will become more self-determined.

As people become more self-determined, they will be more likely to assume greater control, make more choices, improve their ability to set goals, make better decisions, enhance their problem solving, and have greater belief in their capacity to influence their lives.

Discussion Questions

1. What is self-determination?
2. Why is self-determination important?
3. What is enjoyment?
4. What is an optimal experience?
5. How can we create conditions to promote flow experiences?
6. How can the environment encourage self-determination?
7. Why is choice important?
8. What is the difference between a preference and a choice?
9. What is perceived competence?
10. Why is perceived competence an important feature of leisure?

Chapter 14
Provide Leisure
Education

*Education is what survives when what
has been learnt has been forgotten.*
-B. F. Skinner

Orientation Activity: Go Beyond
Recreation Activity Skills

Directions Alone: Select one of the following recreation activities: hiking, reading, playing tennis, playing chess, rock climbing, eating out, playing Frisbee, sketching, doing yoga, playing a musical instrument, and lifting weights. Answer the questions listed below to assist you in developing a comprehensive leisure education program.

Directions with Others: Find other people who chose the same recreation activity as you. If no one else identified your activity, find another person who has identified an activity similar to yours. Once groups have been formed, share your ideas about leisure education with the other person(s) in your discussion group. After a specified time, discuss what you have learned with the entire group.

- How can we encourage participants' *awareness of preferences* related to the activity?
- How can we develop a *sense of appreciation* of the value of the recreation activity?
- How might we encourage development of *self-determination* with this activity?
- How could we encourage *decision making* within the context of this recreation activity?
- How might we teach people about *resources* associated with this recreation activity?
- What *social skills* could we encourage so that participants may be successful in this activity?

Debriefing: Limited leisure awareness, knowledge, and skills become major barriers for many individuals in making successful transitions into active community living. To overcome these barriers, it can be helpful to provide systematic and comprehensive leisure education. Attempt to answer the following questions related to the orientation activity:

- What is the value in addressing the questions listed in the orientation activity?
- What are the implications of offering a leisure education program?
- How might you incorporate leisure education into your current or future position as a leisure service provider?

Introduction

Leisure describes a person's perception of freedom to choose to participate in meaningful, enjoyable, and satisfying experiences. As people experience the positive feelings associated with leisure engagement, such as a sense of control, competence, relaxation, and excitement, they will be intrinsically motivated to participate. When people are *intrinsically motivated*, they will participate in leisure simply to be involved in the experience, not for some tangible outcome or external reward.

This chapter describes the content of a leisure education program that develops opportunities for all people to experience leisure. Leisure education programs designed with the goal of facilitating the leisure experience are needed.

Also, this chapter provides a rationale for leisure education for all people, especially those who will benefit from systematic instruction. The structure and content of a leisure education model are presented to assist professionals in providing comprehensive leisure instruction. The model for leisure education presented in this chapter focuses on facilitating inclusive community leisure experiences.

Within this chapter, a structure and content of a leisure education curriculum is proposed. The chapter contains leisure participation evaluative procedures that can be used as indicators of participants' successful community adjustment. The model emerged in response to the clear need for leisure education and is based on previous suggestions identified in articles and texts reported throughout this chapter. In this chapter the following questions are addressed:

- What is leisure education and why is it important?
- What content could be included in leisure education?
- How can we deliver leisure education?
- What are examples of leisure education?

What is leisure education and why is it important?

The term *leisure education* refers to the use of educational strategies to enhance a person's leisure lifestyle; it is designed to develop awareness of recreation activities and resources and for acquiring skills needed for participating in leisure pursuits throughout the life span. Charlie Bullock, Mike Mahon, and

Charles Killingsworth (2010, p. 412) proposed the following definition of person-centered leisure education:

> *An individualized and contextualized educational process through which a person develops an understanding of self and leisure and identifies and learns the cluster of skills necessary to participate in freely chosen activities which lead to an optimally satisfying life.*

Although leisure education is important to everyone, it assumes an added significance in the lives of individuals who are experiencing constraints to their leisure participation. Many individuals not only have to cope with the constraints that are a direct result of their specific limitations such as a low income, language limitations, age, and ability, but they experience constraints of various kinds imposed by our society. These constraints include physical, attitudinal, and programmatic barriers that work against the achievement of full and satisfying involvement in many aspects of life, including leisure.

Some individuals across the globe are confronted with larger amounts of unobligated time than other people because of the scarcity of education and economic opportunities available to them. These large blocks of time can be both unfilled and unfulfilling. This free time may be unfulfilling because people may lack knowledge, skills, abilities, and awareness associated with leisure participation. Without these abilities, individuals can be prevented from experiencing meaningful involvement in leisure. An effective leisure education program lessens these problems and has the potential to result in development of skills, competencies, and attitudes.

To formulate a common international platform for leisure education, the World Leisure Organization created the Commission on Leisure Education, which was charged with extending global efforts in the development of leisure education in school and community systems, as well as in the training of human resources. The World Leisure Organization (2010) reported that:

> *Leisure education aims to assist children, youth, and adults, to reach the good life and the best usage of leisure through the cultivation of their personal intellectual, emotional, physical, and social development. Going through the process of leisure education can develop an all-round individual, who holds values, attitudes, interests, motivation, habits, knowledge, appreciation and skills which are useable throughout life.*

The need for incorporating leisure education into leisure services for people who have been oppressed is strong. Some people lack adequate knowledge and skills needed to participate in activities that allow them to experience leisure. Leisure education programs that teach such knowledge and skills can prepare individuals for a more enjoyable life in their communities.

What content could be included
in leisure education?

Leisure education provides individuals the opportunity to enhance the quality of their lives in leisure; understand opportunities, potentials, and challenges in leisure; understand the impact of leisure on the quality of their lives; and gain knowledge, skills and appreciation enabling broad leisure skills. Therefore, as illustrated in Figure 14.1, an effective leisure education program could include, but is not limited to:

- awareness of self in leisure
- appreciation of leisure
- self-determination in leisure
- decision-making skills
- knowledge and utilization of resources
- social interaction skills
- recreation activity skills

Awareness of Self in Leisure

An important aspect of developing a meaningful leisure lifestyle is to engage in self-examination. According to Barry (1997, p. 6).

> *Basic to all learning, growth, and positive behavioral change is awareness; therefore an important ingredient of leisure education programs is in assisting participants to explore, discover, and develop knowledge about themselves in a leisure context.*

To facilitate recreation participation, people must possess knowledge of their preferences. When people become aware of what they prefer, they are more likely to select and do the things that they enjoy.

> For example, small groups go for a brief walk outside and are instructed to identify objects or activities they enjoy. Participants collect objects or the leader records the communicated preferences. Upon returning, each group shares the findings. Another learning activity might involve use of equipment used with recreation activities, such as baseball bats, ice skates, or skateboards. Participants are asked to choose equipment associated with their favorite activities. Opportunities for participation in those activities, characteristics of the activities, and previous experience with these activities are explored.

Examination of personal attitudes toward leisure may provide individuals with information about their own barriers to leisure participation. One way to have people examine their attitudes is to place them in a forced-choice situation.

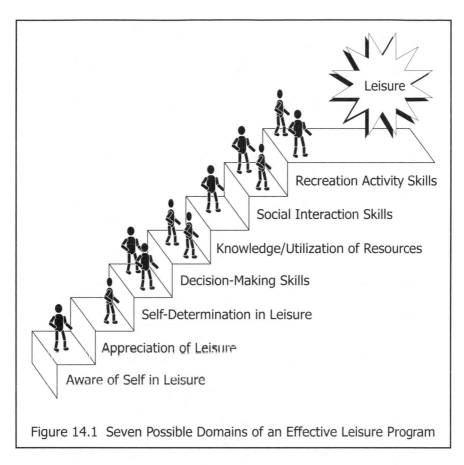

Figure 14.1 Seven Possible Domains of an Effective Leisure Program

To illustrate, a room can be divided in half with one half of the room representing one way of approaching leisure participation, and the other half of the room representing a different approach, such as exciting versus relaxing, outside versus inside, alone versus with others. Participants must go to one side of the room or the other as the leader places large posterboard pictures associated with these concepts on each side of the room. When they arrive at their chosen destination, they are asked to talk about the reasons for their selection.

For some people, considering leisure patterns and desires can be valuable. Reflecting on past leisure pursuits may permit people to gain insight into skills they possess. Analyzing individuals' current leisure involvement will assist them in identifying activities they enjoy, as well as determining barriers they would like to overcome. We can also encourage participants to look beyond their past and present leisure participation patterns, and to consider areas for future discovery to enhance motivation for leisure participation.

For instance, to help people focus on what makes them happy now and what could make them happy in the future, a learning activity can be conducted requiring participants to identify as many enjoyable recreation activities as possible. They could identify these activities by pointing to them in a book, verbalizing them, or drawing them. After they complete this task, materials associated with one activity chosen by each person are gathered. Participants are encouraged to observe or join each individual participating in a chosen activity. Following demonstrations, participants' desire to learn any of the activities presented is assessed. Exploration of what activities they have yet to master but are motivated to learn about is often helpful.

Appreciation of Leisure

To gain an awareness of leisure, it is useful to develop an appreciation of the concepts of leisure and leisure lifestyle. When people understand these concepts, their ability to participate in satisfying and enjoyable recreation activities will be enhanced.

For example, to help participants gain an understanding of the difference between work and leisure, they can be divided into two groups. One group is given paints and brushes and required to paint a specific object on a large piece of paper, such as a car. The other group is provided with the same materials and permitted to paint anything they like. After 10 minutes, the groups switch tasks. Questions and statements are made about the differences between the activities and the role freedom plays in leisure participation. By focusing on leisure appreciation, participants can begin to develop sensitivity for the uniqueness of leisure.

Because many people who have limited skills have been overprotected, their ability to take personal responsibility for leisure involvement may be reduced. Most people are capable and can be responsible for their own leisure, and they can change and improve their present leisure status.

As a case in point, to encourage a sense of responsibility within individuals, leisure education sessions are divided into two parts. One portion of the session involves instruction to teach individuals how to participate in specific recreation activities such as table games. The following portion allows them to engage in socially acceptable activities of their choosing. During this time they are in control and responsible for their participation. The amount of time individuals are placed in this situation varies according to their skills.

Self-Determination in Leisure

As discussed in previous chapters, self-determination occurs when people take control of their freedom. Self-determination involves acting as the primary causal agent in one's life by making decisions free from external influence or interference, which includes the perception of freedom to make choices and the ability to initiate chosen leisure activities.

Self-determination is an important consideration in facilitating leisure. By creating option-rich, responsive, and informative environments, both participants and professionals increase the likelihood of becoming self-determined.

It is helpful to consider leisure education that emphasizes choice and the facilitation of self-directed activity, along with direct skill instruction. Unfortunately, choice and self-determination have been rarely addressed when facilitating leisure for many people who have been oppressed, such as people who have low incomes, those with disabilities, and older adults.

Development of a sense of self-determination facilitates the ability of individuals to make choices and sets the stage for acquisition of more complex decision-making strategies. Leisure education can be effective if it encourages participants to go beyond mere leisure awareness and instill the ability and confidence to take personal action and choose to participate independently in meaningful experiences. See earlier chapters for specific ways to promote self-determination.

Decision-Making Skills

Some individuals have difficulty making decisions related to many aspects of their lives. Based on observations that many people who have been oppressed frequently fail to adjust to community living as a result of inappropriate use of free time, it is useful to encourage responsible decision making and selection of recreation activities. Making a decision related to leisure participation is facilitated by individuals' awareness of themselves relative to leisure, appreciation of leisure, and their sense of self-determination in leisure involvement.

> One way to teach people decision-making skills is to involve them in a cooperative small-group activity. For example, participants attending a leisure education session related to camping are divided into small groups. Each group is given one backpack as they enter a storage area containing camping equipment, food, clothing, and other supplies. Ask members to prepare for an overnight hike to a particular location. Participants must select items they will take; however, they can only take what can fit in the backpack. Each group must keep a list of the items they include and identify why they chose the selected items.

Knowledge and Utilization of Resources

Difficulty in making appropriate leisure decisions may result from people's lack of knowledge about leisure resources. A reason some people experience problems adjusting to life in their communities is their lack of awareness of recreation resources.

Knowledge of leisure resources and the ability to use these resources appear to be important factors in establishing an independent leisure lifestyle. It can be helpful to teach individuals not only how to participate in an activity but also how to answer questions about leisure options, including:

- Where can one participate?
- With whom can one participate?
- How much does participation cost?
- What type of transportation is available?
- Where could one learn more about a recreation activity?
- What equipment is required?

> For example, to help people learn about the equipment needed for participation, they can participate in a matching game that stimulates their memory and concentration, and provides information on recreation activities and equipment. Two sets of cards, one with names and pictures of activities and one with names and pictures of equipment are placed face down on a table. The number of cards varies according to participants' skills. The object of the game is to match an activity with the equipment used in the activity by turning over the related cards. A discussion regarding the equipment needed occurs after each match is made, accompanied by exposure to the actual equipment and activity whenever possible.

In addition to the need for people to acquire knowledge of community leisure resources, they must be able to utilize these resources. To encourage use of leisure resources, it is helpful to inform families and friends about the leisure resources available within their community.

Social Interaction Skills

A lack of social skills prevents many people from developing a satisfying life. An absence of social skills is particularly noticeable during leisure participation and frequently leads to isolation and an inability to function. Lord (1997, p. 35) made the following comment:

> *The lack of social competencies is in fact the greatest barrier to full inclusion. . . . This is due in a large degree to associated communication deficits, as well as the lack of social training and opportunities.*

Because peer relationships during childhood and adolescence are critical, social skill instruction is important. Development of social skills used in leisure situations appears to be valuable because acquisition of these skills promotes inclusion. Successful inclusion of participants into leisure services may occur by teaching people how to make verbal statements, maintain eye contact, maintain appropriate physical proximity, make appropriate physical contact, share equipment and materials, cooperate and develop friendships.

> For instance, people can be instructed to participate in an activity to help them practice how to introduce themselves to a group. In turn, participants tell the group their first name, and for 30 seconds share with others positive information about themselves such as accomplishments, desirable personal traits, or friendships. Participants are instructed to communicate only positive information during this time. Leisure education learning activities such as this are designed to encourage social inclusion.

Recreation Activity Skills

Since choice is critical to leisure participation and choice involves options and alternatives, people must possess a repertoire of recreation activity skills and related interests. A *repertoire* involves the range of techniques, abilities, skills, or knowledge that a person possesses relative to an identified topic.

We can encourage participants to select and develop recreation skills having the most potential for enjoyment and satisfaction. Therefore, it is valuable if the recreation activity skills that an individual is taught are based on the person's:

- needs
- interests
- motivations
- preferences
- aspirations

Another consideration when selecting which recreation activity skills to teach is the availability of the activity within a person's community. It can be helpful for people to learn kills and develop knowledge that allow their participation in activities that are easily accessed near their home. Also, it is helpful to consider resources that are available to a person such as money, equipment, or clothing needed to participate.

Recreation-activity skill development can provide physical and emotional support assisting participants, family members, friends, and community professionals to overcome fears of the unknown and failure. Reduction of fears associated with leisure participation should reduce hesitancy of people to become active participants in community life, as well as develop support systems comprised of family members, friends, and professionals.

Overall, it is helpful if the selection of recreation activity skills a person is taught results from participants' preferences, as well as their ability to engage in the recreation activity in the near and distant future.

How can we deliver leisure education?

Leisure education can contain three components designed to facilitate meaningful leisure participation (see Figure 14.2). One component involves development and implementation of a leisure education course. It can be helpful if this component is supplemented with community support through leisure coaching and family and friend support for leisure participation. Systematic follow-up on community leisure participation facilitates generalization and maintenance of leisure skills and knowledge. This section addresses the following processes:

- leisure education course
- community support through leisure coaching
- family and friend support for leisure participation
- words of caution

Leisure Education Course

A leisure education program can include a structured course that teaches participants skills that can assist them in actively participating in meaningful and enjoyable experiences. A detailed curriculum for leisure education is identified in *Leisure Education Program Planning: A Systematic Approach* (Dattilo, 2008).

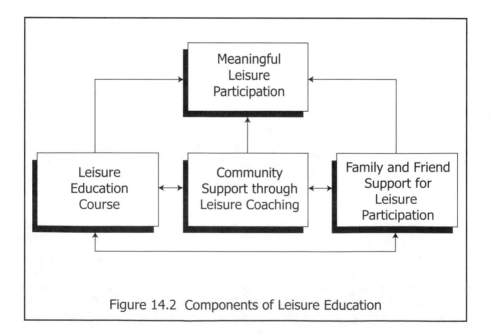

Figure 14.2 Components of Leisure Education

Goals written as general participant outcome statements can guide course development. The course goals can be divided into a number of behavioral objectives with corresponding performance measures. A *performance measure* is a statement of the exact behavior that will be taken as evidence that the intent of the objective has been achieved.

The majority of information contained in the course describes content and process required to conduct the program. Each program's content specifies what is to be done in the program to achieve the intent of the objectives.

Community Support through Leisure Coaching

A leisure education course can be supplemented with systematic community-based leisure instruction and support by a leisure coach. The primary purpose of a leisure coach is to help participants become actively involved in existing community leisure services. Initially, leisure coaches can meet with professionals delivering recreation programs to provide collaboration, consultation, and support for inclusion.

As indicated in Figure 14.3 (p. 278), leisure coaches are available to respond to questions and concerns of the community recreation professional, to act as advocates for both recreation professionals and participants, and to provide assistance to these participants as needed while they engage in inclusive community recreation activities.

A leisure coach can help identify existing community recreation activities that are compatible with interests and skills of the individual. It is helpful if the leisure coach determines requirements of an activity, assesses the skills of the participant, and identifies if specific accommodations are required.

Leisure coaching can occur in conjunction with a formal leisure education course, permitting skill enhancement and alleviation of identified barriers to leisure participation. To facilitate participant autonomy, as well as create a more cost-effective system, the presence of the leisure coach is phased out systematically as the participant gains skills and confidence.

In summary, the leisure coach acts as a support person. This person gives support to other leisure service professionals conducting inclusive programs, while providing support directly to participants to help them engage in community recreation programs of their choosing.

Family and Friend Support for Leisure Participation

Parent, guardian, spouse, sibling, child, and friend participation in the process of leisure education can be stimulated by providing workshops. Workshops are designed to increase the ability of friends and family to work together with the individual to facilitate leisure participation for everyone.

Barriers can occur to people's leisure due to such conditions as chronic pain, cultural clashes, unique religious practices, and limited language competence. The workshops can highlight information communicated in the leisure education course, focusing on identifying leisure resources available in the community.

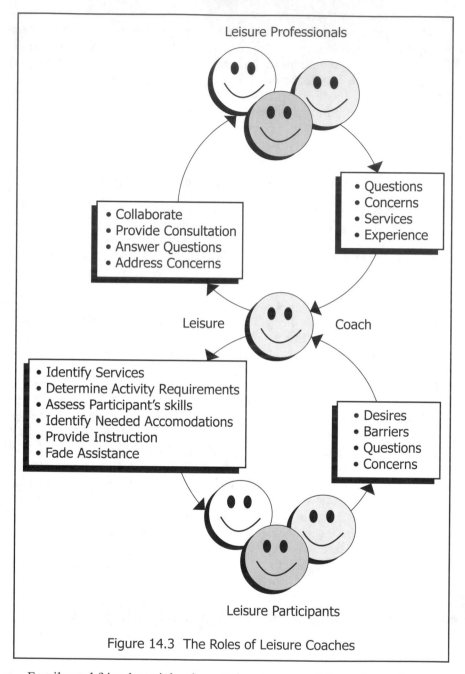

Leisure Professionals

- Questions
- Concerns
- Services
- Experience

- Collaborate
- Provide Consultation
- Answer Questions
- Address Concerns

Leisure   Coach

- Identify Services
- Determine Activity Requirements
- Assess Participant's skills
- Identify Needed Accomodations
- Provide Instruction
- Fade Assistance

- Desires
- Barriers
- Questions
- Concerns

Leisure Participants

Figure 14.3 The Roles of Leisure Coaches

Family and friend participation can be encouraged through regular contact that informs them of accomplishments and problems experienced by their family member or friend. Strategies encouraging continuation of participants' successful efforts and methods for reducing barriers to community leisure involvement can be addressed.

Words of Caution

Although seven components of a leisure education program are identified in this chapter, more or less of these components could be used in any leisure education program. The examples in the next section demonstrate how some professionals have chosen to focus on various components of leisure behavior, given the challenges that are experienced by their participants. What is important is to consider the needs and interests of each person or group to determine how to move forward with a leisure education program.

Even though these components were presented in a sequence, I do not mean to infer that they need to be presented in this particular order when educating participants. I concur with Bullock and colleagues (2010, p. 416) that:

> *[a]ny leisure education process must allow the unique needs of the individual to dictate the order in which different components or elements are introduced and, indeed, whether one, some, or all of the components are necessary for the given individual. Though in many cases people will want or need to proceed through the leisure education process in an order that is quite normative, it is dangerous to assume that all individuals should or must proceed along the same path.*

It is helpful when formulating leisure education programs to consider relevant characteristics of participants that have been addressed previously in the book. The *socio-economic status* of people influences greatly the barriers they encounter to meaningful leisure and the types of leisure pursuits in which they engage. *Age* is another variable that is important to think about; for instance, the focus of a leisure education program designed for adolescents would be different from a program designed for older adults because of various challenges, motivations, and interests they have. Another important consideration for offering leisure education programs is the need for professionals to be culturally competent given the variability of leisure desires across *cultures*.

As an illustration, Rod Dieser (2002) reported on two personal narratives of cross-cultural experiences with a man who was an American Indian and another who was African American. He reported that many leisure education programs are based on Western values such as individualism and independence, which can create problems for people who were raised in cultures that emphasize other values such as cooperation and harmony. Consequently, he recommended that we become culturally competent so that when we develop leisure education programs, we will be more likely to meet the needs of diverse participants.

What are examples of leisure education?

The programs described in this section are just a few examples of how leisure service providers have begun to develop leisure education services for people experiencing a variety of challenges. Great value exists in community leisure service providers offering programs that go beyond recreation activities and incorporate efforts to systematically provide leisure education. The programs described here include ones that:

- promote health
- decrease stress
- increase satisfaction
- contribute to development
- enhance lives
- decrease boredom

Promote Health

It is helpful if leisure service providers offer community-based leisure education programs that focus on health promotion. Besides being affordable, accessible, and attractive, local community leisure service agencies offer a variety of programs and facilities that make them ideal for offering health promotion programs. To illustrate the possibility of using leisure education to promote good health, Payne and colleagues (1999, p. 74) provided the following example:

> For an older person who is recovering from a health problem, initial involvement in community recreation and park services may be limited to physical activity programs. However, to ensure long-term adoption of enjoyable physical activity, recreation and park staff could conduct individualized or small-group leisure education counseling sessions. In these sessions, staff could help older people identify and encourage involvement in other self-chosen, meaningful, enjoyable, and beneficial sponsored recreational activities.

Decrease Stress

With the increasing number of older adults in our society, especially those residing in their communities, many people experience caring for an older adult at home. As more adults are in need of long-term assistance, the people providing their care experience stress. Hagan, Green, and Starling (1998) proposed a leisure education program designed to decrease stress associated with caring for an older adult.

The leisure education program proposed by Hagan and colleagues included personal time management, information about leisure activities, information about leisure support resources, ways to develop leisure appreciation, and ways to develop awareness of self in leisure.

Increase Satisfaction

Although leisure education is often considered to be for children and youth, many adults and those considered older adults can benefit from leisure education. The process of transitioning into older adulthood can bring with it challenges, such as a new living environment, health problems, and an increase in free time. These challenges can be addressed by leisure education.

As reported in previous chapters, aging involves many life transitions that require adjustment and development of new coping strategies. Leisure education can be an effective technique to assist older adults with these changes.

For example, Mahon and Martens (1996) demonstrated that adults enhanced their leisure satisfaction and increased their community adjustment as a result of participating in a leisure education program that included leisure awareness, personal futures planning, and action planning. Mahon and Goatcher (1999) observed that after involvement in a program that helped participants plan for later life, adults increased their leisure and life satisfaction significantly more than their peers who did not participate in such a program.

Contribute to Development

Since leisure provides opportunities to experiment with self-expression and various roles, it is an important context for adolescent development. However, this same leisure context is where many unhealthy behaviors occur, such as cigarette smoking, alcohol and other drug use, and early promiscuous sexual intercourse.

There is value in developing leisure education programs for adolescents that teach them about leisure opportunities in their communities. These programs can identify and promote alternatives to high-risk behaviors like promiscuous sexual behavior.

As an example, Risisky and colleagues (1997) suggested that a leisure education program for adolescents emphasize leisure-skills building, decision making, and enhancing self-esteem.

Enhance Lives

A primary goal of leisure education in schools is development of free time and leisure-related skills that enhance the quality of daily life for children and youth. Provision of leisure education in the school setting can create optimal environments for achieving students' goals related to inclusion.

> Specifically, Heyne and Schleien (1997) suggested that leisure education can encourage refinement of social skills, promote social interactions, and develop friendships in inclusive classrooms. Since recreation and play are important aspects of the socialization and education of children, leisure education can play a vital role in the growth, maturation, and quality of life of all young people.

Decrease Boredom

Leisure education programs can be developed that encourage individuals to explore, discover, and develop knowledge about them in a leisure context. Within the context of such educational programs, practitioners may find it helpful to assist participants to explore new alternative values, goals, and leisure activities.

> For example, Lee, Mittlstaedt, and Askins (1999) encouraged leisure service providers to design leisure education programs for people experiencing free-time boredom, focusing on enhancing participants' awareness of self in leisure. Participation in meaningful leisure education programs can help people experiencing free-time boredom to make important, positive changes to their lifestyles.

Final Thoughts

A primary purpose of leisure services is to meet the leisure needs of participants. Our ability to meet these needs is impaired without effective service delivery systems. This chapter identified the rationale for including leisure education in inclusive leisure services. The suggestions for leisure education are intended to encourage participants to develop skills and knowledge that facilitate successful inclusion in community life.

Across the past three decades, many authors have made general recommendations for planning, implementing, and evaluating leisure education programs. A variety of contexts in which leisure education sessions can be effectively implemented include schools, community agencies, retirement communities, and individuals' private residences. Across all contexts, it is helpful to access supports when implementing leisure education programs, such as family members and friends in the educational process. Volunteers can be a helpful addition to effective service delivery as well.

Leisure education is far from stagnant; it is a *dynamic process* involving continuous enhancement of leisure-related knowledge, skills, and awareness. The process requires presentation of information intended to help individuals identify and clarify their leisure participation patterns. A purpose of leisure education is to instill a leisure ethic within people, so that they may freely and willingly participate in activities that can bring them satisfaction and enjoyment, with the ultimate goal of having their participation in these activities enrich and enhance their lives.

Discussion Questions

1. What is leisure education?
2. What is meant by awareness of self in leisure?
3. How could people attending a leisure education program develop an appreciation of leisure?
4. Why is self-determination an important component of a comprehensive leisure education program?
5. What are some components of the decision-making process?
6. What are some questions relative to leisure resources that are important for people to be able to answer?
7. What are some examples of important social interaction skills when participating in inclusive leisure services?
8. What are some guidelines to follow when teaching recreation activity skills?
9. What are some actions that could be taken to develop a course on leisure education?
10. What are the primary responsibilities of a leisure coach?
11. How could family and friends be included in leisure education?
12. What are some examples of leisure education programs?

Chapter 15
Promote Social
Interaction and Friendships

A candle loses none of its light by lighting another candle.
-Anonymous

Orientation Activity: Connecting People

Directions Alone: Choose an agency with which you are familiar or imagine an ideal job. List at least five different ways you could encourage participants to get to know one another and promote friendships between participants.

Directions with Others: Move about the room with your list, find a person, and introduce yourself. Discuss one idea you had about encouraging friendship and have the person identify one different idea. Record the person's name and her or his idea on your list. Once you have discussed the information move to another person. Continue this process until you have shared all the items on your list. See how many different ideas you can list by talking to as many people as possible.

Debriefing: If given the choice, most people want to participate in inclusive recreation activities. Often the degree to which people enjoy an activity is based on their social interactions with other participants. Continued participation is often linked to the relationships they have developed with their peers involved in the same activity. Consider the following questions when thinking about connecting people:

- How might we prepare a situation to help people interact?
- How can we encourage social interactions between participants?
- How might we help to develop friendships among participants?

Introduction

Development of relationships, the core of inclusion, involves providing support to foster relationships between people who have been devalued and valued members of their community. For people to have access to valued social roles, it is helpful for them to have the chance to grow and learn with their peers. Emphasizing the importance of social interaction, one of my students, Zack Emery, stated:

> *For someone like my brother, who has Asperger's Syndrome,*
> *having social interactions with other children his age is a*
> *critical piece to helping him learn how to behave in public,*
> *in the classroom, and around other people in general.*

There is a growing preference among participants and their families for inclusive leisure programs. In the United States, legislation supports and mandates services for all people in inclusive community environments.

Leisure professionals must be prepared to provide services to people in inclusive settings. Unfortunately, despite research showing benefits of people developing relationships through inclusion, implementation has been slow and has sometimes been met with resistance.

This chapter includes two major areas. The first section addresses information about benefits of inclusive leisure services that primarily relate to the provision of opportunities for social interaction and development of friendships. A variety of groups of people can benefit from inclusive leisure services.

The second major section of this chapter focuses on ways to foster social interactions and ultimately to encourage development of friendships. Prior to offering leisure services, we can prepare people and situations so that positive interactions between all participants are encouraged. In addition, we can take various actions while an activity is occurring to promote positive contacts between participants. The following questions will be addressed:

- What are benefits of inclusion for participants?
- What are benefits of inclusion for leisure service providers?
- How can we prepare people to promote social interactions and friendships?
- How can we encourage social interactions?
- How can we promote and friendships?
- What are examples of inclusive leisure programs that promote social interaction and friendships?

What are benefits of inclusion for participants?

Inclusive leisure participation prepares all people for life in a diverse society and prepares society to accept individual diversity. While there are many benefits of inclusion, greater social acceptance by peers and social inclusion into the community may be the most important.

> After reviewing the literature on inclusion, Ryndak and colleagues (2010) noted that research reveals benefits of inclusion to include appropriate social behaviors, increased interactions with others, more positive feelings, increased friendships, and improved communication.

When discussing benefits of inclusion, people often focus on benefits experienced by people who have been oppressed in some manner, such as individuals who are not members of the dominant race or religion. Although benefits to these individuals are numerous, benefits to people who are privileged are also plentiful.

Learning to live, work, and play with people who are different is a critical part of a person's development. When discussing inclusive communities, Vandercook and colleagues (1989, p. 19) reported that:

> *[p]eople are enriched by having the opportunity to learn from one another, grow to care for one another, and gain the attitudes, skills, and values necessary for our communities to support the inclusion of all citizens.*

By including all people in community programs, people who have been oppressed prepare for life in their community, practitioners improve their professional skills, and overall society makes the conscious decision to operate according to the social value of equality for all people. Some of the benefits of inclusion are that participants:

- cultivate friendships
- acquire social skills
- develop life-long skills
- enhance image
- improve academic performance
- improve attitudes
- increase understanding
- develop acceptance

Cultivate Friendships

People can develop friendships with others when they participate in inclusive community leisure programs. After studying almost 1,000 adolescents across two distinct cultures, Shokoohi-Yekta and Hendrickson (2010, p. 24) defined *friendship* as:

> *[a] social relationship between two people that is reciprocal, rewarding, and fun for both parties; it is a relationship that is characterized by multiple, voluntary contacts, and shared experiences across time.*

Similarly, Sciberras and Hutchison (2004) identified the following qualities associated with friendships:

- reciprocity and mutuality
- voluntary and freely chosen
- enjoyment of one another's company
- share similar interests

Research supports the conclusion that quality friendships are associated with positive attitudes and reduce the chance of being victimized by peers. Often participants develop spontaneous friendships that emerge out of shared interests identified during inclusive leisure experiences.

> For example, Dwayne and Marcia reported that as a result of developing friendships during participation in a community recreation program, their daughter Sasha was invited to birthday parties, received telephone calls from friends, and had friends visit her house to play.

When parents are asked about what they want for their children, often they indicate that they want their child to have friends. In a report to the U.S. President (U.S. Department of Health and Human Services Administration for Children and Families, 1994, p. 2) Linda Charlton talked about her dreams for her young daughter, Katie, who has Down's syndrome, a condition that frequently leads to an intellectual disability:

> *Our goals for Katie include wanting her to feel loved, to give her a sense of high self-esteem so that she can experience life with confidence. She is a very social child and while I think she has a great capacity to make friends, I wonder how other children will accept her.*

Recreation activities that permit interaction with a person's peers provide opportunities for shared interests, a sense of accomplishment, feelings of belonging, formation of a personal identity, and mastery over the environment. Inclusive leisure services help to reduce barriers and create a forum for emerging relationships.

Acquire Social Skills

People are more likely to develop social skills needed to develop relationships when participating in inclusive leisure opportunities. Since having friends is important to the quality of every person's life, people learn best when learning what their friends are learning. Inclusive environments give people a chance to learn to get along with others, interact, seek and lend assistance, understand when assistance is needed, make sense of changing contexts, ask questions, communicate with others, and behave appropriately.

When people who have been *disenfranchised*, those who have been deprived of certain privileges or rights, are congregated in a particular area, there is a tendency for them not to learn social skills associated with the mainstream of society. However, when people are enjoying leisure participation in inclusive environments, they tend to interact with one another and develop relationships with their peers.

> For example, Dreimanus and colleagues (1992) reported that children interacted more often with other children when they were in inclusive environments, and that preschoolers exhibited more socially advanced skills in inclusive settings. Guralnick and Groom (1988) observed play groups and concluded that inclusive play groups facilitated peer interaction, whereas segregated play groups constrained peer interaction and promoted adult-child interaction. Schleien, Ray, Soderman-Olson, and McMahon (1987) observed that social interactions of children increased during an inclusive art education program.

Researchers have consistently found that inclusive environments improved participants' feelings of self-worth, communication and interaction abilities, leadership skills, and tolerance of diversity.

Develop Life-Long Skills

The presence of appropriate inclusive options promotes development of life-long functional recreation skills. People can learn interdependent behaviors such as asking for assistance as needed by experiencing challenges that are part of inclusive community life. Behaviors are *interdependent* when they require people to rely on one another and there is mutual support for each person's efforts.

Enjoyment associated with leisure participation can reward different levels of ability, if professionals encourage valuing each individual's contribution. A variety of life-long recreation activity skills can be developed in inclusive situations.

> For example, martial arts including tae kwon do, karate, or judo are activities that can be engaged in across the life span. Various forms of creative arts such a playing a musical instrument, painting, and sculpting are all activities that can be enjoyed throughout one's life. Additional life-long recreation activities that promote fitness include playing golf or tennis, swimming, and walking.

Enhance Image

Placement of people in a segregated context can result in people being viewed negatively. Conversely, when people are included, their image is enhanced since they become part of a community that is representative of a society.

> As an example, Storey, Stern, and Parker (1991) examined attitudes of college students toward a woman participating in either Special Olympics or in typical recreation activities within an inclusive setting. In the Special Olympics presentation, the

woman was regarded as younger and more in need of assistance than in the typical activities presentation. This study lends support to the belief that the image of a person is more positive when the person is associated with participating in an inclusive context as opposed to a segregated one.

Improve Academic Performance

Many individuals who are involved in inclusive programs do better academically and socially than comparable individuals in segregated environments.

For instance, after conducting longitudinal observations of the performance of students in public schools, Rankin and colleagues (1994) concluded that children who were in inclusive classrooms were doing better than they did in previous years when they were in self-contained classrooms. Ryndak and colleagues (1995) reported that parents stated that for their children, inclusion resulted in removing barriers to learning and their children began using increased vocabulary, employing coping strategies during difficult situations, being less dependent on parents, being more interactive with peers, and reducing inappropriate behaviors.

In summary, people accrue many benefits from participating in inclusive leisure services. The most prominent benefits associated with inclusion relate to participants' abilities to engage in social interactions with their peers and develop meaningful friendships.

Improve Attitudes

People often positively alter their attitudes about diverse individuals as a result of joint participation in selected activities.

For example, McLean and Hanline (1990) concluded that carefully planned inclusive programs result in positive developmental and attitudinal outcomes for young children. Schleien and colleagues (1987) reported that after participation in an inclusive art education program, the attitudes of children toward their peers changed positively.

If the attitude of people toward others who differ from them in some manner is positive because of joint participation, it is likely that the person will participate in recreation activities with these people again. These people will bring to the activity a positive attitude, resulting in them confidently influencing the attitudes of other participants, thus creating a cycle of positive attitudes.

Increase Understanding

Enjoyment of recreation opportunities that reward different levels of ability can occur when people value each individual's contribution. Exposure to inclusive leisure services results in a greater understanding and acceptance of individuals with varying backgrounds and ability levels. This exposure creates the potential for inclusion to have a positive impact on the social development of all individuals.

When involved in inclusive programs, people become more accepting of differences and begin to appreciate the capacities of persons with disabilities. The following quote from the Georgia Advocacy Office (1992, p. 4, 9) illustrates the benefits people receive when participating in inclusive programs:

> Our world includes a vast array of people who, we believe, are more alike than different. We believe that what children learn from each other about difference and acceptance is equally as important as the technical education that they receive. We all need to learn how to live and work together. Students develop more fully when they welcome people with different gifts and abilities into their lives and when all students feel secure that they will receive individualized help when they need it.

Develop Acceptance

Leisure service professionals can take an active role in reducing social stigmas associated with various individuals by emphasizing similarities rather than differences.

> For example, after conducting multiple interviews with 22 middle- and high-school students, Devine and Wilhite (2000) found that the youth reported positive results when the leisure context emphasized similarities in participants' abilities.

Long-term interactions between different groups of people facilitate development of skills, attitudes, and values that prepare these groups to share, participate, and contribute to their communities. As a result of participation in inclusive leisure services, people who have not been disenfranchised learn new ways to solve problems and adapt to difference, develop more positive attitudes toward people who are different from them, and increase acceptance of people in general.

> For instance, after surveying almost 1,500 high school students from two high schools—one inclusive and one segregated—Fisher, Pupian, and Sax (1998) found that youth educated in an inclusive setting expected and recommended inclusion. However, if youth attended a school that provided limited inclusion, they expected and recommended segregation; it

> seemed that as a group, youth who had the inclusive experience are better prepared for their adult life, since they will encounter diverse people in their community and jobs.

As a result of participating in inclusive leisure opportunities, many people report that they experience personal growth and increased social sensitivity, including improved capacity for compassion, kindness, and respect for others. Others report that they develop skills and attitudes needed to live harmoniously in communities that include people with and without disabilities.

> As an example, after a review of the research literature, Kliewer (1998) concluded that children in inclusive classrooms achieved at levels equal to or above their peers in classes that were not inclusive. Helmstetter and colleagues (1994) interviewed 166 high school students; the adolescents reported that inclusive experiences:

- increased responsiveness to the needs of others
- encouraged valued relationships
- increased tolerance of other people
- developed personal values
- increased appreciation of human diversity
- promoted positive changes in status with peers

In summary, benefits of an inclusive leisure opportunity extend beyond leisure services providers and the participants who have been disenfranchised. All people benefit from inclusion (Figure 15.1).

What are benefits of inclusion for leisure service providers?

Leisure service providers also experience benefits associated with having diverse people access services together. As leisure service agencies embrace the concept of inclusion and respond to the needs of a diverse participant group, they comply with various civil-rights legislation. By providing inclusive programs, service providers are exposed to and educated about individual needs, and subsequently they increase their acceptance of people in general.

There are many benefits to inclusion from educational, social, and psychological perspectives. Benefits of inclusion are also realized from an economic standpoint. Many professionals have learned that inclusive services are less expensive than contracting for segregated services. Referring to the economic benefit of inclusion, Tiersten (1994, p. 4) made the following statement regarding one particular oppressed group, people with disabilities:

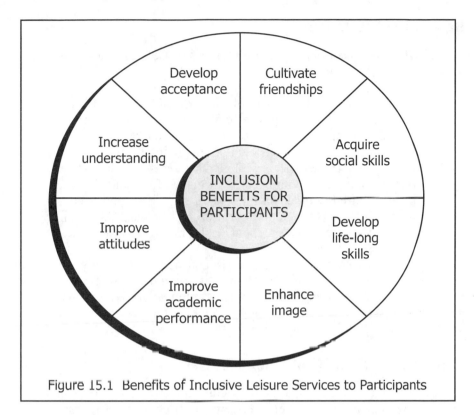

Figure 15.1 Benefits of Inclusive Leisure Services to Participants

Ultimately, inclusion could help, rather than harm, the bottom line. In ignoring people with disabilities, organizations are missing a superb business opportunity. "Americans with disabilities are an emerging market," according to Steven Hacker, president of the Dallas-based International Association for Exposition Management.

How can we prepare people to promote social interactions and friendships?

Many programmatic strategies can be used to encourage the inclusion of all people into community leisure programs. This section highlights the following strategies to prepare people to help encourage social interaction and develop friendships:

- be aware of isolation
- learn about benefits of friendships
- assess participants' interests
- include people in planning and decision making
- teach leisure service providers

Be Aware of Isolation

People who have been oppressed are most often isolated from their peers if interactions are left to chance.

> For example, Favazza and colleagues (2000) observed that children without disabilities do not interact with their peers with disabilities unless they are supported and encouraged to do so. Hanline (1993) reported that children without disabilities tend to communicate with peers without disabilities more often than they communicate with peers with disabilities. They choose other children without disabilities as playmates and friends more often than they choose children with disabilities and prefer to sit next to peers without disabilities in group activities.

Typically, people who have limited social networks usually spend their free time alone or with family. Therefore, it is important that we encourage interactions at a very young age and help people who have been privileged to understand and respond to the unique behaviors of their peers so that they may develop meaningful friendships.

Learn about Benefits of Friendships

The impact of leisure participation on social support is likely to be significant for those who have limited friends or few social contacts. Friendships serve many important functions for people, including:

- learn social skills
- engage in reciprocity
- develop a sense of autonomy
- enhance self-esteem
- instill a sense of belonging
- experience intimacy
- feel valued and loved

Regular social contact through recreation activities can help individuals overcome a considerable deficit in perceived social support for people who are isolated. By engaging in leisure pursuits conducive to social interaction, people are more likely to make friends and develop closer friendships (Figure 15.2).

Assess Participants' Interests

The practice of *administering surveys and questionnaires* to obtain input from potential participants about their interests and desires can be useful. However, to discover people's needs and interests, it is also helpful for professionals to *conduct observations* of participants' expressions and ways of communicating as they participate.

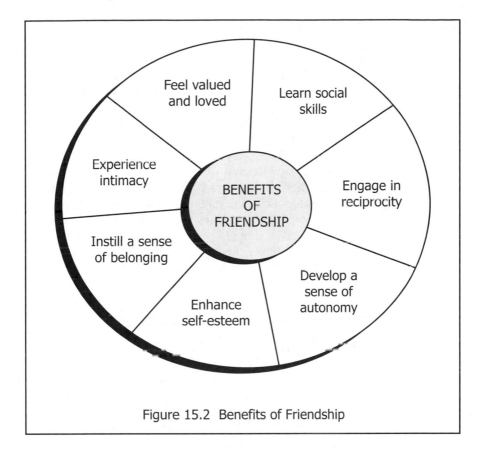

Figure 15.2 Benefits of Friendship

Once preferences are identified, we can encourage people to act on their interests and provide opportunities to learn and to practice leisure skills in various settings. Grouping people by mutual interests rather than by characteristics helps to increase acceptance of all people by their peers and promote social connections.

Include People in Planning and Decision Making

Some professionals have found value in involving participants and families when promoting social interaction and participation in inclusive programs. The act of soliciting feedback can facilitate inclusion and identify ways to promote social interactions.

An invitation to participants and their family members to assist in staff development can be an effective way to promote social interactions and develop a context for friendships. The designation of a staff person to be a facilitator of inclusive experiences and to promote positive social interactions may also be useful. Another approach involves including statements in promotional literature on policies of inclusion, giving potential participants someone to contact.

Teach Leisure Service Providers

Another way to prepare people for inclusion is to provide training for all leisure service personnel. Possible topics for training include presentations on the rationale for inclusive leisure that address the benefits of inclusive leisure services for all people, information about civil-rights legislation and how it supports inclusion, and information on the value of social interactions, friendships, and inclusion.

Roles and responsibilities of people who contribute to inclusive services, such as parents, participants, advocacy groups, schools, and leisure service professionals, can be identified through staff trainings. It can be helpful to describe strategies that promote social interactions between participants, ways to develop meaningful friendships, and how to design services that foster inclusion. These strategies are designed to encourage accepting attitudes, implement program methods to attract and support individuals, evaluate and solicit feedback, and develop networks and resources.

How can we encourage social interactions and friendships?

Positive interaction between diverse groups of people can be increased by limiting space, selecting materials and activities that promote social interaction, and rotating and limiting materials. To address the issue of how to prepare the situation so that it will foster social interactions and the development of friendships, this section is divided into the following areas:

- design cooperative activities
- increase opportunities for active participation
- select interactive materials and equipment
- teach social skills
- promote friendships

Design Cooperative Activities

Activities that require cooperation can facilitate inclusion. A cooperative learning structure can create interdependence between people, because completion of a task by a group requires that everyone contribute in some way. The activity encourages each person to support all other participants to achieve realistic group goals. After a review of the literature of cooperative learning, Jenkins, Antil, Wayne, and Vadasy (2003, p. 279) stated that:

> *Although researchers differ on the exact features that define cooperative learning, they generally agree that students must work together in small groups, make explicit effort to help each other learn, and share in the evaluation.*

Participation in joint activities may result in peer acceptance and inclusion. It is helpful if we encourage positive interactions when these behaviors are not occurring, reinforce positive interactions as they occur, and redirect behaviors if cooperation does not occur.

Increase Opportunities for Active Participation

There are a variety of ways to promote active participation for everyone. Two such techniques include dividing participants into small groups and providing a small area for participation.

As the number of people becomes smaller in a group, the opportunity for expression is typically enhanced, and thereby creates situations conducive to social interaction. Also, a small area in which activities are enjoyed stimulates interaction and inclusion. Small areas result in more peer interaction than large play areas.

Select Interactive Materials and Equipment

Limiting the number of materials tends to promote sharing and positive peer interaction. Specific types of toys such as cars, games, socio-dramatic materials, blocks, dress-up clothes, dolls, dollhouse, housekeeping materials, puppets, and vehicles tend to promote social interaction, whereas other toys such as clay, books, puzzles, LEGO toys, books, paints, paintbrushes, paper, scissors, crayons, markers, and puzzles tend to isolate children.

> Ivory and McCollum (1999) compared behaviors of young children involved in an inclusive playgroup; they noted that cooperative play occurred significantly more often with social toys as compared to the isolating toys.

Teach Social Skills

Placing people in the same physical environment without any assistance does not necessarily lead to social interaction or social acceptance between individuals. Structured programs that teach individuals social skills or how to initiate and respond to peers' social contacts can promote positive peer interactions. Systematic efforts to allow participants to interact frequently with a small, stable group of peers are likely to lead to an increase in interaction between people.

It is helpful to treat all participants the same as others their age by expecting them to be as independent as possible, encouraging others to interact with them, supporting and assisting only when necessary, and encouraging accomplishments. One way to proceed is to compare a participant's abilities to what is expected of all participants, and if there are aspects of the activity that a person cannot perform independently, problem-solve to determine what types of supports are needed.

Promote Friendships

Leisure is an excellent social context for the development of friendships and for the expression of social identities. Friendships developed and fostered through leisure participation and the perceived availability of social support generated by leisure engagement help people cope with stress, as well as maintain or improve health.

Inclusive leisure participation can play an important role in facilitating friendships. The leisure context can encourage friendships because it gives people something to do together, a reason for spending time together, and a way to get to know one another through shared experiences.

To facilitate friendships, it is important for us to provide needed social supports. Supports can range from incorporating volunteers, to providing helpful reminders, to assisting people with equipment, to providing help during some aspects of participation. Regardless of the level of support, it is helpful if participants learn to become independent and interdependent in recreation activities.

Although independence is discussed frequently as a goal for all people, another important goal associated with development and maintenance of friends is interdependence. As discussed in previous chapters, *interdependence* implies a reciprocal relationship where we depend on another person as that person helps us and, in turn, that person depends on us as we help that individual.

> Rossetti and Goessling (2010) reported that research on children and adolescents identify that the most important preconditions for friendship are proximity and familiarity.

Participation in inclusive leisure services can promote both proximity and familiarity. *Proximity* is associated with how near something or someone is to another thing or person, especially in this context, related to distance. *Familiarity* infers a level of closeness and friendliness in a personal relationship.

> To promote proximity, participants in a photography class can be asked to work in small groups at tables to develop an integrated layout of their collective pictures. A way to encourage familiarity is to conduct discussions among participants regarding leisure interests that might include favorite physically active pursuits, sport teams they may enthusiastically support, and preferred musical performers. These types of discussions allow people to learn about each other, and they create opportunities to develop meaningful connections.

See Figure 15.3 for a summary of ways to prepare and encourage social interactions and friendships among all participants.

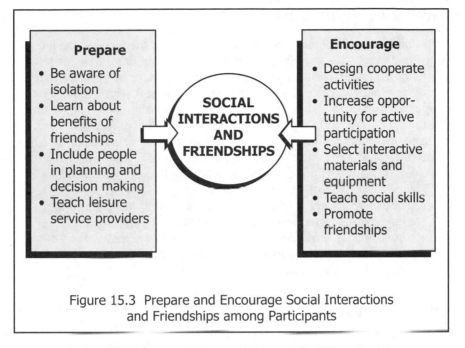

Figure 15.3 Prepare and Encourage Social Interactions and Friendships among Participants

What are examples of inclusive leisure programs that promote social interaction and friendships?

There are numerous examples of leisure programs that encourage interaction between people with and without disabilities and the subsequent development of friendships, including:

- Every Buddy
- Shared interest at home
- Acting Together

Every Buddy

Ledman, Thompson, and Hill (1992) reported on a cost-effective program, Every Buddy, developed to provide supervised after-school services to children of all ability levels. Participants were included in the YMCA programs by adding trained staff to three of the YMCA's after-school program sites. These personnel provided individualized support needed by children to participate in the program alongside their peers. Parents strongly agreed that the environment was safe, children were eager to attend the program and were participating in activities, and the needs of families and children were being met. The YMCA staff felt that all participants benefited from the effort and that there had been no negative response to the program from any participants or family members.

Shared Interests at Home

When children meet others who are different from them, they are naturally curious and may ask a variety of questions. Some children may not have the experience to handle the situation, and they may not have had much experience meeting new people. One way to help children connect with one another is to arrange for children to visit each other's homes. Once children visit their home, parents advise that the child show their peers where they play. Once there, their toys become the center of attention, rather than other characteristics such as the color of their skin, the family's income, their religion, or disability. As interests are shared, or skills identified, acceptance and inclusion is enhanced.

> For example, Olivia, who knows sign language, can teach some simple signs to her new friends, Lydia and Donald. In another situation, an adolescent, Hadar, who is competent with the computer or playing video games, might invite a couple of his peers to play with him.

Acting Together

Miller, Rynders, and Schleien (1993) reported on results of a project entitled *Acting Together*, an inclusive drama class incorporating theater games and improvisational acting experiences for children. Acting Together demonstrated the value of creative drama as an approach to promote inclusion. Since drama is a social art, it exists with an audience and with a society of players, otherwise known as actors. This quality may make it a particularly useful medium when participants have limited social skills.

Final Thoughts

At the center of feeling included in one's community is the ability to experience leisure with friends. Mahon and colleagues (2000, p. 28) quoted Martin, a man with an intellectual disability, as saying:

> *I know what integration means! It means coffee with friends, walks to the mall with friends, getting together with people who like to do stuff you like, having a good time, and being included.*

There are many social benefits that are realized when inclusive leisure services are provided. As an example, Linda Preston made the following statement about her 12-year-old son (U.S. Department of Health and Human Services Administration for Children and Families, 1994, p. 36):

> *We went to a forest preserve one weekend and a group of young people had an impromptu concert with bongos, drums, and other instruments. We went over to listen. One of them gave Elisha some maracas. And for the next hour, Elisha was just one of the band, making music, dancing and keeping the beat. They didn't see his disabilities. They just saw the music in him.*

In the end, what seem to matter most to people, are the relationships we develop over our lifetime. John Sanford (2002, p.3) quoted Richard Rodriguez, an author and journalist, who was a member of a panel attempting to address why Americans have trouble nurturing a healthy relationship with leisure. Rodriguez had just spent a day looking at gravestones where his parents were buried, and he made the following observation:

> *So I was looking at the ways the dead are remembered by the living or the ways the dead wanted to be remembered. In an afternoon of looking, I did not find a single gravestone that referred to a person's occupation. Every single life in the cemetery was remembered through relationships.*

Discussion Questions

1. What are some benefits of inclusion for people with disabilities?
2. What are some benefits of inclusion for people without disabilities?
3. What are some benefits of inclusion for leisure service providers?
4. How can cooperatively structured leisure activities be designed to promote social interactions?
5. What are the benefits associated with developing friendships?
6. Why is it important to foster age-appropriate behaviors to stimulate social interactions?
7. How does the size of a group influence social interactions?
8. What kinds of play and recreation materials promote social interactions?
9. What is the value of including people in the leisure services planning process?
10. What are some examples of successful inclusive efforts?

Chapter 16
Employ Principles of
Universal Design

All the world's a stage, and all men and women merely players;
They have their exits and their entrances.
-William Shakespeare

Orientation Activity: Test Design Awareness

Directions Alone: Read each statement below and decide if they are true or false. Once you have finished, read the debriefing to check your answers.

Directions with Others: Move about the room and find another person to share one aspect related to accessibility that you have learned. Continue this process until a signal to end the activity has been given.

1. Ramps are easier for everyone to use than stairs.
2. Most guide dogs stop at intersection curb cuts.
3. Universally designed buildings should have heat-sensitive elevator controls (touch the number and it lights up).
4. Most people with visual impairments can understand direction signs in Braille.
5. Even short-nap carpets can cause barriers for wheelchairs.
6. Public bathroom signs marked "Ladies" and "Gentlemen" may pose barriers to some people who may not read.
7. If a door is wide and has no threshold, it is accessible to wheelchairs.
8. A person with epilepsy should have many bathroom grab bars.
9. Many older adults and people with disabilities should have a telephone in their bathrooms.
10. Some people experience heat stroke in their shower or bathtub.
11. Rooms for people with limited mobility should be furnished with soft, overstuffed furniture.
12. Round doorknobs are generally the most difficult kind to use.
13. A dark sign with light lettering is generally easier to read than a light sign with dark lettering.

Debriefing: This Design Awareness Test has been adapted from an exercise developed by Interface, Human Factors Design Consultants in Raleigh, North Carolina. Answers to the statements follow.

1. False: Some people prefer stairs and can use them more easily than ramps.
2. False: Dogs are trained to stop at curbs; they may lead their masters into traffic if a curb ramp is in their direct line of travel.
3. False: They are nearly impossible for people who are blind to use; they may be especially deadly if used for wheelchair evacuation during a fire. Raised buttons must be placed on elevators to be accessible to persons with visual difficulties. They must be placed at a height that is accessible to people of small stature, and to those using wheeled assistive devices.
4. False: At least 90% of people who are blind cannot read Braille.
5. True: Some short-nap carpets have a tendency to pull wheelchairs to one side as they roll.
6. True: Some people learn to distinguish between restroom facilities by the length of the word on the door; short word means MEN, long word means WOMEN.
7. False: Doors can have many barriers: door handles may be difficult; doors may close too fast and too hard; doors may be too heavy to push open.
8. False: Grab bars may be a dangerous obstruction during a fall. Cushioning the fall would be more effective.
9. True: The bathroom is the most dangerous room in your house, and phones are often used to call for help.
10. True: The heat from bath or shower water can cause heat stroke, especially in older adults. Lowering the hot water thermostat may prevent this.
11. False: Soft furniture does not support the spine adequately; it may be nearly impossible for some people to get up.
12. True: Lever handles require much less hand and wrist action.
13. True: That is why most interstate freeway signs are dark green or blue with white letters.

Introduction

During an average day, most people give little thought to how they get around in their environment. Mobility concerns arise, however, when people are confronted with personal limitations such as broken bones, sprains, or even pregnancy. We also may experience challenges to our mobility when we encounter external hindrances such as carrying heavy packages or using a baby stroller.

A variety of health impairments and disabling conditions can also result in people having substantial challenges accessing recreation facilities and leisure pursuits. Susan York (2009, p. 201) spoke about this issue:

> *The difficulties experienced in mobility, communication, social interactions, and sensory input of an individual's impairment can be exacerbated by additional environmental and attitudinal barriers that may restrict one's ability to access the world around them.*

At some point in our lives, most of us acquire a temporary or permanent limitation. When this occurs, the issue of accessibility or usability suddenly becomes important. McGill and Holden (1995, p. 11) wrote about a man's struggles with access:

> *In the midst of his struggles, the simplest things became issues. He says, "My house, for example, had the wrong doorknobs." One day, he saw the doorknobs as symbols of independence. "If I just had the right kind of doorknobs, I could open more doors for myself—both literally and figuratively. I could take more responsibility for myself.*

The chapter addresses the following several questions:

- What is meant by universal design?
- What is meant by the International Symbol of Access?
- What types of access barriers exist?
- Which access guidelines should we follow?
- What is the impact of universal design?
- How can leisure contexts be universally designed?
- What are examples of universally designed leisure contexts?

What is meant by universal design?

Access is the freedom or ability to obtain or make use of something or the ability to get into, approach, communicate with, or pass to and from somewhere. Access is also associated with social expectations. Positive or negative feelings and attitudes influence these experiences.

Accessibility or usability of a facility is the degree to which a person can get to, enter, and use a building or surrounding area. The term *barrier* implies that there is an obstruction that impedes an individual's progress. A single stair can allow an individual to move from one level to another level with ease. However, that same stair can deny a person using a wheelchair or a parent with a child's stroller the ability to enter that facility.

The National Center on Accessibility (2010, p. 4) provides a helpful clarification of an often misused term, "ADA Approved":

> *Do not rely on manufacturer or verbal claims that their product meets or complies with the ADA. Ultimately, the owner of the facility is responsible for the accessibility of the facility and its programs, not the vendors who sell the products. Many advertisements claim products to be "ADA Approved" or call the product itself "ADA Table" or "ADA Surface." There is no organization or governmental body that reviews products for compliance of ADA or that has the authority to give "ADA Approval" for any product. This*

wording is misleading and may cause you to end up with products that do not provide optimum access. Be sure to compare products with accessibility guidelines and standards before you make a purchase.

Although the term *accessible* suggests that something is made usable through some adaptation, the term universal design moves beyond the idea of being accessible. *Universal design* involves the formation of an inclusive environment that combines a variety of design concepts, including accessibility, into a range of meaningful options for all people. Sharon Jones (2009, p. 158) stated that:

Universal design is unobtrusive, even invisible. If you've ever been through an automatic door, you've experienced a version of Universal Design. A ramp or curb cut is just as welcome to someone with a baby stroller as it is to someone in a wheelchair. In addition to those whose mobility is limited, the design is intuitive to those who cannot read or hear or those who speak a foreign language. These examples of universal design provide the little of no difference in the manner in which they are experienced for the greatest number of people possible. No one is stigmatized or inconvenienced by their use.

'Universal design' refers to attempts to make all products and environments accessible and usable to all people. In describing the design of his home (built and designed by him and his wife), William Rush (1999, p. 1) taught readers about universal design:

Universal design is making products and environments to be usable by all people, to the greatest extent possible, without the need for adaptation or specialized design. The idea of universal design is to simplify life for everyone by making products, communications, and the built environment more usable by as many people as possible at little or no extra cost. We could see that universal design benefits people of all ages and abilities.

Often, universal design can benefit many individuals other than those who have a disability. For example, Minkoff (1997, p. 22) described the use of a surf chair on the beach of Ocean City, New Jersey:

Initially, it was thought that the chairs would provide assistance for individuals with disabilities; in most cases that is true. However, the chairs have proven to benefit a variety of individuals who have difficulty maneuvering through the city's soft, wide beaches ... senior citizens, pregnant women and people recovering from surgery are just some of the beachgoers who have taken advantage of the program.

A team composed of architects, product designers, engineers, and environmental design researchers came together at the Center for Universal Design to identify the following ***principles of universal design*** (Connell et al., 1997):

- equitable
- flexible
- simple and intuitive
- perceptible information
- tolerance for error
- low physical effort
- size and space for approach and use

Universal design is *equitable*; that is, it results in something useful, and is marketable to any group. *Flexibility* is important in that the design should accommodate a wide range of individual preferences and abilities. Universal design implies that the design is *simple and intuitive*; it is easy to understand for any user. When there is *perceptible information*, the design communicates information needed to operate.

Another aspect of universal design is *tolerance for error*: the design minimizes hazards and any adverse consequences that might occur as a result of accidental or unintended use. The design requires *low physical effort* so that it can be used comfortably and efficiently with minimum fatigue. Universal design incorporates appropriate *size and space for approach and use,* which makes things available to people, with allowances made for moving, reaching, and manipulating within an environment independent of a person's size, posture, or mobility. Figure 16.1 (p. 308) provides a summary of the principles of universal design.

It is important that the principles are applied during all stages of building and purchasing including:

- research of purchases or designs
- procurement of equipment
- construction
- installation of equipment
- maintenance of equipment or building
- periodic testing
- personnel training

What is meant by the International Symbol of Access?

The International Symbol of Access (ISA) represents the hope of independence and mobility to people with disabilities. Wherever it is displayed, people can be assured that obstacles will not prohibit them from participation.

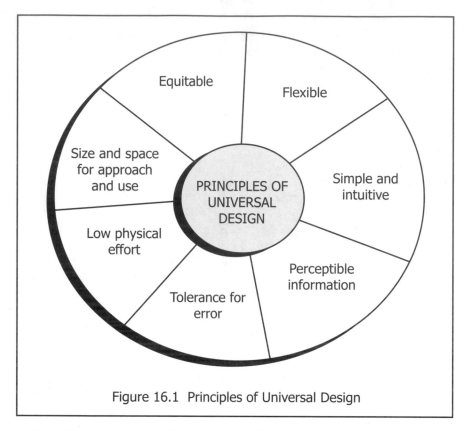

Figure 16.1 Principles of Universal Design

Use of signs to convey information to visitors and participants is an important consideration in the provision of access. The ISA is often used in parking lots to indicate reserved stalls and in buildings to indicate accessible bathrooms. It can also be used in conjunction with directional symbols or a written message such as "Ask for Information Here," which tells the visitor that there are other services available. Such services may include interpretive audio recordings, availability of a wheelchair for loan, and accessible transportation services.

The Symbol, as depicted in Figure 16.2, is used in informational materials such as maps, program announcements and information, and registration brochures, to indicate accessibility. Care should be taken in the use of these symbols. For instance, a building that has an accessible entrance should not have the access symbol displayed unless the facilities and services inside the building are also accessible. The 1975 Assembly of Rehabilitation International meeting presented the following policies to govern the use of the ISA:

- the Symbol shall always be used in the design and proportions approved by the Assembly, reproduction of which shall be disseminated with this resolution
- the colors used shall always be in sharp contrast and, unless there are compelling reasons to use other colors, the Symbol and its background shall be reproduced in either black and white or dark blue and white
- no change in or addition to the design shall be permitted; and

Figure 16.2 International Symbol of Access

- the Symbol shall be used only to mark or show the way to facilities that are accessible to persons whose mobility is restricted by disability

The ISA is to be displayed properly at all times to preserve the meaning of the ISA, to maintain the dignity of individuals for whom the Symbol was designed, and to avoid confusion to the general public. Any organization is permitted to display the Symbol in published material relevant to services for people with disabilities.

The Symbol must be clearly identified as the ISA. It must always face to the right, unless it is meant to be a directional signal, such as identifying that an accessible restroom can be found down a particular hallway.

The ISA was *not* intended to identify a person who is disabled, and it should not be used in that manner. The Symbol is intended to *mark facilities* that use universal design and are usable by people with disabilities.

The ISA tells people that they can enter a building or facility without fear of being blocked by architectural barriers. To use the ISA for reasons other than to denote an accessible building or facility for use by persons with disabilities is prohibited.

The ISA is frequently overused because it should only be used to lead a person to an accessible facility that may not be obvious. As a result, the National Center on Accessibility (2010, p. 7) identified that the ISA is only required at:

- parking spaces designated as reserved for people with disabilities
- accessible passenger-loading zones
- accessible entrances when not all are accessible
- accessible elevators when not all are accessible
- accessible toilet and bathing facilities when not all are accessible
- accessible checkout aisles when not all are accessible

Take care not to overuse the ISA. Overuse can draw unwarranted attention and stigmatization to the user rather than highlighting the availability of the accessible feature.

What types of access barriers exist?

When many people think of access, they often think of physical access—installing a ramp or renovating bathrooms for wheelchair users. But access does not end there. Consider the situation presented by Laird (1992):

> What about people who have a hearing impairment? They can enter a building, but once they are inside, the information being transmitted when a leader is giving directions, a play is performed, or information discussed at a meeting is inaccessible to them because a sign-language interpreter or an assistive-listening device has not been provided. What about people who have a visual impairment? Again, people can enter the building, but if it is a meeting in which information is being distributed on paper and must be read, then the meeting is inaccessible to these individuals. It is inaccessible because the information has not been produced in an alternate format such as Braille, large print, or on an audiophile. What about people who have an intellectual disability? These people may require the assistance of a support person to participate in community activities.

A variety of people encounter architectural and attitudinal barriers every day. Although much of this chapter will focus on physical access, barriers that prevent people from participating in activities on a daily basis can be eliminated if attitudes are improved. It is hoped that people change their attitude from one where implementing changes to structures or producing or providing information in alternate formats is considered to be special treatment, to one where making these changes benefit the entire community. Our willingness to actively make our communities accessible can be the driving force for the removal of barriers to access.

Architectural barriers consist of structures constructed by humans that present an obstacle for people who have a mobility, visual, or sensory disability. Architectural barriers not only inhibit people with disabilities, but also affect older adults, parents with carriages, and people with temporary disabilities.

> Devine and colleagues (1998) reported results of a survey of park and recreation agencies across the United States. They identified environmental and structural areas that presented obstacles to leisure participation for people with disabilities. Of the agencies surveyed, 75% had either not retrofitted existing sites or had made renovations for access but felt more were needed. They identified problems such as baseball dugouts

> with narrow openings, tennis courts with lips or steps or a difficult-to-manipulate latch at the gate, outdoor racquetball courts with narrow and short entrances, or the lack of Braille signage at facilities.

Attitudinal barriers tend to be the most difficult to identify and overcome. As discussed in previous chapters, an attitude is a way of thinking or feeling. Thinking or feeling negatively about a person creates an attitudinal barrier. Attitudinal barriers often arise from fear, lack of knowledge, or lack of communication. To rectify this problem, it is important to consider an individual's capabilities and potential rather than the person's limitations.

Which access guidelines should we follow?

Changes in both federal and state laws have indicated an increased societal commitment to universal design. These laws led to the development of standards and creation of agencies charged with implementing the legislative mandate for access. We must review all federal, state, and local requirements. It is critical that we adhere to the most rigorous and specific standard, evaluate regulations for all items, and implement the regulation that provides the greatest amount of accessibility.

The 2010 Standards for Accessible Design provide guidelines for recreation facilitates. In addition to the fact sheets and description of the final ruling reported by the U.S. federal government, several organizations such as the National Center on Physical Activity and Disability, the National Recreation and Parks Association, and the National Center on Accessibility provide summaries of relevant changes. These standards apply to recreation facilities and locations that offer access to water-based activities. Such activities include boating, swimming, wading, and fishing.

> For example, for *boating*, the minimum number of boat slips that must be accessible depends on facility size dispersed throughout various slip types. Where boarding piers are provided, at least 5% must be accessible. For *swimming pools*, there must be accessible means of entry and exit for pools that include such methods as pool lifts, sloped entry, transfer wall or pool system, and pool stairs. Also, *wading pools* must provide sloped entry and *spas* must have a pool lift, transfer wall, or transfer system. Newly designed, constructed, or altered *fishing piers and platforms* must provide accessible routes and at least 25% of guard- or hand rails must be no higher than 34 inches and dispersed, with clear floor space provided at each railing and turning space on the pier.

In addition to water-based activities, the standards apply to traditional golf facilities, as well as those facilities associated with miniature golf.

For instance, newly constructed and altered golf facilities must have either an accessible route or golf cart passages with a minimum width of 48 inches connecting accessible element and spaces with the golf course boundary, and an accessible route provided to the elements outside the boundary. Also, one or two teeing grounds per hole must be accessible, a golf cart must be able to enter and exit existing weather shelters, and certain percentages of practice teeing grounds, practice teeing stations at driving ranges, and putting greens must be accessible. For miniature golf, at least 50% of all holes must be accessible and must be consecutive, and the last accessible hole must be an accessible route that connects to the course entrance or exit.

Standards for a variety of other recreation sites are stipulated in the 2010 standards. There are guidelines for amusement rides, exercise machines and equipment, play areas, and saunas and steam rooms.

As an illustration, newly designed or constructed amusement rides must be accessible and located on an accessible route. Also, at least one of each type of exercise equipment must be on an accessible route and must have clear floor space positioned to enable a person with a disability to use the equipment. Finally, sauna and steam rooms must be accessible, having sufficient turning space, doors that do not swing into clear floor space, and, where provided, an accessible bench.

The 2010 revised Title II and Title III of the Americans with Disabilities Act (ADA) require, among other things, that newly constructed and altered state- and local-government facilities, places of public accommodation, and commercial facilities be *readily accessible* for all individuals. Recreation facilities, including play areas, are among the types of facilities covered by the ADA.

Guidelines are provided for *construction* associated with exterior facilities, new buildings, additions to and alterations of buildings, and historic preservation of buildings. In addition, guidelines are provided to *permit entrance* to a building.

Examples of entrance considerations include: provision of accessible routes, ground and floor surfaces, parking and passenger loading zones, ramps, protruding objects, curb cuts, stairs, doors, elevators, windows, and platform or wheelchair lifts.

There are guidelines for *restrooms* and related areas that include drinking fountains and water coolers, toilet stalls, urinals, sinks, mirrors, bathtubs, shower rooms, handrails/grab bars, dressing and fitting rooms.

Safety considerations are also addressed by guidelines, such as detectable warnings and alarms. There are also guidelines associated with *other areas*, such as telephones, fixed or built-in seating, and tables. The description of accessible elements and spaces is followed by detailed ADAAG guidelines for restaurants and cafeterias, medical-care facilities, businesses, libraries, accessible transient lodging, and transportation facilities.

Although it is important to know what access guidelines have been established by the ADA, it is valuable to work to embrace the spirit of the ADA and work to exceed the identified standards. For instance, Billy Sassi, the aquatics program manager for the City of Tucson Parks and Recreation, was quoted in *Parks & Rec Business* ("Adaptive and accessible," 2005, May):

> *We're beyond ADA standards. Even though we have a beach entry into the pool, and it meets accessibility, we go beyond that and provide a mechanical and water-powered lift.*

Play areas designed and constructed for *children age two and over* are addressed in the guidelines. There is insufficient information to develop guidelines for children under age two. The Access Board will provide technical assistance materials to help small entities understand the play-area guidelines.

The Access Board also has accessibility specialists who can answer questions about the guidelines. Many companies that sell playground equipment adhere to the guidelines and can be used as a resource. The 2010 revised ADA Standards for Accessible Design stipulated that any play area designed, constructed, and altered for children ages two and over must have accessible ground and elevated play components; accessible routes, ramps, and transfer systems, and accessible ground surfaces must be provided. The guidelines include provisions for:

- ground-level play components
- elevated play components
- accessible routes
- transfer systems
- ground surfaces
- self-contained play structures

Ground-Level Play Components

A ground-level play component is a play component approached and exited at the ground level. Examples include spring rockers, swings, sand-digging toys, and stand-alone slides. The intent of this provision is to ensure that these components, which can be accessed by all children, are integrated with other ground-level play components.

Grouping all ground-level play components that can be accessed by all children in one part of the play area would not be considered inclusive. Where certain types of ground-level play components are separated for safe use, the integrated provision can be met.

> For example, if one part of the play area has activity panels and another part has swings, as long as an accessible route connects to both parts of the play area and at least one activity panel, and at least one swing is located on the accessible route, the ground-level play components would be integrated.

Elevated Play Components

An elevated play component is approached above grade and is part of a composite play structure consisting of two or more play components attached or functionally linked to create an integrated unit providing more than one play activity. Generally, there must be access provided by a ramp or transfer system to at least *one fourth to one half* of the elevated components of a play area. To clarify this revised definition, Hendy (2001, p. 114) identified the following example:

> A horizontal ladder that is free standing with no platform access is considered a ground-level play component. The same horizontal ladder attached to a platform as part of a composite play structure is then considered an elevated play component, and not a ground-level component, even though it can be reached and used from the ground.

Accessible Routes

This guideline stipulates that an area has ***accessible routes*** if there is at least one accessible route within the boundary of the play areas, as well as one connecting the play areas to parking, drinking fountains, rest rooms, and other elements. Accessible routes provide children who use wheelchairs and other mobility devices the opportunity to access play components. Accessible routes should coincide with the general circulation path used within the play area.

When possible, designers and operators are encouraged to provide wider ground-level accessible routes within play areas or *to consider designing the entire ground surface to be accessible*.

> To achieve the goal of accessible routes, transitions at the boundary of play-area accessible routes and site-accessible routes exceed 1/2 inch, such as where a rubber surface is installed on top of asphalt to reduce effects of impact, then a *sloped surface* must be installed with a maximum slope of 1:12. This means that for every inch that a ramp rises above the ground, there are 12 inches of ramp length. This prevents the development of ramps and transitions that are too steep for people who use wheelchairs.

A maximum slope of 1:16 is required for ground level ramps; however, a lesser slope will enhance access for those children with limited strength. Ramps are preferred over transfer systems, since not all children who use wheelchairs or other mobility devices may be able to use or may want to use transfer systems.

Where a stand-alone slide is provided, an accessible route must connect the base of the stairs and the exit point on the slide. Where a *sandbox* is provided, an accessible route must connect to the border of the sandbox. Accessibility to the sandbox is enhanced by providing a transfer system into the sand or by providing a raised sand table with knee clearance.

Transfer Systems

Transfer systems are ways to access play structures that generally include a transfer platform and a series of transfer steps. Children who use wheelchairs or other mobility devices transfer from their wheelchair or mobility device onto the transfer platform and lift themselves up or down the transfer steps and scoot along the decks of platforms to access elevated play components. Some children, however, may be unable to use a transfer system or choose not to leave their wheelchair or other mobility devices.

The distance between the transfer system and the elevated play component should be kept to a minimum, since moving between the transfer platform and a series or transfer steps requires extensive exertion. Transfer supports are required on transfer platforms and transfer steps. Transfer supports allow people an opportunity to use their upper body to make a transfer, and include items such as a rope loop, a loop-type handle, a slot in the edge of a flat structure, and the use of poles or bars.

Ground Surfaces

Ground surfaces must be accessible, as determined by measuring the amount of work required to propel a wheelchair straight ahead and to turn across the surface. The force is measured using a force wheel on a rehabilitation wheelchair as the measuring device. It is required to be less than that required to propel the wheelchair up a ramp with a 1:14 slope. Ground surfaces must be inspected and maintained regularly and frequently to ensure the continued compliance.

Generally, for a play component to be accessible, it must be located over an accessible surface, such as rubber tile, poured-in-place rubber, or engineered wood fiber. Companies that produce accessible playground surfacing should provide verification that their product adheres to accessibility and impact-absorption guidelines. When using a combination of surface materials, careful design is necessary to provide gradual transition between surfaces.

Self-Contained Play Structures

A self-contained play structure is composed of one or more components where people enter a fully enclosed play environment that uses pliable materials such a plastic, netting, or fabric. If four or more entry points are used, at least two must be located at accessible routes. See Figure 16.3 (p. 316) for a summary of ADA standards for accessible design application to play areas.

What is the impact of universal design?

In the opinion of the Access Board, the civil-rights benefits of the guidelines ensure that all children and adults who supervise children on play areas have an equal opportunity to use and enjoy play areas. Many groups of individuals benefit from following the ADAAG guidelines.

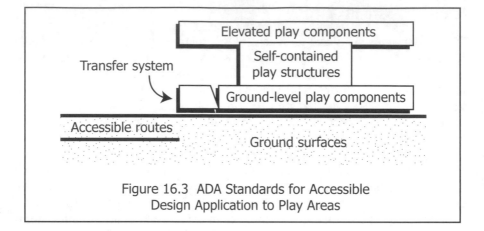

Figure 16.3 ADA Standards for Accessible
Design Application to Play Areas

Children with disabilities benefit from increased opportunities to play and to have social interactions with other children. Children without disabilities may also benefit from this diversity. Crawford and colleagues (2004, p. 39–40) described the importance of accessing play areas:

> *[p]laygrounds represent an important opportunity for inclusion into the natural day-to-day life of community living.... The playground subenvironment fulfills the major characteristics of inclusion, including opportunities for choice, social connections, and peer group belonging while providing skill development.*

Parents of children with disabilities will benefit from lower travel costs to transport their children to accessible play areas. Businesses that provide play areas as part of their facilities may benefit from increased profits, as families with individuals with disabilities are more likely to patronize their establishments. Hendy (2001, p. 109), made the following observation:

> *One of the most frequently asked questions during the National Playground Safety Institute's training is "Do I have to make all my playgrounds accessible?" It is time as a society that we realize that by making our playgrounds and recreation areas accessible to persons with disabilities, we are making them enjoyable for people of all ages and abilities.*

The letter written by "a friend from Springfield" was printed in *Parks and Recreation Magazine* in an article written by Oestreicher (1990). The letter (Figure 16.4) helps to illustrate the importance of accessible recreation environments and the need for access.

Dear Playground Director:

I was told about the playground you want to build for kids like me and regular kids, and that you were looking for ideas from handicapped kids. We really need a place to play, and maybe, if I tell you about my normal day in the summer, you will understand.

I lie in bed an hour to an hour-and-a-half, after I wake up, while Mom makes breakfast. I can help Mom make breakfast. I just don't do it as fast as Mom, and with two brothers and sisters, I "get in the way."

After breakfast, I roll out to the sun porch, while Mom cleans the house, or does the laundry. I could help with the cleaning, but Mom can do it faster, and . . . I "get in the way."

Most days, I go outside in the backyard and play by myself, or with our dog. We have a basketball hoop on the garage, and I'm pretty good, especially my hook shot. I know I could play with my brothers and their friends, but I slow down the game, so most days I sit in the backyard reading or playing with the dog. It seems to me, we are both put out here so we won't be in the way. The only difference is the dog can run off and play with his friends when he wants . . . I can't . . . Deep down inside I know I can do just about anything anyone else can do, just a little different, just a little slower. It just seems I don't get a chance very often . . . or at all.

For a week every summer I go to camp for special kids. It's fun, but it's only for a week a year, and even when I enjoy playing and winning against another handicapped kid, it would be much better to play and win against a regular kid.

So Mr., I'm sorry I don't know how to spell your name . . . it's too long, but if you build a playground where I can go anytime and can play with regular kids, and not be in anyone's way, I'll play in it and I'll buy you a "Big Mac" with cheese and a Coke.

I won't sign my name, because it might hurt my family a little, and they do love me, very much . . . so do your best please.

Yours truly,

A friend from Springfield

Figure 16.4 Letter by a Friend from Springfield

In another example, a woman went to a basketball game with her husband, who uses a wheelchair. She accompanied her husband to the wheelchair section and was told by the attendant that she could not remain there— the area was reserved for people in wheelchairs. This situation is repeated all too frequently at coliseums, sports arenas, and stadiums.

Implementing principles of universal design means more than just providing an entrance ramp and a section with seats removed to accommodate wheelchairs. Often these sections are situated in areas with the poorest view of the event. This practice also segregates people, separating them from their friends or families and setting them apart from the other spectators. *Seating sections* are to be arranged so as to provide people a choice of seating locations and ticket prices. Portable chairs should be used in these sections to allow people who are family and friends to enjoy the event together.

Universal design influences the way we purchase equipment or services. The National Center on Accessibility (2010, p. 2) emphasizes that buyers are responsible for determining which product will work best and are advised to ask the following questions before making a purchase:

- What product or service will create an accessible environment?
- Does the product or service meet all applicable accessibility guidelines and/or standards?
- Does the product facilitate dignified and independent use?
- Does the marketing literature use "People First" language?
- What are other consumers saying about this product?
- Can the sales rep provide a list of nearby installations to visit?
- Can a sample or demo product be installed for user testing before committing to purchase?
- What are the installation and maintenance requirements?
- What does the warranty and service agreement cover?
- If the product doesn't quite meet your needs, is the manufacturer willing to make modifications?

How can leisure contexts be universally designed?

In addition to following the principles of universal design, leisure service professionals are encouraged to consider adopting several strategies (Figure 16.5) that can improve the process of removing barriers to accessibility, such as:

- follow universal design principles
- know laws and standards
- include diverse people in planning
- include access specialist
- exceed standards whenever possible
- extend access past parking
- design outdoor access
- have continuous travel path
- consider aesthetics and environmental values
- ensure materials comply with standards

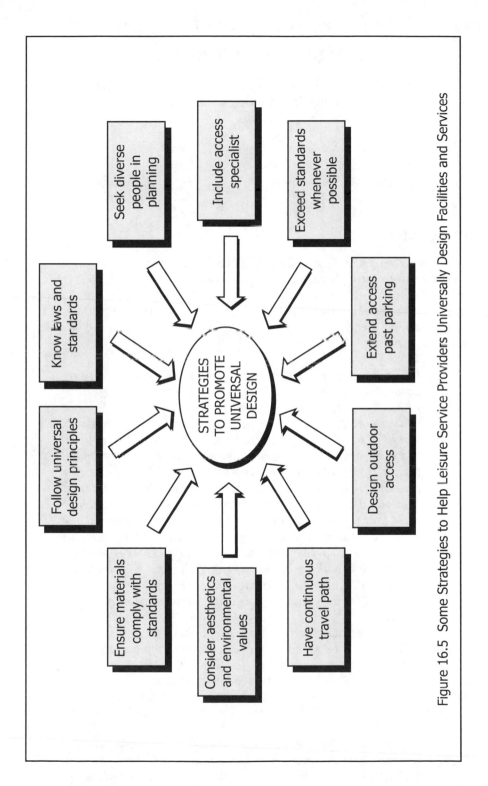

Figure 16.5 Some Strategies to Help Leisure Service Providers Universally Design Facilities and Services

What are examples of universally designed leisure contexts?

There a many different contexts in which leisure services are provided. Examples of the application of principles of universal design to the following contexts are presented in this section:

- playgrounds
- outdoor recreation
- restrooms and locker rooms
- special events

Playgrounds

People who design and purchase playground equipment and play areas have a responsibility to provide safe, challenging play environments that do more than simply comply with safety standards. When choosing playground equipment and associated components to be placed on a play structure, there are many considerations. Hendy (1999, p. 87, p. 90) provided the following suggestions regarding access:

> *When designing a structure for the preschool age group, an appropriate means of access is critically important. A wheelchair-accessible ramp with a slope of 1:12 is the least challenging form of access. A ramp should not be the only means of accessing a play structure, as the distance required to move from one point to another via a ramp is not practical for all users. A ramp that is not intended for wheelchair access, with a slope that does not exceed 1:8, is the next level of challenge. . . . Most transfer platforms enable a wheelchair child to transfer from the chair to the platform to access the equipment, then back to the chair. These transfer platforms are very easy to access and are considered a minor challenge. When a child with limited mobility exits a slide, it is important to provide a way back to the wheelchair or walker. The location of access components is an important issue.*

In honor of her daughter, Caitlyn, Stephanie Munson worked with the Broward County, Florida, Parks and Recreation Department to develop a universal-access playground called Caitlyn's Corral. A *universal access playground* exceeds the minimum standards stipulated by the ADA, with all development personnel working to provide as much accessibility to play structures as possible. Rachel Roberts (2009, p. 44) wrote that Caitlyn's Corral:

> *[i]ncludes equipment such as swings with extra head and leg supports and an interactive maze that can be navigated by a child who is running or one who is in a wheelchair. Aron*

Hall, director of services at the nonprofit National Inclusion Project, says beside it being "the right thing to do," universal design in playgrounds really brings the community together. "If someone in your community can't play, it really isn't a community playground, is it?" he asks.

Outdoor Recreation

One outdoor recreation that is pursued by many people is hiking. The National Center on Accessibility reported on the Accessibility Guidelines for Federal Outdoor Areas. Jennifer Skulski (2010) provided these insights specifically focused on hiking trails:

There are new requirements for trailhead signage to provide users with more objective information on the trail conditions. The provisions require new signs provided at the trailheads on newly constructed or altered trails to include information on the length of the trail or trail segment; surface type; typical minimum tread width; and typical and maximum running slope and cross slope. Communicating the trail conditions will give users the ability to make informed decisions on which trails and trail segments are appropriate in relation to their own individual ability.

The Association for Experiential Education has established standards with the intent of transcending disability rather than compensating for the lack of ability. This approach is solution-oriented and ability-focused and emphasizes socially meaningful roles.

People of all abilities can participate safely in outdoor recreation programs such as ropes challenge courses. Programs can be designed to be inclusive, suggesting that they are accessible to community members of all ability levels. To illustrate this point, Curulla and Strong (2000, p. 49) provided the following example of Martha, a 35-year-old social worker:

She found herself very nervous. Having seen a video of what was in store—climbing 30 feet up a Douglas fir tree and then sliding across a system of cables and ropes on a small platform called "the Stagecoach"—she didn't think it would be possible for her since she used a wheelchair. Her fears were genuine, but unfounded. By the end of the day, she had not only climbed the tree, she had assisted others in climbing, traversing, and succeeding in their challenge course efforts. At the group debriefing following completion of the course she proudly expressed the empowering sense of accomplishment she felt after completing a full day of emotional, social, and physical challenges. With the group's support, she felt she had broken through some of her own personal barriers. She was sure that reflecting on what she had accomplished that day would boost her confidence in the future when she or others doubted her capabilities.

Rogers (2000, p. 85) provided several illustrations of the application of the principles of universal design to challenge courses. One specific example identified was related to horizontal components:

> Incorporate parallel components that anyone can use. A traverse element may have a log and a cable that run next to each other and participants choose how they want to negotiate it, or there may be very large climbing holds that constitute a route up a climbing wall with small ones next to them. This approach allows for exciting two-person team experiences on a variety of elements.

Bernie Mulville was an architect who had a deep admiration for nature. As a result of multiple sclerosis, Bernie experienced a steady decline in his mobility from walking with a cane, to walking with a walker, to using a manual wheelchair, to finally using a motorized chair. In spite of Bernie's physical challenges, he and his wife, Sheryl, with the support of friends continued to visit parks and access as much outdoor recreation as possible.

Sheryl Billman (2007) provided several suggestions to outdoor recreation service professionals that were based on the shared experience of being involved in outdoor recreation pursuits as much as possible with her Bernie.

- Have an all-terrain wheelchair available for use
- Have a paved area for at least one picnic area and campsite
- Have a pontoon boat with a lift
- Offer a boardwalk to the water's edge
- Have entrances without doors such as privacy barriers
- Provide access information on web pages, signs, and brochures
- Place parking lots close to restroom facilities
- Train staff to respect all people

In conclusion, Billman (2007, p. 30) left the reader with this final message:

> *The fact that our parks, campgrounds, and other public facilities are becoming more accessible makes us a less exclusive society. It opens our children to the idea that people with differences are valuable. It refreshes the hearts of adults to see there are people who care and do something about these problems.*

Rest Rooms and Locker Rooms

Important features of any recreation and park facility are the restrooms and locker rooms. An example of how universal design can solve many problems is by including family locker rooms. *Family locker rooms* are self-contained rooms, about 60 square feet, with a toilet, shower, and changing area that can be used by an entire family. Family locker rooms provide privacy and safety for children accompanied by a parent of the opposite sex. People with disabilities desire them, especially those accompanied by a caregiver or family member of the opposite sex.

Ahrwciler (2000, p. 14) provided the following statements about universal design, quoting frequently from William Tracey, a manufacturer of plumbing fixtures:

> *Hand controls, which use sensors to turn water on and off, gained prominence in locker and restroom facilities for the benefit of disabled users but are now popular with a broad spectrum of users and facility operators as well. "Hands-free controls are valuable for the maintenance and sanitation end," Tracey says. "Able users appreciate the fact that they don't have to handle the controls, and the facility managers find they keep restrooms cleaner." ADA requirements have led to greater interest in universal design, where facilities are designed to accommodate all users, disabled or not. "As facilities began switching over to ADA-compliant designs, more and more people realized that instead of installing one or two special areas just for disabled users, it makes sense to create fixtures that can be used by everyone—handicapped or not," Tracey says.*

Special Events

When planning conferences, workshops, and special events, it is helpful to recognize the need to plan ahead for attendance of people with disabilities. It is useful practice to include people with disabilities when planning services and events. The questions presented in Table 16.1 (p. 324) can be used as a general guide when surveying a potential meeting site for accessibility.

When visiting the potential location of a special event, we can ensure doorways are wide enough to accommodate wheelchairs, check for handrails and raised toilet seats in the bathrooms, and look for ramps, parking spaces, and fire alarms with audio and visual notification systems. When considering travel arrangements, questions such as the following can be asked:

- Is there a lift-equipped van for transportation from the airport to the conference?
- What are local taxi service policies about transporting passengers with disabilities?
- Will these services transport people who use wheelchairs?
- Will these services assist the passenger who is disabled?

Table 16.1 Guidelines for Surveying a Potential Meeting Site

Parking
- Are parking spaces available for individuals with physical disabilities?
- Are parking spaces near the building entrance?
- Are parking spaces easily accessible to the front entrance by a level or ramped path at least 4 feet wide and free of obstructions?

Route
- Is the surface of the parking lot smooth and firm but not slippery?
- Are walks leading to the facility level or nearly so?
- Are there curb cuts at crossways?

Entrance
- Is at least one primary entrance usable to individuals who use wheelchairs?
- Do all doorways have a clear opening of at least 32 inches?
- Are doors operated by a single effort?
- Is the door light enough for the person with a disability to open it?
- Are sharp inclines or abrupt changes in level avoided at thresholds?

Ramps
- Are ramps provided where there are stairs?
- Do ramps conform to standard of no more than 1:12 slope?
- Do ramps have non-slip surfaces with a 32-inch handrail on at least one side?

Elevators
- Are guest elevators accessible and usable by people with physical disabilities?
- Are all elevator controls 48 inches or less from the floor?
- Are tactile identifications located beside elevator operating buttons?

Bathrooms
- Do all bathroom doors provide a minimum of 32 inches of clear opening?
- Is the bathroom floor the same level as the floor outside of the bathroom?
- Does the bathroom contain a floor clearance area of at least 5 feet by 5 feet to permit a person in a wheelchair sufficient turning space?
- Is there at least one bathroom stall usable by a person who uses a wheelchair?
- Are sinks, mirrors, and dispensers usable by people in wheelchairs?
- Are there handrails in the toilet and shower area?
- Is there sufficient turning space and maneuvering in the bath for a wheelchair?
- Are hanging rods for clothing located within 48 inches of the floor?

Telephones
- Are there conveniently located public phones 48 inches or less from the floor?
- Do public telephones have volume control devices?
- Are TTYs available?

Miscellaneous
- Are water fountains available and have a clearance of 28 inches?
- Are tables convertible to wheelchair use with floor clearance of 28 inches?
- Is the meeting space accessible and usable by persons with disabilities?
- Are all common areas accessible to all people?
- Is help available for those who might need assistance?
- What is the general attitude of personnel towards persons with disabilities?

Final Thoughts

Universal design is a critical step to inclusion. People must be able to get to a desired recreation activity, interact with the equipment, and interact with other participants if they are to engage in community leisure pursuits. When we start with universal design, we often end with unanticipated desirable outcomes. A case in point is described by Hitchcock, Meyer, Rose, and Jackson (2002, p. 9):

Consider television captioning. When these captions first appeared, individuals who were deaf had to purchase expensive decoder boxes, retrofitting their televisions so that they could access the captions. Later, decoder chips were built into every television, making captions available to all viewers. This universal design feature now benefits exercisers at health clubs, diners at noisy restaurants, people working on their language skills, and couples who go to sleep at different times.

By being creative and persistent, we can expand the leisure options for people by applying principles of universal design. A brief story by 11-year-old Lucas Parker (1998, p. 250) illustrates this point:

One day, when I was five, I went to a local park with my mom. While I was playing in the sandbox, I noticed a boy about my age in a wheelchair. Since I was only five, I couldn't understand why he couldn't just get in the sandbox and play with me. He told me he couldn't. I talked to him for a while longer then I took my large bucket, scooped up as much sand as I could and dumped it into his lap. Then I grabbed some toys and put them in his lap, too. My mom rushed over and said, "Lucas, why did you do that?" I looked at her and replied, "He couldn't play in the sandbox with me, so I brought the sand to him. Now we can play in the sand together."

Lucas can teach us a valuable lesson about bringing the leisure experience to people. Some professionals argue, however, that they rarely, if ever, observe people with disabilities in their community accessing their facilities. Therefore, they conclude that even if they made their facilities and programs accessible, people with disabilities would not attend.

The information presented in this chapter encourages us to apply principles of universal design and thereby create opportunities for people with disabilities to engage in community leisure pursuits. It follows then, that *if you build it, they will come.*

Discussion Questions

1. What is the meaning of universal design?
2. What types of access barriers exist?
3. What are some principles of universal design?
4. What access guidelines have been established by the ADA?
5. What access guidelines have been written specifically for recreation facilities?
6. What is the potential impact of universal design?
7. What is the meaning of the ISA?

8. How can playgrounds be universally designed?
9. How can outdoor recreation programs be universally designed?
10. What are some considerations for universal design when planning special events?

Chapter 17
Advocate for Services

*How wonderful it is that nobody need wait a single
moment before starting to improve the world.*
-Anne Frank

Orientation Activity: Be an Advocate

Directions Alone: Identify 10 of the following advocacy actions that you would
like to adopt as personal goals. Prioritize these 10 actions, assigning the number
1 to the most important and the number 10 to the least important.

Directions with Others: Move about the room and find another person who
chose one of the same activities as you. Introduce yourself, find out the person's
name, and discuss why you each chose the item. Once you have finished, find
another person and continue the process.

1. Invite people with diverse backgrounds to attend programs.
2. Ask adults from typically underrepresented groups to serve as leaders.
3. Organize a Diversity Awareness Day.
4. Survey architectural barriers and share results.
5. Write news releases about barriers facing various groups of people.
6. Educate people about recreation services available to all people.
7. Talk with people with diverse backgrounds to learn more about them.
8. Discuss the problems attitudinal barriers create.
9. Develop public service announcements for radio and television.
10. Contact organizations for ideas about their work with diverse groups.
11. Write letters to newspapers urging changes to attitudinal barriers.
12. Plan exhibits to create awareness about oppressed groups.
13. Ask people who are typically underrepresented in recreation programs
    to appear in advertisements for leisure services.
14. Conduct an evaluation or research project about people who have been
    oppressed and share results.
15. Teach awareness activities to community groups.
16. Keep the media informed of successes obtained by various individuals
    who are members of an oppressed group.
17. Volunteer at an agency that provides services to people who encounter
    various challenges throughout their day.
18. Develop services to assist families who are oppressed.
19. Form an advocacy committee to work on removal of barriers.
20. Meet with a legislator and learn about civil rights policies and laws.

21. Write to media outlets complimenting them on positive portrayals of diverse individuals.
22. Invite a person with an auditory impairment and an interpreter to talk to your agency.
23. Sponsor an idea exchange on ways to promote inclusion.
24. Discuss ways to involve people in activities and remove barriers.
25. Read children's stories and discuss how people with diverse backgrounds are portrayed.
26. Identify different forms of transportation that might be available for people who do not drive an automobile.
27. Learn about technology that assists people in recreation activities.
28. Select a recreation activity, choose a group of people who have been oppressed in some manner, and identify helpful accommodations.

Debriefing: Most attempts at advocacy, by and on behalf of people experiencing oppression, have been to urge opportunities for all people to participate as fully as possible in community life, and to end discrimination based on disabilities. The demands for community inclusion and civil rights have been widely recognized as just.

Advocates are needed not because some people are inherently weak and incapable, but because they are members of a group that has been oppressed. All people should receive community services because they have a right to them. The services are provided because these people are deserving citizens.

If various conditions interfere with citizens' rights, then society must make the changes that will enable them to enjoy those rights—regardless of costs. Ultimately, people become their own advocates. The advocate lets people manage their own affairs. As you reflect on the orientation activity consider the following questions:

- What is an advocate?
- How can advocate for those who have been oppressed?
- Why is advocacy necessary?

Introduction

In describing educating citizens in a pluralistic society, Colby and colleagues (2003, p. 7) stated:

> *If today's college graduates are to be positive forces in the world, they need not only to possess knowledge and intellectual capacities but also to see themselves a member s of a community, as individuals with a responsibility to contribute to their communities.*

At times, people are socially isolated and disconnected; consequently, they have difficulty getting their voices heard by members of their community. Some people are devalued in our society and are cut off from social roles that bring power, status, influence, and opportunities. Sometimes people who have been privileged find it difficult to accept people who have been disenfranchised as equal members of society.

Some people do not have the skills to communicate their wishes effectively and may need a spokesperson. Many people need services and supports to facilitate participation in society. Unfortunately, the systems to provide these are often complex, segregated, and controlling.

Liebe Geft, who grew up in Zimbabwe and has lived on four continents, is the director of the Simon Wiesenthal Center's Museum of Tolerance in Los Angeles. Geft (Breed, 2010, p. A6) stated that:

> *There are limits to what a civil society should tolerate. And when the human sights and dignities of others are being trampled and denied, that's not acceptable in a country that advocates rights and freedoms and dignity for all.*

Advocacy is an important means to facilitate inclusion because it is concerned with securing rights, encouraging full participation, promoting access, and empowering people. This chapter will address the following questions:

- What is advocacy?
- Who is responsible for advocacy?
- How can we become advocates?
- How can self-advocacy be encouraged?
- What are examples of advocacy?

What is advocacy?

To *advocate* means to recommend, to be in favor of, or to plead for. An advocate pleads the cause or gives support to a particular cause. The word "advocate" is derived from the Latin *avocare,* "to summon." The advocate is called upon to provide assistance and this person seeks to correct situations in which discrimination, disempowerment, or disconfirmation occurs, and to remove barriers.

As an example, Saied is preparing the equipment to conduct and indoor rock-climbing clinic. As he is working, he overhears Stella telling Brianne that she is not welcome here. Immediately, Saied moves between Stella and Brianne and asks if there is a problem. Once the situation is resolved, Saied reminds all participants that one part of rock climbing is for people to work together so that everyone can participate and experience the exhilaration of a climb.

Advocacy is required when ordinary actions have been unsuccessful in ensuring that a person's rights are being met. To illustrate this point, Hutchison and McGill (1992) developed a list of characteristics that distinguish between advocacy and other everyday activities, stating that advocacy:

- involves in-depth feelings and commitment to a cause
- calls for doing more than what is done routinely
- involves risk: advocates' actions are open to criticism
- must be structured to be free from conflict of interest

As stated in previous chapters, a *barrier* is any obstacle or obstruction that is natural or man-made that impedes progress but is not necessarily impassable. An *architectural barrier* is any feature of the physical environment constructed by humans that impedes or restricts the mobility of people to the full use of a facility. The most devastating and common barrier is an *attitudinal barrier*, a way of thinking about or perceiving diversity in a restrictive, condescending or negative manner.

To *empower* someone is to give control or authority to that person, increasing their confidence and self-esteem. All people have the right to live life to the fullest and experience leisure, but many people face barriers that prevent them from doing so. These barriers may be in the form of limited access to facilities, transportation, information, programs or job opportunities. Whatever the reason for the barrier, *advocacy*—the process of speaking up and working for changes in policies, opportunities, and attitudes—can help.

Who is responsible for advocacy?

A major role of professionals who provide public services is to advocate on behalf of people who have been oppressed in a variety of community forums. According to Peniston (1998, p. 84):

> *Advocacy is a vehicle for change, whether the change is on a singular level affecting one person or on a multiple level affecting an entire country; change generates progress.*

In addressing the importance of advocating for people who have experienced challenges in receiving community services, Bieler (2000, p. 18) provided the following analogy:

> *In Brazil, we tell a story of a hummingbird that, during a very big fire in the forest, was seen coming back and forth, carrying water in his beak and dropping it over the fire. The other animals, most of them bigger and stronger than the hummingbird, were all running away as fast as they could, thinking only to save their own skins. While running, a lion watching the hummingbird asked him if he had not yet*

realized that he would not extinguish the fire with such drops of water, but instead, he would get himself killed. Without stopping to rest, the tired hummingbird told the lion, "I'm just doing my part."

Heyne and Schleien (1997, p .77) encouraged leisure services professionals to work to facilitate inclusive leisure participation and spoke about our responsibility for advocacy:

Many recreation professionals . . . recognize that parents are often our strongest allies in promoting inclusive services. Yet, the responsibility for advocating for and facilitating inclusion must shift from parents to recreation providers who are competently equipped to offer inclusive services. . . . the readiness and willingness to provide inclusion must be adopted by recreation providers to the extent that, even before a parent or a person . . . approaches a recreation facility, the door to inclusion is open.

Leisure services providers are encouraged to view advocacy as a responsibility associated with their jobs. We must see ourselves and be seen by others as advocates as well as services providers because advocacy is a force for change rooted in our values and beliefs. deLisle and Parr (2005, p. 20) suggested that:

The role of the recreational service provider creates a unique opportunity to become an agent for change and catalyst within our community, regarding tolerance for the belief and interests of others. It allows us to be leaders in realizing and celebrating the inherent diversity within our communities to the benefit of all.

So, it is probably clear to you as you read this book that I believe all of us who have been privileged in some way have a responsibility to advocate for people who have been oppressed and continue to experience prejudice and discrimination. The Dalai Lama (1999, p. 138) speaks to this responsibility:

I, for one, strongly believe that individuals can make a difference in society. Every individual has a responsibility to help move our global family in the right direction and we must each assume that responsibility.

I have found when faced with these types of ethical challenges, looking to people who throughout their lives have repeatedly embraced such ideals is instructive and motivating. One such person is Kofi Annan.

Kofi Annan is a highly regarded diplomat from Ghana who served as the seventh Secretary-General of the United Nations from 1997–2006. As a result of founding the Global AIDS and Health Fund, Annan and the United Nations received the 2001 Nobel Peace Prize for his support of developing countries in their struggle to care for their people.

In her book *Profiles in Courage of Our Time*, Caroline Kennedy (2002, p. 352) reported that Kofi Annan made these remarks as he reflected on the genocide in Rwanda and the massacres in Bosnia:

> *When we recall tragic events such as those in Bosnia and Rwanda and ask "Why did no one intervene?" the question should not be addressed only to the United Nations or even to its member states. Each of us as an individual has to take his or her share of responsibility. No one can claim ignorance of what happened. All of us should recall how we responded, and ask, "What did I do?" "Could I have done more?" "Did I let my prejudice, my indifference or my fear overwhelms my reasoning?" Above all, "how would I react next time?"*

In concluding her remarks about Kofi Annan and his 2002 Profile in Courage Award, Kennedy (2002, p. 252) made the following statements that illustrate why he is an important role model for those of us attempting to acknowledge our advocacy responsibilities and be conscientious advocates for people who have been oppressed:

> *As Secretary-General, Kofi Annan has provoked the powerful and the powerless. He has stood fast for the principles of human dignity and the quest for a peaceful world. A soldier without an army, he must depend on the power of moral leadership. His consistent career of conscience has made him a true Profile in Courage, not just for our time but for all time.*

How can we become advocates?

Since advocacy is an important component of professional behavior it may be helpful to consider ways to advocate for people who have been oppressed in various ways. The following questions will be addressed in this portion of the chapter:

- Prepare for advocacy
- Become an advocate
- Evaluate advocacy

Prepare for Advocacy

Establishing advocacy goals, becoming informed about people's unique needs, being honest, and listening to potential and current participants are all helpful ways to prepare for advocacy.

As we become informed about the rights and desires of people whom we serve we are taking an important step toward advocacy. Credibility is lost when we are unable to answer pertinent questions. Failing to be aware of significant events relating to the issue being pursued can be equally problematic.

An honest response that a topic has not been studied and that the answer is not known can be disarming—and helpful. There is not a need to become an expert, just the desire to be resourceful and know where to find information.

It is important that advocates listen to people's perspectives about inclusion and ways to provide a supportive environment for all people. Resistance to inclusion may be an indication of negative feelings or fears. It can be helpful if we respond by listening to concerns, opinions, and fears of others to keep communication open.

Become an Advocate

Presenting information that is clear, tactful, and contains humor may be useful when advocating for people who have been oppressed. In addition, we may try to make suggestions to help people improve their approach to interacting with people with disabilities. The following techniques are described:

- present information clearly and tactfully
- use humor effectively
- be ethical

Present Information Clearly and Tactfully

Present information about the rights and desires of diverse groups of people. An informal discussion emphasizing how inclusion can benefit all people is often a good beginning. We can provide examples of successful attempts at inclusion that have been achieved within an agency or program.

Based on basic principles of communication, it must be clear whose interests we are representing. We can talk with people who have been oppressed to verify if they agree with our perspective of certain issues. Advocates should define and present the issue in a comfortable way.

Be tactful and avoid being unnecessarily confrontational when serving as an advocate. A situation is ***confrontational*** when an encounter becomes challenging and hostile and is characterized as being a conflict. Leach (2010, p. 38) had this to say about being civil while being an advocate:

> *Civility is not simply about manners. It doesn't mean that spirited advocacy is to be avoided. What it does require is a willingness to consider respectfully the views of others, with an understanding that we are all connected and rely on one another.*

Remain consistent and present facts accurately. Demonstrate appreciation to people and organizations that are helpful and willing to listen, show concern for problems, and show enthusiasm for solutions.

When addressing people, we can demonstrate that we will provide assistance if we are aware of the problems and understand methods for remediation. We can offer to show others how to comply with the ideals of inclusion and the spirit of civil rights legislation.

Sometimes direct information or responding to feelings is not enough to break through rationalizations. We can suggest alternatives to people after initial dialogue and negotiations. Alternatives to time and financial constraints are often appreciated.

Use Humor Effectively

Advocates who have gained acceptance often use humor effectively. If done appropriately, humor can dissipate tension and lead to common understanding. If we are playful, we can often put people at ease and create an environment where they may be receptive to change. However, many of us struggle with using humor in a respectful manner and encounter people who may be using humor in a disrespectful way.

As advocates for people who have been disenfranchised in some manner, we are committed to ending oppression and to educate the public about relevant civil rights issues. Humor can be helpful when we engage in advocacy and that it is important to laugh and not take issues too seriously.

Several questions can be asked when trying to decide how we might feel about specific jokes related to people affiliated with any group that has been stigmatized in some manner:

- In the presence of a person who is the focus of the joke, would you feel comfortable telling this joke? Hearing this joke?
- Does this joke make you feel you have something in common with the person described in the joke and more understanding?
- Does this joke make you feel "they" are different and distant from you? That "they" are somehow less than human?
- Does this joke provide incorrect information about a group or make you tense in the presence of a person with that characteristic?
- Is this joke laughing *at* people or *with* them? Is the joke exploitative? Who benefits from humor of this type?

The above questions can be applied to just about any interaction we might have with other people. Although raising these questions can help us decide how comfortable we are about specific jokes, the question still remains: "What do we do when we are uncomfortable with a joke?"

In any advocacy situation carefully consider the context of the situation. Thinking about where the conversation is occurring, our relationship with the person talking, and people present all play a role in how we might handle a situation.

> For example, if in a group situation Slater uses terminology that some people might find insensitive, Josie decides to wait and speak with the person individually.

Once the context of the situation is assessed there are various strategies that might be helpful in determining what to do when we consider certain humor to be inappropriate, including:

- Ask the joke-teller a question such as "I have heard that term used before and I wonder why people use it; what do you think?"
- Say "Did you know that . . .?" Sharing information presented in this course may help, especially if the joke teller is misinformed.
- Simply do not laugh or smile.
- If asked why you did not laugh, explain: "Did you know that what you said offended me and would probably offend other people?"

Direct methods of interaction might create a negative experience and result in the person becoming defensive. It is helpful to consider the context to determine when to use a particular advocacy strategy and realize that many people are simply not aware of what is sensitive behavior (Figure 17.1, p. 336).

Be Ethical

As expressed in the first chapter, being an advocate for people who have been oppressed requires ethics. Charles Sylvester (2010), a respected historian and philosopher in our field, has developed a model of ethical action called *ACCCCT Right*:

- Awareness
- Convictions
- Competence
- Character
- Courage
- Trust

Each of the components of ACCCCT Right is intended to contribute to a systematic approach to acting ethically in everyday professional practice.

Awareness. As discussed in the initial chapters of this book, gaining knowledge about our beliefs, attitudes, intentions, and behaviors is helpful when attempting to engage in ethical thinking and behavior. It can be valuable

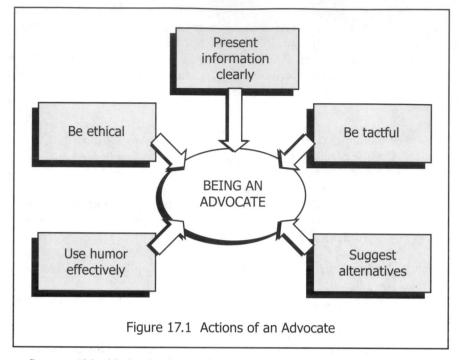

Figure 17.1 Actions of an Advocate

to reflect on ethical behavior by reading and engaging in thoughtful discussions. Awareness also involves reflecting seriously and at length on courses of practical action that match our ethical ideals related to advocacy.

Conviction. A conviction is a belief or opinion that is held firmly. As I shared some of my ethical assumptions in the first chapter; developing key principles that provide guidance for "acting" ethically can be useful. In this way we move beyond awareness to internalizing values and principles such as honesty, respect, responsibility, fairness, and compassion.

Our principles provide us with direction for ways to behave. Again, engaging in thoughtful reading and discussions about these values and principles can help to clarify such convictions.

Competence. As has been discussed previously in this text, a professional's confidence in being able to effectively provide inclusive services is critical in addressing the challenges people experience associated with oppression. So too is it important to become competent in acting ethically. It is helpful to develop the ability to engage in ethical reasoning that involves critical and constructive thinking skills (as discussed in Chapter 1) that encourages us to make ethical decisions.

One way to develop these skills is to share moral dilemmas with others and discuss how to address these dilemmas. It is helpful to practice how to act ethically by listening to others' explanations of how they might respond to ethical dilemmas and then engaging in constructive confrontation, conflict resolution, and solution negotiation. These actions can help us focus our thinking and influence our interpersonal behaviors that reflect ethical thinking.

Character. Character consists of moral habits or qualities that enable individuals to act in ways that are consistently ethical. With character comes the shift from knowing how to behave to actually acting and being a particular kind of person.

Moral character involves being a person who acts in a way that, in addition to other qualities, is honest, just, respectful, compassionate, wise, and trustworthy. Supported by reading, reflection, and discussion, character is most especially developed by practice and experience, enabling character to become a reliable set of personal qualities.

Courage. To live ethically by engaging in actions that are honest, just, respectful, responsible, and compassionate requires courage. Courage involves the ability to be brave and be willing to behave in a manner that addresses situations that are difficult, uncertain, and even dangerous.

To behave in an ethically courageous way requires us to overcome fears that may prevent us from living in a manner that is consistent with our character. There are times when our peers, colleagues, family, friends, and others might encourage us to be unethical. It is during these times that it is important to have courage to confront these situations and be willing to be consistent in our beliefs and avoid succumbing to such peer pressure.

Trust. The final component of Sylvester's model involves reliance on and a confidence in the demonstration of good qualities such as fairness, truth, honor and the ability to act in an ethical manner. As we become ethically competent, develop the character to consistently act in an ethical manner, and demonstrate courage to be ethical, we must trust ourselves, as well as others, to follow the ethical path.

Professionals who deliver inclusive leisure services are placed in a privileged position giving us the ability to help or harm our constituents. As professionals, we are expected to act responsibly and honorably. If we follow the ACCCCT model we begin to trust ourselves in acting ethically (Figure 17.2, p. 338). This sense of trust assumes an element of risk and has been identified as the currency of courage as we come to trust in our convictions and ourselves. As we trust in ourselves, the people we serve and our colleagues will come to trust us as well.

Evaluate Advocacy

Leisure services providers often take pride in their ability to effectively evaluate their services. Evaluation of advocacy efforts that include analyzing the content presented, examining the presentation style, and identifying successful advocacy attempts may be useful. The following techniques are presented:

- analyze informational content
- examine the process
- identify successful advocacy attempts

It is helpful for advocates to closely analyze the content of the information we present. We can consider if people understand what we attempt to convey. It is also useful if we determine if other, more helpful information may be available.

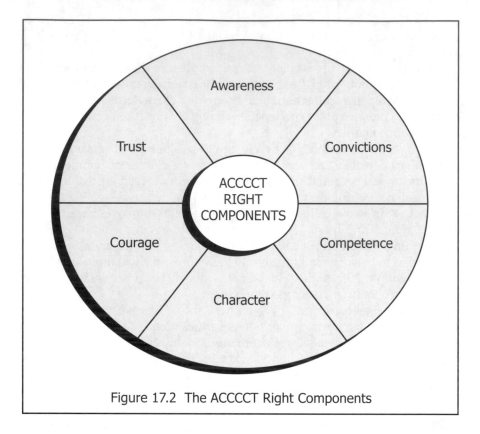

Figure 17.2 The ACCCCT Right Components

Examine the process in which the information was presented. Considering the limitations as well as the strengths of the different advocacy approaches can be useful. We can consider the effectiveness of the approach and if it reached the intended audience.

We can identify successful attempts at advocacy and celebrate these successes. It is important for us to reward ourselves and others associated with these efforts. We can use our successes as examples in future advocacy efforts.

How can self-advocacy be encouraged?

Advocacy has traditionally meant speaking on behalf of others. In recent years the term *self-advocacy* has been coined to refer to individuals and groups who have traditionally been powerless and largely voiceless speaking up on their own behalf to try to change their social status and situation. To be an effective self-advocate, people must be able to understand their own needs and interests and clearly communicate those needs and interests to other people. The self-advocacy movement has been influential in improving opportunities and is an important part of the civil rights movement.

Advocates and advocacy groups that act on behalf of others risk becoming *paternalistic* by defining what is in the best interest of the individuals or groups and working for that without really stopping to ask the people what they want.

To avoid this, the actions of advocates must reflect the expressed wishes of the individuals or groups they are representing, not what others believe is best for them.

It is helpful to initiate advocacy efforts with an honest and open approach and to be willing to negotiate and to compromise when necessary. If we are serious about empowering people who have been powerless, we need to recognize that a certain amount of confrontation and a certain adversarial relationship will always be part of advocacy.

Empowering people inevitably means taking some power away from one person, or group, to give it to another. Neither individuals nor organizations typically relinquish power willingly. Some advocates will need to be adversarial, others cooperative. These two approaches complement each other and are necessary for the social change that people who have been oppressed seek.

Self-advocacy groups are often based on the belief that together people help each other become more independent, learn to speak for themselves, and gain a measure of self-respect and confidence that they did not have in the past. Regardless of what self-advocacy groups do, the important thing is that the activities grow out of the needs of individuals who have been oppressed, and they promote independence and the ability to speak and act on their own behalf.

> Sebag (2010, p. 24) reported that research on self-advocacy demonstrates the effectiveness of placing a person in charge of identifying goals, devising strategies to achieve them, and reflecting on as well as making adjustments on progress.

The underlying assumption in self-advocacy is that dependence encourages dependence, and independence encourages independence. Thus, self-advocacy groups seek to provide peer support that can help break established patterns of dependency.

People become self-advocates because they want to become more independent. Parents, friends, and organizations often encourage self-advocacy because they recognize that as people learn to make decisions and accept greater responsibility for their lives, everyone in society benefits.

Extensive personal contact with diverse individuals within a leisure context creates opportunities for individuals who have been oppressed to inform people who are privileged about how negative attitudes might inhibit them in their pursuit of enjoyable and meaningful recreation activities. For example, after conducting face-to-face in-depth interviews with leisure participants, Devine and Lashua (2002, p. 76) provided this quote by one respondent:

> *I use education as my tool for being accepted. I believe that people will respond to a "put yourself in my shoes," type of information. I have typically found that technique useful to counter someone who feels I don't belong in a restaurant or at a concert or at my painting class. I just try to initiate some conversation and see what happens.*

What are examples of advocacy?

There are many examples of ways to advocate. The list provided in the orientation activity of this chapter is just a sample of the many actions we can take to advocate for people. The following are ways that some people and companies have begun to advocate for people who have been oppressed, including:

- speaking up
- creating access
- making toys
- reading the newspaper and writing letters

Speaking Up

There are moments and situations when advocacy opportunities come to us. Unfortunately, we many not believe that the actions of one person can have much of an impact. Throughout this book, there are examples of how one person can make a difference in the lives of many. Here is one such example. The following is an email message I received from one of my students enrolled in a course based on this book:

> *Hi Dr. Dattilo! I just wanted to share with you some good news I have received. After completing the wheelchair assignment, I approached my apartment complex's organizers to make them aware of some difficulties I had. Today, I received a letter in the mail explaining some changes they are planning to make to some apartments in order to make them more accessible. Changes include: repaving patios so that they are not more than ½ inch below the level of the interior, widening doors to 32", providing grab bars in restrooms, providing an additional bathroom which will comply with HUD (Fair Housing Accessibility Guideline 7), and modifications on entrances (thresholds and width). They are also providing retrofits for any current resident, future resident, or close friends or family members and are promising the project to be completed in 45 days of the written request. I don't think this is a direct cause of my action in making them aware, but I think that could have helped. Thanks for the encouragement to do so! Hopefully this will help many people!*

Creating Access

In the late 1980s, the Durham, North Carolina, Parks and Recreation Department worked to create inclusive opportunities at two of their existing facilities. By 2009, participants could choose from among all 11 facilities and receive the inclusive services they deserve and desire. Miller (2009, p. 40) quoted some of the staff of the department:

> **"We will serve anybody anywhere," says director Rhonda Parker. "We will make support available to help anyone succeed in any program." "We believe it to be the best practice," says Sarah Hogan, Durham recreation manager. "All people benefit when no one is left out."**

Making Toys

Mattel formed a not-for-profit corporation called "For Challenged Kids" to produce and market toys specially designed for children with disabilities. All profits from the sale of these toys will be dispersed among organizations that work with children with disabilities.

The first "For Challenged Kids" product line, "Hal's Pals," consisted of five, 19-inch soft-sculptured dolls, each with a different disability. Hal, who is one of the best skiers in Colorado, is a ski instructor with one leg. Bobby is an athletic little boy who uses a wheelchair for mobility. Suzie is an adventurous girl who is sight-impaired and uses her cane and guide dog to explore her neighborhood. Laura is a ballerina who wears hearing aids. Kathy is a little girl wearing a party dress, a big smile, and leg braces.

Mattel believes "Hal's Pals" are really mainstream toys and not just for children with disabilities. Each doll portrays its disability in a familiar, comfortable way, focusing on ability and strengths. The dolls have been identified as useful educational tools, providing insight and improved understanding into what it is like to have a disability.

Reading the Newspaper and Writing Letters

An editorial appearing in a college newspaper is featured on p. 342, and it is followed (p. 343) by a response entitled "All or None" which was prepared by three students majoring in Recreation and Leisure Studies.

Final Thoughts

Developing an understanding of actions relevant to advocacy can help encourage us to become advocates. As we learn more about ways to promote self-advocacy and are exposed to different examples of how to be an advocate we can become more empowered to advocate for inclusive leisure services. At the time of the opening of the national monument honoring Martin Luther King Jr. in Washington, D.C., Gregory Clay (2011, p. C1) reported:

> *. . . legacies are open to interpretation. But one aspect of King's persona is finite, that is to say, in his own words, "The time is always right to do the right thing . . ."*

Once we gain knowledge about a topic relevant to our professional duties we then have the responsibility to share this information with others who may be naïve about the information we have acquired. We have the social obligation to act in a responsible way and be an advocate.

Dunn (2001, p. 7) commented on the importance of taking action when we see injustice occurring:

> *Have you seen what they're doing to Atherton Hall? They're destroying it. They are going to build up the front courtyard and level it off so that wheelchairs will be able to get to it easier. I'm not against the idea that buildings should be accessible to the handicapped, but Atherton is not the building to do it to. Every floor except the second has some levels that are connected by stairs. This means that the only places that a wheelchair could get to once it was inside the building was the lobby, the TV room, the second floor, and the parts of the others that the elevator is level with (and that elevator only goes to the ground, first, and second floors).*
>
> *Another problem is the bathrooms. Every bathroom in the building has a step at the doorway that you have to step over to get in. Also, there are no handicapped toilets, showers or sinks. There is going to have to be a lot of work done just to make the University and a couple of senators or representatives who want to make this building accessible happy. Again, I'm not against the idea in general, but it is not a feasible option in the case of Atherton. Besides the monetary and time expenditures, there is the problem of a major inconvenience to the inhabitants of the dorm (e.g., noise, privacy, physical inconveniences of closing the front entrance when they rebuild parts of the interior) and even more importantly is the historical nature of Atherton Hall. It is one of the older and most beautiful dorms on campus. Its beautiful main entrance has greeted many dignitaries and honored guests of the hall and this "remodeling" will destroy the original landscaping and architecture of this building. After considering limitations of this project and the inconveniences and the problems it will cause, I have to conclude that the work currently being done to Atherton Hall is inappropriate, unnecessary, and should be halted before any further destruction takes place.*

To speak out might not do any good, but to remain quiet sure does a lot of bad. When no one challenges wrong then wrong doers gain strength and confidence. They can go beyond speaking harmful words to committing harmful actions . . . speaking out against injustice opens a person to isolation and ridicule. Been there, done that. But, I'd rather be attacked proudly for standing up for what's right than to be ashamed of myself for not speaking at all. So, I'd like to encourage you to stop standing in silence as you witness discrimination, intolerance, and erosion of programs designed to level the playing field.

A fundamental aspect of being an advocate is to perceive a sense of responsibility for the way the world is. As we take more responsibility for our actions, we become more likely to be an advocate for people who are in need of our support. Harvey Fierstein (2007) warned us:

You cannot harbor malice toward others and then cry foul when someone displays intolerance against you. Prejudice tolerated is intolerance encouraged. Rise up in righteousness when you witness the words and deeds of hate, but only if you are willing to rise up against them all, including your own. Otherwise, suffer the slings and arrows of disrespect silently.

> *We would hardly refer to a building that is being altered for better accessibility as a building that is being, as you stated, "destroyed." You seem to only be concerned about the minor inconveniences that the inhabitants of the dorm will experience during the construction period. You complain of the "physical inconvenience of closing the front entrance" to the building. Did you ever stop to consider the constant inconvenience people who use wheelchairs face daily because they can not get into a building that has only stairs as a means of entrance? Typically, it would only take a couple of months of "inconvenience" to make a building accessible, yet it would provide a lifetime of accessibility to people who use wheelchairs. You refer to the "many dignitaries and honored guests" that this hall has greeted. Speaking of dignitaries, do you realize that one of our presidents, Franklin D. Roosevelt, used a wheelchair? In addition, you also stated that you are "not against the idea that buildings should be accessible to the handicapped, but Atherton is not the building to do it to." Isn't this a bit contradictory? If you are going to support a cause, you must support the entire cause—it is not right to exclude a portion just because it may cramp your lifestyle for a brief time. This reminds us of those people who used to say, "I'm not against blacks riding buses, but not my bus." If your description of how making Atherton Hall accessible is accurate, it is possible that the University is not going about it in the most efficient manner. However, this does not suggest that Atherton Hall is not a feasible building to make accessible. We suggest that rather than focusing your efforts on condemning accessibility to Atherton Hall by people using wheelchairs, that you focus your efforts on examining the plan for accessibility. In the past few years considerable strides have been made which have provided individuals with disabilities access to buildings. These breakthroughs have enabled integration into the mainstream of society a reality instead of only a dream.*

I began this chapter quoting Anne Colby and her colleagues (2003) as they discussed the importance of college graduates possessing a sense of moral and civic responsibility, and I would like to close with another one of their passages. These authors (pp. 17–18) describe the need for advocacy and the significance of learning values such as those presented in the first chapter of this book.

> **We believe that a morally and civically responsible individual recognizes himself or herself as a member of a larger social fabric and therefore considers social problems to be a least partly his or her own; such an individual is willing to see the moral and civic dimensions of issues, to make and justify informed moral and civic judgments and to take action when appropriate. A fully developed individual must have the ability to think clearly and in an appropriately complex and sophisticated way about moral and civic issues; he or she must possess the moral commitment and sense of personal responsibility to act, which may include having moral emotions such as empathy and concern for others; moral and civic values, interests, and habits; and knowledge and experience in the relevant domains of life.**

Discussion Questions

1. What is meant by the term *advocacy*?
2. How does advocacy relate to barriers experienced by people?
3. How does empowerment relate to advocacy?
4. What methods can you use to help prepare yourself to be an effective advocate?
5. When presenting information to other people on behalf of other people, what should you consider?
6. What are some ideas to consider when evaluating your ability to be an advocate?
7. What is the value in encouraging people to be their own advocates when possible?
8. What is one action you could take today to advocate for people who experience discrimination?
9. Why is advocating for the rights of people who have been oppressed your responsibility?
10. Who benefits from advocacy efforts?

Chapter 18
Use Sensitive Terminology

More people are blinded by definition than by any other cause.
-Jahoda

Orientation Activity: Change Terminology

Directions Alone: Write a substitute word or phrase for those presented that communicates a more positive attitude toward people with disabilities. Circle the numbers of the words or phrases most difficult to change.

Directions with Others: Divide into small groups and discuss the words or phrases that posed the most difficulty for each participant. Allow members of the group to explain the rationale for their choices. After a specified time, discuss your responses with the entire group.

1. a special kid
2. crippled
3. the retarded
4. autistic people
5. the blind
6. AIDS victim
7. the deaf
8. a CP
9. those MDs
10. wheelchair bound
11. dependent on crutches
12. suffers from MS
13. mental age of 3
14. confined to a wheelchair
15. stricken with epilepsy
16. borderline retarded
17. dummy
18. feeble-minded
19. a nervous breakdown
20. a spinal-injured man
21. maniac
22. crazy
23. deaf

24. dumb
25. deaf mute
26. handicapped person
27. normal
28. able-bodied
29. a paraplegic
30. afflicted with autism
31. imbecile
32. the amputee
33. the special woman
34. lunatic
35. moron
36. deformed person
37. a spina bifida child
38. the schizophrenic
39. a neurotic person
40. psycho

Debriefing: Language and words are probably the most severe handicaps facing people with disabilities. Although breakthroughs in technology, medical treatment, and legislation are opening doors to meaningful lives for people with disabilities, language persists in developing barriers. To illustrate this point, Erin Texeira (2005, p. A10) quoted Luke Visconti of DiversityInc, which advises business on racial issues:

> *Modern-day discrimination is more subtle than in years past, he said, and "language is the dominant way today of expressing oppression."*

The use of insensitive language to describe other people often creates tension. To reduce this barrier to interaction, we can use clear and accurate communication. To improve attitudes we can stop using words that convey fear, insensitivity, stereotyping, and discrimination.

This chapter supplies information on terminology that encourages communication of positive attitudes toward people with disabilities. As you examine the words and phrases you substituted for the previous words, consider the following questions:

- In what situations are you not sure of how to refer to people with disabilities?
- What general rules can you offer when attempting to describe people with disabilities?
- Why is it important to focus on the words you use to describe people with disabilities?

Introduction

Young children recite the phrase "Sticks and stones may break my bones, but names will never hurt me." Agreed, words might not physically harm individuals, but the words we choose in our interactions with others can have an impact on how people feel about themselves and us. Abu-Tahir (1995, p.2) responded to criticisms about trying to use the most sensitive terminology when he stated:

> *Some say, "What's the big deal? What's all the fuss about what we call them." We need to remember that how we refer to a people has everything to do with how we treat those people. The early African-Americans were labeled "slaves" thereby justifying their inhumane treatment. The original Americans were called "savages," not "people." Women were called "girls." Today, labels are used to disregard people's beauty and value.*

The suggestions provided in this chapter primarily come from recommendations from people from the United States (U.S.) and, therefore, are generated from a particular perspective that does not encompass preference of all people across the globe. For example, some people associated with the British disability movement use the phrase "disabled people;" however, most people with disabilities in the U.S. prefer using people first terminology resulting in a preference for the phrase "people with disabilities."

The following questions are addressed in this chapter:

- Why is it helpful to use sensitive terminology?
- How can we use words that are sensitive?
- Why does sensitive terminology change?
- Why do we consider perspectives of people who are oppressed?

Why is it helpful to use sensitive terminology?

It is important for leisure service providers to express acceptable attitudes that demonstrate respect for participants and all people. One way to achieve this goal is to become aware of behaviors that offend different individuals.

Terminology should reflect equality of all citizens and sensitivity to the situation. An important aspect of selecting terminology is to ensure that *respect* toward members of the group is communicated. Scully (2008, p. 33) stated that:

> *The words people elect to use demonstrate their respect, or lack of it, for members of other groups. This matters because particular words cause offence, to women or ethnic minorities, for example, but also because their use engenders alienation, contempt, or hatred in those who use them ... examining the language of disability is ethically important. Language not*

only affects the everyday treatment of disabled people, it also
determines the technical capacity to conceptualize in moral
terms the agents and situations . . .

Our behaviors toward participants can affect their quality of life, self-concept, and acceptance. Since leisure services providers frequently interact with participants, it is critical to project a positive attitude through the use of sensitive terminology.

> For example, Byrd, Crews, and Ebener (1991) reported that students who were briefed on appropriate use of language when referring to people with disabilities performed significantly better than students who did not. They concluded that there is benefit to providing this instruction to students.

By advocating for sensitive terminology, people who have been oppressed have stimulated some professionals to rethink old assumptions and redefine ways to address needs identified by participants. According to Smith (1992, p. 1):

Laws, such as the Americans with Disabilities Act, approved
in July 1990, bar discrimination of people with physical
or mental disabilities in public accommodations, private
employment, and government services. By passing laws, the
federal government hopes to empower people with disabilities,
but the battle for access may be better fought on the
communication front. Educators can help the next generation
of writers and the working press learn to use language that
promotes the notion that people with disabilities are entitled
to access. The day the ADA bill passed, The Atlanta Journal
and Constitution announced, "Handicapped Rights Bill
Awaits Final Approval" (1990, p. 11.). This usage may seem
innocuous enough, but it is off the mark. The preferred usage
is "people with disabilities."

How can we use words that are sensitive?

This chapter suggests ways to use sensitive terminology that communicates positive attitudes toward all people, including the following (see Figure 18.1):

- focus on people's similarities
- consider the person first
- emphasize each person's abilities
- communicate respect for each person
- use consistent terminology
- refer to people without disabilities

The following sections of this chapter encourage professionals and students to act as agents of change to help other people use the most appropriate terminology to describe individuals with disabilities.

Focus on People's Similarities

Focusing on a person's uniqueness can be a positive way to view the individual. However, an emphasis on unusual traits might become so overwhelming that the similarities shared by all people are ignored.

Failure to recognize that all individuals have the same basic needs can set people apart from one another and create barriers to interpersonal relationships. Typically, it is easier to interact with a person if we initially concentrate on similarities we share with this person as opposed to differences. People's attitudes tend to be more positive when they focus on similarities.

One way that people mistakenly focus on differences rather than similarities between people is by identifying some individuals as being "special." Typically, people who have been oppressed in some manner express the desire to be treated with the same respect as any person. Charles Greenlaw, an official associated with the Boy Scouts, summarized the involvement of Tim Fredricks (1987, p. 27), a scout who happens to have an intellectual disability, in a community Boy Scout program.

> *The other scouts see nothing unusual about having Tim in the group, nor do they treat him as "special." The only way that Tim is 'special' is that he is an Eagle Scout.*

When people are identified as "special" as a result of having a characteristic that is different such as being the only boy in a dance class, being the only person in a wheelchair in a billiards tournament, or being the only Native American on a cruise, the implication may be that their difference limits them. When this generalized impact of their characteristic is accepted, people tend to lower their expectations of these individuals. McFadden and Burke (1991, p. iii) stated:

> *We're trying to prevent use of the word "special," because every time you have a "special" person, you make that person different. We must have the dream and the hope that our future will be inclusive of everyone.*

When a person identifies with someone because of similarity, there is a tendency for that person to like the other person. However, primarily focusing on individuals' differences could be perceived in as a way that promotes prejudice. Therefore, when we use terminology to describe people, it is helpful if we consider only using a label when absolutely necessary.

For example, Sinead, a supervisor who is educating her staff about the needs of Anthony who is being included in a leisure

> program may say, "Anthony may have some difficulty with abstract concepts; so, it may be useful to provide demonstrations when giving verbal directions."

When writing about people who have been oppressed, journalists and others are encouraged to avoid referring to a person's characteristic such as race, religion, or ability unless it is critical to the story. Emphasizing the worth of all people, rather than differences between people, encourages portrayal of people in a positive fashion.

Consider the Person First

When relating to people who have been grouped together for whatever reason, consider these individuals as people first and then, if relevant, consider their group affiliation. According to Luckasson and Reeve (2001, p. 47):

> *. . . first and foremost, we emphasize that the term given to any disability is not the essence of any individual who has the disability. Individuals are people first.*

If it is relevant to use a label, emphasize the person's humanness. This can be achieved by not making stereotypic generalizations about people who, in addition to many of the other characteristics that affect their humanness, such as a sense of humor and honesty or that they happen to be Asian, or gay, or Jewish, or have a disability.

People first language describes what a person *has*, not what a person *is* and therefore puts the person before the condition. Snow (1998, pp. 15–16) provided insight about the use of people-first language:

> *My son, Benjamin, is 11 years old. He loves the Lone Ranger, ice cream, and playing on the computer. He has blond hair, blue eyes, and cerebral palsy. His disability is only one small piece of his life. When I introduce myself to people I don't tell them I'll never be a prima ballerina. Like others, I focus on my strengths, the things I do well, not on what I can't do. I don't say, "My son can't write with a pencil." I say, "My son uses a computer to do his school work." I don't say, "My son can't walk." I say, "My son uses a walker and a wheelchair."*

By making reference to the person first, respect for the worth of the person is demonstrated. Use of disability-first language such as "the disabled" or "disabled kids" can be interpreted as demonstrating a lack of respect for people with disabilities. Another way to focus on the individual is to avoid labeling people into groups according to medical diagnoses or disabilities such as "the blind" or "the amputee." Focus on people first, such as "individuals with visual impairments," or "people with amputations."

In general, it is helpful to avoid using acronyms such as "CP" for cerebral palsy, "MS" for multiple sclerosis, or "MD" for muscular dystrophy. The use of such acronyms emphasizes the condition rather than the person. In addition, use of acronyms may create confusion and make some people feel ignorant because they are unaware of the meaning of some acronyms. This breakdown in communication can limit our ability to present a positive image of people with disabilities. However, if it is relevant to identify the person's medical diagnosis, the name of the condition is lengthy, and there is high recognition of the acronym within a given society, the acronym may be appropriately used.

> For example, Acquired Immune Deficiency Syndrome is most frequently identified as AIDS because the acronym has a higher recognition rate. Therefore, in some limited situations, use of an acronym may be accepted.

When identifying individuals, it is useful to recognize their humanness and address them as "people" or "program participants" rather than "patients" or "cases." The use of the words "patients" or "cases" implies that individuals are ill and in need of medical assistance. Many participants including older adults and people with disabilities are not receiving medical care, are in excellent health, and therefore should not be identified as patients.

Most of us, at some time, will be receiving medical care and be identified as a patient in the context of the medical environment; however, this does not imply that we should then be identified as a patient in all contexts of our lives.

The condition of being a patient or a case varies according to the situation and, therefore, the use of these terms as a label for people with disabilities is often inaccurate. The word "client" may be used to describe people participating in a variety of leisure services. If the word "client" is used consistently to describe all participants, then it is more acceptable than when client is used only to describe those individuals with disabilities.

> An example of people first terminology occurred years ago on May 10, 1988, when former President Reagan signed Executive Order 12640 establishing the President's Committee on Employment of the Handicapped as the President's Committee on Employment of People with Disabilities. People working to improve the language concerning disability enthusiastically supported the name change (*Rag Time,* 1989). Chairperson Harold Russell stated that the new name demonstrated that the President's Committee was sensitive to the desires of people with disabilities. In addition, other legislation such as the Individuals with Disabilities Education Act (formerly known as the Education of the Handicapped Act) and the Americans with Disabilities Act, clearly demonstrate a focus on people first terminology.

Inclusion encourages people to focus on similarities and to accept differences. When disabilities are seen as secondary to the overall humanity of the person attitudes may change to reflect a greater openness to the person and a greater optimism regarding the amelioration of the disability.

Emphasize Each Person's Abilities

It is important for us to emphasize individuals' abilities rather than focusing on limitations. For example, it is more accurate to say "a woman who uses a wheelchair" rather than "she is confined to a wheelchair" or "she is wheelchair-bound." The use of the phrase "he walks with crutches" is more accurate than "he is dependent on crutches."

Typically, when people access forms of transportation other than walking such as an automobile, bicycle, or skateboard, they are not described as being "confined to" or "dependent on" that particular means of transportation. It is helpful to be consistent with this line of reasoning when describing people with disabilities who use alternative forms of transportation or mobility.

Many words used to describe individuals who have been oppressed reflect concepts of dependency and helplessness that perpetuate negative attitudes and corresponding patterns of response and expectation. At times, fundraising efforts have employed the use of counterproductive terminology intended to evoke impressions of needy, fragile people requiring special treatment. Organizations using such tactics to raise funds intended to promote independence may in fact foster a sense of dependency through the fundraising campaign.

It is helpful to describe people as simply having a disability rather than using words that imply pain and suffering. Phrases such as "afflicted with... suffers from...a victim of...crippled by...stricken with..." sensationalize the disability and tend to evoke sympathy toward individuals. Instead, it would be more appropriate to say "the person has...the condition is caused by...a disability resulting from..."

> In a February 1988 issue of *Time* magazine entitled "Roaming the Cosmos," the lead sentence to the article describing the renowned physicist Stephen Hawking was: "*Physicist Stephen Hawking is confined to a wheelchair, a virtual prisoner in his own body.*" This description can be contrasted with the lead sentence in the article entitled "Black Holes Figured Back in Time" reported in a June 1988 issue of *Insight* magazine: "*Through the intricate equations devised over two decades, cosmologist Stephen W. Hawking has advanced intriguing visions of the universe's origin and structure.*" The differences between the two representations are striking.

Frequently, sympathetic views evoked by such words as "confined" or "prisoner" restrict people's independence by limiting other people's tendency to treat individuals who have disabilities with dignity and respect.

For instance, at the second AIDS forum in Denver back in 1983, individuals with AIDS condemned attempts to label them as "AIDS victims." People attending the conference stated that the phrase AIDS victims implied defeat and identified the phrase "persons with AIDS" as the most preferred terminology.

Communicate Respect for Each Person

The practice of classifying individuals according to mental age has been drastically reduced in recent years. It is important that we avoid using the phrase "mental age," because the label tells us nothing about the person's cognitive strengths and areas to develop.

For instance, when discussing the implications of following written directions by a woman, say "a woman who is 35-years-old and currently identifies a few words" as opposed to stating "the woman who has the mind of a 3-year-old."

Use of the phrase "mental age" may result in mistakenly treating a person with a mental impairment such as Alzheimer's disease or an intellectual disability as a child. In her book, *Riding the Bus with my Sister: A True Life Journey*, Rachel Simon (2003, p. 10) had the following reaction when someone would inquire about her sister's "mental age:"

Mental age. It was as if they thought that a person's daily passions – and literacy skills, emotional maturity, fashion preference, musical tastes, hygiene habits, verbal abilities, social shrewdness, romantic longings, and common sense could fit neatly into a single box topped, like a child's birthday cake, with a wax 7, or 13, or 3. It would become clear to me that their understanding of mental retardation had never moved beyond the stereotype of the grinning, angelic child.

Using terminology that labels adults with intellectual disabilities as children, such as "he is childlike" or "our kids" can show disrespect. Instead we can communicate dignity provided to other adults in our society by using age-appropriate terminology to describe individuals. Age-appropriate terminology involves the use of words that are typically used to describe people of similar ages to the person being identified. Age-appropriate terms encourage development of programs that are appropriate for the age of the participants and do not require participants to compromise their dignity.

Many words that have been used in the past to describe people with disabilities have communicated ideas of deviancy, helplessness, and dependency. Words such as imbecile, lunatic, moron, borderline, dummy, feeble-minded, maniac, crazy, deaf and dumb, or deaf mute are no longer acceptable because of their strong negative overtones. Instead, we can use phrases such as people with developmental disabilities, individuals with intellectual disabilities, people with psychological disorders, individuals with communication disorders, or people with speech and hearing disorders. Through the use of these words and phrases, we will better communicate a positive attitude about people with disabilities.

Use Consistent Terminology

Impairment, disability, and handicap are three distinct words defined in different ways. Unfortunately, many people use the words interchangeably and often inaccurately.

The word *impairment* means to diminish in strength and refers to identifiable organic or functional conditions that may be permanent (such as an amputation) or temporary (such as a sprain). When an individual possesses an impairment, the focus is on the problem—a disease or injury with a specific portion of the body.

> For instance, a visual impairment involves a deficit with the eye, such as that caused by clouding of lenses resulting in cataracts. When cataracts are mentioned, the problem with the eye is emphasized. Another example may be that a person has a neurological impairment, such as cerebral palsy, that prevents independent leg movement. In this situation, when the phrase "neurological impairment" is used, attention is directed toward the central nervous system that was damaged.

The focus of the discussion related to impairment is not on the person; rather, the discussion is directed to the actual condition. Impairment can result in a disability and a person being handicapped in particular situations.

Able is defined as having sufficient power, skill or resources to accomplish a task. When the word able is combined with the prefix dis, which refers to being deprived of, the definition of the word disability becomes apparent. The word *disability* describes the reduction or deprivation of a skill or power. This reduced ability is a result of a particular impairment, as mentioned previously.

> For instance, Rocardo, a man with cataracts has a visual impairment that may result in a reading disability even when corrective lenses are used. When the word disability is used, attention is given to the interaction of the visual impairment with the functioning ability of the individual.

When discussing a person's disability, it is necessary to examine the individual and the effect that the impairment has on that person. However, according to Whyte and Ingstad (1995, p. 3):

> *A preliminary common-sense definition of disability might be that it is a lack or limitation of competence. We usually think of disability in contrast to an ideal of normal capacity to perform particular activities and to play one's role in social life. Sickness also inhibits ability, but we distinguish between*

sickness, which is temporary (whether ended by healing or death), and disability, which is chronic.

Although, at first glance, this definition might seem harmless, this notion of disability is reflective of a belief of social inferiority or stigma.

The word *handicap* was originally used to denote a disadvantage in sport (Hale, 1979). A handicap is a game in which forfeits were held in a cap (hand in cap), a content in which artificial advantage is given (or disadvantage imposed) on a contest to equalize chances of winning. The word *"handicap"* has been linked with the practice of beggars who held cap in hand to solicit charity. These definitions demonstrate that the labeling of people as handicapped represents an impression of society that these individuals are dependent on others.

The important aspect of the word handicap is that it varies from one situation to another. In effect, a handicap is an interaction between environmental conditions and the individual, rather than simply inherent in the person.

> For instance, Yanlin, a woman with a visual impairment may be handicapped when going to the theater to watch a movie but may not be handicapped when listening to music on the radio. Andy, a man with a neurological impairment who uses a wheelchair may be handicapped when playing soccer but may be extremely skilled at billiards.

Because a person may be handicapped in one situation and not handicapped in another, it is inaccurate to label the person as handicapped. The word handicap implies that the person is handicapped in every situation. This generalization of a condition to all life situations imposes unnecessary restrictions on the individual.

Since being handicapped is a social phenomenon influenced by our society, people with disabilities can handicap themselves by believing that they cannot do something and society can handicap people with disabilities by denying them opportunities to participate. The term "handicap" is reserved for describing obstacles that lessen a person's chance of success. These obstacles often will prevent people from doing something. Jack Kemp (1994, p. 28), an attorney and an advocate for people with disabilities who was born with multiple limb anomalies stated:

> *One day I came home crying that these kids had been making fun of me. They said I had wooden arms and wooden legs and a wooden head—which probably isn't too far off the mark! My dad said, "Well, those kids have a handicap too." He told me that I might have a disability, but other people who don't accept me have a handicap. A handicap is something external to me that interferes with my freedom to be a part of my community. A curb without a curb cut is a handicap to someone in a wheelchair. People's negative stereotypical thinking about individuals with disabilities is a handicap to our acceptance. That was the first time someone had lifted*

*the burden of "handicapism" off of me. I got teased, but my
dad put it into perspective.*

Miller and Sammons (1999) identified four types of handicaps: social,
personal, physical and those associated with resources.

- *Social handicaps* are associated with other people's negative attitudes toward people with disabilities.
- *Personal handicaps* occur when people lack adequate information about their disability or about ways participate in activities.
- *Physical handicaps* can include inaccessible buildings, parks, or transportation.
- *Resource handicaps* are when people have insufficient funds, training, and people to assist them.

To illustrate the point that these handicaps or obstacles can shape a person's
quality of life as much or more than a person's specific medical, physical, or
cognitive disability, Miller and Sammons (1999, p. 29) provided the following
example:

> Imagine that you have arthritis (impairment) and cannot climb
> stairs (disability). You want to go to a concert, but the theatre
> has no elevator or ramp. You have a handicap because of the
> architectural inaccessibility of the theatre. Similarly, a person
> who is deaf has a handicap while watching television without
> closed captioning; a person who is blind has a handicap in
> an elevator without Braille signs; and a person who uses a
> wheelchair has a handicap when shopping in a store that does
> not have accessible parking entrances, restrooms, and aisles.

Many people have stated that they want to be identified with a disability
rather than a handicap. For instance, Karol Davenport, a leisure services provider
who also happens to use a wheelchair, explained that she prefers to be referred
to as a "person with a disability" rather than "handicapped" (Jesiolowski, 1988).

> Ms. Davenport's preference was supported by a survey
> conducted by *The Disability Rag* ("The results are in!" 1986)
> reporting the preferences of the magazine's readership. Nearly
> three-fourths of the respondents with disabilities stated that
> they would prefer the phrase "a person with a disability" when
> referring to them, while only 3% preferred "handicapped
> person."

Shapiro (1993) stated that the term "disabled" has replaced "handicapped"
and is becoming the first word to emerge by consensus from people with
disabilities.

Refer to People without Disabilities

The word "normal" is acceptable when referring to statistical norms and averages; however, this term is demeaning to people with disabilities when used in reference to people with no disability (National Easter Seals Society, 1981). The use of the word normal to describe people who do not possess an apparent disability implies that a disability is the one distinguishing factor that separates people into two primary categories: normal and disabled.

Not only is the word normal demeaning to many people with disabilities, but also many people without disabilities resent being labeled as normal. Normal implies that people act similar to many other people in almost all aspects of their lives. This view stresses conformity and ignores individuality, creativity, and diversity.

When describing people without disabilities, it is helpful to apply the same principles described earlier in this chapter. If not having a disability is irrelevant to a particular situation then we can simply avoid labeling the individual. However, if it is important to identify the person as not having a disability we can use the phrase "people without disabilities" to refer to people who do not possess an apparent disability. Some people use the phrase "able-bodied" to describe individuals without disabilities. This phrase can cause confusion, however, because individuals with disabilities may also possess bodies that are very able such as people with intellectual disabilities, autism, and learning disabilities. See Figure 18.1 for a summary of guidelines that promote sensitive terminology.

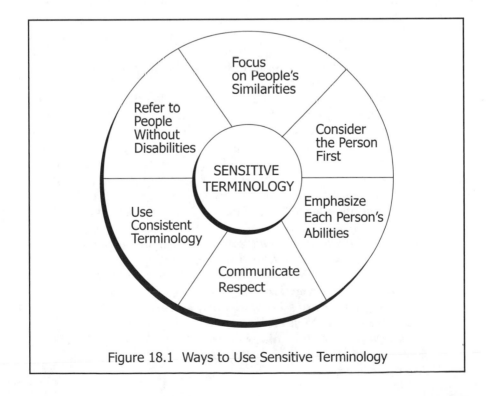

Figure 18.1 Ways to Use Sensitive Terminology

Why does sensitive terminology change?

Language is the means by which we attempt to accurately communicate with others. Over time our words change to reflect changes in attitudes, thinking, and expression. People who have been stigmatized are in a continuous and evolutionary process of choosing language they prefer to be used to describe themselves and their experiences. Words identified today as being sensitive may no longer be responsive tomorrow.

History has shown us that acceptable terms in the past often are no longer acceptable today. Crouser (1999) provided the following example when discussing the American Association on Mental Retardation:

> *We were founded to serve idiotic and feebleminded persons and eventually we moved on to serve imbeciles and morons. Decades later our constituency was described as mentally deficient and now we support people who are mentally retarded. And now we must ask ourselves, again . . . Is it time to change our terminology?*

The term *mental retardation* is a social invention resulting from many factors, including the human tendency to label people based on perceived differences and development of standardized intelligence tests (Warren, 2000). According to Warren, the term mental retardation has been attacked as promoting stigma and negative stereotyping in our society, many people with disabilities hate it and consider it demeaning, and other point out that it lacks sufficient specificity for meaningful professional applications. As a result, people with disabilities, family members, and professionals have asked that we find a more contemporary, less pejorative term to describe this group of individuals (Crouser, 1999).

As an illustration, based on the experiences of an elementary-aged girl, Rosa Marcllino, and her family on October 5, 2010 U.S. President Obama signed S. 2781: Rosa's Law that replaces the term "mental retardation" with "intellectual disability" in specific federal, health, education, and labor laws. The law does not expand or diminish services, rights, or education opportunities; rather, it requires federal language consistent with that used by organizations such as the World Health Organization and the U.S. Centers for Disease Control. At the time the bill was introduced Susan James (2009) provided this description:

> *On any given day at the mall, the sports field or the movies, 8-year-old Rosa Marcellino hears people say, "That's so retarded," or "You're such a retard." "Even good kids use the word, not realizing that they're talking about people like my sister," said Rosa's brother, Nick, a Maryland 14-year-old. Rosa -- who Nick calls the "smartest person I know" -- has Down syndrome and is now at the center of a bill in Congress to strike the term "mentally retarded" from the federal lexicon.*

Given that the words "retard" or "retarded" have taken on such a negative connotation, people are now using the phrase "intellectual disability" instead of saying "mentally retarded." Callaway (2010) interviewed Greg Coni, a high school senior who has a sister with Down syndrome. He reported on people's desire to end the use of the 'R-Word.'

> *I hear it all the time. A lot of people, they just use it. It's really not known too widely that it is such a derogatory word. People have come to use it so freely with such a negative connotation that it is really hurtful. If people use it properly, I wouldn't mind, but it is the fact that it's come to have such a horrible usage.*

Speaking of the R-Word, another word that has an extremely negative connotation is the word "nigger." The N-word is a word that not only offends African-Americans but offends most people across the globe. Leonard Pitts (2009, p. 115-117) has this to say about the use of the N-word.

> *As Richard Pryor told it years ago, he was sitting in a hotel lobby in a trip to Africa when he heard a voice within. "What do you see?" It asked. "Look around." I looked around and I saw people of all colors and shapes. And the voice said, 'Do you see any niggers?" I said, "No." It said. "Do you know why? There aren't any." Pryor told an audience that he started crying then. The comedian, whose speech had always been peppered with the ugly word, abruptly realized that it had not passed his lips in the three weeks he'd spent among the blacks of Africa. Pryor subsequently renounced the word altogether. . . But I haven't seen anybody say a damn thing about black comics who fly it like a dirty flag. Haven't heard a peep about the tiny talents of raunch rap who spill it into the ether like sewage. Haven't heard anyone say the obvious: that if African-Americans truly abhor this word then the protest ought to begin on our own s doorstep. . . So the last word some beaten black man heard before gravity yanked him down and the rope bit into his neck becomes a shock tactic for a callow youth. The word that followed his torn corpse as it was dragged down dusty roads behind the bumper of a car now serves some oafish rapper who can't find anything to rhyme with trigger. That's grotesque. It is obscene.*

Changes in the way we think about people result in changes in the terms we use. However, changing terminology that describes certain people every few decades is no solution and that ultimately we must find a way to somehow transcend the issue of terminology.

Some other terminology that describes people with visual impairments, such as "partially sighted," has met controversy. Some individuals feel the phrase "partially sighted" implies an avoidance of the acceptance of having a disability, while others feel it accentuates positive aspects (sight). Rana Arnold reported that when polling members of the Sight-Loss Support Group of Central Pennsylvania views regarding the phrase "partially sighted" varied from person to person.

Another controversy relates to ways to describe people who are deaf. Some people who are deaf reject "people first" terminology and prefer being described as "Deaf people."

> According to Dolnick (1993, p. 38), "the upper-case D is significant. It serves as a succinct proclamation that the deaf share a culture rather than merely a medical condition." The argument of deafness as culture relates to the belief that over a half a million Americans who are deaf share a common language (American Sign Language) and as a result share a common identity. However, the view that deafness is akin to ethnicity is far from unanimously held.

Considering people who have a hearing loss, the particular phrase that was acceptable previously but is no longer suitable is "deaf and dumb." Related to this idea, Williams and Finnegan (2003, p. 40) stated that:

> *"Dumb" referred to inability to speak, as well as inability to think. Researchers in the field of deaf education have consistently emphasized that people who are deaf posses the same range of intellectual potential as those who here. Therefore, the phrase "deaf and dumb" is arguably inaccurate and unacceptable terminology.*

One problem that arises when using phrases that have yet to receive general support from people associated with a particular group is the difficulty in receiving services such as financial aid, education, and recreation. Although phrases such as "partially sighted" and "physically challenged" seem to accentuate the positive for some people, these same phrases may create problems in acquiring services and seem to offend other individuals. In describing the perceptions of the hundreds of people with disabilities whom he interviewed, Shapiro (1993, p. 33) wrote:

> *Concoctions like "the vertically challenged" are silly and scoffed at. The "differently-abled," the "handi-capable," or the "physically and mentally challenged" are almost universally dismissed as too gimmicky and too inclusive. "Physically challenged doesn't distinguish me from a woman climbing Mt. Everest, something certainly I'll never do," says Nancy Mairs, an essayist and poet with multiple sclerosis. "It blurs the distinction between our lives." Only by using direct terminology, she argues, will people think about what it means to be disabled and the accommodations she needs, such as*

wheelchair accessible buildings or grab bars in bathrooms. Dianne Piastro, who writes the syndicated column "Living with a Disability," complains that such terms suggest that disability is somehow shameful and needs to be concealed in a vague generality. "It's denying our reality instead of saying that our reality, of being disabled, is okay," says Piastro.

At this time it is difficult to recommend the consistent use of such phrases. It is important, however, for us to realize that identification of the most preferred terminology to describe persons with disabilities is a continuously evolving process.

Why do we consider perspectives of people who have been oppressed?

If we are unsure of which words to use when we make contact with people, we can ask the person what terminology he or she prefers. Words that are currently creating controversy and have yet to receive a general consensus may be the words of choice in the future.

In all situations, listen to people to determine the terms and phrases they most prefer and attempt to understand their reasons for these choices. This sentiment is reflected by Coulter (1992, p. 2):

I believe that people have a right to call themselves whatever they want, and that others should respect their choice. We should not be surprised when these choices change over time. We have seen several such changes recently: people preferring to be called gay or lesbian instead of homosexual, or people preferring to be called African-American instead of colored or black, for example. If this choice reflects a reasonable consensus of those who may be so described, then I believe we should respect it. People with disabilities have made it perfectly clear that they want us to use people-first language, and so we should.

In the same way, although many people express a desire for the use of people first terminology, as with any labels, there is not total support for its use. For example, Hartman (1998, p. 10) described Carol Gill, who, based on her research, private practice as a psychotherapist, and experiences as a woman with a disability, stated that:

I don't mind people-first language; I do mind the insistence on it. My disability is an integral component of who I am—I am incredibly proud to be a disabled woman.

Dr. Gill's statements illustrate the point that, although many suggestions are provided on sensitive language by many people with disabilities, a critical suggestion to follow is to learn what each individual desires and to respect the right of that person to name him or herself. As further illustration of this suggestion, Nancy Mairs (1992, pp. 56–57) takes the extreme position as she writes the following:

> *I am a cripple. I choose this word to name me. People—crippled or not—wince at the word "cripple." Perhaps I want them to wince. I want them to see a tougher customer, one to whom the fates/gods/viruses have not been kind, but who can face the brutal truth of her existence squarely. But I don't care what you call me, so long as it isn't 'differently abled,' which strikes me as pure verbal garbage designed, by its ability to describe anyone, to describe no one. I would never refer to another person as a cripple. It is the word I use to name myself.*

Similarly, it is helpful for us to remember that interpretation of the meaning of words is based on our perspective, which is strongly influenced by our culture. Words and sentences used in one culture may demonstrate respect; however, use of the same words in a different culture may be viewed as offensive.

Fernald (1995, p. 99) compared language preferences of people with disabilities among English-speaking countries and stated: "some terminology that Americans assume to be sensitive and stigma-free was, in fact, offensive to British colleagues."

Therefore, it is important to consider that the information presented in this chapter is one perspective of sensitive terminology and, when in doubt, ask individuals what they most prefer.

Final Thoughts

Crabtree (1994) presented a quote by Judy Clouston, a recognized poet, who demonstrated how she felt about sensitive terminology:

> *When the clerk shouts, "Hey, Joe, there's a crippled lady up here who needs some sour cream," I wince. When a stranger says, "My aunt is an invalid . . ." I can't hear the rest of the sentence. When I hear the phrase "confined to a wheelchair" I want to jump out of mine. They're words, but they make a difference.*

One way to communicate respect for people is to avoid using words that offend them and to use words that make them feel valued. The use of sensitive terminology can set the stage for a positive interaction that lead to successful, meaningful, and enjoyable leisure experiences for all. The use of language is an ethical issue since the language we use to describe people influences the treatment they receive on a daily basis.

Based on the premise that changing social attitudes through language has been a powerful tool for the civil rights movements, it is important to use terminology describing all people that is empowering rather than demeaning. Use of empowering terminology establishes groups of people as a social and economic force to be considered and respected.

Use of insensitive terminology may occur because well-intentioned people are not aware of the most accurate words or phrases to describe people. Do not assume that the person using insensitive terminology was purposefully being offensive—the person may be using them out of ignorance and does not intend to be disrespectful. After reading this chapter and gaining knowledge of the most appropriate terminology, consider the perspective of the people using the inappropriate terminology when educating them about the most desired behaviors to exhibit as they interact with or represent individuals with disabilities.

We can become change agents within society. Although this chapter is intended to describe what many people with disabilities and professionals espouse as sensitive terminology, consider that the use of terminology is an evolving process. It is helpful if we continuously respond to the most recent information presented, demonstrate a willingness to listen to and consider other people's perspectives, and revise our terminology to best represent the desires of the people we serve.

I think it is fitting to close this chapter by reporting the sentiments of Benjamin Saenz (2010, p. B44), a professor of creative writing:

> *Today, in the Americas, we live in an age of violence and suspicion. Rather than thoughtfully solve issues that confront us, many choose to speak a language that divides us. There is much talk about building walls. Where is the talk about building bridges?*

Discussion Questions

1. What is the people first philosophy?
2. What are six general suggestions for using sensitive terminology?
3. Why is it important to focus on individuals' similarities?
4. Why is it best to avoid the use of the term "special?"
5. Why should acronyms be avoided? When is it appropriate to use acronyms?
6. What is the difference among the terms "patient," "client," and "participant?" Which term is preferred and why?
7. What are two ways the federal government acknowledged the importance of people first terminology?

8. Why should we avoid using terminology that sensationalizes or exploits people with disabilities?
9. What is meant by the terms "impairment," "disability," and "handicapped?"
10. What is the best way to refer to people who do not have disabilities?

Chapter 19
Support Families

Families are not defined by genetics.
Families are defined by your commitment and love.
-Denise Bierly

Orientation Activity: The
Family Balancing Act

Directions Alone: Collect 10 empty cardboard boxes. Read the following list of possible problems a family might experience. All families may experience these situations; however, families that have a member who has a disability or health impairment are more likely to experience these situations. As you read each situation, pick up one of the boxes. Continue reading and adding boxes until you drop a box.

Directions with Others: Divide into small groups and discuss how you felt when you were attempting to carry as many boxes as possible. Describe how you felt when one or more boxes fell. Discuss your perception of the responsibilities of family members of individuals who may be experiencing a variety of challenges. Generate some ideas on how leisure service providers may be able to alleviate the stress experienced by these families.

1. Since there is no afternoon recreation program for your child to attend, you must hire someone to be with your child.
2. The person you have scheduled to be with your grandmother is sick and you must take a day off work to care for your grandmother.
3. Since there is no summer recreation facility open to your sister, you must watch her instead of working and earning money.
4. Because of the unwillingness of the senior center to accommodate your grandfather, you must stop working and stay home with him.
5. A member of your household becomes ill and you must take care of her.
6. Your father is injured while working and now needs some assistance while he is healing.
7. A person working at the bowling alley tells you that you should not bring your brother there in the future.
8. You decline an invitation to a party because the last time you were there, people did not make your family feel welcome.
9. You are unable to afford to go on a family vacation this year because of the medical expenses you incurred.
10. Your friends make fun of you because a member of your family has a disability.

Debriefing: Families must respond to many circumstances that influence their lives. Each circumstance requires the family to make an adjustment.

In the orientation activity, taking on a cardboard box represented the family circumstances. As families acquire "boxes," they must readjust their strategy of working together to keep them from falling and to maintain an intact family. Through a life cycle, the family accumulates numerous boxes, which they attempt to share and carry as a group.

Eventually, this simulation required the addition of so many adjustments that the boxes could no longer be carried. When some boxes fell, this was a time of crisis and the family could not remain stable without outside community support and intervention. With assistance from others, however, the crisis was managed. Consider the following questions when thinking about the orientation activity:

- How did you feel while participating in the activity?
- What did you learn from this activity?
- How can leisure service providers support families who have a member who has a disability?

Introduction

Behind most every person who receives leisure services is a family. Home-based activities and family-oriented activities outside the home are common contexts for leisure. In considering the definition of "family," Hibler and Shinew (2002, p. 32) provide the following recommendation:

> *Very deliberate efforts to include broad definitions of family educational and recreation programs are necessary. Further, depicting multiracial families in promotional materials would send the message to all participants, mainstream or otherwise, that all types of families are valued.*

A *family* may be generally defined as all members of a household under a roof who have a common interest and commitment to its members. Families are extremely diverse.

> For example, in the United States, the traditional family that consisted of a father who worked outside the home and a mother who stayed at home with the children is now the exception rather than the rule. Instead, families have become increasingly diverse. Social and economic conditions have led to multigenerational families. Immigrants may bring with them living arrangements that are typical in their country of origin, including division of household tasks by gender and arranging marriage for young adults.

Given the diversity associated with the construction of families, it is helpful
be sensitive to individual differences as people discuss their home, spouse,
artner, parents, or family.

> As a case in point, people who refer to themselves as *single,*
> may in fact, be involved in discreet gay or lesbian relationship.
> Such partnerships may function very much as do heterosexual
> couples; they may raise natural or adopted children, maintain
> solid relationships with their biological families, and create
> a network of friends and others who serve as social support.
> Another example of family diversity is those families who
> have children living in the custody of one or more of their
> grandparents. In addition, some children may live in a homeless
> shelter with one or more of their adult siblings or in a foster
> home.

Each family tries to manage the needs of each member of the family, as well
their collective needs. At times, families are placed in a position of having
choose between which needs are met and which ones will not. For instance,
ık (1988) stated

> *Because we could not find after-school care and daily respite
> care, we had to place our son in a group home. We want him
> home now, and I cannot bring him home because there is no
> place for after-school care, vacation, etc.*

Another consideration specific to people with disabilities is the trend within
ᴇ last couple of decades of moving people out of large residential institutions,
ᴇntified as the **deinstitutionalization movement**, has resulted in an increased
mber of people with disabilities residing in their communities. Families have
come the major source of care and support for these individuals. Attempts
provide this care are associated with major challenges and conditions that
ı produce stress.

Although there can be considerable stress placed on a family that has a
ᴇmber who is disabled, families also report experiencing personal growth
ᴇociated with the experience. This growth occurs as a result of family members
ining insight into what really is important to them, such as being sufficiently
ılthy to enjoy free time together with family and friends.

So, it not only can be a challenging balancing act to manage a family who
ᴇ a person with a disability, but it is also is a balancing act to provide effective
vices for that family member. On the one hand, it is helpful to consider the
ᴇss under which some families operate. On the other hand, it is useful to
ısider that the family member with a disability can transform the lives of
 other members of the family in a constructive manner. Keeping in mind
 challenging as well as the transforming effects experienced by families can
 p provide us with insight into the lives of these families.

The attitudes, values, and behaviors of family members are very important in shaping the leisure decisions of individuals. The following questions will be addressed in this chapter:

- What is the value of inclusive leisure services for families?
- Does a family member with a disability cause stress?
- What are examples of supports for leisure and family stress?
- Who is responsible for providing inclusive leisure services?
- What can we do to help families cope with stress?
- Are there benefits to having a family member who is disabled?

What is the value of inclusive leisure services for families?

I wanted my child to have the same experiences as other kids and to learn to live in the real world with its joys and frustrations, and the inclusion program has allowed her to do that. She has learned to be more independent, which will be helpful for preparation for later life. I don't believe that isolating her from other children is better for her or for classmates. I want my child to learn from other kids, and they can learn from her.

This comment was reported by Salend and Duhaney (2002, p. 62). Since leisure occurs more within the family context than any other, for many people, their home is their center for leisure and their family the primary leisure group.

According to Townsend and Zabriskie (2010, p.15), most research findings on family leisure has identified positive relationships between family leisure involvement and family outcomes, such as family closeness, family functioning, communication, and family and marital satisfaction.

Despite the growing support for inclusion, ample evidence exists that families and communities experience significant barriers to accomplishing successful inclusion. Working with families to help foster inclusive programs is an important challenge for leisure service professionals.

Since many people spend much of their free time at home with their families, families are natural partners in leisure education. Many families are aware of the value of inclusive services. For example, when researchers have asked parents to identify the most significant benefit associated with inclusion, most parents refer to:

- acceptance by others
- participation in typical activities with peers
- exposure to ordinary expectations
- membership in a typical community group

Participation in "special" programs may actually contribute to a family's sense of isolation from their community, while participation in inclusive community programs allows families to build relationships that do not focus on a person's difference. Umstead, Boyd, and Dunst (1995, p. 36) provided the following example to illustrate the value of inclusive leisure services:

One parent said she particularly enjoyed the friendships she made while waiting for her daughter, Lakeisha, at swimming and gymnastics classes. She told us that when she ran into these other parents at the supermarket or mall, they had many things to talk about, including their children's accomplishments and activities. Parents also talk about the benefits of giving other community members the chance to know their child and family. Other children come to understand that children with disabilities share many of their own talents and interests. Children who play and learn together develop respect for each other's abilities.

Does a family member with a disability cause stress?

Parenting is a vital and difficult task under any circumstances. While parents of children with disabilities and special health-care needs confront the same challenges as other parents, many of the challenges can be more complicated due to a child's unique needs and because, until recently, the world has not welcomed children with disabilities.

These words by Klein and Kemp (2004, p. xiii) identify the complications that can result from added stress associated with having person with a family member with a disability. Although people with disabilities contribute in positive ways to their families, they have daily care needs and associated problems that create challenges for families.

Quintero and McIntyre (2010) interviewed over 40 families, some who had a member with a disability and some who did not and found that mothers of children with autism spectrum disorder (ASD) reported more daily hassles, life stress, and depression than mothers who did not have a child with ASD. These findings support conclusions by Hoffman, Sweeney, Hodge, Lopez-Wagner, and Looney (2009), who reported that over 100 mothers of children with autism identified higher levels of stress than over 350 mothers of typically developing children. After interviewing 20 culturally diverse groups of family members, Fox, Vaughn, Wyatte, and Dunlap (2002) concluded that assistance is needed for families whose children have disabilities because they experience extreme challenges with limited support. Roach, Orsmond, and Barratt (1999) observed that family members become frustrated because they feel there are few resources to help them care for their family member. After interviewing families, Rowitz (1992) concluded that many families with a member who has a disability perceive they do not have control; often do not know how to access resources, and feel intimidated by the system. Saetermoe, Wideman, and Borthwick-Duffy (1991) reported that many parents who have a child with a disability are working, have no free time, and are barely able to care for their own responsibilities; these families often struggle with rising service costs such as respite care, transportation, and medical support.

For some people, having a relative with a disability alters family roles. Children may feel anger and loss when a parent no longer functions in an accustomed manner as a result of a disability or caring for a family member with a disability.

Struggles faced by families of people with disabilities include financial and time constraints, lack of resources, fatigue, and social isolation. Family duties and responsibilities may change from member to member as the realities of living with a person with a disability become apparent.

A physical or mental disability is regarded as a considerable stress potential for families. Many families of people with disabilities experience challenges regarding long-term support for their family member with a disability and may become exhausted over time.

What are examples of supports for leisure and family stress?

Mary Ulrich has been an active advocate for people with disabilities. She is a contributing member of her community and a leader in several national organizations. In addition, Mary is a wife and a parent. One of her children happens to have a severe disability. Based on her personal experiences, Mary made a valuable contribution to this section of the chapter.

Community Support for Beverly

Many local communities have responded to the needs of typical families. For example, Beverly's parents had access to daycare services for Bev when she was younger. Currently, they piece together public and private community programs to help support their family. During the summer, when school is not in session, Bev, who is 13 years old, rides her bike to the community recreation center at 8:00 a.m. when her mother and father go to work. She begins diving lessons at 8:30 a.m., swim team practice at 9:30 a.m., and free swim with her friends until noon. She then rides her bike to a nearby park for tennis lessons from 1:00–3:00 p.m. After a short bike ride home, Bev calls her mother or father at work to provide them with an update on her status and then starts a few chores before dinner.

When examining Bev's life during the school year and in the summer, the time blocks appear similar: classes, free time, home, and chores. During the summer, Bev's family adjusts their routines to accommodate their needs. As a result of a little creative planning, the availability of financial and community resources, and Bev's growing skills and independence, Bev's family maintains a balance between their needs and community support.

Community Support for Karen

Now, let us examine the balance of family needs and community supports for the family of a person who requires extensive support. Karen is 13 years old and lives in the same neighborhood as Beverly. She goes to the same school, and her mother works with Bev's mother in the same business. Karen, however, cannot go alone to the community recreation center. The swimming program for youth with disabilities is only on Thursdays from 3:00–4:00 p.m. Karen is currently not able to ride her bike to the park independently and is not eligible for tennis lessons because of her disabilities. The sports leagues, Bible schools, Scout camps, and community camps either have no programs for children with disabilities or they schedule programs at times that are inconvenient for Karen's family. Daycare centers will not accept Karen. Although Karen's family contacts many social service agencies, they are unable to locate programs that meet Karen's needs. Though professionals are sympathetic, it is clearly the family's problem. A lack of community leisure services adds more stress to the family.

The family worries about Karen's future. They know she is going to learn fewer skills than most of her peers. Karen is also going to need an increased number of teaching trials to learn those few skills. She frequently will forget skills she does not practice, and then it takes her longer to relearn these skills. Karen has problems with transfer of skills from one place to another. The family is also aware that Karen enjoys recreation activities and wants to be with other people. Unfortunately, instead of engaging in opportunities for growth and enjoyment, frequently Karen finds herself alone wasting time.

Karen's mother and father have taken their vacation days on Mondays during the summer and count on different babysitters for the remainder of the week. They resent that they cannot plan an extended, relaxing, and fun vacation. The additional emotional stress affects their jobs and other relationships. Karen's mother also is upset that the care-giving responsibility for Karen is almost totally hers.

Karen's life during the summer is dramatically different than during the school year. Karen has little to do during her free time. She has no friends and spends a great deal of time engaging in self-stimulatory and destructive behaviors. Her behaviors reflect an attempt to communicate her desire to actively participate in enjoyable and satisfying activities. Because Karen's schedule during the summer is not physically demanding, she does not sleep through the night. During the summer, Karen had not received opportunities to practice many of the skills she mastered during the school year. Karen also has no one in her life, except a very exhausted family, who sees her strengths, gifts, and talents. It appears there is no one who wants to be around Karen in the beginning of the summer, and now that Karen's skills regressed throughout most of the summer and her inappropriate behaviors increased, the likelihood of finding someone who would care about Karen seems remote. Although Karen's family tries to listen to her and make many attempts to meet her needs, in the end they realize they are failing the young woman for whom they care so deeply.

Karen's family is under tremendous stress and feels extremely frustrated with their lack of options, community support, and their inability to support Karen. They began to see themselves not as a "family with one member who happens to be severely disabled," but rather as a "handicapped family." Karen's family began to question their parenting skills and their ability to meet Karen's needs. They sadly joke that in their county, the only way to receive after-school, school holiday, or summer vacation programming was to place Karen in an institution. Unfortunately, if Karen's family does become dysfunctional through divorce, abuse, or other tragedies, some people in the community will conclude they failed because a member of the family had a disability, rather than attributing the failure to a lack of community resources and supports.

Community Support for Aaron

Public schools are designed to support families in educating their children. Unfortunately, many people perceive the support of public schools as all that is necessary for families with children with disabilities. However, it is important for us to keep the amount of support received from the public schools in perspective.

For example, Aaron, who is 15 years old, has a life expectancy of 74 years. His school has a responsibility for his education for approximately 22 years. In a calendar year, the school year is usually about 180 days, and the school day is approximately 8:00 a.m. to 4:00 p.m. (including transportation), which totals eight hours or one third of a 24-hour day. The school has responsibility for one third of the 180 days of the 22 years, a total of 1,300 hours. Aaron's family's responsibility totals 25,700 hours, or approximately 20 times the amount of time their child is under the supervision of the public schools.

During the 8 hours of the school day, Aaron has a large support staff composed of teachers, aides, therapists, administrators, maintenance and transportation staff, cafeteria workers, and clerical personnel, but the other 16 hours, he has only the support of his family. Although there are exciting reports of inclusion facilitators, community developers, and leisure and recreation support staff, the only way that Aaron can be in any extracurricular activity is for one of his parents to attend and assist him. Although there are some positive trends for connecting people to their communities, in Aaron's last evaluation, his circle of friends was desperately small. There are some resources to help families learn to choose their priorities, address stress, and manage their problems. Yet, many family members pray that their child dies before they do, because even with their strongest advocacy efforts they cannot meet their child's needs, especially if they choose the value system that embraces inclusion.

Who is responsible for providing inclusive leisure services?

Eisenman and colleagues (2009) interviewed family members of 45 young adults with significant intellectual disabilities and found that families continue to provide the primary supports for participation and jointly participated in activities with their family member with a disability. The families stressed the importance of increasing the young adults' access to peer networks. Schleien and Werder (1985) asked professionals from community education as well as parks and recreation agencies: "Who should be responsible for the educational and recreational programs of their students on weekends, holidays, and in the summer?" They found that 93% of community education agencies named the parks and recreation staff, and 78% of parks and recreation staff chose community education agencies.

This unwillingness or inability of professionals to assume responsibilities for meeting the leisure needs of youth with disabilities is disconcerting. Families are often forced to compromise needs of family members with disabilities to access leisure programs and services.

To illustrate the many frustrations parents feel toward the absence of adequate community leisure support, consider the following dream that haunts Mary Ulrich:

> The dream begins in a recreation center. She is with her husband, Tom, and sons, Tommy and Aaron, along with their friends, and they are playing in the water. The pool is painted with black lines across the bottom, and professionals with "LG" (lifeguard) on their shirts are stationed between each black line. LGs have been told to save lives of people drowning in their area that are divided by the large black lines. As the families swim, the pool water starts to change. Instead of calm water, there are swift currents. The water rises and whirlpools are pulling them under. Tom and Mary try to keep Aaron and Tommy above water. The other families are struggling. Participants paddle and try to go to the side of the pool, but they are thrown back into deeper water. They cry to the LGs, but the LGs do not seem to hear. Each time a family member sinks to the bottom, they land on a black line. Finally, families all gather in the middle of the pool and shout in one loud voice, "Please help, we cannot do it ourselves." The LGs look at the family members but they are confused because participants continue to land on the black lines, and the LGs cannot decide whose territory the family members are in. A couple LGs throw life preservers into the pool or shout encouragement such as "Swim faster," and "It is up to you, parents, you can do it!" The water begins moving more swiftly and the families become weaker. As the families sink into unconsciousness, the LGs shake their heads as they frantically page through a rule book.

What can we do to help families cope with stress?

Meeting the needs of family members who are disabled may contribute to the family's sense of competence. To involve families in our services, we can:

- create family-centered leisure services
- develop cross-cultural competence
- avoid overprotection
- relieve family stress
- communicate with family members

Create Family-Centered Leisure Services

Family-centered leisure services focus on realizing the visions of individuals and their families through collaborative partnerships with the individual, family members, friends, professionals, and the community. These services typically concentrate on strengths of individuals and their families and on development and maintenance of relationships that enable them to be integral parts of their communities.

As professionals develop family-centered leisure services, they commit to a partnership with families that promote their engagement in the process of planning and developing leisure services. The key to promoting engagement of families is development of *trusting relationships* between families and professionals. Muscott and colleagues (2008, p. 9) reported that people involved in such relationships:

respect one another, believe in each other's ability and willingness to fulfill their responsibilities, have high personal regard for one another, and trust each other to put children's interests first.

Family-centered approaches to leisure-services delivery require support by each professional to help families overcome barriers to leisure participation. After reviewing trends in family support programs, Terrill (2001) reported considerable support for the following strategies:

- provide user-friendly approaches so programs are easily accessed
- be flexible to accommodate diversity in family configurations
- encourage families to play a leading role in identifying supports

Family-centered leisure services focus on helping the family experience leisure together, rather than focusing on only one family member. Services identify the importance of individuals and families receiving social support from key members of the community, such as leisure service providers.

Social support is an important aspect of family-centered leisure services that involves people helping to maintain a person's participation in their home and community. Providing social support emphasizes personal interactions that lead a person to feel cared for, valued, and included in mutually dependent relationships. Social support influences families' ability to cope and adjust. It is important for public agencies such as leisure service departments to emphasize family-centered approaches to services.

Research has consistently demonstrated that family time and family leisure are highly valued.

Agate, Zabriskie, Agate, and Poff (2009) surveyed almost 900 U.S. families and found that family leisure involvement is an integral component of satisfaction with family life, which supported previous research identifying benefits of family leisure that also included increased communication skills and development of life and social skills. In a review of family leisure and leisure services, Susan Shaw (1992, p. 13) reported that, "family leisure is an important aspect of leisure and an important part of life for many people in our society." She noted that family-oriented activities within and outside the home are the most common forms of leisure. Shaw suggested that recreation programming for families represents a challenge because of the mix of ages and both sexes, and because of the varied interests, skills, and needs that each family member has.

Develop Cross-Cultural Competence

The presence of a culturally diverse society has implications for developing inclusive programs. Current best practices in offering inclusive services are family-focused with emphasis on diversity and cultural issues. With each passing day, professionals are increasingly providing services for culturally diverse people and their families. These families may have beliefs, values, and customs that are different for members of the dominant culture.

Addressing the needs of culturally diverse individuals and their families in the development of programs requires that service providers recognize and respect the cultural differences of people with disabilities. Since all families differ, even ones from the same cultural group, it is helpful if leisure service providers anticipate differences, value these differences, and incorporate the family's perspective into actions.

Various issues are interpreted in a variety of ways by people from different cultures. Views related to disability, and causes of these conditions, range from those that emphasize the role of fate to those that place responsibility on the person or the person's family.

> For example, people who ascribe to the more fatalistic view of disability may see little recourse or remedy to their condition, feel they have little power to escape their fate, and therefore, seek to achieve harmony in this life. In other cultures, people believe that they are responsible for their own conditions and may attribute the cause of a disability to the parents who are being punished or who had taken inappropriate actions while the mother was pregnant. In some cultures, the person with a disability can be viewed as being possessed by evil spirits or having a mind-body imbalance.

The cause of a disability can be a result of a variety of factors, including disease, brain injury, genetic disorders, chemical imbalances, or environmental factors such as child abuse. Some disabilities are caused by many factors, while for others no single factor of causation can be identified. The views held by families concerning disability and associated causes influence the degree to which a family will participate in leisure services.

> For instance, some families may be uncomfortable about discussing ways to make adaptations that facilitate inclusion of a family member into a recreation program, while others might be very eager to do so.

As we become more effective at working cross-culturally, we will be able to tailor services to address these cultural differences. For families of all backgrounds, subtle ethnic and social class differences exist, and imposing our own ethnically influenced standards about a variety of issues may limit our ability to provide meaningful services. Reiter (1999, p. 334) concluded:

> ***Respect for the client means that he or she also has an opinion, a recommendation, a vision. Cultural sensitivity***

should lead to a dialogue based on mutual respect and open communication and assist in avoiding any power struggles.

It is important for us to move beyond cultural awareness and work to develop cultural competence. *Cross-cultural competence* refers to our ability to respond optimally to all participants and their families and to understand the cultural contexts of participants and their families. Hernandez and colleagues (1998) suggested that cultural competence is characterized by:

- accepting and respecting differences
- continuing self-assessment regarding culture
- attending to dynamics of difference
- expanding cultural knowledge and resources
- adapting service models

Although cultural awareness and sensitivity are necessary elements of cultural competence, these approaches are not enough to alter the practices and perceptions of many delivering leisure services. Lynch and Hanson (1998, p. 48) stated:

> *Achieving cross-cultural competence requires that we lower defenses, take risks, and practice behaviors that may feel unfamiliar or uncomfortable. It requires a flexible mind, an open heart and a willingness to accept alternative perspectives.*

To be culturally competent, we must become knowledgeable about the unique characteristics and backgrounds of participants and their families. We must be committed to changing services so that our programs are sensitive to the perceptions of participants and their families. Also, being culturally competent implies that we develop skills that allow us to work effectively across a variety of cultural situations (see Figure 19.1, p. 378).

Avoid Overprotection

Professionals and families report that families facilitate opportunities and situations where social inclusion can occur across the life span. However, families restrict inclusion by being overprotective and not allowing their family members who are disabled to make independent decisions. Therefore, Minow (1990, p. 39) raised the following question and attempted an answer:

> *Shielding a minority or disabled child from community dislike may allow her to develop a sense of self-esteem but disable her from coping with that community—or from recognizing hostility when it comes her way. Experience with community hostility may injure the child's sense of self, yet such experience could also itself be the best educator and*

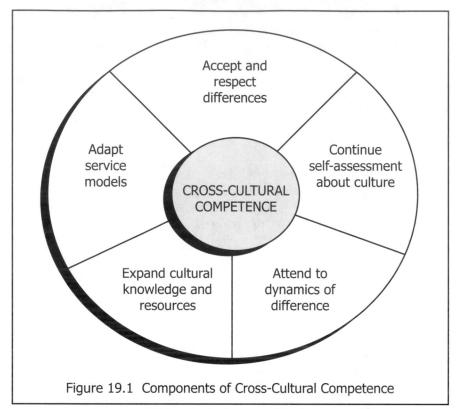

Figure 19.1 Components of Cross-Cultural Competence

strengthen the child to deal with a world where her difference has been made to matter.

Because peer relationships during adolescence serve as foundations for relationships with spouses, neighbors, and future coworkers, it is critical that social opportunities of youth with disabilities be broadened. Overprotective parental practices and limited friendships restrict opportunities for adolescents with disabilities to learn social skills necessary to establish and maintain intimate and mutually responsive relationships.

> Turnbull, Blue-Banning, and Pereira (2000) reported that several parents of children with disabilities discussed overprotection as a barrier that prevented them from giving their children sufficient freedom to explore friendships.

Overprotection can be a major problem for children. Janet Davis, the mother of Scott, who is a friendly boy who happens to have cerebral palsy and uses a wheelchair that he calls "Mad Dog," talked about how overprotection can deprive children of experiences needed to enrich their lives and stated (Rugg & Weber, 1995):

You have to let them experience the perks and frustrations that a kid not in a wheelchair is going to experience. You have to step away enough and let them do that.

While overprotection can stifle a person, Janet Davis reported that inclusion nurtures friendships, and in the end friendships are what count. To illustrate, she described a roller-skating party with Scott's schoolmates:

He gets out there on the rink in his wheelchair with 10–15 kids hanging on behind him in a train. He'll go as fast as he can and then stop and they all come together like an accordion. They say, "Come skate with me, Scott" and "Scott's skating!" And the only ones who are surprised to see him out there are the parents.

Relieve Family Stress

Leisure service professionals are in an excellent position to develop services that can be enjoyed by participants with disabilities and be beneficial to their families. One benefit is the knowledge that the family member with a disability is involved in an enjoyable and safe program.

> In describing the "Respite and Recreation Project," Lashua, Widmer, and Munson (2000) suggested that leisure service professionals may use recreation not only to provide participants with enjoyable and meaningful experiences but also to offer families with a temporary reprieve from demands of caring for a family member with disabilities.

To effectively provide a respite situation for families that have a member who has a disability or health impairment, it is critical that leisure service providers develop a trusting relationship with family members. The importance of developing trust is supported by research.

> For instance, Stoner and Angell (2006) conducted face-to-face interviews with parents of youth with autism spectrum disorders and reported that the parents described the importance of trust as critical to them developing effective relationships with professionals. This degree of trust strongly influences the degree to which parents and families participate in available services.

Communicate with Family Members

Researchers have asked parents about their frustrations about not being heard when speaking with professionals. As a result, suggestions have been made to develop channels of communication among parents and professionals if service delivery is to improve.

A characteristic of an effective communicator is that the person is a skillful listener. It is critical that leisure service providers listen closely to the family members. Sebald and Luckner (2007, p. 54) spoke to this issue:

> *Listen to families as they share, complain, argue, or question. This will help establish a trusting relationship. When families know they can share in a safe and supportive environment they are more likely to collaborate.*

Given that an important aspect of communication involves our willingness to listen to the desires, concerns, and dreams of family members, Marcia Rock (2000, p. 30), commented on the value of being a good listener when meeting with families:

> *I conferenced extensively with parents regarding the wonderful educational programs I had created for their children. The parents nodded and smiled in agreement. In fact, they were quite appreciative. Yet they said little about their child. At the time, I was perplexed and often bewildered about their reluctance to contribute to the dialogue. In retrospect, how could they have responded any differently? I was the one monopolizing the discourse.*

One way to increase communication with families is for professionals to use technology to provide these families with information about available services. Parette, Meadan, Doubet, and Hess (2010) presented the following examples of technology that has successfully been used to communicate with families:

- informational Web sites
- listservs
- discussion forums
- social networks
- blogs

Communication is critical to any meeting between service providers and service recipients, and including families in these communications is extremely helpful. We can connect with families if we respect, acknowledge, and learn more about their family patterns and values (Figure 19.2).

Are there benefits to having a family member who is disabled?

In his compelling book, *Man's Search for Meaning*, Victor Frankl (1984) documented how his time as a prisoner of war transformed his life. Other survivors of major crises have identified positive changes and personal growth as a result of these experiences.

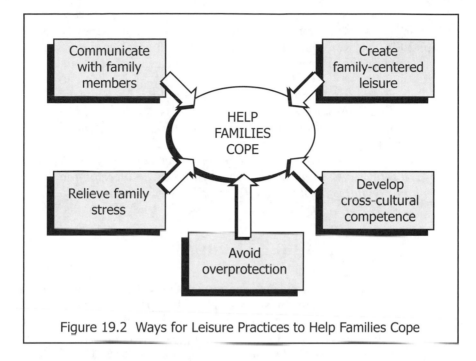

Figure 19.2 Ways for Leisure Practices to Help Families Cope

Such a *transforming experience* involves a life event that causes substantial and lasting psychological change. *Transformation* involves letting go of a previous way of life in favor of a new and clearly better way of living.

Similarly, many families who have family members with a disability assert that though the challenges in their lives have been great at times, they have not only merely coped successfully with them, but they have experienced beneficial outcomes.

For example, Taunt and Hastings (2002) interviewed almost 50 families who had a member with developmental disabilities and found that family members reported a range of positive experiences for themselves and other family members. Also, after surveying 80 parents of children with disabilities about their experiences, Scorgie and Sobsey (2000, p. 205) reported that they are experiencing positive changes in their lives, many of which would not have occurred apart from parenting a child with a disability. Based on their research the authors stated:

Some parents resent the assumption that living with a child who has disabilities must be a distressing and difficult experience. Although they would be the first to admit that there are times when life is exceedingly difficult, and want others to recognize how difficult parenting a child with a disability can be, they also ardently attest to ways in which they have been transformed . . . through their parenting experience.

A more personal testimony was provided by Barbara Jordan (Jordan & Dunlap, 2001, p. 287) who spoke about her daughter, Cassandra, who has profound cognitive impairments, a visual impairment, cerebral palsy, and autism:

> *My relationship with Cassandra, my daughter, is one of the most intimate and fulfilling relationships I have had the pleasure of experiencing. She has a gentle spirit that has a calming effect on me whenever I am close to her. She has a sweetness, innocence, and vulnerability that are coupled with an amazing strength of character. She has a sincerity and honesty that is hard to match.*

Final Thoughts

If we truly embrace inclusion and if we really want families to promote inclusion, then stronger support systems must be developed. Supportive leisure requires professionals to examine the individual desires and needs of individuals and their families and to concentrate on coordination of resources and development of community support systems. Consider the statement of Jeff and Cindy Strully (1989, p. 61) about their daughter, Shawntell:

> *There are a number of skills in which Shawntell needs to show improvement—toilet training, eating properly, verbal communication, and walking stability. However, despite our active efforts to help her in these areas, whether Shawntell achieves such skills during her lifetime is not what concerns us most as parents. It is that there will be no one in our daughter's life who will want to be with her . . . that people will not spend the time to get to know Shawntell; that she will be isolated, lonely, and without friends.*

As exemplified at the beginning of this chapter, through a cooperative approach to meeting individual leisure needs, professionals will be in a position to assist family members, such as Cindy Strully, with managing some of their *boxes*. Clearly, one important aspect in facilitating inclusion is working with family members. Families can be a valuable resource for leisure service professionals in determining ways to promote inclusion.

In summarizing her feelings about pursuing inclusion for her child, a mother interviewed by Turnbull and Ruef (1997, p. 225) stated:

> *You're untrained and unskilled to meet the enormous needs of your child; but, boy, do you try, even when you don't sleep enough or eat your "balanced" meals. You live with the fears, frustrations, and lots of sacrifices, but you just never give*

up. For this is your child, and the love and commitment will
see you through. Parents need support and encouragement.

Considering the cultural background of family members can help to determine effective ways to communicate with them. In addition, an understanding of the impact of overprotective family members can help in determining ways to promote inclusion. By listening to the desires and dreams of families, we can gain considerable insight into ways to enhance their leisure.

> After interviewing 40 mothers, of which half had a child with a severe disability, Lehman and Baker (1995) concluded that all the mothers expressed the same hope: that their children would achieve independence from their family.

The following statement illustrates the value of participating in community recreation with one's family. Wanda made this response when discussing how she felt when going to an amusement park with her family. The trip to the amusement park occurred soon after Wanda returned to her community following completion of a treatment program conducted at a rehabilitation center.

> *I just had so much fun; I loved it. I was out with my family*
> *and I had aunts and uncles and cousins there with my parents*
> *and brothers and sister, and it was really fun . . . we just had*
> *a great time and didn't care about anything and it was just*
> *terrific.*

Discussion Questions

1. What is the value of inclusive leisure services for families?
2. How does having a member of a family with a disability place stress on a family?
3. What are five suggestions for community support that could help Karen and her family?
4. Why is it important for community education agencies and parks and recreation staff to work together to meet the leisure needs of individuals with disabilities and their families?
5. What can be done to help families alleviate their stress?
6. What is a family-centered approach to leisure services?
7. What are cultural considerations when involving families in leisure services?
8. What can be done about overprotection of individuals with disabilities?
9. What are the benefits to having a family member who has a disability?
10. How does the concept of transformation relate to families with a member who has a disability?

Chapter 20
Make Reasonable Adaptations

The more things change, the more they are the same.
-Alphonse Karr

Orientation Activity: Be Flexible and Change

Directions Alone: Record the name of a recreation activity that requires materials or equipment for participation. As you keep this recreation activity in mind, answer the following questions to encourage you to make adaptations to your programs.

Directions with Others: Attempt to find other people who chose the same recreation activity as you. Share your ideas about making adaptations with the other person(s) in your group. After a specified time, discuss what you have learned with the entire group.

- What materials or equipment can be changed to promote inclusion?
- What aspects of the activity can be changed to promote inclusion?
- What about the environment can be changed to promote inclusion?
- What can be changed about how we teach to promote inclusion?

Debriefing: When attempting to adapt existing recreation programs to meet the needs of current participants, many facets of a given program can be considered. As you reflect on the orientation activity, respond to the following questions:

- What is the value of making adaptations for people with disabilities that provide them with the opportunity to participate in community recreation programs with their families and friends?
- What can you do in your current or future position to encourage personnel to make adaptations that facilitate participation by people with disabilities?
- What can you do to maintain the enjoyment of all participants when making adaptations for one person or only a few people?

Introduction

Making *adaptations* involves changing materials, activities, the environment, participants, and instructional strategies so that all participants can engage in recreation activities and pursue leisure. Adaptations can make the difference between a person being excluded from participation or being included.

It is clear that adaptations can have a positive impact on individuals' leisure participation. There are many examples of how simple and creative adaptations have resulted in successful leisure participation.

Leisure service providers must possess the knowledge and skills needed to make adaptations and be prepared to make accommodations based on the individual's abilities and limitations. Adaptations are a vital component in effective inclusion efforts. Appropriate activities draw on individual's strengths and allow participants to learn from each other.

Making adaptations to skills, rules, and equipment makes it possible for us to meet the needs of the range of individuals participating in inclusive settings. It is important that people not be separated from their peers and friends because the program requires adaptation and modifications; rather, these adaptations must be made so that inclusion can be achieved.

> Devine and colleagues (1998) reported results of a survey of park and recreation professionals and found that difficulty with program modifications was the fourth most common problem encountered when implementing inclusion in recreation. When interviewed about inclusion practices, instructors reported that they frequently modified instructional plans, equipment used, and opportunities for practice (LaMaster et al., 1998). After surveying 484 community leisure service agencies, Schleien, Germ, and McAvoy (1996) reported that rural and urban agencies cited adaptations of program materials and environments and partial participation strategies as the techniques most frequently implemented to support inclusion.

This chapter, devoted to adaptations, encourages us to modify our programs as necessary. When needed, these adaptations should permit us to meet the varying needs and abilities of the people receiving leisure services.

The suggestions presented in this chapter for adaptations are not intended to be complete. They are, however, intended to communicate some options to make accommodations that can facilitate active leisure participation for everyone. Questions addressed in this chapter include:

- What aspects can be adapted?
- How can materials be adapted?
- How can activities be adapted?
- How can the environment be adapted?
- How can participants be adapted?
- How can instruction be adapted?
- How can we evaluate adaptations?
- What are examples of adaptations?

What aspects can be adapted?

The following information encourages leisure service providers to consider a variety of aspects when attempting to make adaptations that facilitate participation. Identification of possible adaptations of leisure services are divided into five major areas:

- materials
- activities
- environment
- participants
- instruction

These five adaptations are not necessarily mutually exclusive and are simply presented as a way to organize suggestions for adaptations. The *materials* used during a recreation program can be adapted to meet the needs of the participants. The specific requirements associated with the learning *activities* may be changed. The *environment* provides another adaptation alternative to facilitate active involvement for participants. Efforts toward adaptation can be focused on the *participants* themselves, to increase the likelihood of their success. Finally, it can be helpful to focus adaptations inward and examine possible ways to modify *instructional strategies* to teach people about leisure.

The descriptions related to these five areas are not intended to be all-inclusive, but to help develop plans for adaptations for recreation programs. Examples given in many of the following situations are made with recreation activities to provide instances that enable visualization of the suggested adaptation.

How can materials be adapted?

Many aspects of materials used in recreation programs can be adapted. Some examples of possible methods for adapting materials are presented below relative to the following areas:

- size
- speed
- weight
- stabilization
- durability
- safety

Size

The size of materials can be adjusted for participants by making objects. Increasing or decreasing the size of equipment and materials can increase participation depending on the skill and limitations of participants.

For example, puzzle pieces can be made larger for those having difficulty grasping small objects. Tape can be wrapped around handles to increase their size and permit manipulation. Conversely, other people may have difficulty grasping larger objects such as felt-tip markers, so smaller ones could be used. The size of objects to be inserted into an opening can be reduced such as a basketball while the opening can be enlarged such as a basketball hoop. Large, colorful cards can assist individuals with visual problems in playing board or card games. For racquet sports, the racquets can be shortened for more control or lengthened to allow participants to cover more ground.

Speed

Some individuals may experience problems associated with gross motor coordination. A coordination problem can be quickly observed as individuals respond to moving objects. One way to increase the success of persons responding to objects is to change the speed of the moving object.

Air can be removed from a ball so when struck it will move at a slower speed. Wedges can be placed under any angled surface to change the incline to decrease or increase the speed of a ball.

Weight

The weight of objects can be adjusted to meet the strength of the participants. Wooden and metal materials can be exchanged for those that are made from plastic or rubber.

For instance, plastic balls, sponge balls, and balloons can be substituted for heavier balls in some situations, while lighter plastic or Nerf bats can be used in lieu of heavier metal or wooden bats.

Stabilization

Sometimes people who have unsteady movements may be prevented from using some expensive technology because they are likely to break the equipment.

Suction cups and clamps can be used to stabilize the material such as a portable music device. In this way, the person can use the material without fear of accidentally damaging it.

People participating in craft projects who possess grasping skills with only one portion of their bodies can be assisted as well. Crafts can be secured to a board or table such as taping paper to a desk for drawing or painting.

Durability

It is helpful that materials for recreation programs be made durable so that they will last as long as possible and expense will be minimized.

> Duct tape is often helpful in reinforcing many different pieces of equipment. Game boards and playing cards can be laminated to increase the ability of the objects to withstand regular use. Velcro can also be used to secure objects that need to be removed at different times.

Safety

When making any adaptations to objects, continuously evaluate each adaptation in reference to safety. If objects change in any way they should be examined closely. Use only nontoxic substances and remove any sharp edges. Possibilities of ingestion of objects and suffocation should be considered and prevented. In all cases, problems should be anticipated and steps taken toward prevention of any injuries. See Figure 20.1 for a summary of ways to adapt materials.

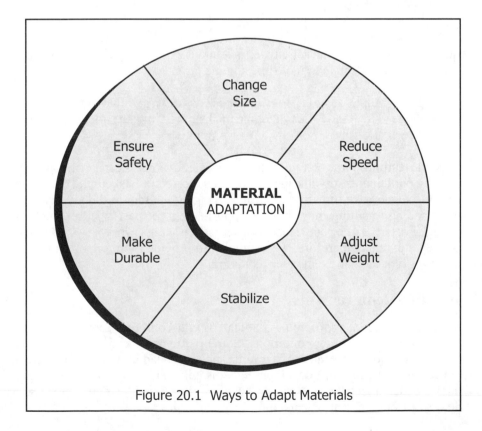

Figure 20.1 Ways to Adapt Materials

How can activities be adapted?

Many traditional recreation activities can be adapted to facilitate more active participation by individuals with disabilities. Some examples of possible methods for adapting activities are presented below relative to the following areas:

- physical aspects
- cognitive requirements
- social conditions

Physical Aspects

Individuals participating in leisure pursuits vary a great deal relative to physical strength, speed, endurance, energy level, gross motor coordination, hand-eye coordination, flexibility, agility, and many other physical skills. To adapt a physical requirement of a program, several adjustments can be made. The typical number of people associated with a game can be changed.

> For instance, the number of people participating in volleyball can be changed from 6 to 10 people for participants with limited speed and agility.

People with limited endurance and strength may benefit from making the requirements to complete an activity less strenuous by reducing either the number of points needed or the length of time a game lasts.

> For example, needing to score 8 points to win a table tennis game rather than 21, or changing the length of time to complete a recreation activity from 30 to 15 minutes.

While learning some activities, the physical movements can be changed by requiring participants to walk instead of run, such as in basketball. For those individuals who have impaired mobility, changing the required body position from standing to sitting may provide opportunities for participation, such as throwing Frisbee. Some people receiving recreation services may possess limited physical endurance; therefore, we may wish to provide more opportunities to rest during a particular event, such as hiking.

Cognitive Requirements

People may encounter problems associated with cognitive requirements as a result of many disabling conditions. Some participants may have impaired cognitive functioning because of a trauma such as a head injury, a neurological disorder such as a stroke, a developmental disability such as autism, a learning disability such as dyslexia, a mental-health problem such as depression, or a side effect from medications taken for physical illness.

To accommodate these individuals' reduced cognitive functioning, the rules associated with different games can be changed.

> As an illustration, if short-term memory appears to be a problem for a person with a traumatic brain injury, the number of cards used in a card game can be reduced. Also, rather than using all cards in a deck in a game of concentration, only the face cards can be used.

People who do not yet possess counting skills may be able to play a game by substituting matching of colors, instead of requiring the recognition of numbers or words to move game pieces. If the requirements for scoring during an activity are too difficult for participants, changes can be made.

Some individuals with learning difficulties may require some minimal assistance with reading cards used for a table game. We may wish to change the game from requiring individuals to play alone to participation with partners. Often, teams of participants can be developed that allow the individual team members to complement each other's skills and abilities.

Social Conditions

As discussed in previous chapters, many people may experience barriers to their leisure involvement. Frequently, these barriers are related to problems encountered in a social context. Some individuals may be intimidated by activities requiring larger groups. A reluctance to participate in larger groups may be a result of previous experiences associated with failure and perhaps ridicule.

To assist people in gaining the confidence needed to participate in large group activities, we may initially choose to reduce the number of people required to participate in an activity and begin instruction and practice of an activity in small groups, or if resources are available on a one-to-one basis.

> For instance, social-skills instruction related to learning how to make friends may be conducted initially with a few individuals. As participants acquire the social skills, the context could be expanded to include more participants.

The pressure involved in some activities involving direct competition against another team may be extremely threatening for some people. A person's failure to perform may result in the entire team losing to an opponent. This failure can decrease confidence and self-esteem and contribute to a reduced motivation to participate.

One approach to adapting an activity could be changing the activity so cooperation is emphasized and direct competition against another team is eliminated. To accomplish this cooperative atmosphere, we may decide to eliminate the opposing team. The opposing team would be replaced by a series of established goals to be achieved by the team.

In lieu of the traditional game of basketball, one team could participate by establishing goals related to making a basket. For example, beginning at the opposite end of the court requiring all five team members to dribble the ball as it is brought down the court while trying to make a basket in the least amount of time.

See Figure 20.2 for a summary of ways to adapt activities.

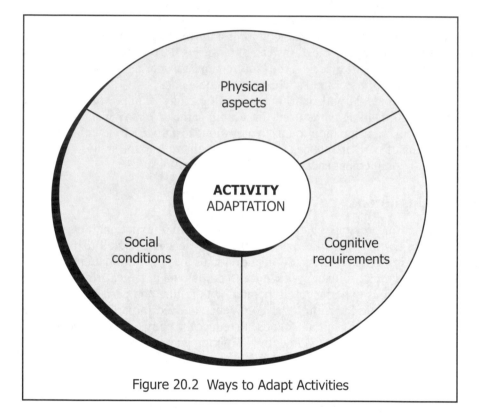

Figure 20.2 Ways to Adapt Activities

How can the environment be adapted?

The environment can play an important role in the ability of individuals to actively pursue leisure involvement. We may be in a position to adapt the environment in which leisure participation is intended to occur or to make recommendations for changing the environment. Because we are often attempting to provide leisure services in a variety of contexts, possible adaptations to the environment are suggested that relate to:

- sensory factors
- participation area

Sensory Factors

Participation can be enhanced for some individuals by simply manipulating the sounds occurring within the environment during participation.

> For instance, when playing a recreation game, some people who are easily distracted may have difficulty concentrating when the game is being played in a multipurpose room with other people talking to one another as they engage in other activities. Moving the recreation game to a small, quiet room where only people participating are present may facilitate more active participation for some individuals.

Some people using hearing aids can experience difficulty when participating in a gymnasium because of the echoing effect that can occur.

> Placement of drapes and sound-absorbing tiles near the ceiling may muffle some distracting sounds and provide persons with hearing impairments the opportunity to attend to directions more easily.

Providing an environment that permits people to see as much as possible is important when attempting to teach people. Therefore, examine the context of an activity to determine if adequate lighting is available. Simply adding a lamp may enhance completion of craft projects.

Some people's vision may be substantially impaired as a result of glare. Therefore, it is helpful if we consider the angle of the lights and realize the possibility that some lights may be too bright and inhibit, rather than enhance, participation.

Participation Area

The area in which an activity is played can be adapted to facilitate more active participation. This can allow participants with limited speed to successfully participate.

> For example, rather than using an entire baseball field to play kickball, participants can be required to keep the ball in play within the infield. In softball, participants can be required to hit to one side of the pitcher's mound, allowing more individuals to cover a small area.

Boundaries designating the end of the playing areas can also be changed to make people more aware of these designations.

> Wider chalk marks can be used on soccer fields to allow people to see more clearly when they are approaching an area designated as out-of-bounds. Ropes can be placed along a walking trail to permit individuals with visual impairments to follow the trail and maintain their awareness of boundaries.

The surface area can also be changed to permit some people to more easily access activities. A person who uses a wheelchair may be able to join a hiking expedition when some firm foundation has been applied to a trail. Changes in textures on the ground and adjacent walls of playgrounds can indicate to children with visual impairments that they are moving toward different equipment.

The facility where the activity is conducted may be also changed.

> For instance, we may place ramps in a swimming pool to permit access for people with limited mobility. The water in the swimming pool can be lowered to only two or three feet to initially accommodate those people with significant fears associated with water.

See Figure 20.3 for a summary of ways to adapt the environment.

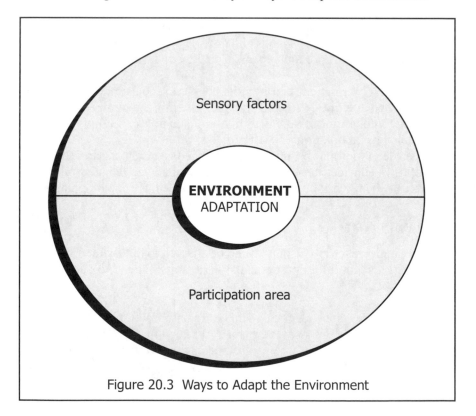

Figure 20.3 Ways to Adapt the Environment

How can participants be adapted?

When considering adaptations, the changes associated with materials, activities, and the environment often come to mind. If, however, adaptations are viewed as changes that are made to facilitate active leisure participation, then another category for making adaptations may be considered. The participants themselves may actually be altered to encourage active participation in those experiences that bring them joy and satisfaction.

This section provides suggestions on how to make some of these adaptations to the participants. Modifications can dramatically influence participants' level of participation. These modifications include:

- position the person
- provide physical aids that support
- recommend evaluations for sensory aids
- provide opportunities for increased mobility
- be open to alternative ways to communicate
- teach skills

Position the Person

The optimal condition in which individuals learn and actively participate is the *ready state*. In the **ready state**, individuals sit or stand as erect as possible, feel comfortable, able to reach materials and objects associated with an activity, and face in the direction of the activity.

Pillows, foam wedges, and support belts can be used to help individuals prepare for activity involvement. If individuals who have limited muscle control wish to read or look at a book or magazine, they can lie on their stomach on the ground. A triangle wedge can be placed under their chest with the larger side close to their neck and the smaller side near their stomach. The book can be placed on the floor and can be controlled with their hands. A person using a wheelchair can be securely fastened into the chair and provided access to toys by placing them directly on a lap tray attached to the chair. For swimming, life jackets can be used to support individuals as they learn to swim. If people using wheelchairs wish to actively contribute to the development of a mural that is being painted, they can be positioned sideways to the wall or easel to allow them to reach the mural.

Provide Physical Aids that Support

Providing physical aids that support the individual can enhance many people's participation in recreation activities.

For instance, people may encounter difficulty grasping a fishing pole because of severe weakness associated with their wrists. A brace may be used to help support the wrist when holding the fishing pole.

Some participants involved in a nature walk may have a limited range of motion. This reduced range of motion would typically limit their ability to bend at the waist and collect samples of leaves, bark, and other items used for debriefing sessions following the walk.

> Providing some people with a scooping device attached to an extended handle would permit them to participate more actively in the walk and accompanying discussion. People who have limited grasping capabilities can paint, if a paintbrush is strapped to their hand by using Velcro.

Recommend Evaluations for Sensory Aids

If we notice that participants appear to have difficulty seeing demonstrations or responding to other visual cues used to facilitate participation, it is helpful if we determine when the person was last seen for an eye examination. If there has not been a recent eye examination, then one can be recommended. The eye examination may result in the prescription of corrective lenses or contacts, which would then promote more active participation.

Some participants may not respond quickly to verbal instructions. At times, they may seem confused or inattentive. These characteristics may be indicative of a hearing loss. It is important that records be checked to determine the most recent audiology examination. Again, if a recent evaluation has not been performed, it would be important to make a recommendation for the person to have a hearing examination completed. The examination may result in people using some form of hearing aid to enhance their ability to hear and thus reduce barriers to leisure participation.

Provide Opportunities for Increased Mobility

Some leisure service participants may have reduced mobility. Mobility may be limited because of a degenerative disease, such as multiple sclerosis; a traumatic accident resulting in injury to the central nervous system, such as a spinal cord injury; or from an orthopedic disorder resulting in reduced range of motion, such as arthritis. In response to this reduced mobility, people may find assistance by using a variety of aids such as wheelchairs, crutches, walkers, or braces.

Although their primary means of ambulation may be effective in the majority of situations across their life experiences, they may be able to participate more actively in some recreation activities with a different variation of the mobility aid. For children who use wheelchairs and are participating in activities in a gymnasium, a scooter board can inject fun and increased speed into the activity.

> For example, when playing kickball, children could use scooter boards to move about. This adaptation could be made in conjunction with an activity modification by establishing the rule that participants use their hands to hit the ball and then move to the bases quickly on the scooter boards.

Personal wheelchairs may be the most appropriate for daily experiences. There are, however, many commercially available sport wheelchairs designed specifically for the requirements associated with particular types of sports.

> As an illustration, there are chairs designed for activities that require a great deal of rapid turning. These types of chairs may be used when participating in activities such as tennis, basketball, and racquetball. Other people may be interested in participating in races on or off the track. These individuals frequently use chairs designed for speed and movement in a forward direction. It is helpful to examine the participation patterns of people experiencing reduced mobility and consider variations to their typical mobility that could enhance leisure involvement.

Be Open to Alternative Ways to Communicate

Some individuals cannot meet their communication needs through standard forms of spoken communication. It is essential that we be willing to modify the required response mode for a particular activity. These individuals may require augmentative and alternative communication (AAC) systems to fulfill their needs.

AAC systems include unaided arrangements, such as gestures, sign language, and finger spelling; aided systems that are not electronic, such as communication boards and books containing symbols, words, or pictures; and computer-based assistive technology, such as speech synthesis and word printouts. AAC systems vary considerably according to message storage and retrieval systems, communication speed, and communication-aid output capabilities.

There is a large range of competencies and abilities across individuals using AAC systems resulting in an extremely heterogeneous group. It is useful if leisure service professionals are open to these alternative forms of communication and are willing to change the required mode of communication for a specific activity to permit active participation by people using communication systems other than speech. Further information about AAC systems is provided in the final chapter.

Teach Skills

As stated previously in this chapter, if an imbalance exists between the degree of challenge of a program and participants' skills, barriers to leisure participation may be created. The majority of this chapter has focused on adaptations that can permit modification of the challenge associated with a recreation program to meet the abilities of the participants.

However, we have another option when trying to help individuals meet the requirements of an activity. Recreation is designed to teach people skills and knowledge that facilitate their ability to meet the challenges encountered when attempting to experience leisure.

> As an example, if people do not possess the skills to access public transportation to go to a fitness club, instruction related to use of public transportation will increase the ability of individuals to meet the challenges associated with enhancing their physical fitness.

See Figure 20.4 for a summary of ways to adapt the participant.

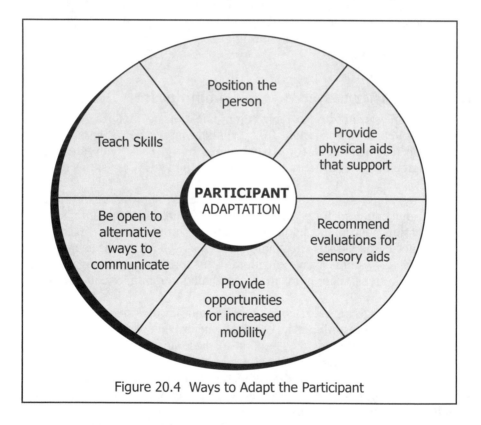

Figure 20.4 Ways to Adapt the Participant

How can instruction be adapted?

The four areas for making adaptations previously mentioned have required us to focus attention away from providers and onto materials, activities, environment, and participants. The fifth area encourages us to consider the way we deliver services and provide instruction.

If people receiving leisure services are not developing leisure skills and knowledge at a rate consistent with their potential, there may be ways to modify the instructional strategies we employ to allow them to more effectively and efficiently meet their needs. The next section will address the following considerations related to instructional strategies:

- establish objectives
- develop instructional steps
- offer opportunities for practice
- include instructional prompts
- provide reinforcement
- consider personnel

Establish Objectives

Some participants in leisure programs may encounter difficulty achieving established objectives. We may continue to focus on the inability of individuals to achieve their objectives and thus create further difficulty. It is important to be willing to reassess the objectives and change them to meet the needs of participants; however, the objectives should still create a manageable challenge for participants. In fact, objectives should be monitored closely for the possibility of retaining objectives that are too easily completed by participants. While overly rigorous objectives can create frustration for both participants and practitioners, development of objectives demanding too little of individuals can create an environment conducive to boredom and apathy.

Develop Instructional Steps

A useful tool in providing leisure services for people with disabilities is task analysis. *Task analysis* involves segmenting a task into components that can be taught separately. The instructional components can then be sequenced together to allow individuals to complete an identified task. The procedure of task analysis is used when attempting to teach a multifaceted task that may appear complex for participants.

Although task analysis requires identification of components that, when accomplished in sequence, permit completion of the task, the number of components identified for any given task may vary considerably.

> For instance, in one situation the act of swinging a table tennis paddle to hit the ball may be divided into 4 steps for someone with fairly advanced skills, while in another circumstance for another person who may have fewer skills, the task may be divided into 10 steps.

The skills of individual participants should determine the level of specificity associated with a task analysis. Therefore, if people experience problems learning a skill, we can examine the components being taught. We can then determine if further delineation is needed for those individuals who are not learning how to complete a particular component, or if some components should be collapsed to accommodate people who feel they are not being sufficiently challenged.

Offer Opportunities for Practice

Sometimes, people enrolled in recreation programs fail to progress at the rate we expect. One reason people may not acquire skills and knowledge associated with a particular aspect of recreation is that they may not have received sufficient opportunity to practice the information presented in the program. Another way to adapt the instructional strategy is to change the amount of practice associated with a particular objective.

Repetition through practice can allow individuals to integrate the newly acquired knowledge and skills into their existing leisure repertoire. Continuous practice of previously learned skills can increase the chance that individuals will maintain the skills over time.

When planning practice sessions, it is important to be creative and make these opportunities as interesting and fun as possible. Frequently, people do not understand a concept the first time they are presented with the idea. Practice provides experiences that permit repetition of concepts and ideas that enable people to retain that information more easily.

Include Instructional Prompts

As we provide instruction, we may observe that participants do not respond to our directions. If this occurs, we may consider the use of prompts to assist participants. Prompts can provide auditory cues for individuals, typically through *verbal instructions*. There are, however, other forms of prompts that can be used.

Environmental prompts can encourage participant involvement by simply manipulating the context in which an activity is provided.

> For instance, one way to encourage use of recreation table games in a recreation lounge may be to place the games on tables in the room, or open the closets where they are stored so that participants entering the area will see the games.

Visual cues may be provided to stimulate participation. *Modeling* appropriate behaviors and providing systematic demonstrations may allow participants to more clearly see the desired leisure behavior. *Hand-over-hand physical guidance* may permit individuals to feel the specific movements associated with participation and thus increase their ability to correctly perform the skill. Because people may respond differently to various prompts, examine the procedures and be willing to modify the way participants are prompted to learn and apply new leisure skills.

Provide Reinforcement

We often provide individuals with reinforcement. Selection of an object or event to serve as **positive reinforcement** means that when that item, activity, object, or social contact is given as a consequence of a behavior, the likelihood of that behavior occurring again is increased.

Positive reinforcement must be person-specific; that is, it must be something that will effectively influence that individual's behavior. Therefore, we must monitor the participants' responses to a consequence to determine if it is truly a powerful enough reinforcement to influence behavior.

If, over time, a person's behaviors do not increase in response to being given a specific item or activity, we must be willing to make adaptations. Testing various items and activities until reinforcements are identified may provide us with a systematic procedure for identification of reinforcements.

Consider Personnel

Interaction between participants and practitioners is highly complex. Some participants may respond to some leisure providers more energetically than to others. Failure of some program participants to progress at an anticipated rate may be influenced by who delivers the services.

It is helpful to closely monitor our interactions with participants as well as other personnel delivering recreation services. In-service training can be provided to improve our interpersonal skills. Adapting schedules to accommodate both staff and participant needs may also encourage more effective implementation of recreation programs. See Figure 20.5 for a summary of ways to adapt instruction.

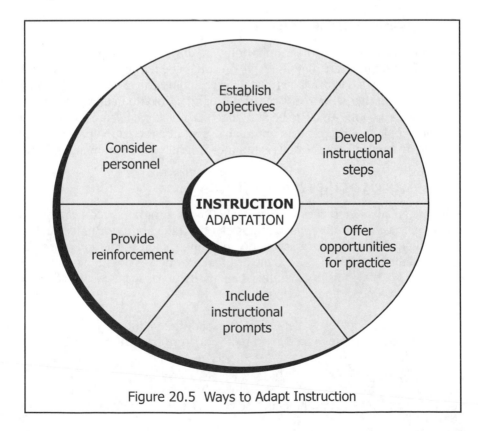

Figure 20.5 Ways to Adapt Instruction

How can we evaluate adaptations?

Competent professionals must continuously evaluate effects of their services. The evaluation process allows us to be aware of our actions, to improve our services, and to respond to the needs of the people we serve. To encourage evaluation of the adaptations made to materials, equipment, activities, people, and environments, the following suggestions are provided:

- conduct continuous observations
- make necessary adjustments
- retain aspects of the original task

Conduct Continuous Observations

When adaptations are made to specific aspects of a recreation program, continuous observation of individuals participating in the program is suggested. Observations of individual participation can allow us to determine if the adaptations are achieving their intended goals.

Observations provide us with a way to examine unanticipated difficulties participants may be experiencing relative to the adaptations. Continuous observations put us in a position to understand the effectiveness of the adaptations.

Make Necessary Adjustments

Observations provide us with the opportunity to discover problems with adaptations. When problems are identified, we must then be willing to respond to any difficulties associated with adaptations. This willingness to change an adaptation must stem from the belief that even if a great deal of time and energy is put into a given task, it may need to be altered to permit active leisure participation for some people. A slight adjustment to an aspect of a recreation program may make the difference between active and meaningful participation and failure.

Retain Aspects of the Original Task

Each time an adaptation is made, that aspect of the program becomes less like the original task. Therefore, adaptations can limit the ability of individuals to participate in different programs that do not contain such adaptations. Keeping features of the program as close to the original program as possible is helpful if to encourage participants to generalize their ability to participate in the activities in other environments and situations.

> As an example, a leader of an afterschool recreation program notices that several participants struggle when playing volleyball. Many serves do not make it over the net and if a serve does make into play, it is rarely returned. The leader decides to lower the net and move the serving line closer to the net. The rules, the ball, and the net remain the same. An

> advantage of this form of adaptation is that the changes can
> easily be adjusted to accommodate participants as they increase
> their skills over time by gradually moving the serving line back
> and raising the net.

Individuals who have experienced a trauma in their lives often want to establish continuity with experiences that existed before their illness or accident occurred. People often strive to achieve positive experiences associated with leisure participation similar to those that they had encountered before the trauma.

The sense of continuity can be fostered by keeping the activity as similar to the original activity as possible yet providing an accommodation that promotes meaningful leisure participation for individuals.

What are examples of adaptations?

Adaptive equipment can be used to help individuals with mobility impairments to experience the excitement associated with many outdoor adventure activities. Activities identified as "extreme" such as skiing, hang gliding, motorcycling, kayaking, skydiving, and mountaineering have generated development of extensive medical adaptive devices and rehabilitation equipment.

Kaminker (1995) described a variety of adaptations that have been made to allow individuals with quadriplegia to participate in physically active recreation activities:

- **Buddy system for scuba diving**. Julia Dorsett, East Coast Director of the Handicapped Scuba Association, explained, "Under water, we're all the same."
- **Chin-activated joystick to fly a plane**. "You have to have arm muscles, but you don't have to have hands." says Ray Temchus, President of Freedom's Wings International.
- **Sip-and-puff-activated switch for sailing**. Sam Sullivan, an engineer with the Disabled Sailing Association, stated, "The exciting thing about sailing is that people of all abilities can compete against each other with no special categories or allowances."
- **Adapted saddle and reins for horseback riding**. "Hand use is not necessary, a horse can be trained to respond to wrist-controlled reins," says Evelyn Refosco, co-chair of the American Handicapped Riding Association's Adult Riding Committee.

There are many examples of adaptations that have facilitated participation. One example is associated with Dennis Walters and his approach to golf, as reported by Perry (1995, p. 65):

> Golf hasn't been the same since Dennis Walters mounted a
> barstool on a golf cart so he could return to the links following
> an accident that left him paralyzed from the waist down. Proving

that a disability doesn't necessarily translate into a big handicap, Walters has received the prestigious Ben Hogan Award for the Golf Writers of America in honor of his remarkable comeback. . . . Walters shows people with disabilities they can enjoy the challenge and satisfaction a good round of golf brings. He demonstrates how to adjust swings to correct any problem—from slices to hooks. But his lessons also have a broader application that extends far beyond the links: Obstacles can be surmounted with a little ingenuity and a lot of hard work.

Final Thoughts

Although there are many commercially available materials that have been developed to facilitate participation in recreation activities by people with disabilities, a critical ingredient in promoting inclusion is to identify barriers. Once these barriers are identified, then we must take on the challenge to make the necessary adaptations to promote inclusion.

These efforts occur not in isolation, but with assistance from participants, families, colleagues, advocates, and experts. When we believe that all people deserve to be included in any program and we are willing to do what it takes to make it happen, inclusion becomes a reality.

This chapter focused on ways to make adaptations. These adaptations should permit us to meet the varying needs and abilities of the people attending recreation programs.

Discussion Questions

1. What is meant by an adaptation?
2. What are different aspects of a program that can be adapted?
3. How can participants be involved in the adaptation process?
4. What are ways to evaluate adaptations?
5. What are possible methods for adapting materials used in recreation programs?
6. How can activities be adapted to facilitate recreation participation by people with disabilities?
7. How does the environment play an important role in the ability of individuals with disabilities to participate in recreation activities?
8. How can the environment be adapted to facilitate inclusion of individuals with disabilities?
9. What are ways of altering the participants to facilitate participation?
10. What are ways instructional strategies can be adapted to promote inclusion?

Chapter 21
People, Inclusion, and Physical Limitations

Jon Franks is a chiropractor who owns a fitness center in Venice, CA. He sustained a spinal cord injury in a motorcycle accident in 1985. Jon is a triathelete who has raced all over the United States, China, and the Virgin Islands.

Photo by Lynda Greer

Jon's Story

It was November, 1985. I was on my way to a UCLA basketball practice (I was working with the team) when the engine on my motorcycle seized up on me, while doing a curve at about 40 mph, and I slammed into a utility pole. As a chiropractor, I do know about the spine, so I knew right away what the score was.

Basketball and fitness have been part of my life since I can remember, so well-meaning people suggested that I go for wheelchair basketball. No way would I settle for less with a sport I excelled in on my feet. So in the hospital I set my mind on the triathalon. I've always been a competitor and the accident didn't kill that spirit. The triathalon is a grueling event . . . just what I wanted. Two months after the accident I was training 15 to 20 hours a week. I'm most competitive in the swimming and running events, weaker in the cycling division. For swimming I wear a wet suit and webbed gloves to give me power, and I do the backstroke . . . breathing's easier. For the run I use a lightweight chair and I use a hand-powered bike designed and built by my friend, Bruce Eikelberger. We're working to develop a better bike.

I love the challenge of racing. But it isn't just for me that I do this. I intend to change the image most adults have of people in chairs. And I'm doing it in an effort to raise bucks as well as consciousness. Attitude-wise I want to teach people that being in a chair isn't the most disabling thing; it's the attitude of others. Sometimes it's very difficult for athletes to participate in certain events. I've had my share of rejection because I'm in a chair and a pain in the butt to work around. This segregating athletic events along able-bodied/disabled lines has to stop. And I'm also racing to get sponsors to help raise money for research and technical advances. I believe I'll be out of this chair someday and that kids . . . anyone with a spinal cord injury . . . deserve the chance of complete recovery.

But as long as I'm in this chair I'm going to prove to others that people in chairs are really no different from them. A lot of people don't feel comfortable with wheelchairs . . . and that's got to change. Believe me, it will be better for everybody.

*Latent abilities are like clay. It can be mud on shoes, brick in a
building, or a statue that will inspire all who see it. The clay
is the same. The result is dependent on how it is used.*

-James A. Lincoln

Orientation Activity: Zhenya, Kostas, and Susan—What to Do?

Directions Alone: Read each of the following situations and answer the questions posed.

- Zhenya, an accountant in your hometown, would like to participate in a tennis program offered by the private country club of which she is a member. As the director of recreation for this country club, what might you do to facilitate participation in the tennis program by Zhenya, who has paraplegia?
- Kostas, a college student, has expressed a desire to participate in a hiking expedition planned for a weekend adventure with a local community outing club. As a member of this club, what suggestions might you make to assist Kostas, who has spina bifida, to successfully participate in the program?
- You are the assistant coach of your sister's softball team. Susan, a 12-year-old, would like to play on the team. Susan has muscular dystrophy and is still able to walk. What are some things you may wish to consider when coaching Susan and what is some information you may wish to discuss with Susan, the coach, and perhaps her parents?

Directions with Others: Move about the room with your answers and share your strategies for including Zhenya, Kostas, and Susan with another person. Record any strategies that he or she identified that you did not. After a specified time, discuss what you have learned with the entire group.

Debriefing: To include Zhenya in the tennis program we can ensure that the parking lot and the path to the tennis courts are accessible to people using wheelchairs. We can advertise that the tennis program is available to every member in the club. Modification to the rules as established by the National Foundation of Wheelchair Tennis will help to assure success for Zhenya. For example, players who use wheelchairs are allowed two bounces of the ball. Ensure that she is able to participate with her friends. If she is a new member, arrange matches with peers of similar ages. We can also identify other resources she could access to improve her skills. If Zhenya has limited strength and endurance, the use of a ball-retrieving basket or a person to pick up the loose balls may be helpful.

To facilitate Kostas's participation in the hiking expedition, we could first talk with Kostas about his skill and experience as a hiker. Also, we can obtain the difficulty level of the trail and match the skill level required to Kostas's skills. We may want to hike the trail in advance conducting an environmental inventory to identify obstacles that will need to be negotiated. It may be helpful if we determine what the weight of his pack should be based on Kostas's endurance, strength, and agility. As with any camping expedition, a communication device that can signal distress to others may be useful. We also will want to determine strategies to accommodate people on the expedition who move at slower speeds. It can be useful to schedule breaks to allow participants who are moving more slowly than others to catch up and rest. We can identify meeting points along the trail to encourage people on the expedition to come together. If Kostas is unsteady on his feet, he may wish to use a hiking stick or cane or he may feel comfortable being paired with someone who can assist him as needed.

To encourage Susan's inclusion on the softball team, we can visit with Susan and her family to discuss her strengths, as well as concerns about participation. We can have her share any adaptations she has already made when playing softball. If Susan has difficulty running, we may suggest she hit and have another player run the bases for her. If she has difficulty moving, perhaps she may prefer to play the position of catcher, pitcher, or first baseman. She may be paired with someone playing other positions that could catch the ball, throw it to her, and then allow her to make the play. Rotating the entire lineup to avoid fatigue may be useful if endurance is a problem. For instance, players only play for two consecutive innings and then are rested for one inning.

Consider the following questions as you think about the orientation activity:

- How can you promote participation of individuals with physical limitations in your recreation program?
- Why is it important for recreation providers to talk to new participants when they begin a program?
- What are some considerations for the inclusion of participants who may have limited strength, balance, or endurance?

Introduction

People acquire physical disabilities in many different ways. It is helpful if we consider perspectives of people with disabilities when attempting to assist them in participating in meaningful leisure pursuits. This chapter presents some information to address these issues.

After surveying over 600 people with mobility impairments who had a diagnosis of spinal cord injury, multiple sclerosis, cerebral palsy, stroke, or polio, researchers Crawford, Hollingsworth, Morgan, and Gray (2008) concluded that providing community-based programs that focus on increasing the level of physical activity of people with mobility limitations may improve their health and community participation.

To set the tone for this chapter and to identify the possibilities for people with physical disabilities, consider the words of Gloria Brawn (1995, p. 13):

> *I am a quadriplegic from a car/moose accident seven years ago. Since my accident, I have been up in a helicopter twice. I also have been on the back of a Harley Davidson and had a wonderful time. I've gone snow sliding with my granddaughters here in Maine. I go swimming in our pool and fishing in our boat in the summer. I have been camping and on a trip to Nashville. Did everything I wanted to do down there. I want to go skydiving this summer. I feel the days of keeping the disabled in the closet are gone.*

- What are characteristics of multiple sclerosis?
- What are considerations for inclusion of people with multiple sclerosis?
- What are characteristics of spina bifida?
- What are considerations for inclusion of people with spina bifida?
- What are characteristics of arthritis?
- What are considerations for inclusion of people with arthritis?
- What are characteristics of spinal cord injuries?
- What are considerations for inclusion of people with spinal cord injuries?
- What are characteristics of amputations or congenital absences?
- What are considerations for inclusion of people with amputations or congenital absences?
- What are characteristics of muscular dystrophy?
- What are considerations for inclusion of people with muscular dystrophy?
- What are considerations associated with wheelchair technology?
- What are characteristics of people using a wheelchair?
- What are considerations for inclusion of people who use wheelchairs?

Meet Joan, Who Has Many Interests

People describe Joan as a lifelong activist, committed to a wide range of issues and interests, such as the peace movement and international affairs. Recently, she has become an activist for the rights of people with disabilities. "When you don't have something wrong, it's not part of your life," she said. "It didn't hit home until it hit me."

Joan's range of interests is obvious in even a quick visit to her apartment. Huge flower boxes made of railroad ties, overflowing with her flowers, flanks the wheelchair ramp to the door. The most prominent object in the living room is a loom—she says she made 10 sweaters one year as Christmas gifts. Delicate Japanese rice-paper cutouts, gifts from a friend, decorate the walls. And of course, there are the books and records. Joan has no intention of slowing down.

> *I have to keep going—there's a lot left to do. There's so much—the homeless, the hungry . . . civil and social rights.*

> *We are not facing the needs of the poor, the homeless, the children . . . These are the problems we need to face as a country, a state, and as a county right down here in the local level. I hate this flag-waving, this superficial patriotism. It's just blinders to cover the real problems.*

Joan has multiple sclerosis. The symptoms became noticeable during her freshman year in college, approximately 20 years ago. In addition to other physical traumas, the multiple sclerosis has weakened her legs so that she has used a wheelchair for the past 13 years. Joan said she has learned from her disability.

> *My aims and goals in life changed a great deal because of my illness. Things that were so important weren't important after all. You learn to smell the flowers, look at the trees. I'm really pretty normal—that's all part of our advocacy, to get people to see that persons with disabilities are just like anyone else.*

What are characteristics of multiple sclerosis?

Multiple sclerosis is a progressive disease affecting the central nervous system, which includes the brain and spinal column. 'Multiple' means many or varying, and 'sclerosis' means scarring or hardening.

Although there is no known cause of or cure for multiple sclerosis, some patterns exist. It affects more women than men and Caucasians more than other ethnic groups. It typically occurs anytime from adolescence until the early 50s, with the average age of the onset approximately age 30.

Multiple sclerosis involves spontaneously appearing lesions at the nerve endings of the central nervous system and the disappearance of the protective nerve coverings. As the lesions heal, the sclerosis (scarring) occurs. The scars prevent neurological impulses from traveling to and from the brain. The result of these damaged transmissions include numbness and tingling of hands or feet, weakness of lower extremities, loss of voluntary movements of muscles, loss of vision in one or both eyes, and facial numbness.

Most individuals with multiple sclerosis will also develop cognitive problems and affective disorders which result in personality changes, memory loss, and decreased planning and organizational abilities. The location and severity of the sclerosis will determine the degree of disability.

For most individuals, multiple sclerosis follows a course of exacerbations and remissions. A new outbreak of lesions, an *exacerbation*, is characterized by increasing severity of the symptoms. When lesions heal, relief of some symptoms may result; these episodes are known as periods of *remission*.

At times, exacerbation is characterized by decreased motor ability and remissions by increased motor proficiency. Periods of exacerbations and remissions are unpredictable, and depression is a common emotional response of individuals with this disease. As the disease progresses, the individual may need to rely upon a cane or wheelchair for mobility.

What are considerations for inclusion of people with multiple sclerosis?

Be Prepared for Fluctuations in Behaviors

Since the skills of people with multiple sclerosis vary from time to time because of exacerbations and remissions, being prepared to deal with fluctuations in performance may enhance a person's success. Some people may require the use of a wheelchair during times of exacerbations and then later be able to walk with assistance during a period of remission.

Some participants may interpret fluctuation in performance as a lack of effort or commitment to an activity. Being aware of this variation in abilities can allow us to make accommodations for the person and facilitate positive interactions between participants.

Provide Support

Fluctuation and reduction in participation skills, as well as the cognitive and affective changes, can be frustrating for a person with multiple sclerosis. Providing support for this person and demonstrating sensitivity to the experience can help us increase the likelihood of successful leisure participation.

> For example, since heat slows reactions of the central nervous system, creating a supportive environment for recreation participation includes working to ensure the person does not get overheated. People with multiple sclerosis can benefit from exercising in cool water.

Meet Chuck, Who Enjoys Lifting Weights

Fabbri (1991) reported that as a youth playing in tackle-football games between neighborhoods, Chuck awkwardly pursued runningbacks and took on blockers. He wore a pair of steel leg braces at his defensive line position. "The offensive linemen looked at me kind of funny and played me namby-pamby. But after the first couple of plays, they realized I could play and started taking clean shots at me."

Chuck progressed from neighborhood noseguard to world-champion weightlifter. He won the gold medal at the Paralympics in Seoul, South Korea, and has won four world titles.

> *I wanted to be a wrestler. When I was a sophomore in high school, I asked the wrestling coach if I could try out for the team. He told me that I couldn't come out because of the handicap, but he asked me if I wanted to be the damn equipment manager.*

Another coach suggested he try the weight room instead. In six months, Chuck was bench-pressing 260 pounds. That year, he finished second in the national championships, and two years later he was the national champion. His national bench-pressing record in the 165-pound division was 485 pounds, and his world record was 462 pounds. Chuck fits his training schedule around a full-time job as a stockroom manager.

Some people may view Chuck's participation and excellence in athletics as unique because he is paralyzed from the waist down by spina bifida. He can walk with the aid of braces and crutches and has made many adaptations to recreation activities of interest, allowing him to continue active participation.

What are characteristics of spina bifida?

Spina bifida means "cleft spine" and is a congenital disability of the spinal column that occurs early in prenatal development, as the central nervous system forms. The defect, usually located in the lumbar area, occurs when the covering of the spinal cord is displaced and forms a sac-like protrusion. The protrusion then causes improper formation of the vertebrae and results in externally exposing the abnormal protrusion. Effects of this congenital disability range from no noticeable effects to paraplegia.

Although there are different forms of spinal bifida, the most severe form of spina bifida is called mylomeningocele. With *mylomeningocele*, a portion of the spinal cord itself protrudes through the back, sometimes exposing tissue and nerves.

Some children born with this form of spina bifida also have *hydrocephalus*, which occurs because spinal fluid is not absorbed properly, and this fluid builds up in a person's head. A surgical shunting procedure can control hydrocephalus by draining the fluid into portions of the body that can dispose of the fluid. Without this procedure, the pressure can cause an enlargement of a person's head, seizures, blindness, and brain damage.

Effects of mylomeningocele may include muscle weakness or paralysis below the affected area of the spine, accompanied by loss of sensation and loss of bowel and bladder control. Children with this type of spina bifida often need mobility assistance in the form of crutches, braces, or wheelchairs. Children with both spina bifida and hydrocephalus may have difficulty attending to tasks, expressing thoughts, and understanding language. This can result in learning problems; however, early intervention can help to reduce the severity.

What are considerations for inclusion of people with spina bifida?

Consider Decreased Sensation

People with spina bifida often have reduced sensation in their legs and may not be able to differentiate between temperatures. Care should be taken in activities to prevent burns from hot water or other sources of heat.

With the loss of pain sensation, people with spina bifida may not feel the friction of their braces resulting in ***decubitus ulcers***, which are sores that occur on the skin as a result of continuous pressure or rubbing on that portion of the body. If a person uses braces, leisure service providers are encouraged to check the braces and any areas of skin that are adjacent to the braces.

Communicate with Participants to Determine Preferences

Keeping open lines of communication with individuals who have spina bifida will help alleviate possible problems. Speak with participants who have spina bifida to determine their interests and preferences. Avoid being overprotective of participants, and do not make assumptions about their interests.

> For example, Zoerink (1988) found that many of the young people with spina bifida in his study preferred active and group-oriented leisure experiences and sports activities. Together with the participant, we can explore ways to facilitate optimal participation with attention to safety and health.

Meet Marty, the "Family Man"

His friends consider Marty a "family man." His wife, Gloria, children, and grandchildren are the most important aspects of his life. He takes great pleasure in spending time with them and talking about their accomplishments. In addition to his family, he has two major leisure pursuits.

Since his retirement, Marty volunteers at a local hospital, assisting nurses with office-management tasks. Although the nurses appreciate his contributions to office operations and his strong work ethic, they value even more his friendship and sense of humor. They characterize him as a person who is playful and fun to be around while he accomplishes a great deal of work.

Walking is another one of Marty's passions. He rises early in the morning to complete a vigorous 30-minute walk. Marty views walking as an activity he enjoys and something that offers him a sense of accomplishment, including significant health benefits. Since developing osteoarthritis, Marty awakens in the morning stiff and in pain. However, after his morning stroll, the pain subsides and he goes about his day with increased range of motion and vigor.

What are characteristics of arthritis?

According to the Arthritis Foundation, arthritis occurs among one in seven people, including children and adults, and one in three families. It affects three times as many women as men, and with over 100 different forms, it is the most common crippling disease in the United States.

While many people will not experience serious physical problems, many people have arthritis that requires medical treatment. A common denominator for more than 100 different forms of arthritis is pain and stiffness in or around the joints of the body. Inflammation of joint tissues or breakdown of joint cartilage often causes arthritis. Joint cartilage is the spongy tissue located at tips of bones that acts as a shock absorber.

The word arthritis is derived from the Greek word arthros, which means joint, and the suffix itis, which is translated to mean inflammation. Understanding the derivatives of this word help define arthritis as a group of conditions that involve an inflammation of the joints, tissue, and bones, which results in stiffness, swelling, redness, and pain. Two of the more recognized types of arthritis are osteoarthritis and rheumatoid arthritis.

The most common form of arthritis, *osteoarthritis*, is a degenerative joint disease, rarely found in people younger than 45, caused by the erosion of cartilage. This degenerative disease creates stiffness, swelling, and pain. As the cartilage erodes, bones begin to rub against one another, resulting in pain, stiffness, and joint deformity. Fortunately, osteoarthritis usually responds to medication and exercise.

Rheumatoid arthritis is one of the more profound forms of arthritis, typically resulting in severe inflammation that attacks primarily the joints. It can also affect the skin, blood vessels, muscles, spleen, heart, and even the eyes. Individuals may report feeling "sick all over," with fatigue, poor appetite, fevers, weight loss, enlarged lymph glands, and excessive sweating or cold tingling hands and feet. It is a progressive type of arthritis characterized by unpredictable fluctuations in the degree of pain and stiffness and can occur at any age.

What are considerations for inclusion of people with arthritis?

Talk with Participants

Since some people with arthritis may be in considerable pain, maintain open communication with them when they are participating in activities. Open lines of communication will increase the likelihood they will feel comfortable discussing with you their mobility limitations in certain situations.

It is often useful to consider the existing weather conditions, because they can affect the extent of stiffness and pain associated with the joints. Typical treatment for many people with arthritis is rest, exercise, and the use of nonsteroid anti-inflammatory drugs such as aspirin.

Consider Using Exercise

Research supports the belief that most people with arthritis who follow a sensible exercise program may ease pain and avoid disability. A routine of walking, swimming, biking, and/or stretching, can help reduce joint and pain stiffness, build stronger muscles and bones, and improve overall health. Aquatic programs such as water walking, swimming, and water aerobics are frequently recommended forms of exercise for people with arthritis. The Arthritis Foundation offers extensive recommendations for activities and exercise programs tailored for people with differing forms and severity of arthritis.

When people experience pain during periods of exercise, encourage them to take a brief rest. If affected joints are hot and inflamed, the activity may be too strenuous. Recommend that they discontinue the exercise at that time. The goal for an exercise program is typically to increase mobility rather than strength. Moving the joints through their full range of motion at least twice daily can help people continue their free movement.

Make Adaptations

There are many benefits of making adaptations to recreation activities so that individuals with arthritis may continue to participate. Buildings meeting the requirements of the ADA in regard to faucet handles, door openers, and ramps enable people with arthritis to move about with dignity and independence.

> Some adaptations require minor adjustments, such as adding a Velcro strap to a lap pillow to help a person hold a book. Cardholders can be improvised as simply as sticking cards upright in Silly Putty or Play-Doh or standing them in a shallow box filled with sand.

Meet Stacy and Jimmy, Who Are Quite in Love

Sleek, aerodynamic racing wheelchairs spin around the practice track, pushed by athletes who are intent on bettering a previous time. As he finishes his last lap, Jimmy rolls to a stop, panting, and gratefully accepts ice water from his coach. "Pretty good time," she says, consulting her stopwatch. The coach is Jimmy's wife, Stacy. The two met at a track meet several years ago when Stacy was a student intern. They hit it off immediately. In one year, they were married.

> *"My parents thought I was crazy," she admits. "They had that old-fashioned way of thinking that people in wheelchairs can't do a lot of things. They said, 'You love scuba diving, dancing, sports—think of all the things you'll miss!'"*

As they got to know Jimmy, Stacy's parents' fears dissolved. And from the many interests the couple share, it appears that neither of them misses out on anything.

"We're both very athletic, and training for wheelchair sports competitions keeps us pretty busy. Often when he's training for a race, I'll ride my bike alongside for exercise," says Stacy.

The two introduced each other to new interests that they now share. Due to Stacy's love of scuba diving, Jimmy got his certification and the two go diving in the Florida Keys almost every year. Jimmy sparked Stacy's interest in deer hunting, and now they hunt together. Jimmy hunts from an all-terrain vehicle that he drives to the spot he chooses after he drops Stacy off at her chosen location. Things were not always picture-perfect for Jimmy.

"I was 23 when I was paralyzed in a car accident. After that, I went into seclusion for about a year. I didn't want to see my old friends because I didn't want them to feel sorry for me. I had been dating several girls, but I dropped them, too. I had no interest in seeing anyone. I thought, 'What would a girl see in me, in a chair?' After he finally started getting out of the house and being active, his confidence returned. "You eventually realize you're the same person you were before. And as you meet people and find that they still find you attractive, your self-esteem comes back. You have to keep believing in yourself in order to be a likable person. No one's interested in being with someone who's having a pity party for himself! When I was injured, it was kind of like I ended one life and started another one. Of course, I'd love to walk again. But honestly, if the choice came down to giving up Stacy and wheelchair sports and going back to my life the way it was before, I'd choose to stay in a chair."

What are characteristics of spinal cord injuries?

The *spinal cord*, contained within the vertebrae, transports impulses to and from the brain. Impairment of the transportation of impulses occurs as a result of the extent and location of an injury to the spinal column. Impairment experienced from a spinal cord injury is permanent because the spinal cord is not able to regenerate.

The degree of disability associated with a spinal-cord injury is classified according to the level of the injury to the spinal column, as well as the severity of the injury. Spinal injuries are classified as complete, resulting in no sensation or movement, or incomplete, resulting in some sensation and motor function.

Paraplegia describes injuries to the sacral, lumbar, or thoracic areas of the spinal column. The *sacral* and *lumbar* regions of the spine are the areas below the waist. Injury to this area may cause some paralysis, which can result in needing leg braces for mobility and some loss of sensation in the lower extremities. People with injuries in the *thoracic* area that result in paralysis between the waist and shoulders can typically live independently in a wheelchair-accessible environment.

Injuries to the *cervical* area or neck are the most serious and result in quadriplegia, which causes the greatest amount of disability. With an injury to the lowest portion of the cervical area, some individuals can live alone, independently, with alterations to their homes. With an injury at the highest portion of the cervical area, individuals can control some neck muscles. They can typically control their wheelchairs with the assistance of a chin control or a sip-and-puff apparatus. They are able to control their environments or work a computer with a mouth stick, but need human assistance for daily care needs.

Traumatic spinal-cord injuries occur in a split second but necessitate a life-long adjustment to almost all domains of life, including leisure. My colleagues and I conducted in-depth interviews with adults with spinal-cord injuries who returned to their communities. Not surprisingly, these people reported how the loss of their physical ability was a constraint to returning to their community. Two of the respondents made the following statements:

> *I like to hunt a lot . . . before I could hold a rifle like this, but now when I hold it I fall forward because I don't have the balance. I haven't been hunting yet.*

> *I tried playing racquetball for the first time two weeks ago; after two or three games I was exhausted, where normally I could go five or six games, so it's definitely more tiresome for me now.*

Although the respondents identified their physical limitations as a constraint to leisure, they reported a strong desire to participate in community-based recreation activities. The social networks and relationships with members of the community were critical. It is helpful if we use strategies that promote inclusive leisure services and use leisure education to help people with physical disabilities become involved in community life.

As an example of the role leisure can play in someone's sense of identity, consider the words of Curtis Lovejoy, who was injured in a car accident when he was 29 years old. Curtis described what he says to people who have recently experienced a severe physical trauma (Grizzle, 1994, p. 5):

> *I tell patients I visit that the sky's the limit, and that they all have the same opportunities I have. When they can't see the light at the end of the tunnel, I tell them to take a look at me. I broke my neck and went from 175 pounds to 85 pounds. Now I can scuba dive, water ski, and I've taken up swimming competitively.*

What are considerations for inclusion of people with spinal cord injuries?

Adapt Activities as Needed

People with spinal-cord injuries have reduced mobility and motor strength. Therefore, some recreation activities that have extensive physical demands may need to be adapted. If an adaptation is required, work with the person to determine the most effective adaptation.

Consider Physical Needs of Participants

Individuals with impaired sensation will need to shift their weight when sitting to avoid developing pressure sores; therefore, inserting breaks into extended activities may be helpful. Many people must attend to bathroom needs on a strict schedule, so it is important to have accessible restrooms near areas where programs are provided. Because individuals with spinal-cord injuries are unable to regulate their body temperatures below the level of injury, it is helpful for us to be sensitive to this condition and provide appropriate means for cooling and warming, such as water spray bottles or blankets.

Get to Know Participants

When they are first injured, some people with spinal-cord injuries think their lives are over. Some think they will never be athletic again, they will never be able to work again, or they will never fall in love again. Hopefully, during the rehabilitation process, these myths are stripped away. They discover that there are many recreation activities available to them, there are many jobs they are qualified for, and relationships can be as meaningful as they ever were. As an example, Zambo (2009, p. 61) provided this statement by Michael, an adolescent with a spinal-cord injury:

> *I don't move like Trevor Ariza or Kobe Bryant, but I can still play basketball. Kids just have to get to know me. They have to get past the typical image of male athletes and see me for who I am and what I can do.*

Avoid Setting Limits on What People Can Do

An important contribution that we can make to the lives of people with spinal-cord injuries is to not set limits on them because of their reduced mobility. Whenever people think an individual with a spinal-cord injury cannot participate in a given recreation activity, such as mountain climbing or hang gliding, people with spinal-cord injuries prove them wrong and successfully participate in these activities. We must work to make our programs available to all people and work with individuals to find ways to foster their ability to experience leisure.

Sadowsky (1997) reported on a four-day adventure skills workshop that focused on introducing people with physical disabilities to water sports and outdoor recreation activities. Of the many people with physical disabilities who participated in the workshop, Tommy Baug, a 28-year-old avid outdoorsman and farmer who sustained a spinal-cord injury three years prior to the workshop, made the following observation:

> *I had never even been on a jet ski until after I was injured. Now I own two, which I use regularly. I feel like the only thing I can't do is stand up and walk. I had a lot more free time after I was injured. [Sports and outdoor activities] have given me something to do instead of sitting around all the time. The most important thing you learn is that there are things you can do and ways you can enjoy life with a spinal-cord injury, or whatever disabling injury you have. There's so much that you can still do.*

Meet Jim, the Big-League Pitcher

Hersch (1991) wrote about the moment for which Jim had long strived. At that time, Jim was a 23-year-old left-hander who had started the baseball season by losing four games for the California Angels. His critics complained that he had no control, no off-speed pitch to confuse hitters, and no minor-league seasoning to draw on. The words missing were the ones Jim was most accustomed to hearing, the ones that said he could not succeed because he had no right hand. "It was all about pitching—this guy stinks. I thought, there it is. Finally, I've arrived."

After untold fastballs in Little League, three successful years at the university, stardom at the Olympics, award-acceptance speeches, and three seasons in the majors, Jim was at last being seen as he had always seen himself—as a pitcher. He was no longer the feature attraction of a media circus or the living embodiment of a made-for-TV movie—he was one-fifth of the Angels rotation.

True, he is visible proof that what appears to some to be a limitation need not be one. But he is equally notable for the commercial ventures he turns down and for the time he takes with the children with physical disabilities who flock to him. Interestingly enough, immediately following his disastrous start, he went on to win 14 games, losing only 4, and becoming one of the best pitchers in the American League.

Since he was 5, Jim has practiced switching his glove from his left hand to his right arm and back again, a maneuver that is now fluid and routine. He can do it in that instant before the bat meets the ball. Jim is living his dream, and he appreciates it. He is also living the dream of many others who aspire to overcome their disabilities, and he appreciates that, too. He still answers more than 300 pieces of mail a week, sometimes giving personal responses to writers who need encouragement or reassurance. In each city he goes to, Jim chats easily with youngsters who come to the park just to see him.

What are characteristics of amputations or congenital absences?

The absence of a portion of a limb is an *orthopedic impairment* since it relates to a disorder of the bone, joints, ligaments, or muscles that can occur in two possible ways. A person who is born with a portion of one or more of their limbs missing is identified as having a *congenital absence*. If, however, a person is born with all their limbs but experiences a trauma or infection that results in the need to remove a portion of a limb, then the person is identified as having an *amputation*.

Sometimes individuals with a congenital absence or an amputation will wear a *prosthesis* which is an artificial body part. Prostheses are customized to the person and, with growing children, need to be changed periodically. John Kemp (2004, p. 195) explained a helpful perspective when discussing his congenital absence and using prostheses in this way:

> *Born with arms ending just above the elbows and legs ending near the knees, I didn't know I was different until about age three, maybe four, when a young boy, very angry at me, said something hurtful. I went immediately to my dad for comfort and protection. For the first of many times, he told me that I was different—not better, worse, or special—than other children and that other children who couldn't accept me for using prostheses had problems, not me. Thank you, Dad, for giving me the gift of pride in being equal as well as different.*

What are considerations for inclusion of people with amputations or congenital absences?

Help Care for Prostheses

In the case of amputation, changes in the residual limb may require adjustment of the prosthesis. Since prostheses are typically expensive, care should be taken not to damage them by exposing them to extreme heat, cold, dampness, or wetness.

Typically, prostheses are removed before entering a swimming pool area and may be covered when participating in recreation activities requiring active physical contact. Individuals with missing lower limbs or an amputation may choose to use a wheelchair for mobility and for sport and recreation participation. As an example, Navarro (2007) wrote about:

> *Kylee Haddad, 40, a mother of two from Walkersville, Maryland, who decorates her prosthetic leg with palm trees, fish, and the American flag. Ms. Haddad, whose right leg was amputated below the knee in 2003 after a car accident, said she has no problem wearing shorts when she goes shopping. Neither does she shy from removing the prosthesis in order to swim at the neighborhood pool. She said people gawk and some have even tapped her on the shoulder to ask her to put her leg back on. She said she's been told, "It is upsetting to my child." But she refuses to hide. "You either accept me as I am," she said, "or you don't have to look at it."*

Promote Active Participation

There is a specific need for many individuals having a loss of some or all of their lower limbs to increase mobility skills for walking on uneven ground during such activities as hunting and fishing. People with amputations and those born without a portion of a limb should be supported to receive the benefits of actively participating in recreation activities of their choosing.

Meet Darren, Who Loves to Travel

According to Gething (1992), Darren, who has childhood muscular dystrophy, attributes much of his success to his parents' support. His motorized wheelchair allows him to be active within his community and facilitates his involvement in travel and tourism.

> *I use an electric wheelchair and my father looks after most of my daily physical needs. Movement is fairly restricted and I must rely on others to hand me things. This does not stop me going out or doing many things. It does mean, however, that activities must be planned in advance. I have gone out with a number of girls, but I have not had a long-term relationship. Nonetheless, I have lots of friends, I have traveled overseas a number of times, I frequently go out socially and I work part time. I really believe that you must live your life, do your best, and experience as much as you can.*

What are characteristics of muscular dystrophy?

Muscular dystrophy is a general designation for a group of chronic, hereditary diseases characterized by the progressive degeneration and weakness of voluntary muscles. It is not typically painful.

Childhood muscular dystrophy, otherwise known as *Duchenne*, is the most common type of muscular dystrophy, displays the most rapid progression, and has a poor prognosis. The condition involves general weakening and loss of voluntary muscle control. It occurs only in males and typically onset occurs prior to age six. The pelvic musculature is affected first, resulting in some loss of independence by age 10.

What are considerations for inclusion of people with muscular dystrophy?

Consider the Condition's Progressive Nature

Since common characteristics of muscular dystrophy include slowness and fatigue, it is important that leisure service providers make adaptations to activities requiring physical participation and incorporate rest periods into prolonged activity. Because muscular dystrophy is progressive and not static, observe participants frequently and make adaptations as skills deteriorate.

Provide Social Support

It is helpful to provide social support to help people with muscular dystrophy adjust to a reduction in skill levels. Attempts to make accommodations that permit continued participation with peers is critical to avoid the possibility of social isolation in response to reductions in physical skills. Development of skills associated with recreation activities that require limited vigorous physical exertion may provide additional avenues for individuals to experience leisure.

People with muscular dystrophy can benefit from social support since they often encounter people who have misconceptions about them and their disability. For instance, Mike Ervin (2009, p. D3), a Chicago writer and a disability rights activist, made the following observations:

> *For decades, disability rights activities have criticized how his [Jerry Lewis] annual telethon for the Muscular Dystrophy Association exploits people with disabilities by making us objects of pity. . . He and his telethon symbolize an antiquated and destructive 1950s charity mentality. This says that people*

with disabilities have no hope and nothing to offer unless we are cured—so the whole focus should be on raising money for behemoth charities that can find a cure. This is a dangerously simplistic outlook. It devalues and dehumanizes people with disabilities by suggesting we can be worthy contributors only if we first shed our disabilities. It gives people permission to avoid addressing the daunting task of creating an inclusive society if they simply make an annual contribution to Jerry.

Meet Roberta, Who Enjoys Her New Image

Roberta was an active girl involved in many activities, including her high-school cheerleading team. At the age of 16, a drunk driver hit the car Roberta was driving, and she sustained a spinal-cord injury that resulted in paraplegia. After months of intensive rehabilitation, she could walk again with the aid of crutches and long leg braces. Roberta soon discovered, however, that walking took considerable time and effort, and despite her early insistence about walking, she began to use a wheelchair for mobility.

Roberta's insurance company covered the cost of her wheelchair: a 40-pound, stainless steel chair with padded armrests. In 1974, this chair was state-of-the-art. By 1991, Roberta's wheelchair was badly worn: the armrests were torn and the broken vinyl covering scratched her arms. One footrest dragged on the ground, impeding her mobility. Although Roberta had a good job at a hospital, she could not afford a new wheelchair. She was embarrassed to go out socially in her worn-out chair, which hindered her leisure lifestyle.

Her only outlet was a new performing arts group that included people with disabilities. This was her opportunity to be able to dance and act in a supportive environment. Dancing and acting were activities she had wanted to participate in since her accident, but had found acceptance in other groups difficult.

Through Roberta's participation in the performing arts group, she learned about a small grant that would buy her a new wheelchair. Roberta applied, and six months later she finally got a new wheelchair. She was ecstatic! She picked a bright red chair built for speed and agility. The new wheelchair weighed only 18 pounds, allowing her to transfer it into the car with much less effort than her old chair. Roberta loved her new-found freedom. She took up tennis, and even went out socially with her friends from work. She claimed:

> *Not only am I able to participate in recreational activities that were almost impossible with my old chair; I feel like I look better. I used to be embarrassed to leave my house, now I feel like a new person. This is better than a new car.*

What are considerations associated with wheelchair technology?

The wheelchair is one of the most commonly used assistive devices for enhancing the personal mobility of people with disabilities. An estimated 1% of the world's population, or just over 65 million people, need a wheelchair. In most developing countries, few of those who need wheelchairs have access, production facilities are insufficient, and wheelchairs are often donated without the necessary related services. Providing wheelchairs that are appropriate, well-designed, and fitted not only enhances mobility, but also opens up a world of education, work, and social life for those in need of such support.

In response to the needs listed above identified by the World Health Organization (WHO, 2010), WHO worked with the International Society of Prosthetics and Orthotics, as well as the Disabled People's International, to create guidelines on the provision of manual wheelchairs in less resourced settings. The guidelines address design, production, supply, and service delivery of manual wheelchairs.

The modern wheelchair has changed considerably from the "*wicker chair on wheels*" used earlier in this century. Today, wheelchairs can be customized to meet individual needs and lifestyles. Wheelchairs can be equipped with seating systems to accommodate individuals with specific positioning needs. Some wheelchairs are designed to be used for specific sports, such as those built for road racing, tennis, or fishing.

People with paraplegia and lower-extremity amputations and disabilities most frequently use lightweight wheelchairs. With aluminum, titanium, or composite frames, lightweight chairs are available with rigid frames and pop-off wheels with an average weight of 20 pounds, or folding frames with fixed wheels with an average weight of 26 pounds. Other optional features include swing-away or removable armrests; flip-up, swing-away, or rigid footrests; push handles; and mag wheels. The presence or absence of these features helps individuals tailor the chair to their work and leisure lifestyle.

Specialized sports chairs for use by athletes, both amateur and professional, came into popular use in the 1980s. Many racing wheelchairs feature aerodynamic, tri-wheel designs for greater stability, cornering, and speed. Court chairs are used for sports such as tennis and basketball, and some feature one central-front caster to facilitate sharp turns and forward stability.

The American National Standards Institute and the Rehabilitation Engineers Society of North America, an interdisciplinary organization that promotes assistive technology for people with disabilities, have developed standards for wheelchairs. The standards address seating, such as dimensions, upholstery, and optional cushions; structure, such as weight, frame material, and casters; performance, such as minimum turn-around width, camber; and safety, such as flammability and tip angles. These standards are voluntary and are designed to help consumers make more educated selections and purchases. For additional information, see the subsequent chapter on assistive technology.

What are characteristics of people using a wheelchair?

Many people choose to use a wheelchair for a variety of reasons. Some people can walk with aids and use a wheelchair because they can conserve energy and move about quickly. However, other people require use of the wheelchair to move about freely. Consider Jenny, who stated,

> *I feel distinctly affectionate toward my wheelchair. I did a lot of falling down and hurting myself and wasted a lot of energy using canes and crutches. When I see a visual image of myself in my wheelchair, I see a handsome, accomplished woman instead of the "fearful-of-falling-down" woman I was when I was struggling to remain standing. Would I be happier if I could suddenly walk and not need the chair anymore? Only if I could keep the attitude toward it that I have gained up until this time as a result of being a wheelchair user. Only if I didn't lose the spiritual growth I have experienced working as a person with a disability. Without this continued growth, I could not be happy.*

One concern common among individuals with obvious disabilities is the fear of being viewed as "an easy target" by individuals looking for someone to victimize. Retzinger (1990) quoted Larry, who realizes that defending oneself on the street is more necessary today than ever before:

> *You hear about muggings every day. People with visual impairments knocked down and robbed while they lie helpless on the ground. Purses snatched from people in wheelchairs as they go about their daily errands. Many people using wheelchairs would go out more if they had some form of self-defense knowledge. To go out by yourself, you must develop confidence that, if confronted with a situation, you can defend yourself. I've always had a strong desire to help other people who use wheelchairs feel that they're not vulnerable or easy targets for muggers. Through wheelchair karate, this has become a reality.*

Jerry, a fourth-degree black belt in karate who runs a karate school, suggested to Larry that a wheelchair did not have to prevent him from protecting himself. Together the two developed a wheelchair karate system. After extensive discussion and training, the two discovered that some techniques would work on the street and others would be important in developing speed and accuracy. Wheelchair karate techniques use various movements involving wheelchair maneuvers, enabling people to defend themselves against possible assailants.

What are considerations for inclusion of people who use wheelchairs?

Speak Directly to the Person

Leisure service professionals are encouraged to speak directly to the person in the wheelchair and not to someone nearby, as if the person in the wheelchair did not exist. If the conversation lasts more than a few minutes, consider sitting down, squatting, or kneeling to get on the same level as the person. It is fine to use expressions like "running along" when speaking; the person likely expresses things the same way.

It is helpful to encourage inquisitive children to ask questions about the wheelchair, because communication helps overcome negative attitudes. Also, it may help to describe physical obstacles that could impede travel when giving directions to an individual who uses a wheelchair.

Consider the Wheelchair as an Extension of the Person

Leisure service professionals are encouraged to avoid classifying people who use wheelchairs as sick because, as stated earlier, wheelchairs are used for a variety of reasons. It is helpful not to assume that using a wheelchair is a tragedy; it is a means of freedom that allows independent movement.

When a person "transfers" out of the wheelchair to a chair, car, swimming pool, or bed, do not move their wheelchair out of reaching distance. John Hockenberry (2005, p. 4) talks about perceptions about him using a wheelchair:

> *Doctors may call me a paraplegic. Strangers might say I am "wheelchair bound." But to my daughters, I have always been a daddy who comes with his own playground apparatus. In their short lives, oblivious of the fears and anxieties of adults, they have known a wheelchair only to represent a warm, safe place.*

Provide Inclusive Services for Children

Children can begin to use a wheelchair for independence as early as 3 or 4 years of age. One wheelchair manufacturer even has a club for children, featuring T-shirts, a newsletter, and summer camping opportunities.

Children's wheelchairs come in child-pleasing colors, ranging from cotton candy pink to neon green, and in manual and power models. See the chapter on people, inclusion, and technology for more information on motorized chairs.

Final Thoughts

The following passage is adapted from the verse entitled "Other People" by an anonymous author.

> *I don't think anybody's ugly. I think that something ugly always has something beautiful in it. I don't judge people by ugliness and prettiness in their faces, in their figure. I don't judge a person like that. I judge a person by talent, by their personality, how they think about other people. A beautiful person smiles. I appreciate people that try to help me. But sometimes they want to help too much. Mostly, I can do everything for myself, going downstairs, for instance. Some people try to carry me all the way. But I can do that mostly by myself unless it's too high. People that know me and are around me often, they know what I can do and can't do for myself. But people that I'm just getting to know, they want to treat me different so I try to tell them. I try to explain what they could do for me, what I appreciate. For example, if I'm getting to know somebody and the ice cream truck comes, they go "I'll buy it for you." I try to explain, "That's okay, I could do that." The way I was raised was to do things for myself. My mother is a very strict woman. I got polio when I was four-and-a-half. She always taught me to do all I could for myself and not to depend on everyone else. It makes me feel useless when people think I can't do nothing myself. I don't like them to treat me nice, or any special way. I like them to treat me like any other kid running around—just like a regular kid.*

It is helpful to consider the perspectives of people with disabilities when attempting to include them in community leisure programs. Think about the ideas expressed by Burstein (1999, p. 9) as she wrote about her initial feelings related to having multiple sclerosis and using a motorized wheelchair:

Entering the room became a command performance, starring my motorized wheelchair. "Hi, I'm The Wheelchair and this is Ellen with me." I could not tolerate the look and feel of my wheelchair and I was devastated by the loss of height. I had two choices: give up and fade into self-imposed oblivion or move on. I chose the latter. A wheelchair would not be a metaphor for my life. Rather, it would be a tool to enable me to enjoy life and participate in it.

Discussion Questions

1. What are characteristics of multiple sclerosis?
2. What are considerations for inclusion of people with multiple sclerosis?
3. What are characteristics of spina bifida?
4. What are considerations for inclusion of people with spina bifida?
5. What are characteristics of arthritis?
6. What are considerations for inclusion of people with arthritis?
7. What are characteristics of spinal-cord injury?
8. What are considerations for inclusion of people with spinal-cord injury?
9. What are characteristics of amputations or congenital absences?
10. What are considerations for inclusion of people with amputations or congenital absences?
11. What are characteristics of muscular dystrophy?
12. What are considerations for inclusion of people with muscular dystrophy?
13. What are characteristics of people who use wheelchairs?
14. What are considerations for inclusion of people who use wheelchairs?

Kate Gainer, pictured with her husband Willie Smith and their son Michael, was born with cerebral palsy. Kate is an active advocate for people with disabilities, serving as a volunteer member of various commissions and advocate organizations. She also works for the Atlanta Center for Independent Living.

Photo by Lynda Greer

Kate's Story

I guess I was one of the pioneer children in special education in Atlanta. In 1953, when I was 4, the first special education class for Black children opened up. It was funded by Easter Seals and 16 of us were selected by doctors at a clinic in Atlanta. When my mother learned of the program she pushed hard to see that I got in; she wanted her baby to go to school. When I went to the elementary program, the teacher from pre-school went with us. Mrs. Muscia White was the only Black teacher in the city with a background in special ed.

More important than her background, though, was her belief that her "babies" deserved the best. She exposed us to a lot of things other kids didn't get . . . all kinds of field trips . . . to a farm . . . the symphony. After all this time she still keeps up with her "babies." This was a very important time in my life; it was during this period that Kate was formed.

In the sixth and seventh grades I was mainstreamed on a partial basis. It was great! Those kids treated me like one of the gang. These same kids were my classmates at Booker T. Washington H. S., the first Black high school built in Atlanta. So I had a support system already. The only real problems I had were architectural barriers.

By the time I got to college those barriers weren't a problem. I wanted to go into marketing. I've always had strong writing skills and wanted to use them in the area of marketing. One of my professors told me that he didn't think I'd make it in marketing because the business world wasn't ready for a severely disabled person who made strange involuntary movements and talked with what I call the "C. P. dialect." And he was right. For every interview I had I got a ridiculous reason I couldn't have the job. None of them had anything to do with my professional ability. I was shocked and angry. Up until college I believed that if a person is smart enough and works hard enough, disability doesn't make any difference.

So I decided I was going to save the world . . . at least for kids with disabilities that would come along later. The first thing I did was serve on the accommodations committee for Federal Section 504 funding qualifications. Since then I have served on a lot of committees, councils, etc. to secure a better life for people with disabilities. The most frustrating thing is that it should be so simple. The basic level of accessibility to life . . . jobs, transportation, housing . . . should be there for all of us without such a struggle. But that's not the way it is. And until that's the way it is, Kate Gainer will be out there, WORKING!

Chapter 22
People, Inclusion, and Cognitive Limitations

Peter Thornburgh lives in Harrisburg, Pennsylvania, and works in nearby Mechanicsburg at the Center for Industrial Training. Peter sustained a brain injury when he was in an accident at the age of 4 months. This picture was taken in Washington, DC, at the home of his parents, Dick and Ginny Thornburgh.

Photo by Lynda Greer

Peter's Story

I'm 31 years old. I live in Harrisburg in a house with Brian, Todd, Ron, Michael, and Tim. Four people come in to help. They don't live there. They help plan, remind people about things . . . just help out. Everyone who lives in the house works.

I work in Mechanicsburg at C.I.T. (Center for Industrial Training). I like my work. . . . I pack boxes, sweep, help people. I have good friends at work. I take four buses to work . . . two over and two back. I like taking buses. I know how to take buses in Pittsburgh, Harrisburg, and Washington. I take Greyhound buses, too. I like to fly.

My church is the Linglestown Church of God. I go every Sunday. The church van picks me up. At church I sit with Carol Grauel. Her husband is Jim. He sings in the choir. They are my church family. I love going to church. I love God. He is in Heaven, so is Jesus. And my first Mom. Mom (Ginny Thornburgh) is my second Mom.

I want to live somewhere else . . . with more room, not so many people. I want more friends my age. I want to do more things . . . shopping at malls and stores, baseball games . . . the Phillies . . . I like the Pirates, too . . . hockey games and the Hershey Bears.

I know how to get up by myself. I know when to pack my lunch. I know how to take a bus. I do a lot for myself. Sometimes I do need staff. Sometimes I don't need staff at all.

Recognizing our common humanity opened all of us to further learning.

-K. E. Eble

Orientation Activity: Bill and Shantel—What to do?

Directions Alone: Read the following situations and write a paragraph describing your reactions.

William, a 38-year-old man interested in joining a competitive softball league, has a wonderful sense of humor and Down's syndrome. The recreation supervisor, Ron Turner, says, "Billy, come into my office. Be a good boy and we will see what it is you want." William is hurt and angry. He does not like being called "Billy" or considered to be a "good boy." He thinks of himself as a man. He works, lives in an apartment, and has a girlfriend. He dislikes being talked to like a child. He wishes Mr. Turner would treat him just like any other adult. William cannot understand why he is called "Billy," while Mr. Turner addresses other men as "Mister."

Shantel, a 21-year-old woman who enjoys bowling, went one night after work with a few women from her office. Afterwards, a bowler told Shantel that she would be better off joining the bowling league sponsored by the Association for Persons with Mental Illness, because her "friends" would be there. Shantel was hurt. She just wanted to bowl and meet new people. The bowler's remark made her feel different—like she did not belong.

Directions with Others: Move about the room with your paragraph and share your reactions with another person. After a specified time, discuss what you have learned with the entire group.

Debriefing: For years people believed that individuals who experienced some disruption in their cognitive process including intellectual disability, cerebral palsy, epilepsy, traumatic brain injury, and mental health problems should be "with their own kind." This belief created many of the problems we are now trying to remedy, including institutionalization, segregated services, and lack of communication.

One way for us to begin to construct ways to promote inclusion is for us to consider the words of James Brady:

> *What's the difference between a stumbling block and a stepping stone? It's all in the way you approach it.*

As leisure service providers, it is our task to include people in programs even though they may not think, learn, act, or respond to situations in typical ways. One way for us to begin is by getting to know people with cognitive impairments, learn a little about their conditions, and be prepared to include them in our programs. As you reflect on the learning activity, consider the following questions:

- How should you talk to recreation participants who have cognitive impairments?
- Why is it important to treat all recreation participants in a similar manner?
- How can you facilitate inclusion of individuals with cognitive impairments into recreation programs?

Introduction

The brain is the master organ of the body. It controls autonomic functions such as heart rate, body temperature, and respiration. An *autonomic function* is one that the central nervous systems control, is not under our voluntary control, is automatic, and does not require any conscious thought.

The brain also controls *voluntary functions*, those actions that require us to think before acting, such as speaking and walking. Damage to the brain can affect autonomic functions, voluntary functions, or both, depending on the location and severity of the injury.

Damage to the brain can occur at any point in the life span—before birth, during childhood and adolescence, or at any time during adulthood—and can be caused by:

- toxic agents such as alcohol, carbon monoxide, or lead
- brain tumors
- infection such as AIDS, encephalitis, meningitis, or rubella
- diseases such as hypertension or sickle-cell anemia
- trauma such as brain surgery, concussion, and skull fracture

This chapter contains a description of various people and impairments caused by damage to the brain. The following questions are addressed:

- What are characteristics of intellectual disability?
- What are considerations for inclusion of people with intellectual disabilities?
- What are characteristics of autism spectrum disorders?
- What are considerations for inclusion of people with autism spectrum disorders?
- What are characteristics of cerebral palsy?
- What are considerations for inclusion of people with cerebral palsy?
- What are characteristics of epilepsy?
- What are considerations for inclusion of people with epilepsy?
- What are characteristics of traumatic brain injury?
- What are considerations for inclusion of people with traumatic brain injury?
- What are characteristics of a stroke?
- What are considerations for inclusion of people who have had a stroke?
- What are characteristics of mental health problems?
- What are considerations for inclusion of people who have mental health problems?

Meet Nancy, Who Is a Strong Advocate

When Nancy received her high school equivalency diploma, it was like getting a key and an eraser. The diploma was a key to further education and a career in a helping profession, and it assisted her in erasing the label that has dogged her for most of her 34 years: retarded.

As a child, she was diagnosed as mentally retarded, now referred to as "*intellectual disability*." That colored the image her teachers, classmates, and even her parents had of her. Teachers' low expectations for her became evident to her when in high school she was still reading from the same textbook she had in fifth grade.

Working in nursing homes, Nancy realized that older adults were also victims of labeling, and she decided to pursue a career in geriatrics. She entered an Adult Basic Education program, and passed the battery of tests for her General Educational Development (GED) diploma. "I loved it," she said, adding that having the GED helped dispel negative stereotypes that have stood in her way. "I feel I was definitely improperly labeled. I know I'm slow, but I don't feel I am retarded."

Nancy plans to pursue an education in human services and obtain a job helping others overcome their labels. As a vocal advocate for people with disabilities, she has had practice doing that. Nancy is a leader of a chapter of People First, an organization promoting the rights of people with disabilities. "We want people to see us as people first and not our disability," she said. "Label jars, not people" is the message on her People First T-shirt.

Nancy has testified before her state legislature on bills related to people with disabilities, and traveled to various states to help organize People First chapters. Through People First, she has worked to eliminate outdated language in state laws that refer to "idiots," "morons," and "imbeciles"—labels that she considers archaic and harmful. The lobbying has been an educational experience for both speakers and listeners, she said. "It shows that people with a disability can speak for themselves, and it also teaches us that we can do it."

What are characteristics of intellectual disability?

There has been a change in the conception of intellectual disability over the past 20 years. It is viewed not as an absolute trait expressed solely by the person, but as an expression of the impact of the interaction between the person and the environment. The change in the way intellectual disability is conceptualized requires that services be provided in inclusive environments. The environments contain necessary supports based on the capabilities of the person, with the purpose of empowering the individual to function within our society.

The current conception of intellectual disability focuses attention on the capabilities of the person related to intelligence and adaptive skills, their environment, and the presence or absence of the supports needed to live a meaningful life. Intellectual disability:

- is characterized by significantly sub-average general intellectual functioning
- results in, or is associated with, concurrent impairments in at least two adaptive skill areas
- is manifested before age 18 (during the developmental period)

Significantly sub-average intellectual functioning occurs when a person's score on standardized measures of intelligence is below the score of the average person taking the test to such a degree (two standard deviations) that society has determined this person requires assistance beyond what is typically provided by the family and community.

The average intelligence quotient is a score of approximately 100. A score below approximately 70–75 on one or more individually administered general intelligence tests results in a determination of significantly sub-average intellectual functioning.

Large individual differences exist in performance on these standardized tests, and the meanings associated with tests results differ across societies and vary with any given society at different times. Since all people require support from other people throughout their lives regardless of disability, identification of a disability such as an intellectual disability is relative.

Although IQ and intelligence are frequently used interchangeably, these concepts are not synonymous. IQ score is an estimate of an individual's rate of intellectual development as compared with the average rate for same-age peers.

A person's lack of performance on a particular standardized measure of IQ can be the result of many factors other than actual intelligence. Some people may not have been exposed to the items presented on the test due to cultural and environmental differences, or perhaps people may have difficulty communicating their response due to physical or neurological impairments. Other people may be experiencing pain and sickness. The attitudes of the examiner and examinee can also influence test scores. These situations may reduce a person's performance on an intelligence test, and perhaps bring the scores into question.

Adaptive skills are a collection of competencies that allows for individuals' strengths, as well as areas for improvement, to be defined. By recognizing strengths and areas for improvement, we can avoid focusing on deficits and emphasize individual competencies and the need for support. Adaptive skills include communication, self-care, home living, social skills, use of community resources, self-direction, health and safety, functional academics, leisure, and work.

For the purpose of this book, the adaptive skill area of leisure is highlighted. The AAMR (p. 41) described the adaptive skill area of leisure as:

> *[t]he development of a variety of leisure and recreational interests (self-entertainment and interactional) that reflect personal preferences and choices. Skills include choosing*

and self-initiating interests, using and enjoying home and community leisure and recreational activities alone and with others, playing socially with others, taking turns, terminating or refusing leisure or recreational activities, extending one's duration of participation, and expanding one's repertoire of interests, awareness, and skills. Related skills include behaving appropriately in the leisure and recreation setting, communicating choices and needs, participating in social interaction, applying functional academics, and exhibiting mobility skills.

Intellectual disability begins in childhood when limitations in intelligence coexist with related limitations in adaptive skills. The *developmental period* refers to the time after conception when growth and change occur at a rapid rate. This rate of development typically begins to slow as the person enters adulthood. Intellectual disability is one particular type of developmental disability. A developmental disability refers to a severe, chronic disability that is attributable to a mental or physical impairment, is manifested before age 18, is likely to continue indefinitely, and results in substantial functional limitations.

Although the phrase intellectual disability is used throughout this section, the label alone means very little. The profile of cognitive, adaptive, educational, and recreational ability, as well as the health status associated with each person, is critical for appropriate planning and implementation of effective services.

Intellectual disability refers to a level of functioning that requires support from society. Therefore, the person with intellectual disability is classified by the extent of support required for the person to learn, and not by limitations as to what the person can learn. The person's level of functioning is determined by the amount of resources society is willing to allocate, and not by significant limitations in biological potential. The intensity levels of support include:

- intermittent supports provided as needed
- limited supports that are not extensive, but consistent across time rather than intermittent
- extensive supports not limited in time and provided on a regular basis in some environments such as at home
- pervasive supports that are constant, intense, and have the potential to sustain life

The classification of intellectual disability in terms of the supports needed focuses our attention on expecting people to grow, believing in their potential, focusing on their personal choice, giving them opportunity and autonomy, and recognizing the need for people to be both in and of their community. This view of intellectual disability results in all people being given the supports necessary to enhance their independence, interdependence, productivity, and community engagement.

What are considerations for inclusion of people with intellectual disabilities?

Suggestions for including people with intellectual disabilities into leisure services can be categorized in the following manner:

- consider the uniqueness of each person
- concentrate on abilities and potential
- provide age-appropriate communication and service
- offer opportunities for serious leisure engagement
- focus on the positive

Consider the Uniqueness of Each Person

As discussed previously in this book, when relating to people who have been grouped together for whatever reason, it is helpful to consider these individuals as people first and then—if relevant—consider their group affiliation. It is much easier to interact with a person if we initially concentrate on similarities we share as opposed to our differences.

As much as possible, attempt to avoid the tendency to make generalizations about people—who, in addition to many of the other characteristics that effect their humanness such as a sense of humor, reliability, or honesty, happen to be identified as having an intellectual disability.

Concentrate on Abilities and Potential

Sometimes people focus on results of individuals' scores on standardized measures of IQ and adaptive behavior scales and determine that the person with an intellectual disability has significant problems, as well as limited potential for growth and development. If this conclusion has been drawn, with the focus of the problem on the individual with intellectual disability, our work has failed.

However, if we view people with intellectual disability—no matter how severe the disability—as having potential for growth and development, then we can continuously attempt to determine the most effective and efficient procedures and assist these individuals in achieving their maximum potential.

Motivational speaker and proclaimed self-advocate, Ann Forts (2009, p. 1), wrote about her keys to opening doors to successful inclusion:

> *I have Down syndrome, which I prefer to call "Up" syndrome. I created the concept of "Up" syndrome to redefine, in a positive way, the image of mental disabilities and to focus on the "ability" portion of the word "disability." [I] live a very happy and satisfying life on the "Up" side of Down syndrome—a life that is filled with lots and lots of friendships, excitement, accomplishments, and acceptance in my community.*

Provide Age-Appropriate Communication and Service

Sometimes people mistakenly treat an adult with an intellectual disability as a child. This occurs when an adult who happens to have intellectual disability is compared to a child because he or she performs some skills, such as reading, at a level similar to some children. Because the adult with intellectual disability has many more years of experience at living and has developed a variety of skills, the comparison to a child is misleading.

We must work to avoid viewing adults with intellectual disability as children, as identified in the orientation activity, and, instead, give them the respect provided to other adults in our society. This view of people with intellectual disability encourages us to develop age-appropriate recreation programs that do not require people with an intellectual disability to compromise their dignity.

Offer Opportunities for Serious Leisure Engagement

Based on numerous research findings, in the 1990s, sociologist Robert Stebbins (e.g., Stebbins, 1992) wrote extensively about the value of engaging in serous leisure pursuits. *Serious leisure* involves those meaningful pursuits that are challenging, require a level of commitment, are valued by the community, contain a status system, and create a network of colleagues and friends.

Stebbins identified three types of activities that are conducive for serious leisure that include volunteering, hobbies, and amateurism. Amateurism involves engaging in a recreation activity for pleasure rather than for pay, although other people might participate in the activity for pay.

Subsequently, Ian Patterson (2001, p. 23) advocated for providing serious leisure opportunities especially for people with intellectual disabilities and suggested the following possible activities:

> For example, whether participating in the making of model airplanes, an artistic performance, an athletic contest, or volunteering at a local supermarket, the person with an intellectual disability is making a positive contribution to the community that is generally appreciated, and at the same time helping develop the skills, abilities and confidence to assist the person with an intellectual disability in the social inclusion process.

Patterson (2000) used a case-study approach by conducting in-depth interviews with three people with intellectual disabilities and found that involvement in serious leisure provided the participants with a sense of purpose and a host of positive results.

Focus on the Positive

Unfortunately, some people with an intellectual disability have been required to participate in recreation activities with only other people with intellectual disabilities. The only viable recreation activities have been those identified as "*special.*" As a result, some people may be reluctant to access community recreation opportunities.

Although some individuals with an intellectual disability might be reluctant to join community recreation programs, there are many examples of success associated with different activities. For example, Lamplia (1998, p. 3) described how Jamie Barth, who has Down syndrome, was only seven years old when she began to attend the community karate school:

> *Today, Jamie holds a black belt in karate. Yes, people with intellectual disabilities can earn black belts, not just gold medals for running faster than other people with Down syndrome.*

Lamplia also described a man with Down syndrome who is now attending her karate school. She stated that the man has expressed to her that when he participates:

> *He feels equal, not special, when he does push-ups, sit-ups and martial arts drills with doctors, engineers, lawyers, business owners, schoolteachers, and college students.*

Some people worry that people with intellectual disability might have difficulty participating in athletics with people without disabilities, because athletics focus on competition against other people and there is a strong chance of failure. It may be helpful to consider that there are many community activities that emphasize competition against a standard or oneself, rather than against other people, such as aerobics, weightlifting, dance, martial arts, rock climbing, and hiking. The words of David Smith (2009, pp. 123-124) might help put into perspective the value of including people with an intellectual disability into leisure services:

> *To be disabled can be a valuable human attribute. People with disabilities can be powerful in the humanizing influence that they have on others. I am glad I have had friends with disabilities for most of my life . . . The power of those who have often been considered to be powerless may be important to our health as human beings and as cultural groups. A person with a disability may temper hateful and prejudicial attitudes. A person with an intellectual disability may soften a heart that has become hardened. A person with multiple and severe disabilities may have much to teach us about love.*

Meet Amanda, Who Enjoys Music

Amanda is a 15-year-old high-school student. Amanda does well in quiet areas with small numbers of students present, but has difficulty in public areas of the school such as hallways or the cafeteria because she does not like loud noises or anyone touching her.

When not at school, she can usually be found in her bedroom. Amanda enjoys listening to music and, although she has many different recordings, Amanda listens to two songs, which she plays repeatedly. She has a book collection displayed in precise order.

Amanda is a proficient swimmer; however, when the pool is crowded, she is too distracted to swim. Recently she indicated that she would like to learn to ride a horse. Because of her problems with communication and other behaviors, Amanda has been diagnosed as having an autism spectrum disorder.

What are characteristics of autism spectrum disorders?

Autism spectrum disorders refer to a wide variety of complex developmental disorders that typically appear during the first three years of life. The three core features of autism spectrum disorder are:

- problems with social interactions
- restrictions in verbal and nonverbal communication
- restricted and repetitive behavior patterns

Many individuals with an autism spectrum disorder may actively avoid social contact, adhere to rigid schedules, and inappropriately focus on objects or topics. The cause of this disorder is unknown.

> The character Raymond in the movie *Rain Man* depicts an individual with autism. Raymond was able to perform many self-care skills. He seemed to take pride in his room and the orderliness he maintained. Raymond had difficulty making eye contact, had poor social skills, could repeat a joke but did not understand the humor, and became upset when his routines were interrupted. He had unusual body posturing and would rock forward and back repeatedly when anxious. Raymond also exhibited characteristics of a *savant*—an extraordinary talent in one precise area, such as music, art, mathematics, or amassing facts on a particular subject. It is important to note that few people with autism spectrum disorders actually have savant characteristics.

Even though individuals with autism spectrum disorder are identified as having deficits related to social interactions, it is important for us to avoid the conclusion that these deficits represent a lack of interest in developing meaningful relationships.

> For example, Causton-Theoharis, Ashby, and Cosier (2009) explored the autobiographies of individuals with autism and reported that these individuals expressed that they are lonely and that their greatest desire is to have a friend.

What are considerations for inclusion of people with autism spectrum disorder?

When promoting the leisure experience for people with autism spectrum disorder it can be helpful to consider the following:

- be consistent
- be open to alternative forms of communication
- celebrate successes

Be Consistent

Consistency with equipment placement and routine is often helpful to develop a positive and relaxed atmosphere. Because individuals may have difficulty processing information, providing consistency within their environment has been found to help the individuals relax and be more at ease.

Be Open to Alternative Forms of Communication

People with an autistic spectrum disorder often use alternative communication techniques, such as electronic communication boards, picture boards, and sign language. Regardless of the method of communication or level of response, it is important for us to speak to the participant with age-appropriate language.

Celebrate Successes

When we encounter people who are having challenges interacting with us and other participants we may tend to view that person in a negative manner since we are not rewarded for are attempts at social engagement. However, it is important that we keep an open mind about the person and consider the challenges they might be dealing with constantly.

When it is difficult for us to engage someone socially it is helpful if we try to find any behaviors that are positive and work to reward and celebrate those positive behaviors. As and example, Lesley Jones (2004, p. 179–182), a college student who has a form of autism spectrum disorder known as Asperger's syndrome, described her struggles and made some recommendations about interacting with people like herself:

> *I couldn't write properly (dysgraphia); I often misunderstood what people were saying to me (central auditory processing disorder); and I sometimes had a hard time recognizing people (mild prosopagnosia). . . . If I could change my childhood, adults would have focused more on the things I could do and spent less time on punishing me for the things I couldn't do. . . . Most important of all, I would have been frequently reminded that I was unique and talented instead of only being told, at school, that I was lazy, willful, and not living up to my potential—and being told, at home, that I was a disappointment and embarrassment to the family.*

Meet Christopher, Who Finds Freedom in the Written Word

Christopher Nolan has an acute mind that has found its liberation in writing, according to Sherrid (1988). Christopher was unable to make a meaningful mark on paper until age 11, when the drug Lioresal helped his muscle spasms. He approached words much as another child might approach an overturned truck of candy, says one critic.

Just four years later, he published a book of poetry, *Dam-Burst of Dreams*, which won him comparisons with such literary giants as James Joyce and the 17th-century poet John Donne. Christopher, who has cerebral palsy, taps out letters on a typewriter with the help of a "unicorn" stick strapped to his forehead. His chin is supported by his mother, who stands behind her son in his wheelchair for hours at a stretch in a study in their middle-class Dublin home.

His autobiography, Under the Eye of the Clock, won Britain's most prestigious literary award and was on the London bestseller list. The autobiography chronicles his ultimately successful struggle to attend high school. While heaping praise upon his family, teachers, and friends, Christopher writes unflinchingly of society's pity and intolerance.

Christopher plans to write a novel, but even some of his supporters are skeptical that his personal experience is wide enough to sustain fiction. His mother does not entertain any doubts. Nodding to a visiting journalist, she asks, "What do you think he is doing with all the people he meets?" Regardless of what the future brings, his work already may have changed attitudes toward people with disabilities. Says his teacher, Brendan: "Christopher experiences life so intensely; no one who reads his book could pity him."

What are characteristics of cerebral palsy?

Cerebral palsy is characterized by the inability to control muscular and postural movement. It is caused by damage to the motor portions of the brain. The condition is *not* degenerative. A *degenerative condition* is one that will worsen over time. There are many causes of cerebral palsy, including prenatal infection, anoxia (a lack of adequate oxygen) before or during birth, fetal cerebral hemorrhage, and metabolic disturbance.

People with cerebral palsy are classified by the muscular condition and degree of bodily involvement they display. People who have *spasticity* display increased muscle-tone stiffness, known as *hypertonia*, and immediate contraction when stretching affected muscles. People with athetosis have difficulty controlling movement associated with affected muscles, resulting in "worm-like" movements. Individuals with ataxia have a more subtle form of cerebral palsy that results in balance problems. Individuals with more than one type are said to have mixed cerebral palsy.

Individuals with cerebral palsy are also classified according to the extremities that are affected. If only one limb is affected, individuals are said to have *monoplegia*. If the person's legs are impaired, the person is said to have *paraplegia*. If one side of the person's body is affected, the person is said to have *hemiplegia*. When all four extremities are impaired as a result of cerebral palsy, the person has *quadriplegia*.

What are considerations for inclusion of people with cerebral palsy?

When providing inclusive leisure services for people with cerebral palsy, it can be helpful to:

- work with participants
- accommodate mobility limitations

Work with Participants

Work with the individual to determine what accommodations they have already devised. When teaching activities, it is helpful to avoid excessively loud sounds and sudden, unexpected motions that may increase uncontrollable movements and trigger the startle reflex. Consider that some individuals may have balance difficulties and be prone to falling. Farris (2004, p. 70) warned not to make assumptions about what people cannot do just because they have been diagnosed with cerebral palsy:

> *When we first saw LaDonna, who has cerebral palsy, and uses a power wheelchair, we would never have thought of putting her in a go-cart or on a roller coaster. But, why not? The*

only accommodation necessary was a bit of help out of her wheelchair and in to the seats. If we had made assumptions that she couldn't participate based on the fact that she used a power wheelchair, where would she have been?

Accommodate Mobility Limitations

It is important to make necessary adaptations based on some people's mobility. Since gross motor coordination can often be a problem, accommodations can be made when introducing physically active activities. Fine-motor activities using hand-eye coordination or delicate finger movements can be very difficult for some people; as a result, efforts to enhance hand-eye coordination can be useful.

> When encouraging the grasping of an object, the use of sponges may help individuals with spastic cerebral palsy. The creation of a firm, hard surface for people with athetosis can also be beneficial.

Meet Jennifer, Who Likes to Climb

Jennifer had her first seizure just before her 13th birthday. Because of initial difficulty in regulating her medications for her epilepsy, she had memory problems that resulted in poor grades. Fortunately, Jennifer's school was understanding and explored options for assisting her to be a successful student. She graduated from prep school with honor grades and left home to attend college and live in a dorm. In the spring, Jennifer went rock climbing with skilled mountaineers. Lovell and Lovell (1993, p. 6) reported Jennifer stated that:

I never thought the best solution was to live a limited life. I'd rather do things and take risks than do nothing at all. Going to college far from home wasn't something I felt afraid of. I felt very capable of taking care of myself.

Jennifer is careful to explain to those around her that she has epilepsy and forewarn them what to do in case she has a seizure.

What to do and what not to do is something I explain to everyone I know. I try to explain what seizures look like, why I have them, what may set them off, what I'm like afterward. (I usually forget things.) Although I've felt frustrated and occasionally angry, I've never felt embarrassed by it. I have epilepsy, but epilepsy doesn't have me.

What are characteristics of epilepsy?

Epilepsy is a common neurological disorder that occurs when there is a sudden brief change in how the brain works. When brain cells are not working properly, a person's consciousness, movement, or actions may be altered for a short time. Epilepsy is therefore called a seizure disorder.

Not all seizures are classified as epilepsy. For example, many young children have convulsions from fevers. These convulsions are one type of seizure. Other types of seizures not classified as epilepsy include those caused by an imbalance of body fluids or chemicals, or by alcohol or drug withdrawal. A single seizure does not mean a person has epilepsy. Epilepsy is classified according to three specific features:

- generalized or partial seizures
- whether the seizures are the primary or secondary disorder
- the age of onset of recurrent seizures

Generalized seizures involve cells from both hemispheres of the brain and result in loss of consciousness. On the other hand, *partial seizures* result when only one hemisphere of the brain is involved and are typically localized in one portion of the body.

One type of generalized seizure consists of a convulsion with a complete loss of consciousness, called a grand mal seizure. A *petit mal seizure*, another generalized seizure, is characterized by brief periods of fixation, called absences, in which the individual appears to be staring into space and does not respond to external stimuli.

An example of a partial seizure is the *Jacksonian*, in which convulsions begin in one part of a limb, such as a foot or hand, and quickly spread throughout that entire side of the body. Other partial seizures may cause periods of automatic behavior, such as rubbing movements with one hand, wandering, or periods of altered consciousness.

What are considerations for inclusion of people with epilepsy?

Since most people with epilepsy have their seizures controlled by medication, it is often not necessary to do anything in addition to creating a welcoming environment. There are a couple suggestions that might be useful in addressing their need:

- consider the nature of epilepsy
- be prepared to treat a person having a grand mal seizure

Consider the Nature of Epilepsy

Frequent occurrence of seizures by a person with epilepsy is very rare. Most people with epilepsy manage their seizures with medication. When people's seizures are controlled with medication, there is very little need to make adjustments to leisure services delivery. People with petit mal seizures can miss part of a sentence that may lead to confusion if instructions were provided at the time of the seizure; therefore, repetition of instructions can be helpful.

Be Prepared to Treat a Person Having a Grand Mal Seizure

Probably the most important consideration in including people who have epilepsy in leisure services is being prepared to follow basic first aid if a person has a grand mal seizure. Treatment during a seizure is the same regardless of the cause of the seizure, and should focus on preventing injury.

When a person has a seizure, keep calm—there is nothing you can do to stop a seizure. Do not try to restrain the person, but clear the area so the person does not injure herself or himself. Do not interfere with movements, unless it is to cradle the head to prevent injury. Do not force anything between teeth or into mouth, but if the person is choking, turn the head to the side. Treat the incident in a calm, matter-of-fact manner, and do not crowd around the individual. Allow the person to rest after the seizure.

An important consideration for first aid for grand mal seizures is whether the person experiences the seizure in the water. O'Dell (2001, p. 86) made the following suggestions:

> First aid steps would include keeping her head above the water; if this is not possible she would have to be removed from the water during the seizure; removing her from the water as soon as possible after the seizure; turning her on her side to facilitate drainage of secretions; keeping her airway open; and observing her closely until she has returned to her baseline level of consciousness.

Meet Tara, Who Helps Others Have Fun

Tara's favorite activity is spending time on cruise ships headed for warm sandy beaches. She loves traveling with friends to remote, isolated islands. Although she enjoys her work as a supervisor of a community recreation and parks department, she is constantly planning, saving for, or going on a cruise.

Tara has always enjoyed traveling. She enjoys meeting new people and seeing new lands. After she received a traumatic brain injury as a result of a car accident when she was in college, she was determined to reacquire skills needed to continue to travel. She used thoughts of beaches and foreign sites to motivate her during rehabilitation.

Although she requires adaptations in many activities, she is able to continue to travel. Tara reports that when hospitality staff members are open to making accommodations for her, she almost always has a great vacation.

What are characteristics of traumatic brain injury?

A *traumatic brain injury* is a physical insult to the brain that may cause problems with physical, emotional, and social functioning. These changes influence not only the present status but also the future status of a person.

A traumatic brain injury frequently means that the person may never quite be the same again. The 1999 National Institute of Health (NIH) Consensus Development Panel on Rehabilitation of Persons with Traumatic Brain Injury (p. 974) provided the following details:

> *Traumatic brain injury (TBI), broadly defined as brain injury due to externally inflicted trauma, may result in significant impairment of an individual's physical, cognitive, and psychosocial functioning. The number of people surviving a TBI with impairment has increased significantly in recent years, which is attributed to faster, more effective emergency care, quicker and safer transportation to specialized treatment facilities, and advanced acute medical management. Although TBI may result in physical impairment, the more problematic consequences involve the individual's cognition, emotional functioning, and behavior, which can affect interpersonal relationships . . . Community-based, nonmedical services should be components of the extended care and rehabilitation available to persons with TBI.*

A variety of community leisure programs can be a part of the nonmedical services identified by NIH Panel to help facilitate the continued recovery process of individuals with traumatic brain injury who are living in their communities. James Brady (1995, p. 4) spoke about brain injuries:

> *Each year, two million Americans sustain brain injuries, all of whom must deal in some degree with the lasting effects of this disability. Whether it be chronic headaches, sleeplessness, memory loss, paralysis or any myriad of symptoms, we all continue on the journey, persevere and gain the experience required to travel a brand new road, to a changed life.*

It may be helpful to consider the words of James Brady when trying to gain insight into the implications of having experienced a traumatic brain injury. The most common cause of such an injury is from a motor-vehicle accident. The onset of traumatic brain injury is more associated with the use of alcohol than any other disability, and males are typically affected twice as often as females. Other common causes include falls and child neglect or abuse. Common cognitive processes influenced by traumatic brain injury are attention, memory, general intellectual performance, language, and perceptual abilities.

Closed-head injury is one type of traumatic brain injury that is often caused by the brain being whipped back and forth in a quick motion. This pull-and-tug places extreme stress on the brain stem—the part that connects the larger part of the brain with the spinal cord and the remaining portion of the body. A large number of functions are packed tightly into the brain stem, such as controls of consciousness, breathing, heartbeat, eye movements, pupil reactions, swallowing, and facial movements. In addition, all sensations going to the brain, as well as signals from the brain to the muscles must pass through the brain stem.

Anoxia results from loss of oxygen to the brain and is another form of closed-head injury. Anoxia may occur following cardiac arrest, stroke or accident such as drowning or choking.

Open-head injury, a second type of traumatic brain injury, is a visible assault that results from an accident, gunshot wound, fall, or other trauma, such as brain surgery to remove a clot or tumor. As with closed-head injuries, symptoms can vary greatly and depend on the extent and location of the brain injury. Physical disabilities, impaired learning ability, and personality changes are common. Physical impairments can include disruption in speech, vision, hearing, and other sensory impairments; headaches; lack of coordination; spasticity of muscles; paralysis of one or both sides; and seizure disorders.

The most common area affected by a traumatic brain injury is memory, especially memory for new information. All types of head trauma may damage that part of the brain crucial to memory. Both short-term (recall of recent information) and long-term (recall of past information) memory may be impaired. *Amnesia* is a common type of memory loss, where the person can only remember bits and pieces of events that occurred in the past. Amnesia does not affect one's ability to learn new information. Other symptoms include difficulty with maintaining attention, problem solving, organizational skills, and recognition of priorities, planning, and acting to achieve a goal.

Seizures, another typical result of traumatic brain injury, may also affect memory and can occur immediately after the injury or may not develop until months, or even years, later. At times, the memory loss may persist because a small seizure, called a partial complex seizure, will originate from the injured area and continue for an indefinite period afterward. This brain damage is often not diagnosed, however, because the identifying seizure is sometimes difficult to recognize. There is only a short staring spell or period of unusual behavior, and only a momentary lapse of concentration occurs. If recognized, however, the condition is often readily treatable with prescription drugs.

A person's emotions can also be influenced by a traumatic brain injury. Some individuals with traumatic brain injury experience severe behavior disorders that disrupt their daily life. Disorders may include mood swings, denial, self-centeredness, anxiety, depression, lowered self-esteem, sexual dysfunction, restlessness, lack of motivation, inability to self-monitor, difficulty with emotional control, inability to cope, agitation, excessive laughing or crying, and difficulty in making choices. These behavior disorders can be treated with behavior management programs and medication.

Any or all of the symptoms of traumatic brain injury may occur in different degrees, and there may be other symptoms not mentioned. Intellectual ability may cease to improve after a period of time, but memory, social, and behavioral functions may improve over long periods of time. For many people, ongoing involvement in activities can decrease the severity of these symptoms. Martin McMorrow (2003, p. 13) concluded:

> *Acquired brain injury is an amazing thing. A life can seem to be headed one way, and in a few brief moments, literally everything can change. A person's ability to move, speak, see, hear, think, feel, engage in personal care, have relationships, work, and much more can be changed in an instant. A person may not even remember what life was like without the injury.*

What are considerations for inclusion of people with traumatic brain injuries?

Often individuals who have experienced a traumatic brain injury encounter challenges organizing their time and understanding abstract concepts. A couple of helpful considerations when attempting to include these individuals into leisure programs include:

- help participants with planning
- use concrete leadership strategies

Help Participants with Planning

Individuals who have had a traumatic brain injury often have impaired planning ability and may need individualized reminders about leisure options. Calendars, notes, and telephone calls may help to increase their attendance and participation in leisure services. Individuals who have experienced a traumatic brain injury may have difficulty working toward long-term goals. To maintain continued interest in a program, we can provide opportunities that include gratifying experiences.

Preparation for participation is just as important as the activity itself. It is helpful to plan activities that encourage social interaction, cooperation, challenge, and success for everyone. Measuring self-improvement is more meaningful to the person's self-concept than is competition against others, especially with people who are less skilled. Individuals may have a slower learning rate, but can still accomplish a great deal.

Use Concrete Leadership Strategies

Abstractions or generalizations often present difficulty for a person who has experienced a traumatic brain injury. It may help to introduce novel activities by relating them to a familiar activity. It is also helpful to conduct a *task analysis* by dividing an activity into its components, teaching small steps, and allowing for additional practice time.

To gain the person's attention, saying the person's name before giving key directions may be helpful. It is useful to consistently model, demonstrate, and provide manual assistance using physical guidance, visual cues, and verbal directions when conducting activities. One-step or two-step directions are more appropriate than a series of commands; however, avoid using more guidance, direction, or cues than necessary to encourage the person to take more responsibility.

If having a short attention span is a problem, it may help to simplify verbal instructions. Often participants will take cues from how something sounds rather than from what is said. Consistency in voice tone, voice quality, and communication pattern is helpful. Keep directions brief and simple to increase the person's attention to the most important parts of the task. Use repetitious, slow, meaningful progression.

Implement rules and procedures, especially as related to health and safety, before the activity starts. Learning by example, repetition, reminders, verbal feedback, and experience will foster an individual's comprehension of instructions.

It can be helpful to vary activities and introduce new skills early in a session. Alternate active and quiet games so that a person is not over stimulated and the person's interest is maintained. Structure the environment so that all participants may become involved. The circle formation is an excellent leadership tool; people are then able to take advantage of modeling, imitation, demonstration, and peer interaction.

Meet Calvin, Who Enjoys Playing Cards

One morning in 1990, Calvin awoke early as usual and swung his legs over the side of the bed. To his surprise, he fell to the floor, unable to speak or move. When his wife, Ruby, awoke, she assumed he had gone for his ritual walk. Not until his grandson came by two hours later did they find Calvin on the floor. The doctor told his family he had experienced a stroke.

After one month in a rehabilitation hospital, Calvin returned home and began a new phase in his life. Many of his favorite pastimes still gave him pleasure: listening to gospel music, enjoying his grandchildren, and attending their Little League baseball games.

Other activities were no longer pleasurable. He no longer enjoyed church due to the emotional arousal that brought on tears and embarrassment. He also had difficulty talking to acquaintances due to the impaired speech caused by the stroke.

One of his greatest pleasures is playing cribbage with his wife and best friend, Charlie. For a long time, Calvin did not think he would ever be able to remember the rules and hold the cards, but with Charlie's patient tutoring and the help of an adaptive cardholder, Calvin is now the reigning cribbage champion of the neighborhood.

What are characteristics of a stroke?

A *stroke* or *cerebrovascular accident* is a form of traumatic brain injury that originates inside the brain itself. A stroke occurs when a portion of the brain is deprived of blood. The incidence of strokes, which is the second leading cause of death in the world, is higher for men than women and higher for African Americans than other racial groups.

Since long-standing hypertension is a major cause of stroke, very few people under the age of 40 experience a stroke. *Hypertension*, otherwise known as high-blood pressure, is a chronic condition that involves elevated blood pressure in the arteries.

The most common form of stroke is a cerebral thrombosis, which occurs when a blood clot forms in an artery that supplies blood to the brain. A *cerebral embolism* occurs when a blood clot travels to the brain from another part of the body, often from the heart. In both instances, the brain is deprived of blood due to the clot, and damage ensues. A *cerebral hemorrhage* is a stroke caused by a blood vessel bursting in the brain. Not only is the area beyond the burst deprived of blood, but also the blood that spilled out puts pressure on the brain tissue in the area of the rupture. A cerebral hemorrhage is the most serious form of stroke, and frequently causes coma and death.

There may be no warning that a stroke will occur, although some individuals may be forewarned by a series of small strokes known as *transient ischemic attacks*—brief episodes of circulatory deficiency to the brain. These small strokes may cause sudden weakness or numbness on one side of the face, in one arm, or in one leg; sudden and sharp dizziness; dimness or loss of vision especially in one eye; or loss of the ability to speak clearly or understand speech. The individual may not realize that a stroke has actually occurred. Transient ischemic attacks are a warning sign that a major stroke may happen if medical attention is not sought. They can occur days, weeks, or months before the major stroke.

The amount of injury caused by a stroke depends on the type and location of the damage. A right-brain stroke affects the left side of the body and may cause hemiplegia, which involves paralysis or weakness, memory loss, and impulsive behavior. Individuals who have had a right-brain stroke often experience inappropriate reflex crying, reflex laughter, or reflex anger. These reflexes occur when some emotion is triggered, and the area of the cerebral cortex that controls emotions has been damaged. A left-brain stroke causes right-side hemiplegia; memory loss; speech and language problems; and slow, cautious behavior. These patterns may be opposite for those who are left-handed.

The brain damage caused by stroke may suddenly alter every aspect of the person's life. In addition to paralysis, some individuals have a condition known as hemianopsia. This condition causes half of the visual field to disappear. The person may eat only the food on one side of the plate and may not be aware of the other food unless the plate is turned. Likewise, the person may only respond to people who approach on one side and seem to ignore those who are standing on the other side. It is helpful to guide an individual who has hemianopsia to a position in the room where he or she will be able to see the most. Take care when approaching the person from the affected side, since it may startle the person when you suddenly appear in the field of vision.

Aphasia is the term used to indicate difficulties in processing language. *Receptive aphasia* means that the person can no longer understand the messages received as either spoken or written language. *Expressive aphasia* describes the condition in which the person can understand what is said or written but cannot respond to it. Some people may be able to sing or count but not speak, or may be able to say only a few words such as "okay," "amen," or "bye." Families are often shocked when their relative is only able to say swear words, which were never used before the stroke.

What are considerations for inclusion of people who have had a stroke?

A stroke can impact people in many ways, including their cognition and their emotional stability. As a result, a few suggestions might assist individuals in providing inclusive leisure service for people who have experienced a cerebrovascular accident:

- give the person time to respond
- understand reflexive behaviors
- encourage physical activity

Give the Person Time to Respond

It is important to treat the individual in an age-appropriate manner and not to respond as though the person is a child. Encouraging the individual to speak and to indicate personal preferences can be helpful. It is useful to be patient and allow the person sufficient time to speak, rather than finishing sentences or thoughts for the person.

Likewise, it is valuable to give the individual opportunities to do as much as possible independently. If we work to enable a person's independence, we often will enhance the dignity of the person.

Understand Reflexive Behaviors

One aspect of maintaining the participant's dignity relates to how we respond to reflex crying. Understand that crying does not necessarily reflect the mood of a person who has had a brain injury. If it is not clear how a person is feeling, ask the participant and respond appropriately.

Reflex crying has a tendency to come and go suddenly and may look different than real crying. It can be helpful to speak with people who are reflexively crying when they are not crying to determine how they would like to be treated when an episode does occur. Similar steps can be taken with reflex anger and laughter as well.

Encourage Physical Activity

Once a person has been medically stabilized after a stroke and returns home, there is a tendency for some people to discontinue physical activity. Unfortunately, this sedentary lifestyle can create a downward spiral of reduced physical activity and depression. Therefore, it may be helpful to offer physically active leisure services to people who have had a stroke and their families.

> For example, Lewis (2006) encouraged leisure service providers to offer programs that involve wheelchair biking, strength training, leisure education, and community reintegration.

Meet Thomas, Who Enjoys the Outdoors

Thomas likes taking long walks in the woods nearby his home. He often brings his binoculars so that he can identify birds and more closely observe other wildlife. Although many may enjoy such an activity, for Thomas it brings a sense of pride. It was not long ago when he had difficulty leaving his home because he experienced hallucinations due to his schizophrenia.

When his schizophrenia emerged during his early 30s, Thomas withdrew from his friends and family, and from activities that brought him joy. He lost his job and finally sought psychiatric assistance. After actively participating in therapy sessions with mental health professionals and following a scheduled plan for taking medication, Thomas has returned to his community. He is now employed and takes advantage of many recreation programs within his community.

Thomas expresses concern about the prejudice he has experienced as a result of his clinical diagnosis of schizophrenia. He hopes that in the future people will keep an open mind about people and focus on them as individuals rather than labels.

What are characteristics of mental health problems?

Many people believe that individuals receiving a psychiatric diagnosis are dangerous and should be incarcerated. As a result of certain news reports and horror movies, many people harbor the misconception that people who are receiving psychiatric care are a menace to society. While it is true that a small minority of people with psychiatric diagnoses have a history of violence, the majority do not engage in violent behavior.

Unfortunately, some people believe that individuals with mental disorders do not really need help. People still have the general belief that others should be able to handle mental health problems by themselves. The view that people should "pull themselves up by the bootstraps" or "talk themselves out of it" closely relates to the belief that problems with mental health are shameful. There is a tendency to think that there is something weak or morally wrong with someone seeking help for a mental impairment. According to Michels (1985):

> *The irony of this popular view is that growing evidence links cancer, heart disease, and other "traditional" health problems to such personal behaviors as cigarette smoking or improper eating habits. In fact, as many as half the deaths from the 10 leading causes of death in our country can be traced to people's lifestyle. It would be fairer to attribute these diseases to "weak characters and poor decisions" than to make the same claim about the most familiar mental disorders, such as schizophrenia or depression, which stem from causes that have little to do with voluntary choice.*

Some mental disorders are identified as those associated with mood problems, such as depression and mania. *Clinical depression* is different than the temporary experience of "everyday" depression that results from such emotions as sadness, frustration, and discouragement, but tends not to significantly impair a person's ability to function over time. Depression becomes a psychiatric diagnosis based on the frequency of the depressed mood, the intensity of the depressed feelings, and the degree to which it impairs an individual's ability to participate in daily activities.

Diminished interest and pleasure in life, fatigue and a loss of energy, and a sense of worthlessness or guilt characterize clinical depression. It is also a common cause of memory loss. The loss of concentration that accompanies depression makes it difficult for the affected person to acquire new information. The slowed thinking process associated with clinical depression makes the retrieval of information more difficult and sometimes even impossible for certain periods of time.

In addition, people experiencing clinical depression may reflect their feelings in changes in their weight, resulting in excessive losses or gains in weight, or sleeping patterns, resulting in insomnia or oversleeping. *Insomnia* involves the repeated inability to fall asleep or to remain asleep long enough to feel rested. At times, severe depression can result in thoughts of, or attempts at, suicide.

Extreme elevated, expansive, or irritable mood states characterize **manic episodes**, another type of mood disorder. During a manic episode, the person may exhibit several of the following behaviors: inflated self-esteem, decreased sleep need, excessive talkativeness, racing thoughts, distractibility, physical activeness, and risk-taking. Individuals who shift between states of depression and mania are often diagnosed as having bipolar disorder.

Schizophrenia, a mental disorder familiar to many people, in truth affects less than 1% of the population and does not refer to someone who has multiple personalities. *Schizophrenia* is a psychotic disorder characterized by an individual who at various times departs from reality. The lack of awareness of reality can be manifested in a variety of ways.

Some individuals with schizophrenia experience hallucinations that involve the perception, through any of the senses, of objects or beings that are not actually there, such as hearing voices telling one what to do. *Delusions* are another symptom of schizophrenia, and involve false beliefs about self, others, or objects that persist despite presentation of facts to the contrary, such as the belief that one's thoughts are not their own, but imposed by some outside force.

Individuals with schizophrenia may have disturbances in speech, motor activity, and expression of emotion. One characteristic of schizophrenia strongly tied to leisure participation is disturbances associated with volition. People who have disturbances associated with volition experience difficulty making a decision that often results in the absence of self-determination.

Anxiety disorders are associated with intense fear or panic of a situation, object, or person that is not justified and should not result in fear. Many situations justify fear; however, a person experiencing an anxiety disorder will have continuous intense fears about something for no apparent reason, such as worrying about the welfare of a loved one. Physical symptoms include shortness of breath, accelerated heart rate, dizziness, abdominal distress, and chills or hot flashes. Anxiety disorders result in a decreased ability to function and relate to other people.

> For example, Michele Meyer (2000) reported that social anxiety disorder, characterized by intense fear of being humiliated in social situations, is the most common anxiety disorder and the leading psychiatric problem after depression and alcoholism.

Closely linked to anxiety disorders is a category of mental disturbances identified as phobias. *Phobias* involve continuous, unrealistic fears and dominate a person's thinking, such as agoraphobia, which is the fear of leaving one's house, or claustrophobia, which is the fear of closed spaces. Other phobias include fear of speaking in public, fear of snakes, and fear of seeing blood. The most common phobia, social anxiety disorder, is characterized by an intense fear of being scrutinized and humiliated by others in social situations that results in trembling, sweating, and racing heartbeat.

Obsessive-compulsive disorders result in people not being able to think clearly because of recurring thoughts and repetitive behaviors. *Obsessions* involve a persistent disturbing preoccupation with unreasonable ideas or feelings. *Compulsions* are irresistible impulses to perform irrational acts. The two conditions are linked in that a person may be obsessed with an idea such as cleanliness, which may result in a compulsion such as washing hands hundreds of times in a brief period of time.

What are considerations for inclusion of people with mental health problems?

People who are experiencing mental health challenges are often working to be on the road to recovery. Leisure service professionals can provide valuable supports for these individuals. Susan Lilly (2010, p. 7) referred to these possibilities in assisting people with their journeys when she stated:

> *What does recovery in mental health mean? It is a self-determined and holistic journey that people undertake to heal and grow. What enables recovery to happen? Relationships and environments that provide hope, empowerment, choices, and opportunities. Through these connections and supportive surroundings, individuals with mental illness can reach their full potential as community members.*

Often the challenges that people with mental health encounter are as a result of negative attitudes of people who they encounter. Some considerations for inclusion that focus on maintaining the dignity of the person can be identified in the following manner:

- see similarities first
- demonstrate respect when speaking and listening

See Similarities First

Many view people who have mental health problems as different from them, so they are uncomfortable in interacting with them. As stated many times throughout this book, if we view all people, including people with mental health problems, as similar to us, we can interact with them more comfortably. With careful planning, activity inclusion can help to enhance self-esteem and provide a sense of well-being for the individual. It is important to establish rapport with all program participants.

Demonstrate Respect When Speaking and Listening

To start a conversation, choose a topic you think people may be interested in, something that has happened to them lately, or a "safe" topic like the weather or sports. If you receive no response, it may be that the person did not hear you or did not understand you. Repeat the question, point to what you are talking about, rephrase the question, and make eye contact. If there is still no response, try to put them at ease by telling about something that happened to you or make light conversation. As with anyone who may have difficulty holding a conversation, the person may still very much like to listen to others and be spoken to.

If we cannot understand people when they speak, we may ask them to repeat themselves, or, if someone is talking about a topic we know nothing about, we may ask to change the subject or just listen politely. Even though we may feel awkward, our listening is often appreciated and we may begin to understand some of the person's speech.

It is acceptable to tell a person we do not understand or ask them to repeat something. If someone responds to us on a totally different topic, it is helpful if we are polite and either bring the topic back, or speak to the new topic. We could say, "That's interesting, but let me ask you again about your interest in swimming." Or you could respond to the new topic.

If someone asks a personal or embarrassing question, honesty is the best way to handle this. A good response is, "That is not something I want to talk about. Let's talk about something else." The person can learn from you that some things are not to be asked.

If someone is extending a conversation beyond a reasonable amount of time, honesty is the best policy. "I'm sorry, but I need to move on. We can talk more another time. Right now I don't have time to listen further." If someone rudely interrupts your conversation, you can say something like, "I'm talking with Mary now; come talk to me some other time."

Final Thoughts

People who meet individuals with cognitive impairments may have incorrect perceptions about their skills and abilities. For those whose brain-related impairment is acquired later in life, there are inevitable changes that people experience as they transition back into their families and communities. With the necessary assistance and support, people with cognitive impairments can live meaningful and often enjoyable lives.

It may be helpful when thinking how we might include people with conditions that affect their cognitive functioning to consider a report in the newsletter *Recreation: Access in the 90s* that described a situation with a child with Attention Deficit and Hyperactivity Disorder ("Oh, so this is the most integrated setting," 1997).

> *This child chose to register for an after-school recreation program, instead of a separate after-school program for youth with disabilities. When the registrant displayed some disruptive behavior, an additional staff member with behavior management training was hired and assigned as a companion or aide to the child. The child's disruptive behavior diminished. Unfortunately the additional assistance was soon terminated. The child's behavior deteriorated and his participation in the program was suspended. The family filed a complaint with the U.S. Department of the Interior, who ordered reinstatement. They decided that the additional one-to-one staff was not an undue burden and did not result in a fundamental alteration in the after-school program.*

This is an example of how leisure service professionals initially responded to the spirit of the Americans with Disabilities Act (ADA) and helped facilitate the inclusion of a youth with a cognitive impairment. The provision of an additional staff member to work with this person was an effective accommodation. However, this is also an instance when a family was required to assert their legal rights achieved by ADA to gain access to an inclusive program and to avoid segregation.

Discussion Questions

1. What are the characteristics of intellectual disability?
2. What are considerations for the inclusion of people with intellectual disability?
3. What is the difference between intelligence and IQ?
4. What are three factors that can affect IQ scores?
5. What are characteristics common to persons with autistic disorder?
6. What are considerations for the inclusion of people with autism?
7. What is the best way to assist a person having a grand mal epileptic seizure?
8. What are behaviors common to traumatic brain injury?
9. What are considerations for the inclusion of people with traumatic brain injuries?
10. How would you determine the best way to proceed with a participant who exhibits reflex crying?
11. What are difficulties in adjustment that may occur following acquisition of a brain-related disability during adulthood?

Pictured from left to right are Kathy Sullivan, Jane Mazur, RoseBary Trammell, and Christine Eckman, who were born with various types of intellectual disabilities. All are employed and live together with a resident manager in a house in Roswell, Georgia.

Photo by Lynda Greer

The Stories of
Kathy, Jane, RoseBary, and Christine

Kathy

My family . . . mother, stepfather, brother, and sister live near in Atlanta, and I live at Barrington Landing. I really love the people here. We mostly get along really well. I'm supposed to move my room into the basement soon . . . and I'll have more privacy. I work at the Haynes Bridge Kroger where I make pizzas in the deli and help Chris [Eckman] in the bakery if I can. Right now we need more people to work at Kroger. I like to ride my exercise bike, listen to music—mostly rock and roll. At night I do what I need to to get dinner ready and clean up. Then I relax, watch TV.

Jane

My sister and brother live in Atlanta; I see them holidays, weekends, sometimes. The rest of the time I live with my friends. I love my friends here! I work at Herman Miller, where they make furniture. Now I am gluing furniture pieces together and I like that job a lot. When I'm not working, I love to look at TV Guide. And I like listening to music and coloring.

RoseBary

Mom and Dad live on E. Wesley Rd. in Atlanta. My brother lives near Atlanta. Whenever I can, I see my family, but we're very busy at Barrington Landing. It's almost three years since I moved here. I love Jane and Kathy and Chris. And I like this house a lot. I work at RRA [Resources for Retarded Adults], helping with the cleaning. I also go to the training center and do different things. This Christmas we're helping the homeless and the needy, giving food; and I took some pennies to school today. I like to read my encyclopedias, Reader's Digest, things like that. I ride my exercise bike sometimes, and when the weather is nice, I like to take walks and talk to the neighbors.

Christine

My parents live in Atlanta and I have a sister in New York. For three years I have lived at Barrington Landing with Sasha, the cat; RoseBary, Jane, Kathy, and now, Tanya [resident manager]. I'm happy here. I work at the Haynes Bridge Kroger. I bake cookies and some bread; I enjoy baking cookies the best. My friend, Kathy, works there, too. We eat lunch together when we can. At night I watch television, listen to music—many kinds of music. I like to sing, too. Every night I write in my diary about my day.

Chapter 23
People, Inclusion, and
Sensory Limitations

Fraternal twins Will (left) and Robby Smith are high school students in Gainesville, Georgia. Born prematurely, they sustained severe hearing losses during neonatal care.

Photo by Lynda Greer

The Stories of Will and Robby Smith

Will

I was born in Augusta, GA. I have a brother who is named Robby Smith. My father is a doctor and my mother deals with art. When I was three years old, the whole family moved to Gainesville, GA. Now I go to a school called Gainesville Middle School. I have some friends named Chip and Justin, and a bunch of others that I cannot remember their names.

I am an editor and a movie reviewer for the Gainesville Middle School's newspaper, "The Mirror." I hate "The Mirror," but I always wanted to be an editor and a movie reviewer, so I got no choice. I always get a feeling like I am a special guest of the newspaper and I try to take a break from it whenever possible.

I have a lot of hobbies. I am not sure exactly how many, but I got comic books, rockets, stamps, books, movie reviews, articles, posters, and role-playing games. I have told you not all, but some parts of my life.

Robby

Hey! Well, my name is Robby Smith and I have a hearing loss and eyesight problem. I love reading books, and usually stake out the local bookstore when I hear that a good book has been published.

I enjoy living life to the fullest and relaxing. I like to go to the beach, the city, and the mountains. I'm going to be a freshman at high school. My favorite movies are the Indiana Jones trilogy, Midnight Run, and Mr. North.

My hearing/sight losses never bother me, and I really don't make a major deal out of it.

Detachment will not do . . . And there ought to be mutual respect, regard for each one's competence and integrity.

-M. Green

Orientation Activity: Silvia and Shavaun—What to do?

Directions Alone: Read the following scenarios and respond to the tasks posed.

Silvia would like to use our cruise line to take a vacation with her husband. She has communicated to you that she has *diabetic retinopathy*, a disorder of the retina due to diabetes. As the recreation director on the ship, identify some adaptations or considerations we may make when attempting to make this vacation one of the best Silvia has ever experienced.

Shavaun, a teenager, would like to participate in the basketball league offered by the local parks and recreation department. Since Shavaun happens to have a *sensorineural hearing loss* caused by a childhood disease, identify some ways we may assist Shavaun in having a successful experience with the basketball league.

Directions with Others: Move about the room with your responses and share your thoughts with another person. After a specified time, discuss what you have learned with the entire group.

Debriefing: To permit Silvia to access the cruise line, we provide her with an orientation to the ship and ask her for suggestions on how we could best serve her. The lighting is often a consideration: natural daylight varies from extremely bright sun that creates glare, to overcast skies that provide insufficient light. These conditions may make it difficult for Silvia to see demonstrations, environmental obstructions, or signage. We can assist Silvia by checking the signs on the ship for compliance with the Americans with Disabilities Act regarding positioning, color, and use of raised letters or Braille. When making visual demonstrations, it can be helpful if we increase the number of verbal instructions and directions. During the evening entertainment, we can reserve a place at one of the front tables for Silvia and her party so that she can enjoy the show. Since Silvia has diabetes, we can work with her to have appropriate refreshments, such as sugar-free options.

To promote Shavaun's ability to play in the basketball league, we could determine the level of his residual hearing and learn how to maximize his hearing abilities on the basketball court. Many athletes with hearing impairments play successfully by using signs to represent verbal instructions. We could work with local basketball officials to educate them on accommodations required for compliance with the ADA. It may help to have a light flash to signal Shavaun each time the whistle is blown. Shavaun's teammates will be an important component in his success. It is valuable to identify a player to be an informer to ensure Shavaun understands verbal discussions. If desired, this person could go to Shavaun each time there is a break in the action and be available to clarify any situation. If Shavaun uses sign language, he may choose to teach the coach and his teammates a couple of signs a day to help with communication. Once some signs have been learned, it will help to always use the sign and the spoken word together. The American Athletic Association for the Deaf, headquartered at Gallaudet University in Washington, D.C., provides additional information on sports for individuals with hearing impairments. Consider the following questions when thinking about the orientation activity:

- Why is lighting an important consideration when working with individuals with visual impairments?
- Why is it important to include Silvia's entire party at a front table if only she is visually impaired?
- What is the purpose of using an informer during activities?
- Why is it important to use sign language and the spoken word together when addressing individuals with deafness?

Introduction

Visual and hearing impairments can be congenital or acquired at any point across one's lifespan. These impairments can affect a person's ability to perform daily tasks at home and in their communities. Sensory impairments can also have an effect on the individual's leisure lifestyle. Without leisure options, the individual may eventually become isolated from other people.

This chapter presents information on the causes and treatments for visual and hearing impairments and offers suggestions for inclusion into leisure services. The following questions will be addressed in the chapter:

- What are terms that describe visual loss?
- What are causes of visual loss?
- How can people with visual impairments be included?
- What are terms that describe hearing loss?
- What are ways of measuring hearing?
- What are types of hearing loss?
- How can people with hearing impairments be included?
- What are characteristics of deaf-blindness?
- How can we include people with deaf-blindness?

Meet Donna, Who Enjoys Nature

The following description is based on the testimony given by Donna Veno back in 1986 before the President's Commission on Americans Outdoors.

I still hear professionals in the recreation field tell me that they do not know why they should make their parks or programs accessible to blind people. How little they know about blind people and our ability to see beauty around us. These professionals ask me why someone with no sight would be interested in seeing mountains, or watching the sun as it rises over the ocean. It is sad that they clearly believe life's beauty can only be experienced through the eyes.

One day I boarded a ski lift and went to the summit of Mount Wild Cat. On the way I leaned as far as I could out of my window and listened intently to the trees passing by me. This ride actually ascends the face of the mountain. That enabled me to sense the rock formations, smell the pines, hear the wind blowing through the trees, and listen to a stream descending the mountain, twisting and curving beneath me.

Then I arrived at the summit. As I moved about, I saw some areas thick with vegetation. The flowers felt beautiful and soft as I looked at them. How can I describe to professionals the joy I felt standing on the top of the mountain, listening to its silence and seeing it not with my eyes, but with every part of me!

Descending the mountain provided me with the opportunity to drop heavy stones from the ski lift's window and listen to them roll down, down, down. The trees rose up to greet me; the air became warmer, and soon I was at the base. I kept a stone from my mountain; it now sits in a dried arrangement I made for my living room. The stone and the cassette tape I made of the mountain's sounds are my photograph!

Those with sight admire the sun as it rises above the horizon; I listen to the sounds created by daybreak, feel the increase of light and warmth, and become part of the total experience. True, I do not see the beautiful colors; but what is color when you have a world of sounds, smells, and feelings around you to absorb?

According to Donna (Veno, 1986), a freelance writer who happens to be blind, people with visual impairments will be best served when service providers stop viewing blindness through their eyes.

Most of us do not feel restricted or disadvantaged; we lead normal, healthy and active lives. We work hard and want to play hard as well. While you who see stand at a distance and view the beauty of the mountain, I go to the top and become one with it.

Meet Alex, Who Likes to Plan His Strategy

Alex is faced with some tough decisions these days. The 17-year-old high school senior has to decide where to go to college next year—University of Pennsylvania, University of Michigan, or the University of California at Berkeley—whether to attend a conference, accept a scholarship he has been awarded, start guide-dog training, or take a computer-training class—all of which start at about the same time.

Not an easy set of decisions for any 17-year-old, but certainly not any less difficult for a teenager who is blind and about to start a new life away from home for the first time. Home for Alex is Staten Island. A town that is miles outside of Manhattan, Staten Island is far enough away to require his daily commute of a bus, a ferry, and a subway to Hunter College High School, one of Manhattan's public schools for children who are academically gifted.

But commutes do not seem to bother Alex. When he is not running uptown to complete his senior-year internship, he is dashing downtown to meet with his chess teacher. Alex has won accolades in both areas. This year, he won a Class-C national chess championship and has garnered top scores in the New York state exams in Spanish.

Alex, who returned from a solo two-week trip to Spain in April, says he has always been interested in Spanish culture and language. "I plan to major in Spanish and other foreign languages, and then go on to law school where I will specialize in international law." Ambitions aside, Alex is not all that different from any other 17-year-old testing new waters as a young adult. Alex's mother would prefer a college closer to home and family, while Alex thinks otherwise. But mother and son are willing to compromise. Says his mother: "After all, this is the beginning of a new life."

What are terms that describe visual loss?

The terms *blind* and *blindness* are typically reserved for persons who have no usable sight. The terms *visually impaired*, *partially sighted*, or *low vision* describe a host of conditions that indicate a serious loss of vision that cannot be corrected by medical or surgical procedures or with conventional eyeglasses.

In the early 1930s, the U.S. federal government developed a "legal" definition for blindness to determine whether individuals are eligible for special benefits. Because of this definition, there is often confusion between the terms blindness and visual impairment. The government adopted the same terms used by medical specialists to describe low-vision acuity and visual field.

Acuity describes the amount of detail an individual sees compared to what a person with normal vision sees. It is the measurement taken of the best eye with the best correction to determine what the individual can see at 20 feet compared to what a person with unimpaired vision sees.

For example, if a person has to be 20 feet away from an object that a person with normal vision can view from at least 70 feet away, the person would be said to have 20/70 vision. The larger the second number, the less vision a person has. The common phrase "20/20 vision" means the individual's sight is normal and needs no correction for distance.

Visual field refers to how great an area a person can see at one time with the fixed eye, measured in degrees (as an angle). The normal visual field is 180 degrees. If a person with normal vision looks straight ahead, that person should be able to see nearly all of the objects in a half-circle (180 degrees), with an equal area perceived on each side of the nose. Both eyes see the central one third of the visual field. A loss of visual field restricts either *central vision* (what is seen in the center of either eye) or *peripheral vision* (side vision). The definition of field used for legal blindness is 20 degrees.

A person is said to have *low vision* if the individual can only see a 20-degree to 40-degree field or less in the best eye. *Legal blindness* occurs when a person's visual acuity is 20/200 or less in the better eye (with the best possible correction) and/or the visual field is 20 degrees or less at the widest point. Seventy-two percent of people identified as legally blind are 65 or older. Eighty percent of people who are legally blind have some degree of usable vision, such as perception of light and dark.

Having low vision or a severe visual impairment means that a person's vision can range between 20/70 and 20/200 acuity or have 30 degrees or less visual field. There are five times as many individuals with low vision as people who are legally blind. People with low vision often encounter reading and mobility problems; however, with the aid of special devices, they are able to read and perform tasks requiring vision.

What are causes of visual loss?

Visual impairments can be *congenital* (present at birth) or *acquired* (acquired after birth). *Rubella* (German measles) is an infectious disease that can cause multiple disabilities in the fetus, including blindness, if contracted during the first trimester of pregnancy. Although once common, rubella can now be prevented by immunizations that are mandatory in the United States and many industrialized nations. *Trachoma* is an infectious disease caused when a microorganism spread by flies enters the eye, producing infection and scarring the cornea or eyelid. Although rare in the United States, trachoma is the major cause of blindness in the world, found most often in areas with poor hygienic conditions.

Accidents are another common cause of visual impairments. Since pieces of flying metal from construction or home workshops cause many eye wounds, safety glasses are strongly recommended when doing projects that include these items. School-aged children sustain sports-related eye injuries that could be prevented with proper headgear and eyewear. For children of preschool age, cigarettes, cigars, and pipes that dangle at eye level cause eye damage as well.

In addition to accidents that puncture, rupture, or burn the eye, two additional accidents are *retinopathy of prematurity* (ROP) and detached retina. ROP is blindness that occurs when premature infants are exposed to 100% oxygen for prolonged periods of time. There is often accompanying brain damage. Detached retina occurs when the retina (the sensory tissue upon which the lens image is formed) detaches and rips a hole in the outer wall. This creates a blind spot as the blood supply decreases. Detached retina can be surgically repaired, often using laser technology. The condition is often associated with trauma.

Diabetic retinopathy is a vascular disease that is a leading cause of blindness in the United States for adults. Retinal blood vessels degenerate due to an imbalance of insulin, the hormone that the pancreas does not secrete in diabetes. There is no cure for this disorder; however, it is possible to slow the loss of sight through laser technology to coagulate and seal off leaking blood vessels.

Glaucoma is a blinding disease caused by increased pressure in the eye. The intraocular pressure is usually due to a malfunction in the system that controls the amount of fluid in the eye. If the pressure is raised enough, it may damage structures in the back of the eye, particularly the optic nerve. Glaucoma may be *acute* (severe and of short duration), but is usually *progressive* (gradual peripheral sight loss) and unnoticed until peripheral vision is lost, causing a condition known as tunnel vision. Glaucoma is most often treated with eye drops or with surgery to drain the excess fluid in the eye to relieve pressure on the optic nerve.

Cataracts describe opacity or fogging of the lens, and are found at the two extremes of the life span: infancy and advanced age. If something is opaque, images cannot be clearly seen through it. Cataracts are usually caused by a breakdown of the metabolic process that keeps the lens transparent. For older adults, vision decreases very gradually as the developing cataract blocks more and more of the light needed for vision. Cataracts can also be caused by external factors, such as electrical shock, wounds, or X-rays. Treatment ranges from the use of prescription eyeglasses and contact lenses to surgically implanted lenses to replace the opaque natural lens.

The *macula* is the region of the retina that is the most important for such activities as reading or sewing. *Macular degeneration*, a leading cause of new cases of legal blindness, is a malfunction of the pigment epithelium that removes waste from the inner fluid of the eye. This condition tends to run in families and is most common in people who have blue, gray, or green eyes. There is little treatment for macular degeneration; however, it usually does not result in total blindness.

Retinitis pigmentosa, another inherited disease, often leads to blindness in adolescence or young adulthood. The cause of the disease has not been fully established; however, the result is the failure of the normal process of rod and cone rejuvenation. Over time, the rods and cones (receptor cells) grow shorter, resulting in night blindness, tunnel vision, and loss of central vision.

How can people with visual impairments be included?

- Communicate with participants
- Provide an orientation
- Act as a sighted guide
- Understand methods of mobility
- Use accommodating teaching methods
- Purchase adaptive equipment
- Modify activities
- Include participants in planning

Communicate with Participants

As always, it is best to ask program participants how best to meet their needs. The individual may disclose information regarding residual vision that will help us to maximize their participation and enjoyment. When first meeting an individual with visual impairments, it is helpful for us to introduce ourselves and let the person know we are speaking to them. Speak directly to the individual rather than through a companion, parent, or sibling. Speak in a normal tone of voice.

Someone who has a loss of vision probably does not also have a loss of hearing. We do not need to hesitate to use "sighted" terms such as "look," and "see." People who are blind usually use such words themselves to help those who are sighted feel more relaxed.

When others enter or leave the room, it is considerate to use their names when greeting them or saying good-bye to help the person who is visually impaired monitor who is in the room. It is helpful to reduce the chances of loud, monotonous noises of prolonged duration because they can interfere with participants' ability to utilize auditory cues.

Provide an Orientation

People with visual impairments often depend on familiar landmarks, sounds, and smells for successful mobility. It may be helpful to provide a person with a visual impairment an orientation to the environment, including touring the facility and describing the location of distinctive landmarks to help them locate restrooms, water fountains, and emergency exits. Environmental barriers such as posts, changes in floor level, and other obstructions can be located and described.

> In his book *Hope Unseen*, Captain Scott Smiley (2010) speaks about the value of having aides provide him with a description of contexts he encounters at work. He also makes the point about the importance of receiving an orientation from his wife, especially when he is changing his son's diaper at home.

For the safety of all participants, it is important for us to keep doors and cupboards either completely closed or open. Some individuals with visual impairment may also have impaired balance and may benefit by knowing the location of hand railings, counters, and other features that can provide support.

Sometimes being placed in a large group of people in an unfamiliar context may overwhelm an individual with a visual impairment.

> For example, a young child beginning a playgroup, a teenager attending a social function, or an older adult joining a senior center may be reticent to interact with available materials or people.

One approach to promote the inclusion of a person with visual impairments is to introduce the person to another individual and encourage their interaction by introducing an activity they might enjoy doing jointly.

> For instance, two young children might like to play together with puppets, teenagers might find it fun to help prepare refreshments for a social function, and two older adults who were raised in the same area might enjoy reminiscing about their childhood together.

Act as a Sighted Guide

For ease in moving through the environment, people with visual impairments often use a *sighted guide*. When assuming the role of a sighted guide, we simply allow an individual with a visual impairment to grasp our bicep. The person with the visual impairment walks beside us about a half-step behind. Communication occurs through subtle movements in the sighted guide's arm.

The advantage of sighted guiding is that it includes and promotes social interaction. As a sighted guide, we can concentrate on orienting the person with a visual impairment to the surroundings and inherent dangers. Also, it is useful to let the person know if you must leave them and make sure they are oriented to their current location. Variations of the concept of sighted guide are present in sports.

> For example, Kim has competed in numerous triathlons and the Chicago Marathon. Kim, who has a severe visual impairment, runs with a guide, swims with a guide using a tether, and rides on the back of a tandem bike.

Understand Methods of Mobility

Canes provide the most independent means of mobility for people with visual impairments. However, some people resist using a cane because of the stigma associated with it. Some parents may be embarrassed if their child were to use a cane, so they may not allow children to learn the procedure.

Some technological developments in the area of mobility are sonic guides and laser canes. Guide dogs assist some individuals with visual impairments to move about their communities and, by law, are permitted to enter most facilities within the community, with hospitals as one exception.

Use Accommodating Teaching Methods

Lighting, color, texture, size of objects and print, space, and boundaries may all be modified for successful participation. If glare is a concern, the individual may wear sunglasses or a hat. Consider the speed of the activity and, if appropriate, slow the action down. Provide auditory and tactile cues that are consistent with material placement. If the person is partially sighted, the teaching techniques can be adapted to make use of the person's residual vision. Consider each person's needs.

> For instance, we would not teach dancing to a person who has been blind since birth in the same way as we would to a person who was previously sighted and has danced or has seen dancing performed

In addition, touch may be helpful when instructing a person with a visual impairment, but it is important to always ask before doing so.

> In teaching golf, for example, we might position the person's fingers and hands around the golf club. Verbal instruction may have to be more detailed and consistent to compensate for lack of vision. Conduct a task analysis by dividing larger skills into smaller ones and teach one skill at a time.

Purchase Adaptive Equipment

Consider equipment requirements to determine if adaptive equipment would be helpful. Beep baseballs and dartboards, raised checkerboards, and Braille sheet music are examples of commercially available adaptive equipment. A catalog of aids and appliances is available in Braille and printed editions from the American Foundation for the Blind.

> Kim, who competes in triathlons with guides as described previously, must access the fitness center resources including the pool, treadmill, or a spin class when she is alone. The fitness center has made helpful accommodations, such as tactile buttons on machines with large print, high-contrast signage, printed materials in alternative formats, and having instructors for classes such as yoga provide detailed, clear descriptions of the movements.

Modify Activities

Making adaptations to the activity and materials is an important consideration when providing leisure services for people with visual impairments.

> As an example, skating requires no more equipment for the person who is blind than for the person who is sighted, but a sighted skating partner might accompany the person who is blind. Music coming from a central speaker may be helpful in giving the person who is blind a sense of direction while moving around the rink.

Likewise, no special equipment is needed for swimming, but the person who is blind must be warned about any hazards in the area. Activities such as wrestling can be successful when competitors who are blind compensate with their senses of touch and balance. In all active sports, athletes should be warned of potential danger.

Include Participants in Planning

Including people with visual impairments in the planning process makes sense and can benefit everyone. We can involve people with disabilities at all levels of recreation, from planning of services to participation in programs. Separate services are discouraged, such as segregated trails in parks or specially designed tactual rooms in museums.

Though opportunities to enjoy services at parks and recreation areas have increased, there are still barriers that must be eliminated. A barrier may be physical, such as a lack of materials in Braille and audio format, or attitudinal. Attitudinal barriers are by far the worst to encounter and the most difficult to dispel. For both types of barriers, planning teams including not only leisure service professionals but also participants with visual impairments are essential. Veno (1986, p. 14) encouraged leisure service professionals to:

> *Look at who we are and what we have, not at what you think we lack. Accept the reality that people with visual impairments are like others, except we do not see with our eyes. Be assured, however, we see with our hands, feet, ears, and minds. Blindness allows me to use the gift of imagination. I create my own beauty in the space around me. You see your world as it is; I see the same world as I want it to be in my own mind's eye. Who can tell, then, whose appreciation is greater?*

Meet Reba, Who Advocates for Rights

Nelson (1987) reported that like most pageant winners, Reba is talented, attractive, and articulate. She has used her status as a pageant winner to advocate for the rights of people with disabilities, especially those with hearing impairments. Reba has asked people she meets to help remove the communication and attitudinal barriers between people who hear and those who do not.

I want people to learn that people with hearing impairments should not be looked upon as having a handicap that cannot be overcome. We must reciprocate the best way we can and overcome communication difficulties.

Reba was raised in a family with parents who are deaf and several brothers and sisters, some of whom hear and others who do not. In response to the varying hearing abilities of her family members, Reba is fluent in oral and manual communication. She has had a severe hearing impairment since birth.

Since her days as pageant winner, Reba has completed her degree in recreation and leisure studies and is a practicing Certified Therapeutic Recreation Specialist. She enjoys helping others, as she recognizes that others have helped her along the way. Reba is not only able to help people with disabilities develop meaningful leisure lifestyles, but also to serve as a role model for them. She continues to be a strong advocate for people with disabilities, educating all citizens regarding the ability of people with disabilities to be successful members of their communities.

Meet John, Who Has Signed His Way to the Top

John founded a high-tech computer company and turned it into a multimillion-dollar enterprise. What is interesting about his company is that more than 12% of the 375 employees have some form of hearing impairment, and at least half of the employees without hearing impairments use sign language (Anderson, 1988). They do so because it is the most effective way to communicate with their boss, John, who is deaf.

John remembers when he was 10 and had just moved to a new community. The neighborhood children decided to test the newcomer by setting a firecracker off behind his back. Of course, he never heard the explosion. The humiliation drew tears. How did John cope with the cruelty? Did he fight back? "No, I made friends with them."

John continues to make friends wherever he goes. He enjoys the social contact and values his relationships. For relaxation, he spends time with his wife and their three children. John feels it is important to advocate for the rights of people with disabilities. "I want the business world to understand that any person has capabilities. They can work and perform well if given the opportunity."

What are terms that describe hearing loss?

A *hearing impairment* is an invisible condition but one of the most prevalent disabilities. Hearing impairments include all losses of hearing, regardless of type or degree. *Deafness* can be defined as the state occurring when a person is unable to understand speech through the ear alone, either with or without a hearing aid. Hearing loss can range from total congenital deafness to mild partial deafness.

Hearing losses are also experienced as people age—almost half of senior citizens have some hearing loss. Although hearing impairments are common, many people who are affected do not fully understand the problem. They may be unaware of the need for (or unwilling to seek) treatment. Those who have adjusted to a gradual loss of hearing through the years often do not realize that the sounds reaching them are greatly diminished.

Hearing impairment is categorized by the degree of hearing loss in one or both ears. *Mild hearing loss* is a loss of some sounds, while *moderate hearing loss* indicates a loss of enough sounds so that a person's ability to understand his or her surrounding environment is affected, including some speech sounds. When both ears have some hearing loss and the better ear has some difficulty hearing and understanding speech, the individual is said to have significant *bilateral loss*. *Severe hearing loss* indicates that many sounds are not heard, including most speech. Finally, *profound hearing loss* indicates the inability to hear almost all sounds. These classifications and their audible ranges are listed in Table 23.1.

Total or partial impairment of hearing may result from a variety of causes. The onset can be either insidious, which is when a condition has a gradual and cumulative effect, or acute, which is when a condition has a sudden onset, sharp rise, and short course.

Table 23.1 Hearing Loss Classifications Based on Audible Decibel Levels

Audible Range	Classification
0–25 dB +	Normal hearing
25–40 dB +	Mild loss
40–55 dB +	Moderate loss
55–70 dB +	Severe loss
90 dB +	Profound loss (deaf)

People are said to be ***hard-of-hearing*** if they have mild to moderate hearing loss, resulting in decreased perception of conversational speech, but sufficient hearing to permit understanding with optimal circumstances. These people have losses that can result in sound distortions or trouble interpreting sounds. Depending on the causes of the hearing loss, some people who are hard-of-hearing can benefit from the use of a hearing aid. Many people who are deaf prefer the term 'hard-of-hearing' rather than the term 'hearing impaired'; however, 'hearing impairment' is the term of choice by the general public.

What are ways of measuring hearing?

Units of sound intensity, called ***decibels*** (dB), are used to measure hearing (see Table 23.2). Zero decibels is the softest intensity of sound or speech that can be heard by a person with normal hearing.

People who can hear sounds from 1–25 dB and up are considered to have *normal hearing*. People who can only hear sounds starting at 25–40 dB are considered to have a *mild hearing loss*, whereas those who begin to hear at 40 55 dB are said to have a *moderate loss*. *Moderately severe loss* occurs when the individual cannot hear at volumes lower than 55–70 decibels. *Severe loss* refers to the inability to hear sounds and speech under 70–90 decibels. Not being able to hear until a sound is at least 90 decibels or above is termed a profound hearing loss. Beyond 90 decibels, many people would be called deaf, but with modern hearing devices, some people can obtain usable sound. People with hearing in the normal range begin to experience discomfort at volume levels of 90–100 dB; danger to one's hearing increases with exposure.

Hertz (Hz), the unit of measurement of the frequency of sound waves, describes pitch. Persons who have difficulty understanding speech generally

Table 23.2 Examples of Sounds at Various Decibels

Decibels	Example
20 dB	Whisper
50–60 dB	Typical conversational speech
80 dB	Alarm clock volume (at two feet)
90 dB	Lawn mower
100 dB	Chainsaw or stereo headphones
120 dB	Music concert (in front of speakers)

have losses of high or low pitch. Some people may find it easier to understand low and deeper voices rather than high voices, or vice versa.

What are types of hearing loss?

There are three basic types of hearing impairments:

- conductive hearing loss
- sensorineural hearing loss
- central hearing loss

Conductive Hearing Loss

With a *conductive hearing loss*, sound waves are blocked as they travel through the auditory canal or middle ear and cannot reach the inner ear. Sounds seem muffled, and an earache may be present. Both children and adults are often affected by conductive hearing loss caused by wax blocking the ear canal, infection, or a punctured eardrum.

Another cause of conductive-type loss is *otosclerosis*. In this disorder, the bones of the middle ear soften, do not vibrate well, and then calcify. This, and other conductive hearing problems, can often be treated successfully with surgery or other procedures.

Sensorineural Hearing Loss

A *sensorineural hearing loss*, commonly termed *nerve deafness*, involves the inner ear and is the result of damage to the hair cells, nerve fibers, or both. Sounds are distorted, high tones are usually inaudible, and *tinnitus* which involves hearing ringing or buzzing sounds may be present. Speech can be heard but is not easily understood.

This type of loss is permanent and irreversible. Infants are born with sensorineural hearing loss caused by genetics, birth injury such as loss of oxygen during labor, or damage to the developing fetus because of maternal infection such as rubella, herpes, or other viral diseases. Other causes include high fevers, excessive noise, heredity, adverse reactions to drugs, head injuries, the aging process, and diseases such as meningitis.

Central Hearing Loss

A third, although rare, form of hearing loss is *central hearing loss*. With this type of impairment, the pathways to the brain or the brain itself are damaged. Sound levels are not affected, but understanding of language becomes difficult. Central hearing loss results from excess exposure to loud noise, head injuries, high fever, or tumors.

How can people with hearing impairments be included?

Inclusion of people with hearing impairments has positive effects on people who do not have significant hearing loss.

> For example, Most, Weisel, and Tur-Kaspa (1999) asked 140 high school students without hearing impairments, half of whom had regular contact with youth with hearing impairments, to listen to the speech of youth with hearing impairments and rate the speakers' personal qualities. Students who had regular contact with youth with hearing impairments reported more positive evaluations of personal qualities of speakers than students who did not have contact.

This finding supports studies indicating that inclusion has positive effects on attitudes towards individuals with hearing impairments. The following are some ways to promote inclusion for people with hearing impairments:

- consider diversity of skills
- use meaningful communication
- understand methods of assistance
- know classifications of hearing impairments

Consider Diversity of Skills

People who access leisure services possess many different types of hearing loss that result in varied skills, abilities, and experiences.

> For example, Easterbrooks and Baker (2001) reported that some people with hearing impairments may have cochlear implants and communicate orally, others may use an English-based sign system of American Sign Language, while others may have additional disabilities or reside in a home where the spoken language is not English.

Use Meaningful Communication

When speaking to a person with a hearing impairment, use a normal tone of voice and speak in complete sentences. We can speak slowly and distinctly, and enunciate clearly without "mouthing" the words. Over articulation does not make it easier to read lips. Look at the person when speaking and maintain face-to-face contact while communicating.

Ensure that adequate lighting is available to facilitate reading the person's lips. When interacting with the person, watch their gestures and face to gain additional cues to understand them. Use demonstration when teaching skills or explaining activities, because demonstrations are often more meaningful to the person who is hearing impaired than lengthy explanations. Individuals who have hearing impairments benefit from communication and information presented visually.

> As an illustration, Easterbrooks and Baker (2001) suggested using charts, graphs, simulations, demonstrations, models, and other forms of visual representations to enhance the chance that a person will learn and understand information that is presented.

Understand Methods of Assistance

Speech reading and sign language are other modalities available to persons with severe hearing loss. Speech reading is a virtual necessity in cases of severe or profound loss and can be self-taught to some extent; however, professional training may be needed for many people. Depending on the degree of impairment and individual needs, each person must decide what options offer the most advantages.

Know Classifications of Hearing Impairments

Consider when the onset of the hearing impairment occurred, if the individual chooses to disclose the information. People are identified as having *pre-lingual deafness* if deafness occurs before language skills have been acquired. The deafness can be congenital or acquired in infancy.

The second category, *post-lingual deafness*, is deafness that occurs after language has been acquired. The most common known causes of post-lingual hearing impairments are high fevers during childhood and certain childhood diseases, such as meningitis, encephalitis, measles, mumps, and influenza.

Meet Lisa, Who Tends the Garden

One look at the flower garden in Lisa's front yard tells you how much she enjoys beauty. Lisa has been blind since birth. She lost her hearing at age 5 from complications of meningitis. She tells all of the people she meets how fortunate she was to have learned to speak.

> *I remember the sound of the piano—my mother was a music teacher when I was a girl. The fragrance of the flowers, the subtle ways they move with the breeze, the delicate, velvety texture of their petals, all remind me of the music that came from my mother's piano. One doesn't need to be able to see or hear to find beauty in the world. My flower garden gives me so much pleasure. I grow different flowers every season. Every type is unique in fragrance, shape, and texture. Of course, the gardenias are my favorite: simple, pungent, and yet delicate.*

Another source of pleasure for Lisa is her imagination. She knows Braille and reads at least one new book a week that she receives from her public library's Talking Book program. Lisa provides us with some insight about her love of reading:

> *The books I enjoy reading the most are the stories with rich descriptions about people and their environment, like Charles Dickens or John Steinbeck. I also love poetry, especially Maya Angelou. The written word can so eloquently convey beauty.*

What are characteristics of deaf-blindness?

Most people who are deaf-blind are over 65 years of age, and most are women, due to the longer life span for women. However, many children who are deaf-blind are born each year due to accidents, diseases, and genetic problems. Prior to the advent of rubella vaccine, incidence of deaf-blindness was much higher. Although some conditions that cause deaf-blindness may cause other impairments, most children with deaf-blindness are just as intelligent as children without disabilities.

Infants who are deaf-blind require immediate and intense stimulation to increase their awareness of the world around them. Without outside stimulation, infants with deaf-blindness often withdraw and develop behaviors such as rocking, finger waving, and eye rubbing.

Play and recreation activities are excellent forms of stimulation. Even though toddlers with deaf-blindness may have balance difficulties, it is important for them to walk frequently, rather than being carried, because by walking they can develop a clear perception of space and its relationship to their bodies.

People who are deaf-blind can learn leisure skills; however, they may learn in different ways and at different rates than people with hearing and vision. Providing educational and leisure services often requires perseverance of the family and professionals.

How can we include people with deaf-blindness?

The family and the individual are the greatest resource for information on how to provide leisure opportunities for the person with deaf-blindness. We can learn how to best communicate with the person to discover their leisure preferences. Recommendations given for providing services to individuals with visual impairments such as assuring there is a barrier-free environment, and those for individuals with hearing impairments such as teaching through demonstration, are helpful when providing services for participants with deaf-blindness.

Final Thoughts

People who have sensory impairments can successfully participate in leisure services when offered appropriate support. When first meeting individuals with sensory impairments, avoid the assumption that they have limited skills and cognitive abilities; rather, consider that these participants may only have difficulty communicating their preferences and needs. It is our responsibility to discover the best way to communicate with each individual who happens to have a sensory impairment.

All participants with sensory impairments have the right to be served with dignity and respect. The National Federation of the Blind has published the following narrative to communicate courtesies to follow when interacting with people with visual impairments. Many of these recommendations are equally applicable to people with hearing impairments.

> *I am an ordinary person, just blind. You don't need to raise your voice or address me as if I were a child. Don't ask my spouse if I want cream in the coffee—ask me. I may use a long white cane or dog guide to walk independently, or I may ask to take your arm. Let me decide. And please don't grab my arm. Let me take yours. I'll keep a half-step behind to anticipate curbs and steps. I want to know who's in the room with me. Speak to me when you enter. And please introduce me to the others. Include the children and tell me if there's a cat or dog. A partially opened door to a room, cabinet, or car can be a hazard to me. Please be considerate.*
>
> *I have no trouble with ordinary table skills and can manage with no help. Don't avoid words like "see." I use them, too. I'm always glad to see you. Please don't talk about the "wonderful compensations" of blindness. My sense of smell, touch, and hearing didn't improve when I became blind. I rely on them more and therefore may get more information through those senses, but that's all. If I'm your houseguest, show me the bathroom, closet, dresser, window, and the light switch. I like to know whether the lights are on, so please tell me. I'll discuss blindness with you and answer all your questions if you're curious, but it's an old story to me. I have as many other interests as you do.*
>
> *Don't think of me as just "a blind person." I'm just a person who happens to be blind. In all 50 states, the law requires drivers to yield the right-of-way when they see my white cane. Only the blind may carry white canes. You see more blind persons today walking alone, not because there are more of us, but because more of us have learned to make our own way.*

Discussion Questions

1. What is the difference between blindness and low vision?
2. What is acuity?
3. What is the visual field?
4. What are considerations for inclusion of individuals with visual impairments?
5. What are the differences among the terms 'deaf,' 'hearing impairment,' and 'hard-of-hearing'?
6. What is the difference between pre-lingual deafness and post-lingual deafness?
7. What are decibels? How are they related to each of the categories of hearing loss?
8. What are the three basic types of hearing impairments?
9. What is a hertz? How does it affect hearing?
10. What are considerations for inclusion of individuals with hearing impairments?

Mary Jane Owen lives in Washington, D.C., where she is Executive Director of Disability Focus, Inc., as well as Executive Director of National Catholic Office for Persons with Disabilities. She also works as a freelance writer and public speaker. Mary Jane's loss of sight in 1972 was the result of a hereditary ophthalmic disorder. An inner ear dysfunction caused hearing impairment and severe loss of balance, which requires her to use a wheelchair.

Photo by Lynda Greer

Mary Jane's Story

I'm a lot of things rolled into one package: laughter and tears; triumphs and defeats; dreams and disappointments; foolishness and wit; self-concern and willingness to sacrifice for others. Sometimes I wonder how I manage to balance so many differing abilities and disabilities. I'm proud of my American heritage and humble before those who have prevailed without my advantages.

I'm a strong, intelligent, principled, articulate, and very stubborn woman (who happens to be blind, partially hearing, and a wheelchair user) who will probably continue to fill roles I consider essential in the struggle to create opportunities and allow my species to fulfill its potential.

I was born to young parents who cared about racism and a religious life. I gained my sense of women's roles when my mother assumed total responsibilities following the death of my father when I was six. From my family I gained an inquiring mind, a strong attractive body, a sense of moral obligation to others, an orientation toward art and literature, and a life-long interest in ideas and education.

Several years ago it became evident to me that the risks and stresses of the living process itself bring assorted impairments but also awaken one of the evolving joys of life. Therefore, I recognize the power of experiences I would never have selected for myself. Through them I have gained a firm knowledge of the power of the human spirit and its drive toward self-determination. The weakest among us is empowered by a dream of possibilities and the gift of "being."

Chapter 24
People, Inclusion, and Assistive Technology

C. Anthony Cunningham is an attorney in Decatur, Georgia. Born with a detached retina and glaucoma, he was totally blind by the age of 23.

Photo by Lynda Greer

In Memory
After the publication of this text's first edition, C. Anthony Cunningham died.
His photo and story are included in the third edition as a memorial.

C. Anthony's Story

My eyesight was never any good, but nobody really knew for a long time. My mother worked in domestic and restaurant service; my father was a heavy equipment operator. They stayed busy, working and raising 10 kids. Of course when I started to school, I had to deal with it. I developed certain "tricks of the trade" to compensate and conceal my poor vision. They worked pretty well most of the time. I went through school as a sighted person and graduated a quarter early. But by the time I was 17, I was legally blind in my left eye and had no vision in my right.

Between 1973 and 1978, my sight deteriorated rapidly, but after working for three years I was finally able to start college . . . while still working, in 1976. In 1978, I began to come to grips with the fact of my blindness. I quit working and took time off from school to do rehabilitation training. During this time I came to the realization that I'm me, blind or not blind, and that was fine. After the time in rehab training, I had the confidence to go back to college full-time.

Since I was young I've wanted to be in a helping profession, to do something socially responsible. I grew up hearing the cries of the sixties and seventies, aware of the need to create social change. So while in college I decided to become a criminal lawyer . . . to help those accused of crimes. I'm not talking about corporate types, rich people who hire big names for big money. I mean the little guy, usually not much money, no real understanding of the system, who is in trouble and scared. For five years after law school I worked on the civil side of poverty law practice for the Atlanta, Georgia, Legal Aid Society and now I'm practicing on my own. I opened my office in early 1990. It was a big step. There were no guarantees it will work out. But it was a step I had to take.

Ability is of little account without opportunity.

-Napoleon Bonaparte

Orientation Activity: What's New?

Directions Alone: Read the following scenario and identify the technological advances that were not available to people just 50 years ago.

> *Carlos leaned back in his chair, took off his glasses, and rubbed his eyes. It had been a productive afternoon at the computer and time had slipped away. Gazing out the window, he was surprised to see that it was dusk and the streetlights were on. A glance at the digital clock confirmed the time as 6:06 p.m. and he had not started dinner. Carlos saved his document and then hurried to the kitchen. This would be a good night for the frozen gourmet dinners. Placing them in the microwave, he turned his attention to the remaining portion of the meal. By the time the aroma of chicken and rice filled the kitchen, Carlos had whipped an instant chocolate mousse in the blender, started the coffeemaker, and put a loaf of brown-and-serve French bread in the oven. Place mats and tableware were put into place just as he heard the automatic garage door begin to open. Carlos rolled his wheelchair into the living room to turn on the CD player and ignite the gas log. At 6:30 p.m., Jennifer walked in the house to find her smiling Carlos, a fire, her favorite music, and wonderful smells. It was good to be home!*

Directions with Others: Move about the room with your list, find a person, and discuss your impression of the paragraph. Once the other person has done the same to you move on to another person until you are given a signal to stop.

Debriefing: Innovations appear so rapidly that we quickly forget the way things used to be. Many people cannot remember or were not born yet when there were televisions without remote controls and kitchens without a microwave oven.

The scenario above has many examples of inventions not available 60 years ago, including the computer, automatic streetlights, digital clock, frozen dinners, microwave oven, instant chocolate mousse, blender, automatic coffeemaker, brown-and-serve French bread, convection oven, automatic garage door opener, CD player, and gas log. Consider the following questions when reflecting on the orientation activity:

- What are some technological advances that may increase leisure opportunities for people with disabilities?
- Why is technology important to consider relative to leisure participation of people with disabilities?
- What is meant by the phrase "assistive technology"?

Introduction

Advances in computers and other technology have helped individuals with disabilities to be included into society by increasing their mobility, communication, and opportunities to learn. Technological supports have come a long way in the past century. Gallagher (1994, p. 31) emphasized this point as he discussed wheelchairs and braces in the 1920s:

> *Wheelchairs were large, bulky, wooden wicker contrivances, which could not be folded for travel, could not be carried up steps, could only with great difficulty be propelled up curbs, and could rarely pass through narrow bathroom doors. It was virtually impossible to live an independent life confined to such a chair. Braces were heavy iron and leather—difficult enough for a limb with normal muscle power to handle, and painful, tiring, and awkward for an impaired limb. Various pieces of iron, cage-like equipment and frames—painful and ugly—were used to prevent increased deformity caused by growth and muscle imbalance.*

People with disabilities can be assisted by technology because in many cases programs are self-paced, provide opportunities for practice, and can be individualized. However, since use of assistive technology is a very individual experience, it is important to think about differences in skills and interests of participants when considering use of different assistive technologies.

Professionals who see the leisure-related potential of computers and adapted devices and who are also interested in advancing the independence of people they serve contribute to a growing interest in assistive technology. Although assistive technology can improve the lives of people with disabilities, its cost is significant and probably many more people could benefit from assistive technology if they could afford it.

Leisure service providers are encouraged to promote the use of assistive technology whenever possible and to seek ways to support acquisition of such devices, systems, and services. By incorporating technology into inclusive leisure services, participants with disabilities can increase their independence, become more expressive and creative, make more choices, and improve their self-images. The following questions will be addressed in this chapter:

- What is assistive technology?
- How can technology improve physiological functioning?
- What are considerations for inclusion with technology that improves physiological functioning?
- How can technology enhance skills?
- What are considerations for inclusion with technology that enhances skills?
- How can technology help to control the environment?
- What are considerations for inclusion with technology that helps to control the environment?
- How can animals be of assistance?
- What are considerations for inclusion with people who use assistance animals?
- How can technology expand experiences?
- What are considerations for inclusion with technology that expands experiences?

What is assistive technology?

Technological developments have made it possible for people with disabilities to participate in previously inaccessible leisure opportunities. *Technology* is the use of systematic procedures to produce outcomes that require less work and that are more uniform and predictable than can be produced by unassisted effort.

Technological changes enhance skills and talents, increase a sense of control, and broaden the scope of activities. Technology can help people overcome barriers by supporting independence and self-reliance and provide opportunities for them to do things for themselves. Many technological advances and conveniences have transformed the quality of life for people who have disabilities.

Assistive technology can help people with disabilities overcome limitations and perform tasks that might otherwise not be possible. *Assistive technology* are devices and services used by people with disabilities to compensate for functional limitations and to enhance learning, independence, mobility, communication, environmental control, and choice. Referencing the Individuals with Disabilities Education Improvement Act of 2004 (IDEA, 2004), Bausch and Ault (2008, p. 6) identified assistive technology as:

> *Any item, piece of equipment, or product system, whether acquired commercially off the shelf, modified, or customized, that is used to increase, maintain, or improve functional capabilities of a child with a disability that does not include medical devices that are surgically implanted.*

Use of assistive technology by individuals with disabilities should increase the likelihood that they will be included in community leisure pursuits. Assistive technologies are devices and techniques used to optimize human function that:

- *enhance existing skills*—computers to help organize thoughts
- *replace missing structures*—prosthetic hand
- *substitute structures*—wheelchairs for mobility instead of legs
- *provide alternative means of function*—speech synthesizer
- *minimize environmental barriers*—universal design of buildings

Technological tools that restore or extend human functions are called **assistive technology devices**. Today many assistive devices exist to help people with disabilities learn more efficiently, communicate more effectively, live more independently, and experience leisure more easily.

Assistive technology devices include adaptive toys, wheelchairs, augmentative communication systems, and many other items that have been modified, or customized to increase, maintain, or improve the function of individuals with disabilities. Mann and Lane (1991, p. 7) offered the following description of assistive devices:

> *New assistive devices for persons with disabilities are based on technologies from many fields. Computer-based devices (hard technology) come from the electronics industry, while applications (soft technology) come from health and education. Controls, switches, and robotics are based on advances in the industrial and aerospace programs. Commercial and military developments generate new composite materials useful for mobility devices. Advances in biotechnology will generate unimaginable devices and functions for persons with disabilities.*

The next section of the chapter examines how assistive technology can enhance independence and promote interdependence and allow people with disabilities to:

- improve physiological functioning
- enhance skills
- control their environment
- utilize animal assistance
- expand their experiences

Meet the Mechanically Inclined Family

Bill likes to tell friends that his family is "mechanically inclined," or, more accurately, they are "mechanical." When his rheumatoid arthritis finally became too painful, Bill had two artificial hip replacements. One year later, he is able to take his grandchildren fishing again.

Bill's wife, Edna, is able to go with them now that she has a heart pacemaker implanted. Their oldest son, Rodney, is also enjoying better health since being fitted with an insulin pump to automatically monitor and treat his diabetes.

Finally, Bill is happy that his granddaughter, Celeste, has received permanent dental implants to replace the teeth she lost in a fall from her bicycle.

How can technology improve physiological functioning?

Devices implanted in or attached to the body to simulate more typical functioning may sound like science fiction, but they are real and making differences in the lives of individuals with disabilities. Since there are too many innovations to discuss them all, and more are being developed rapidly, this section only provides an overview of only some of the many advances. Technology designed to improve physiological functioning can help to:

- manage health problems
- control one's body
- improve muscle tone
- promote hearing

Manage Health Problems

Neuroimplantation is a procedure that implants electrodes on the spinal cord, in limbs, or directly in the brain. The electrical impulses generated help to alleviate dysfunctions such as seizures and spasticity that are found in individuals who have cerebral palsy, closed head injuries, spinal-cord injuries, and multiple sclerosis.

To benefit people with heart problems, the *artificial pacemaker* is a small device permanently implanted under the skin of the chest wall. A pacemaker regulates the heart rate by sending out electrical impulses that force the heart to contract rhythmically.

Control One's Body

Technology has enabled people with disabilities to have more control over their bodies. Personal *cooling systems* help individuals with spinal-cord injuries to regulate body temperature. Custom-made *gloves* assist those who use wheelchairs to experience less strain on their hands and wrists.

People with disabilities may need assistance with personal care, and so they may welcome products that enable more privacy and independence. An instrument is available that uses completely external *ultrasound* to inform individuals who have no lower body sensation when it is appropriate to mechanically empty their bladder. Technological advances have made it possible for men with paralysis due to spinal-cord injury to father children and for women with disabilities to conceive and carry pregnancies to term.

Improve Muscle Tone

Research continues on ways people with paralyzing disabilities might be able to walk. *Neurorehabilitation* is an experimental system of stimulating muscles to contract by sending electrical impulses to them through surface electrodes. In addition to enabling a few people with partial paraplegia to walk again, the technology has greater potential for the improvement of muscle tone and circulation in many people with paralysis. The alternate contracting and relaxing of the muscle via electrical impulse helps to build muscle mass, which improves the health of the skin, helps to build bone, and increases cardiovascular health.

Promote Hearing

Several instruments have been created to assist hearing processes. Approved by the U.S. Food and Drug Administration in 1985, *cochlear implants* are electrode devices that are surgically implanted in the mastoid bone behind the ear to stimulate the hearing nerve. Although they do not restore total hearing, they have helped some people to gain some understanding of spoken words.

What are considerations for inclusion with technology that improves physiological functioning?

Biotechnology holds enormous potential for increasing leisure experiences for people with disabilities. Often we are unaware that participants are using biotechnological aids. The key is a willingness to work with individuals and facilitate their leisure involvement.

Meet Stephen, Who Enjoys a Joke and an Occasional Dance

Berger (1992) wrote about Stephen, possibly the world's most brilliant physicist and best known as the developer of the black hole theory.

> *Stephen, who has amyotrophic lateral sclerosis (Lou Gehrig's disease), rolled noiselessly into the darkened conference room accompanied by two nurses. Fingering a control panel with the partial motion remaining in his left hand, he positioned himself at the back of the center aisle, quietly attended the lectures of his fellow physicists, and took in their illustrative slides. When he had a comment to interject, he fingered the same panel, triggering an artificial voice that emanated from somewhere beneath him.*

Over lunch a friendly discussion ensued about why Americans often groan rather than laugh at puns. Was it back-handed appreciation or were they seriously offended? As the debate proceeded, Stephen began fingering his panel and gazed around the table, eyes sparkling mischievously, and a voice beneath him said, in elevated tones, "I am trying to get my synthesizer to groan."

During the last night of the conference, participants were bused to a flamenco club for dinner and entertainment. Guitarists, singers, and dancers took to the stage, gave an accomplished performance, and then invited the physicists to dance with them. When one of the dancers made her way through the tables to dance in front of Stephen, I thought it might cross that nebulous boundary into bad taste. Here was a young woman stomping her feet in front of a man who could barely move. Other physicists stood aside to make room. Grinning asymmetrically, Stephen programmed his chair to move back and forth in synchronicity with the dancer. As correctly as his fellow physicists, Stephen ended the conference by dancing flamenco.

The impact of assistive technology on an individual's life is immediately apparent when noting the accomplishments of this world-renowned physicist who uses a motorized wheelchair to help him with mobility and a computer and voice synthesizer to facilitate his communication. In covering one of his lectures, the following report was published in the *Athens Daily News* ("Salt Lake City" 1995, p. 2A):

Leave it to Stephen Hawking to pack a stadium with talk of quantum physics and black holes. A record 9,185 people flocked to the University of Utah's Huntsman arena Monday night to hear the physicist discuss those subjects and more. "It's a bit like a rock concert, and shows physics can be as popular as heavy metal," Hawking said at a reception.

How can technology enhance skills?

Stephen is able to continue his work because he has a combination of human and technological assistance. For a person with severe disabilities, no amount of computerized, robotic, or biomechanical equipment can completely substitute for human assistance with activities of daily living. People, not machines, make technological adaptations work for people with disabilities. The application of technology is especially meaningful for people with severe disabilities. Assistive technology can provide new ways to:

- move better
- speak better
- hear better
- see better

Move Better

For people who cannot see, technological advances such as laser canes and other electronic travel aids help to lead the way. *Electronic travel aids* provide information about objects in the vicinity, including distance, direction, and surface characteristics. The electronic travel aids are most useful in unfamiliar areas but are not preferred in rainy, snowy, or noisy conditions. Sometimes these applications are accessed via a smartphone.

Power wheelchairs have undergone major improvements since the first motor was attached to a manual chair. Lightweight materials, improved shock-absorbing features, better batteries, and other advances have created more reliable, customized chairs. Individuals who have cervical spinal-cord injuries, severe developmental disabilities, post-polio weakness syndrome, or other degenerative disease processes typically use power chairs.

Power chairs have been developed that roll forward and back and raise the individual to a standing position, because periods of standing can have positive mental and physical effects. An individual with such a chair could stand to work at a drawing board, or stand facing others at a party. Manual and power chairs are not the only option for moving about the community. To illustrate the capacity of some power wheelchairs Claudia Paniagua (2000, p. 13) stated:

> *Because of the severity of my disability (my bones break easily), I am unable to walk. So I use an assistive technology device, which is a power chair. This chair is not like you might think of a wheelchair. It has a neat feature which allows me to go up to five feet high and all the way down to the floor. It's a great help because now I can reach for things that are up on a counter, and I can reach for things that I drop on the floor. I can also look people in the eye.*

Individuals who have arthritis or multiple sclerosis often use *battery-powered scooters*. These compact scooters in which a person sits are often collapsible to fit into the trunk of a car. In addition, specialized *battery-operated cushions* are available that automatically shift the pressure points of the cushion at regular intervals to prevent skin ulcers.

To transport a power chair requires a van with specialized lifts and other equipment. Under the requirements of the ADA, metropolitan areas have power-wheelchair-accessible buses and vans.

Individuals with disabilities are also able to operate their cars and vans with adaptations. *Automobile hand controls* installed on the steering column can brake and accelerate the vehicle. For those who do not have the range of motion to turn a standard steering wheel, there are *miniature wheels and joysticks* as substitutes. There is a joystick-type invention that replaces the steering wheel, throttle, and brakes of a converted van. A person who can move a joystick only three inches is able to drive independently.

Speak Better

We communicate in a variety of ways, including vocalizations, hand gestures, body movements, and facial expressions. Acquisition of speech allows people to join the community of language users who share conversation about objects, actions, and events. When children fail to develop functional spoken language, their access to topics and partners is limited.

Freedom of expression is a highly prized right for many. However, many people with significant speech disabilities routinely experience isolation, discrimination, segregation, illiteracy, institutionalization, unemployment, poverty, and despair. Due to the lack of understandable speech, these individuals are perceived to be unable to direct their own lives—a perception that often leads to deprivation of their most basic civil rights and liberties.

To address the challenges experienced by people with speech impairments, they can be encouraged to use augmentative and alternative communication devices, services, and supports. Since speech alone may not be a viable mode of communication for many people with disabilities, the use of these systems should be welcomed so that individuals can express preferences, make choices, and gain some control over their daily activities and events.

An *augmentative and alternative communication* (AAC) system describes the symbols, aids, strategies, and techniques that are used by individuals whose disabilities prevent typical communication. Systems can be simple paper charts or elaborate computers. Systems can utilize pictures in the form of simple line drawings, full-color photographs, or picture symbols. Information can be recorded into these systems via keyboard or by touching the display on the monitor.

AAC systems are typically about the size and shape of a large computer keyboard and can be mounted on a wheelchair, desk, or table in front of the individual. Several models of AAC systems are the size of an electronic organizer and can fit into a person's pocket. Some units even come in a choice of colors. Once the device is selected, the communication options are customized to the needs of the person.

Some AAC systems operate as a simple *visual display format* projected when a person activates the system. The advantage of such a system is that it is silent and can be used anywhere. One disadvantage is the tendency of the listener to focus on the system, rather than the face of the person who is communicating. Another disadvantage is that the person cannot communicate with anyone who is not able to read the screen, such as a young child, someone in another room, a person who has a visual impairment, or one who is not literate.

It is important to consider the appeal of the AAC system.

For example, Light, Drager, and Nemser (2004) suggested that if these systems are highly appealing, they are more likely to: be used by children with communicate needs, enhance a person's self-esteem, and facilitate interactions with other children.

Other AAC systems have auditory output in the form of digitized speech that converts the written message to sound. Manufacturers of AAC systems offer a choice of different male and female voices with some sounding like children and others like adults. Digitized speech can enable people to participate in discussions and to have a voice and speak for themselves. For active people, small, portable devices are available that can be used for both receptive and expressive communication.

Romski, Sevcik, and Wilkinson (1994) found that individuals with speech impairments eagerly integrated the use of AAC systems into their repertoire of vocalizations and gestures. Subsequently, Romski and colleagues (1999) reported that use of speech-output communication systems had a positive effect on the communication of people with speech impairments.

Statements of a man interviewed by Bryen and colleagues (1995, p. 85) who has a significant speech disability and who began using an AAC system called a TouchTalker support this conclusion:

> *I am very active in my church. Up until the time when I got my TouchTalker, most of the people in the church never interacted with me. I think they were intimidated because they had a very difficult time communicating with me. But now, everybody is very friendly with me.*

Hear Better

Technology has drastically changed the way people with hearing impairments socialize and experience leisure. The ADA has helped support many advances in technology that have allowed people to hear better. Walker (2001, p. 4) spoke to this idea:

> *The 1990 Americans with Disabilities Act, which outlawed discriminatory practices against the disabled, gave deaf people the legislative muscle to make headway as never before. A new "can-do" attitude and sense of pride soon emerged. Then, as the 1990s saw a virtual explosion of technological advances; deaf people finally had the tools to fully enter the mainstream.*

Individuals who have natural speech but are not able to produce volume may be assisted with a ***personal amplifier***, a small, portable, battery-powered device with adjustable volume. The amplifier enables the person to carry on conversations, speak up in class, or make public presentations. If the larynx, a person's voice box, is removed, speech is still possible with an electronic device held against the throat that converts vibrations into sound. In addition, there are cordless infrared headsets that allow people to listen to a television or radio at a higher volume than others nearby.

Another innovation, ***computerized eyeglasses***, converts spoken language to print and display it at the bottom of the lens. This technology is most useful for individuals whose hearing loss occurred after their spoken language had developed.

The most common and best-known assistive hearing device, the ***hearing aid***, improves hearing in many instances, but it does not correct hearing nor does it necessarily restore hearing to normal levels. A hearing aid will, however, lessen the degree of severity of hearing loss and enable the user to hear many previously inaudible sounds.

If a hearing aid is recommended, there are many types from which to choose. These range from tiny, all-in-the-ear models for mild to moderate losses, to large body aids for profound impairments. Hearing aids may also be worn in eyeglasses or behind the ear. Some people require only one aid that is identified as ***monaural*** while others gain the most benefit from two that is known as ***binaural***. Many hearing aids are equipped with a telephone switch, which enables the sound from the telephone to go directly into the hearing aid, greatly increasing clarity. Also, for people who require two hearing aids there are now systems that allow the hearing aids to share sonic information and automatically send the appropriate sound to each ear.

The ***ear mold*** is a vital component of any hearing aid. Some ear molds are made from a solid plastic material, others from a more pliable substance. Some are simple tubular inserts, while other molds fill the entire cavity of the outer ear. They are made in a manner similar to taking an impression for dentures. Like hearing aids, ear molds eventually need replacement. Danger signs are whistling noises indicating the ear mold no longer fits snugly in the ear.

In various situations, and especially with a severe to profound loss, a hearing aid may not be enough. In addition, technology has been helpful for those who have hearing impairments but are not candidates for implants. While hearing aids are helpful for some individuals, others find the background noise that is picked up to be very distracting. ***Amplification systems*** consist of a wireless microphone worn by the speaker, and a headset or insert ear mold worn by the listener. This may be the ideal solution in an instructional situation, allowing the instructor to move about freely, all the while "broadcasting" to an audience of one.

Another instrument, an ***electronic metronome device*** worn outside the ear, has been successful in reducing stuttering for some individuals. Finally, a hearing-aid-type device is available to mask the ringing of the ear caused by tinnitus. The device produces a soothing white noise, which makes the ringing less distracting for many individuals.

Modern technology has provided a variety of ***assistive listening devices*** for telephones, conference rooms, classrooms, theaters, and places of worship. They include portable and permanent telephone amplifiers, direct audio-input devices, personal infrared systems, alarm systems, and telecaptioning devices. The many devices available for people with hearing impairments allow them to be included in interactions with other people.

Alerting systems, also identified as "signalers," allow people with hearing impairments to be aware of audible sounds or warnings such as those generated from telephones, smoke alarms, and timers.

> For example, a flashing signaler can consist of a single lamp attached to a receiver or several lights strategically placed in a building that flash in response to an alarm. As another option, a vibrating signaler can be used to notify a person.

Text telephones, often referred to as TTYs, were invented in 1964 and enable people who have severe hearing impairments to use the telephone. The TTY resembles a small computer keyboard with a telephone modem and a small liquid crystal display (LCD) screen to transmit coded signals across the standard telephone network. To use the TTY, a person dials the telephone and places the handset on a couple (modem) which then transmits an electronic signal across the phone line to another person who has a TTY. Once a connection is made, the individuals type their messages to each other and the messages are displayed on the LCD panel. If a person who has a TTY wants to contact a person who does not have a TTY, then the person dials a specific number that connects the person to an operator equipped with a TTY. The operator then contacts the person to be called and acts as a relay as the operator listens to the person who does not have a TTY and then types the message to the person using the TTY. The ADA stipulates that telephone companies provide telecommunication relay services 24 hours a day, seven days a week, at no additional charge.

As some technology advances, the need for other technology wanes. For example, there are now telephones that are captioned; that is, they display on a lighted screen written word-for-word text of everything the caller speaks.

See Better

Computers hold promise for people who have visual impairments. Characters can be displayed on the computer screen in very large type and with varying degrees of color and contrast to assist readers who have reduced vision. *Video magnifiers* can be used with computers but also are available in self-contained portable units that can be more easily transported than an entire computer system. Printers are also available that produce messages in Braille or raised standard print.

A variety of assistive technology devices available do not necessarily help a person to see better, but improve the ability of people with severe visual impairments to experience leisure. In addition to services that place books on to audiotapes, *reading scanners* can convert text to verbal output and allow individuals to acquire the information presented in books.

Cell phones keep people in touch with their families and friends are available that vibrate to notify a person of a message and then present the message verbally. Written material can be presented in alternative formats.

The computer can be an effective way to disseminate information to people with visual impairment as long as sites follow ADA access guidelines. *Video and audio recordings* can be used to present information to people that has typically only been presented in text. Videos on television and radio advertisements inform people who may not be able to read flyers and notices placed in the newspaper.

> For example, Menacker and Batshaw (1997, p. 235) reported that text can be converted to Braille using a machine that scans typed text and converts it into a tactile stimulus of vibrating pins. Another system converts material received by a computer into Braille. Computer printouts can be converted into speech, and software programs provide speech capacity to a personal computer. There are verbal note-taking devices and talking calculators. Audio books are generally available at bookstores and libraries.

What are considerations for inclusion with technology that enhances skills?

Many people with a significant hearing loss will not choose to participate in activities where conversation is an important element unless they know that there will be others who use the same communication mode with whom they can communicate. Oliva and Simonsen (2000) offered the following suggestions to leisure service providers:

> For people who are deaf and hard of hearing, the concepts of right to leisure, quality of life, and barrier removal involve much more than just removing barriers between leader and follower, providing a TTY, or employing a person who signs at the community center. Instead of only concentrating on making the facility accessible so that people who are deaf and hard-of-hearing can recreate alongside their hearing counterparts, the professional might consider expending more energy in the area of social accessibility—that is, promoting social interactions with others.

People of all levels of cognitive ability have used technological systems with positive results. However, simply providing an individual with an AAC system, a mobility aid, or a sophisticated piece of sports equipment does not enable them to have a better quality of life if they have not learned how to use the device. It is helpful for us to ask about the skills and interests of the participant who uses assistive technology.

For example, if a participant enjoys playing video games, an AAC might be programmed to say, "I want to play video games." Other words to include in an AAC system might be the names of the leisure service providers, activities the participant enjoys, rooms or spaces in recreation centers such as the pool and baseball field, and personal needs, such as going to the restroom.

We can use computers to assess the preferences of program participants, such as the toy preferences of children with severe disabilities. Such information is useful in both the recreation setting and in the home to provide the individual with satisfying choices.

If people use assistive technology that results in their communicating in different ways, it is critical to give them adequate time to engage in meaningful dialogue. We must learn to give people our attention, wait for their contribution, listen to them, and respond accordingly.

Often when people use alternative forms of communication there are times when silence occurs. We must resist the temptation to fill that silence with our words; rather, we should remain silent and allow the person adequate time to contribute. Crossley (1999, p. 9) described Joe, a person with cerebral palsy, who wrote that:

> *Some people have asked me questions and walked away before I point to a word or answer.*

Meet J. D., Who Makes His World Move

Hallem (1991) reported on J. D., who has quadriplegia and is unable to move his arms or legs yet can walk his dachshunds, escape a house fire, answer the phone and set his burglar alarm—all without any assistance. These tasks are completed with the assistance of an electronic box the size of a clock radio.

The high-tech device rests on his bedroom dresser, lighting up in red. This environmental control unit is a sophisticated, centralized system that is connected to his wheelchair and almost every electronic device in his home—from his TV, video player, and personal computer to the back door that swings open for his dogs. Using either a mouth stick or a sip-and-puff mechanical straw attached to his wheelchair, he can activate these systems and function without someone constantly at his side. That independence is important to J. D.

How can technology help to control the environment?

Environmental control units can increase independence and personal safety. Manufacturers advertise the following capabilities: control lights, electric beds, electric doors, appliances, and TVs; make and answer phone calls; detect intruders; activate an alarm to wake you in the morning; and awaken an attendant if you fall out of bed. These services can be controlled by the owner's voice in any language. The Prentke Romich Company (1992) that manufactures environmental control devices sums up the advantages of their system with the words:

> *If you can move your head . . . you can move your world.*

Technology is advancing at an extremely fast pace, and there are numerous tools available to equip homes to be *smart*. Tony Gentry (2009, p. 210) provided a definition of *smart homes*.

> *Within the disability community, the term "smart home" typically refers to the use of electronic assistive technology, including electronic aids to daily living, assistive technology for cognition, wireless connectivity, and other tools that provide support to people with disability in the home setting.*

The following is a listing of classes of technology identified by Frances Aldrich (2003) that can be used as resources for developing *smart homes*:

- *intelligent objects*—doors or window shades that open with a remote control switch or motion-activated lighting
- *wired or wireless networks for information exchange*—computer controlled thermostat or lighting
- *electronic networks reaching beyond home for information exchange*— automated billing
- *computers that analyze activity patterns and manage appliances accordingly*—a wrist-worn sensor that monitors vital signs and falls that trigger messages to off-site caregivers

Technology can help people to find their way around public buildings. One such system consists of small transmitters placed throughout public buildings such as shopping malls and museums. Individuals with visual or cognit̶i̶v̶e̶ impairments obtain a pocket-size receiver when they enter the building.

As the person moves through the environment, the transmitter provi̶d̶e̶s̶ information in multiple languages, as needed on the location of the near̶e̶s̶t̶ exit, public phone, elevator, restroom, or office. A typical message might̶ "Welcome to the City Hall Second Street entrance—nine steps up to dou̶b̶l̶e̶ door entry, Verbal Landmark Directory to your right." The person may rep̶e̶a̶t̶ the message as often as desired and at the desired volume.

Dan Sadowsky (2002, p. 6) reported on the impact of environmental con̶t̶r̶o̶l̶ systems on the life of Jimmy Brooks:

> *When the phone rings at Jimmy Brooks' home in Montgomery, Alabama, he needs only to say the word "hello" to answer it.*

Assistive technology devices are essential to Jimmy's lifestyle. He gets around in a joystick-controlled power wheelchair and relies on friends to drive him in his life-equipped van. He uses the latest voice recognition software to surf the Internet and send email, and [with assistive technology he] controls everything from the temperature of his apartments to the channels on this television with mouth stick-operated remote control units. "All these little gadgets," he says, "make it possible for me to live on my own."

What are considerations for inclusion with technology that helps to control the environment?

Technological advances have greatly improved opportunities for individuals with disabilities to enjoy a wide range of recreational and leisure choices. For young participants, toys and games have been adapted to utilize switches and computers.

Interactive computer programs allow children to touch the computer screen and have immediate results. Popular children's books are available in interactive computer versions with voice narration and sound effects. When the child touches the portion of the screen that shows a bird in the tree, for example, the bird chirps and flies away. Touching the mailbox causes it to open, allowing a frog to jump out one time, an ocean wave to roll out the next. The random display of these many interactive choices and finding unexpected things in unexpected places entertains and teaches young children.

Older children enjoy making popcorn, using a blender to make a milkshake, watching videos, and playing video games using electronic adaptations. Adult hobbies can be made more accessible by use of such devices as a battery-powered card shuffler for card enthusiasts who have some use of their hands. Poker, blackjack, bridge, and chess are also available in computer versions for one or more players to enjoy. For those who like to sew, electric scissors, and chin-controlled sewing machine power units are a couple of the adaptations available.

Meet Kim and Her Best Friend, Sophie

Kim and Sophie are a familiar sight around the university campus. Like other best friends, they share a dorm room, rely on each other, enjoy ice cream, and spend time together outdoors whenever possible. Sophie walks to class with Kim and waits quietly during the lecture. She always seems to know when Kim is feeling sad and does her best to let her know that she is there for her.

Kim is proud to be seen with Sophie, who always attracts admirers with her golden hair and big brown eyes. Kim likes to tease her boyfriend Lee by telling him that he only hangs around her because he has a crush on Sophie. Lee laughs and responds that he is not interested in younger females, especially the four-legged type who get fleas. Kim's best friend, Sophie, is a 5-year-old golden retriever trained as a dog guide for Kim, who is blind.

How can animals be of assistance?

In addition to the companionship that pets provide, animals can help people with disabilities in a variety of other ways. Animals can assist people with:

- visual impairments
- hearing impairments
- physical limitations
- mental health problems

Assist People with Visual Impairments

Although dogs have aided humans for thousands of years as watchdogs and farm helpers, they have only recently been trained to guide owners who are blind. *Dog guides* for people with visual impairments have enabled thousands of individuals to move about their communities in confidence and safety. To qualify for a dog, an applicant must be between the ages of 16 and 55, be in good health, have good hearing and at least average intelligence, and possess the temperament, emotional stability, and responsibility to maintain a working relationship with the dog. The applicant must be totally blind or without any useful vision that might interfere with reliance on the dog and must also like dogs.

Dog guides require daily exercise and grooming. Generally, dogs are not suitable for children, who may lack the necessary maturity. The applicant and the dog must train together for four weeks at a dog guide school. For these reasons, only 1% of people who are blind actually use a dog.

Assist People with Hearing Impairments

Hearing-ear dogs are trained to assist people who have hearing impairments. Such dogs are often obtained from animal shelters and may be almost any breed.

During a six-month training program, hearing-ear dogs are taught to alert the owner to such sounds as the doorbell ringing, a pot boiling over on the stove, a baby crying, or a smoke detector alarm. The dogs respond to these noises going to the owners and leading them to the cause of the sound. Hearing dogs can be recognized by an orange collar and leash.

Assist People with Physical Limitations

Assistive dogs, who are also called *helper dogs* or *service dogs*, to accompany individuals who have disabilities that affect their balance, such as multiple sclerosis or spinal cord injury. Each dog is trained to help with the specific needs of its owner.

The dogs may be fitted with backpacks to carry objects, or trained to pick up dropped objects, such as pencils and keys. They can turn light switches on and off and provide a stable support for the person when transferring from wheelchair to bed or car. Some dogs can answer the phone and bring it to the owner, change the television channel, push elevator buttons, and pull wheelchairs up the curb. Canine Companions for Independence of Santa Rosa, California, breeds dogs and trains them to respond to approximately 100 instructions before they are placed with the new owner.

Lesser-known animal helpers are *simian aides*, capuchin monkeys that are trained to perform activities of daily living for owners with disabilities. The owner must be able to operate a motorized wheelchair and to operate the equipment needed to signal the monkey. Three-year-old female monkeys receive extensive training in the activities of daily living that are difficult for the owner.

The 5-pound, 18-inch capuchins can retrieve a snack from the refrigerator, open it, feed it to the owner, wipe the owner's mouth, and put the dirty container in the sink. They can brush the owner's hair, hold up a mirror, and return the brush and mirror to the bathroom. The owner directs the monkey through verbal commands or by pointing with a light beam attached to a mouth stick. Fruit-flavored pellets are dispensed from a device attached to the owner's wheelchair to reward the monkey for tasks completed. Only the imagination and patience of the owner and trainer limit the possibilities for simian help. As an added bonus, the little monkeys are affectionate, playful, and fun to watch.

Assist People with Mental Health Problems

Dogs have been trained as companion animals, otherwise known as *therapy dogs*, for some people with depression and mental illness. The affection that an animal gives the person helps to enhance the self-esteem of the owner. Knowing that the dog depends on the owner for food, water, and care can be therapeutic and can encourage the owner to develop relationships.

What are considerations for inclusion with people who use assistance animals?

The ADA guarantees use of animal assistants in public. Leisure service providers responsible to educate all participants about proper etiquette with animal s. The owners can help everyone understand how their animals have been d to respond in public. Most animal aides are very protective of their but will enjoy a kind word and pat when they are not working—only owner has given you permission to approach the animal.

Meet Calandra, Who Enjoys being Creative and Playing with her Friends

Calandra enjoys spending time at the recreation center with her friends. Often she makes her way to the computer lounge where she finds several of her friends playing computer games. They talk about various ways to improve their scores and succeed in the games. One particular game requires the operator to move through a series of mazes. Calandra has studied a magazine that explains strategies for this game. As a result of her preparation and practice, Calandra is very skilled at this game and her friends seek her advice on ways to solve various problems.

After some socializing and playing, Calandra begins using the Internet to complete a school project that requires her to report on birds of South America. She visits several websites that provide her with ample information for her report. While she is on the Web, she checks her e-mail and jots off a quick note to her new pen pal in Argentina.

Before she leaves the recreation center computer lounge, Calandra tries the new painting program that was recently installed on the computers. She loves to use the computer to create artwork. She enjoys the new program and uses it to try a variety of techniques that resemble her favorite type of art, French Impressionism.

Calandra has worked with members of the recreation staff who have been very helpful in finding ways for her to access the computer. Because Calandra has quadriplegia and uses a motorized wheelchair, she is able to access some programs using a sensitive simple switch and other programs she operates more effectively using a joystick. She states that if it were not for the helpful staff, she probably would not come to the recreation center and would go home to do her homework and watch television alone.

How can technology expand experiences?

Many positive experiences associated with leisure involvement have been influenced by technology. Most leisure pursuits contain an element of socialization. Since humans are social creatures, we tend to pursue activities that allow us to interact with other people. Many consider writing to be a form of leisure because it allows us to express ourselves and can bring meaning to our lives. The ability to be creative and engage in artistic endeavors is also considered to be leisure. Virtual reality may simulate various experiences that may not be available at a particular time or place. Finally, technology can help improve people's ability to engage in recreation activities and have fun. This section examines technology's influence on our ability to:

- socialize better
- write better
- create better
- learn and remember better
- recreate better

Socialize Better

A critical aspect of the inclusion of people with disabilities into community recreation programs is the chance to interact with other participants in a socially meaningful way. Computer-based activities can be used to facilitate positive interactions between participants, such as initiating and terminating turn-taking, attending to an object or person, and following instructions. Social skills can be modeled and reacted to by computer simulations, and information can be recorded in portable computers and analyzed quickly for decision-making purposes.

> For example, Simpson, Langone, and Ayres (2004) examined effects of combining video- and computer-based instruction and found that youth showed rapid improvement in social skills. Lau (2000) suggested that practitioners who incorporate computers into their services can facilitate social interactions by modeling social behaviors, praising positive social interactions, structuring cooperative activities, and establishing a system of peer tutoring. Howard, Greyrose, Espinosa, and Beckwith (1996) observed that computer activities facilitated by a practitioner enhanced social play and positive affect of young children with disabilities. Hutinger, Johanson, and Stoneburner (1996) conducted a case study of a child with multiple disabilities and found that using computers was associated with social interactions, cooperation, and exploratory play. Similarly, Margalit (1991) found that children with cognitive limitations who received computerized instruction scored higher on classroom adjustment and social skills than peers who did not receive such instruction.

Write Better

Computers enable people to write more rapidly and legibly than by hand. Individuals who have difficulty manipulating the letters on a keyboard can benefit from software that uses a *scanning system* to help a person write. With one such device installed, the computer displays the alphabet, numbers, and important symbols on the bottom of the screen and slowly moves the cursor across the display. The person hits the switch when the desired letter is highlighted and it is then pasted on the screen.

By selecting one letter at a time, the person can type an entire document by pressing one switch. The switch could be placed under a person's hand, foot, elbow, or against the cheek. Blowing air through a sip-and-puff control also trigger the switch.

Computers are also able to respond to speech. People who cannot access ard because of physical limitations, or people who have attention s, can enter their thoughts through speech. This allows participants it option and can create situations that help the people express their ugh the written word.

Electronic notetakers allow people who have severe visual limitations to type in their notes. The notes are then converted to Braille or to speech that will allow individuals with limited sight to access their notes.

Create Better

Computers provide people with a way to experience leisure by offering an outlet for creative expression through the development of artwork. When computers are used, people with a variety of physical and cognitive limitations can participate. People of all ages can enjoy exploring the creative possibilities of a computer.

The computer can help all people, including people with disabilities, draw, paint, and sculpt, thereby promoting their inclusion. The time, energy, and expense associated with purchasing, setting up, and cleaning art materials can be significantly reduced if computers are incorporated into a person's artistic repertoire.

Learn and Remember Better

Virtual reality can be used to help people with disabilities simulate experiences they may encounter when pursuing leisure opportunities in their community. These computer simulations can help people to anticipate and practice how to handle challenging situations that may arise while they are in an environment that social pressure may not be present. Broida and Germann (1999, p. 95) described virtual reality in the following way:

> *Virtual reality refers to an alternative world filled with 3-D computer-generated images that respond to human movements. These simulated images can be enhanced through the use of stereoscopic goggles and fiber-optic-data gloves. Virtual reality integrates computer graphics, body-tracking devices, visual displays, and other sensory input devices to immerse a participant in a computer-generated environment.*

The intent of the project for people with severe physical disabilities described by Broida and Germann was to provide virtual reality situations so that participants' fears could be alleviated and their access enhanced. They reported that comments by participants indicated the value of the virtual reality project in helping them overcome their apprehension of new places. Yang and Poff (2001) expanded the definition in the following way:

> *[virtual reality] also comes in a "nonimmersive" form in which sensory aspects of the virtual environment are presented on a conventional computer monitor and the individual controls his or her movements by means of a joystick or other control devices.*

A variety of personal digital assistants and smartphones can provide people with picture, text, auditory, and video cues. These devices can serve as self-prompting systems for people who may experience challenges remembering to complete tasks or following complex and extended directions.

> Exercising at a fitness club is a leisure pursuit that often presents numerous tasks that contain many steps. Electronic devices can be programmed to remind people of the various steps and repetitions, as well as to identify when it is time to move on to the next exercise station.

Self-prompting systems are designed to help individuals remember to perform and complete tasks without having to rely on external prompts delivered my other people.

> For example, Mechling, Gast, and Seid (2010) examined effects of a personal digital assistant (PDA) on adolescents with moderate intellectual disabilities and found that youth there independently used the PDA (to self-prompt completing cooking recipes and maintained use of the device over time). These findings extend previous research by Mechling and colleagues (Mechling & Gustafson, 2008, 2009; Mechling & Stephens, 2009) who examined video-prompting strategies for youth completing cooking recipes.

Recreate Better

Wheeled sports are enjoyed by people of all ages. Bicycles have been adapted to allow individuals to pedal with the hands instead of the feet, and are available in three-wheel and tandem models. Wheelchair wheels with carbon fiber spokes offer less resistance and facilitate faster acceleration than conventional wheels. Throwing events such as discus, shot put, and javelin are benefiting from an anchor system that utilizes four strong suction pads to hold wheelchairs in place instead of the traditional ropes and rigging systems.

Sailors with disabilities are assisted by specialized systems to adapt racing boats. Those who prefer to spend their time on the water fishing, rather than racing, can do so with a push-button drive system to operate a fishing reel. To facilitate boating, a weatherproof, salt-water resistant portable lift device has been developed to transfer sailors from their wheelchairs on and off watercraft. Mono-skis, sit-skis, and bi-skis enable both water and snow enthusiasts who have physical limitations to enjoy skiing.

For those who want to participate in rigorous outdoor activities, all-terrain cles can be adapted. Golf, scuba diving, fencing, and archery—the list of ties transformed by technology continues to grow.

hletes are being equipped with artificial limbs that rely on various ogies such as Bluetooth to help the prostheses respond more effectively to the desires of the individual. In an article in the *ESPN Magazine*, Eric Adelson (2008, p. 53–54) reported that:

> *Soon, prosthetics wearers will be able to turn, cut, and twist, motions difficult with current technology but essential in most sports. Next-gen research will shift from replacing the human leg to improving it, just as pharmaceuticals have shifted from restoring to enhancing. Sports have always been about progress: higher, faster, stronger. Technology, though, is quickly outpacing evolution, and few know how to respond.*

In the article titled *Let 'Em Play*, Aldeson profiled eight athletes who are benefiting from new technologies associated with prosthetic limbs.

- Jarrod Fields, who lost his leg in Iraq, learned to use his prosthetic leg to allow him to dunk a <u>basketball</u>.
- Anthony Burruto is an adolescent who can hurl a <u>baseball</u> fast and is learning how to use his prosthetic legs so he can quickly field bunts.
- Jeff Skiba, at age 23, has learned to use his leg prosthesis to <u>high jump</u> almost 7 feet.
- Willie Stewart helped develop a prosthetic arm with a supple wrist that could hold an oar, allowing him to <u>kayak</u> the Grand Canyon rapids. Then he developed a bike arm with a rigid wrist that rotates to a handlebar, permitting him to be a competitive <u>mountain biker</u>.
- Alex Zanardi worked with his crew to develop a <u>race car</u> that accommodates his prosthetic legs, resulting in two World Touring Car Championships.
- Goalie Mike Ginal used a leg prosthesis that distributes energy from heel to toe to tend goal for Harvard and now plays <u>hockey</u> in a Chicago recreation league.
- Sarah Robertson uses her prosthetic leg to help her win <u>triathlons;</u> her athletic success has been a spring board for her motivational speaking and modeling, resulting in celebrity status.

Although these prostheses are providing a technological solution for athletes with disabilities as they participate competitively in sports with people without disabilities, there are people and organizations that are restricting the use of such advances. The other athlete profiled by Adelson (2008, p. 54) was Oscar Pistorius. The article included a description of Pistorious' unfortunate and ironic journey to be an Olympic sprinter:

> *On January 14, the IAAF banned South African sprinter Oscar Pistorius from the Olympics because tests found that his Cheetah Flex-Foot legs, which look like J-shape spatulas, give him an advantage over runners with human legs. Sprint on his carbon prosthetics, Pistorius looks to be bounding springs. The IAAF study says the Cheetahs are more e than human legs, so Pistorius uses less oxygen than s*

fast able-bodied runners. In essence, the IAAF's contention is that running is too easy for him, so the governing body banned "any technical . . . device that provides the user with an advantage over another athlete." Pistorius was crushed before he had a chance to qualify at his country's trials.

Another way for people to recreate who have physically disabilities is through virtual reality.

Reid and Campbell (2006) used virtual reality with children who had cerebral palsy and noted the potential of virtual-reality video games to create a context for these youth to play virtual games such as volleyball or snowboarding with their peers. This study extended the findings of Harris and Reid (2005), who found that children with cerebral palsy indicated that virtual-reality play was extremely motivating.

What are considerations for inclusion with technology that expands experiences?

Technology contributes to the leisure experiences of all people. Computers are being used in a variety of ways that allow people to pursue leisure activities. Some agencies have labs containing computers available to the public on a drop-in basis, and conduct different instructional classes.

The computer can be used as a means to *socialize* through discussions via e-mail, chat rooms, and numerous messaging systems. Socialization can also be encouraged by having participants work jointly on projects completed with the computer. Specific software that allows people *to create visual art as well as music* can be used to allow participants to be creative and to socialize with one another.

Technology can be acquired that allows people to simulate experiences through interaction with virtual-reality hardware and software. Leisure service providers are encouraged to work to use assistive technology to help people participate in recreation activities and enjoy themselves through active participation.

Most people have a limited awareness of assistive technology. A fundamental ˍblem is the misconception that individuals with disabilities cannot be ˍctive and capable citizens. It is important to increase awareness that people ˍisabilities have widely ranging skills and capabilities.

ˍterm '*reasonable accommodation*' suggests that there is an expanding ˍptions and resources available to integrate people with disabilities into ˍ The role that assistive technology can play in inclusion of people ˍopportunities needs to be more widely known and understood. ˍectly impacts the delivery of assistive technology services.

Technological advances do not solve all problems for people with disabilities and are only as helpful as the people who design them for the user. Anyone who has used a computer knows that systems must be programmed, debugged, and updated. Some products just do not perform as advertised or do not work. Even the best advances are often a bit temperamental and will not always work the first time they are used.

Advanced technology can be costly. A device that looks as if it should cost hundreds of dollars usually costs thousands. Sometimes it can be a challenge for families to acquire the funds to obtain such helpful technology. The story of Max Frazier (Bradley, 2000, p. 10) illustrated this point:

> *Max Frazier, 4, grabbed the Dyna Myte 3100 off the coffee table and punched a couple of pictures on the keyboard. "Hi, my name is Max," an electronic voice said, "and this is my talking device." His parents smiled. His parents said that the smile is worth the yearlong fight they waged with their insurance company to get their son the speech-communication device.*

The Assistive Technology Act of 1998, formerly known as the Technology-Related Assistance for Individuals with Disabilities Act, does not directly provide technological systems to individuals, but it does enable states to set up information and referral centers. In some states, for example, individuals have the opportunity to borrow a system for a four-week trial period before making a decision to purchase it. Unsatisfactory systems can be returned and another tried until the best possible match is determined.

Technology can greatly enhance a person's abilities and may open new ways to explore his or her world. However, using these new technologies can be frustrating and difficult for some people with disabilities.

> For example, there are word-processing systems that can be activated by merely sipping and puffing on a straw connected to a special switch. Such devices make it possible for people who are immobile and lack speech to communicate in ways that were not previously possible. Yet, sipping and puffing through the 2,000 characters of a short one-page letter is laborious and mentally demanding. For every other similar technological solution, there is a corresponding challenge.

Technology enables many people with disabilities to exercise control over their lives and to become more fully integrated into society. Assistive technology extends the same options commonly available for people without disabilities by offering tools necessary for access.

Unfortunately, persistent misconceptions about assistive-technology services and devices limit their use as a solution for people with disabilities. As a result, this great equalizer is underutilized, despite the growing number of technology-related options currently available.

Technology can provide a means for people with disabilities to experience enjoyment facilitated through the leisure experience. Construction of a supportive environment responsive to people using assistive technology is needed in the area of leisure service delivery. Leisure service providers are encouraged to:

- develop a position statement on assistive technology
- initiate discussions about assistive technology related to recreation
- develop a public awareness campaign on assistive technology
- conduct surveys on technology and resource availability
- establish a peer-support network for sharing ideas and resources
- document technology resources related to recreation participation
- identify participant needs and prioritize assistive technology
- secure appropriate technology devices to meet priority needs
- compile a "wish list" for devices and target funding groups
- become familiar with participant needs and technology possibilities

Final Thoughts

Assistive technology can make a considerable difference in the leisure participation of many people. Technology originally intended for other uses can support people with disabilities in their pursuit of leisure experiences. For example, personal computers can help people compensate for cognitive impairments that can impede independence, self-determination, and inclusion. Kaminker (1995, p. 47) noted:

> *Though not designed solely for recreational use, environmental control units, infrared remote devices and voice- or head- or eye-controlled computers all increase leisure options—both indirectly, by offering greater independence and privacy, and directly, by providing access to computer games, TVs, VCRs, and CD players.*

Assistive technology can open many doors for various individuals; however, there are some challenges with assistive technology. For instance, some people who experience economic challenges find it difficult to access technology because of the expense associated with various devices and systems. Also, people who use assistive technology may be stigmatized because the technology provides a signal that this person is different in some way.

Parette and Scherer (2004) provide an example of the stigmatization of older adults. Such adults may avoid using assistive technology that is not routinely used by the general public, such as wheelchairs, walkers, or hearing aids, given the message communicated to others that they are vulnerable.

The following statement by Matt Boyer (2000) identifies the extent to which a person with a disability can use assistive technology and illustrates the impact that assistive technology can have on an individual's life:

> *My current arsenal of tricks includes a Braille-n-Speak Classic (which is an electronic talking Braille note-taker with a built-in calculator, clock, calendar, stopwatch, and countdown time); a MultiVoice (a device that takes the output of what I write on the Braille-n-Speak and speaks it in a more intelligible voice); an IBM-compatible computer with a variety of speech-output programs, screen readers, and a Braille translator; and a Hewlett Packard 5200 scanner that reads print. I use the Braille-n-Speak to keep a diary, do my math more easily, keep an appointment calendar, keep track of names and e-mail addresses, write some of my programs on, and keep a log of what we're doing on trips. I use the MultiVoice to communicate with people who don't understand my speech or the Braille-n-Speak's speech.*

Discussion Questions

1. What is meant by 'assistive technology'?
2. What are some examples of assistive technology devices?
3. What are some ways that assistive technology can improve people's abilities to write, work, hear, communicate, speak, see, move, and participate in recreation activities?
4. What do the initials "AAC" represent?
5. What are two mobility aids for individuals who are visually impaired or blind?
6. What are four recreation activities available to people with disabilities through the use of assistive technology?
7. How could environmental-control devices influence leisure participation for some people with disabilities?
8. How can animals be used to assist people with disabilities in participation in recreation activities?
9. What are some advantages and disadvantages for people with disabilities using assistive technology?
10. What can be done to encourage the use of technology that increases leisure participation for people with disabilities?

Paul Guest lives in Fort Oglethorpe, Georgia, with his parents and younger brothers Chan, Bo, and Clay (pictured here). He is currently a sophomore in high school. When he was 11, he sustained a spinal-cord injury in a bike accident.

Photo by Lynda Greer

Paul's Story

Several years ago, when I was hurt, the other kids didn't make a big deal of it when I went back to school. They still don't. I have some really great friends and we have great times together. But there are a number of things that I like about being in high school . . . this year I'm a sophomore. So . . . I'm on the editorial staff of our yearbook, THE WARRIOR. I'm one of the people responsible for the design of the yearbook; I also design motifs, do a little editing . . . whatever is needed.

The yearbook work is really good, but I especially like being on the Toss-Up Team . . . that's our academic competition team. We meet twice a week to practice, but mostly you just have to read a lot and keep up with current events to prepare for matches with other teams. We have to try out every year for Toss-Up. I hope I can make it every year until I graduate, and then I'd like to continue in college on a college bowl team. I guess I have to say that the competition is what I really love about it.

Another thing I really like is basketball . . . professional basketball. My teams are the Detroit Pistons and the Atlanta Hawks. I guess home state loyalty gives the Hawks an edge on the Pistons for me, but they're both great teams . . . very different teams.

When it comes to academics, the areas that interest me most are biological science and computer science. Working with computers seems to come easily to me most of the time; when it doesn't, I enjoy the challenge. Computer science is definitely a career choice I consider for the future. BUT my first love is writing . . . science fiction, fantasy. Right now I keep my stories to myself, but someday I want to be a published writer. I wouldn't mind a career like Stephen King's! Of course, I could do something in the field of computer science AND be a writer. Well, I've got a little while to think about it!

References

Abdullah, H. (2011). Asserting their identity: American Muslims face changed climate since 9/11. *Centre Daily Times* D7.

Adaptive and Accessible: Tucson's new adaptive recreation center meets the needs of the entire community, while especially addressing those with special needs. (2005, May). *Parks & Rec Business*, 10–15.

Adelson, E. (2008, May 5). Let 'em play. *ESPN, 11*(9), 52 65.

Adler, P. (1975). The transitional experience: An alternative view of culture shock. *Journal of Humanistic Psychology, 15*(4), 18–28.

Agate, J. R., Zabriskie, R. B., Agate, S. T., & Poff, R. (2009). Family leisure satisfaction with family life. *Journal of Leisure Research, 41*(2), 205–223.

Albom, M, (1997). *Tuesdays with Morrie*. New York, NY: Doubleday.

Alcoff, L. M. (1995). The problem of speaking for others. In J. Roof & R. Wiegman (Eds.), *Who can speak: Authority and critical identity*. Champaign, IL: University of Illinois Press. 97–119.

Alcoff, L. M. (2007). Epistemologies of ignorance: Three types. In S. Sullivan & N. Tuana (Eds.), *Race and epistemologies of ignorance*. Albany, NY: State University of New York Press. 39–58.

Aldrich, F. (2003). Smart homes past, present and future. In R. Harper (Ed.), *Inside the smart home*. London: Springer.

Allport, G. W. (1954). *The nature of prejudice*. New York, NY: Addison-Wesley.

Allsop, J. A., & Dattilo, J. (2000). Tai Chi Ch'uan. In J. Dattilo (Ed.), *Facilitation techniques in therapeutic recreation* (pp. 245–271). State College, PA: Venture Publishing, Inc.

Amir, Y. (1969). Contact hypothesis in ethnic relations. *Psychological Bulletin, 71*, 319–342.

Amir, Y. (1976). The role of intergroup contact in change of prejudice and race relations. In PA Katz (Ed.), *Towards the elimination of racism*, (pp. 245–280). New York, NY: Pergamon.

Aronson, E., & Patnoe, S. (1997). *The jigsaw classroom* (2nd ed.). New York, NY: Longman

Associated Press. (2009). *Elder Bush completes birthday parachute jump*. Retrieved from http://www.msnbc.msn.com/id/31301377/ns/politics-more_politics/

Baker Collins, S. (2005). An understanding of poverty from those who are poor. *Action Research, 3*, 9–31.

Baker, D. A., & Palmer, R. J. (2006). Examining the effects of perceptions of community and recreation participation on quality of life. *Social Indicators Research, 75*, 395–418.

Baker, P. E. (1934). *Negro-White adjustment*. New York, NY: Association Press.

Baltes, P. B., & Baltes, M. M. (Eds.) (1990). *Successful aging: Perspecti from the behavioral sciences*. New York, NY: Cambridge Universit Press.

Bausch, M., & Ault, M. J. (2008). Assistive technology implementation plan: A tool for improving outcomes. *Teaching Exceptional Children, 41*(1), 6–14.

Bialeschki, M. D. (2005). Fear of violence: Contested constraints by women in outdoor recreation activities. In E. L. Jackson (Ed.), *Constraints to leisure* (pp. 103–114). State College, PA: Venture Publishing, Inc.

Billman, S. (2007). Bernie's legacy: And what parks and recreation pros can learn from it. *Parks & Rec Business, 5*(11), 26–30.

Boone, C. G., Buckley, G. L., Grove, J. M., & Sister, C. (2009). Parks and people: An environmental justice inquiry in Baltimore, MD. *Annals of the Association of American Geographers, 99*, 767–787.

Breed, A. G. (2010, August 22). N.Y. mosque flap tests the limits of U.S. tolerance. *Centre Daily Times*, pp. A1, A6.

Brehm, J. W. (1966). *A theory of psychological reactance*. New York, NY: Academic Press.

Brown, S. (2009). *Play: How it shapes the brain, opens the imagination, and invigorates the soul.* New York, NY: Avery.

Brown v. Board of Education of Topeka. 347 U.S. 483. (1954).

Bui, Y. N., & Turnbull, A. (2003). East meets West: Analysis of person-centered planning in the context of Asian American values. *Education and Training in Developmental Disabilities, 38*(1), 18–31.

Bullock, C. C., Mahon, M. J., & Killingsworth, C. L. (2010). *Introduction to recreation services for people with disabilities: A person-centered approach* (3rd ed.). Champaign, IL: Sagamore.

Bunch, G., & Valeo, A. (2004). Student attitudes toward peers with disabilities in inclusive and special education schools. *Disability and Society, 19*(1), 61–76.

Burns, R. C., & Graefe, A. R. (2006). Toward understanding recreation fees: Impacts on people with extremely low income levels. *Journal of Park and Recreation Administration, 24*(2), 1–20.

Callaway, B. (2010). Pa. teens help raise awareness of 'R' word. *Centre Daily Times, March 7th*, C2.

Carruthers, C., & Hood, C. D. (2007). Building a life of meaning through therapeutic recreation: The leisure and well-being model, Part I. *Therapeutic Recreation Journal, 41*(4), 276–297.

Cartledge, G., & Kourea, L. (2008). Culturally responsive classrooms for culturally diverse students with and at risk for disabilities. *Exceptional Children, 74*(3), 351–371.

Causton-Theoharis, J. N., Ashby, C., & Cosier, M. (2009). Islands of loneliness: Exploring social interaction through the autobiographies of individuals with autism. *Intellectual and Developmental Disabilities, 47*, 74–96.

~enter for Immigration Studies (2007). Immigrants in the U. S., 2007. From http://www.cis.org/articles/2007/back1007.html

~ters for Disease Control. (2010).

~ness, N., & Boot, W. R. (2009). Aging and information technology use: ~otential and barriers. *Current Directions in Psychological Science,* ~(5), 253–258.

Chiang, I., Lee, Y., Frey, G., & McCormick, B. (2004). Testing the situationally modified social rank theory on friendship quality in male youth with high functioning autism spectrum disorder. *Therapeutic Recreation Journal, 38(*3), 261–274.

Chirkov V. I. (2009). A cross-cultural analysis of autonomy in education: A self-determination theory perspective. *Theory and Research in Education, 7*(2), 253–262.

Chubb, M., & Chubb, H. R. (1981). *One third of our time.* New York, NY: John Wiley & Sons.

Clay, G. (2011, August 28). A "Dream" remembered: As a national monument honoring Martin Luther King Jr. opens in Washington, D.C., a look back at his legacy and his star power. *Centre Daily Times,* C1.

Coffroad, K. G. (2005). Diversity in action. *Parks & Recreation, 40*(10), 20–23.

Colby, A., Ehrlich, T., Beaumont, E., & Stephens, J. (2003). *Educating citizens: Preparing America's undergraduates for lives of moral and civic responsibility.* San Francisco, CA: Josey-Bass.

Coleman, D., & Iso-Ahola, S. E. (1993). Leisure and health: The role of social support and self-determination. *Journal of Leisure Research, 25(2),* 111–128.

Conatser, P., & Block, M. (2001). Aquatic instructors' beliefs toward inclusion. *Therapeutic Recreation Journal, 35*(2), 170–184.

Connell, B., Jones, M., Mace, R., Muellar, J., Mullick. A., Ostroff, E., Stanford, J., Steinfeld, E., Story, M., & Vanderheiden, G. (1997). *The principles of universal design.* Raleigh, NC: North Carolina State University, Center for Universal Design.

Connor, D. J., & Behoian, L. M. (2006). Pigs, pirates, and pills: Using film to teach the social context of disability. *Teaching Exceptional Children, 39*(2), 52–60.

Cooke, C. A. (2004). Diversity in therapeutic recreation: Why now? *American Journal of Recreation Therapy, 3*(3) 25–29.

Crawford, A., Hollingsworth, H. H., Morgan, K., & Gray, D. B. (2008). People with mobility impairments: Physical activity and quality of participation. *Disability and Health Journal, 1,* 7–13.

Crawford, D. W., & Godbey, G. (1987). Reconceptualizing barriers to family leisure. *Leisure Sciences, 9,* 119–127.

Crawford, D. W., Jackson, E. L., & Godbey, G. C. (1991). A hierarchical model of leisure constraints, *Leisure Sciences, 13,* 309–320.

Crawford, M. E., Livingston, C., & Swango, A. (2004). Developing age appropriate playground skills in children with developmental disabilities. *Annual in Therapeutic Recreation, 13,* 38–58.

Dalai Lama. (1999). *Ethics for the new millennium.* New York, NY.

Dattilo, J. (2008). *Leisure education program planning: A systematic approach* (3rd ed.) State College, PA: Venture Publishing, Inc.

Dawson, S., & Liddicoat, K. (2009). "Camp gives me hope": Exploring the therapeutic use of community for adults with cerebral palsy. *Therapeut Recreation Journal, 43*(3), 9–24.

Deci, E. L., & Ryan, R. M. (1985). *Intrinsic motivation and self-determination in human behavior.* New York, NY: Plenum.

Deci, E. L., & Ryan, R. M. (2008). Facilitating optimal motivation and psychological well-being across life's domains. *Canadian Psychology, 49*(1), 14–23.

Delany, S. L., Delany, A. E., & Hearth, A. H. (1993). *Having our say: The Delany sisters' first 100 years.* New York, NY: Dell.

deLisle, L. J., & Parr, M. (2005). Understanding tolerance, embracing diversity. *Parks & Recreation, 40*(5), 20–27.

DeNavas-Walt, C., Proctor, B. D., & Smith, J. C. (2010). *Income, poverty, and health insurance coverage in the United States: 2009.* Current Population Reports, P60-238. Washington, DC: U.S. Government Printing Office.

Devine, M. A. (2004). Being a "doer" instead of a "viewer": The role of inclusive leisure contexts in determining social acceptance for people with disabilities. *Journal of Leisure Research, 36*(2), 137–159.

Devine, M. A., & Lashua, B. (2002). Constructing social acceptance in inclusive leisure contexts: The role of individuals with disabilities. *Therapeutic Recreation Journal, 36*(1), 65–83.

Devine, M. A., & O'Brien, M. B. (2007). The mixed bag of inclusion: An examination of an inclusive camp using contact theory. *Therapeutic Recreation Journal, 41*(3), 201–222.

Devine, M. A., & Wilhite, B. (2000). The meaning of disability: Implications for inclusive leisure services for youth with and without disabilities. *Journal of Park and Recreation Administration, 18*(3), 35–52.

Dieser, R. (2002). A personal narrative of a cross-cultural experience in therapeutic recreation: Unmasking the masked. *Therapeutic Recreation Journal, 36*(1), 84–96.

Dixon, J. C. (2006). The ties that bind and those that don't: Toward reconciling group threat and contact theories of prejudice. *Social Forces, 84*(4), 2179–2204.

Dixon, J. C., & Rosenbaum, M. S. (2004). Nice to know you? Testing contact, cultural, and group threat theories of anti-black and anti-hispanic stereotypes. *SocialScience Quarterly, 85*(2), 257–280.

Dovidio, J. F., Gaertner, S. L., & Kawakami, K. (2003). Intergroup contact: the past, present, and future. *Group Processes and Intergroup Relations, 6*(1), 5–21.

Dred Scott v. Sandford. 60 U.S. 393. (1857).

Dresser, N. (1996). *Multicultural manners: New rules of etiquette for a changing society.* New York, NY: John Wiley & Sons.

Drum, C., McClain, M. R., Horner-Johnson, W., & Taitano, G. (2011). *Health disparities chart book on disability and racial and ethnic status in the United States.* Durham, NH: University of New Hampshire Institute on Disability.

Dudziak, M. L. (2002). *Cold War civil rights: Race and the image of American democracy.* Princeton, NJ: Princeton University Press.

Dwyer, J. F., & Gobster, P. M. (1992). Recreational opportunity and cultural diversity. *Park and Recreation, 27*, 22–31.

Easterbrooks, S. R., & Baker, S. K. (2001). Enter the matrix: Considering the communication needs of students who are deaf and hard of hearing. *Teaching Exception Children, 33*(3), 70–76.

Edmundson, W. A. (2004). *An introduction to rights*. Cambridge, UK: Cambridge University Press.

Eisenman, L. T., Tanverdi, A., Perrington, C., & Geiman, A. (2009). Secondary and postsecondary community activities of youth with significant intellectual disabilities. *Education and Training in Developmental Disabilities, 44*(2), 168–176.

Emerson, M. O., Kimbro, R. T., & Yancey, G. (2002). Contact theory extended: The effects of prior racial contact on current social ties. *Social Science Quarterly*, 83 (3), 745–761.

Engelbrecht, P., Swart, E., & Eloff, I. (2001). Stress and coping skills of teachers with a learner with Down's syndrome in inclusive classrooms. *South African Journal of Education, 21*, 256–260.

Engh, F. (2007, June). Why Johnny hates sports: When competitive parenting and youth sports mix, the result can be ugly. *Parks & Rec Business*, 55–56.

Erickson, B., Johnson, C. W., & Kivel, B. D. (2009). Rocky Mountain National Park: History and culture as factors in African-American park visitation. *Journal of Leisure Research, 41*, 529–545.

Ervin, M. (2009, March 1). No Oscar for Jerry Lewis. Pittsburgh Tribune-Review, p. D3.

Evans, G. W., & Kantrowitz, E. (2002). Socioeconomic status and health: The potential role of environmental risk exposure. *Annual Review of Public Health, 23*, 303–331.

Farhney, S., Kelley, C., Dattilo, J., & Rusch, F. (2010). Effects of goal setting on the physical activity of walkers with osteoarthritis. *Therapeutic Recreation Journal. 44*(2), 87–104.

Farris, B. (2004). Programming for mixed ability recreation. *Parks & Recreation, 39*(11), 70–72.

Fierstein, H. (2007, April 13). Our prejudices, ourselves. *New York Times*. Retrieved from http://www.nytimes.com/2007/04/13/opinion/13fierstein.html

Fischer, R., Maes, J., & Schmitt, M. (2007). Tearing down the 'wall in the head'? culture contact between Germans. *International Journal of Intercultural Relations, 31*, 163–179.

Flower, A., Burns, M. K., & Bottsford-Miller, N. A. (2007). Meta-analysis of disability simulation research. *Remedial and Special Education, 28*(2), 72–79.

Forts, A. M. (2009). My keys to opening doors to successful community inclusion. *DDD Express, 20*(2), 1.

Fox, C. (2004). The changing color of welfare? How Whites' attitudes Latinos Influence support welfare. *American Journal of Sociology* 580–625.

Fox, L., Vaughn, B. J., Wyatte, M. L., & Dunlap, G. (2002). "We can't expect other people to understand": Family perspectives on problem behavior. *Exceptional Children, 68*(4), 437–450.

French, S. (1996). Simulation exercises in disability awareness training: A critique. In G. Hales (Ed.), *Beyond disability: Towards an enabling society* (pp. 114–123). Thousand Oaks, CA: Sage.

Freysinger, V. J. (2000). Acting our age: The relationship between age and leisure. In M. T. Allison & I. E. Schneider (Eds.), *Diversity and the recreation profession: Organizational perspectives* (pp. 139–155). State College, PA: Venture Publishing, Inc.

Friedman, T. L. (2008). *Hot, flat, and crowded: Why we need a green revolution—and how it can renew America.* New York, NY: Farrar, Straus, and Giroux.

Gamberini, L., Alcaniz, M., Barresi, G., Fabregat, M., Prontu, L., & Seraglia, B. (2008). Playing for a real bonus: Videogames to empower elderly people. *Journal of CyberTherapy & Rehabilitation, 1*(1), 37–47.

Gardner, H. (1995). *Leading minds: An anatomy of leadership.* New York, NY: Basic.

Gentry, T. (2009). Smart homes for people with neurological disability: State of the art. *NeuroRehabilitation, 25*, 209–217.

Godbey, G., Graefe, A., & James, S. W. (1992). *The benefits of local recreation and park services: A nationwide study of the perceptions of the American public.* Washington, DC: National Recreation and Park Association.

Gonzalez-Balado, J. L. (1996). *Mother Teresa: In my own words.* New York, NY: Random House.

Graham, J. A., & Cohen, R. (1997). Race and sex as factors in children's sociometric ratings and friendship choices. *Social development, 6*, 355–372.

Halberstam, D. (2004, April 18). *Brown v. Board of Education*: What it means to every American. *Parade*, 4–6.

Hansma, A. H. G., Emmelot-Vonk, M. H., & Verhaar, H. J. J. (2010). Reduction in falling after a falls-assessment. *Archives of Gerontology and Geriatrics, 50*, 73–76.

Harnik, P. (2010, August). Secrets of the private sector. *Parks and Recreation*, 32–35.

Harris, K., & Reid, D. (2005). The influence of virtual reality play on children's motivation. *Canadian Journal of Occupational Therapy, 72*(1), 21–29.

Henderson, K. A., Stalnaker, D., & Taylor, G. (1988). The relationship between barriers to recreation and gender-role personality traits for women. *Journal of Leisure Research, 20*, 69–80.

Hendrie, H. C., Albert, M. S., Butters, M. A., Gao, S., Knopman, D. S., Launer, L. J., et al. (2006). The NIH cognitive and emotional health project: Report of the critical evaluation study committee. *Alzheimer's and Dementia, 2*, 12–32.

ndy, T. (1999). Beyond public playground safety standards. *Parks and Recreation, 34*(4), 87, 90.

nann, D. (1998). *Helen Keller: A life.* Chicago, IL: University of hicago Press.

G. (1991). Leisure and aging. *Physical & Occupational Therapy in iatrics, 9*(2), 55–78.

Hibbler, D. K., & Shinew, K. J. (2002). Moving beyond our comfort zone: The role of leisure service providers in enhancing multiracial families leisure experiences. *Parks and Recreation, 37*(2), 26–35.

Histerberger, A. (2007). Feminism and the politics of representation: Towards a critical ethical encounter with "others." *Journal of International Women Studies, 8*(2), 74–83.

Hitchcock, C., Meyer, A., Rose, D., & Jackson, R. (2002). Providing new access to the general curriculum: Universal design for learning. *Teaching Exceptional Children, 35*(2), 8–17.

Hockenberry, J. (2005, July 24). Yes, you can. *Parade Magazine*, 4–5

Hoffman, C. D., Sweeney, D. P., Hodge, D., Lopez-Wagner, M. C., & Looney, L. (2009). Parenting stress and closeness: Mothers of typically developing children and mothers of children with autism. *Focus on Autism and Other Developmental Disabilities, 24*(3), 178–187.

Hood, C. D., & Carruthers, C. (2007). Enhancing leisure experience and developing resources: The leisure and well-being model, Part II. *Therapeutic Recreation Journal, 41*(4), 298–325.

Hsu, E., Davies, C. A., & Hansen, D. J. (2004). Understanding mental health needs of Southeast Asian refugees: Historical, cultural, and contextual challenges. *Clinical Psychology Review, 24,* 193–213.

Huntington, S. P. (1996). *The clash of civilizations and the remarking of world order.* New York, NY: Simon & Schuster.

Hwang, W., & Ting, J. Y. (2008). Disaggregating the effects of acculturation and acculturative stress on the mental health of Asian Americans. *Cultural Diversityand Ethnic Minority Psychology, 14*(2), 147–154.

Iso-Ahola, S. E. (1980). *The social psychology of leisure and recreation.* Dubuque, IA: W.C. Brown Co.

Jackman, M. R., & Crane, M. (1986). "Some of my best friends are black...": Interracial friendship and whites' racial attitudes. *Public Opinion Quarterly, 50,* 459–486.

Jackson, E. L., Crawford, D. W., & Godbey, G. (1993). Negotiation of leisure constraints. *Leisure Sciences, 15,* 1–11.

James, S. D. (November 18, 2009). Rosa's Law to End Term 'Mentally Retarded:" Mental Retardation Slurs Have Long History, but Cost Nothing to Change, Say Advocates. *CNS News/Health.* http://abcnews. go.com/Health/rosas-law-asks-senate-kill-slur-mentally-retarded/ story?id=9109319

Jang, Y., Kim, G., & Chiriboga, D. (2005). Acculturation and manifestation of depressive symptoms among Korean-American older adults. *Aging & Mental Health, 9*(6), 500–507.

Jenkins, J. R., Antil, L. R., Wayne, S. K., Vadady, P. F. (2003). How cooperative learning works for special education and remedial students. *Exceptional Children, 69*(3), 279–292.

Johnson, D. C. (2007, March 29). Income gap is widening, data shows. *The New York Times.* Retrieved from http://www.nytimes.com/2007/03/29/ business/29tax.html

Johnson, H. M. (2006). *Too late to die young: Nearly true tales from a life.* New York, NY: Picador.

Jones, D. B. (2004). "Denied from a lot of places": Barriers to participation in community recreation programs encountered by children with disabilities in Maine: Perspectives of parents. *Leisure/Loisir, 28*(1–2), 49–69.

Jones, L. A. (2004). As much love as you can muster. In S. D. Klein, & Kemp, J. D. (Eds.), *Reflections from a different journey: What adults with disabilities with all parents knew* (pp. 179–183). New York, NY: McGraw-Hill.

Jones, S. (2009). Enhancing quality of life through universal design. *NeuroRehabilitation, 25*, 155–167.

Jordan, B., & Dunlap, G. (2001). Construction of adulthood and disability. *Mental Retardation, 39*(4), 286–296.

Kaplan, M. (1979). *Leisure: Lifestyle and lifespan.* Philadelphia, PA: W. B. Saunders.

Kazui, P. (2002). The advantages of using a wheelchair. *Active Living: The Health, Fitness and Recreation Magazine for People with a Disability, 10*(6), 20.

Kemp, J. D. (2004). Afterword: Disability culture. In D. Klein & J. Kemp. (Eds.), *Reflections from a different journey* (pp. 195–199). New York, NY: McGraw-Hill.

Kennedy, C. (2002). *Profiles in courage for our time.* New York, NY: Hyperion.

Kennedy, M., & Lewin, L. (2010). *Fact sheet: Summary of self-determination.* Syracuse, NY: National Resource Center on Supported Living and Choice, Center on Human Policy.

Kessler Foundation/The National Organization on Disability. (2010). *The ADA, 20 years later: Survey of Americans with disabilities.* New York, NY: Harris Interactive.

Kessler Foundation/The National Organization on Disability. (2010). *The ADA, 20 years later: Survey of Americans with disabilities.* New York, NY: Harris Interactive.

Kim, J., Dattilo, J., & Heo, J. (2011). Use of leisure education and recreation activities associated with Asian cultures to promote older Asian immigrants' well-being. *Educational Gerontology.*

Kim, O. (1999). Predictors of loneliness in elderly Korean immigrant women living in the United States of America. *Journal of Advanced Nursing, 29*(5), 1082–1088.

Kitayama, S., Markus, H. R., & Kurokawa, M. (2000). Culture, emotion, and well-being: Good feelings in Japan and the United States. *Cognition and Emotion, 14*(1), 93–124.

Klein, S. D., & Kemp, J. D. (2004). *Reflections from a different journey.* New York, NY: McGraw-Hill.

Krishnankutty, N. (2007, February 7). Sharing smiles and sharing stereotypes. *Centre Daily Times*, p. A6.

Lai, D. W. (2004). Impact of culture on depressive symptoms of elderly Chinese immigrants. *Canadian Journal of Psychiatry, 49*(12), 820–827.

Laurin, D., Verreault, R., Lindsay, J., MacPherson, K., & Rockwood, K. (2001). Physical activity and risk of cognitive impairment and dementia in elderly persons. *Archives of Neurology, 58*, 498–504.

Leach, J. (2010). *Civility in a fractured society. AARP Bulletin, 51*(8), 38.

Levy, B. R., Slade, M. D., Kunkel, S. R., & Kasl, S. V. (2002). Longevity increased by positive self-perceptions of aging. *Journal of Personality and Social Psychology, 83*(2), 261–270.

Lieberson, S. (1980). *A piece of the pie: blacks and white immigrants since 1880*. Berkeley, CA: University of California Press.

Light, J. C., Drager, K. D., & Nemser, J. G. (2004). Enhancing the appeal of AAC technologies for young children: Lessons from the toy manufacturers. *Augmentative and Alternative Communication, 20*(3), 137–149.

Li, J., Scott, D., & Floyd, M. (2001). Structural inequalities in outdoor recreation participation: A multiple hierarchy stratification perspective. *Journal of Leisure Research, 33*(4), 427–449.

Lilly, S. (2010). Recovery: A vision of hope. *Pennsylvania Recreation and Parks, 41*(3), 6–9.

Livengood, J. S., & Stodolska, M. (2004). The effects of discrimination and constraints negotiation on leisure behavior of American Muslims in the post-September 11 America. *Journal of Leisure Research, 36*(2), 183–208.

Lloyd, K. M., & Auld, C. J. (2002). The role of leisure in determining quality of life: Issues of content and measurement. *Social Indicators Research, 57*(1), 43–71.

Logan, J. (2001). *Ethnic diversity grows, neighborhood integration lags behind*. Albany, NY: State University of New York at Albany, Lewis Mumford Center.

Long, T. (Winter, 2005). Constructivists teaching in parks and recreation classrooms. *Issues and Innovations*, 1, 3–4.

Markus, H. R., & Kitayama, S. (1991). Culture and the self: Implications for cognition ,emotion and motivation. *Psychological Review, 99,* 224–253.

Martin, M. E. (2006). *Residential segregation patterns of Latinos in the United States, 1990-2000*. New York, NY: Routledge.

Mason, C., Field, S., & Sawilowsky, S. (2004). Implementation of self-determination activities and student participation in IEPs. *Exceptional Children, 70*(4), 441–451.

Massey, D. S. (2007). *Categorically unequal: The American stratification system*. New York, NY: Russell Sage.

May, K. (2011). Increasing access to parks for all community members. *Parks and Recreation, 46*(5), p. 33–34.

McDowd, J. M., & Shaw, R. J. (2000). Attention and aging: A functional perspective. In F. I. M. Craik & T. A. Salthouse (Eds.), *The handbook of cognition and aging* (pp. 221–292). London, UK: Psychology Press.

McGuire, F. A., Boyd, R. K., & Tedrick, R. E. (1996). *Leisure and aging: Ulyssean living in later life*. Champaign, IL: Sagamore.

McGuire, J., & McDonnell, J. (2008). Relationships between recreation and levels of self-determination for adolescents and young adults v disabilities. *Career Development for Exceptional Individuals, 31*(3), 154–163.

McLaren, L. M. (2003). Anti-immigrant prejudice in Europe: contact, threat theory, and preferences for the exclusion of immigrants. *Social Forces, 81*(3), 909–936.

McLean, D. J., & Yoder, D. G. (2005). *Issues in recreation and leisure: Ethical decision making.* Champaign, IL: Human Kinetics.

McMorrow, M. J. (2003). *Getting ready to help: A primer on interacting in human service.* Baltimore, MD: Paul H. Brookes.

Mechling, L. C., Gast, D. L., & Seid, N. H. (2010). Evaluation of a personal digital assistant as a self-prompting device for increasing multi-step completion by students with moderate intellectual disabilities. *Education and Training in Autism and Developmental Disabilities, 45*(3), 422–439.

Mechling, L. C., & Gustafson, M. (2008). Comparison of the effects of static picture and video prompting on completion of cooking related tasks by students with autism spectrum disorder. *Journal of Special EducationTechnology, 23(3),* 31–45.

Mechling, L. C., & Gustafson, M. (2009). Comparison of the effects of static picture and video prompting on completion of cooking related tasks by students with moderate intellectual disabilities. *Exceptionality, 17*(2), 103–116.

Mechling, L. C., & Stephens, E. (2009). Comparison of self-prompting of cooking skills via picture-based cookbooks and video recipes. *Education and Training in Developmental Disabilities, 44,* 218–236.

Meneses, C., & Monroe, J. E. (2007). Health inequities in long-term care: Through the eyes of the consumer. *American Journal of Recreation Therapy, 5*(1), 20–26.

Meyer, M. (2000, December 17). There's help for social phobia. *Parade Magazine,* 10–11.

Miller, K. D. (2009). Something for everyone. *Parks & Recreation, 44*(2), 36–41.

Miller, K. D., & Schleien, S. J. (2006). Inclusive recreation: The tipping point is within our sights. *Parks & Recreation, 41*(10), 8–10.

Miller, K. D., Schleien, S. J., & Bowens, F. (2010). Support staff as an essential component of inclusive recreation services. *Therapeutic Recreation Journal, 64,* 35–60.

Mills, C. W. (2007). White ignorance. In S. Sullivan & N. Tuana (Eds.), *Race and epistemologies of ignorance.* Albany, NY: State University of New York Press. 11–38.

Mio, J. S., Barker-Hackett, L., & Tumambing, J. (2008). *Multicultural psychology.* New York, NY: McGraw-Hill Higher Education.

Mishkin, J. R., & Schill, M. (1973). *The complete belly dancer.* Garden City, NY: Doubleday.

berg, S. (2003). Education for all in the North and South: Teacher's attitudes towards inclusive education in Finland and Zambia. *Education nd Training in Developmental Disabilities, 38*(4), 417–428.

Montuori, A., & Fahim, U. (2004). Cross-Cultural encounter as an opportunity for personal growth. *Journal of Humanistic Psychology, 44*(2), 243–265.

More, T. (2002). "The parks are being loved to death" and other frauds and deceits in recreation management. *Journal of Leisure Research, 34*, 52–78.

Morgan, T. (Ed.). (2001). *A simple monk: Writings on his holiness the Dalai Lama.* Novato, CA: New World Library.

Mowen, A. J., Payne, L. L., & Scott, D. (2005). Change and stability in leisure constraints revisited. *Leisure Sciences, 27*, 191–204

Multinational study of attitudes toward individuals with intellectual disabilities: General findings and calls to action. (2003, June). Washington, DC: Special Olympics.

Muscott, H. S., Szczesiul, S., Berk, B., Staub, K., Hoover, J., & Perry-Chisholm, P. (2008). Creating home-school partnerships by engaging families in schoolwide positive behavior supports. *Teaching Exceptional Children, 40*(6), 6–14.

NAACP (2012). Our mission. http://www.naacp.org/pages/our-mission

National Archives, The. (n.d.) *Teaching with documents: The Civil Rights Act of 1964 and the Equal Employment Opportunity Commission.* Retrieved from http://www.archives.gov/education/lessons/civil-rights-act/

National Center on Accessibility. (2010, August). *Choosing products to improve access to parks and facilities.* Bloomington, IN: National Center on Accessibility, Indiana University-Bloomington. Retrieved from www.ncaonline.org

Navarro, M. (2007, May 13).Clearly, frankly, unabashedly disabled. *New York Times.* Retrieved from http://www.nytimes.com

Navarro, M. (May 13, 2007). Clearly, frankly, unabashedly disabled. Retrieved from http://www.nytimes.com/2007/05/13/fashion/13disabled.html?pagewanted=all&_r=0

Obama, B. (2010, July 26). Remarks by the President on 20th anniversary of the Americans with Disabilities Act. Retrieved from http://www.whitehouse.gov/the-press-office/remarks-president-20th-anniversary-americans-with-disabilities-act

Oh, Y., & Sales, E. (2002). Acculturation, stress, and depressive symptoms among Korean immigrants in the United States. *The Journal of Social Psychology, 142*(2), 511–526.

Older Americans Act, The (OAA). (2006). *The Older Americans Act of 1965, Public Law 109–365, as amended through 2006.* Washington, DC: U.S. Government Printing Office.

Olzak, S. (1992). *The dynamics of ethnic competition and conflict.* Standford, CA: Stanford University Press.

Parette, H. P., Meadan, H., Doubet, S., & Hess, J. (2010). Supporting families of young children with disabilities using technology. *Education and Training in Autism and Developmental Disabilities, 45*(4), 552–565.

Parette, P., & Scherer, M. (2004). Assistive technology use and stigma. *Education and Training in Developmental Disabilities, 39*(3), 217–226.

Park, S., & Bernstein, K. S. (2008). Depression and Korean American immigrants. *Archives of Psychiatrics Nursing, 22*(2), 12–19.

Parks, R. (1992). *Rosa Parks: My story*. New York, NY: Puffin.

Patchen, M. (1999). *Diversity and unity: Relations between racial and ethnic groups*. Chicago, IL: Nelson-Hall.

Patterson, I. (2000). Developing a meaningful identity for people with disabilities through serious leisure activities. *World Leisure Journal, 2,* 41–51.

Patterson, I. (2001). Serious leisure as a positive contributor to social inclusion for people with intellectual disabilities. *World Leisure Journal, 3,* 16–24.

Pausch, R. (2008). *The last lecture*. New York, NY: Hyperion.

Pegg, S., & Compton, D. M. (2004). Creating opportunities and ensuring access to leisure and recreation services through inclusion in the global community. *Leisure/Loisir, 28*(1–2), 5–26.

Peregoy, J., & Dieser, R. (1997). Multicultural awareness in therapeutic recreation: Hamlet living. *Therapeutic Recreation Journal, 31*(3), 173–187.

Pettigrew, T. F. (1998). Intergroup contact theory. *Annual Reviews Psychology, 49,* 65–85.

Pettigrew, T. F., & Tropp, L. R. (2006). A meta-analytic test of intergroup contact theory. *Journal of Personality and Social Psychology, 90*(5), 751–783.

Pitts, L. (2009). *Forward from this moment: Daily triumphs, tragedies, and curiosities*. Chicago, IL: AGATE.

Pivik, J., McComas, J., & LaFlamme, M. (2002). Barriers and facilitators to inclusive education. *Exceptional Children, 69*(1), 97–107.

Plessy v. Ferguson. 163 U.S. 537. (1896).

Police say coach paid player to hurt teammate. (2005, July 16). *Centre Daily Times*, p. A5.

Quintero, N., & McIntyre, L. L. (2010). Sibling adjustment and maternal well-being: An examination of families with and without a children with an autism spectrum disorder. *Focus on Autism and Other Developmental Disabilities, 25*(1), 37–46.

Raymore, L. A., Godbey, G. C., & Crawford, D. W. (1994). Self-esteem, gender, and socioeconomic status: Their relation to perceptions of constraint on leisure among adolescents. *Journal of Leisure Research, 26,* 99–118.

Reid, D., & Campbell, K. (2006). The use of virtual reality with children with cerebral palsy: A pilot randomized trial. *Therapeutic Recreation Journal, 40*(4), 255–268.

Reilly, R. (2003, October, 20).Worth the wait. *Sports Illustrated.* Retrieved from http://sportsillustrated.cnn.com/vault/article/magazine/ MAG1030174/index.htm

Rimmer, J. (2007). Emphasis on winning banishes many youth, with and without disabilities, from playing fields. The National Center on Physical Activity and Disability. Retrieved from http://www.ncpad.org/director/ fact_sheet.php?sheet=527

Riordan, C. (1978). Equal-status interracial contact: A review and revision of the concept. *International Journal of Intercultural Relations, 2,* 161–185.

Roberts, R. (2009). Universally loved: Universal access allows children of all abilities to have fun. *Parks & Recreation, 44*(12), 43–45.

Rodrifuez, G. (2010, March 22). The white anxiety crisis. *Time*, 175 (11), 52.

Rosenzweig, R., & Blackmar, E. (1992). *The park and the people: A history of Central Park*. Ithaca, NY: Cornell University Press.

Rossetti, Z. S., & Goessling, D. P. (2010). Paraeducators' roles in facilitating friendships between secondary students with and without autism spectrum disorders or developmental disabilities. *Teaching Exception Children, 42*(6), 64–70.

Rothart, M., & John, O. P. (1988). Social categorization and behavioral episodes: A cognitive analysis of the effects of intergroup contact. *Journal of Social Issues, 41*(3), 81–104.

Ryan, R. M., & Deci, E. L. (2000). Self-determination theory and the facilitation of intrinsic motivation, social development, and well-being. *American Psychologist, 55*, 68–78.

Ryan, R. M., & Deci, E. L. (2006). Self-regulation and the problem of human autonomy: Does psychology need choice, self-determination, and will? *Journal of Personality, 74*(6), 1557–1585.

Ryan, R. M., Lynch, M. F., Vansteenkiste, M., & Deci, E. L. (2011). Motivation and autonomy in counseling, psychotherapy, and behavior change: A look at theory and practice. *The Counseling Psychologist, 39*, 193–260.

Ryndak, D. L., Ward, T., Alper, S., Montgomery, J. W., & Storch, J. F. (2010). Long-term outcomes of services for two persons with significant disabilities with differing educational experiences: A qualitative consideration of the impact of educational services. *Education and Training in Autism and Developmental Disabilities, 45*(3), 323–338.

Ryndak, D. L., Ward, T., Alper, S., Storch, J. F., & Montgomery, J. W. (2010). Long-term outcomes of services in inclusive and self-contained settings for siblings with comparable significant disabilities. *Education and Training in Autism and Developmental Disabilities, 45*(1), 38–53.

Sadowsky, D. (2002, Spring). Living solo. *Spinal Column*, 6–7.

Saenz, B. A. (2010, September 24). Where Spanish and English are good for each other. *The Chronicle of Higher Education*, B43–B44.

Salend, S. J., & Duhaney, L. M. G. (2002). What do families have to say about inclusion? *Teaching Exceptional Children, 35*(1), 62–66.

Sanford, J. (2002, February 19). U.S. culture's focus on work leaves Americans in a quandary over leisure time. *The Stanford Report*. Retrieved from http://news.stanford.edu/news/2003/february19/work-219.html

Scalzi, J. (2005). *Being poor*. Retrieved from http://whatever.scalzi.com/2005/09/03/being-poor

Schooler, C., & Mulatu, M. S. (2001). The reciprocal effects of leisure time activities and intellectual functioning in older people: A longitudinal analysis. *Psychology and Aging, 16*(3), 466–482.

Sciberras, J., & Hutchison, P. (2004). Close friendships of integrated youth: Parents as partners. *Leisure/Loisir, 28*(1–2), 87–114.

Scott, D. (in press). Race, ethnicity, and leisure services: Can we hope to escape the past? In M. Stodolska, K. J. Shinew, M. F. Floyd, & G. J. Walker (Eds.), *Race, ethnicity, and leisure*. Champaign, IL: Human Kinetics.

Scott, D., & Munson, W. (1994). Perceived constraints to park usage among individuals with low incomes. *Journal of Park and Recreation Administration, 12,* 52–69.

Scully, J. L. (2008). *Disability bioethics: Moral bodies, moral difference.* Lanham, MD: Rowman & Littlefield.

Sebag, R. (2010). Behavior management through self-advocacy. *Teaching Exceptional Children, 42*(6), 22–29.

Sebald, A., & Luckner, J. (2007). Successful partnerships with families of children who are deaf. *Teaching Exceptional Children, 39*(3), 54–60.

Seligman, M. E. P. (1975). *Helplessness: On depression, development, and death.* San Francisco, CA W. H. Freeman.

Shafer-Landau, R. (2010). *The fundamental of ethics.* New York, NY: Oxford University Press.

Shay, A., & Seller-Young, B. (2003). Belly dance: Orientalism: exoticism: self-exoticism. *Dance Research Journal, 35*(1), 13–37.

Shelton, J. N., & Richeson, J. A. (2005). Intergroup contact and pluralistic ignorance. *Journal of Personality and Social Psychology, 88,* 91–107.

Shinew, K. J., Glover, T. D., & Parry, D. C. (2004). Leisure spaces as potential sites for interracial interactions: Community gardens in urban areas. *Journal of Leisure Research, 36*(3), 336–355.

Shokoohi-Yekta, M., & Hendrickson, J. M. (2010). Friendships with peers with severe disabilities: American and Iranian secondary students' ideas about being a friend. *Education and Training in Autism and Developmental Disabilities, 45*(1), 23–37.

Shores, K. A., Scott, D., Floyd, M. F. (2007). Constraints to outdoor recreation: A multiple hierarchy stratification perspective. *Leisure Sciences, 29,* 227–246.

Simon, R. (2003). *Riding the bus with my sister: A true life journey.* New York, NY: Plume.

Simpson, A., Langone, J., & Ayres, K. M. (2004). Embedded video- and computer-based instruction to improve social skills for students with autism. *Education and Training in Developmental Disabilities, 39*(3), 240–252.

Simpson, S. (2003). *The leader who is hardly known: Self-less teaching from the Chinese tradition.* Oklahoma City, OK: Wood 'N' Barnes Publishing.

Skulski, J. (2010). Access board issues draft final rule for outdoor developed areas. Bloomington, IN: National Center on Accessibility. www.ncaonline.org/

Smart, J. (2009). *Disability, society, and the individual* (2nd ed.) Austin, TX: Pro-Ed

Smiley, S. M. (2010). *Hope unseen: The story of the U.S. Army's first blind active-duty officer.* New York, NY: Howard Books.

Smith, T. L., Polloway, E. A., Smith, J. D., & Patton, J. R. (2007). Self-determination for persons with developmental disabilities: Ethical considerations for teachers. *Education and Training in Developmental Disabilities, 42*(2), 144–151.

Sohng, K., Sohng, S., & Yeom, H. (2002). Health-promoting behaviors of elderly Korean immigrants in the United States. *Public Health Nursing, 19*(4), 294–300.

Soonthornchaiya, R., & Dancy, B. J. (2006). Perceptions of depression among elderly Thai immigrants. *Issues in Mental Health Nursing, 27*, 681–698.

Spivak, G. (1999). *A critique of postcolonial reason: Toward a history of the vanishing present.* Cambridge, MA: Harvard University Press.

Spousta, T. (2005, February 10). Martin says this might be his last season if game falters. *USA Today*, p. 6C.

Stebbins, R. A. (1992). *Amateurs, professionals, and serious leisure.* Montreal, Canada: McGill-Queen's University Press.

Stephan, W. G., & Stephan, C. (1985). Intergroup anxiety. *Journal of Social Issues, 41,* 157–176.

Stephan, W. G., Ybarra, O., & Bachman, G. (1999). Prejudice toward immigrant: An integrated threat theory. *Journal of Applied Social Psychology, 29*, 2221–2237.

Stern, K. S. (2002). *Why campus anti-Israel activity flunks Bigotry 101.* New York, NY: The American Jewish Committee.

Stodolska, M. (2010). Providing leisure service for diverse populations. In *Inclusive Recreation: Program and services for diverse populations* (pp. 93–118). Champaign, IL: Human Kinetics.

Stone, C. F. (2003). Exploring cultural competencies of certified therapeutic recreation specialists: Implications for education and training. *Therapeutic Recreation Journal, 37*(2), 156–174.

Stoner, J. B., & Angell, M. E. (2006). Parent perspectives on role engagement: An investigation of parents and children with ASD and their self-reported roles with education professionals. *Focus on Autism and Other Developmental Disabilities, 21*(3), 177–189.

Sullivan, A. K., & O'Brien, M. B. (2001). Inclusive programming at summer camp. *Parks & Recreation, 36*(5), 66–72.

Sylvester, C. (2010). ACT Right: Overcoming Ethical Barriers. National Recreation and Park Association Congress. October, 2010, Minneapolis, MN.

Taunt, H. M., & Hastings, R. P. (2002). Positive impact of children with developmental disabilities on their families: A preliminary study. *Education and Training in Mental Retardation and Developmental Disabilities, 37*(4), 410–420.

Taylor, M. (1998). How White Attitudes vary with the racial composition of local populations: number count. *American Sociological Review, 63,* 512–535.

Taylor, P. (2010, July 5). A gift from the game. *Sports Illustrated, 112*(28), 80.

Taylor, P. (March 22, 2010). A life in balance. *Sports Illustrated.*

Terrill, C. F. (2001). Presidential address 2001—You can change the world. *Mental Retardation, 39*(5), 391–400.

Texeira, E. (August 19, 2005). 'Minority' at odds with demographic data: Words fall from favor, criticized as outdated and inaccurate. *Centre Daily Times*, A10.

The Dignity Project, Crown Prince Haakon of Norway, John Bryant from Operation HOPE, and Professor Pekka Himanen, University of Art & Design Helsinki and Visiting Professor at Oxford University.

Thun, B. (2007). Disability rights framework in Canada. *Journal of Employment Rights, 12*(4), 351–371.

Tilly, C. (1999). *Durable inequality.* Berkeley, CA: University of California Press.

Townsend, J. A., & Zabriskie, R. B. (2010). Family leisure among families with a child in mental health treatment: Therapeutic recreation implications. *Therapeutic Recreation Journal, 64,* 11–34.

Trussell, D. E., & Mair, H. (2010). Seeking judgment free spaces: Poverty, leisure, and social inclusion. *Journal of Leisure Research, 42,* 513–533.

Turner, R. N., Hewstone, M., & Voci, A. (2007). Reducing explicit and implicit prejudice via direct and extended contact: The mediating role of self-disclosure and intergroup anxiety. *Journal of Personality and Social Psychology, 93,* 369-388.

Ulrich, M. E., & Bauer, A. M. (2003). A closer look at communication between parents and professionals. *Teaching Exceptional Children, 35*(6), 20–24.

United Nations. (1948). *The universal declaration of human rights.* Retrieved from http://www.un.org/en/documents/udhr/

United Nations. (2002). *World population ageing: 1950–2050.* Retrieved from http://www.un.org/esa/population/publications/worldageing19502050/

U.S. Census Bureau. (2008). U. S. census bureau news. Retrieved May 1, 2008, from http://www.census.gov/Press-Release/www/releases/archives/population/011910.html

U.S. Census Bureau. (2009). *American community urvey demographic and housing estimates: 2009.* Retrieved from http://factfinder.census.gov/

U.S. Department of Health & Human Services. (2009). *The 2009 HHS poverty guidelines.* Retrieved from http://aspe.hhs.gov/poverty/09poverty.shtml

Voelkl, J., & Aybar-Damili, B. (2008). Aging and the life span. In T. Robertson & T. Long (Eds.), *Foundations of therapeutic recreation* (pp. 185–198). Champaign, IL: Human Kinetics.

Ward, C., Bochner, S., & Furnham, A. (2001). *The psychology of culture shock.* Philadelphia, PA: Routledge.

Weybright, E. H., Dattilo, J., & Rusch, F. (2010). Effects of participation in an interactive video game (Nintendo Wii) on attention and positive affect in older adults with a mild cognitive impairment. *Therapeutic Recreation Journal, 44*(4), 271–287.

Williams, C. B., & Finnegan, M. (2003). From myth to reality: Sound information for teachers about students who are deaf. *Teaching Exceptional Children, 35*(3), 40-45.

·lliams, J. (1998).*Thurgood Marshall: American revolutionary.* New York, NY: Three Rivers Press.

ʒ, K. (2006). Life as he knows it: Michael Bérubé is an ardent voice for ·isability rights. *Penn State Outreach, 9*(2), 12–13.

World Health Organization (WHO). (2010). New guidelines released on wheelchairs to support users in developing countries. Retrieved from http://www.who.int/disabilities/publications/technology/wheelchairguidelines/en/

World Leisure Organization. (2010). International position statement on leisure education. Retrieved from http://worldleisure.org/about/publications/position_statement.php

Yancey, G. A. (1999). An examination of the effects of residential and church integration on the racial attitudes of Whites. *Sociological Perspectives, 42*, 279–304.

Yang, H., & Poff, R. (2001). Virtual reality therapy: Expanding the boundaries of therapeutic recreation. *Parks and Recreation, 36*(5), 52–57.

Yoo, E. E., & Buzinde, C. N. (2012). Gazing upon the kingdom: An audience reception analysis of a televised travelogue. *Annals of Tourism Research, 39(1)*, 221–242.

York, S. L. (2009). Residential design and outdoor area accessibility. *NeuroRehabilitation, 25*, 201–208.

Yu, M. (1997). Mental health services to immigrants and refugees. In T. R. Watkins & J. W. Callicut (Eds.), *Mental health policy and practice today* (pp. 164-181). Thousand Oaks, CA: Sage

Zambo, D. M. (2009). Using visual literacy to help adolescents understand how images influence their lives. *Teaching Exceptional Children, 41*(6), 60–67.

Zhang, D., Landmark, L., Grenwelge, C., & Montoya, L. (2010). Culturally diverse parents' perspectives on self-determination. *Education and Training in Autism and Developmental Disabilities, 45*(2), 175–186.

Index

Other Books by Venture Publishing, Inc.

Therapeutic Recreation: Cases and Exercises, Second Edition
    by Barbara C. Wilhite and M. Jean Keller
Therapeutic Recreation in Health Promotion and Rehabilitation
    by John Shank and Catherine Coyle
Therapeutic Recreation in the Nursing Home
    by Linda Buettner and Shelley L. Martin
Therapeutic Recreation Practice: A Strengths Approach
    by Lynn Anderson and Linda Heyne
Therapeutic Recreation Programming: Theory and Practice
    by Charles Sylvester, Judith E. Voelkl, and Gary D. Ellis
The Therapeutic Recreation Stress Management Primer
    by Cynthia Mascott
Tourism and Society: An Introduction
    by Robert W. Wyllie
Trivia by the Dozen: Encouraging Interaction and Reminiscence in Managed Care
    by Jean Vetter